AutoCAD in 20 Hours
AutoCAD and AutoCAD LT

Version 2020

James Beebe
Building Designer, Drafter,
Building Contractor,
Construction Consultant

Structural Press

ISBN 978-0-9848631-5-0

Preface to AutoCAD in 20 Hours

Try the first chapter for free at: www.AutoCADin20Hours.com

This book is for all types of 2d drafting—mechanical, circuitry, as well as **architecture**. It uses a project—**drawing a set of house plans**—as a format for learning AutoCAD. This is an excellent way to learn because this project utilizes all the features that are necessary for drafting any object. After completing this course you will be able to draft anything in 2d and print it to scale. This is an enjoyable way to learn because it is project orientated and the drafting begins immediately. The drawing evolves quickly; this creates a feeling of rapid progress. This is quite different from other manuals that require many hours of learning in preparation for drafting.

This book is a carefully designed **programmed learning system** where every sentence has been crafted to fall into the proper order. The instructions build upon each other, step by step, to make the process flow naturally. Great attention has been paid to including every step of each process in plain English. Jargon has been avoided as much as possible. It is designed for people who wish to learn how to draft, not for the computer wunderkind.

Many of you will agree with the statement that help menus are often of little help. The same can be said of many software manuals. There are several reasons for this.

First, the language is often incomprehensible. The writers know how to use the software, but they don't know how to speak in plain English.

Second, steps are omitted from the instructions, often the first step(s). The writer assumes that the reader knows some of the steps.

Third, many manuals are presented in encyclopedic format. They list the various procedures, commands, and functions in sections without context. And they try to cover the entire program even though only a portion of the program is essential to most users. The essential information is buried in a sea of relatively unimportant information. **We don't need to know how to do everything in these programs; we just need to know enough to get the job done.**

Fourth, because we don't know the jargon, we can't ask for help. Without the words we can't formulate the questions.

This book addresses all of these problems. It goes straight for the **goal: how to draw any 2d object in AutoCAD**. It does this by guiding the reader through the creation of a set of house plans with every step illustrated and described in plain language.

This makes for a dynamic learning experience because the drawing begins to take shape in the first pages and progresses at a rapid pace. The floor plan in Chapter 1 is completed in four to six hours.

But don't take my word for it—try it for free and decide for yourself. Find it on the book website.

Visit the book website at: **www.AutoCADin20Hours.com**

I hope you enjoy this experience, it is meant to be fun. That is: if drawing stuff is your idea of a good time.

Note on appropriate version: This is the updated **2020** version of **AutoCAD in 20 Hours**. AutoCAD doesn't change a lot from year to year so this version is adequate to learn Autocad for most versions of the software after 2006. The ribbon was introduced in 2008 and that was a major change in interface, but other than that the functions have changed little over the years. I have some older versions of the book starting with 2006. They are available upon request through AutoCadin20Hrs.com. Use the contact form to request older versions.

Table of Contents

Introduction

READ THIS BEFORE YOU BEGIN

Often we skip the introductions because they contain a lot of promotional material and not a lot of substance. **This introduction contains important information.** Take a few minutes and read through it.

This book can be used to learn all types of 2d drafting—mechanical, circuitry, as well as architecture. It covers all of the procedures and commands to draw anything. It uses Imperial measurements because that is (unfortunately) what is still used today in the United States for Architecture. This should not be an impediment for metric drafters. All of the measurements are called out in exact numbers and **no math is required**. The conversion to metric is not difficult and is explained. It is the **drawing skills** that are important and this is an excellent method to learn those skills as architectural drafting covers almost every situation that will be encountered by any drafter.

The house drawn in this book is designed to facilitate the learning process. It is not meant to be an award winning design. Some design components are less than optimal to speed up the drawing process. It is a very small house so that each view can be printed on 8.5 x 11 paper and on a typical small printer. But the home is fully functional and could be built. The completed plans would pass inspection in any building department, though additional drawings and notes could be requested. Some jurisdictions would require engineering.

AutoCAD is a huge system. It can perform very complicated operations. But most of us do not need all the complex features. This book teaches the essentials, based on the concept that the drafter can then draw anything in 2d. More complex methods and procedures can be learned later.

The huge size of the AutoCAD program causes **glitches**. There are hundreds of system variable settings that can change through some glitch. Sometimes the program locks up. Sometimes, when opened, the settings from prior sessions will be lost. Sections of the drawing can become locked up and "unselectable". The command line can disappear. It would take an entire book to catalog all of these possible glitches. This creates a problem for an instruction manual because it is not possible to predict when these glitches may occur.

Usually if things are not working, it is because the instructions are not being followed to the letter. But if there is a glitch, it can be difficult for the reader to evaluate.

If you are unable to obtain the demonstrated results, start by assuming that you have left out some part of the procedure. Read the text carefully and try again. Read the command line to see if the system is picking up on your input. If you still have a problem, see if there is an appendix listing for the command. Read Appendix I—Glitches. If you have access to the videos (see www.AutoCADin20hours.com), you can review the procedures there. If all else fails and you think that it might be a glitch, try restarting the program. If that fails you will have to research online for your problem. That should eventually produce the solution.

A very common glitch is that the system does not recognize the selection of a command when you click on a button. This seems to run in shifts—it happens for a while and then ceases to be a problem. When this happens **double click** the buttons. The problem should pass after a while and you can go back to a single click.

The system is setup for automatic saving. When the system **saves**, it **freezes** all actions. This can take a minute or more depending on the size of the file and the power of the computer. So, if you are drawing and the system freezes, wait a minute, it is probably saving your file.

Often, in the beginning, you will get stuck in the middle of some procedure and nothing seems to work; when this happens, use the escape button on your computer and start again. The escape button is a major tool in AutoCAD.

Often you will see a blue or green rectangle on the screen and nothing will respond, use the escape.

Read the command line as you go through the different procedures. The prompts tell you what to do and you can see if your input matches the prompts.

All of the drawing in this book is done in one file. In other words: **do not create a new file for each chapter**. Open the same file each time and do all your drawing in the same workspace.

Enter means to hit the enter button on your keyboard (see Appendix I—Keyboard). **<e>**, **ent** and **enter** are all the same: press the enter key.

In the Imperial system the quote symbol (**”**) means **inches**, the apostrophe symbol (**’**) means **feet** as in 10’ 4” (ten feet four inches).

You can **type commands** instead of clicking on the buttons. But if you do this you will have to type the command and then **enter**. Clicking on a button **equals** typing the command **and** hitting the enter key. This can be confusing because some procedures require clicking a button and then hitting the enter key. For these procedures, if you type that command, you will need to enter twice. You'll figure it out now that you have read this.

Many of the parts of the drawing are created **off to the side in open drawing space**. This means anywhere on the screen. These are meant to be copied or moved later, so the original location of these parts of the drawing is not important. Similarly a lot of the instructions indicate an approximate location for certain objects or text. **Approximate** means put it anywhere close to where it is depicted in the figure.

Don't worry about making things really precise. That is not an important aspect of this learning process. The idea here is to learn the drafting methods and procedures; precision is something that you can work out later. So if you are uncertain exactly where to place something, or exact dimensions, let it go and just keep moving forward with the lesson. Of course precision is essential to drafting, but that is something you can work out on your own.

The **Osnap** or Object Snap feature places your objects in a precise location that is marked by an icon that appears when your cursor approaches certain predetermined points. You don't need to understand this now; you will understand when it happens. If an Osnap icon is highlighted, your object will **attach to that point**. Sometimes this is not what you want and you will want to turn off the Osnap feature to resolve this problem.

Sometimes AutoCAD **switches layers automatically** (you will understand this later, also). Watch for this in the Layer Control window displayed on the first page of Chapter 1.

This book is meant to be used in a variety of ways. The two main distinctions are between the readers who want to just learn AutoCAD and those who wish to draft a full set of plans. The difference is mainly in Chapter 15. That chapter is for those who wish to complete the plans, everyone else can skip it. The book without Chapter 15 takes about twenty hours. The reader should be able to learn all of the skills for 2d drafting (of anything) in about that amount of time. The complete set of plans takes an additional fifteen to twenty hours because of the drafting labor.

Another variation in how this book can be used is that some readers will want to rely mostly on the illustrations and skip from one to the next. If you choose to use the book this way, you should still skim the **bold text** to make sure that you have not skipped over something essential.

Try to complete the entire book in as short a time frame as possible. This will insure that you retain the previously learned material as you move forward. If the study is stretched out over weeks or months it may require review or even starting over with the process. The best method would be to take a four day period and spend five hours a day. If you can learn AutoCAD in four or five days, it will be an accomplishment. It takes most people months or even years.

Draft long and prosper!

Chapter 1—Setup and Floor Plans

Read the Introduction, before you begin, for some important general information.

1.1 Setup

Most books on CAD design begin with an extensive set up. This book takes a different approach. We will do the minimal amount of set up and start drawing. This will get things moving along and the set-up will be introduced as it is necessary to continue drawing. If you are unable to perform any of the tasks refer to Appendix I for trouble shooting.

When you first install AutoCAD click on the box that reads **Start Drawing**. You will see the screen in Fig 1-1. Yours will be black. This doesn't matter. I set my color scheme to white so it can be seen more clearly.

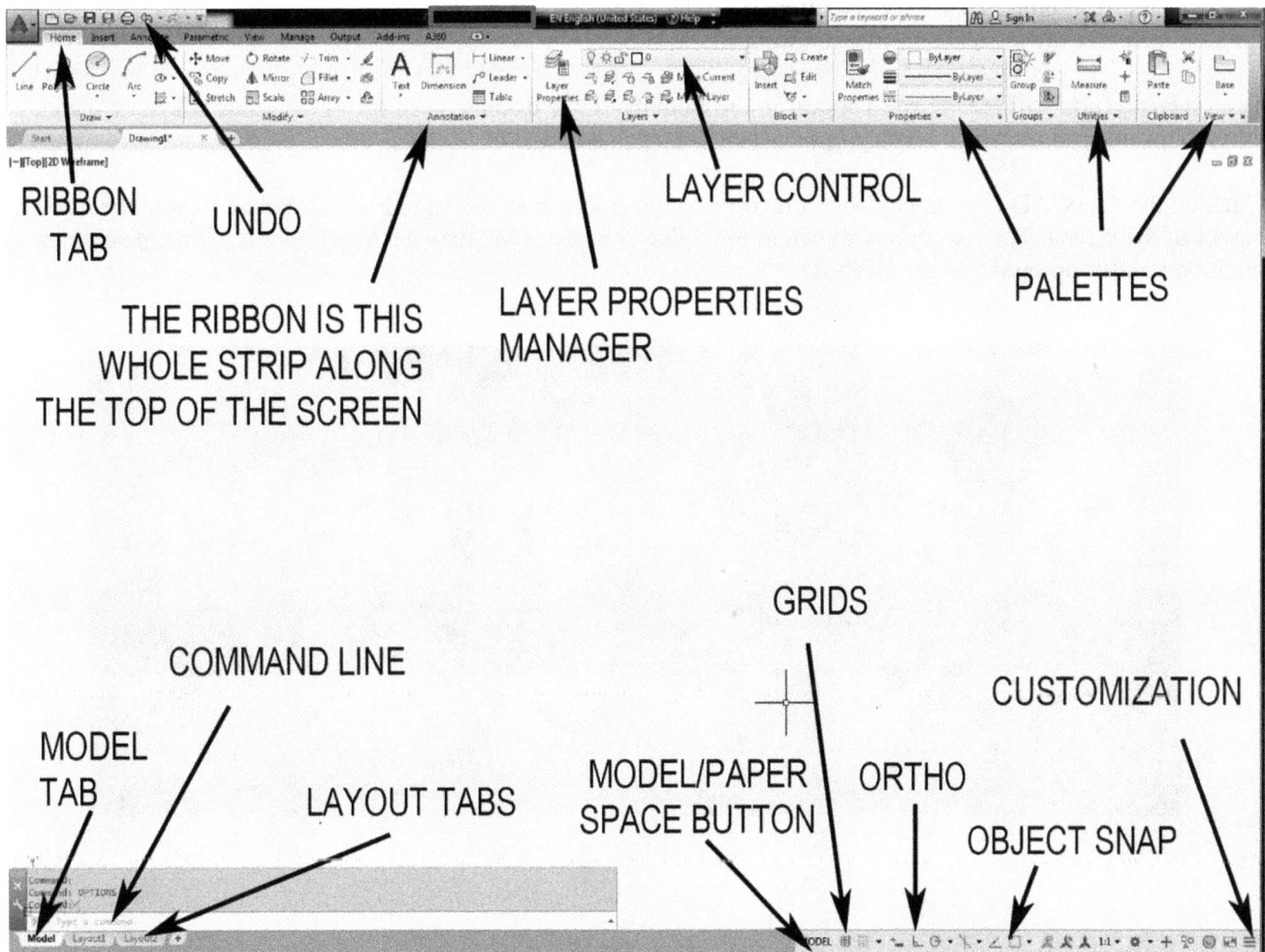

RIBBON TAB — UNDO — THE RIBBON IS THIS WHOLE STRIP ALONG THE TOP OF THE SCREEN — LAYER PROPERTIES MANAGER — LAYER CONTROL — PALETTES — COMMAND LINE — MODEL TAB — LAYOUT TABS — GRIDS — MODEL/PAPER SPACE BUTTON — ORTHO — OBJECT SNAP — CUSTOMIZATION

Fig. 1-1

If your screen displays boxes (not shown here) in the drawing area, close them by clicking on the x's.

If you see a different ribbon at the top of the screen, click on the Home tab. You may have more tabs than are shown here, don't worry about that for now. (If you want to add or eliminate tabs right click on a tab and select Show Tabs, then check or uncheck the tabs you want on the ribbon.)

The ribbon is the row of tools at the top of the screen as shown in Fig 1.1. There are a number of tabs along the top of the ribbon (Home, Insert, Annotate, etc.). If you click on these tabs you will see that a section of the ribbon opens that relates to the tab label. Within each section there are buttons associated with each command.

You do not need to know about these commands at this time as we will present them as they are needed to draw.

First we must set the measurement units to imperial standard for architectural drawing. AutoCAD will draw in metric or Imperial units. This book is written using the **imperial standard**—feet and inches. That is what is used for architectural drawing and construction work in the U.S.

Type **startup** (you will see the word appear in the Command line display, see Fig 1-1), hit **enter**. Type **1** then **enter**. This determines which menu you see when you open a new file.

Click on the AutoCAD icon in the upper left corner of your screen as shown in Fig 1-2. Select **New** at the top left corner of the screen. The pop up box shown in Fig 1-3 will appear (you may get a different box first, if so, click on the **quick set up** option to get this box).

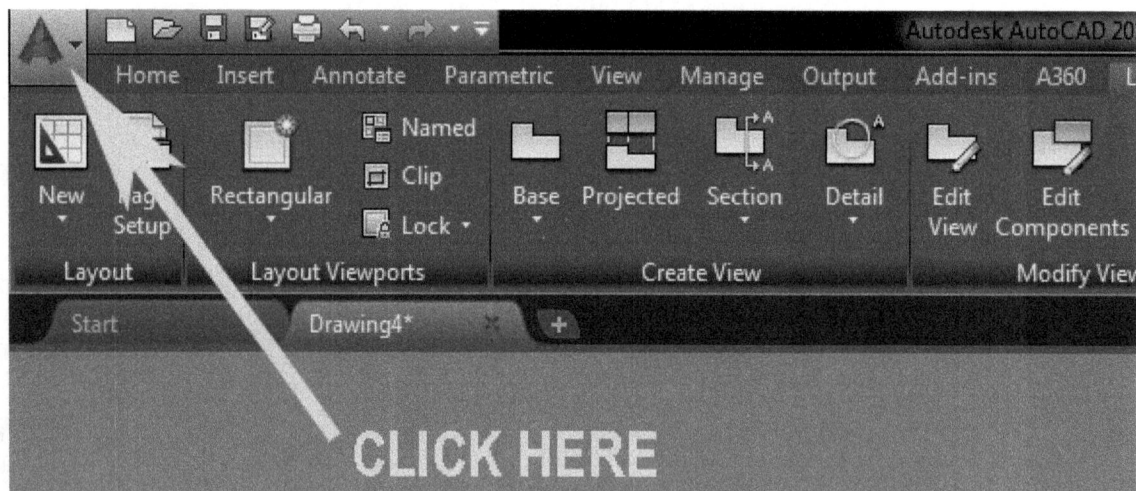

Fig. 1-2

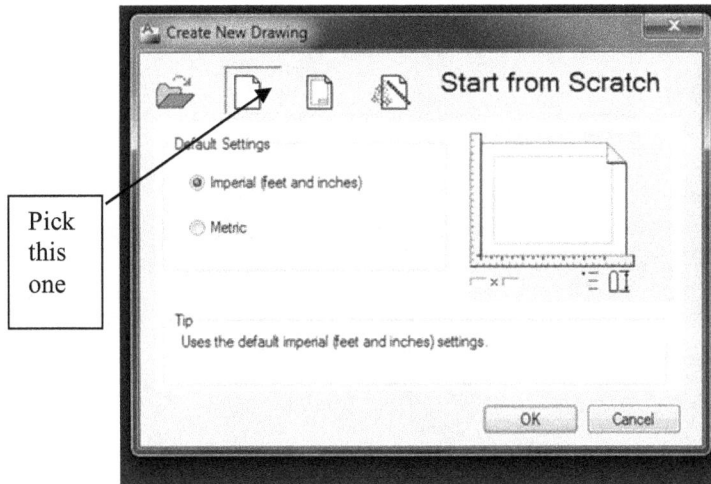

Fig 1-3

Click on the button shown in **Fig 1-3**.

Select the **Imperial (feet and inches)** button as shown.

Click **OK**.

If you need to know where to find a particular button use the F1 button, or type help. In the help homepage window that opens select **Commands**. There you will find an alphabetical list. Select the first letter of your command and scroll down until you find the command you are searching, click on that command and a box will open that shows the location of the button explains the process for its use.

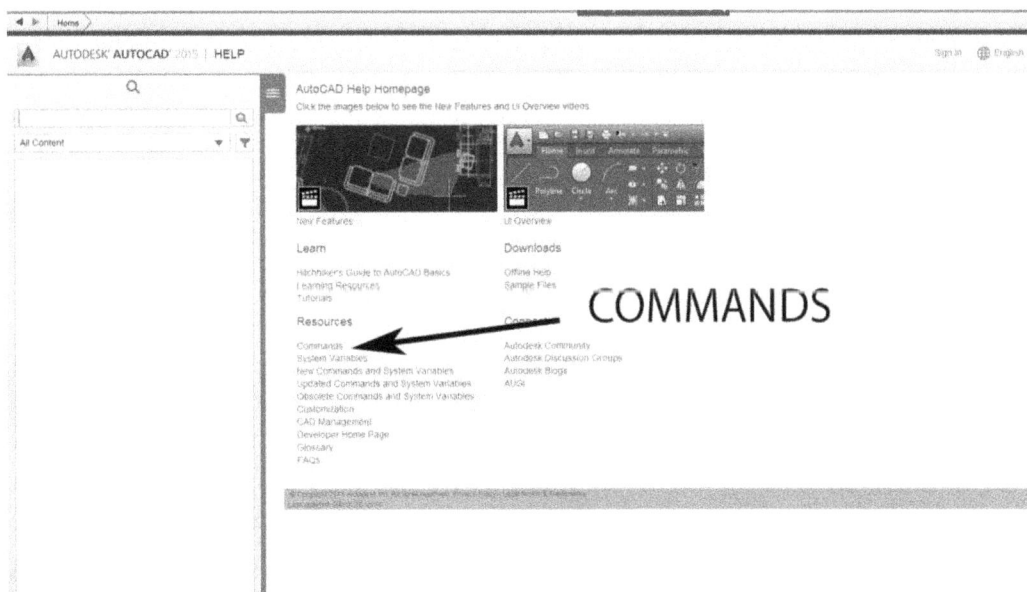

Fig 1-4

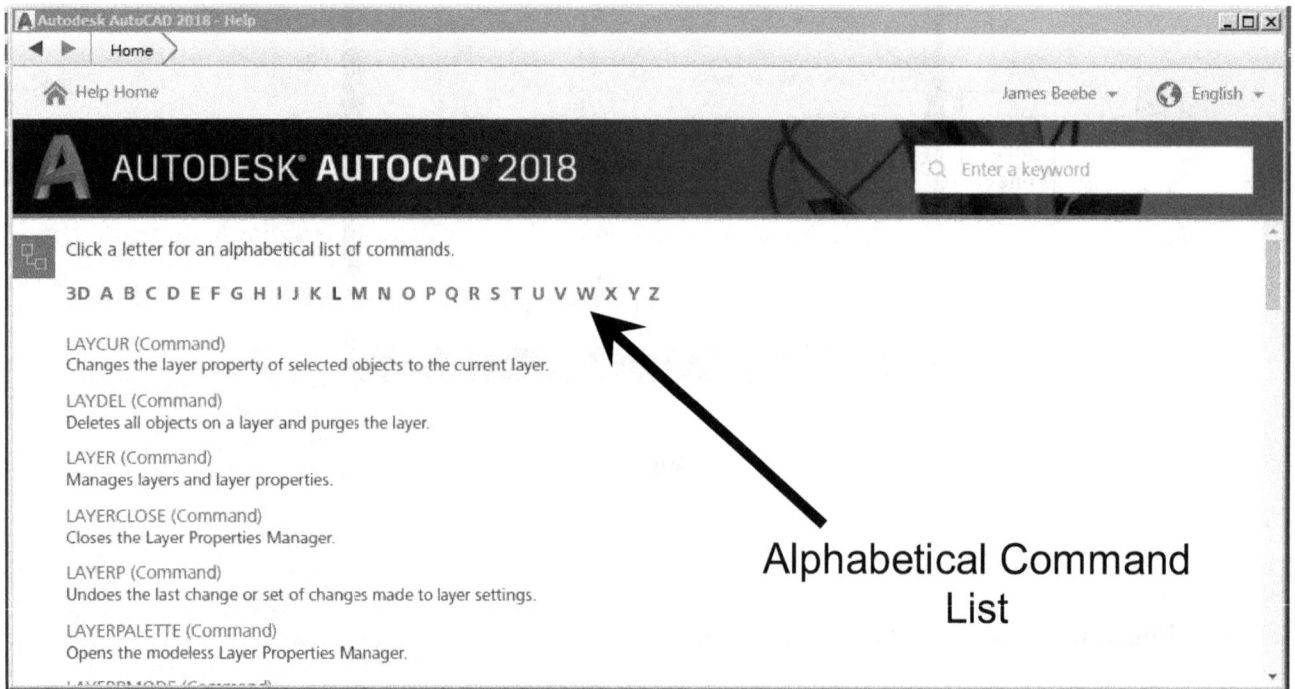

Fig 1-5

All the commands can be typed instead of clicking on the buttons (type the word for the command: **Line**, **Trim**, **Erase**, etc). However, if you type a command the procedures may be different than as described in this book. Most commonly you will need to press the enter key on your keyboard after you type the command. The **buttons equal: typed command + enter**. In this case the "enter" key sets the command in motion. Otherwise the typed command just sits in the command line waiting for some action.

If you lose the command line hold down the control button on your keyboard and press 9 on your keyboard. If this does not work type commandline and enter.

Down at the bottom of the screen you will see a row of buttons. If you **position** your **cursor** arrow **over** any of **them** and **do not click** (this is called: **hovering**) they will **tell you their names** (Fig 1-1). **Turn them** all **off, except** the **Ortho** and the **Object Snap** (we want these two turned on).

You can turn **Object Snap** on and off by pressing the **F3** key on your keyboard. The **Ortho** command can be turned on and off with the **F8** key. Object Snap is also called **Osnap**.

Now right click the **Object Snap** button. A selection box will open. Click on: **Open Object Snap Settings**.

A dialog box will open called **Drafting Settings** as shown in Fig 1-5A. Take a moment and look at the tabs at the top of this box. Here are the settings for the commands that are controlled by the buttons at the bottom of your screen as shown in Fig 1-1.

Select the **Object Snap** tab at the top. Turn on the following: **Endpoint, Midpoint, Intersection, and Perpendicular** (as shown by the leader arrows in **Fig 1-5A**). Turn off all other object snaps.

Click on the **OK** at the bottom to close the menu box.

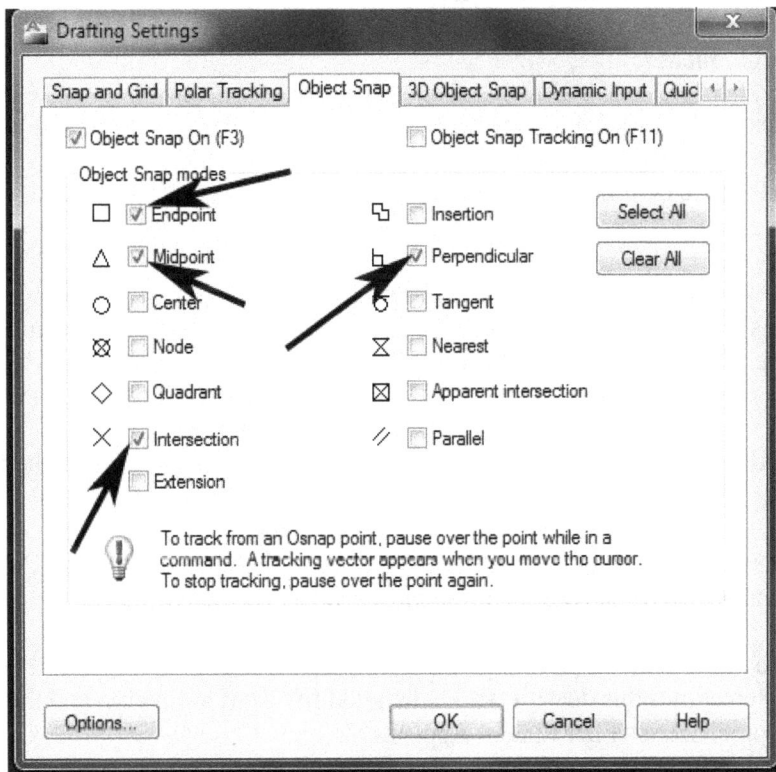

Fig 1-5A

Turn off the grids by clicking on the **Grid display** button in **Fig 1-1**.

1.2 Line

We are ready to draw the floor plans. Before we begin take a quick look at the completed floor plan so you know what we are doing. You will find them at the rear of this book in Appendix IV. Look at the last figure in this chapter (Fig 1-63) to see the drawing we are going to draw in this chapter.

Before we begin an **important notice**: the apostrophe symbol (') represents feet in the Imperial system. The quote symbol (") represents inches. As an example 12 foot is 12' and 6 inches is 6". 12 foot 6 inches is 12'6". **You must type the foot symbol after a number that represents feet** or you will get the default (which is inches). It is not necessary to type the inches symbol (") because **inches is the default** (though it won't hurt to use this symbol).

Let us take a moment and turn off the **UCS**. This is the X and Y coordinates graphic in the lower left of the screen.

On the ribbon click on the View tab. All the way to the left you will see the UCS Icon button. Click on it. The USC will disappear from the screen.

Often AutoCAD does not set the units that you select in the start-up. Check to make sure they are set correctly by typing the word: **units**. When the Drawing Units window opens set the **Type** to **Architectural** and set the **Units to scale inserted content** to **inches**.

On the **Draw** palette click on the **Line** button (click the Home tab to see the Draw palette).

If strange things start to happen, or you get into trouble, hit the **Escape** on your keyboard, or click on the Undo button (Fig 1-1), and try again.

After you click the **Line** button, move your cursor over into the drawing area. It will turn into a cross. (If it doesn't look like a cross see Appendix I—Cursor.) Click anywhere in the drawing area and move the cursor down. You will see a line. (This line should be locked into the vertical—straight up and down—if it is not, you must turn on the Ortho as detailed above). Now type: **27'** and press the **enter** key. Press **enter** a second time.

Type: **zoom** (all you need to do is type the first letter **z**—many commands only require the first letter of the word) and Enter (press the enter key on the keyboard).

At the **Command line** (Fig 1-1) at the bottom of the screen you will see a list of options. Type: **a** and **enter**. (As you type, look at the command line and read the prompts: **a** = all.)

Use your mouse wheel to zoom out a bit (see Appendix I—Mouse Wheel). You will see the vertical line you drew. It is 27 feet long. Sometimes this doesn't work when you first start a drawing and the line disappears when you enter. If you have a problem, see First Line in Appendix I.

Click on the **Line** button again. Position your cursor (the cross) at the upper end of the line and an object snap box will appear (Object Snap must be turned on). Click on this box. Move your cursor to the right a short distance. You will see a horizontal line. Type: **22'** then **enter**. Do not enter a second time as you did before.

You will see a 22' line. Move your cursor down and pull out a line. (If this doesn't work click on the Line button again). Type: **27'** and **enter**.

Now position the cursor near the bottom of this line and draw towards the left. When you get near the end of the original first line you should see a snap object icon. Click on this icon and hit **enter**. You should see Fig 1-6.

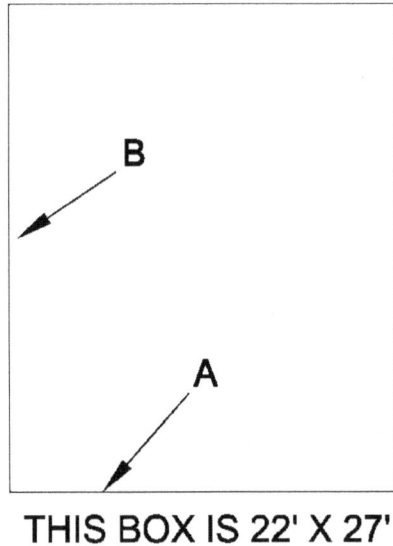

THIS BOX IS 22' X 27'

Fig 1-6

You do not need to click the Line button each time as long as the next line starts at the end point of the line you just drew. Just position the cursor near the end of the last line and pull out a new line in the direction that you want to draw. Watch the prompts that appear in the command line to see where you are in the sequence.

1.3 Offset

Click on the **Offset** button in the **Modify** section of the Home ribbon.

Type **5'** then **enter**. (Look down at the Command line when you type and read the prompts.) The cursor will turn into a box. Place that box over the lower horizontal line A in Fig 1-6. The line will illuminate; click on it. The cursor will turn back into a cross. Move the cursor up above line A a bit and click (anywhere above is fine). A new line will appear. It is 5 ft from the lower line. Press the escape key on the upper right corner of your keyboard.

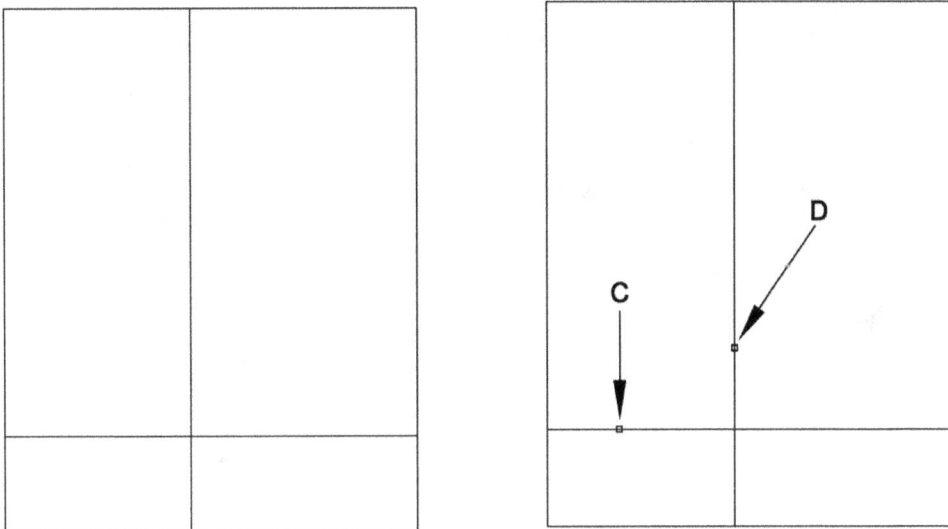

Fig 1-7

Click on the **Offset** button again. Type **10'** and **enter**. The cursor will turn into a box again. Position the box over the vertical line B in Fig 1-6. The line will illuminate. Click on that line. Move the cursor to the right a bit and click. A new vertical line will appear. Press the Escape key on your keyboard again. You will see the drawing on the left in Fig 1-7.

1.4 Trim

Click the **Trim** button on the Modify palette (it is co-located with Extend, see Appendix II for help). Press **enter** **(from here on <e> will mean to hit the enter key).** The cursor will turn into a box again. Position the box on the center vertical line somewhere near the middle as in D in Fig 1-7. It will illuminate. Click on it. It will erase the upper part of the line, leaving the lower five foot section.

Press the Escape key on your keyboard. The cursor will return to a cross. (Note: you must press the **enter** key on your keyboard immediately after you click the **Trim** button for it to function in this manner. If you do not hit enter right after you click on the Trim button it works in a different way—see Appendix I-Trim for an explanation.)

Click on **Trim** then <e> again and this time click on the point indicated by **C** in **Fig 1-7.**

Click on the **Line** button again. Position the cursor (cross) over the upper right corner (E in Fig 1-8) of the rectangle and click. Move the cursor to the right a little and type: **12' <e>**. A new horizontal line will appear.

Move the cursor down from the far right of that new line a bit and type: **22' <e>**. From the bottom of this line move the cursor to the left and when it gets near point F in Fig 1-8 click on the osnap icon that appears. Press the **Escape** key again. You will have a drawing that looks like Fig 1-8.

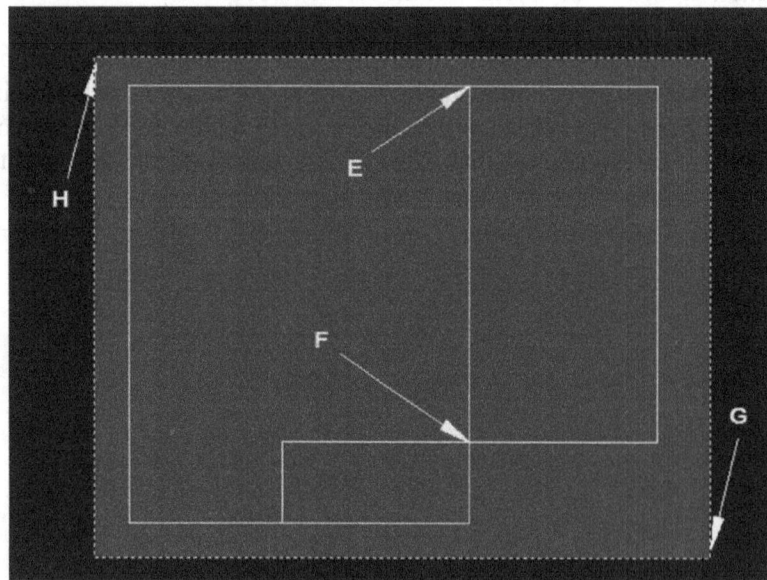

Fig 1-8

Zoom out by using the wheel on your mouse. (Sometimes AutoCAD locks up and won't scroll out. If this happens type: **zoom <e>** then: **a <e>**. Now the wheel should work.) Zoom out until the drawing is about a quarter as tall as the drawing area (see Fig 1-9).

Click on the **Copy** button On the Modify palette. The cursor will become a square (box). Position this cursor box to the right of the drawing a bit and down below the drawing a bit as shown by **G** in Fig 1-8. Press the left button on the mouse, release the mouse button (the cursor box will disappear) move the mouse up and to the left. A **green** window will form. Enlarge the green box until it covers the entire drawing and **click at approximately H** in Fig 1-8. Completely cover the drawing with the green box before you click the left mouse button again. The lines covered by the green selection window will be highlighted and the little cursor box will reappear. This indicates that all the lines that were inside the green selection window have been selected. Press **<e>** (enter). Read the prompts.

Now position the cursor somewhere in the center of the drawing you just selected and click. **Move** the cursor to the left of the drawing a distance more or less as you see in Fig 1-9 and click then <e>. Use the mouse wheel as needed to zoom out. This will make two separate views of the drawing. Press the **Escape** key. You will have two drawings and they will look (more or less) like Fig 1-9.

1.5 Selection windows

When you cover items with the green shadow box, like we just did, you must include all the parts of the drawing to be selected within the green shading. See Appendix I—Selection Window for an explanation of this. (There are other ways of selecting elements to be copied that we will discuss later.) If you end up with only part of the drawing copied then you will need to erase or undo the flawed copy and try again. Use the Undo button at the top of the screen (or Ctrl Z which is the typed command for Undo).

This second copy of our drawing will be used later to create other views of the plans (ie: Foundation).

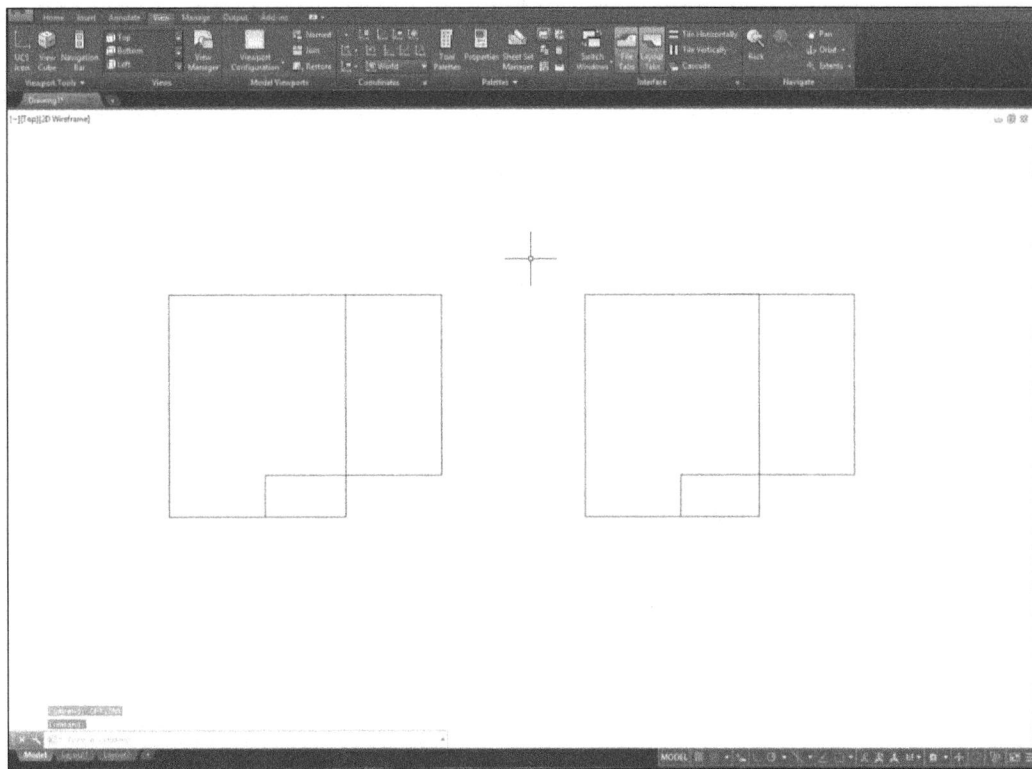

Fig 1-9

You can move around in the drawings by holding down the mouse wheel and **Panning** (Appendix I—Panning). Try this. Escape from all commands, place the cursor in the drawing area, hold down the mouse wheel and move

the mouse around. If you don't have a mouse with a wheel, buy one. It makes life so much easier in AutoCAD land. If you can't afford one then use the zoom features to move around (described a little later).
Let us return to our original drawing. Zoom in on the drawing to the right. Use the mouse wheel (place the cursor in the center of the drawing then turn the mouse wheel) to scroll in and enlarge it until it fills the page (see Appendix I—Zoom if you do not have a mouse wheel). Hold the mouse wheel down and pan the drawing until it is centered in the drawing space.

Let's add a new line. Click the **Offset** button. Type **6'6 <e>**. Position the cursor on the top horizontal line (**I** in Fig 1-10) and click. Move the cursor down below the line a bit and click. A new line will appear. Press the **Escape** (from now on to be abbreviated to **Esc**) button on the keyboard.

Add another line (for the stairwell—see the final floor plan if you need a reference). Click the **offset** button. Type **5' <e>**. Center the cursor box on the middle vertical line (J in Fig 1-10). It will illuminate. Click. Move the cursor to the left a bit and click. A new line will appear. Press **Esc** on the keyboard. Now the screen should look like Fig 1-10 (your drawing will not show the little boxes).

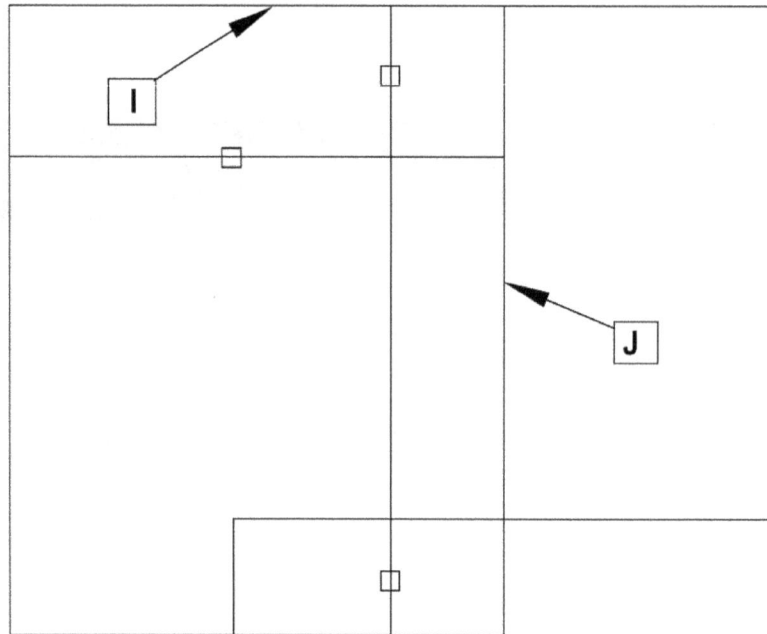

Fig 1-10

Now we will trim some more lines.

Click on **Trim** then immediately **<e>**. Position the cursor over one of the lines indicated by the **little boxes** as shown in Fig 1-10, click (do not enter after clicking on each of these points—just go on and click all the trim points). Click on all the points indicated by the boxes in Fig 1-10. Press the **Esc** button on the keyboard. You should now see Fig 1-11.

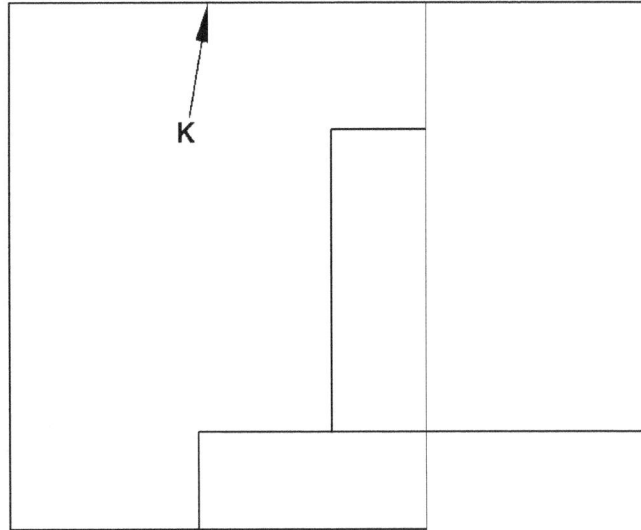

Fig 1-11

1.7 Walls

Figure 1-11 shows the outline of the first story floor plan. Now we will draw the wall thickness. Click the **Offset** button. **Type 3.5 <e>**. AutoCAD uses inches as the default. So if you enter feet you must designate this by using the feet sign: ('). For inches no sign is necessary. This measurement is inches.

Position the cursor on the top horizontal line (K) and click. Move the cursor down below this line and click. A new line will appear 3.5 inches below the top horizontal line. This is the thickness of that wall (nominally a 4" wall—but drawn at 3.5" because they are framed with 3.5" wide lumber).

Now let's repeat this process with all of the walls. Click Offset, position the box cursor over the far left line and click. It becomes highlighted. Move the cursor to the right of that line (any distance will do) and click. Repeat this process by drawing parallel lines on the sides of the single lines as shown in Fig 1-12. You will see that it is not necessary to hit the Offset button each time. The tool remains active until you press <e> or ESC. We are creating the thickness of the framed walls. Continue until you see Fig 1-12.

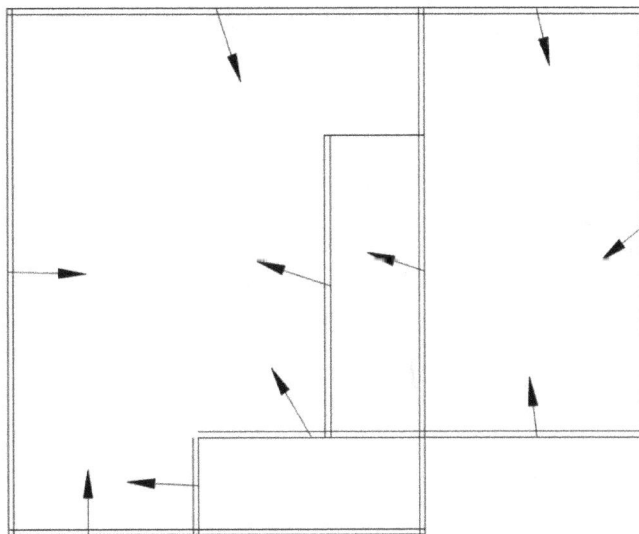

Fig 1-12

As always, do not get too caught up in the perfection of the details, if you miss something, or draw it incorrectly, you can fix it later. The main thing is to keep moving along and learn the commands and procedures. Precision and accuracy will come with practice.

Next we are going to clean up the inside corners of the walls. Click on **Trim <e>**.

Sometimes the buttons don't respond; if this happens double click them. Also you can always type any command.

Use the mouse wheel to zoom in on the upper left corner of this plan drawing. **Click** on the point indicated (approx.) by **L** in **Fig 1-13**.

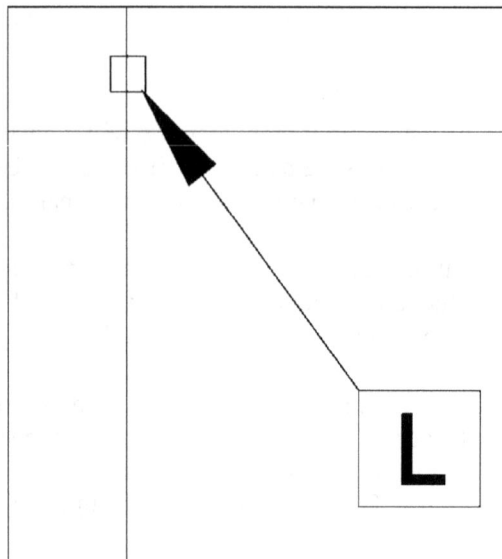

Fig 1-13

This will trim the line to the lower intersection of the lines as in Fig 1-16.

Use the **Trim** tool, position the cursor box over the lines in the rest of the corners, and trim the lines so that they all look like **Fig 1-16**. Remember to hit the enter key <e> **immediately after clicking** on the **trim button**.

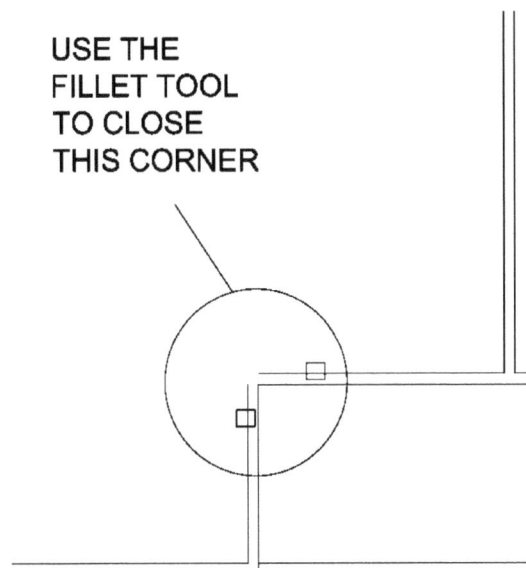

USE THE
FILLET TOOL
TO CLOSE
THIS CORNER

Fig 1-14

1.8 Fillet

To close up the open corner in Fig 1-14 use the **Fillet** tool on the modify palette.

Click the **Fillet** button on the Home ribbon. At the command line it will prompt you for options. Read the Command Line. Type: **r** <e>. This selects the radius setting.

With many of these prompts typing the first letter of the word is sufficient to choose that option. The command line will ask you to specify radius. Type **0** (zero) <e>.

 Now it will prompt you to: **select the first object or**... Type **m** (for multiple) <e>. The cursor will change to a selection box again. Click on each of the two lines at the boxes shown in Fig 1-14. The corner will close (square). **ESC**.

Let's make a copy of this working drawing, as we did before. Click the **Copy** button. Enclose the main drawing that you have been working on with a **green selection** window and make a copy to the right so that the screen looks like Fig 1-15. To do this click **copy**, then click the cursor to the **lower right** of the floor plan, then **draw** the **green shading** up and to the left until the entire floor plan is covered, **click again** to select the floor plan. Next **click** the cursor in the middle of the floor plan and then **click** again in the **open space to the right**. This is an approximate location (the exact location is not important). We will use this new copy for the second story floor plan and the framing plans.

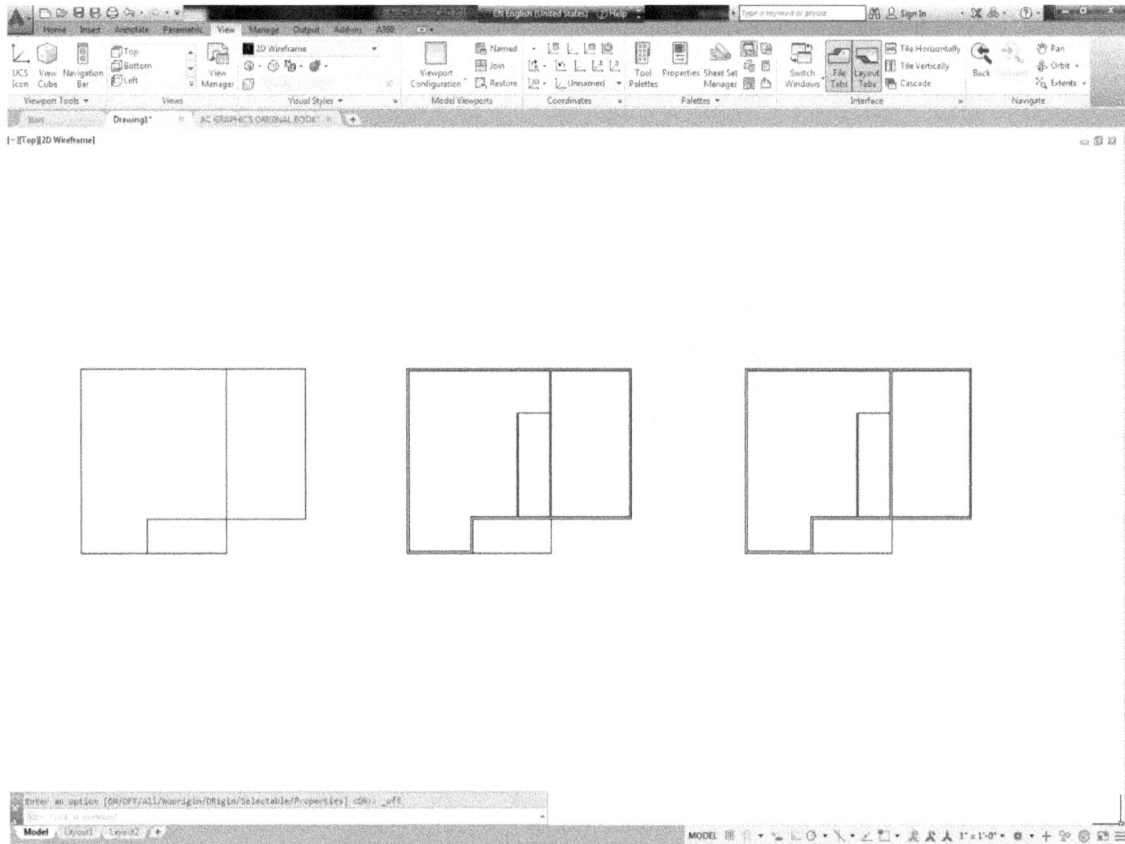

Fig 1-15

Sometimes the mouse wheel zoom will lock up and not zoom out enough. If this happens use the **Zoom** command –type **z<e>** then type **a <e>**. Now the mouse wheel should work.

1.9 Zoom

Take a minute and play around with the zoom options. Try some of the buttons on the **Navigate** panel. Click on the **View** tab. Right click anywhere on the panel and select **Show Panels**. Select the Navigate option. The navigate panel will appear on the ribbon. Click on the arrow in the lower right corner. Click on the **Extents** button. The entire drawing should appear. (There is a drop down menu next Extents, click it to see options.)

Now click on the **Window** button in that same menu. Then click the mouse at the lower corner of one of your three drawings. Use the mouse to create a selection box around a part of the drawing by clicking on the screen and moving the cursor up diagonally and click. You can always use the ESC button and the Undo button at the top of the screen to go back if you get in trouble.

It is faster to type these commands. Type z for zoom (read the Command Line) and then the first letter of the type of zoom (as in w for window).

The Zoom Window is useful, especially when used with Zoom All. But ninety percent of the time I use the mouse wheel for zooming. See the info in Appendix I—Zoom for more on the subject of Zooming.

Your working drawing should now look like Fig 1-16 (minus the text—the text is for temporary reference).

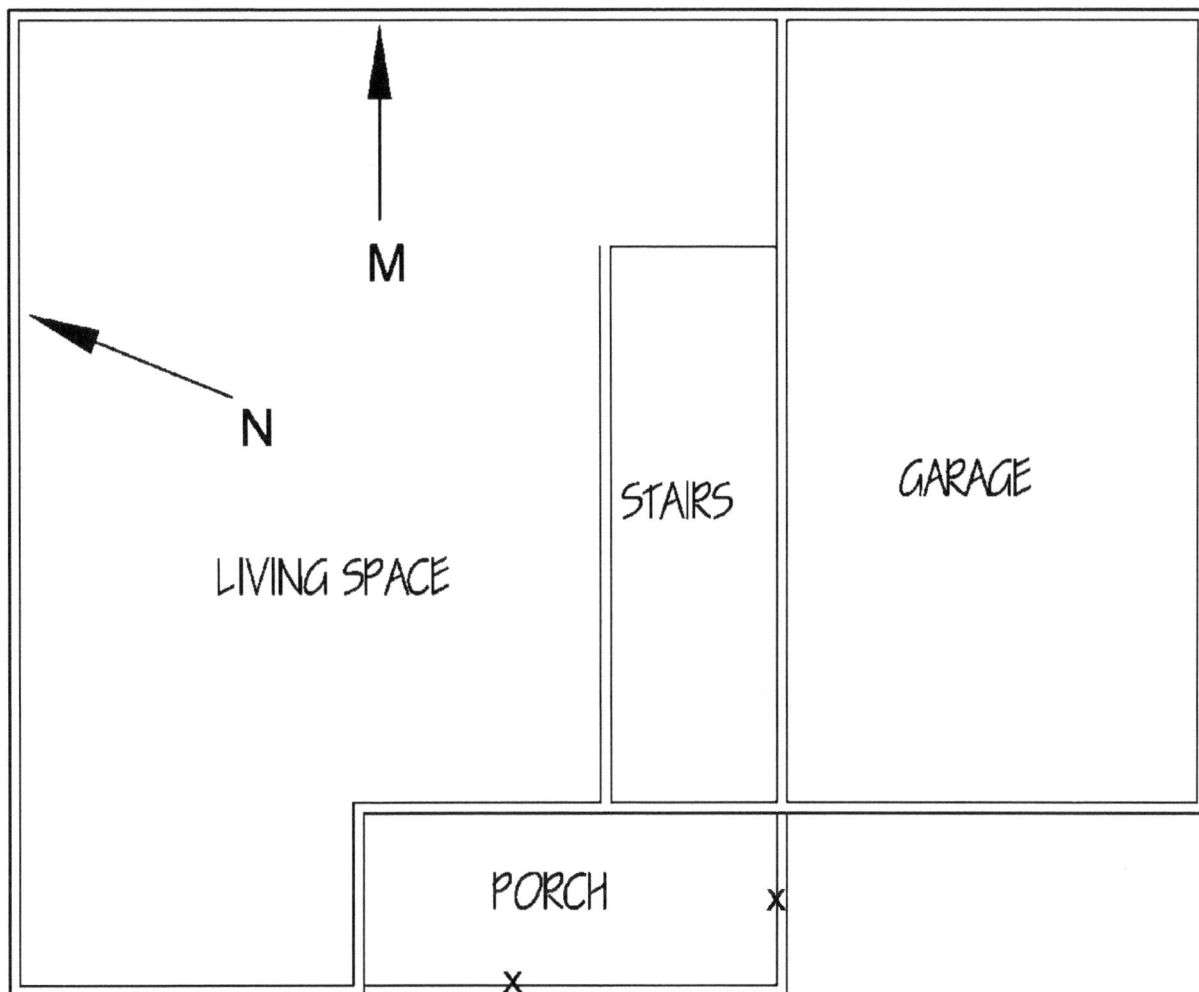

Fig 1-16

Erase the **lines** marked with **X's** in Fig 1-16. Click on them and then click the right button on the mouse. Select **Erase** from the menu that appears.

You can erase in a number of different ways. You can use the **delete** key on your computer keyboard, or click the **Erase** button in the Modify panel or enter erase at the command line. You can also select an item then right click and select the erase option.

You can select multiple objects and erase them in a group.

1.10 Kitchen

Click on the **Offset** button (Home tab/Modify palette). Type **24 <e>** (this will indicate inches—the default). Click on the inside line of the wall at the top of the living space shown as **M** in **Fig 1-16**. Move the cursor down and **click inside** the living space. Repeat the process with the wall to the left of the living space (N in Fig 1-16). **Esc**.

Click on the Offset button again and type **8'8 <e>**. Click on the new horizontal line (O in Fig 1-17) and click below that line to create new line (P).

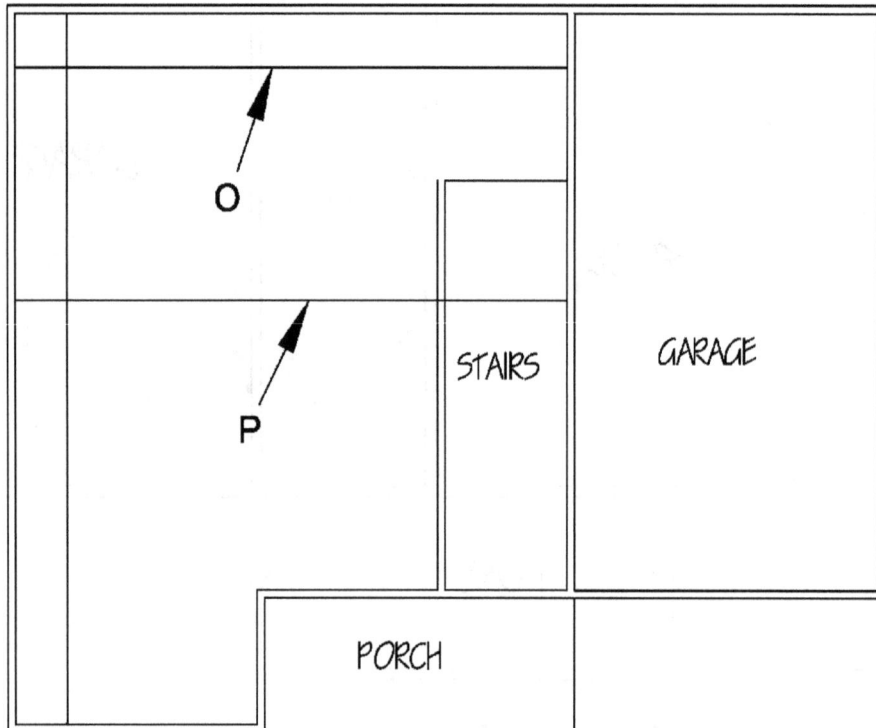

Fig 1-17

Click on **Trim <e>**. Trim the lines so that they look like **Fig 1-18**. If you make a mistake, use the Undo button and try again.

Escape.

Click on the line marked with an **X** in Fig 1-18 and **erase** it.

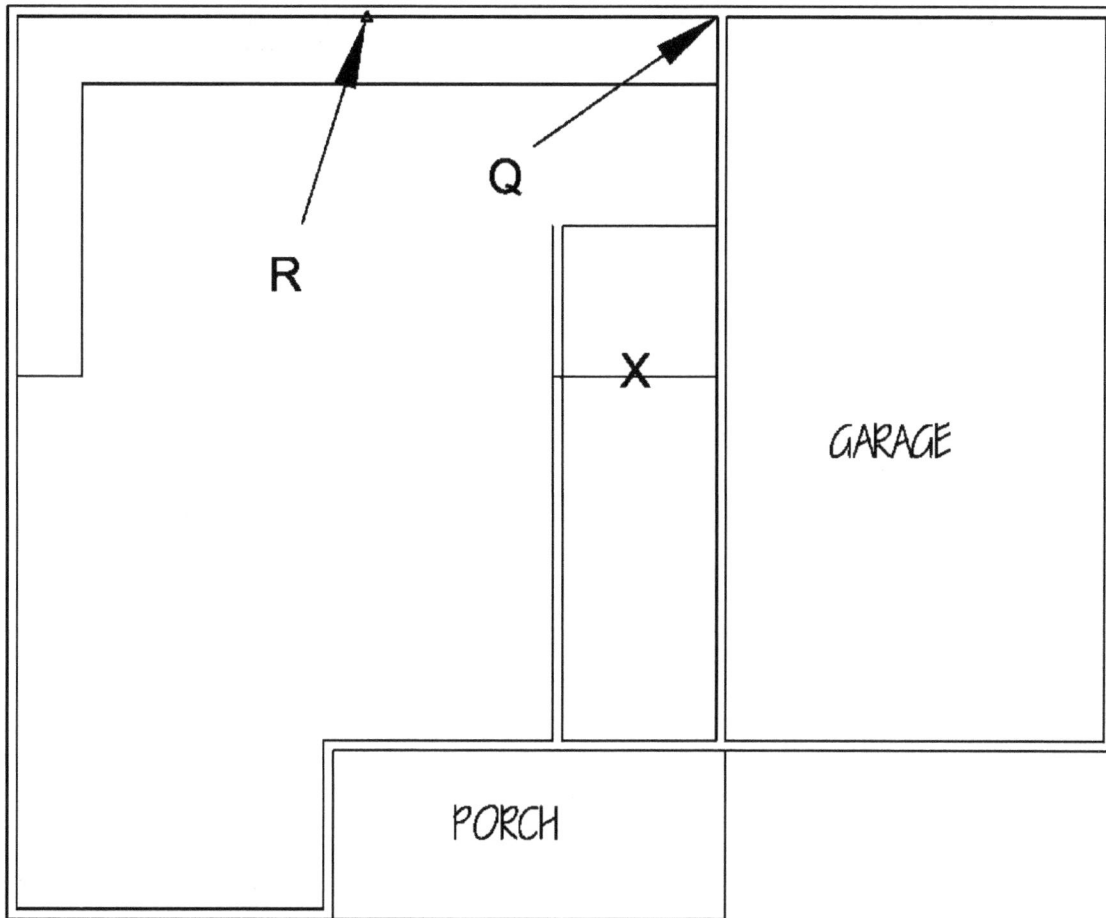

Fig 1-18

1.11 Offset Start Point of Line

Click on the **Line** button. Hold **down the Shift key on your keyboard and right click the mouse**. Click on the **From** selection. Now **click** on the inside corner point as marked **Q** in **Fig 1-18**. **Move** the cursor (now a cross) to the left along the horizontal line to point **R** and you will see a triangle icon (this is a snap object icon indicating the **midpoint** of this line). Do **not click on point R**, just let go of the mouse and let the cursor hover over the triangular Osnap icon. Type **7'5 <e>**. **Move** the **cursor down** the screen and **a line will appear** with a starting point at 7'5" from point Q. Pull the line down a ways, **do not click**. Type **3' <e>**. Hit **ESC**.

Sometimes when you make lines using the From function they do not attach correctly to the intended starting point. Zoom in and see if the line is attached to the horizontal wall. If it is not attached then undo and try again or see the Appendix I—Snap From.

Click on the **Offset** button. Type **3.5 <e>**. Click on the line that we just drew and click to the left of it to create a new short wall. At the bottom connect the ends to create the wall end as in **Fig 1-19** (use the Line button).

Trim the lines at the **X**'s in **Fig 1-19** (**you must press enter right after you click the trim button or it will not work as a trimming tool**). Escape and **erase** the line marked with an **O**. It will now look like Fig 1-20.

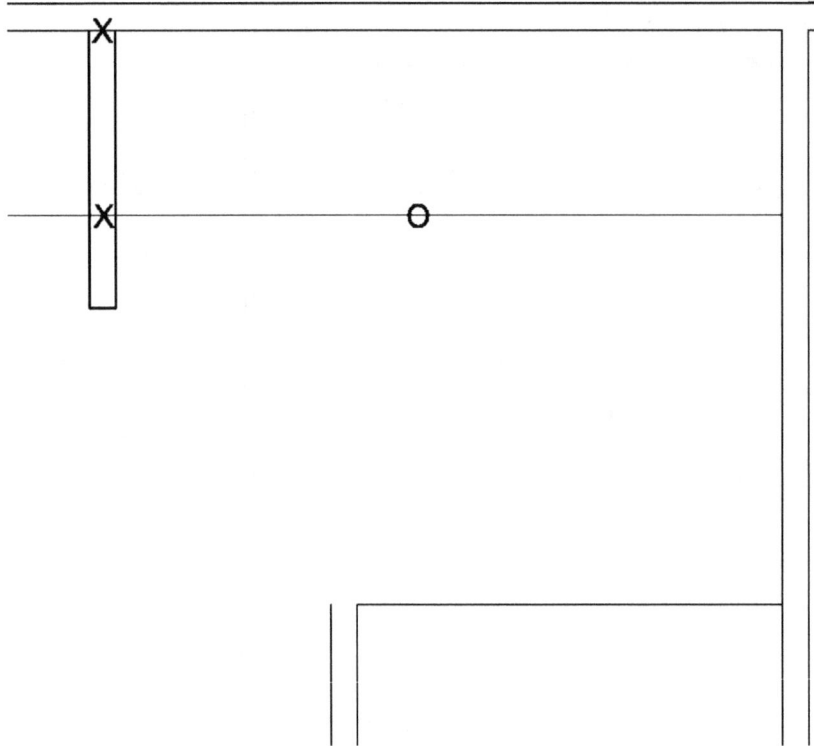

Fig 1-19

The new lines inside the living space at 24" offset represent the lower kitchen cabinets. Look at the finished floor plan in Appendix IV (or Fig 1-63) to see what we are drawing.

1.12 Rectangle

Now we will create the sink and the range.

Click on the **Rectangle** button on the **Draw** palette. It is in the upper right corner and shares a button with Polygon.

Click on the empty space somewhere in the middle of the living space (see Fig 1-20). Look at the command line. It prompts for a response (Area/Dimensions/Rotation). Do not move the mouse—your typing will automatically be entered into the Command line window. **Type d <e>. Type 30 <e>. Type 24 <e>. Click** (this last click sets the rectangle in place). **Make a copy** of the **rectangle**—so we have two as in Fig 1-20. Read the prompts as you follow these instructions. The **d** selects the **Dimensions** option (this is the most common method to create a rectangle). Then the numbers you enter are the dimensions (with the horizontal dimensions first, then the vertical).

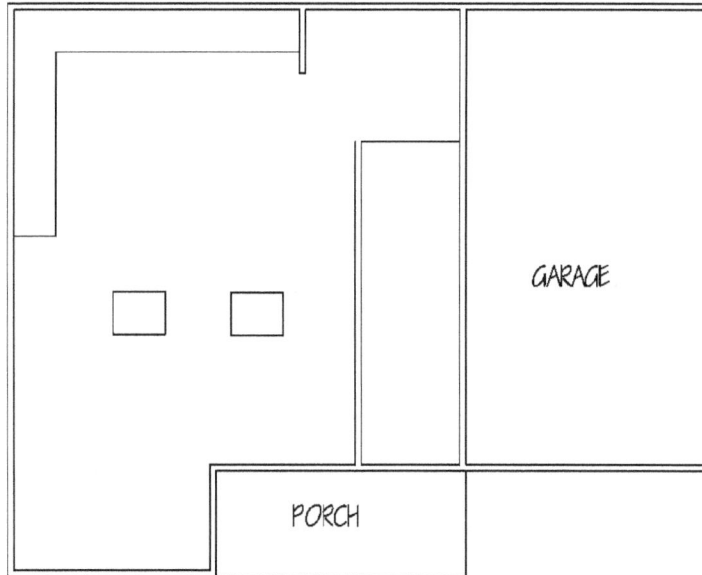

Fig 1-20

1.13 Rotate

Click on the **Rotate** button on the **Modify** palette. **Click on any line** of the rectangle on the left to select it and <e>. Read the prompts. The command line will read: **Specify base point. Click** (anywhere) **inside** the selected rectangle. **Type 90 <e>**. The box will now be at a 90 degree angle to its original orientation.

1.14 Move

Click on the **Move** button on the **Modify** palette. **Click on any line** of the box you just rotated, then <e>. **Click** on the **mid point object snap icon** as shown in step 1 of **Fig 1-21**. Move the rectangle around a bit. You will see that it will only move at right angles. We want to release the box to move free from this right angle constraint, so we will turn off the **Ortho**. Press the **F8** key. This will turn off the **Ortho** function (and the Ortho button at the bottom of your screen will un-highlight or pop out).

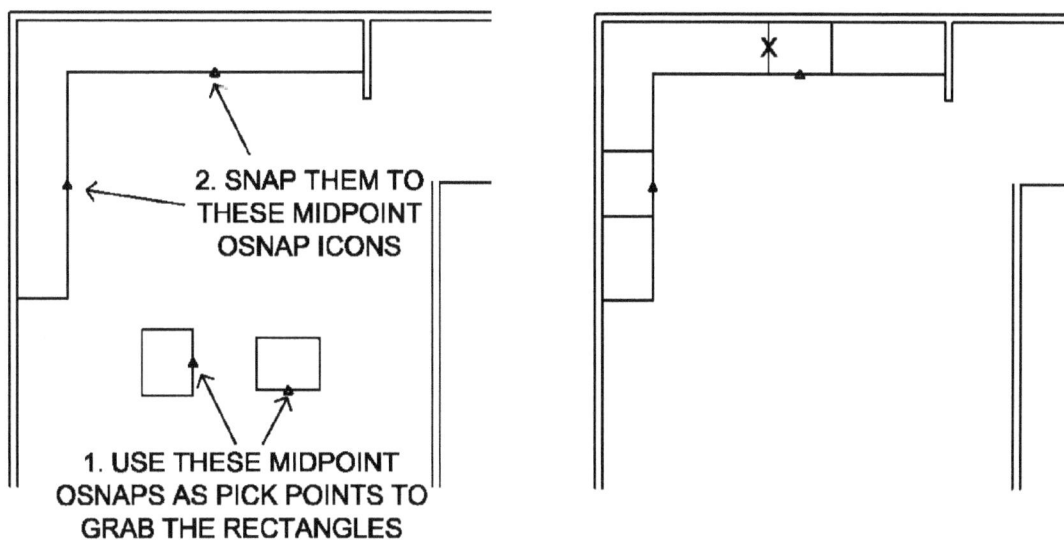

Fig 1-21

Move the rectangle and **snap it** to the kitchen counter at the center of the vertical section of the kitchen counter (the triangle to the right shown as step 2 in Fig 1-21) snap to the object snap **triangle icon** at the midpoint of the line shown. When you approach the midpoint of a line (with the midpoint osnap turned on) a small green triangle will appear. Click on this and the rectangle will copy to this point. It will **"snap to"** this point.

Now click on the **Move** button again and **select** the other **rectangle** (not rotated). **Grab** it by the middle of the lower line by clicking on the **triangle** icon (midpoint icon as shown in step 1). **Move** it up and place it on the center of the horizontal cabinet line at the midpoint icon for that line. Your kitchen cabinets will look like the right half of Figure 1-21 (minus the triangles).

Click on **Offset**. Type **3 <e>**. Click on the left vertical line marked X in the right drawing of Fig 1-21. Click in the center of the rectangle. **Esc**. This will create a parallel set of lines inside the rectangle as in Fig 1-22.

Click on the **Fillet** button on the **Modify** palette. Type **r <e>**. Type **2 <e>**. Then **m <e>**. Read the Command Line as you type, you will see that you are choosing the **first letter** of the various options offered. Click on the corners of the inside rectangle that you just created as shown in Fig 1-22 to create a radius corner at each corner.

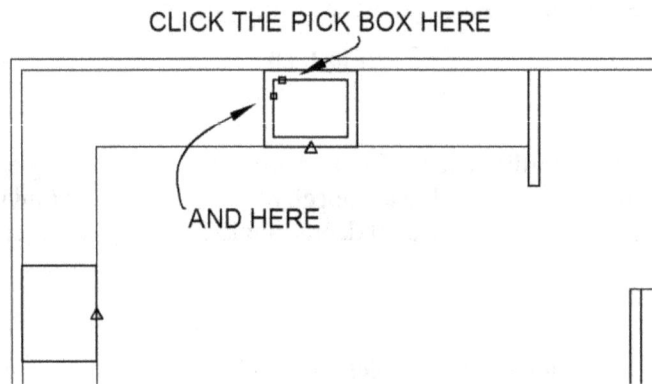

Fig 1-22

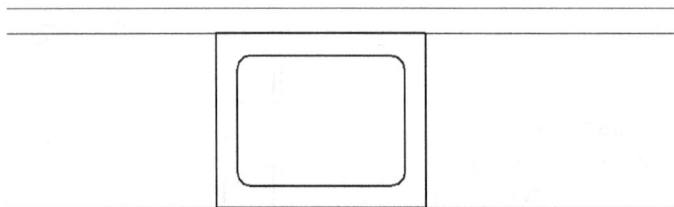

Fig 1-23

Click on the other corners of the rectangle; continue until the rectangle looks like Fig 1-23. This is the sink.

Now let's make the other rectangle into a stove. Let's find the center of the rectangle by drawing two lines that start and end at the midpoints as in Fig 1-24.

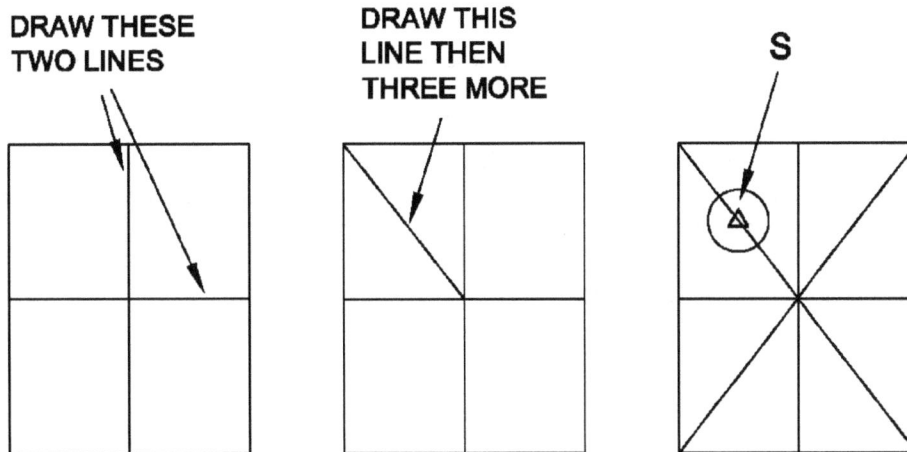

Fig 1-24

Now draw **four separate diagonal lines** as shown to the right in Fig. 1-22. (***They must be four separate lines to make this work, so don't cheat by drawing this with just two lines***). We will use these diagonal lines to find the center of each quarter of the rectangle by snapping to the center of each diagonal line.

Click on the **Circle** button on the **Draw** palette. Click on the **midpoint osnap icon** at S in **Fig 1-24**. Type **d <e>**. Type **6 <e>. ESC.**

Click on the **Copy** button and then **click** on the **edge** of your new **circle** and **<e>**. Grab the circle at the **center** by clicking on the **triangle** icon. Now copy the **circle** to the **center** of the other **three diagonal lines. ESC.**

Now **erase** the **diagonal lines** and the lines that cross the center of the rectangle. Your drawing will look like Fig 1-25.

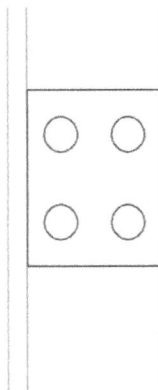

Fig. 1-25

1.15 Chimney

Now we are going to create the chimney and fireplace. Click on **Offset**. Type **8' <e>**. (Don't forget the ' symbol—you will get inches by default—you want feet.) **Click** on the lowest horizontal line at **T** in **Fig 1-26**. Move the mouse **up** and **click.** Right click the mouse and select **Enter** from the short cut menu box. This is a quick way of doing Enter. If no short cut box appears or one that doesn't include an **Enter** option then you can just press **<e>** on your keyboard (and see Appendix I—Mouse settings).

Click **Offset**. Type **12'** **<e>**. Click on the lowest horizontal line (**T** in **Fig 1-26**) again and then click again **up above** it and **<e>**.

Click **Offset** again. Type **18** **<e>**. Click on the vertical line to the left (**U** in **Fig 1-26**) and then to the **left** of that line and **<e>**.

There is another way to do repeated tasks, like three offsets in a row. Instead of the final enter in the above steps right click the mouse and a shortcut menu will give you some options, the top option will be **Repeat** the last command, click on it. You can also use this to access a list of other commands. Check it out.

Using this flyout menu can speed up your drawing.

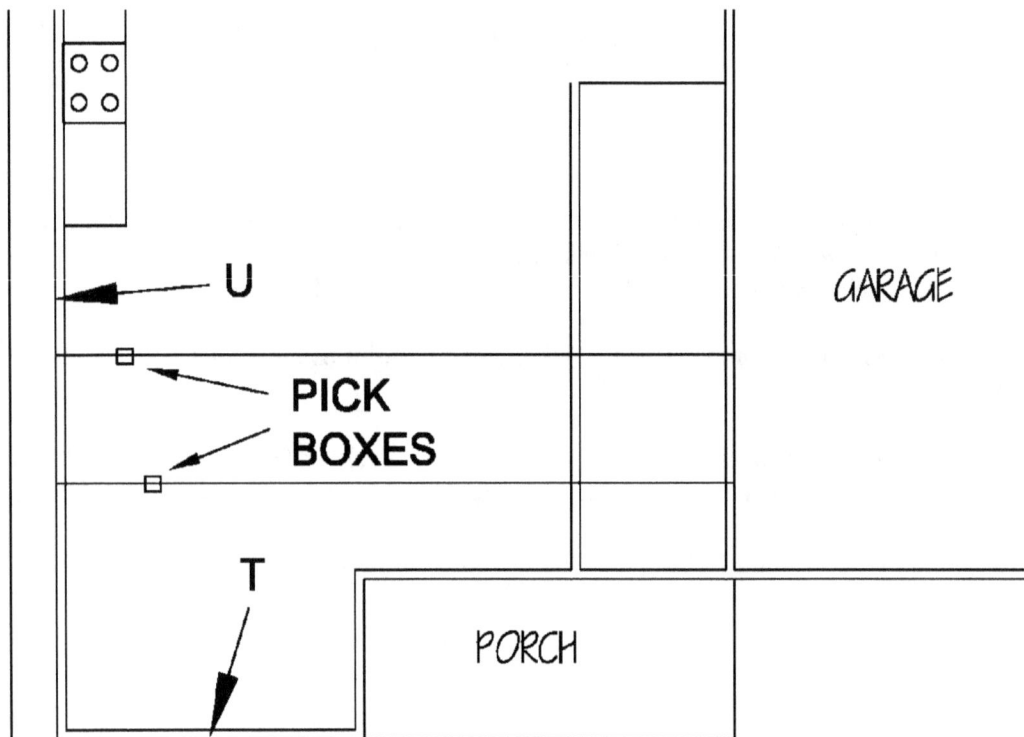

Fig 1-26

Your drawing should now look like Fig 1-26 (minus the references, pick boxes, and leaders).

1.16 Extend

Click on the **Extend** (co-located with trim) button on the **Modify** palette then **<e>** (you can right click the mouse to **enter**—with this function—if your mouse is set up this way. See Appendix I—Mouse settings). Click on the **lines** shown in **Fig 1-26** by the pick boxes. **ESC**. The lines should extend over to meet the new vertical line at 18" beyond the wall line as in Fig 1-27.

Extend is one of the more persnickety of the commands and sometimes it does not work the first time. If it doesn't work try clicking closer to the end of the line and, if that doesn't work, try again by escaping and re-clicking the Extend button then immediately press the enter key. See Appendix I—Extend for help.

Now your drawing should look like Fig 1-27.

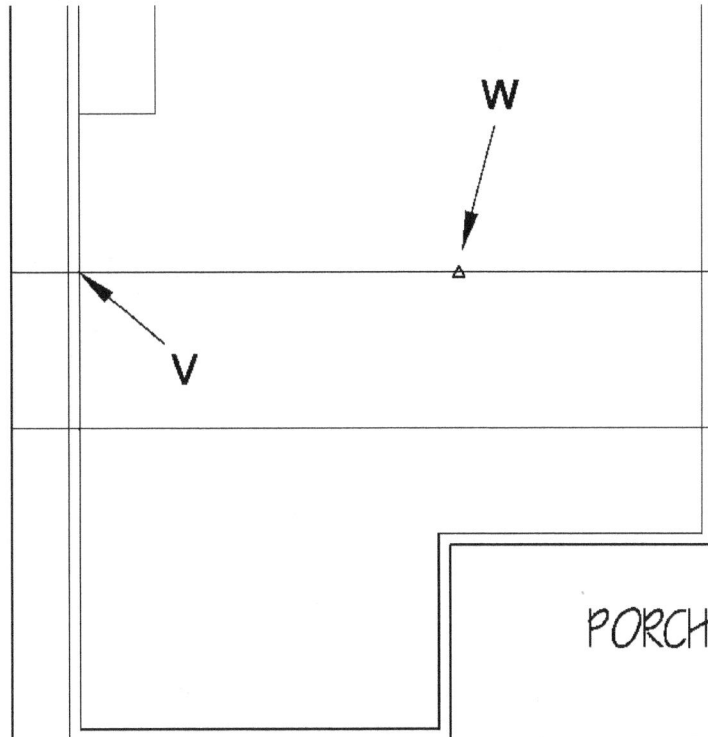

Fig 1-27

Click on **Line**. Hold down the Shift key on your keyboard and right click the mouse to bring up the Osnap menu. Select **From**. Now **click** on the intersection at **V** in **Fig 1-27. Move** the **cursor** to the **right along line W** in **Fig 1-27** until you **hover (don't click)** over the **midpoint** Osnap icon (triangle). Type **8.5 <e>**.

Turn the **Ortho on** (F8). Move the **cursor down** and to the **left** until a **vertical line appears**. You should have a stretchy line that **starts** at 8.5 inches to the right of point V. Pull the line down until you intersect with the line below. A **perpendicular osnap icon** should appear. **Click** on it. Then **ESC**. Now it will look like **Fig 1-28** (minus the text and boxes).

Sometimes the line created with the From command doesn't attach to the perpendicular line at the starting point. Then when you try to trim (as you will in the next step) it doesn't trim. If this happens erase the new line and try again or use the Extend command to attach it.

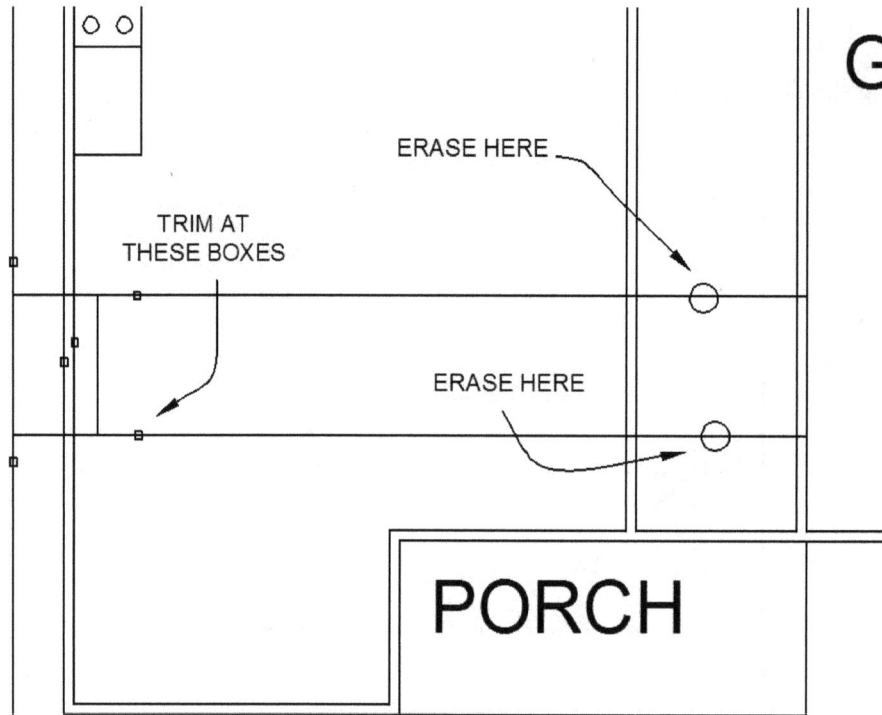

Fig 1-28

Click on **Trim <e>** and trim the **lines** at all the little boxes as shown in **Fig 1-28**. After you trim, **erase** what is left of the lines as shown in **Fig 1-28**. You will see Fig 1-29.

Fig 1-29

Click **Offset**. Type **5 <e>**. Click on the **top horizontal line** of this rectangle. Click below that line and **<e>**.

Right click and a menu will appear. Click on **Repeat Offset** (or use the old method and just click Offset). Type **14 <e>**. Click on the **top horizontal line** of the rectangle again. Click below. **Esc**. You will now see the two offset lines shown in Fig 1-30 (minus the diagonal line).

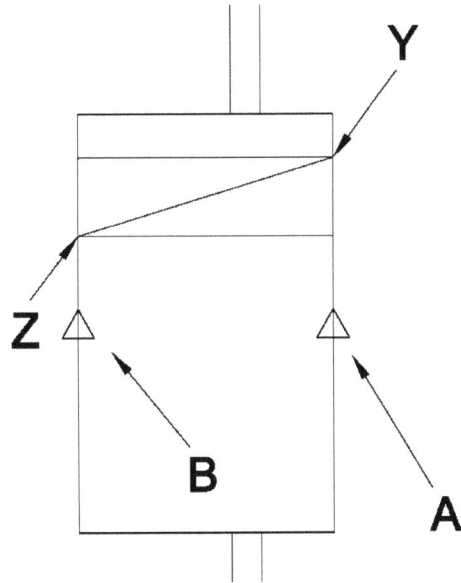

Fig 1-30

Turn the **Ortho off**. Draw a **line** from **Y** to **Z** in **Fig 1-30**. **Esc**.

Click on the **Mirror** button on the **Modify** palette. The Command Line reads: **Select Objects**. Click on the new diagonal **line YZ**. Then **<e>**. The Command Line reads: **Specify first point of mirror line**. Click on the middle of the right side of the rectangle on the **midpoint icon** that will appear when your cursor approaches the point shown as **A** in **Fig 1-30**. Move the cursor to the left and **click** on the middle of the other side of the rectangle (**point B**). Then **<e>**. You will see Fig 1-31.

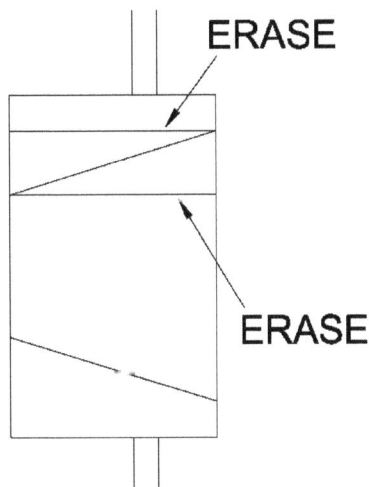

Fig 1-31

Erase the **lines** as shown in **Fig 1-31**. Click **Offset**. Type **3.5 <e>**. **Click** on the **sides** of this **rectangle** and create walls inside the rectangle to look like **Fig 1-32** (minus the boxes).

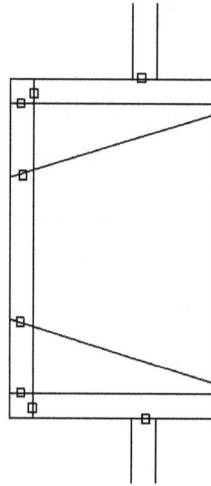

Fig 1-32

Trim the lines at the points marked with the **boxes** shown in **Fig 1-32**. The fireplace will now look like it does in Fig 1-34.

1.17 Door Openings

Now we will create the door openings. Click **Line** then hold down the shift key and right click the mouse. **Select From in the menu that opens. Click** on the upper left corner as marked **C** in **Fig 1-33**. Move the cursor down that same line to where it shows an **endpoint** icon at the chimney (point **D**). Hover over this icon, **do not click.** Type **11'6 <e>**. Turn the **Ortho on**. Draw a line to the right and connect to the **perpendicular** point icon on the other side of the wall at **E** in **Fig 1-33**. **Esc.** Zoom in. Click **Offset.** Type **32 <e>**. Click on the line you just drew and **click below** to draw the line at **F** in **Fig 1-33**.

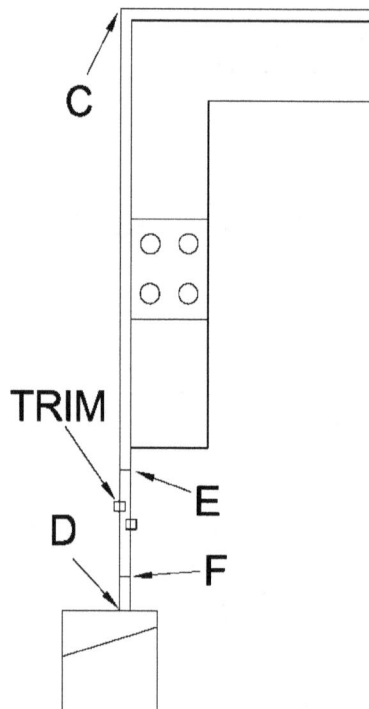

Fig 1-33

Trim the lines at the boxes shown in **Fig 1-33**. This is a door opening. Now we will **repeat** the process to create the door openings as shown here in **Fig 1-34**.

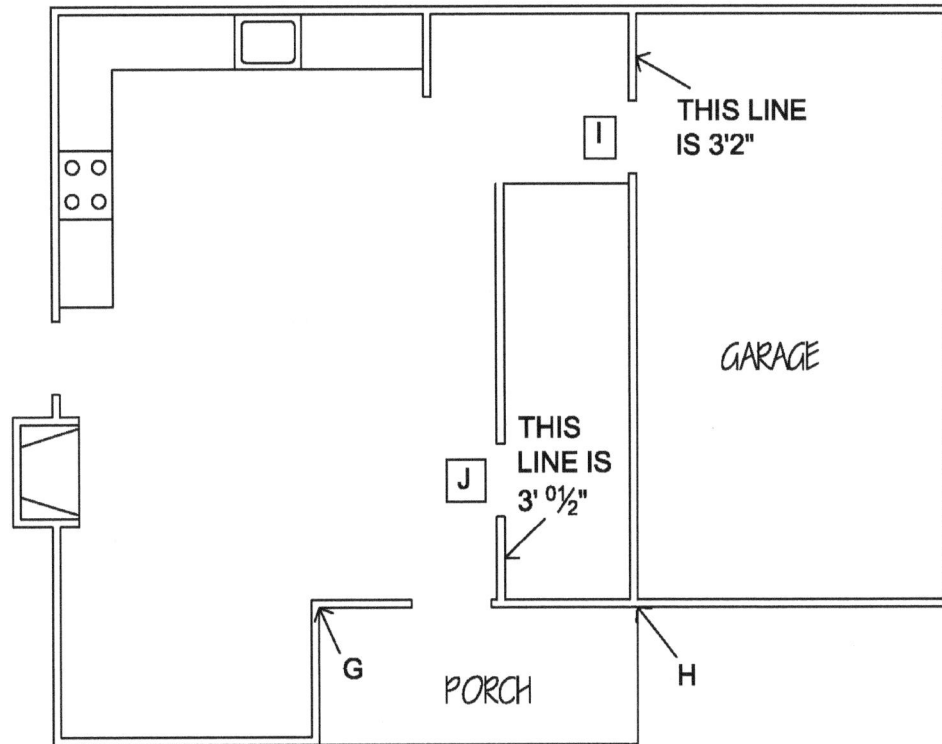

Fig 1-34

To create the lower door opening use **Line** then **From** (Shift + right click) and click on point **G** in **Fig 1-34** then **hover** over the osnap icon that appears when you approximate point **H** (do not click here—just hover). Type **6'6** <e>. Attach the line to the other side of the wall as shown. Use the **Offset** tool to draw the other side of the door opening at **36 inches** offset, then trim the opening. This is the front door to the house.

Use the **Line** and the **From** buttons for the first line of all the openings. Use the **measurements** shown in **Fig 1-34** to draw the first line of each door opening. The dimensions shown are the offset for the first point of the door opening lines. They indicate the length of the lines shown after you trim for the opening.

The dimension that reads 3'-0 ½" is typed 3'0.5 <enter> (also 36.5 or 3' 01/2 works). Draw the first line, then use the Offset button to create the line at the other side of each door opening. The **door opening** sizes are all **32"** except the lower (**front**) **door** which is **36"**. Use the **trim** to remove the **lines** inside the door openings.

Now let's add the doors. Turn the **Ortho off**. Click **Line**. Click at point **K** in **Fig 1-35**. **Type: @32<315** <e>. **ESC.** This is a new way to draw a line. The **32** is the **length** of the line and **315** is the **angle**. This is the easiest way to draw lines that are a specific length and at a specific (non right) angle. (See Appendix I—Polar Coordinates for an explanation).

Let's create the door swing arc. Click on **Circle** on the **Draw** palette. **Click** on **K** then **L** in **Fig 1-35**. You will see Fig 1-35. Make sure you click on the intersections and not the midpoints.

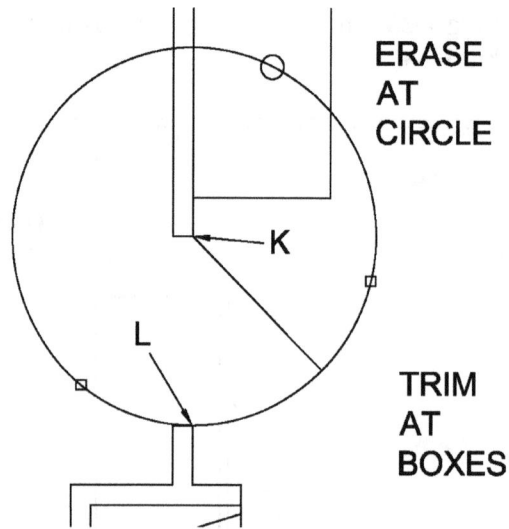

Fig 1-35

Trim the circle at the **boxes** and **erase** the remaining line at the **circle**. Now repeat this process for the other doors.

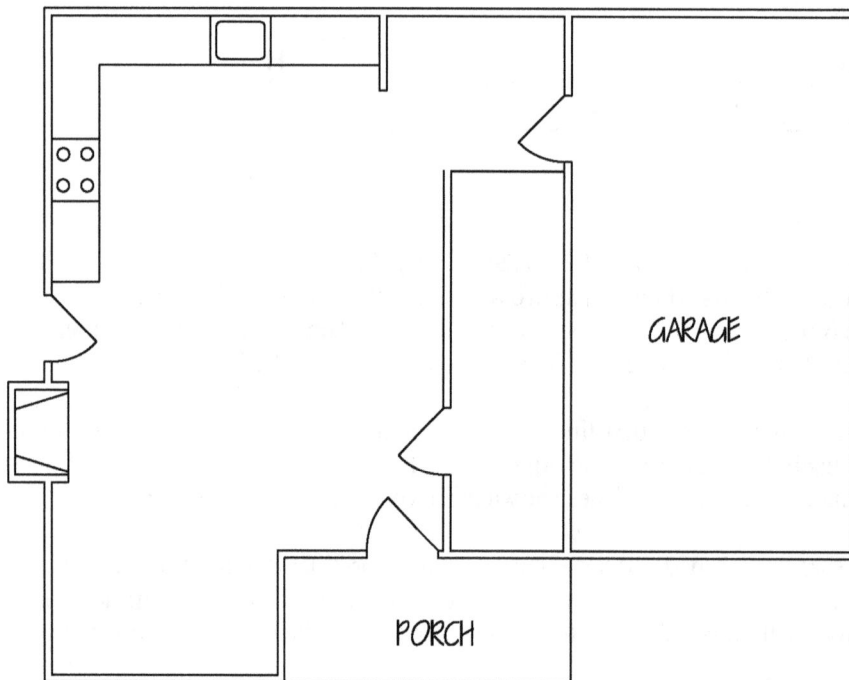

Fig 1-36

Remember the front door is 36". The measurements and angles that you need are: **@32<225** then **<e>** at the upper garage door **I** in **Fig 1-34**, **@32<225** then **<e>** for door **J** in **Fig 1-34**, and **@36<135** then **<e>** for the **front door**. Create the **arcs** for each door following the steps as before. You will see Fig 1-36.

When you input measurements you can always enter them as inches (you don't need to use feet). So the Offset from measurements that we used here for the first line of the bath door opening could be **36.5** or **3'0 ½ or 3'0.5**. **Remember inches** do **not need to be identified** because inches is the **default unit** of measure—no entry for units means inches.

1.18 Windows

Now we will draw the windows. First we will create a new layer. **Layers** in AutoCAD (as in a number of different graphic programs) are essentially a series of transparencies overlaying each other. They can be turned on and off for a variety of purposes, some of which we will explore as we go along.

To create a new layer find the **Layer Properties** button (see **Fig 1-37**). **Click it**. It may take a moment to respond. A **dialog** box will open that looks like **Fig 1-37**. You can expand this window by grabbing the side border when a double arrow line appears, hold down the left mouse button and pull. Also the border at the bottom down.

Fig 1-37

Click on the **New Layer** button as shown in **Fig 1-37**. A new line will appear. In the **Layer Name** window type: **windows <e>** to give it a name. Click on the **Line Color** where it says **white** or **w….** A **Select Color** box will open. Click on the **Index Color** tab at the top and select a **red box**. Click the **Okay** button at the bottom. Close the Layer Properties Manager by clicking on the x in the upper left corner.

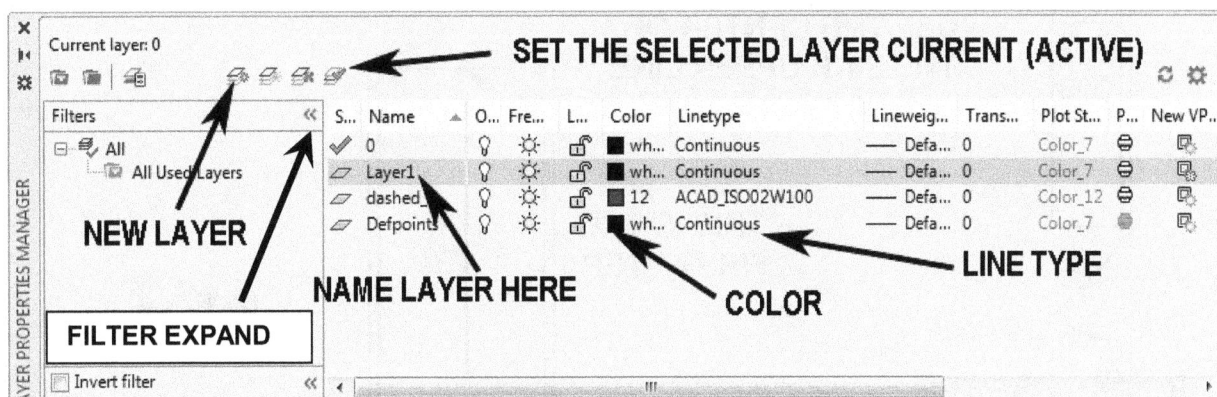

Back in the AutoCAD main screen click on the **Layer Control** window as shown in **Fig 1-38**.

Fig 1-38

A drop down box will appear. **Click** on the **Window** line. Now the layers box will show the **Windows layer**. It will be set as the **current layer** (to use the correct jargon). If all layers are not shown expand the Filter window (Fig 1-37), click All, then All Used Filters.

Fig 1-39 contains all of the information that you need to draw the windows. In each case, start with the center line as indicated. They are all located on the **midpoint** of a line; except the window over the sink, it is located on the **midpoint** of the **sink rectangle** upper line. Locate the **midpoint osnap** icons at the points indicated. Start the line at the midpoint icon then attach the other end of the line to the opposite side of the wall (at the **perpendicular osnap** icon).

Use the **Offset** to draw the lines **parallel** to the **center line** to create the ends of the windows (over the sink that will be 24 inches each way from the center, the **5'0"** window will be **2.5'** each way from center, the **2'6"** window will be **1'3"** each side of center, the **6'0"** window will be **3'** each side of center). Then use the **Line** tool and snap to **midpoint** again to create the line running the length of each window.

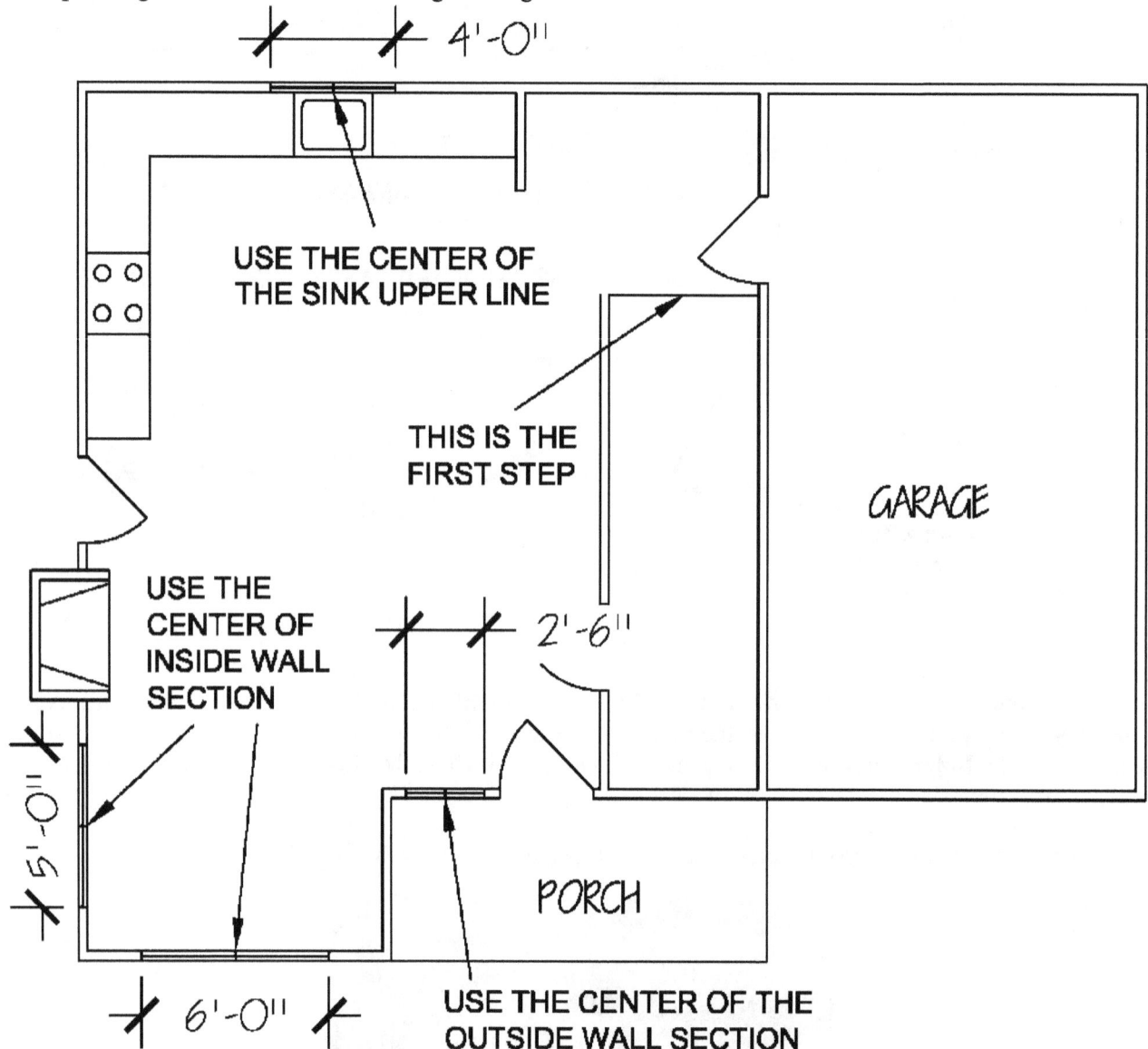

Fig 1-39

Now let's create the stairs. Click **Offset**. Type **10 <e>**. Click on the **FIRST STEP** line shown in **Fig 1-39**. Then type **m <e>** at the prompt. **Click** below that line and then below the new line and **repeat** until you have **11 lines**. This set of stairs will have 14 steps but we will only show 11 lines (including the first line) on this first story floor plan view because a portion of the bathroom is located below the stairs).

1.19 Design Center

We will now draw the bathroom fixtures. Start by creating a **new layer**. Go to the **Layer Properties Manager** again. **Create a new layer**. Name it **Fixtures**. Click on the Colors Designation and set it to white. **Close** the dialog box. In the **Layer Control** drop down box click the little arrow and select the **Fixtures** line. This will make the Fixtures layer the **current layer**. It will say: Fixtures in the Layer Control window.

Now on the **Palettes** palette on the View ribbon there is a button titled **Design Center;** it looks like this: Click on it and the **Design Center dialog box** will open. You can also type: adcenter.

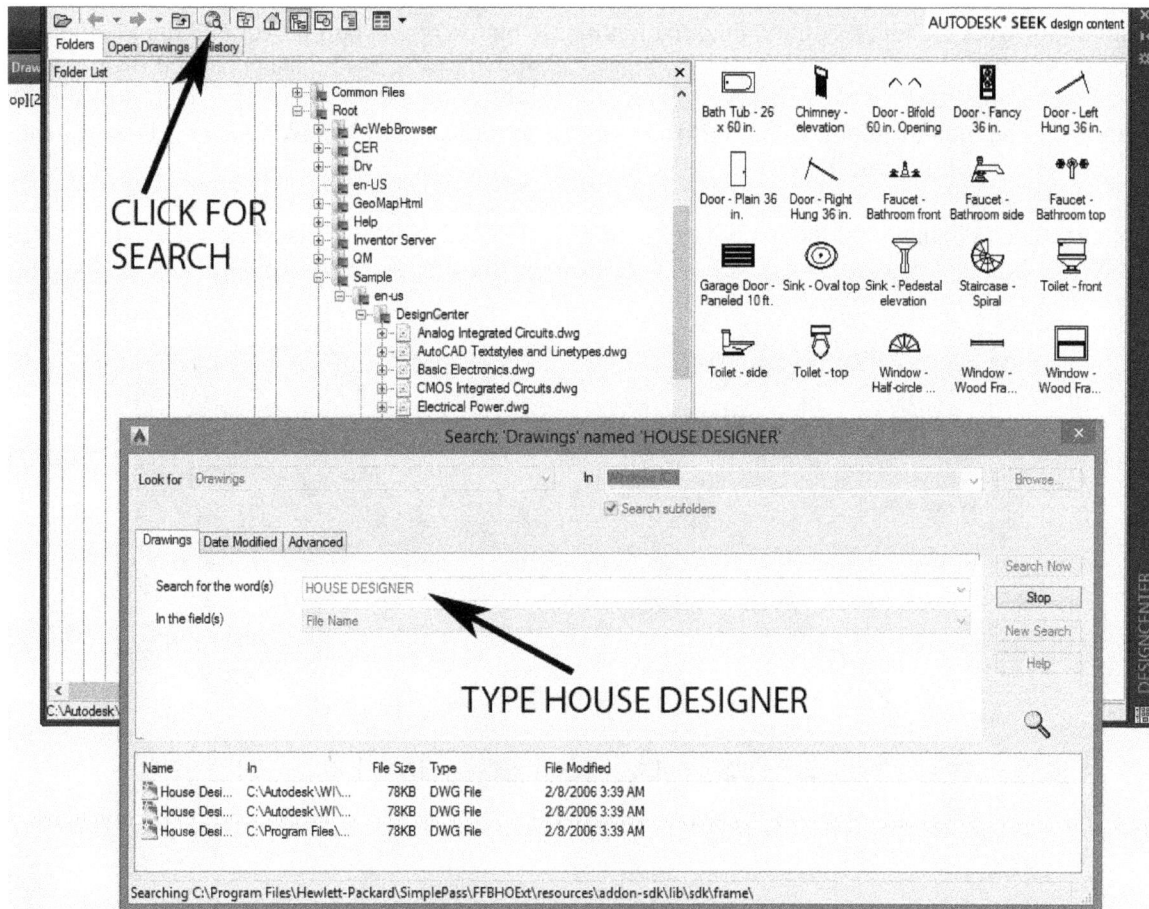

Fig 1-40

Click on the **Search** button as indicated in **Fig 1-40**. In the search window type: **house designer**. And Select the first search result below.

When the House Designer folder opens double click on the Blocks icon as in Fig 1-41.

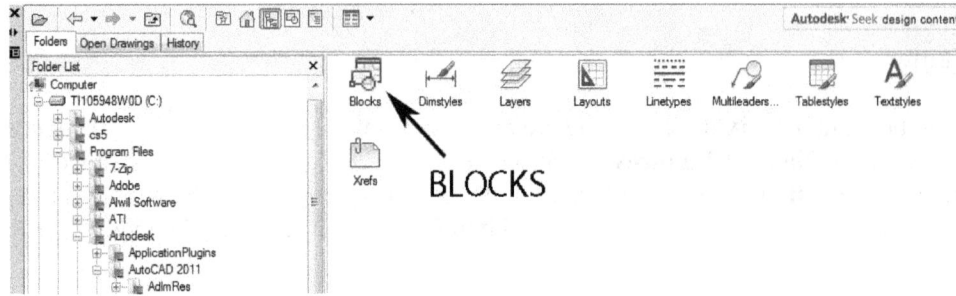

Fig 1-41

Center the **cursor** over the **toilet symbol**, hold the left mouse button down, pull it over and release the button on the AutoCAD drawing screen (not too close to the house) as shown in **Fig 1-42**. (This is called **drop and drag**.)

Do the same with the **Sink** symbol and the **Bathtub** symbols as indicated in **Fig 42**. **Close** the Design center box (click the x at the upper left corner).

An alternate method is to highlight the symbol (ex: toilet) right click, select the **Insert Block**, click on **Okay** in the **Insert dialog box** that pops up, then place the cursor on the drawing screen and click.

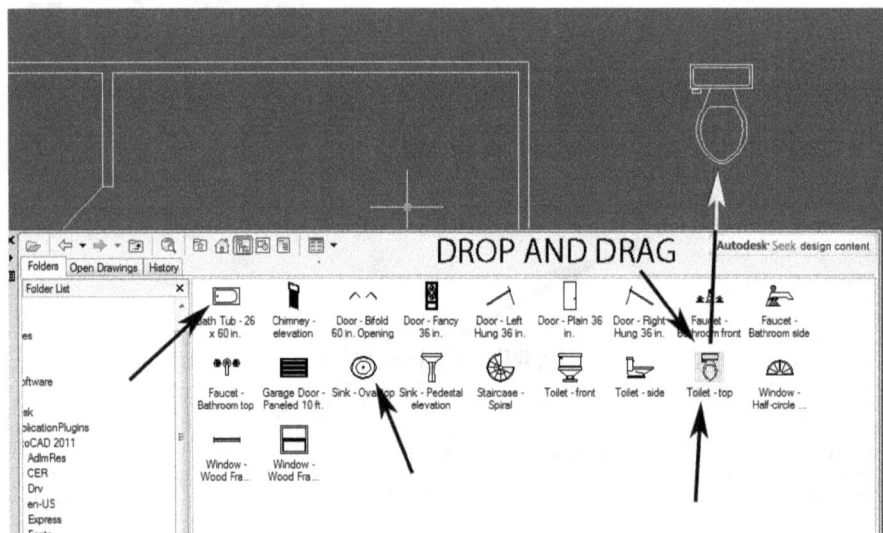

Fig 1-42

Now we will place the toilet and sink. Rotate the toilet. Click on the **Rotate** button on the Modify palette. **Click** on the **toilet** <e>. (Sometimes when you click on an object it will show little blue boxes and triangles, *you do not want this*, so escape and try again until the toilet appears as a highlighted line drawing as in Fig 1-44.) The prompt will read: **Specify base point**. This is the point you will rotate around. **Anywhere on the toilet** symbol is fine. **Click** and the prompt will read: **Specify rotation angle**. **Type 180** <e>. Now rotate the sink—enter **90** <e> for the angle of rotation for the sink.

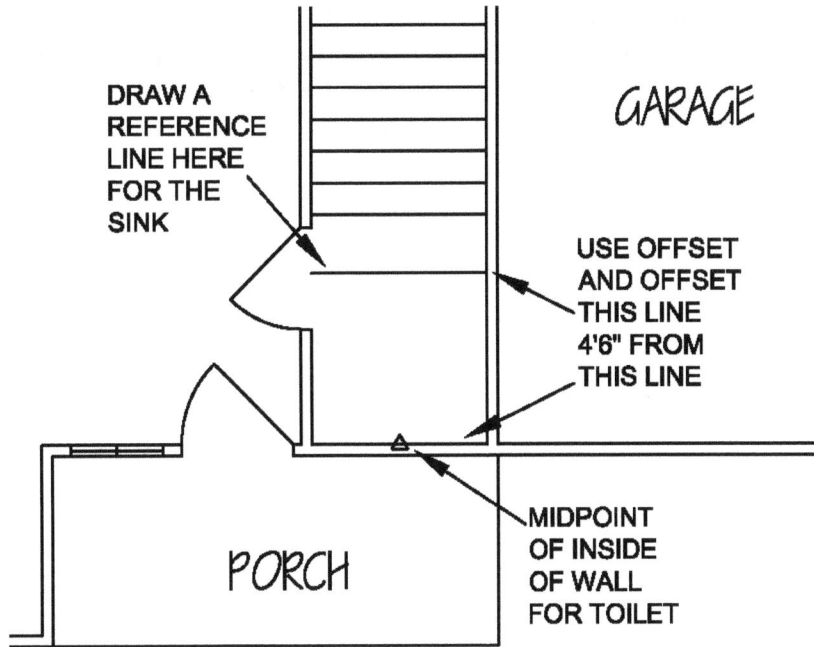

Fig 1-43

Move the toilet. Click on the **Move** button on the Modify palette. **Click** on the **toilet** <e>. The command line will prompt for: **Specify base point**. This is where you will grab the toilet. Grab it at the **midpoint** of the back of the toilet as in **Fig 1-44**. Make certain that the **Ortho** is turned **off**. Drag the toilet and place it as shown in **Fig 1-45**. This is the midpoint of the inside wall section indicated in Fig 1-43.

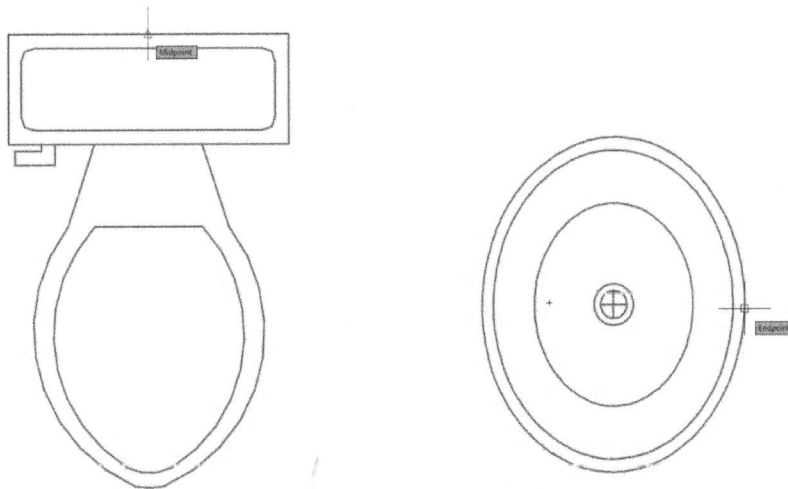

Fig 1-44

Create the **line** shown in **Fig 1-43** as a reference point for placing the sink. It is **offset 4'6"** (use the **Offset tool**) from the inside of the bathroom wall (see Fig 1-43). This a temporary line to mark a point on the bathroom wall—the point on the wall where we will snap the copy of the sink.

Now **move** the **sink**. Place the sink as shown in **Fig 1-45**. Snap the sink to the intersection of the wall and the reference line that you created. When you go to grab the sink you may notice that the icon you want is a box (endpoint as shown in Fig 1-44) and not a triangle (midpoint). This is because the sink is made up of series of arcs and lines. Erase the reference line when you have placed the sink.

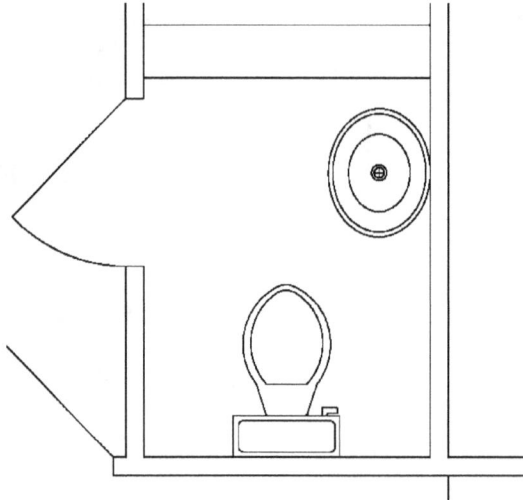

Fig 1-45

You can move the toilet and sink away from the walls with the Move button. Click **Move** then **select** the **toilet** <e>. Turn the **Ortho on**. **Click** on the **toilet again** anywhere. **Move** the toilet **away from the wall** a bit and **type 1** <e>. It will move it 1 inch away from the wall. Repeat for the sink.

1.20 Washer and Dryer

Now draw the washer, dryer and water heater and then our graphics will be nearly complete for the first floor.

Set the **0 Layer current**.

Create a square anywhere in open space that is **30" x 30"**. Click on the **Rectangle** button then **click** in open space. Follow the prompts at the command line (**d** <e> for dimensions at the prompt, then **type** the dimensions **30** <e> and **30** <e>, then **click** on the screen to set the rectangle. If you have forgotten how to do this, review section 1.12.

Now **copy** the **square** to the places shown in **Fig 1-46** by **snapping** the **corner** of the box to the **inside corners** of the **walls**. Turn the **Ortho off** and the **Object Snap on** (F3). You will need to do two different copies: one for the right hand corner and another for the left hand corners. Click the **Copy** tool, then on the rectangle, then grab it by the corner osnap icon, snap this to the inside corner icon where you wish to copy.

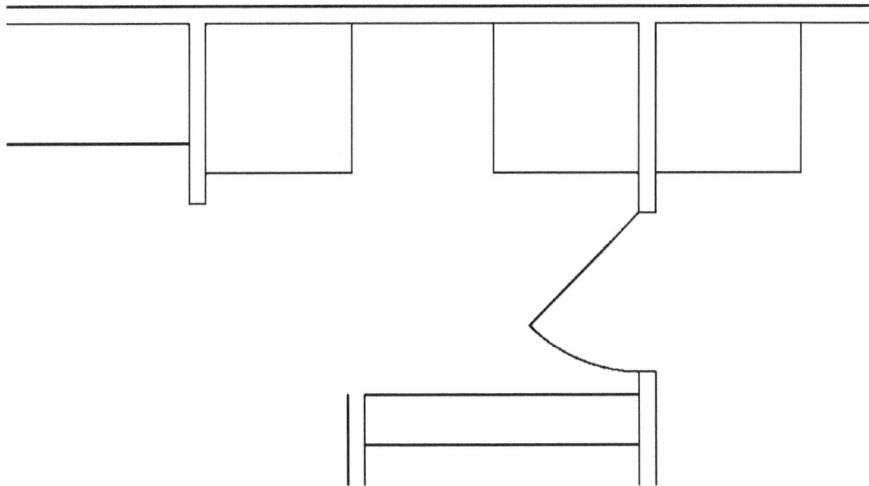

Fig 1-46

Now move the boxes representing the washer and dryer away from the walls one inch by using the **Move** button as we did with the toilet. Turn **Ortho on**. At the prompt for: **Specify base point**, show which way you want to move the rectangle by clicking on the rectangle, holding down the mouse button, moving it a bit in the direction you want it to move, and type **1 <e>**. Repeat in the other direction until it looks like Fig 1-47.

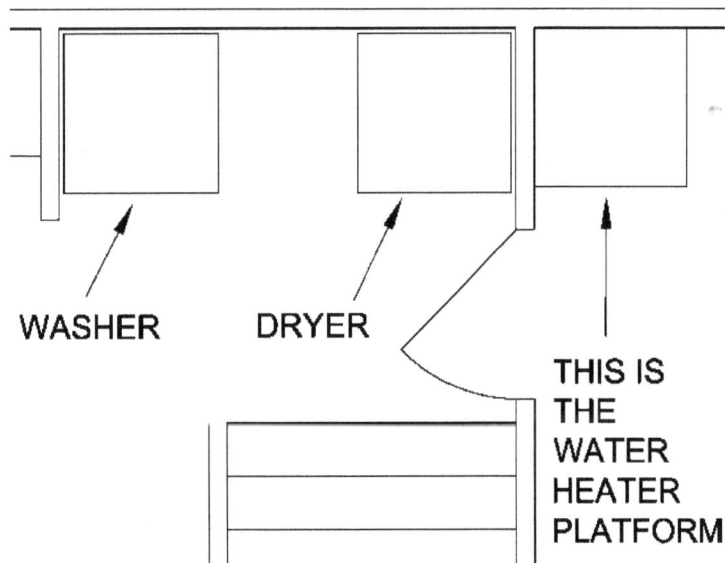

WASHER   DRYER

THIS IS
THE
WATER
HEATER
PLATFORM

Fig 1-47

Now place the water heater on the platform (see Fig 1-49). Find the center of the square in the garage by drawing a **diagonal line**; draw a **24** inch diameter **circle centered** on the **midpoint** of the **diagonal line**. This is the same procedure that we used for the stove in Fig 1-24. **Follow the prompts**. If you are not finding the right osnap points, turn them on in the Object snap settings (see Appendix I—Object Snap).

Erase the diagonal **line**.

1.21 Text

We are ready to enter our text into the drawing. First **create** a **new layer** in the **Layer Properties Manager** and call it **Text**. Leave it white for now. **Set** this **Text** layer as the **current** layer.

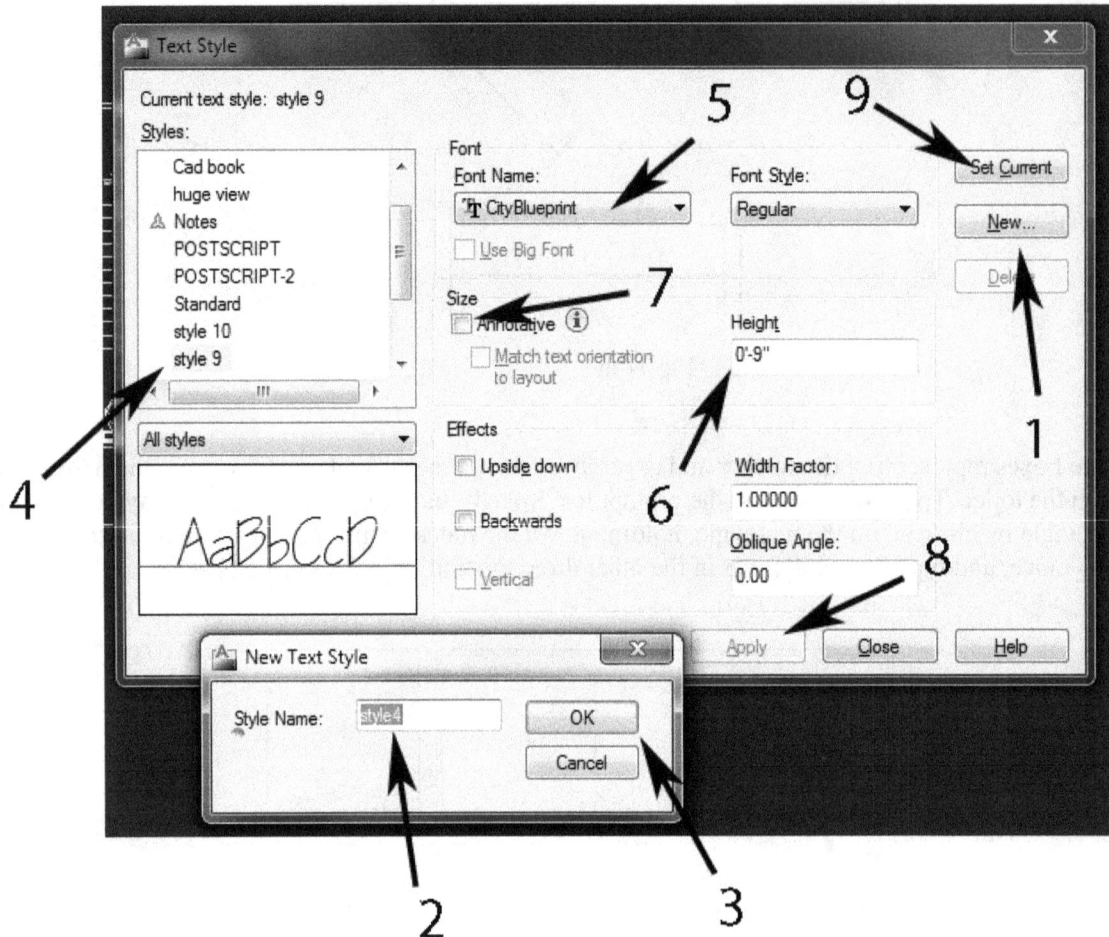

Fig 1-48

Now we must **create a text style**. Type: **style**. The **Text Style dialog box** will pop up (**Fig 1-48**). Click **New** (1 in Fig 1-48). **Name** the **style** in the window (at 2 in Fig 1-48), type: **style 9**. Then click **Okay** (3).

Back in the **Text style dialog** box **click the style 9 selection** (4). **Click** on the drop down menu under **Font Name** (5) and **select City Blueprint**. **Highlight** the **Text Height** (at 6 in Fig 1-48) and **over type**: **9**. **Uncheck the Annotative** box (7). Click **Apply** (8), then **Set Current** (9), then **Close** (see Appendix I—Text for more info).

Type mtexttoolbar in the command line and enter a value of 1. This will turn on the text formatting tool bar.

We will begin with the room/space designations. Type **mt <e>** (mt stands for Multi-line text).

Click on the **space** in the **middle** of the **kitchen** and move the mouse up and to the right to **create** the (approximate) **text box** that is shown in **Fig 1-49**. **Click** for the second corner. The exact size and placement are not important.

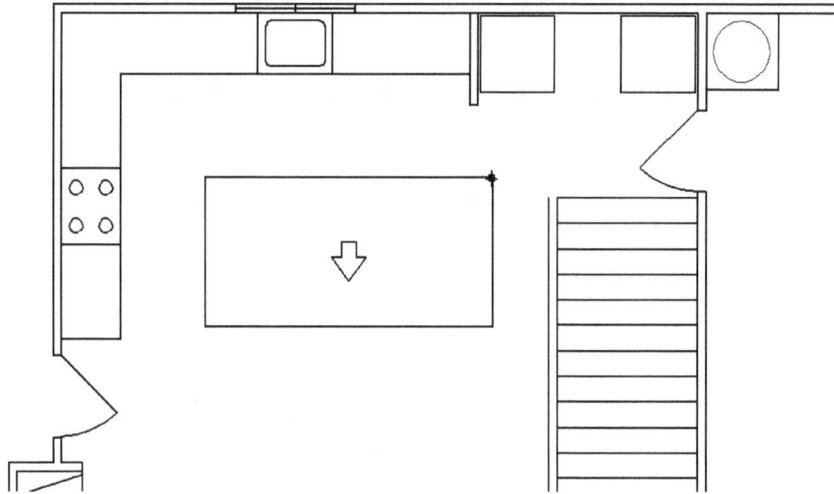

Fig 1-49

The **Text formatting bar** shown in **Fig 1-50** will appear.

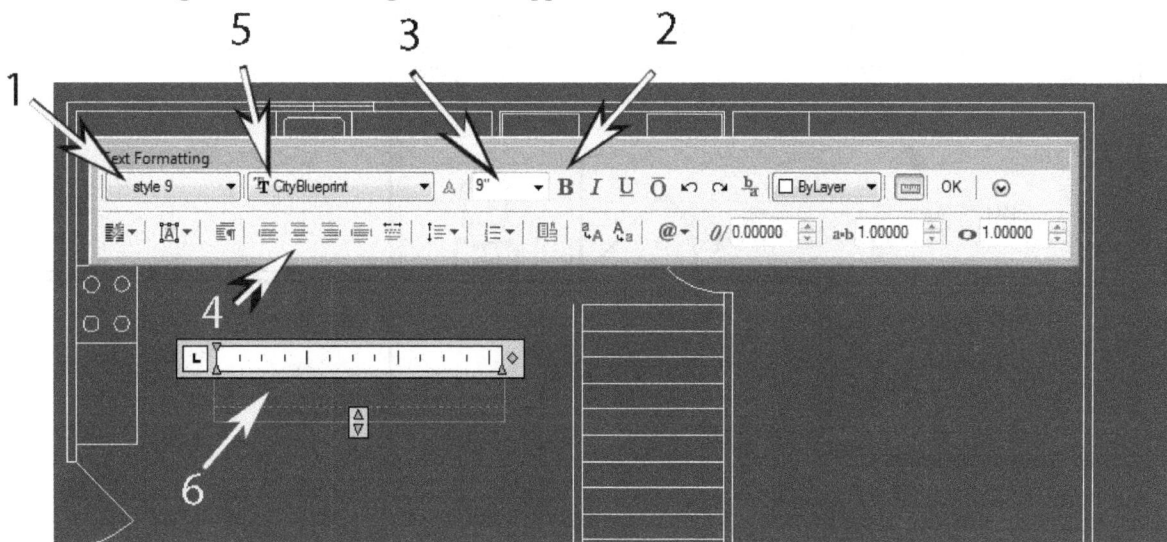

Fig 1-50

Set the **Caps Lock** on the computer keyboard (see Appendix I—Keyboard). **Select** your **style 9** (at **1** in **Fig 1-50**). **Click** on the **Bold** (2) button at the top of the bar. **Check** the **size** box (3) to make sure it reads **9**. If there is another number in this box then click on the number in the box, when it turns blue, **overtype** it with a **9**. Click on the **Center Text** (4). Check that the Font reads **City Blueprint** (5). If it is something different then you can change it in this window, but it is better to close this box, go back to Text Styles dialog box, and set it there.

Now type **KITCHEN** in the text box (6) on the screen. Click **OK**.

Click on the **Copy** button and then **click on** the word **Kitchen** <e>. The text (KITCHEN) must highlight before you can select it (if you have trouble selecting it then hover over it and move the mouse; you will see it change to a highlighted lettering—this means it can be selected). Now copy the word to the (approximate) locations shown in **Fig 1-51**. (Turn the **Ortho off** and **Object Snap off**). **Esc** when you have copied them all.

If your text doesn't highlight, then see Appendix I—Selection Problems. Your system settings might be wrong.

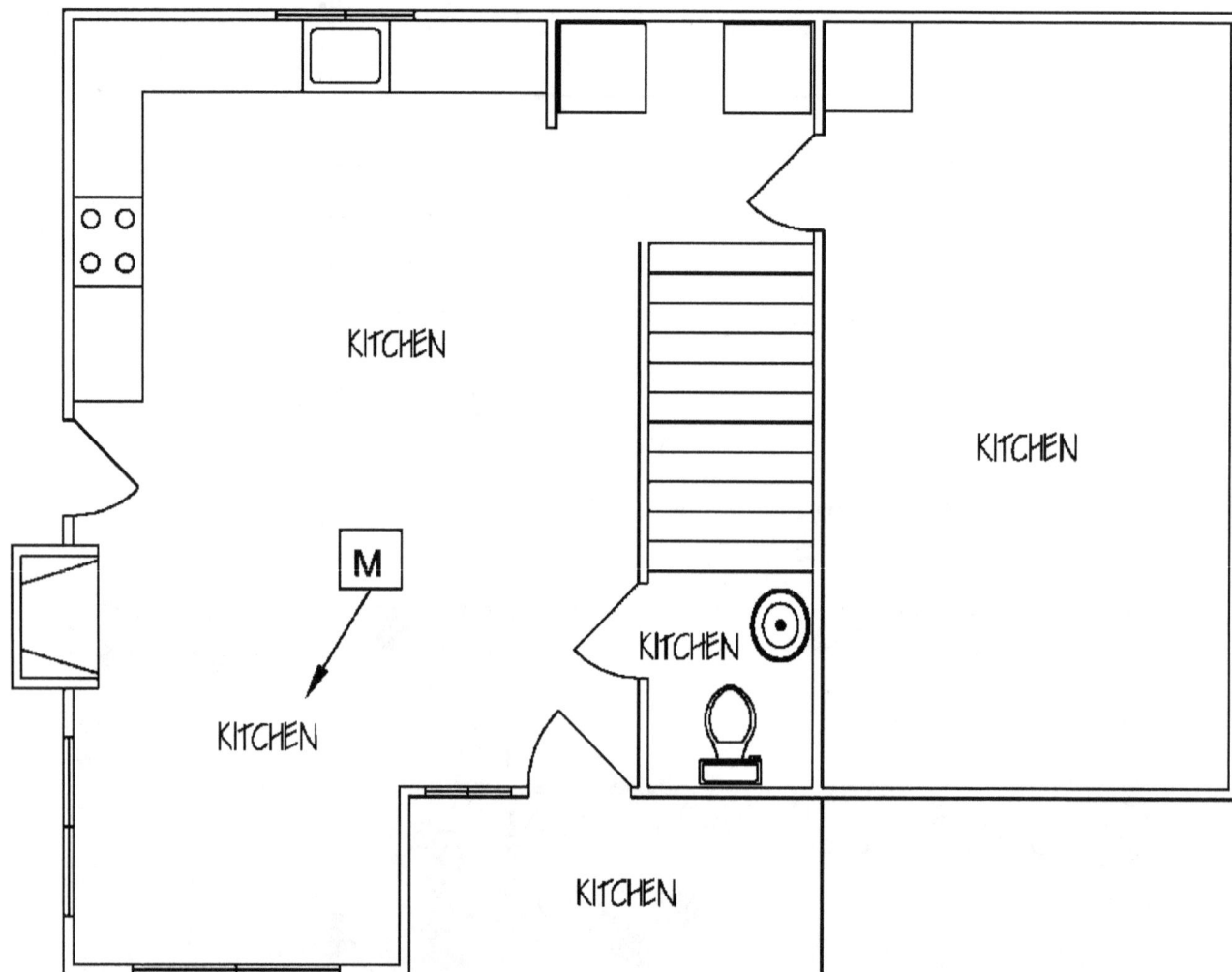

Fig 1-51

Now **click on** the lower left **KITCHEN** text at **M** in **Fig 1-51**. **Right click** and a drop down box will appear, choose **Mtext Edit**. The **Text Formatting** window will open as in **Fig 1-52**. **Highlight** the text (**KITCHEN**) by placing the cursor in the text box at **O** in **Fig 1-52** and press down on the left mouse button, hold it down, and scroll to the left. It will create a **blue selection window over the text**. Leave it blue and **overtype it with: LIVING ROOM**. Click **OK**.

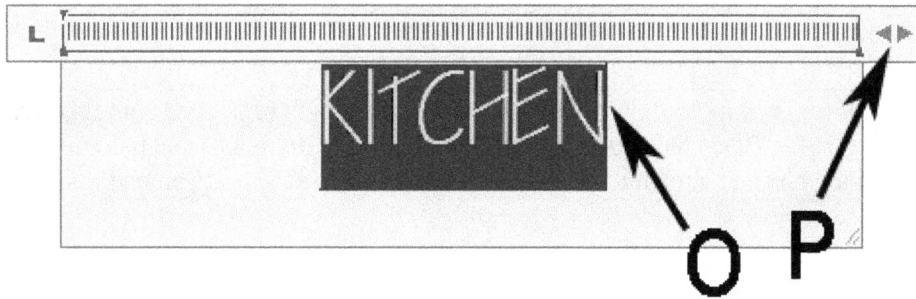

Fig 1-52

Repeat the **text edit process** with the rest of the text until the drawing looks like **Fig 1-53**. Click on each of the Kitchen texts, open the Text formatting box, highlight the text and over write it with the text shown in Fig 1-53.

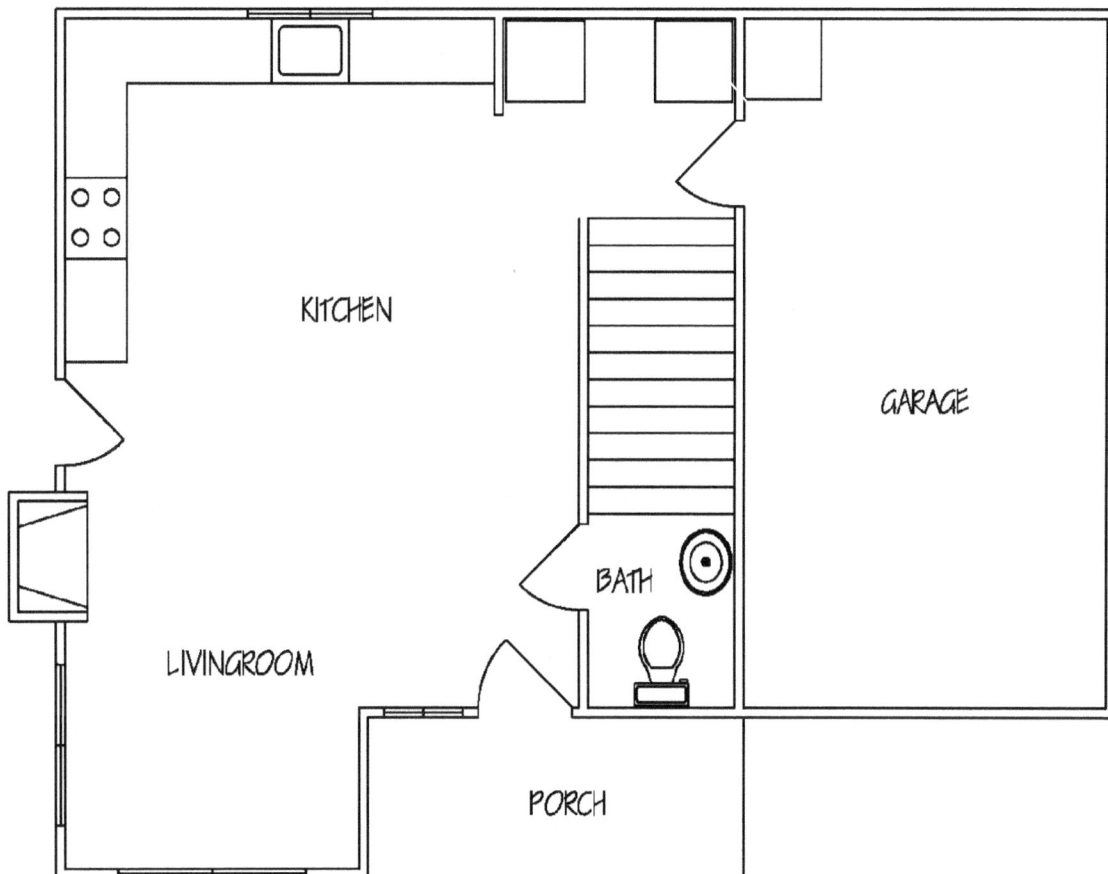

Fig 1-53

There are a lot of different ways to do each thing in AutoCAD. You can experiment with the different ways to approach the Text. I find this to be the easiest way to create multiple labels with the same properties. The standard way would be to open a new text dialog box for each piece of text. It is fine if you prefer that method.

Now we will create the window information text. Type **mt <e>**. Open another text box above the kitchen window at **Q** in **Fig 1-54**. **Highlight the 9"** in the text size box by clicking on it (it turns blue) and overwrite it with: **6** (see

Fig 1-50). Turn on the **Bold** button. Click in the text box (where the cursor is blinking) and type: **4-0 x 3-6 SLD**. Then OK.

If the text doesn't appear in a single straight line then adjust the length of the box using the grip at **P** in **Fig 1-52** at the right side of the **ruler**. Place the cursor on the little arrows (or diamond) and hold down the left hand button on the mouse to grip the box and stretch it out to the right until the text appears on one line.

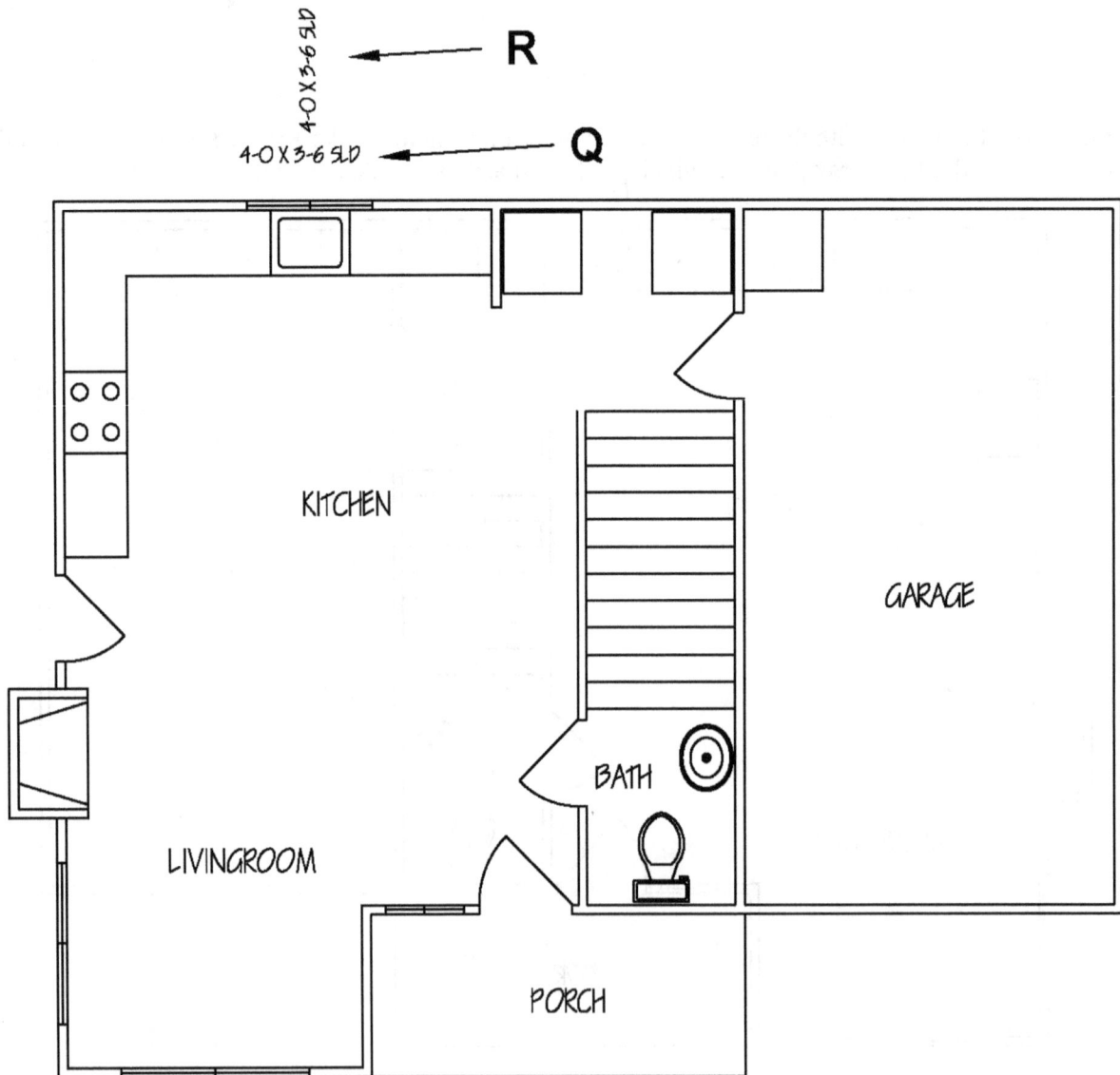

Fig 1-54

We are going to copy and rotate this text. **Copy** this text to the empty space above it as at **R** in **Fig 1-54** (this Fig shows it after rotation). **Esc**. The exact location of the copy is not important.

Click the **Rotate** button and then **click** on the **text** that you just copied <e> (at **R** in **Fig 1-54**). **Click** again on this same **text**. (Read the prompt: **Specify rotation angle or...**) type **90** <e>. This will rotate the copy to 90 degrees as it appears in Fig 1-54. Now **copy** these two versions of the text to the places shown in **Fig 1-55** (**Object snaps off**). Place the **text** by **hand** (no snap points—just place it by eye), roughly centered on the windows. Don't worry about placing it exactly for now—you can do that on your own drawings later if you choose. I place most of my text by eye—just as long as it looks good it is fine. Setting text to precise points is covered later.

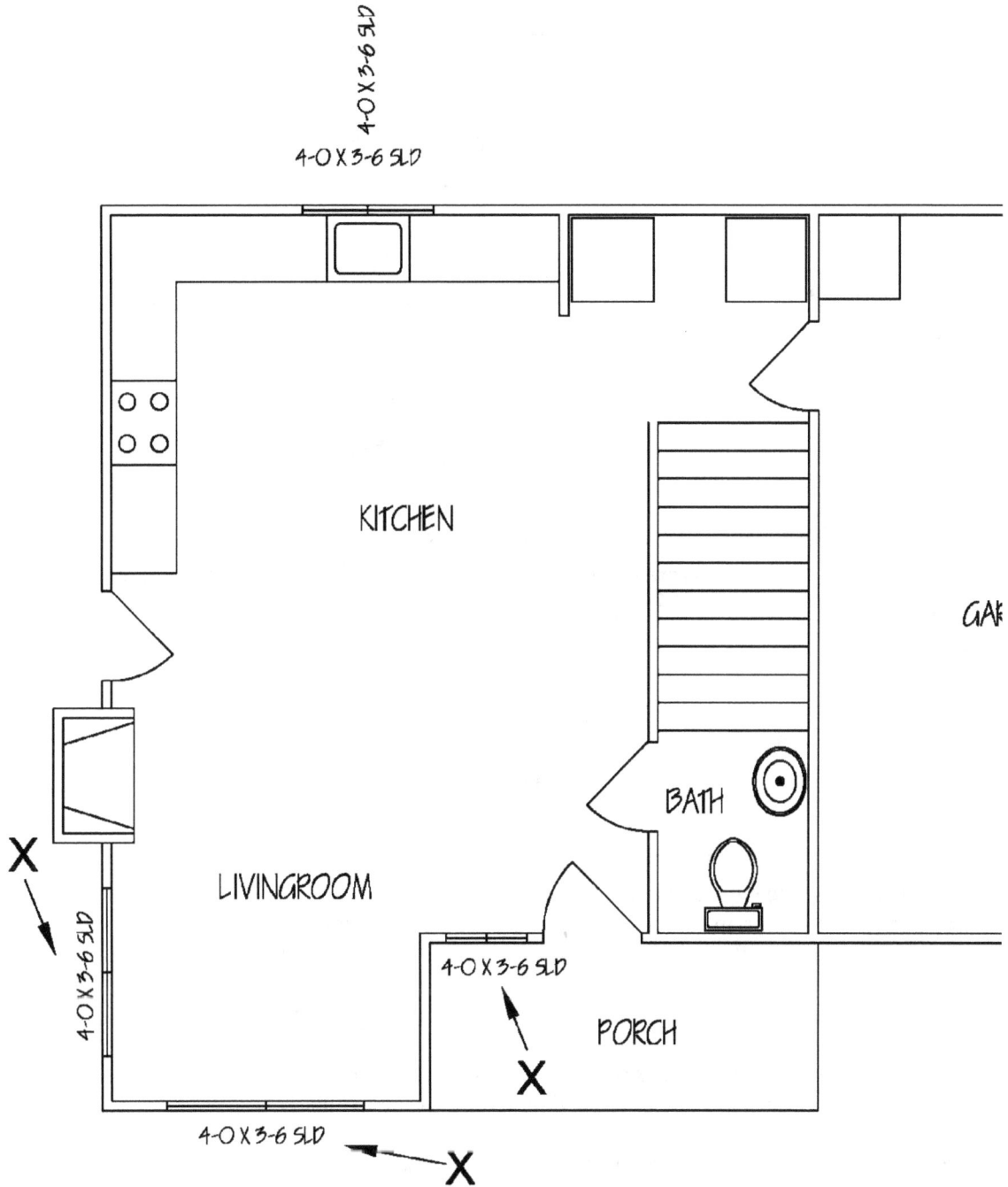

Fig 1-55

Click on each of the window size **texts** and edit them (highlight the text and overwrite it) to read as in **Fig 1-56**.

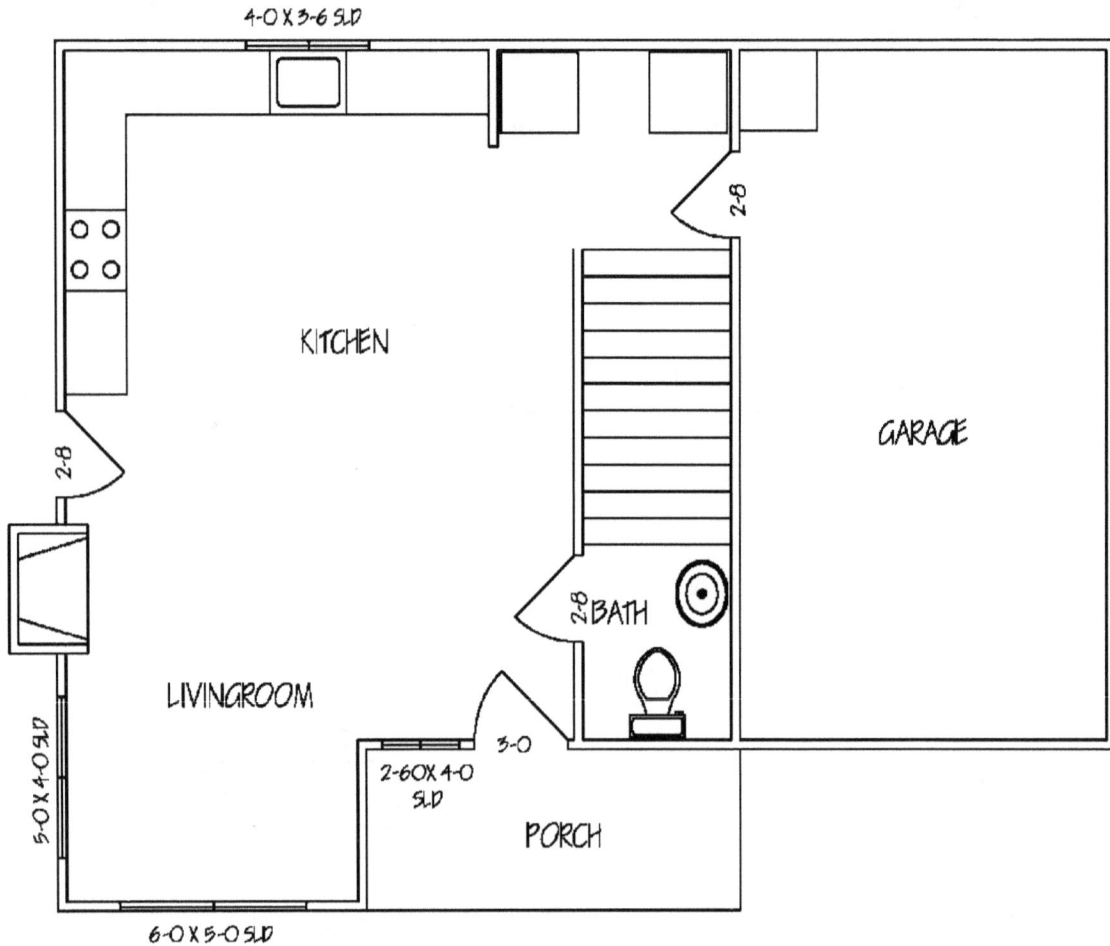

Fig 1-56

Use the **ruler** at the top of the **Text box** (**P** in **Fig 1-52**) to change the window label text on the porch to two lines as shown (you can also use the enter key between the numbers and the letters SLD to move them to a new line, as you would with any typing program). Check to make sure the **Text Centered** button is on (4 in Fig 1-50). If the text is not where you want it, click on the Move button on the Modify palette then use it to position the text where you want it (Ortho and Object Snap off). This doesn't always respond as it should, if you have troubles try stretching the text into one line, press the Center Text button, then shorten the box again.

Now **repeat** the process with the **door sizes** (use **6"** letter size and **Bold**); and with the washer (**W**), dryer (**D**) and water heater (**HW**) as shown in **Fig 1-57**. Use the **9"** text for these and **Bold**.

Now **add** a **note** for the **fireplace** as shown in **Fig 1-57**. Open a **mt** box and enter the information from the drawing below. Use **6"** letters and **Bold**. Use the Move command to position the text.

1.22 Odds and Ends

Okay we have just a few more items to add and the floor plans will be complete. Let's wrap up a few odds and ends. Turn on the **0 Layer**. Turn the **Ortho on** and the **Object Snap on**.

Close off the end of the wall at the stairwell with a short line (**Fig 1-57**).

Now open up the front of the garage with a **nine foot opening** as shown in **Fig 1-57**. Use the **exterior wall midpoint** as the center of the opening. This **opening is 9'**, so it will be 4.5' offset each way from the center line. Enter the garage **door size text** as shown below (use **6" font** and **bold**). You will need to have the Midpoint and Perpendicular Osnaps turned on.

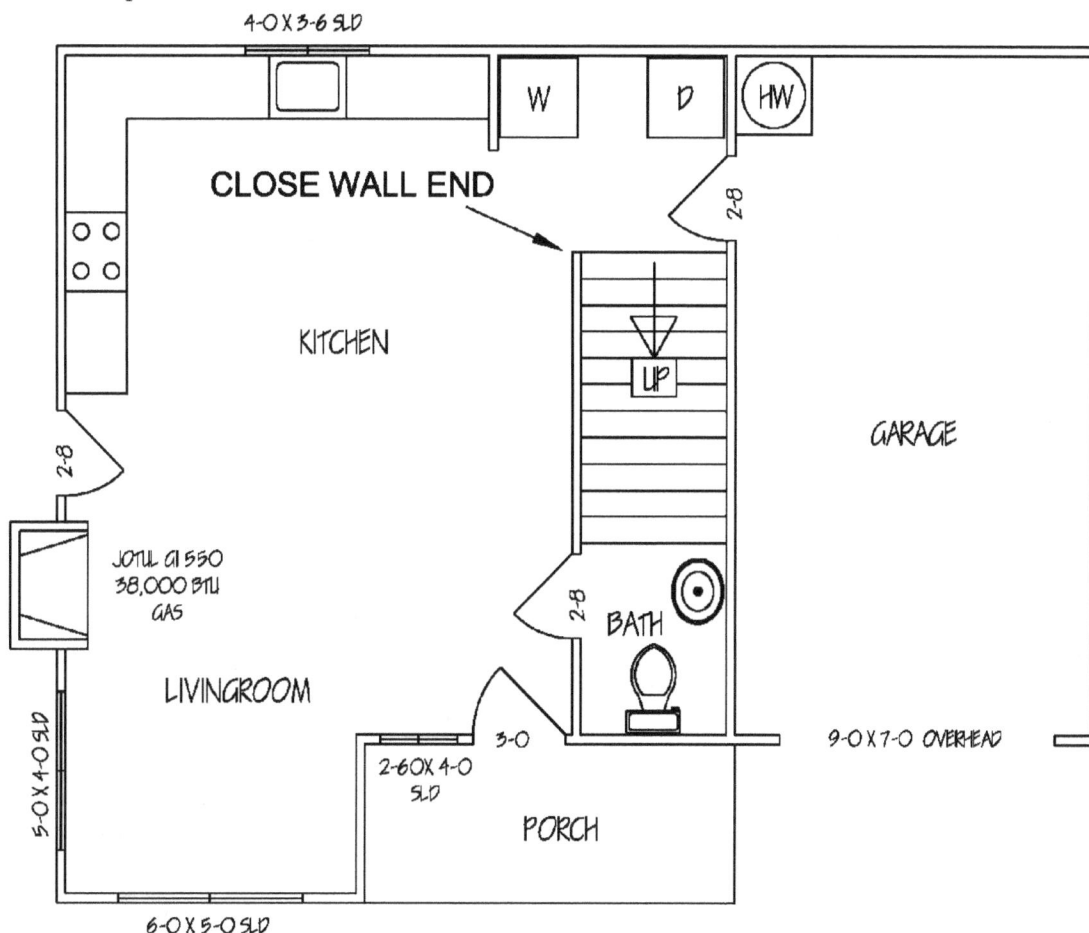

Fig 1-57

Make an UP arrow for the stairs (**Fig 1-57**). Out in open space (anywhere on the screen) draw a vertical **line 36"** with the **Ortho on** (see **Fig 1-58**). Now turn the **Ortho off.**

Click on the **Line** button and snap the start point of a new line to the bottom of the 36" vertical line as in **S** in **Fig 1-58**. **Type @18<60 <e>. Draw** another **line** from the top of this angled line back to the vertical line **T** and attach it at the **perpendicular** osnap point (left side drawing in Fig 1-58).

Use the mirror tool to create the other side with the mirror line being the 36" vertical line (T in fig 1-58). Click on the **Mirror** tool then **read the prompts**. When it says to **select an object**: select the **angled line** and the **horizontal line** and **<e>**. When it says: **select first point of mirror line**, snap to the **top** of **line T**. When it prompts for the **second point** click on the **bottom** of **line T** and **<e>**. Don't forget to enter.

Move this arrow and place it on the **midpoint** of the fifth step line using the **tip of the arrow** as the base point as in Fig 1-57.

Now in open space again, open a **mt** box (**type mt <e>**) and **type: UP**. Use **9"** and **Bold**.

Use the **Rectangle** tool and **create** a **box around the UP text** like the one in **Fig 1-57**. **Move** the **box** (just the box for now *not* **the UP text**) and place it on the end of the arrow (use the Osnap at the top midpoint on the rectangle). Now use the **Trim** tool (Trim + rt click or <e>) to erase the line inside the box. Now **move** the **UP** text and place it in the **center** of the **box**. Do this by eye for now, we will discuss precision text placement later. **Erase** the **box** and **trim** the **arrow** to appear as shown in **Fig 1-63**.

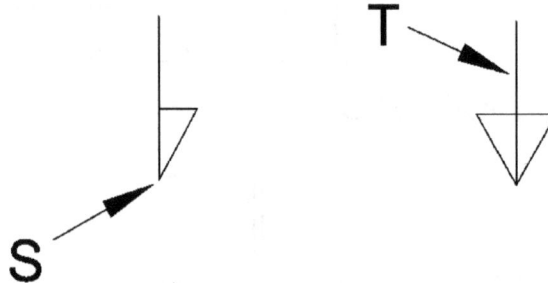

Fig 1-58

1.23 Dimensions

Now we are ready to enter the dimensions. We are going to use the non-annotative method. Annotative text is covered in Chapter 16.

To begin, create a **new layer** in the **Layer Properties Manager**. Name it **Dimension**. Leave it **white** (you can always change the colors of the layers at anytime). **Set** it as the **current layer**.

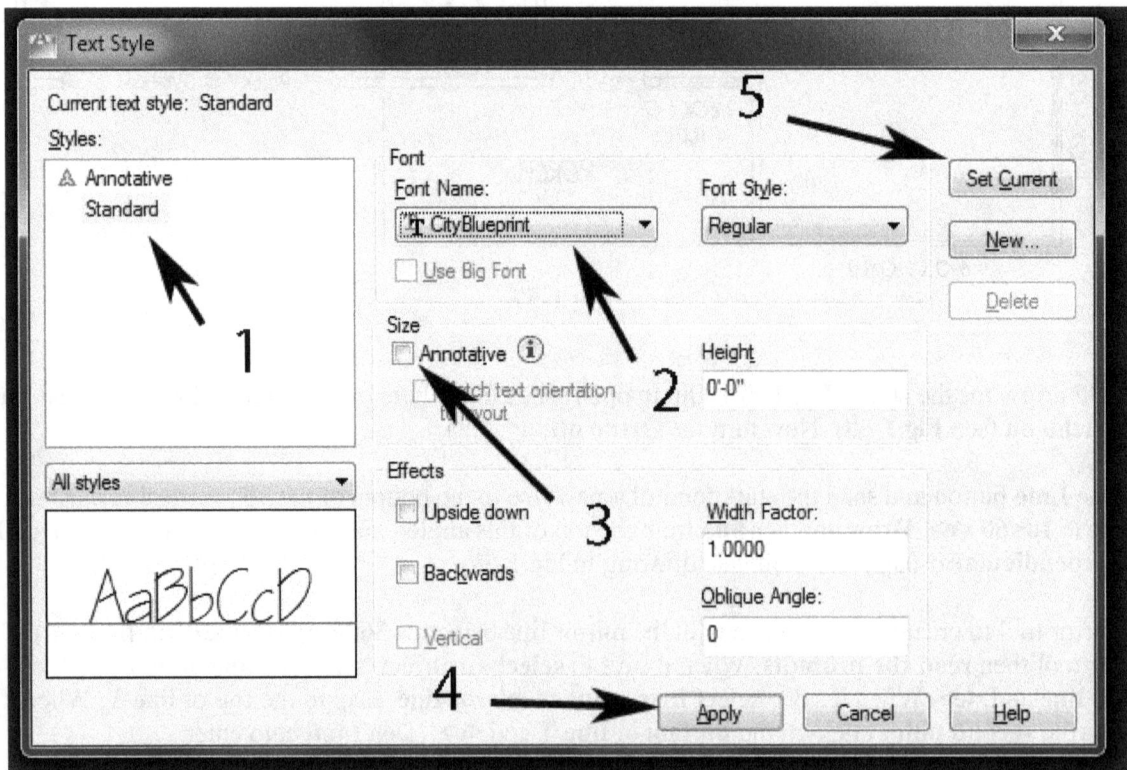

Fig 1-59

Type: **style** <e>. The **Text Style** dialog box will open as in **Fig 1-59**. Click on **Standard** (1 in Fig 1-59). In the window at **Font Name** (2 in Fig 1-59) scroll to **City Blueprint** and click. **Uncheck the Annotative** box. Click **Apply** (4) (if the **Apply** box is not highlighted then skip this step), then **Set Current** (5), and **Close**.

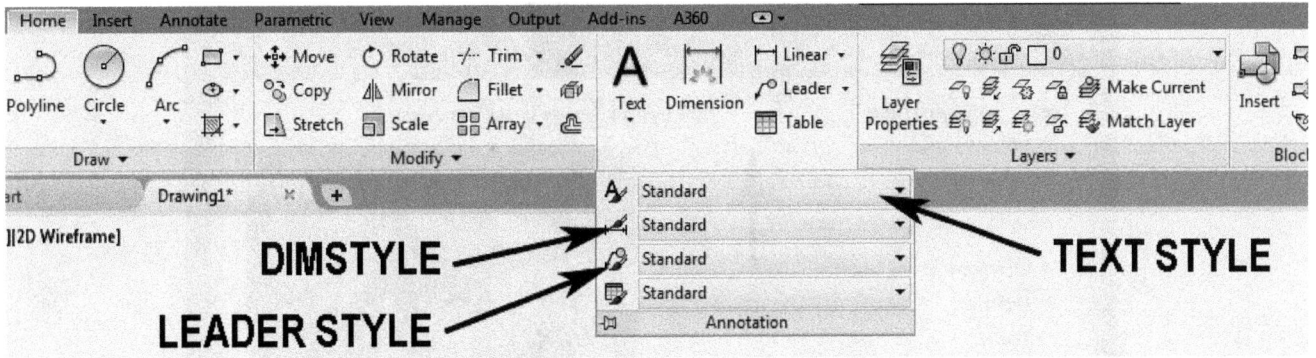

If you hover over the icons it will reveal their names.

Fig 1-60A

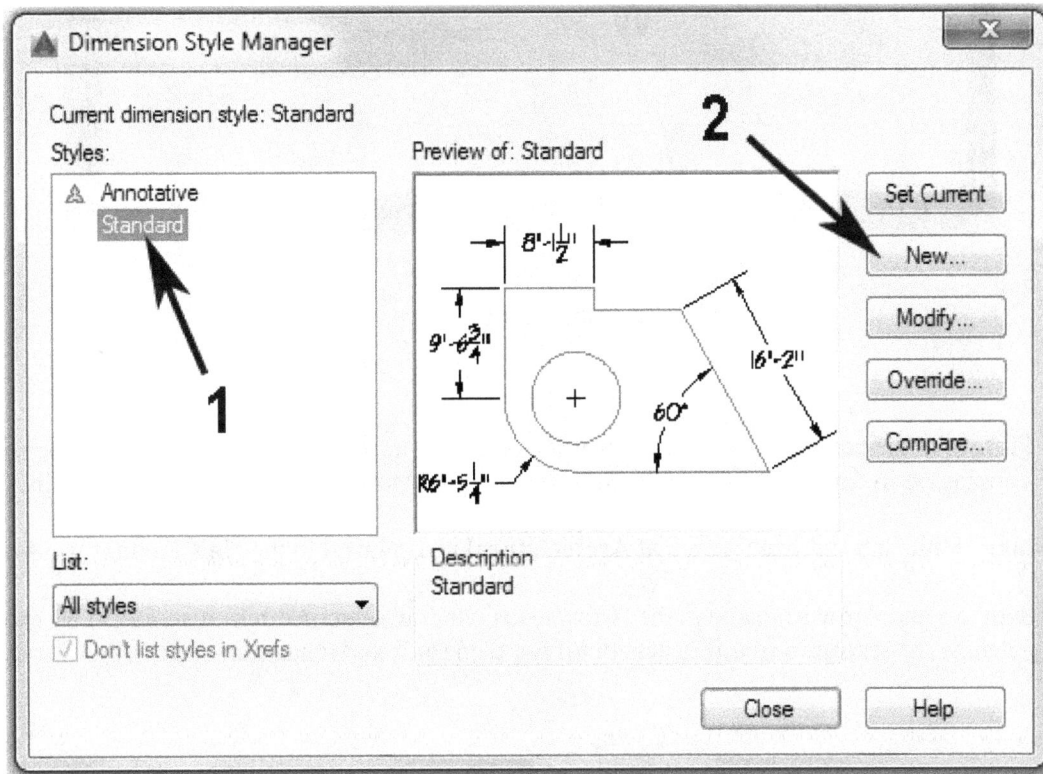

Fig 1-60B

Click on the **Dimension Style** button by clicking on the down arrow at the bottom of the **Annotation** palette next to the word Annotation (or type **dimstyle**). A dialog box will open. **Select** the **Standard** style as shown in **Fig 1-60A**. **Click New** (**Fig 1-60B**). When the **Create New Dimension Style** box appears **name** this new style **Quarter**. Then click on **Continue**. The **New Dimension Style: Quarter** box shown in **Fig 1-61** will appear.

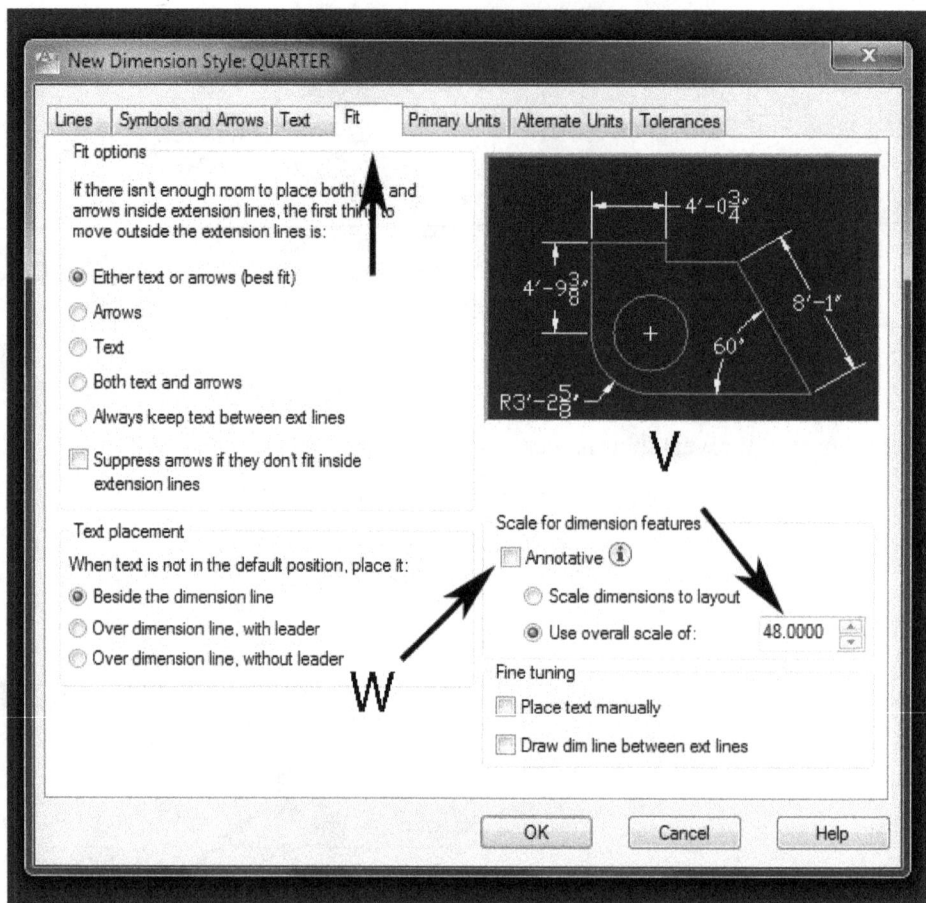

Fig 1-61

Click on the **Fit tab**. In the box that says: **Use Overall Scale of: (V** in **Fig 1-61**) highlight the number in the box (double clicking on it) and overtype it with **48**. Make sure the **Annotative is turned off** at **W** in Fig 1-61.

Click the **Primary Units** tab and make sure that **Architectural** is displayed in the **Unit Format** window.

Click on the Symbols and Arrows tab and in the Arrowheads window select Architectural tick. This should automatically change the second to read the same but if not then set it to Architectural tick in the second window also.

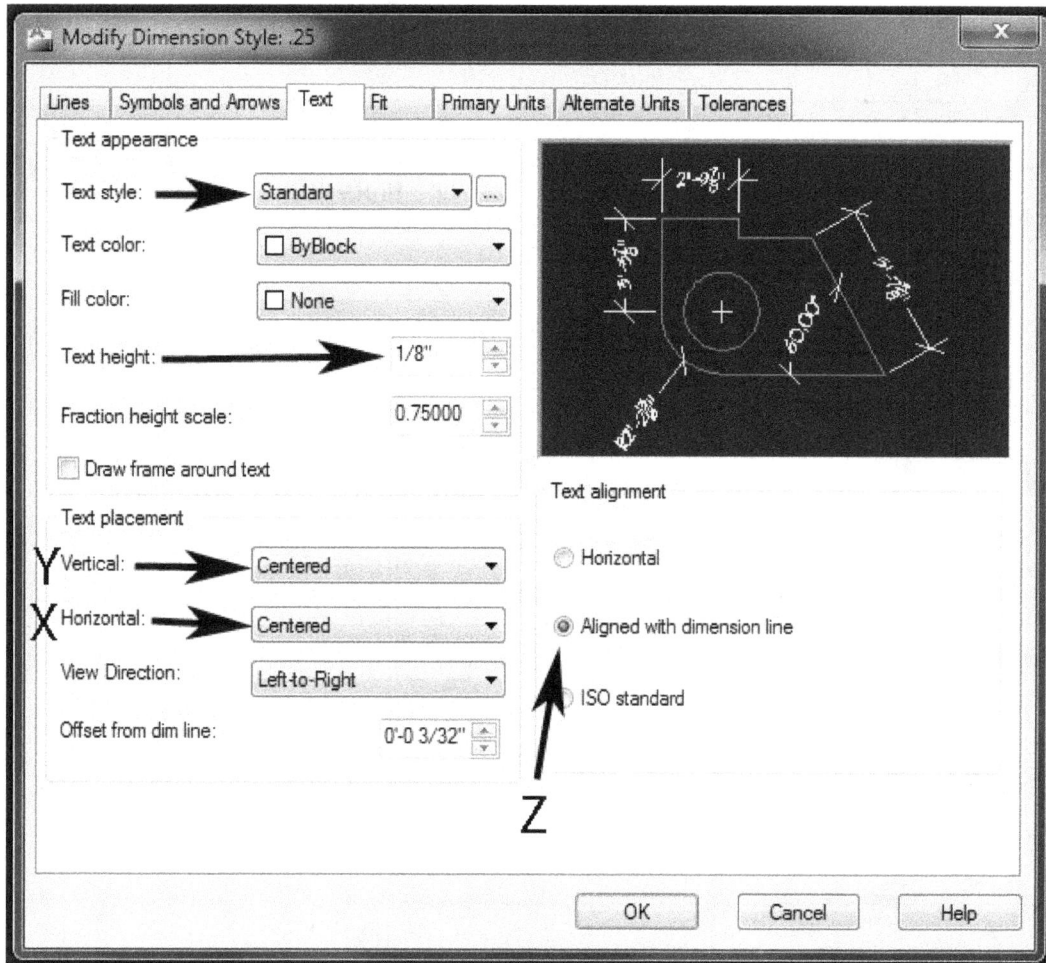

Fig 1-62

Click on the **Text** tab at the top of the box (Fig 1-62). Make certain that **Standard** appears in the **Text Style** window. Set the **Text height** to **1/8"**. Then below in the **Text Placement** box open the **Horozontal** drop down menu (**X** in **Fig 1-62**) and click on **Centered**. In the **Vertical** box (**Y**) select **Centered**. Turn on the button for: **Aligned with dimension line** (**Z**). Click **OK**.

Back at the **Dimension Style** box click on the **Quarter**, then **Set Current**, and **Close**.

In architectural design it is common to have the text (the dimension) above the line, but here we are centering to keep the drawings more compact so that these drawings will print out on a home/office printer.

This setup is for a dimension style using a quarter inch to the foot scale (¼" = 1'). Later we will set up dimension configurations for other scales. Scales are discussed throughout the book and in detail in Chapter 13. You can read that chapter at any time for more info, but it may be a bit confusing without some more practice— this is a learn by practice method—so you can just follow along and all will become clear.

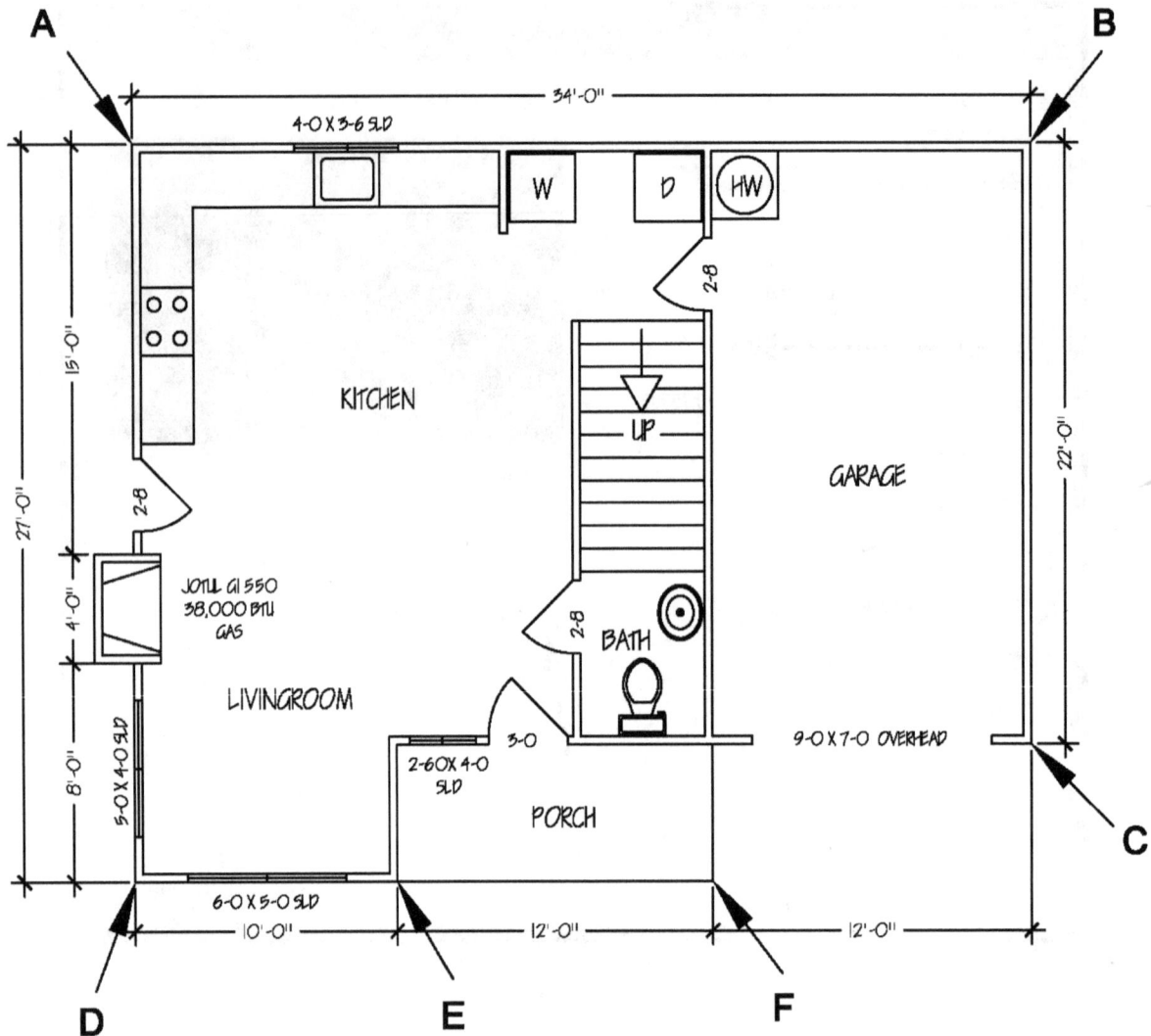

Fig 1-63

Now click on the **Linear** button on the **Dimensions** palette (on the Annotate ribbon co-located with Aligned, Angular, Arc Length, Radius, Diameter, Jogged and Ordinate—it could read any of these—click on the down arrow to see the list or type: dimlinear). Turn the **Object Snap on** and snap to the upper left corner of the building (**A** in **Fig 1-63**). Now snap to the upper right corner (**B**) of the building and move the mouse up. When the dimension line is approximately where you see it in Fig 1-63 **click** and it will set it in place. Keep these dimensions close to the building if you want to be able to print this out on a 8.5 x 11 paper (it just fits). You may want to move the kitchen window text—4-0 x 3-6 SLD—closer to the building first.

Now repeat this process on the garage wall to the right. **Click Linear** then point **B** then **C** in **Fig 1-63**, pull it out to the right, and **click** to set it in place.

You must be careful to **Osnap to the corner** of the building and **not to the end of the dimension indicator**. If you get a weird measurement that is probably what is happening. Zoom in if needed to differentiate.

Click on the **Linear** command and then click on the front of the living room, snap to the lower left corner of the building first (**D**) and then to the corner of the 10 ft pop out section (**E**). Pull it down and **set it** with a **click**. Now **click** on the **Continue** button on the **Dimensions palette** (co-located with the Baseline button) and snap to the corner of the porch (**F**). **Do not enter or right click.** Continue on and snap to the outside corner of the garage (**C**) then **<e>**.

You should see the dimensions shown in **Fig 1-63**. This is the continuous tool that automatically aligns a string of dimensions.

At the left side use the **Linear** command to create the 8'-0" as shown in Fig 1-63, then the **Continue** button to create the 4'-0" and the 15'0". Use the **Linear** button to create the 27' dimension.

The Continue command saves you from having to click the Linear repeatedly when there is a continuous line of dimensions and it lines them up perfectly.

Congratulations you have finished the first floor plans!

If you are going to produce the complete set of plans then you will add some more details to this drawing in Chapter 15.

2nd Story Floor Plan

It is not necessary that you draw the second story floor plans. The dimensions and information that you need to continue this course are provided so that you can complete the chapters without drawing the second story.

If you want to draw the second story floor plans look at Fig 15-5 (in Chapter 15) and at the completed plans in Appendix IV, and repeat the steps in this chapter. The Index identifies where to find all of the necessary commands and processes if you forget how you did something.

If you are going to draw the second story floor plan, use the copy that you made of the drawing (Fig 1-15) and **make a new copy**. You will need more copies of this for other views later.

A Few Notes

Here you have a completed floor plan and you now know a lot about how to use AutoCAD for drawing in two dimensions. There are a number of different ways to draw any particular object in AutoCAD. None of them are wrong. Readers of this book will develop their own style of drawing as time goes on. Some of what I have demonstrated here is not the easiest or fastest (or best) way, but rather the easiest to explain. The idea is to get you drawing what you need as quickly as possible and then you can fine tune your methods as you go along. Alternate methods for many of these techniques will be discussed as we go along.

Remember that all the commands can be typed in (as opposed to using the mouse and clicking buttons).

Take some time and look at the **Options** dialog box. Type options and **<e>**. Here you will find dozens of settings for many parts of the system. You can change the size or shape of the pick boxes for example. You can set the default for something other than inches (feet perhaps). You can set the default for line weight. Lots of options, most of which you will never need, but it is good to know what is available in case you find yourself looking for some esoteric setting.

Remember to **save your work often** as you draw. It is a (minor) tragedy to lose hours of work because of some strange computer glitch. Name this file **Paradise** (the fictional street name of our project) and save it to your computer. The desktop is a good place if you are going to be going at this course intensively.

There is an automatic save function find it in the **Options** dialog box (type **options**), then the **Open and Save** tab. Check the box next to **Automatic save** and set the **time between saves**—not too often because the program freezes while it saves your work—20 minutes is a good compromise. Check the box next to **Create backup copy with each save.**

Explore using right clicks as you draw. Use it to repeat commands and enter. Right clicks do a variety of things so the best way to learn about this is to right click at each stage of any process to see what happens.

Chapter 2—Elevations

2.1 Story Pole

If you completed Chapter 1 you have acquired many of the skills that you need to draw with AutoCAD. I will not repeat the individual steps to perform the functions that you have already learned (Line, Rectangle, Move, etc.). For much of the elevation drawing you will be instructed simply to draw what you see in a particular figure. Only new skills will be fully detailed. If you have forgotten how to do something look in the **Index** for the location of the instructions for each command.

All the drawing in this book is performed in one file. If you are reopening AutoCAD, then select your Paradise file (that you saved from Chapter 1) from the menu under the File tab. In other words: **do not create (open) a new file for each chapter**.

Remember that we are using the shorthand symbol **<e> to represent** pressing the **enter** key on your keyboard.

Look at the completed elevations in Appendix IV. These are the elevations for this house. In this chapter we will draw the east elevation shown here (this is the front of the house that faces the street).

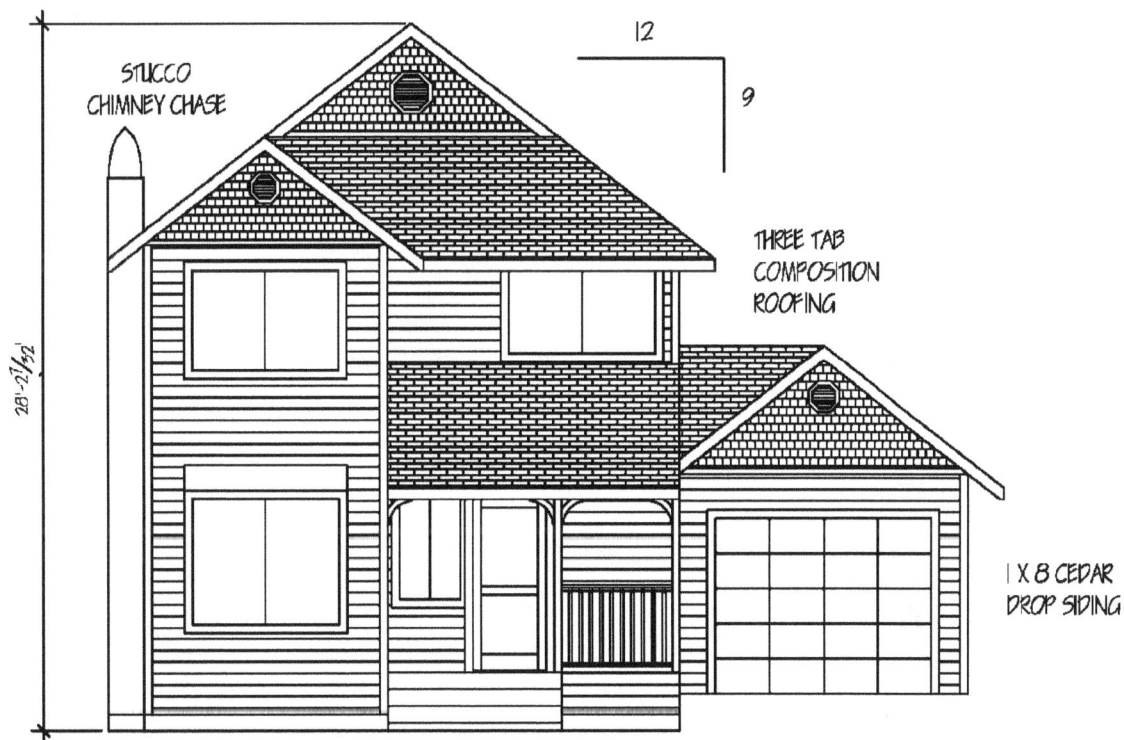

A good place to start when drawing elevations is to **create** a **story pole line**. This is a reference that defines the various elevation levels of the structure: the exterior ground level, the floor levels, the top of wall levels, etc. Fig 2-1 depicts the story pole for this design.

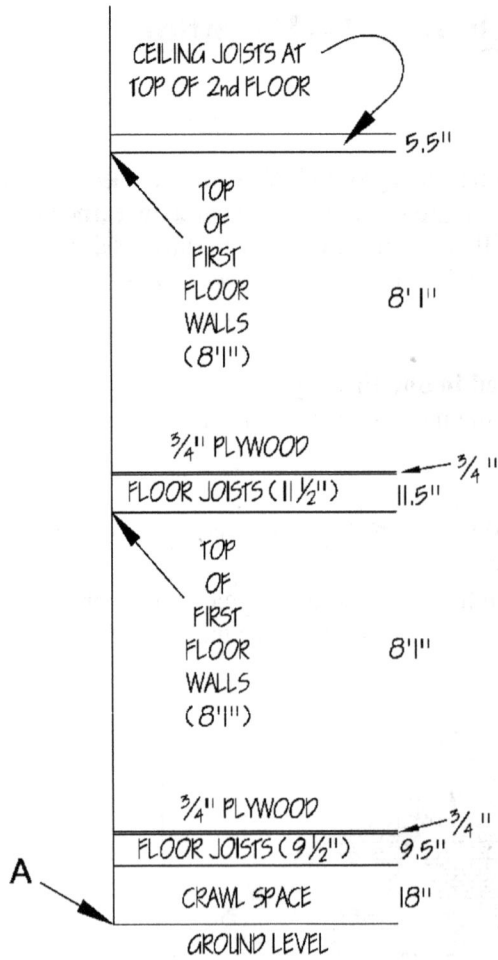

Fig. 2-1

First, create a new **Layer**, make it **orange** in color and name it **Construction**. **Set it current**.

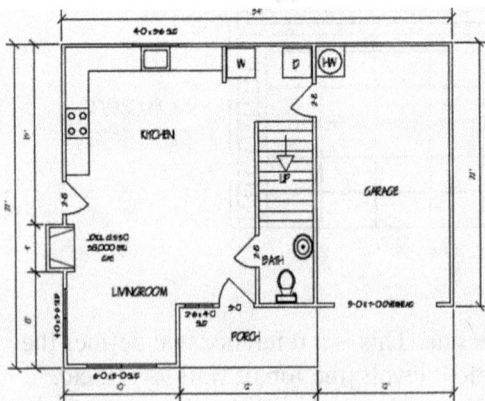

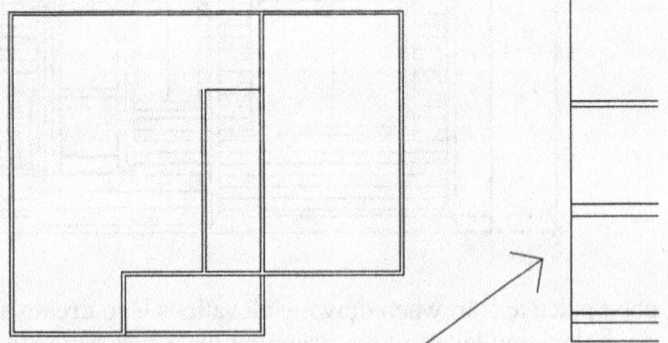

DRAW THE STORY POLE SOMEWHERE
TO THE SIDE IN OPEN SPACE

Fig 2-2A

Zoom out and **pan** to the right of your drawing as in **Fig 2-2A**. The exact placement is not important—anywhere in open space will work. With the **Ortho on** draw a **vertical line 34 ft** long.

Now **draw** the **horizontal lines** shown in **Fig 2-1**. Make them **8 ft** long. Draw **line A** (make it 8' long) at the bottom, then use **Offset** to create the other horizontal lines. The **offset measurements between each line**, starting at the bottom, are as follows: **18 / 9.5 / .75 / 8'1 / 11.5 / .75 / 8'1 / 5.5**. These are the measurements from line to line—*not from line* **A** in Fig 2-1.

Fig 2-1 details what each measurement represents. Starting at the bottom moving upward, the 18" at the bottom is the **crawl space**, above that is the 9.5" height of the **floor joists**, above that is the ¾" **plywood** subfloor, next the 8'1" represents the distance between the floor and the **first story ceiling**, etc.

Draw a 14' line at the top of the story pole as in Fig 2-3A.

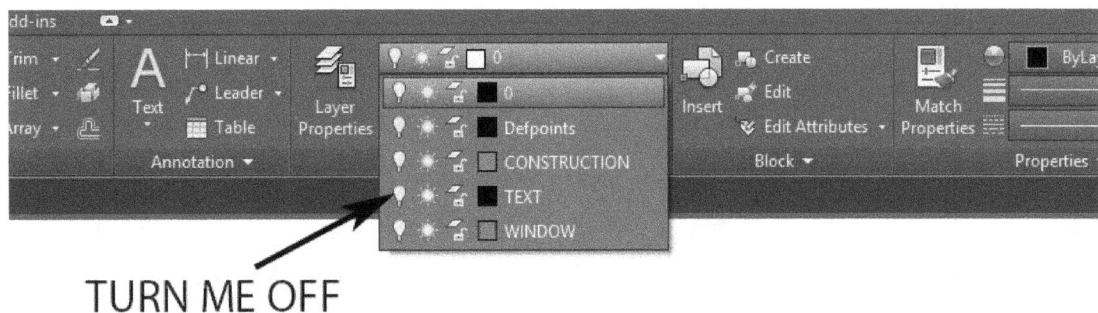

TURN ME OFF

Fig 2-2B

Turn off the **Text layer** and the **Dimension layer**. To do this go to the **Layer Control** window and click on the **little light bulb** next to the **Text Layer** (see **Fig 2-2B**) and again next to the dimension layer. When you do this the text and dimensions will disappear (we will bring it back later). You cannot turn off the current layer.

At the top of the Story Pole draw a **horizontal line** to the right **14'** long (**Fig 2-3A**).

Copy the **first story floor plan** to the end of the **14'** line as in **Fig 2-3A**. Use **Copy** and select the **lower left corner** osnap icon of the floor plan as the **base point**. Read the prompts at the command line. Snap this to the endpoint of the top horizontal line (14' line) as in **Fig 2-3A**.

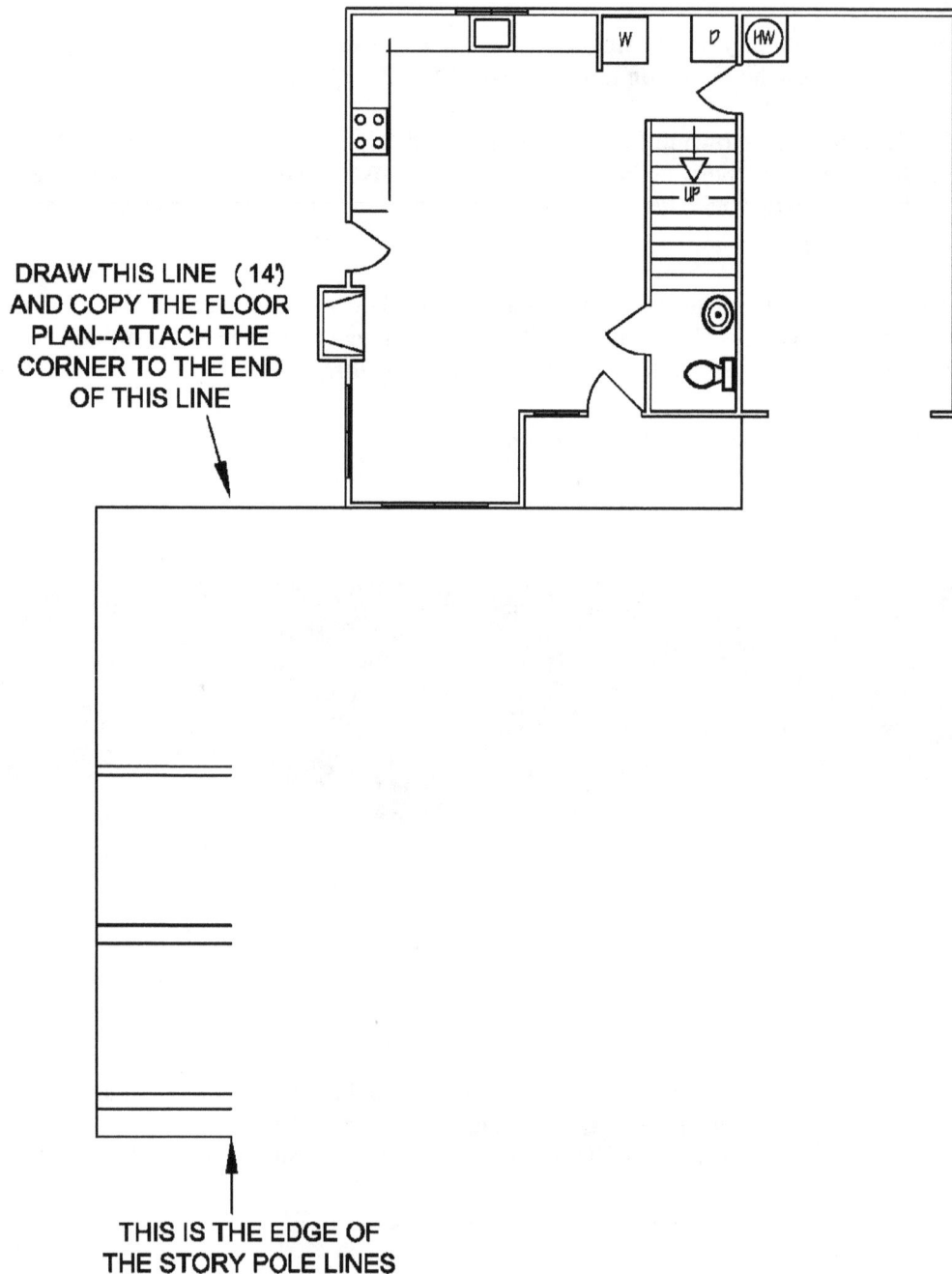

**DRAW THIS LINE (14')
AND COPY THE FLOOR
PLAN--ATTACH THE
CORNER TO THE END
OF THIS LINE**

**THIS IS THE EDGE OF
THE STORY POLE LINES**

Fig 2-3A

Select the **0 Layer** from the **Layer Control** window. Draw the **lines** shown in **Fig 2-3B**.

Draw the **horizontal lines** first as you see in **Fig 2-3B**. Draw them with the **Line** tool. Attach the starting point to the appropriate end of the story pole line then, with the **Ortho on**, end them in the space to the right of the floor plan—don't worry about the exact length as we will trim them back later. Make them extra long so they end well beyond the floor plan (we will trim them back later). Just click in open space for the second point of each line. Now add the vertical lines. As you can see the **vertical lines** are **drawn down from**: the **exterior corners** of the floor plan, the **edges and centers of the windows**, and the **sides of the doors**.

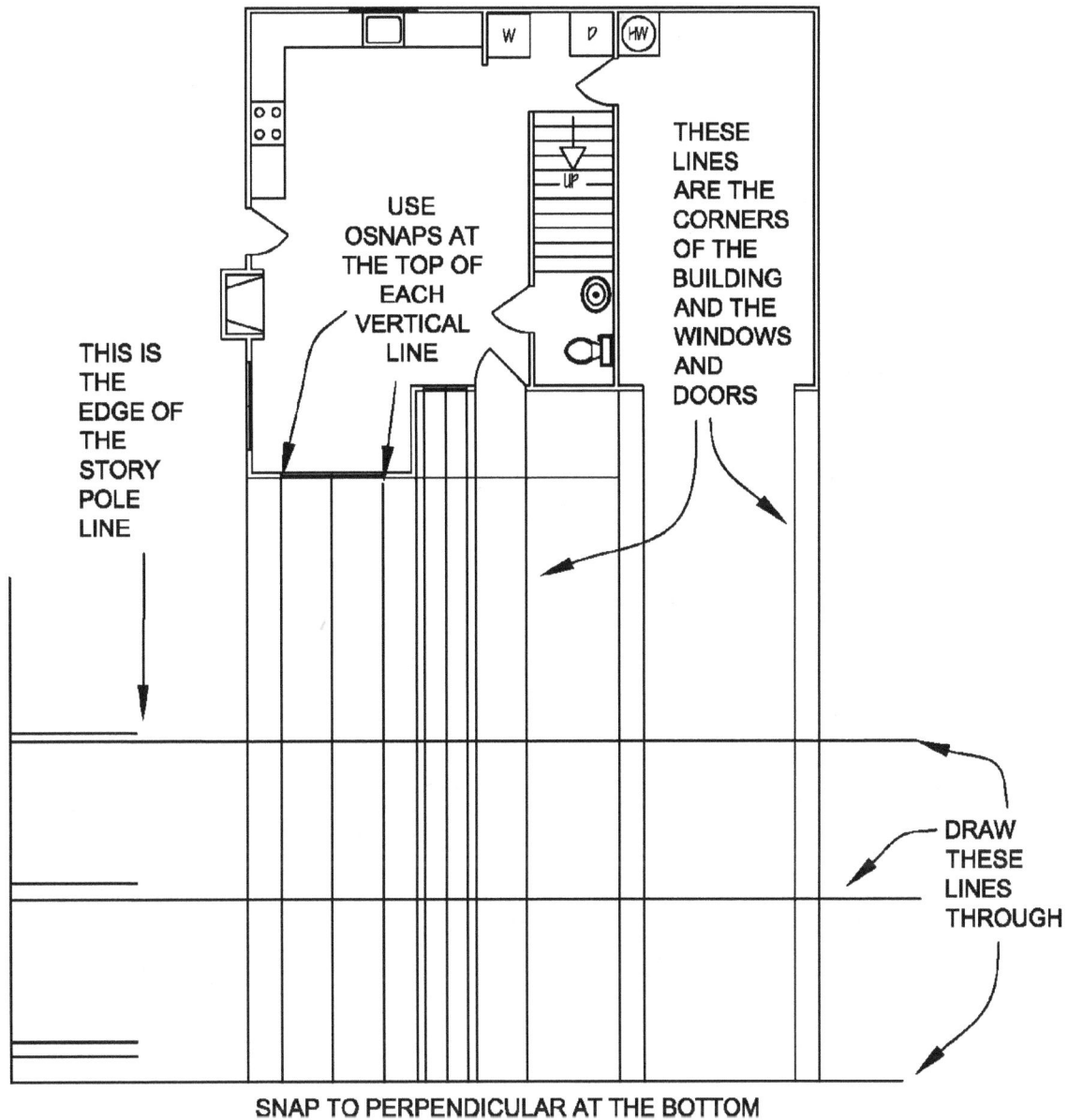

Fig. 2-3B

Use the **Object Snap** to attach the lines at the top (at the floor plan). With the **Ortho on** draw the lines down and attach them to the **Perpendicular Osnap** icon at the bottom.

We are using the floor plan as a template to measure the lines for the elevation (You could just use measurements to get the same results, but this is faster). If you have trouble understanding what we are doing look ahead at the figures to see how the drawing develops.

The vertical lines that we drew down from the windows and doors represent the windows and doors of the *first story* (the second story will be added later), so we will **trim** these lines at the **top** of the **first story** elevation and separate them from the second story as in Fig 2-4. **Trim** them to **line B** in **Fig 2-4**. Leave the corners as in Fig 2-4.

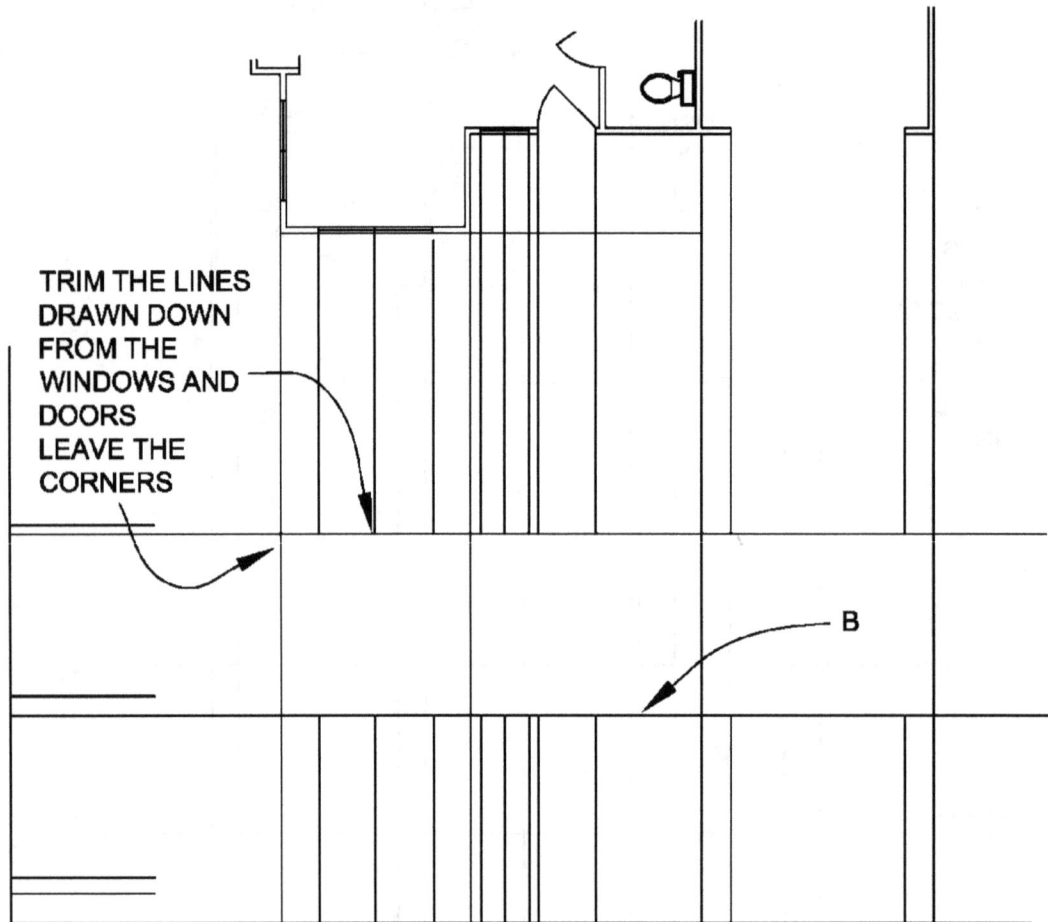

TRIM THE LINES DRAWN DOWN FROM THE WINDOWS AND DOORS LEAVE THE CORNERS

B

Fig 2-4

Now let's draw the line for the top of the doors and windows. It is offset down from the ceiling line (**B** in **Fig 2-4**). Use **Offset** and draw a line **14.5** inches **down** from line **B** (the top of the wall line) to create line **C** in **Fig 2-5**. **Trim** the lines at the **X**'s in **Fig. 2-5**.

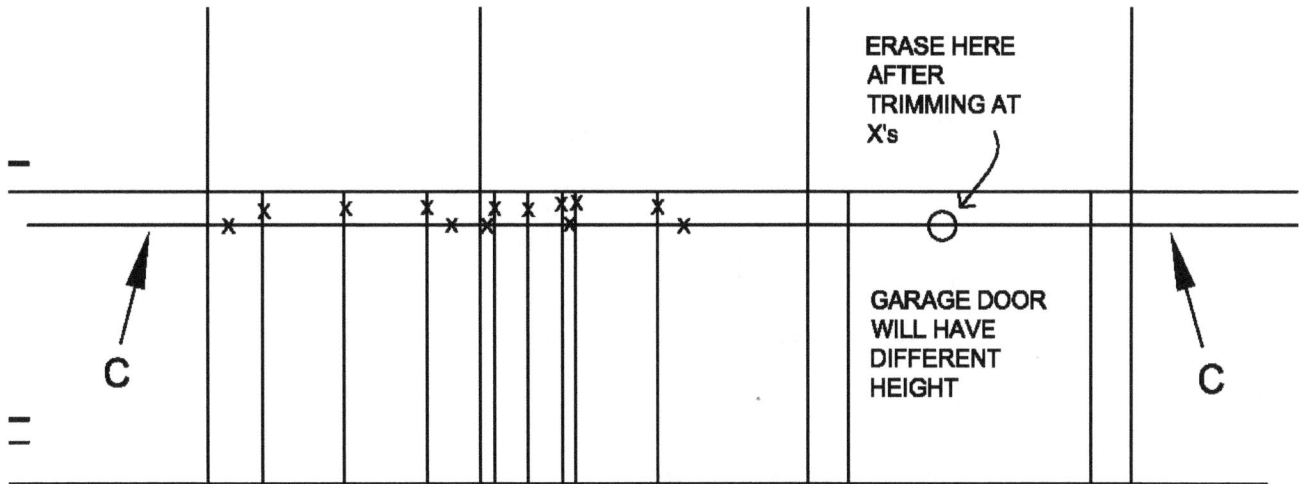

Fig. 2-5

Once trimmed you will see the **top line** and **sides** of the first story **windows** and **doors**. Your drawing will look like Fig 2-6. Look ahead a few figures and it is clear what we are doing.

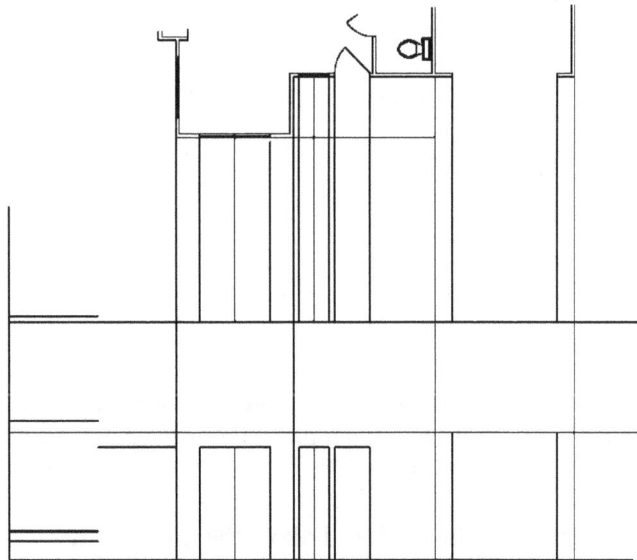

Fig 2-6

Now draw the **bottom** line of the **windows** using **Offset** as in **Fig 2-7**. The big window is **5** ft tall the small is **4** ft. The **bottom** of the **door** is drawn from the **plywood line** of the **story pole** (the bottom of the door is the ¾" **plywood line** on the story pole). **Trim** the lines from the corners and **Erase** everything else until you see **Fig 2-7**. Leave the line shown in Fig 2-7 as a marker.

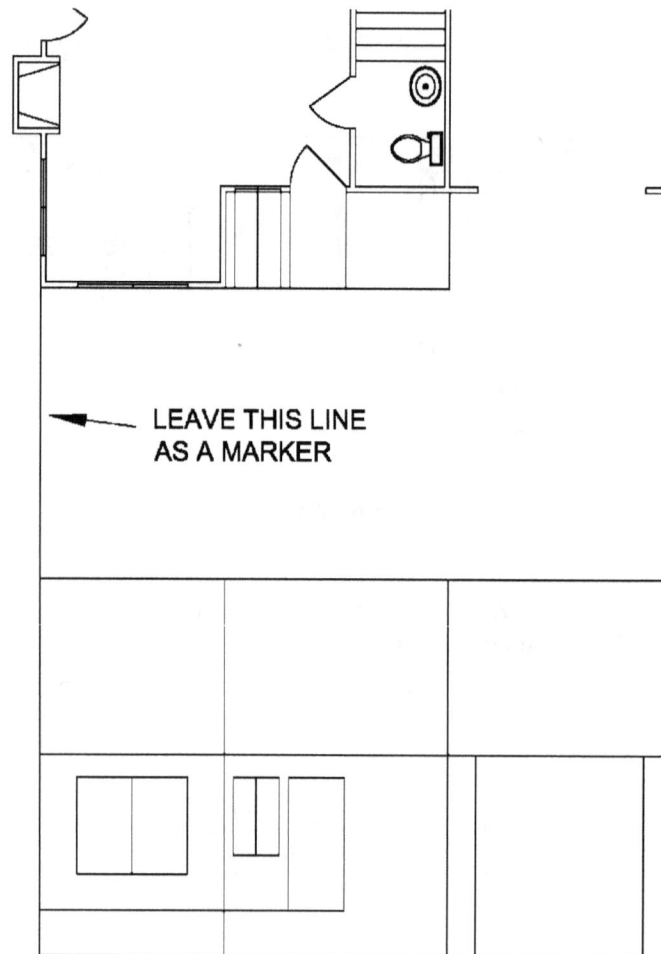

LEAVE THIS LINE
AS A MARKER

Fig 2-7

This is all of the information that we can obtain form the first story floor plan. **Erase** this copy of the **1st floor plan.** If you have drawn the second story floor plan then **place** the **second story floor plan** in its place as in **Fig 2-8**. Copy the second story floor plan as shown in Fig 2-8.

You do not need to draw the second story floor plan. Follow the directions.

If you have not drawn the second story floor plan, all you need are the six lines that delineate the sides of the windows shown in **Fig 2-8**. Use the information indicated in Fig 2-8A. Look ahead at the figures to see what we are doing.

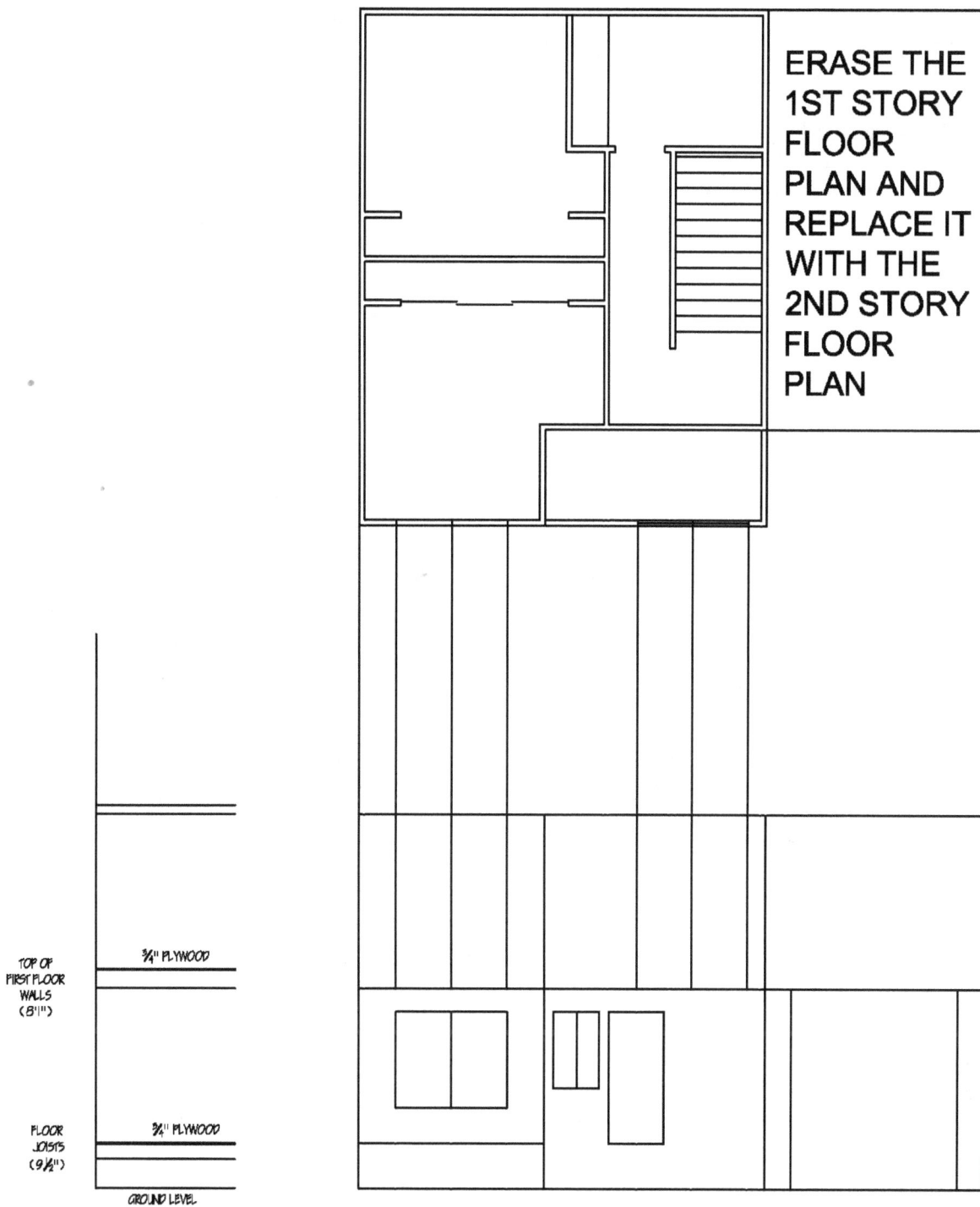

TOP OF
FIRST FLOOR
WALLS
(8'1")

¾" PLYWOOD

FLOOR
JOISTS
(9½")

¾" PLYWOOD

GROUND LEVEL

ERASE THE
1ST STORY
FLOOR
PLAN AND
REPLACE IT
WITH THE
2ND STORY
FLOOR
PLAN

Fig. 2-8

Line D (the vertical line is line D) is **12 inches from E**. Use **Offset** from the corner (E) to create D. Then **offset** again **3'** to create the next line to the left, and again (**3' offset**) to create the next line from that. The window is 6'-0" as shown in **Fig 2-8A**.

The **three lines marked F** in **Fig 2-8A** can be drawn up from the first story window lines below as they are in the same lateral position as the first story window (We could have left them from the first story, but we are doing it this way to demonstrate the concept).

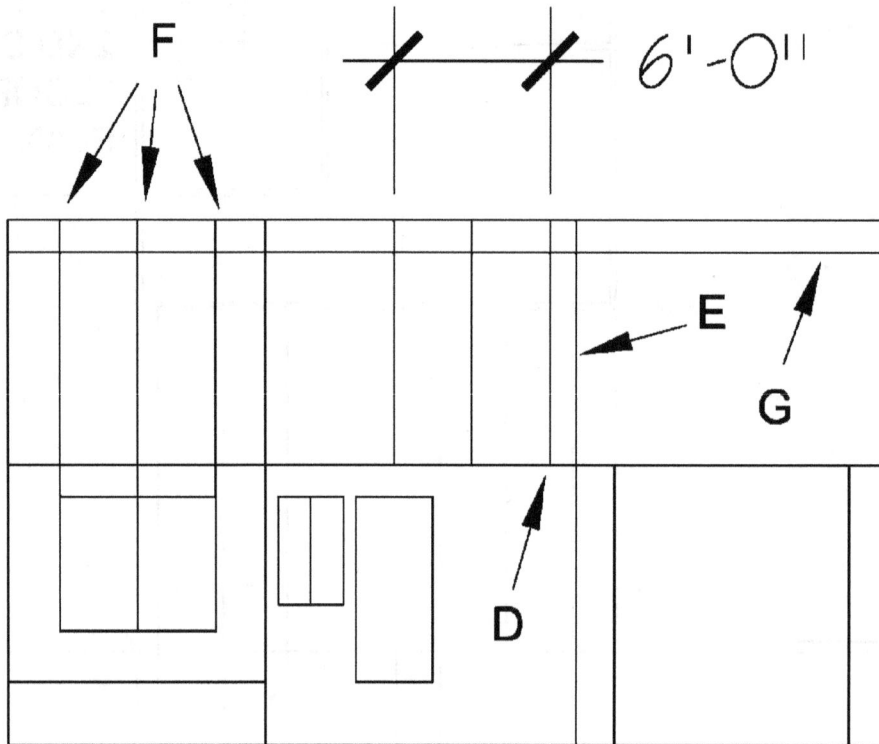

Fig 2-8A

After you draw the lines for the second story windows as in Fig 2-8, create a top of window **line** (**G in Fig 2-8A**). It is **14.5** inches below the top of the second story wall line as shown in **Fig 2-8A**. **Trim** these windows as before and use the **Offset** to create the **bottom line** of the **windows**. (**4'** for the window on the left and **3'4"** for the window on the right).

Now add the **lines** for the garage as in **Fig 2-9**. Use **Offset 2'** and **7'** as indicated. **Trim** at the **X**'s and then **erase** at the **O**'s.

Look at the completed drawing at the beginning of this chapter if you need a reference as to what the various lines represent (or flip forward through the Figures to see the progression).

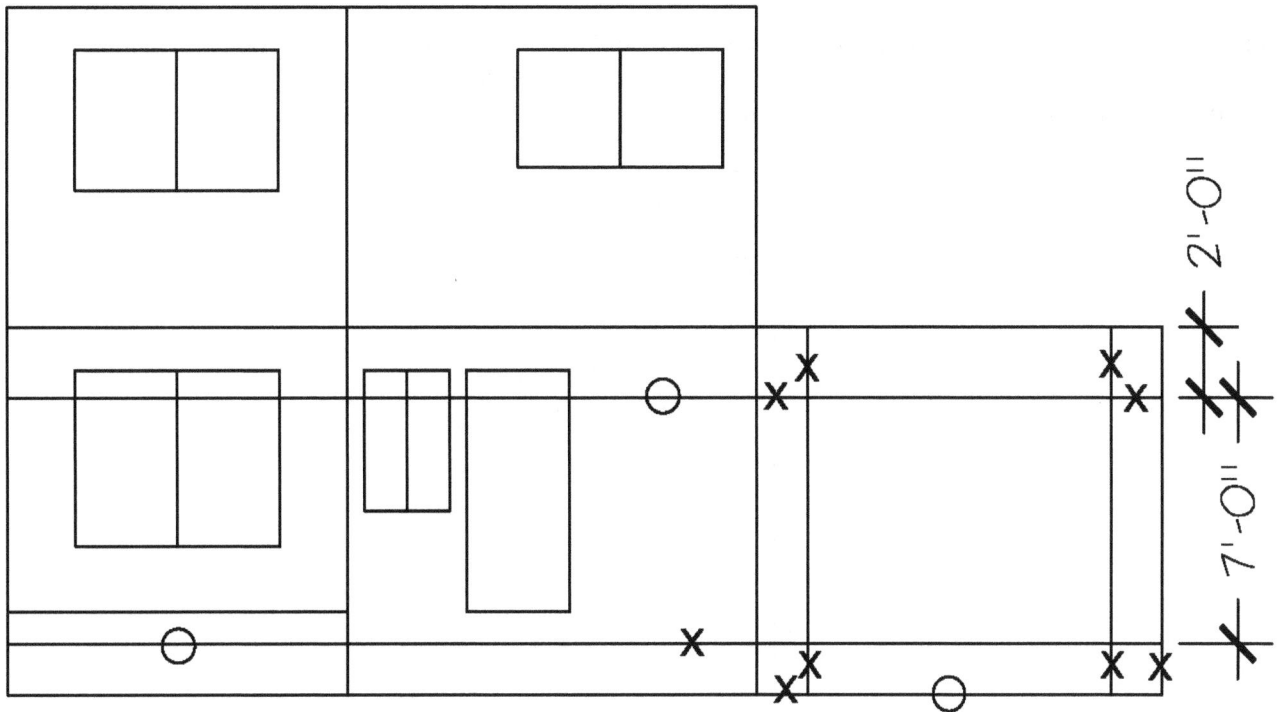

Fig 2-9

Trim the lines to look like **Fig 2-9A**.

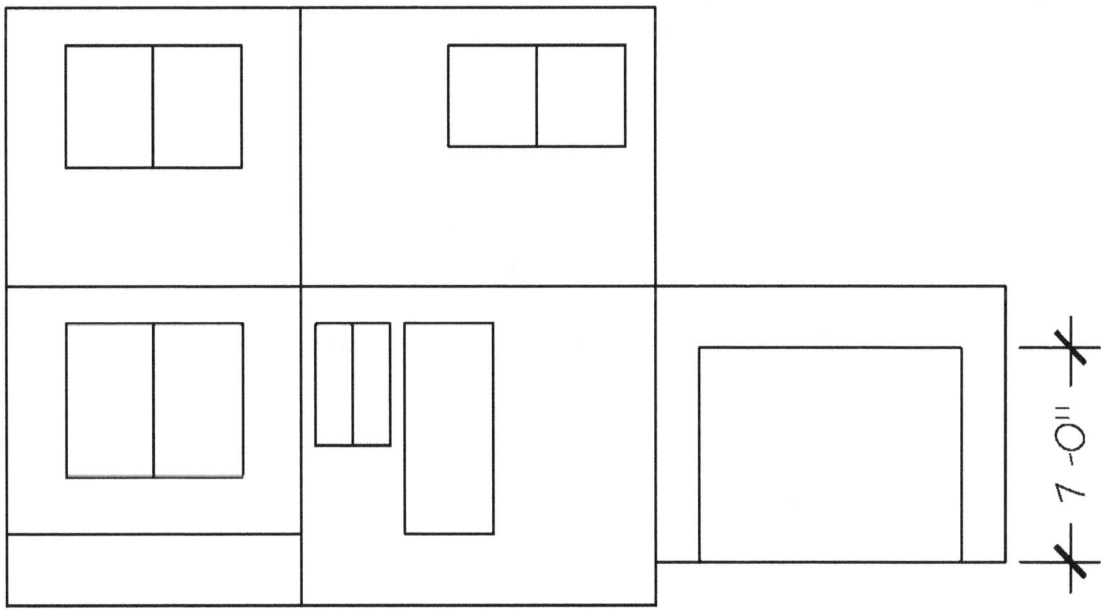

Fig 2-9A

Move the **story pole** away from this drawing so it doesn't crowd the elevation drawing. You will use it for some of the other drawings.

2.2 The Roof Lines

I like to draw a graphic of the roof where it meets the wall. It is a good way to establish precise rooflines. **Draw the figure in Fig 2-10** somewhere in empty space to the right of the elevation. Use **four separate lines** (*not the rectangle tool*).This represents the **wall** that the rafters sit on.

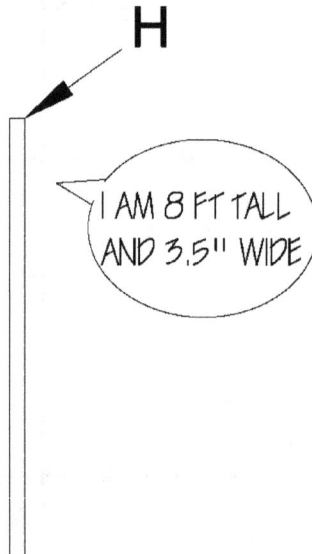

Fig 2-10

Turn on the **Object Snap** and turn off the **Ortho**. Click **Line** and then click on point **H** in **Fig 2-10** (*do not enter*). Now **type: @20'<37 <e>**. You will see a line appear that is twenty feet long at an angle of 37 degrees as in Fig 2-11. Thirty-seven degrees is the angle of our roof slope (9 in 12 slope in construction terms).

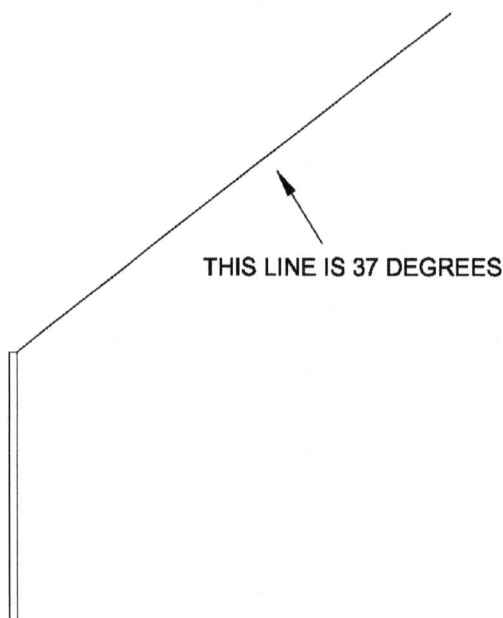

Fig. 2-11

Now we will draw Fig 2-12. Look at **Fig 2-12** then **read** through the **steps** in Figures 2-12A through 2-12D.

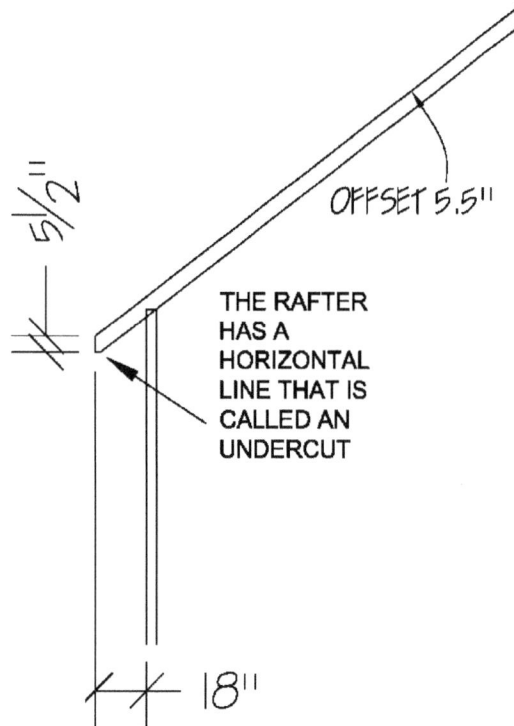

Fig. 2-12

First, **Offset** the **angled line** by **5.5"** as in **Fig 2-12A**.

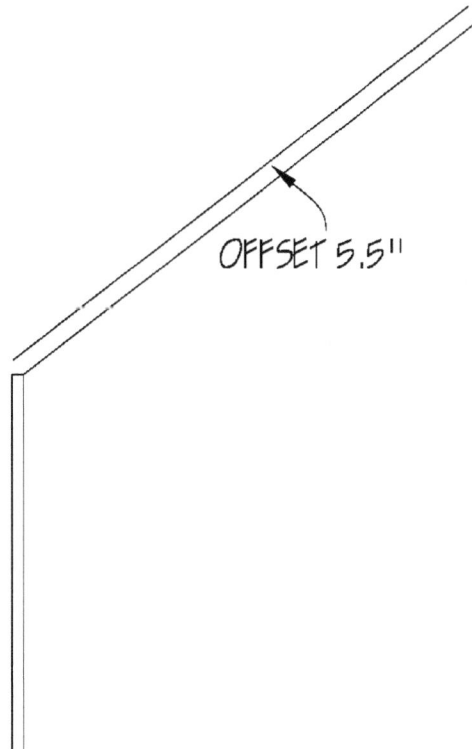

Fig. 2-12A

Use **Offset** to draw the line that is **18"** to the left of the wall in **Fig 2-12B**.

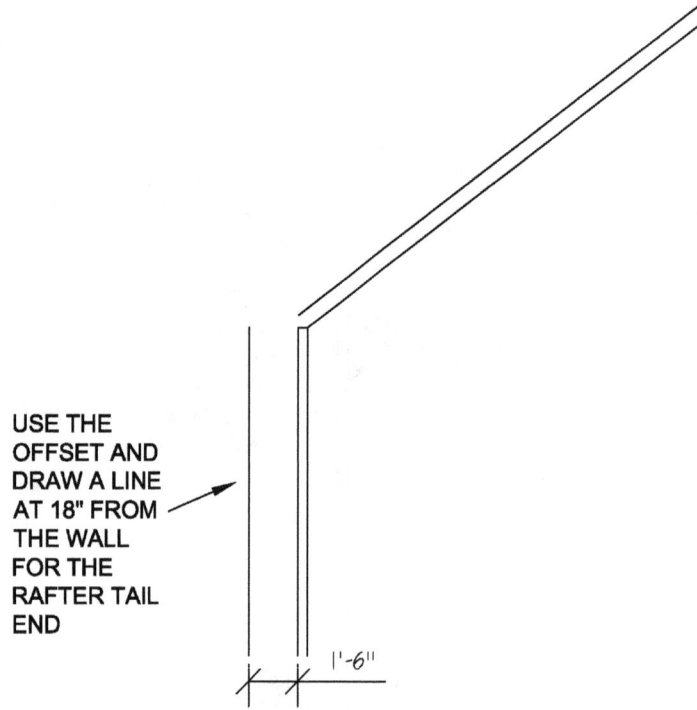

USE THE
OFFSET AND
DRAW A LINE
AT 18" FROM
THE WALL
FOR THE
RAFTER TAIL
END

1'-6"

Fig. 2-12B

Extend the **angled lines** to meet this 18" offset line as in **Fig 12-2C**.

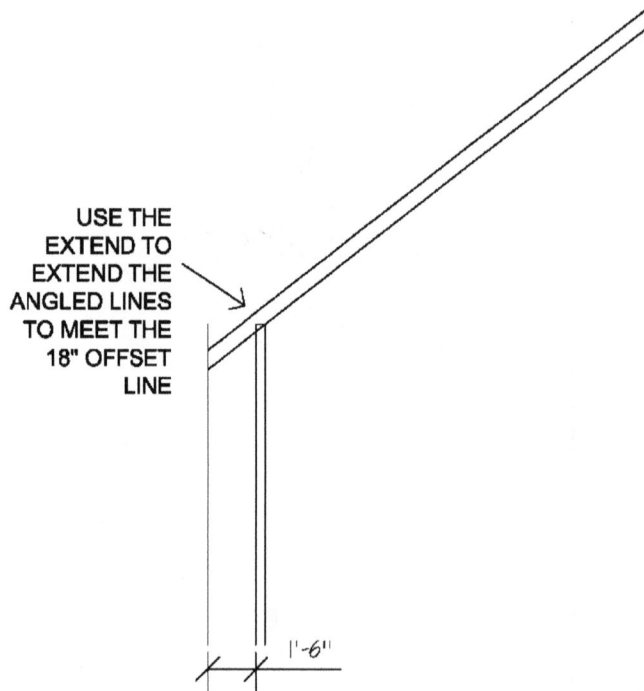

USE THE
EXTEND TO
EXTEND THE
ANGLED LINES
TO MEET THE
18" OFFSET
LINE

1'-6"

Fig. 2-12C

Click on the **Line** button then hold down the shift button on your keyboard and right click the mouse. Select **From** then **click** on the **point** indicated in **Fig 2-12D** then **hover** (*do not click*) over the icon at the bottom of this line, **type 5.5 <e>**, this will attach the **first point** of a new line to this vertical line. **Draw** the line out to the **right** (Ortho on) and **click** in open space to create the line shown in **Fig 2-12D**.

Use the line tool, click **Line** then use **From** (click the Line button then hold down the shift key and right click—select From) click the top point of the vertical line (at arrow), hover over the bottom of that vertical line (do not click) type 5.5. Then stretch the line to the right and click as shown.

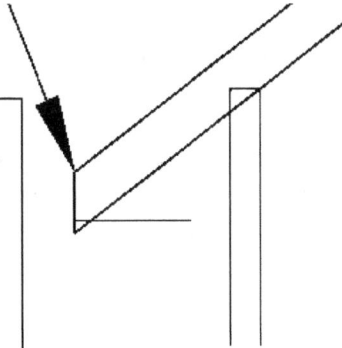

Fig. 2-12D

Trim the end of the rafter to look like **Fig 2-13**.

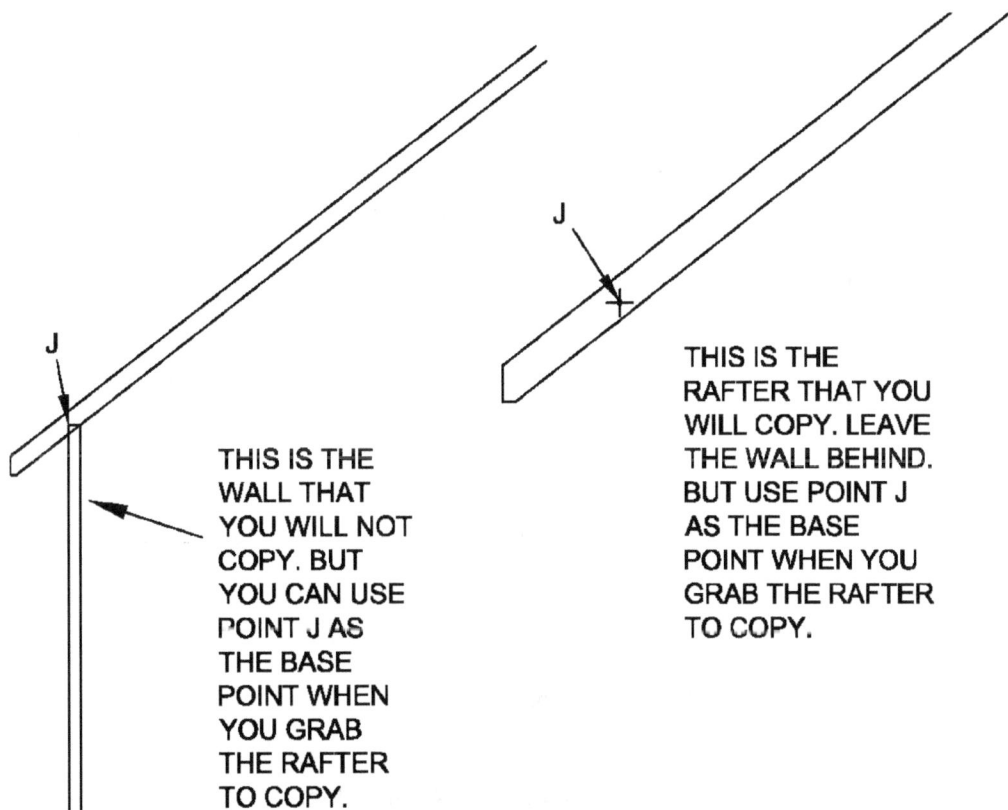

THIS IS THE WALL THAT YOU WILL NOT COPY. BUT YOU CAN USE POINT J AS THE BASE POINT WHEN YOU GRAB THE RAFTER TO COPY.

THIS IS THE RAFTER THAT YOU WILL COPY. LEAVE THE WALL BEHIND. BUT USE POINT J AS THE BASE POINT WHEN YOU GRAB THE RAFTER TO COPY.

Fig. 2-13

Copy the roof **rafter** but **not the wall**. Read the prompts in the Command Line window. When it says: **Specify base point**, **click** on the upper wall corner at **J**, and **snap it** to **point K** on the elevation drawing as in **Fig 2-14**.

You will notice that the base point (for copying, moving, etc) need not be part of the items to be copied. The base point can be anywhere on the screen (point J in this case). This is very useful for many applications. In this case point J represents the top outside corner of the wall; the rafter has a notch (called a bird's mouth cut or seat cut) that sits on the corner of the wall frame.

One of the concepts in AutoCAD that is difficult to explain is: when you **copy (or move, rotate, etc)**, the **point at which you grab** the object to be copied **does not need to be copied** with the object. This is called the base point.

In the example of the rafter in Fig 2-13, we are **copying only** the **object shown to the right** (minus the cross that represents the cursor), but we are using **point J** (the intersection of the horizontal and vertical wall lines) as a **base point** (the point where we grab the object to be copied). This is the point we wish to snap to the new destination point of the copy (as at K in Fig 2-14).

This same principle applies to the Move command, Rotate, any command that requires a base point.

The base point for these commands can be anywhere in the workspace.

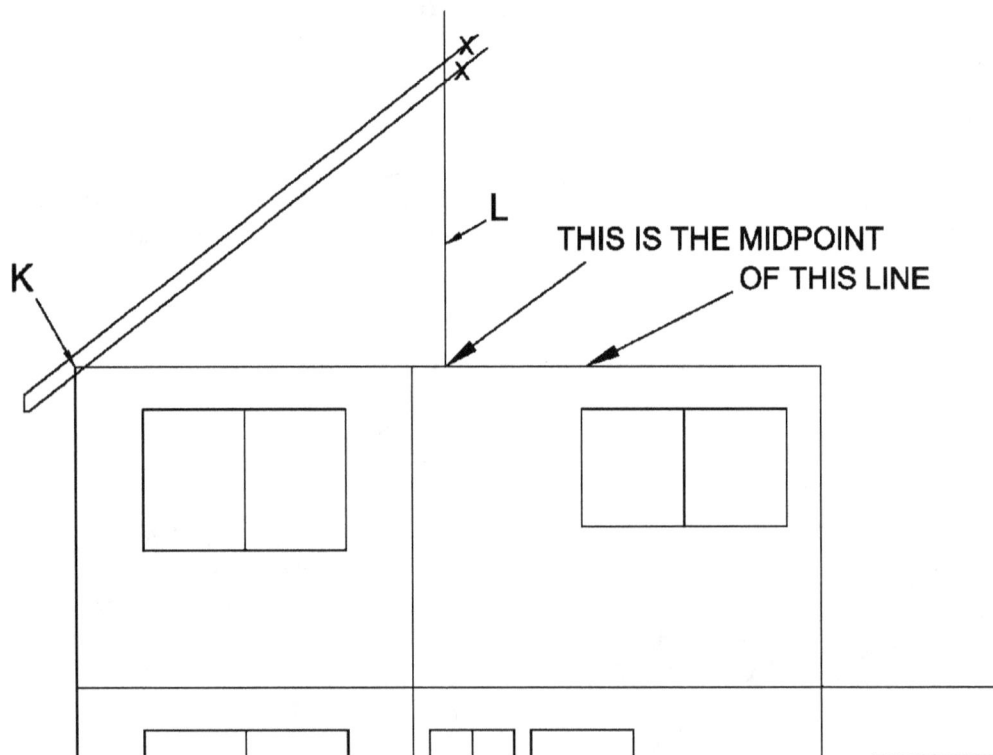

Fig 2-14

Find the center of the top wall line as in **Fig 2-14** and draw a **line** straight up (L) with the **Ortho on**. End the line in open space above the rafter (just click the end of this line in open space). **Trim** the rafter at the **X's** shown in **Fig 2-14**.

Now click the **Mirror** button on the Modify palette and **select** the **rafter** (only the rafter)—*do not select the top of the wall*. **Enter** and **read** the command line **prompt**. It asks for the first point of the mirror line. Click the **bottom** and **then** the **top** of **line L** <enter>. You will see Fig 2-15.

Fig. 2-15

Now **repeat** the process to **create Fig 2-16**. You can click on the center of the window for the first point of the mirror line (you do not need to actually draw a line with the line tool—the **mirror line** is an invisible line drawn between **any two points** you choose to click on). Use **Ortho**, **click** on **Mirror**, then **select** the **rafter** to the left <e>, **click** on the **middle** of the **window** and then **click anywhere above** the drawing (anywhere in the open space for the upper end of the mirror line).

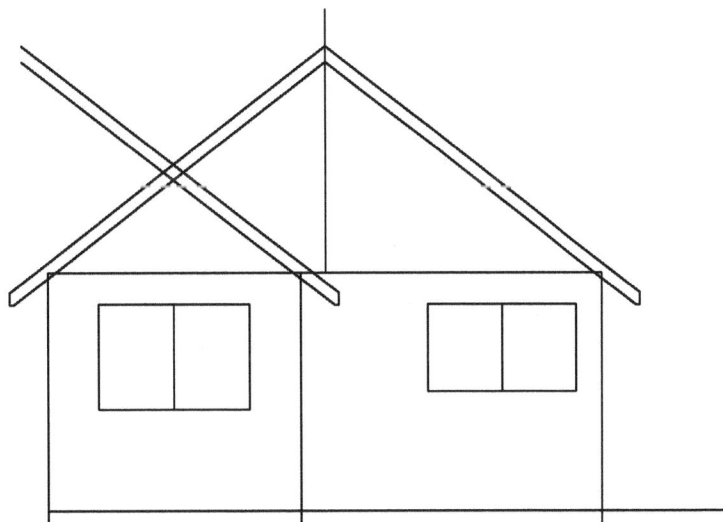

Fig 2-16

Mirror lines are not lines drawn on the screen. Mirror lines are a boundary between the two mirrored images. See Appendix I—Mirror for an explanation of this concept.

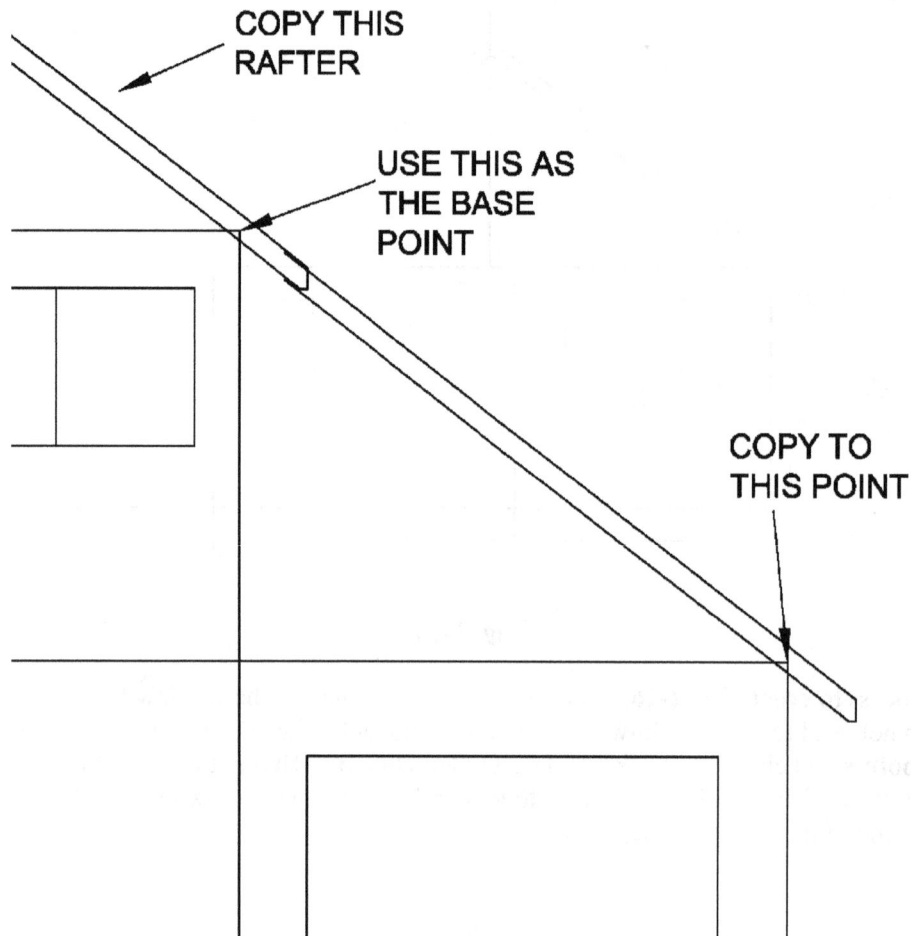

COPY THIS
RAFTER

USE THIS AS
THE BASE
POINT

COPY TO
THIS POINT

Fig. 2-16A

Copy the rafter to the right side of the garage (**Fig 2-16A**). Now draw the roof on the garage using the mirror tool. Use the **midpoint of the top line** of the **garage door** as the **mirror** line. Start the mirror line at **M** in **Fig. 2-17** and draw the line straight up with the **Ortho on**—**click** in the open space **above** for the upper end of the mirror line.

Draw a **line** from the top of **T** in **Fig 2-17** to the left and attach it to the vertical line of the house as shown.

Trim line **L** (Fig 2-14) **above** and **below** the **rafters** to look like **Fig 2-17**.

Make a **copy** of this **elevation** before proceeding and set it to one side for use in the cross section drawing in Chapter 5.

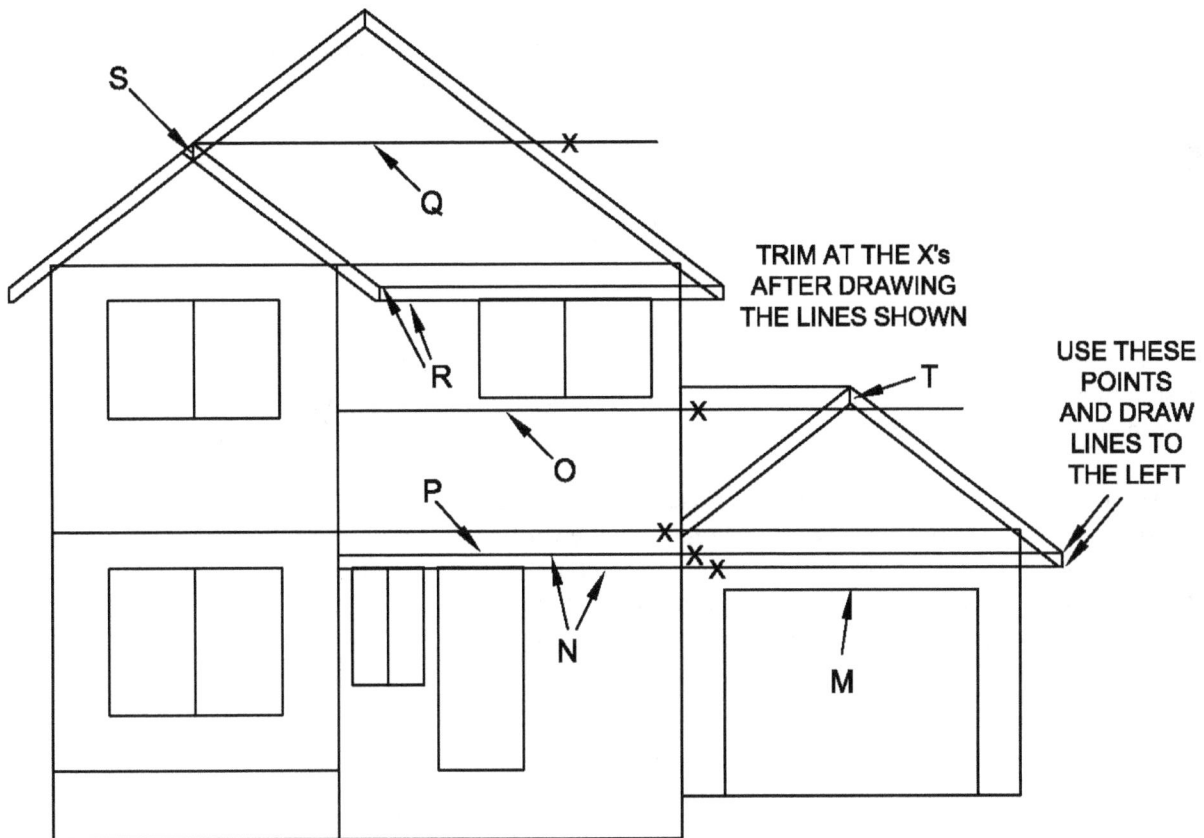

Fig 2-17

Draw the fascia **lines** of the front porch roof (**N in Fig 2-17**) using the garage roof overhang as a template as shown in Fig 2-17. Draw the **line** at the top of the porch roof (**O**) with the **Offset** tool at **4'11"** from line **P**.

Draw **line Q**. Start the line at the small ridge shown in Fig 2-17 and draw it through into open space (no object snap at the right end of this line). Then **trim** it at the **X** shown. Draw the **lines** for the fascia for this roof section by connecting the overhangs as shown at **R**. Add **lines S** and **T**. Then **trim** at the **X**'s. **Trim** and **erase** to look like **Fig 2-18**. You will see a house.

Fig 2-18

That was a lot of steps. Don't worry if your drawing is not exact, or if you missed a trim here or there. You can trim and add lines later. The idea is to learn how to draw, not to create a perfect copy of this drawing.

2.3 Porch

Next we will add the front porch posts. First draw the **line** for the porch deck (the floor) as in **Fig 2-19**; it is ¾" **below** the **bottom** of the **door**.

> The exact locations and sizes are not really important; we are learning drawing techniques and not trying to create a perfect drawing. So don't spend too much energy trying to be super precise at this point in the process. For now it is best to move along as quickly as possible in order to learn the drawing techniques. You can make your drawings precise after you learn how to draw.

Use **Offset** to establish line **U** in **Fig 2-19** it is offset **5'2"** from the (corner) line **V**. Use **Offset** again to create the **lines** marked **W** (there are two lines W—these represent the width of the posts for the porch—look ahead in the figures to see what these lines represent) these are the porch posts. They are **offset 3.5"** from U on the left and **3.5"** from V on the right as shown. Then **trim** at the **X**'s and **erase** at the **O**'s to **see Fig 2-20**. Look at the completed drawing on page 51 to see what this should look like.

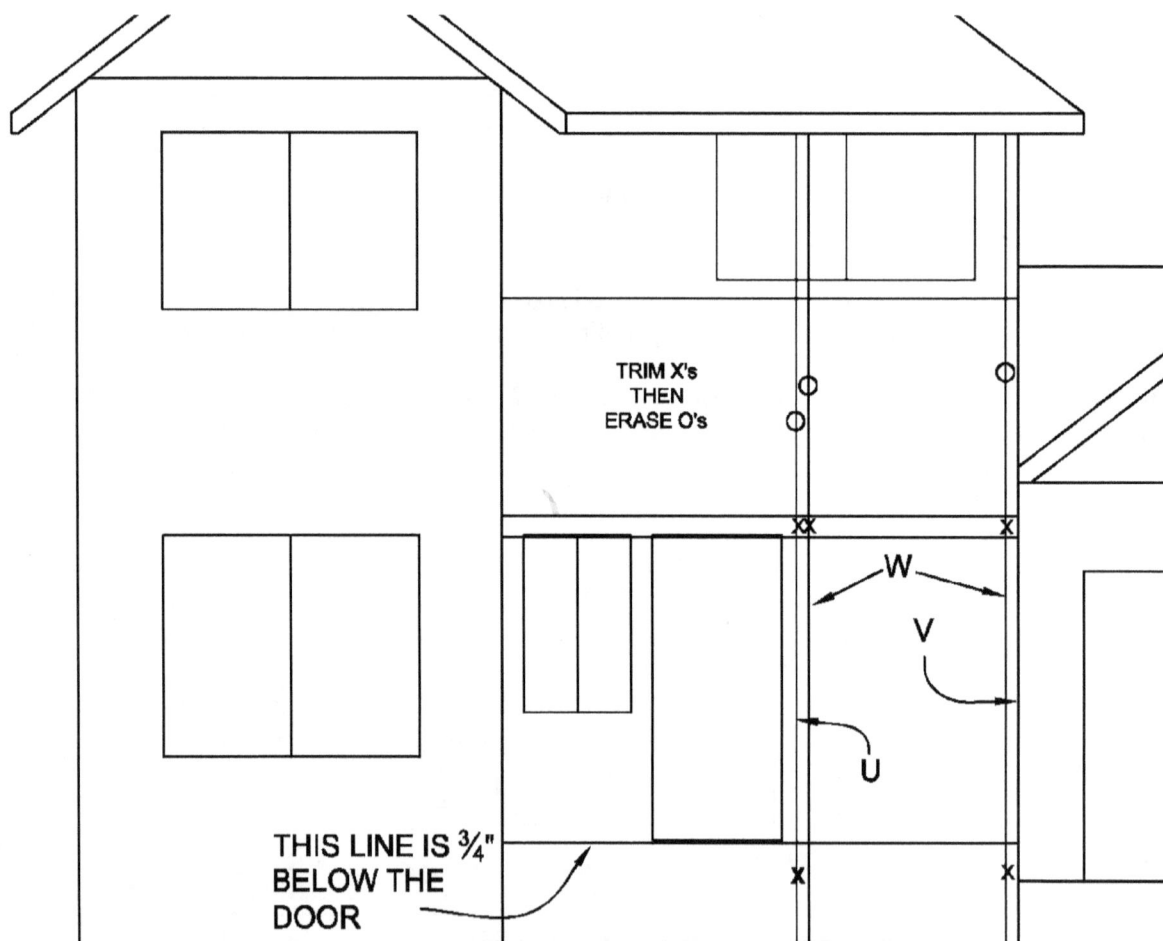

Fig 2-19

If you zoom way in and look at the top of the door and the window next to the door you will see that the lines cross over the porch fascia. **Trim** them back to line **Y** in Fig **2-20**.

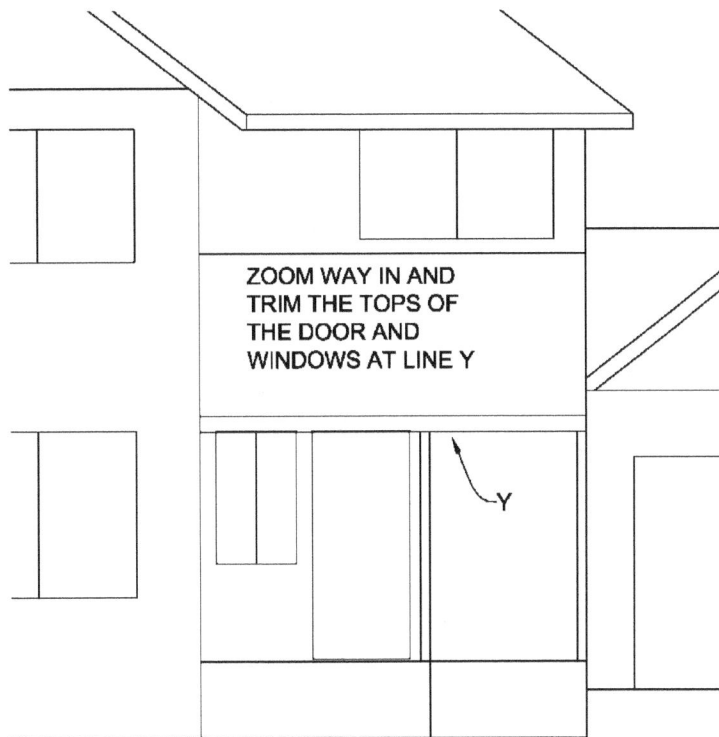

Fig 2-20

2.4 Knee Braces

Now we are going to do something a bit more complicated: draw the knee braces on the porch (Fig 2-21).

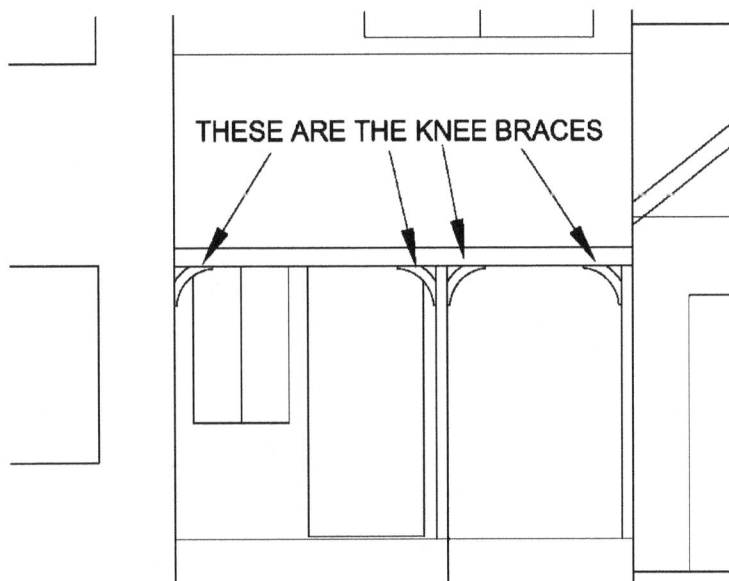

Fig 2-21

Fig 2-22 shows the steps for drawing a knee brace. Off to the side of the elevation—in open space, draw the first **rectangle** at **13"** x **13"**. Use the **rectangle** tool. You must click the screen at the end to set the rectangle.

Now click the **Circle** button on the Draw palette and click at the point shown as **A** in **Fig 2-22**. Follow the prompts at the Command Line. It asks for a **radius** or diameter—select radius). Type **12 <e>**. **Trim** and **erase** as shown to get **FIG B**.

Use **Offset** to make another larger arc (**3" offset**) as in **FIG C** in **Fig 2-22**. **Trim** as shown to get **FIG D**.

Add a **Point** to the corner **E**. **Click** on **Point** (same as Multiple Points) on the **Draw** palette (click the down arrow next to Draw or type point) and then **click** on the corner **E**. This point is called a **Node** when we snap to it. **Trim** the knee brace to get **FIG E**. *Your point at E will be very small*.

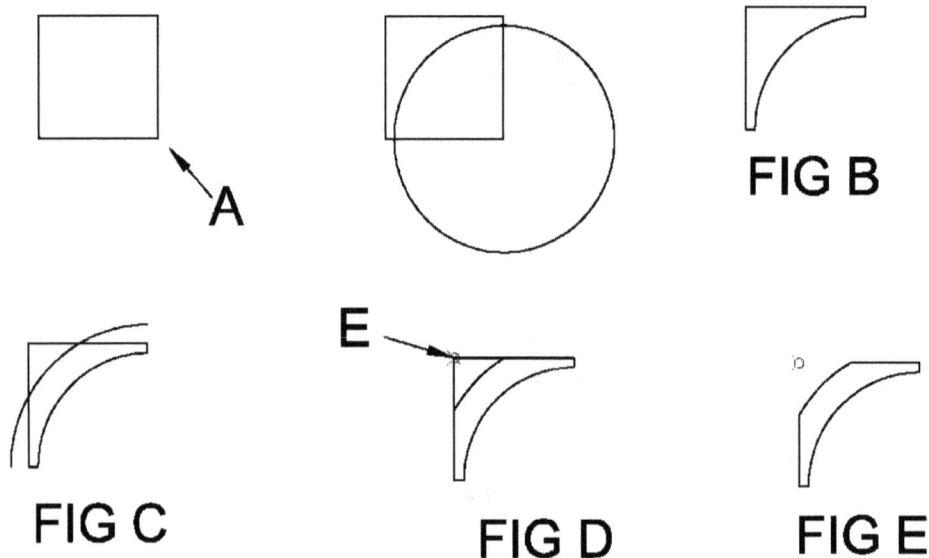

Fig 2-22

Copy this knee brace. The **base point** (where you grab it) is at the **node** point **E** that you created. First you must go to the **Osnap** settings and select the **Node Osnap**: right click in the Osnap button at the bottom of your screen, select settings and turn on the Node Osnap (See Appendix I—Object snap settings for help). **Copy** the knee brace to points **F** and **G** in **Fig 2-23** using the node at point E as the base point for the knee brace.

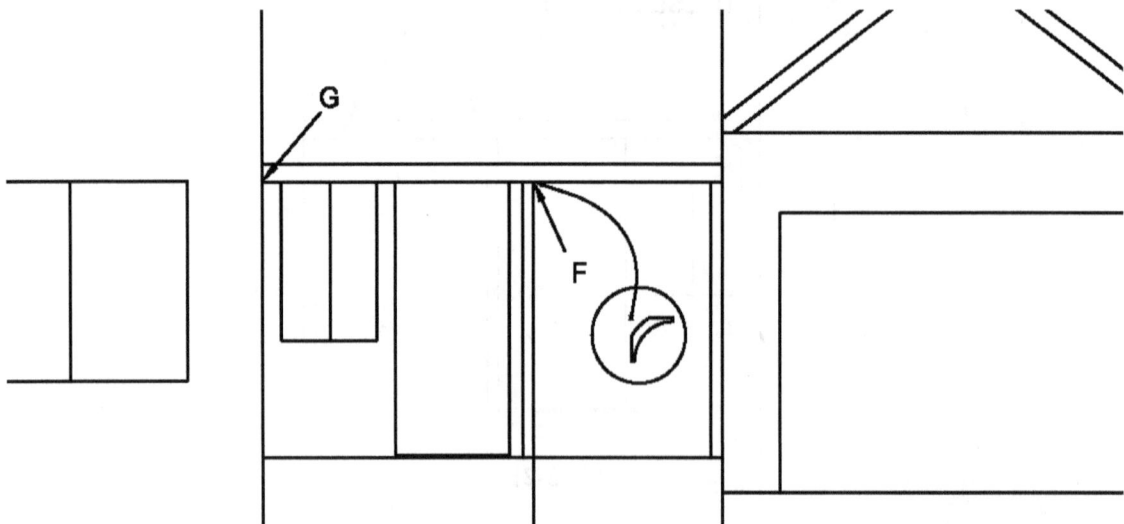

Fig 2-23

Make a **copy** of the **knee brace** in open work space. Include the point/node in this copy. Use the **Mirror** command to create a **mirror image** (see Appendix I—Mirror if you need help). **Copy** the mirror image knee brace to the other two **inside corner points** to get **Fig 2-21**. These are the intersections of the lines that represent the posts—not the door or the outside corner of the porch.

2.5 Gable Vents

We will now draw the gable vents. Click on the **Polygon** button on the **Draw** palette (co-located with Rectangle). The command line will ask for the **number** of **sides**. Type **8 <e>**. Off to the side of our drawing a bit, in open space as in **Fig 2-24**, **click**, you will see nothing, but the Command line will read: **Enter an option…** the default is **Inscribed (I)** so just hit the **<e>** to select this option. Now it asks for the **radius**, type **9 <e>**. An octagon will appear where you clicked in the open space. **Make a copy** of this (so you have two).

We are going to scale down one of these copies of the octagon. Click on the **Scale** button on the **Modify** palette. **Select** the **copy** of the **octagon** and **<e>**. The **base point** can be anywhere in the octagon, **click**. Type **.66 <e>**. This will now be 2/3 (66% or .66) of the original copy.

Draw the **lines** in **Fig 2-24** down from the **bottom** of the ridges. **Copy** the large octagon to the bottom of the **18"** line and the smaller octagon to the **12"** lines as in **Fig 2-25**.

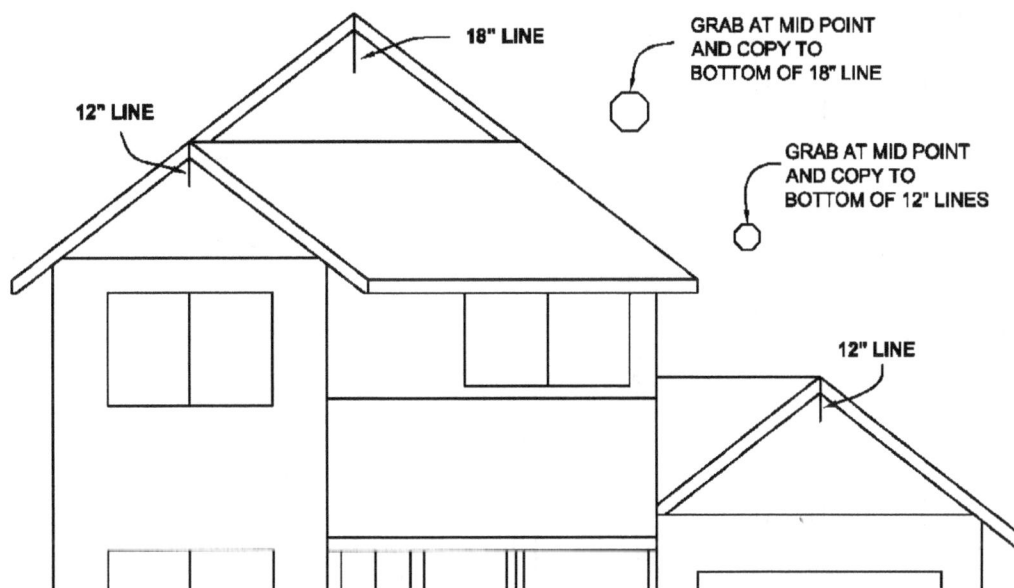

Fig 2-24

2.6 Trim

Let's put some trim on the building. Draw **line H** at the bottom of **Fig 2-25**. Offset it **7.5"** from **I**. Trim it at the **X**. This is the bottom of the siding.

Draw the **lines J** (there are three). **Offset** this from the existing gable lines **2.5** inches, below for the garage and small gable, and above for the large upper gable. **Extend** these lines to meet the vertical lines at the edge of the building (see **Fig 2-25**).

Offset the corners **4"**, and **Extend** these **lines** up to meet the lines **J**.

Offset the windows to the outside **4"** to create the window trim. **Offset** the front **door** and the **garage door 4"** to the **outside**.

Use **Fillet** (set radius to **0"**) to close up the **corners** of the window and door trim. Read the prompts. Make sure you catch the **third prompt** and enter **M** for multiple. That way you don't have to restart the command for each corner.

Extend the window **trim** next to the **door** over to meet the door trim at **K**. **Extend** the side of the door and the door trim down to the deck at lines **L**.

Offset the octagons by **2"** to the outside. **Trim** at the **X**'s and then **erase** at the **O**'s as shown in **Fig 2-25**.

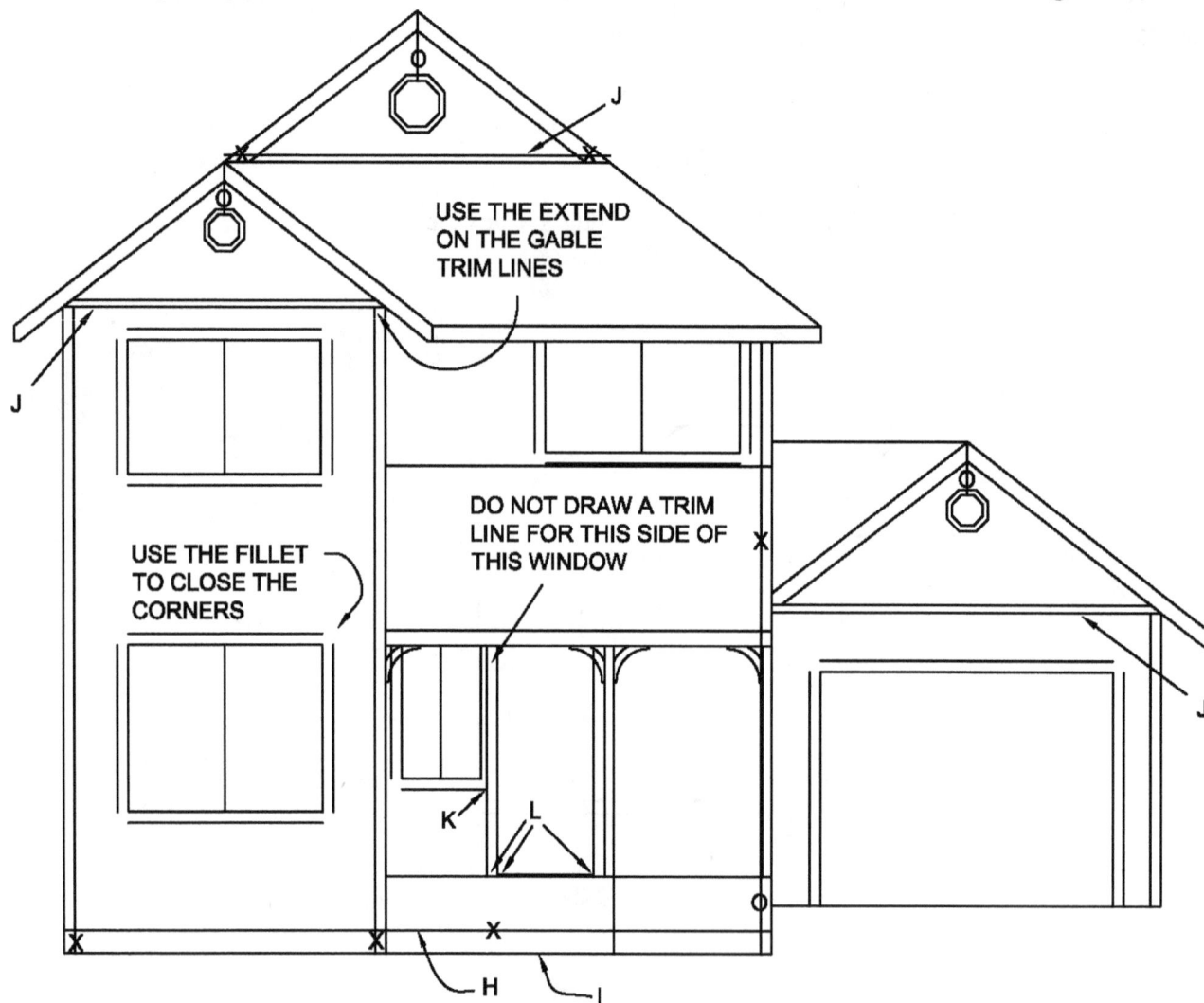

USE THE EXTEND ON THE GABLE TRIM LINES

DO NOT DRAW A TRIM LINE FOR THIS SIDE OF THIS WINDOW

USE THE FILLET TO CLOSE THE CORNERS

Fig 2-25

Draw the top of the lower left window at **M** in **Fig. 2-26**—this a small roof cap over the box window. The **offset** for this is **12"**. Clean up any loose ends to see Fig 2-26 (minus the grids on the garage door—they are next).

Trim the lines inside the porch **knee braces**.

2.7 Garage Door and Porch Rail

Now we will draw the lines on the garage door.

Type **divide** <e>. **Select** the right side of the garage door <e> (at **N** in **Fig 2-26**). Type **5** <e>. **Read the Command Line** as you do this so you can see what is happening. You are dividing this line into five sections. Each section is marked by a **node** that you will only see if you try to snap something to it (or if you set your nodes to a larger size—see Appendix I—Nodes and Points). Make certain that the **Node Object Snap** is turned **on** in your Osnap settings window.

Click **line** and then attach the **first point** of the line to a **node** on **line N,** draw a line to the left and attach it to the perpendicular osnap on the other side of the garage door (you will need to move your cursor up and down the line N until you locate a node Osnap—the same type of osnap point/node that you used to copy the knee braces at E in Fig 2-22). See **Fig 2-26**. **Repeat** this process for each of the four horizontal lines. Don't mistake the midpoint osnap for a node.

Now **repeat** this process for each of the three vertical lines—use **Divide** then **select** the **line (P)** at the top of the door opening as the **select object**, at the prompt type **4** divisions and <e>. The midpoint and the middle node will be the same point this time—pick either osnap for the center line.

Fig 2-26

Next we will draw the **deck rail**. Look at **Fig 2-32** to see the completed deck rail.

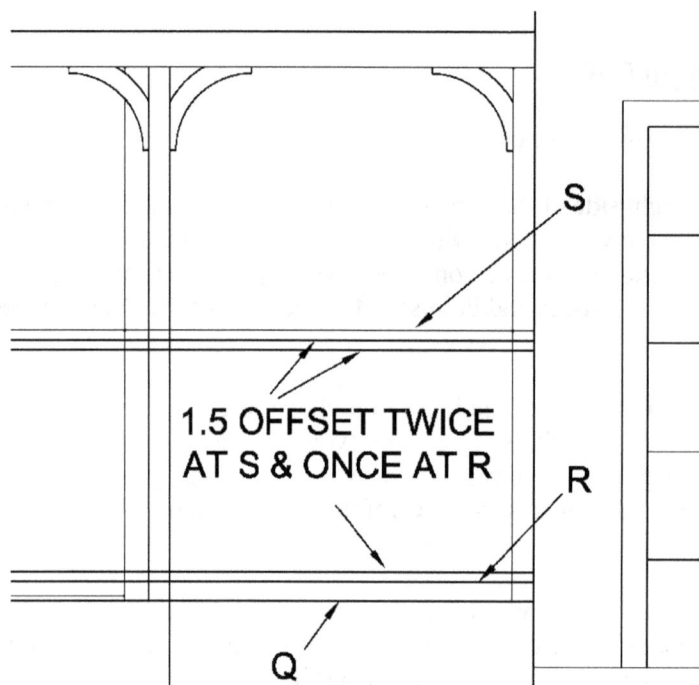

Fig 2-27

Offset the deck line (**Q** in **Fig 2-27**) **3"** to draw line **R**. Offset **Q** again **42"** to create **line S** in **Fig 2-27**. Create the **thickness** of the **rails** (single at the **bottom** and double at the **top rail**) using **1.5 offset** as in **Fig 2-27**.

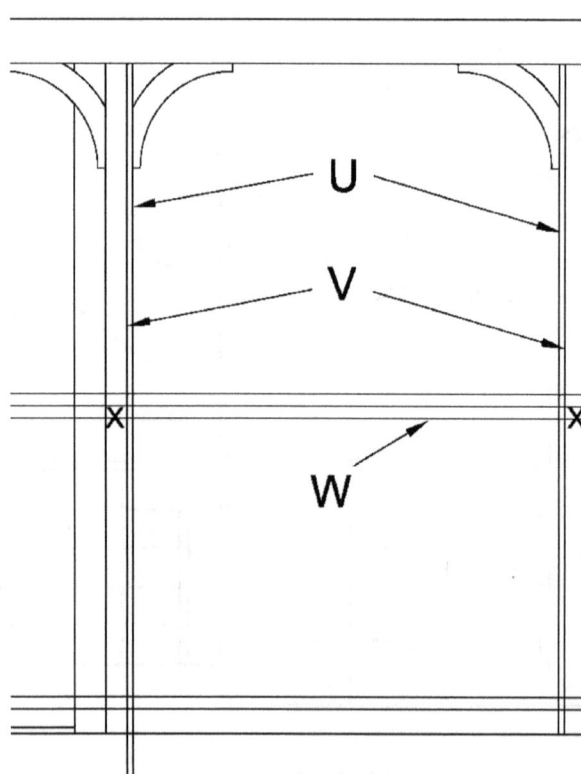

Fig 2-28

Draw **lines V** in **Fig 2-28**. They are **offset .75"** from the lines marked **U**. **Trim** Where you see the **X**'s. This will extend line W beyond lines U by ¾" both sides.

Set the **Construction layer current**.

Type **divide <e>**. **Select** the line **W** in **Fig 2-28**. **Type 11 <e>**. **Set the 0 layer current**.

Now draw lines as you did with the garage door using the **nodes** at the top (line W) and the **perpendicular osnap** at the bottom. **Offset** all of these lines by **.75"** to **both sides** as in **Fig 2-29**. Select all of the middle lines at once and **erase** them. These are the balusters. **Erase** the **V** lines in Fig 2-28. **Trim** the rail lines back to the posts (**U**).

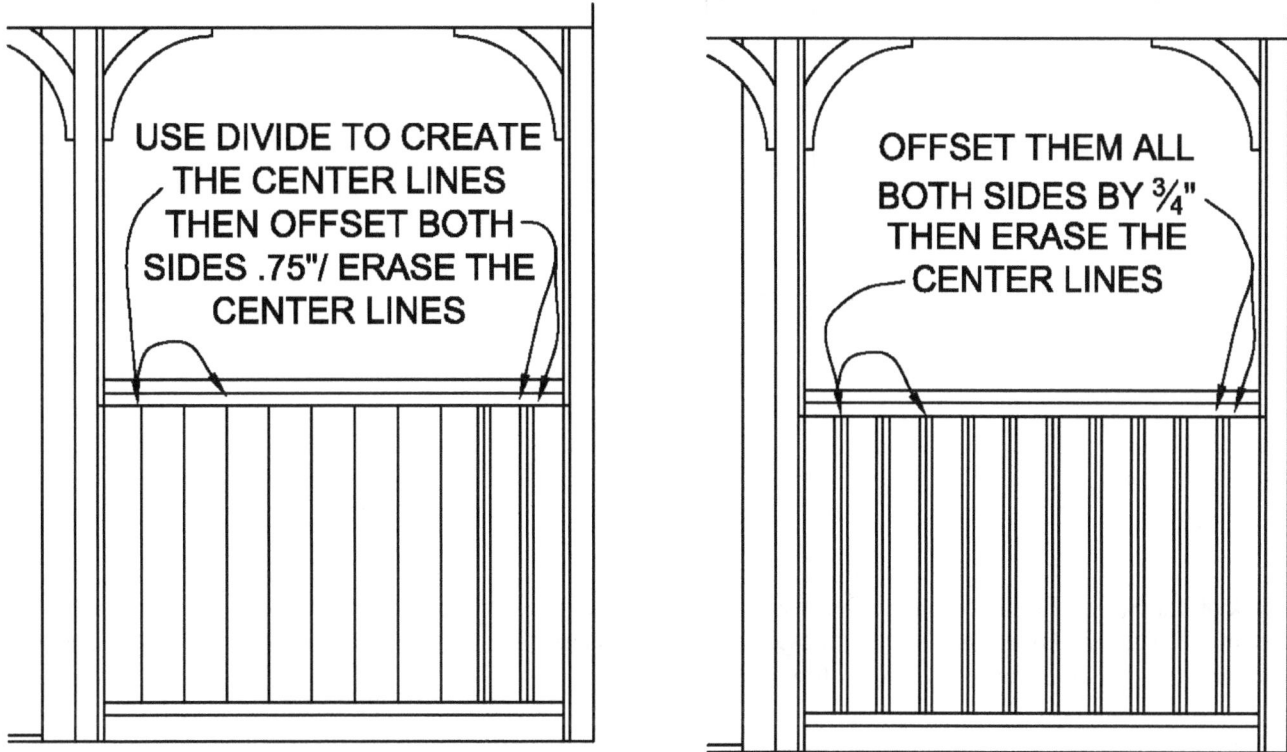

Fig 2-29

There are a number of ways to create rails. We did it this way to demonstrate a method of drawing. It would be faster to create the first baluster and then copy it to the other nodes using the top of the center line as the base point (but not copying the center line).

2.8 Chimney

Draw a line to represent the chimney at **18" offset** from the left exterior wall (see **Y** in **Fig 2-32**). **Click** on the line **Y** and use the **blue grip box** at the top of this line (turn the box red first by clicking on it) to stretch the line up a bit (**do not click** for the **second point**), with the **Ortho on**, then type **30 <e>** (See Appendix I—Line for more on this.) The line will extend upward by 30". ESC.

Draw a **line** from the top of this line to the right **18"**. Then draw a **line** down to the rafter. Use the **Ortho**. **Turn off** the **Osnap** and extend the line down below the roof rafter into the open space (random length) then **trim** it back to the roof line.

Let's draw the chimney cap. Draw a **line** from the midpoint of the top of the chimney chase (**Z** in **Fig 2-30**) up **24"**. Offset this line at **5", 7"** and **8"**.

Offset the top line Z of the chimney chase **6" four times**. It should look like **Fig 2-30** without the dimension lines.

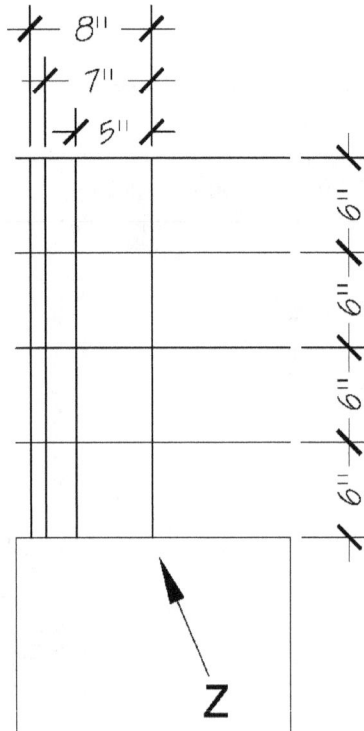

Fig 2-30

Click on the **Spline Fit** button on the **Draw** palette (find it under the little down arrow next to Draw). Turn the **Ortho off**. Turn the **Osnap on**. **Attach** the spline to the points in **Fig. 2-31**. **Start** at the **bottom** and **click** each **successive point up**. After you click the top point **enter**.

Splines can come out with a weird loop or curve at the top. To see how to remedy this, undo the spline and start again. This time, after you click the final point, stretch the spline up and away from the final click point—do not click—move it around until you see the curve that you want and (do not click) **enter** to set the spline. Sometimes the spline will disappear at this point and you will need to enter twice. Occasionally it will not appear even after you enter and you must click on the undo button to make it appear (don't ask).

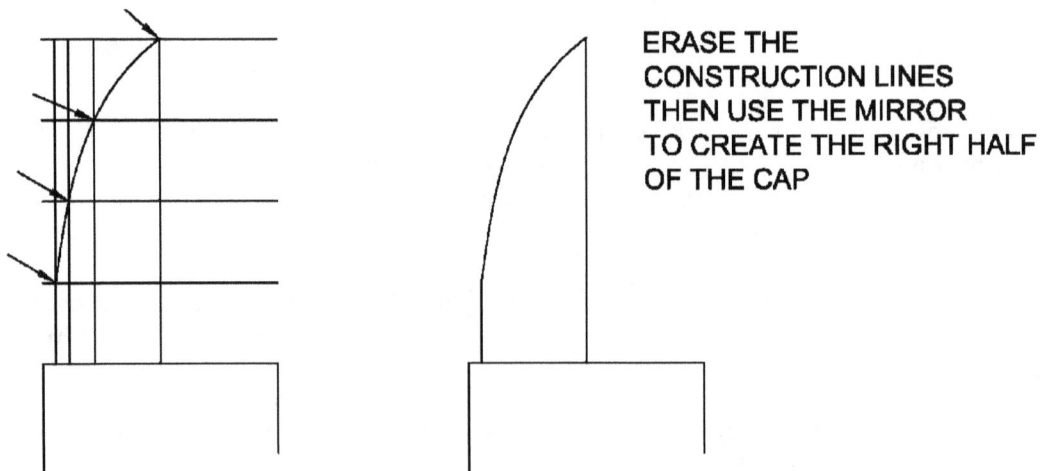

ERASE THE
CONSTRUCTION LINES
THEN USE THE MIRROR
TO CREATE THE RIGHT HALF
OF THE CAP

Fig 2-31

Now use **Mirror** tool and create the other side of the cap (see **Fig 2-32**). Use the center vertical line as the mirror line. **Erase** the center line.

Finish off the chimney chase by drawing **line A** in **Fig 2-32** at the ground level (close off the bottom of the chimney).

Draw in the front steps. Use **8"** and leave the bottom line at **3.5"** to represent the concrete walkway. See **Fig 2-32**.

Clean up the drawings to appear as shown in Fig. 2-32.

Fig 2-32

2.10 Hatch

Now the **Hatch** function will finish off the graphics for this elevation view. Hatch is very useful, but it can be confusing. If you just follow along here you will learn the basic concepts, later we will explore it in more detail.

Set a new layer in the **Layer properties** manager. Name it **Hatch**. Give it a **green** color. Then **Okay**. Back in the main display, select the hatch layer from the drop down menu from **Layer Control** (set it as the current layer).

Click on the **Hatch** button on the **Draw** palette (co-located with Gradient and Boundary). The ribbon shown in Fig 2-33 will appear.

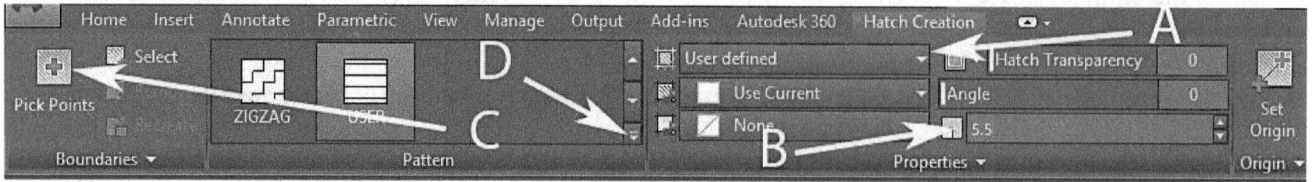

Fig 2-33

Make the following adjustments (follow the letters in Fig 2-33):

A   Select "User defined" (click the arrow to see the options).
B   Hatch Spacing: highlight and type in 5.5". (This window identifies as Hatch **Scale** with other settings.)
C   Click on "Pick points".

In the drawing area, **click at points B** in **Fig 2-34**, then <e>.

Fig 2-34

You should see the horizontal lines in **Fig 2-35**.

Fig 2-35

If you have problems read more in Appendix I—Hatch.

You may have to wait a minute after you click the Add Pick points button: *the cursor needs to become a cross before you can select the pick points.*

Now create the roof hatch and try a few different settings to see how hatch functions.

Click **Hatch**. Select **"Pattern"** at **A** in Fig **2-33** (click the arrow to see the options). **Click** the little down arrow at **D** in **Fig 2-33**. Here you will see a bunch of hatch patterns (Fig 2-36).

Scroll down and look at the patterns. Ar-con is concrete. Ar-sand is sand. Etc. **Select AR-BRSTD** by clicking on it. (AR=BRSTD is actually bricks, but it will work for three tab roofing.) Leave all of the settings as you find them. Click on: **Pick points (C in Fig 2-33)**. In the drawing area click in the roof spaces (**C**) shown in **Fig. 2 35** and <e>.

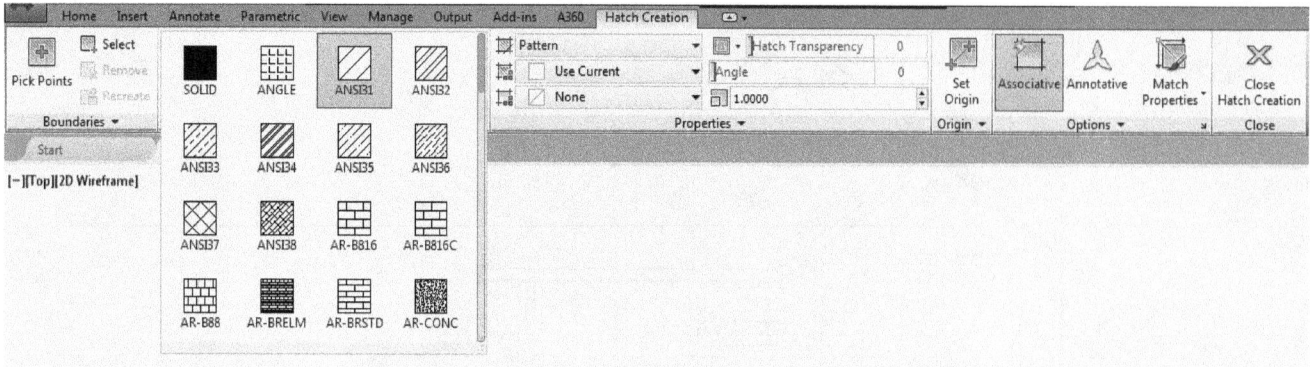

Fig 2-36

Let's play around with the settings a bit to further explore the hatch settings. **Select** the roof hatch (that we just created) by clicking on one of the roof hatch areas (C in Fig 2-35). ***You must click on a hatch when it is highlighted to select it.*** If it is not highlighted at first, then move the cursor around a bit and it should highlight; click to select it (see Appendix I—Hatch if you have problems). **Right click** and **click** on **Hatch Edit** (if you have trouble with this you can type **hatchedit** at the command line). Sometimes this is a bit persnickety and you will have to ESC and start again. When the **Hatch Edit** box opens change the **scale** to **2.000**, then click **OK**. The roof shingles just got huge. You will play around with this setting often when using hatch. Sometimes the scale will be so out of whack that you will see nothing when you OK the hatch. In that case **Undo** and try a different scale. This process will lead you to the right scale.

Do another the **Hatch Edit** on the roof hatch and set the **scale** back to **1**, then **OK**. Or use Undo to get back to the original hatch scale.

Now let's take just a moment to look at a different function. Click on the **Match Properties** button on the **Properties** palette (Home ribbon). The command line reads: **select source object**. The source object is the object whose properties you wish to match. With the pick box (cursor) run over the roof hatch (any section marked C in Fig 2-35) until it lights up and then click on it. A **little paint brush** will **appear** next to the pick box. Now **click** on a section of the siding hatch (any section marked B in Fig 2-34). It will change to a brick hatch like the roof. **ESC** and **Undo** and **change** it **back** to the **siding pattern** (Undo will revert it to the siding hatch pattern).

Match Properties is very useful.

Let's finish up the hatches. Click **Hatch** again. Click **pattern** and then the little box next to the pattern window as before. From the drop down menu choose **AR-B88**. Set the **scale** at **.5**. The **Pick points** now are the three gable ends outside of the octagons at **F** in **Fig 3-37**.

Fig 2-37

These are shingles on the gable ends.

One more Hatch and we are done. Open the **Hatch** dialog box. This time select the **"User defined"** option. In the **Scale** window type **1.5**. For the selection of the **Pick points** click on the **insides of the octagons** (all three), <e>. Look at **Fig 2-38** for the results of all this hatch work.

2.11 Text and Dimensions

That is it for the Front Elevation graphics. We need a few **notes** as in **Fig 2-38**. Select the **Text layer** in the **Layer Control** (the layer we created in Chapter One). **Turn it on** (little light bulb). Use **mtext** and **9"** for the height of the text. Use **bold.** If the text comes out wrong then type style and check to make certain that the **Style 9** is selected—set it current. You can also set this style after you open the Mtext box—set it in the **Text Formatting** bar that opens at the top (to open it type: mtexttoolbar and set the value to 1) or use the ribbon. Add the notes you see in Fig 2-38.

We want an overall height dimension. Select the dimension layer from the Layer control.

Set the Dimension layer current. **Turn it on** (little light bulb). **Click** on the **Dimension Style** button on the **Annotation** palette (click the down arrow next to Annotation). Make certain that you have the **Quarter** style selected, then press **Set Current** and **Close**.

Click the **linear** button on the **Annotation** or **Dimensions** (it is located on both) palette and then the points shown in **Fig 2-38** (the bottom of the chimney and the peak of the roof).

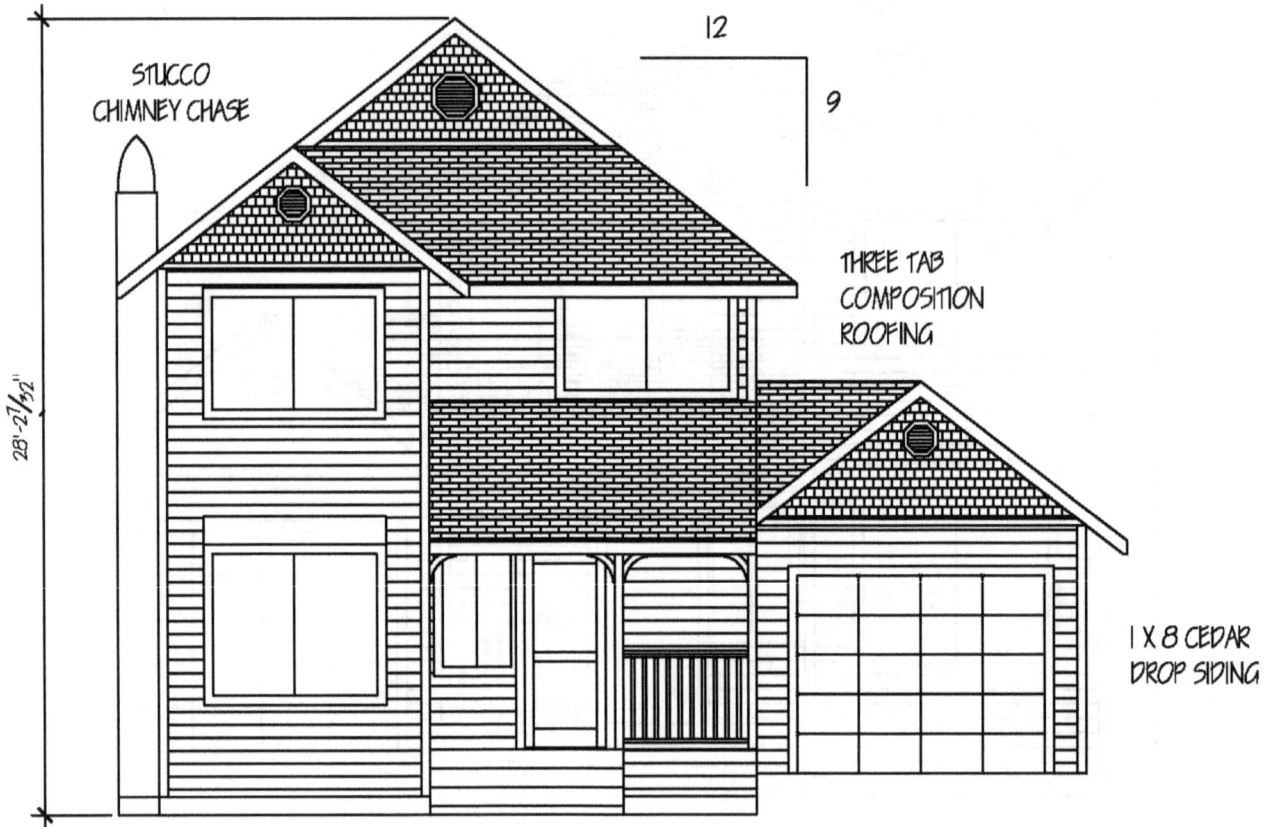

STUCCO
CHIMNEY CHASE

12

9

THREE TAB
COMPOSITION
ROOFING

28'-2 7/32"

I X 8 CEDAR
DROP SIDING

Fig 2-38

Mine reads 28' 2 7/32". That is a bit cumbersome. Let's round it up to the nearest inch.

Click on the **dimension** (click on the number—called the **text**—**of the dimension**). When the **blue grip boxes** appear **right click**. In the **drop down box** that appears select **Properties**. The **Properties** box will appear as in **Fig 2-39**. This is a very useful tool for all kinds of things.

Look down the line items in the box. From here you can change the layer, the color, the weight of the line, the angle of lines can be adjusted, most qualities of an object can be edited here. This can be used for recalling the properties of hatches (if you forget the settings) and editing them. Play around with the Properties dialog box and see what it can do for you.

One of the most useful functions of the **Properties** box is to edit dimensions and their text.

Make sure you see the properties box for the dimension—it is labeled at the top. It is easy to click on the wrong object after you open the properties box. You can leave the properties box open and click on different objects. Use the ESC to unselect an object before selecting another object.

Use the **slide bar** on the **left** of the **Properties box** to **scroll down** until the **Text** section is fully displayed. Click in the empty box next to **Text override** (you may need to widen the Properties box to read the options: place the cursor on the right edge of the box until it changes shape and pull it out/do this at the bottom of the box to make it longer). **Click** in the Text Override box a second time to get the cursor line pulsating. Now type: **28' 3"** (**here you must enter** the **"** for inches) <e>. It should change the dimension to read just that.

While you are here, try a few other things. At the **Text position vert**, click in that box where it says "Centered". Change the settings from centered to "Above". These settings can be very useful when you have trouble placing the dimension text in tight spots and need to be creative about the placement of text. **ESC** and **Close** the Properties box.

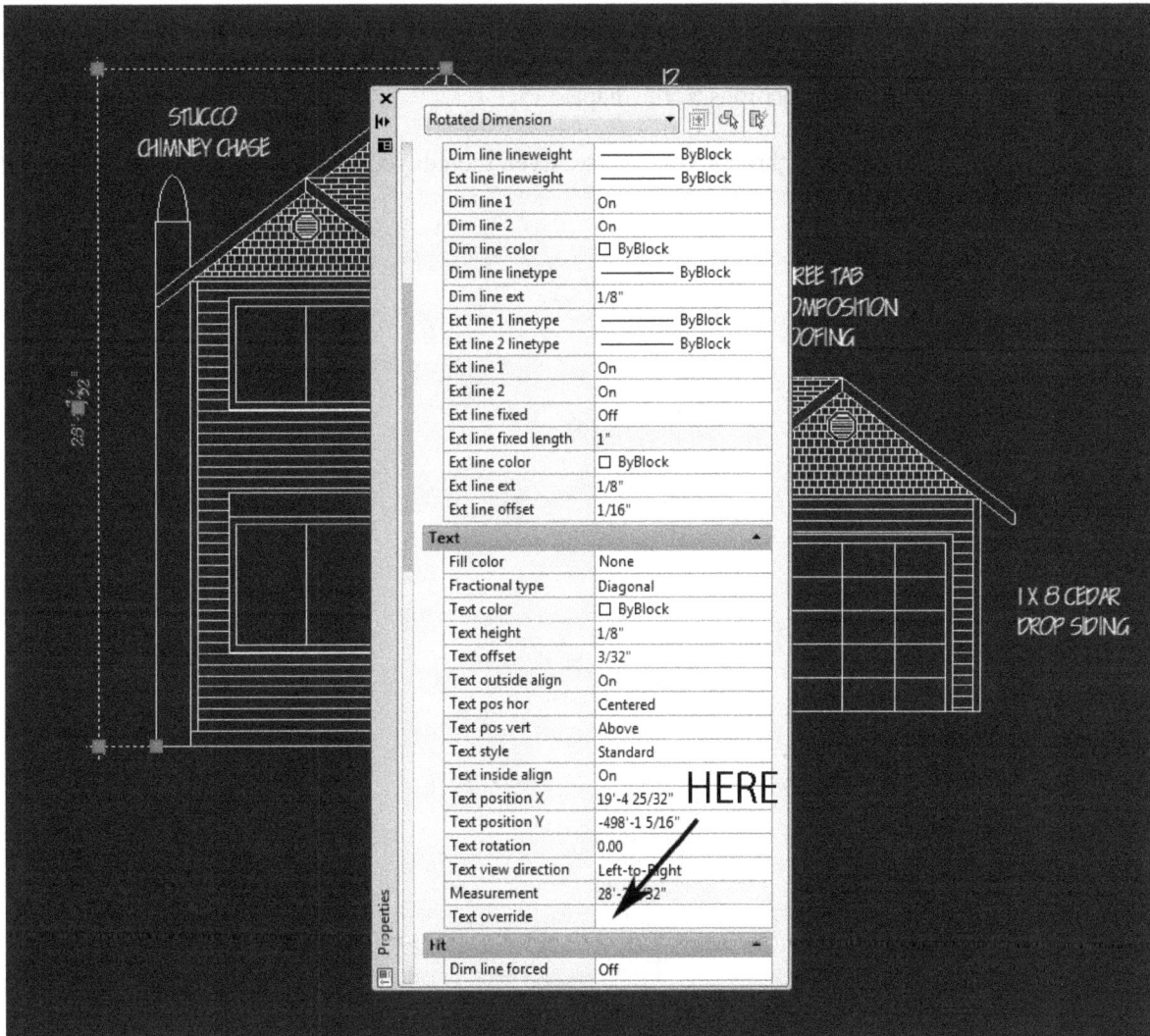

Fig 2-39

Set the **0 Layer** current and draw the door details. Use **4" offset** for the styles and rails (these are the lines in the door). Use **Offset**, **Extend** and **Trim** to get the lines you see in Fig 2-38. You are done with this view!

The Rest of the Stories (Elevations)

The other three elevations of this set of plans can be drawn using the same techniques that we have used in this chapter; so I am not going to reiterate those steps.

You do not need to draw the other elevations to continue (and you can always draw them later). If you choose to draw them now, draw them according to the elevation drawings in Fig 6-1 and in Appendix IV. Use the story pole for heights and get the window positions from Chapter 15.3.

There you go. You are about half way through this course. Even though you are only a third of the way through the pages, the process accelerates as you go along.

Chapter 3—Foundation Plans

3.1 FOUNDATION

The next part of the building we are going to draft is the foundation. This will allow us to explore some different types of lines and address some of the issues regarding drawings of different scales presented on the same page.

The learning process accelerates now. The main reason for the acceleration is that you have already learned how to do most of the drawing that is required. For this reason I will not reiterate how to draw lines or offsets, rectangles or how to mirror or trim. I will, for the most part, only describe how to do **new procedures**. If you have forgotten how to do something go to the **Index** to find where a particular command was introduced and look in Appendix I.

Before you start look at **Fig 3-10** and **Fig 3-24**. This is what we will draw in this chapter.

To begin, **copy** (do not move it, copy it) the floor plan that you saved in **Fig 1-9**. Drag it over and place the copy to the side of your drawing as in **Fig. 3-1**. As always, when no specific place is designated, the exact location is not important.

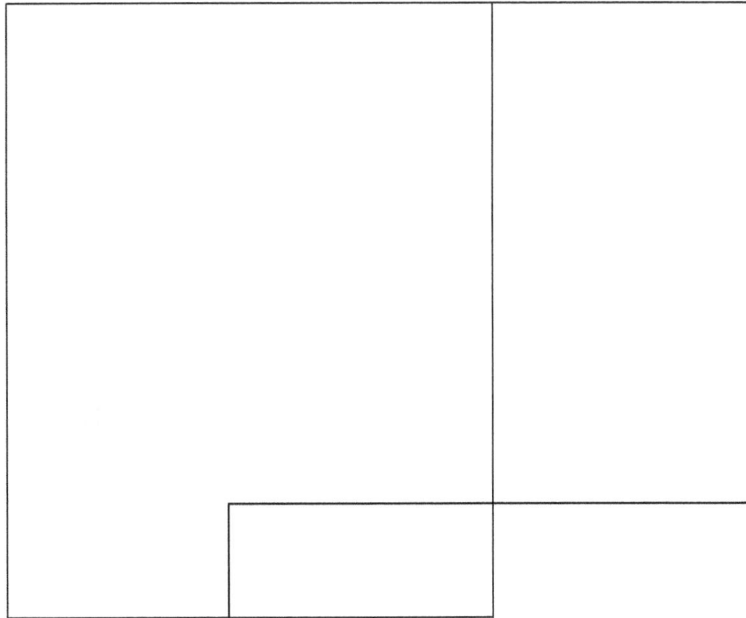

Fig 3-1

Use the **Offset** to draw a **line** at **B** (**Fig 3-2**). It is offset **5'** from line **A**. **Trim** it at the **X**. This is our outline for the foundation.

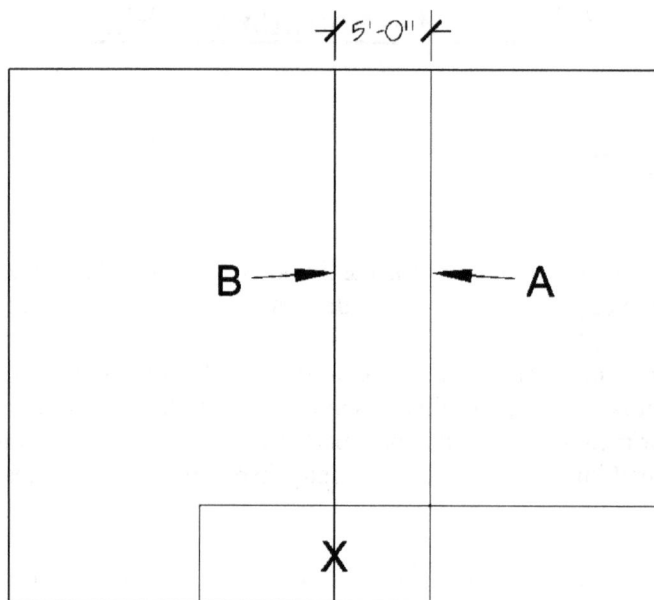

Fig 3-2

First we are going to draw an eight inch wide foundation wall (concrete stem wall) for the two story part of the structure. Use the **Offset,** set it to **8"** and draw **lines** inside the building perimeter as in **Fig 3-3**. **C** is to the left of line **B** (in Fig 3-2).

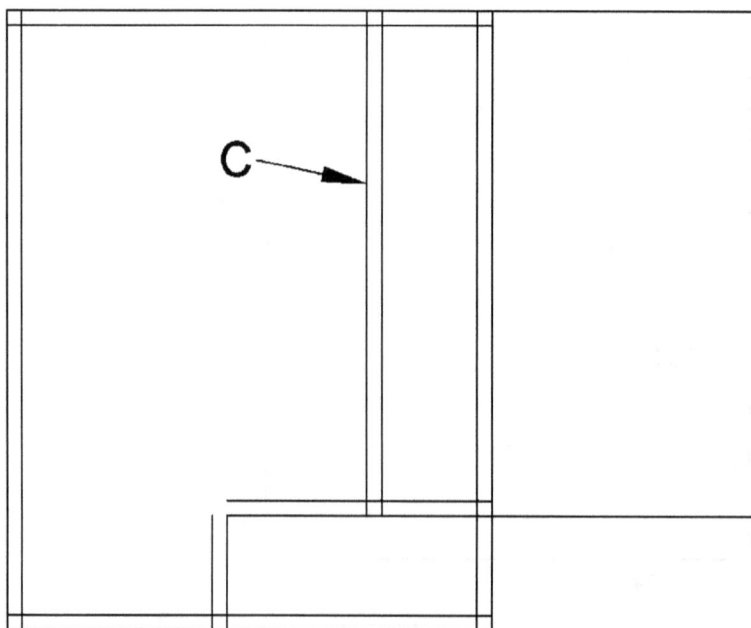

Fig 3-3

Trim and use the **Fillet** command to create **Fig 3-4**. **Watch the prompts** when you use the Fillet command.

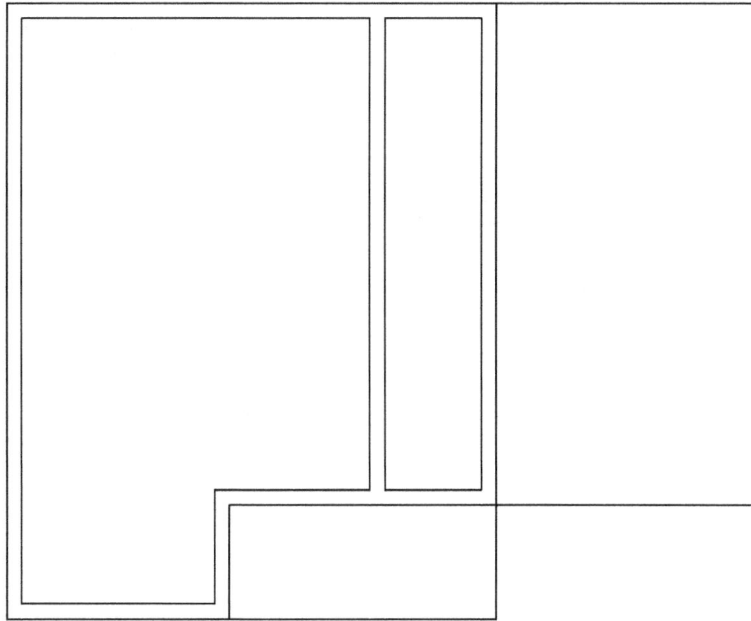

Fig 3-4

Draw a **six inch** wide stem wall for the one story garage and the porch as in **Fig 3-5**. Trim the corners. **Fig 3-8** shows these lines after they have been trimmed.

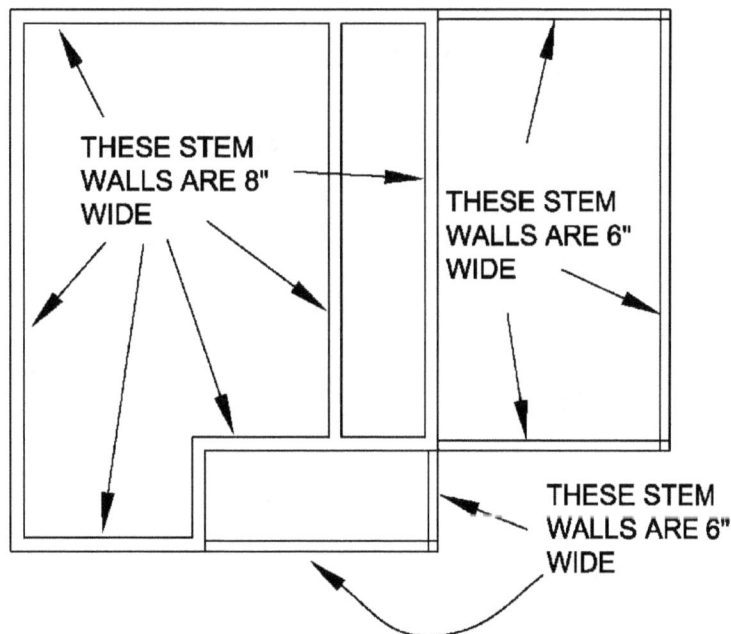

Fig 3-5

Now we will draw the footings—18" for the two story and 12" for the single story components. Or stated in another way, the eight inch stem walls get an 18" footing and the six inch stem walls get a 12" footing. For this we will create a dashed line.

3.2 Dashed Lines

Create another layer in the **Layer Properties Manager**. Name it **dashed_1**. Make it **blue** by clicking on **D** in **Fig 3-6.**

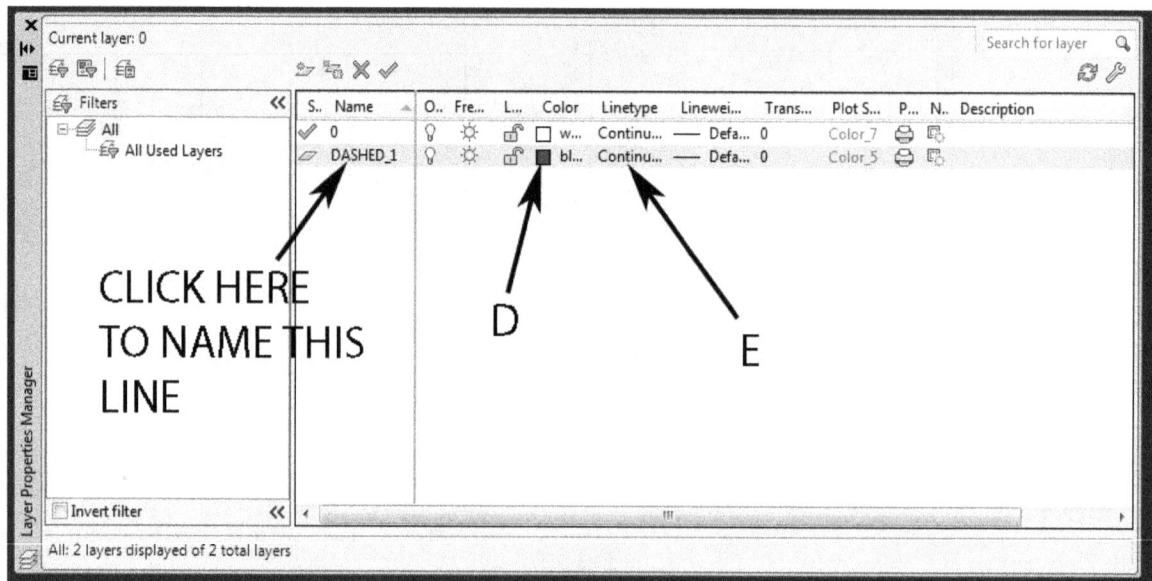

Fig 3-6

Click on the **Linetype** designation where it says **Continu...** at **E** in **Fig 3-6**.

A **Select Linetype** box will appear as in **Fig 3-7**. **Click** on the **Load** button at the bottom.

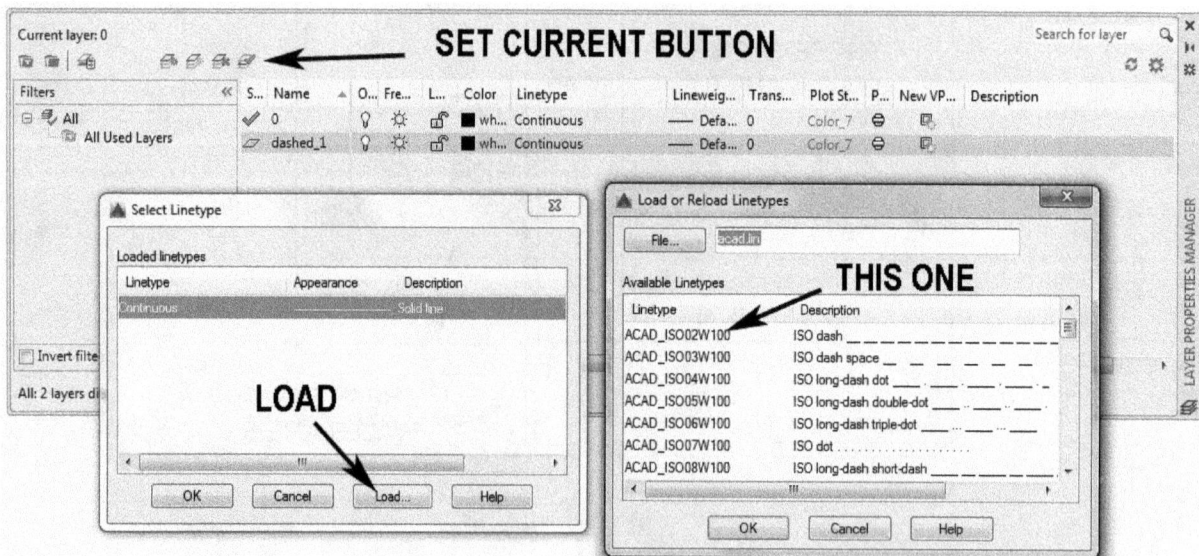

Fig 3-7

Select the **ACAD_ISO02W100** by clicking on it (**Fig 3-7**). **Click OK**. Back in **Select Linetype** window highlight the **ACAD_ISO02W100** and then **OK**.

Back in the **Layer Properties Manager** box you will see the designation for **linetype** now reads: **ACAD IS...**

Set this as **the current layer** by **clicking** on the **check** mark at the top of this box (Fig 3-7) and close the dialog box. You can also just close this box, and back in the main drawing screen, click on the **Layer Control** and **select dashed_1**.

Back in the main screen type **LTScale** in the Command Line. It will display the current **Line Type Scale**. **Type: 1** and **enter**.

Offset the eight inch stem wall each side by **five** inches (Fig 3-8). The new lines will show up as a solid white (0 Layer) because they are matching the lines you are offsetting (which are on the 0 Layer).

Highlight them and then **select** the new **dashed_1** layer from the **Layer Control**. They will all turn blue and they should turn into dashed lines. If they do not, then read the section in Appendix I—Dashed Lines.

> If you find these blue lines too difficult to see then go back into the Layers Properties Manager box and click on the blue box. The Select Color box will open. Select the True Color tab. Change the Luminance to 75. Click OK. Close the Layer Properties Manager box. Your dashed lines should now be brighter.

Trim these footing lines and use the **Fillet** tool to create the drawing as in **Fig 3-8**.

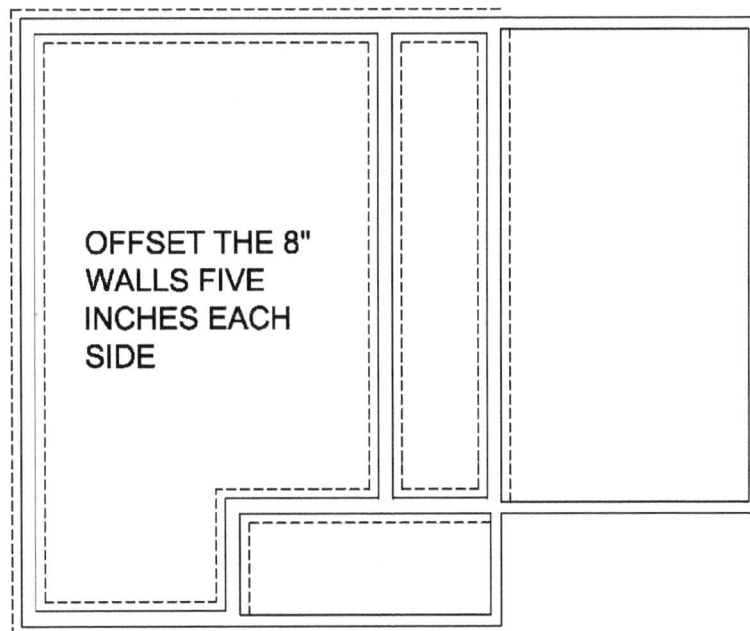

OFFSET THE 8"
WALLS FIVE
INCHES EACH
SIDE

Fig 3-8

Now **offset** the **six inch** stem **walls** (Fig 3-5) by **three** inches **each side** to create the twelve inch wide footings. **Trim** and use **Fillet** to get **Fig 3-9**.

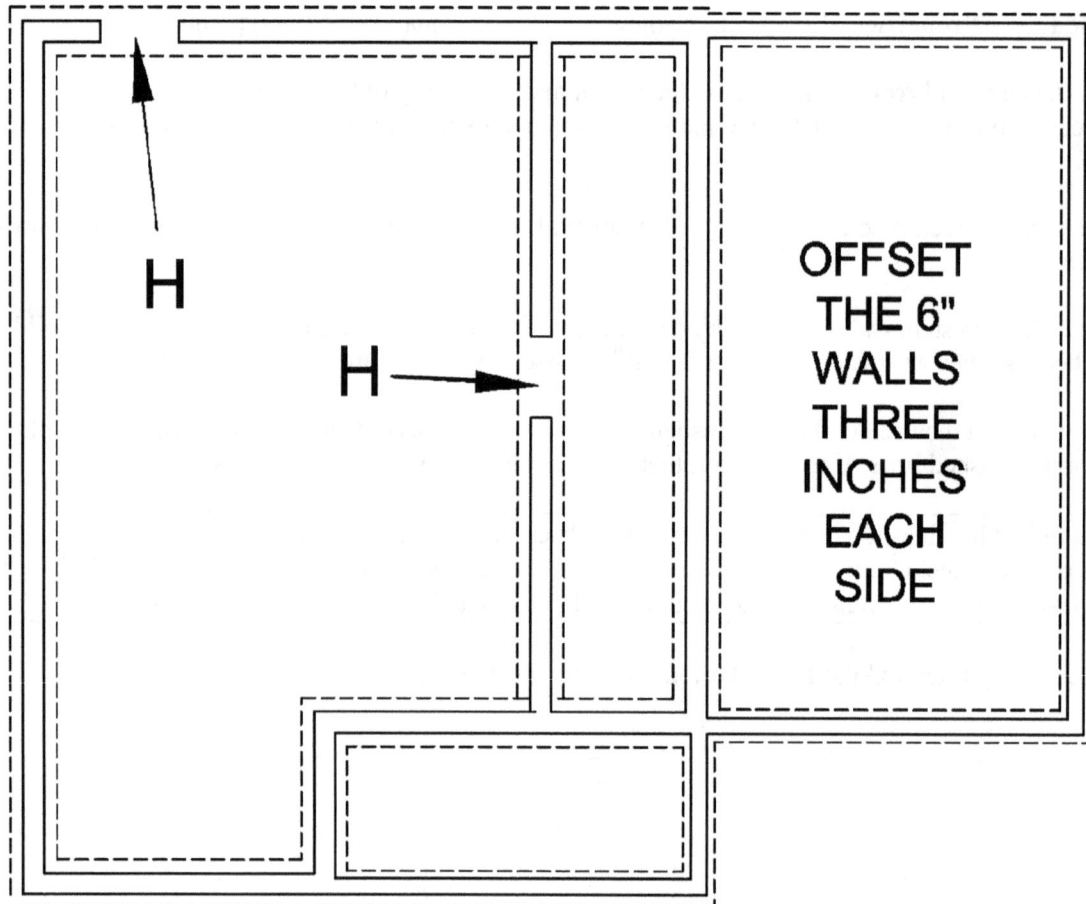

Fig 3-9

We need to create **openings** for access to the crawl space and we need an access for the area under the stairwell. These are designated **H** in **Fig 3-9**.

Use the **0 layer** and make them **30"** wide. Their **positions** are **32"** from the top left corner, and **centered** in the **wall** for the opening to the right, as shown in **Fig 3-9** (their exact placement is not important).

AutoCAD switches the layers on you sometimes. The reason for this is complex. But if this happens, select the lines or objects that need to be changed to a different layer, then open the Layer Control drop down menu and select the layer you want to place the lines on. This will change all of the selected lines and highlighted objects to the layer that you click on. This is something that requires constant vigilance with AutoCAD and it is one reason for using different colors with different layers—it is easy to catch any incorrect attributions.

This is all the graphics for this simple Plan View of the foundation. We just need to add notes and dimensions.

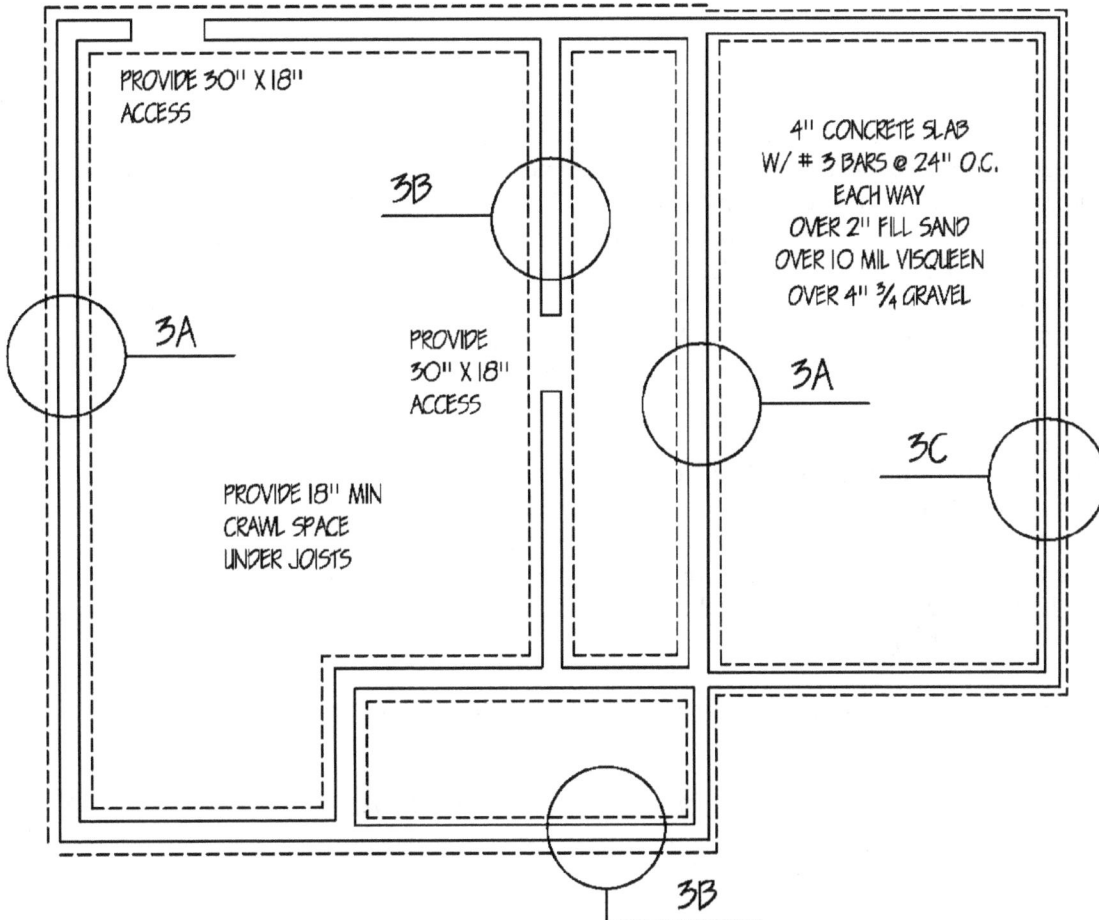

PROVIDE 30" X 18" ACCESS

3B

4" CONCRETE SLAB
W/ # 3 BARS @ 24" O.C.
EACH WAY
OVER 2" FILL SAND
OVER 10 MIL VISQUEEN
OVER 4" ¾ GRAVEL

3A

PROVIDE
30" X 18"
ACCESS

3A

3C

PROVIDE 18" MIN
CRAWL SPACE
UNDER JOISTS

3B

Fig 3-10

Let's add some reference graphics as in **Fig 3-10**. Make the **circles 4 foot** in diameter. Make one and **copy** it to the other locations (these are approximate locations—set them by eye).

Right click on the **Object Snap** button at the bottom of the screen. In the settings box, turn on the **Quadrant** Osnap. Now turn the **Ortho on** and create the **lines** under the **text** 3A, 3B and 3C as in **FIG 3-10**. Make the **lines** approximately **4'** long—except the **lowest line**—make that one **5'** with a **1' vertical line** to attach it to the circle.

Type **mt**. You should still have the **Style 9** selected. If not, then set it from the **Text Style** options that open by clicking on the Text Style button that appears after you open the mt box (upper left corner). Or you can set it in the Text Formatting Toolbar if you have set it to open (See Appendix I—Text).

Type the **text** for the reference designations shown in **Fig 3-10** (**3A, 3B, 3C**). Make the letter size **12"** and **Bold**. Turn the **Object Snap off** when you **Copy** this text. **Copy** it and **edit** it in each location as necessary.

This Foundation Plan View will be printed at ¼" scale. So 12" letters will be ¼" when they are printed on the page. More on this later.

Add the rest of the **text** that is shown in **FIG 3-10**. Make it **7.5"** and **Bold** (I always use bold with the lighter fonts like City Blueprint). The text in the garage is center justified, so after you type it, highlight it and **center** it using the **text justification** button on the Ribbon or the Text Formatting bar. **Ok.** See Appendix I—Text for help.

That is it for the plan view of the foundation (for now). Next we will draw the detail views.

3.3 Details

Details and cross sections are commonly drawn in a larger scale than the plan views or the elevations. This allows for precise reading and finer detail depiction. Many designers like to put the foundation details on the same page as the foundation plan view so that the constructor doesn't have to flip back and forth between pages. This means that one page will have drawings printed (called plotted) in different scales. The foundation plan that we just drew will be printed at a scale of ¼" = 1'. The detail we are about to draw will be printed at the scale of 1" = 1'. In order to have two or more different scales on the same page we have to employ one of several methods. In this chapter we will employ the simplest method. We will draw the cross section details for the foundation to plot at one inch scale (1 in. = 1 ft); that means that one inch on the paper will equal one foot in the actual building. This is explained in more detail later.

Draw the **lines** in view **A** of **Fig 3-11**. Do not draw the dimensions yet. I have put them there so you can see the dimensions you need to draw. Your drawing will look like **FIG 3-11 B**. There is no need to use anything but the **line** tool. **Turn** the **Ortho** and **Osnap on**. Start at the top and draw a horizontal line 8" (8" is the same as 8 inch or 8in.). Draw a line down from each end 20" long (shown here as 10" and 10"). Draw the lines out from the bottom of these two lines 5" each way. Draw lines down from the outside endpoints of these lines 8". Draw a line between these at the bottom.

Add the two 6" lines shown in **Fig 3-11B**. They are located at the midpoint of the 20" lines.

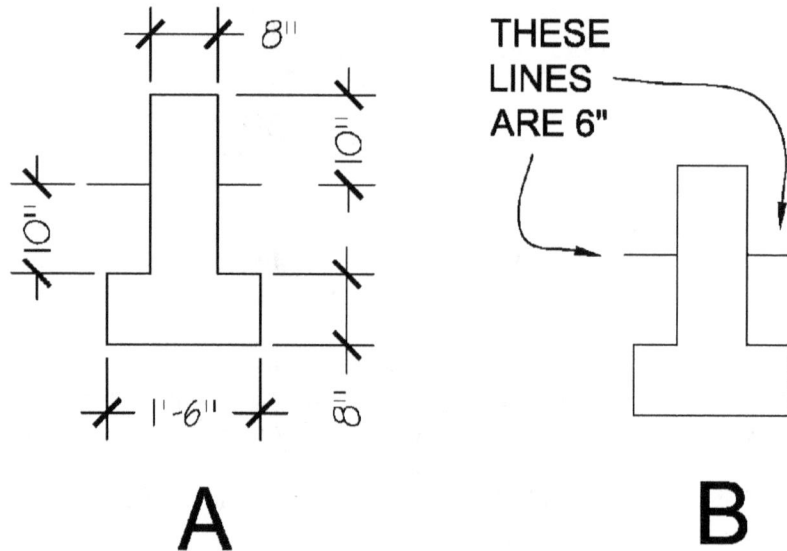

Fig 3-11

Draw the two **rectangles** shown in **Fig 3-12.** Draw the **5.5 x 1.5 inch rectangle** and copy it to the location shown in **Fig 3-12**. Draw the **3.5 x 7.5 rectangle** on top of that.

Next draw the lines above that as shown in Fig 3-12. The **9.5 offset line** represents the floor joists (**approx. 24"** long). Add a line **.75** above that for the plywood floor (**approx. 22"** long).

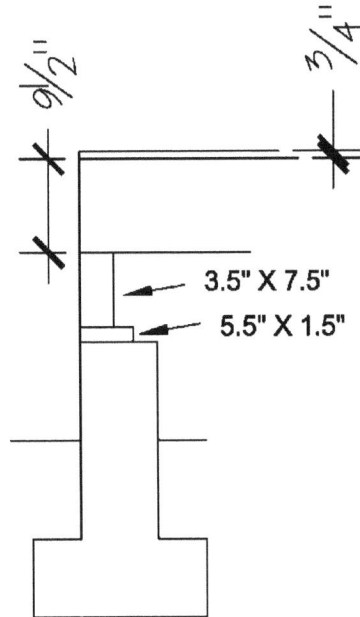

Fig 3-12

We need an anchor bolt. Follow the steps in **Fig 3-13**. Draw the two perpendicular **lines** at **12"** and **2"** (**1** in Fig 3-13). Use the **Fillet** tool to round the corner (**2**) off—use a **1" radius**. Use the **Offset** set to **.5"** to make the other side (**3**) to the right. Draw the ends (**4**). **Offset** the top end line by **.5"** (**J** in **5**). J is below the top line.

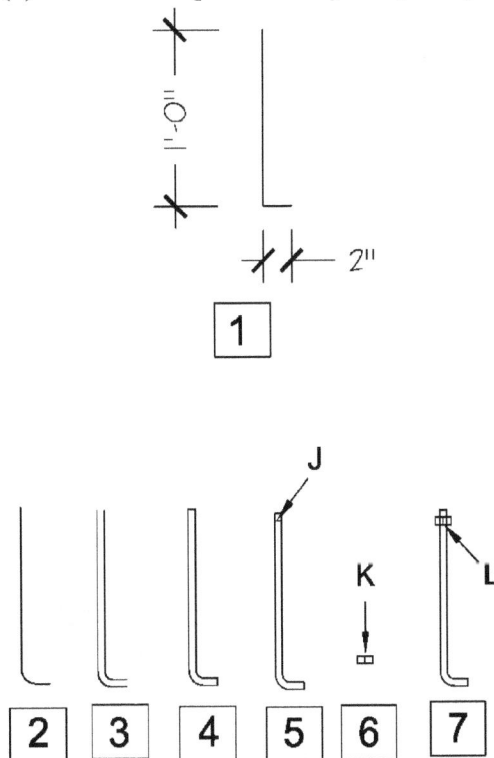

Fig 3-13

Now draw the nut for the bolt—**1.25" x .5"** (**6**). Draw a **line** down the **middle** at **K**. **Copy** the nut. Grab it by the **top** of this **middle line K** and snap it to the **midpoint** of line **J** (**7**).

Make a **copy** of the bolt and place it as shown in **Fig 3-14**; use the point L in Fig 3-13 as the base point and osnap it to the midpoint at **M** in Fig 3-14. Add the **line** at **N** in **Fig 3-14**. It is **offset 1.5"**.

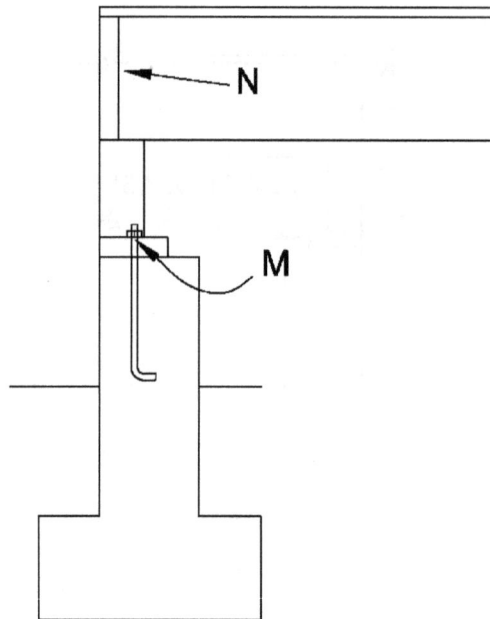

Fig 3-14

Add the **diagonal lines** shown in **Fig 3-15 (P)**.

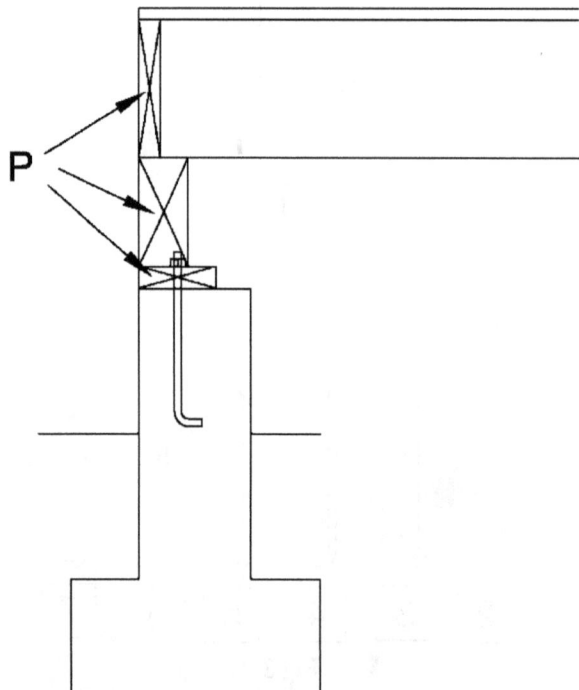

Fig 3-15

We need some rebar (reinforcement steel) in the foundation. To draw the rebar use the **circle** tool and make a circle with a **.5" diameter**. Draw a cross **1.5" x 1.5"** and **snap** it to the **center** of the **circle** as in **Fig 3-16**. You will need to have the **Center Object Snap turned on** (right click the Object snap button for settings).

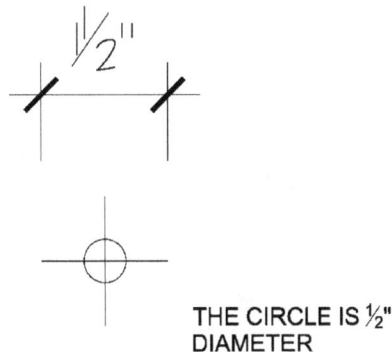

THE CIRCLE IS ½"
DIAMETER

Fig 3-16

Use the **Offset** tool to **create** line **Q** at **3"** from the **bottom** line of this detail drawing (Fig 3-17). Use **Offset** again and create line **R** at **3"** from the **top** of the stem wall as in **FIG 3-17**. **Copy** the rebar object from **Fig 3-16** and snap it to the **midpoint** of these lines as shown by **S** in **Fig 3-17**. **Erase** the lines **Q** and **R**.

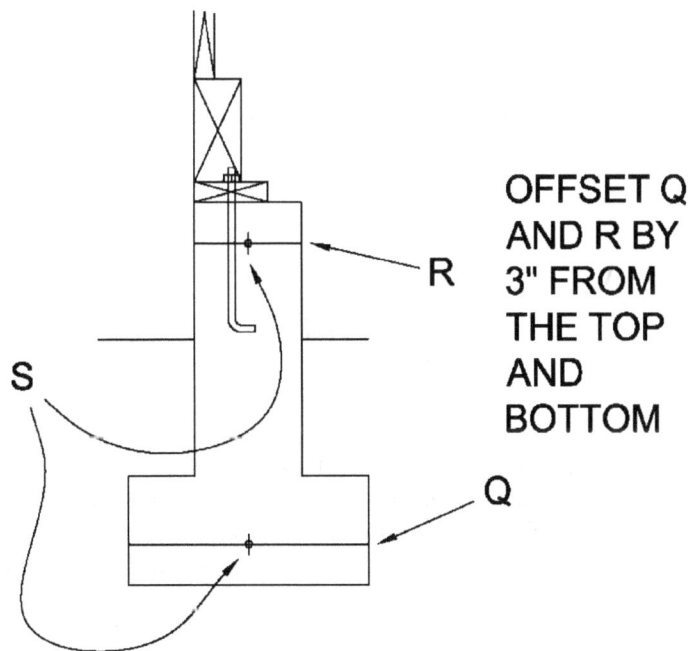

OFFSET Q
AND R BY
R   3" FROM
THE TOP
AND
BOTTOM

Fig 3-17

Make a **copy** of the detail as shown in Fig 3-17 and set it to the side somewhere in open space for later use.

We are going to draw the earth using the Hatch tool on the Draw palette. First we must enclose the space we wish to hatch. **Extend** lines **T** in **Fig 3-18** out to look approximately like **Fig 3-18**. They are about 12" long. Do this by turning the **Osnap off** and **clicking** on a **line** once (a single click). **Blue grip boxes** will appear. **Click** on the outer **grip box**. It will **turn red**. **Pull** it out a ways and **click**. Alternately you can just begin to move it and type in a number (in this case 6 because it is already 6 inches long).

I put a slight angle on the line to the left to depict the slope as required by the building code. If you want to do this turn the Ortho off, highlight the line to bring up the blue grip boxes. Click again on the box on the left end of the line. When it turns red grab it and swing the line down a bit and click. Just do this by eye for now (you could use the rotate tool to get a precise angle, but this way demonstrates how to use the grip boxes).

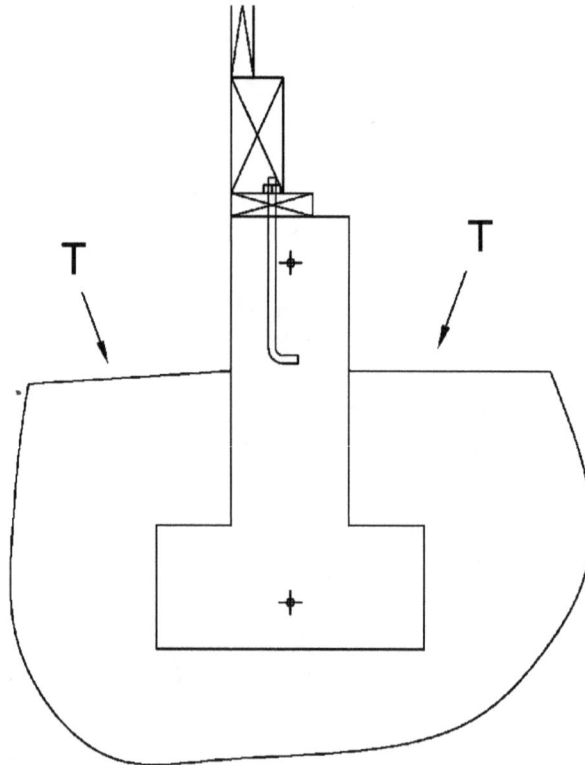

Fig 3-18

Next click on the **Spline Fit** tool and draw something roughly like you see in **Fig 3-18**. Don't worry about the shape—just don't make it too big. This type of object is not meant to be precise. **Start** the **spline** on the outside end of one of the lines **T**. Then **click** on **five** or **six points** in the space around the foundation. Finally, **osnap** the **end** of the **spline** to the other line **T**. Sometimes you have to enter twice with the Spline tool to get it to set. See Appendix I—Spline if you have problems.

Set the **Layer** to **Hatch**. Then click on the **Hatch** button in the Draw palette. Click the **Pattern** button at **U** in **Fig 3-19**. Click on **the down arrow** to the left of the **User Defined/Solid/Gradient** button to find it. In the Pattern section of the ribbon scroll down and click on **Earth**. Then back in the Hatch Pattern Scale window set **Scale** to **10**. Click on **Pick Points**. **Click** in the space shown at **A** in **Fig 3-20**. **Enter**. This is what architects think earth looks like.

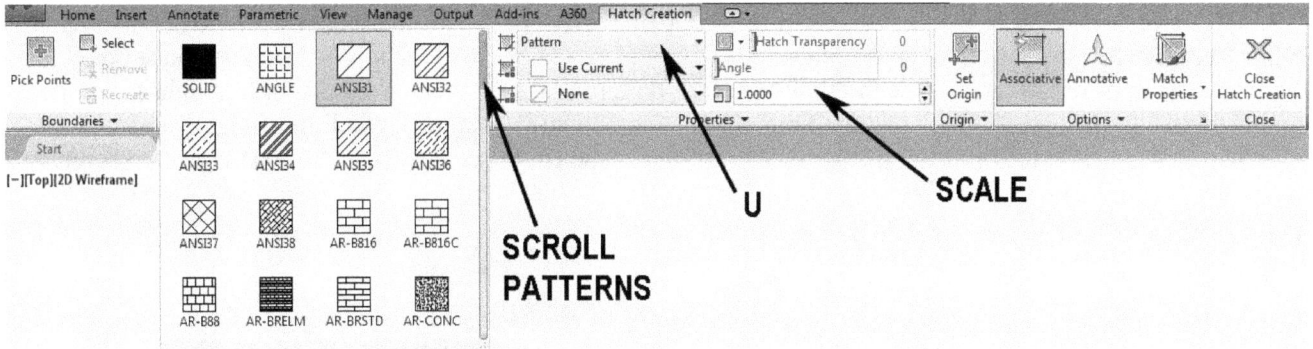

Fig 3-19

Let's add the concrete in the stem wall. Use **Hatch** again: **Pattern/AR_CONC/** Set **scale** to **1. Pick points. Click** at inside the space designated **B** in **FIG 3-20** then **<e>**.

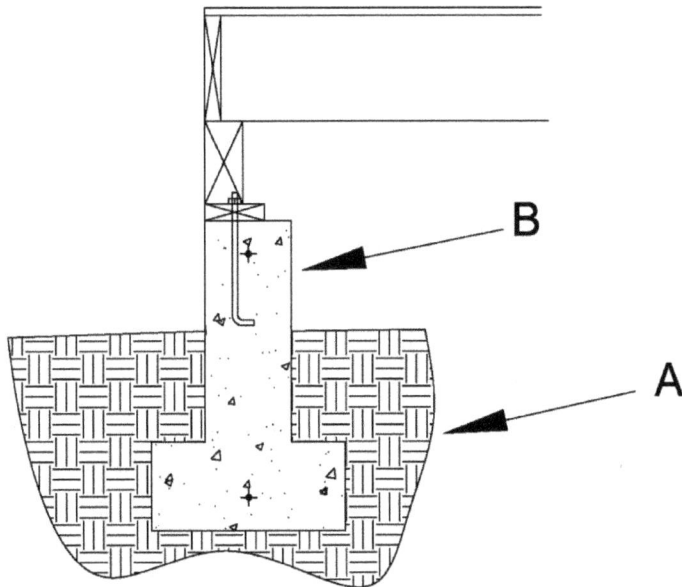

Fig 3-20

Fig 3-21

The rebar is a bit hard to see so we will use a new tool and **fill** the circle. Click on **Gradient** which is co-located with Hatch on the **Draw** palette (click on the down arrow next to the Hatch/Gradient button). Click the button at **C** in **Fig 3-21**. Then select **Solid**. Click on the down arrow next to Use Current (the button under Solid, it may read By Layer or By Block—it is a co-located button). Click on More Colors at the bottom of the box that opens. When the Select Color box opens select blue then click on True Color tab at the top. Select blue and set the luminance to approximately 50 (Use the slide bar at the bottom of the luminance column or highlight the number and over type it). Click OK. Click on Pick Points. Now zoom in and click inside the little circles as in **Fig 3-22**. You will have to click **four times**: once for each quadrant of the circle because there are four separate quadrants. <e>.

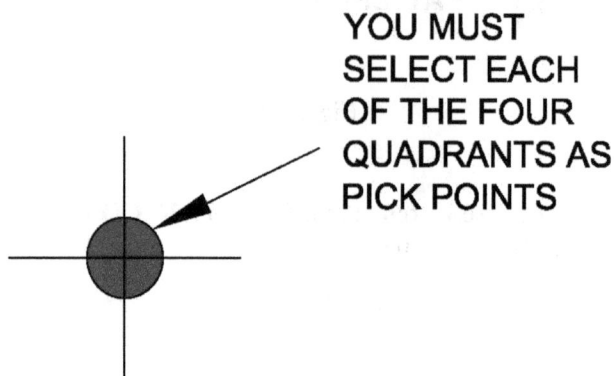

**YOU MUST
SELECT EACH
OF THE FOUR
QUADRANTS AS
PICK POINTS**

Fig 3-22

3.4 Scale Drawing

We are going to **scale** the **foundation detail** drawing (Fig 3-20) up to print out at **1" scale**. Click on the **Scale** tool on the **Modify** palette. Start at the lower right of this detail and encompass it in a **green selection window** (move the cursor up and to the left until the entire detail is covered with a green selection box) then **click**. The detail should turn into a bluish highlighted line drawing. The **prompt** will ask you to **select objects** again. <e>. Now it **prompts** for a **base point**. Click **anywhere** in the **middle** of the **detail**. It asks for the **scale factor**. Type: **4 <e>**. The detail is now 4 times the original size.

> If you don't have enough room for the scaled up drawing, then Undo and move the detail further away from the other graphics and scale it again.

This is four times the size of the foundation plan view. You can see on the finished page in Appendix IV, Page 4, or go to the website at www.autocadin20hours for a pdf of the plans (there you can view it in detail).

Now we need dimensions. **Click** on the **Dimension Style** button dialog box (the down arrow next to Annotation on the Annotation palette opens a drop down menu with four buttons, the second is the Dimension Style—click the dimension symbol to the left). Select the **quarter** scale, then **click** on the **New** button. **Name** this **quarterx4**. Under the **Fit tab** set the **Use Overall Scale of**: to **48**. **Uncheck the Annotative**.

Under the **Primary Units** tab set the **Scale factor** to **.25**. Make sure it is set **Architectural** under the **Unit format** setting. Click **OK**. Click **Set Current** and **Close**. You can review all of this in Chapter 1, section 1.23.

Set the **Dimension Layer current in the Layer control on the Layers Palette**. Click on the **Linear** dimension tool on the **Annotation palette** and **create** the **dimensions** shown in **Fig 3-23**. Linear is co-located with Aligned/Angular/Arc Length/Radius/Diameter/ Ordinate/Jogged. So the button may read any of these, though it should reset to Linear each time you turn on AutoCAD (AutoCAD doesn't always do as it is told).

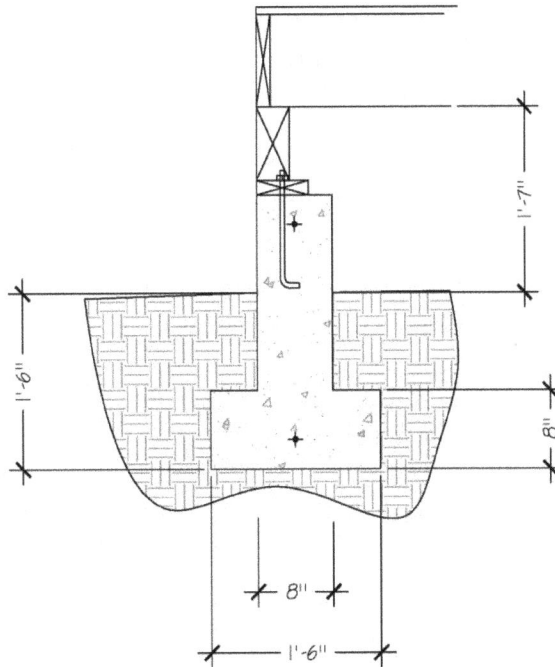

Fig 3-23

If you have **problems** getting the numbers right it may be because the linear dimension tool is snapping to the hatch. If this is the case you can **turn off the Hatch layer**. To do this, use the Layer Control: click on the down arrow and click on the little light bulb next to the hatch layer. Click back in the drawing area and the hatch should vanish. Add the dimension lines and then turn the hatch back on by clicking on the little light bulb again.

I moved the dimension extension lines for the 8" and the 1'6" down from where they originally appear. If you want to do this, then use the **Move** command to move the dimension text down, then highlight the dimension by clicking on it and use the **grip boxes** to shorten the dimension lines.

This detail now only needs notes and it is done.

We have already scaled the detail to four times original size, so the **text** we add will be the same as we used for the plan views, because they are both to be plotted on the same page and in the same viewport. Don't worry if you don't understand everything right now. It is difficult to explain with words and much easier to demonstrate. It will become clear as we proceed and Chapter 13 is all about scales.

Set the **Text layer** current. Type **mt <e>**, select the **style 9**, and type the text shown in **Fig 3-24**. Use **7.5" letters** and **Bold**. Set the size of the text in the **Text Height window** that appears when you create a Mtext box (on the Style Palette). **Highlight** the 9" and over type it with **7.5"**. Do this before you start typing the text as shown in Fig 3-24.

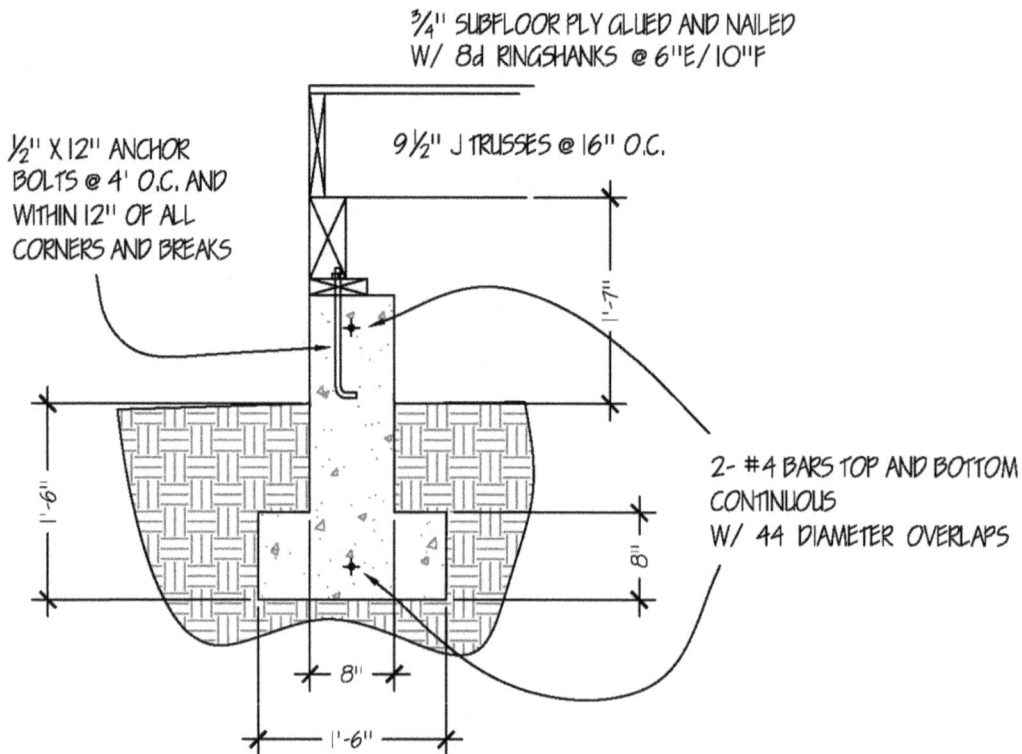

¾" SUBFLOOR PLY GLUED AND NAILED
W/ 8d RINGSHANKS @ 6"E/10"F

½" X 12" ANCHOR
BOLTS @ 4' O.C. AND
WITHIN 12" OF ALL
CORNERS AND BREAKS

9½" J TRUSSES @ 16" O.C.

2- #4 BARS TOP AND BOTTOM
CONTINUOUS
W/ 44 DIAMETER OVERLAPS

Fig 3-24

3.5 Leaders

Now we are going to add the **leaders** in **Fig 3-24**. These are the lines with the arrows on them. Leaders are a bit tricky in AutoCAD. The setup is difficult to find. In this book we will use exclusively Qleaders. Qleaders are set up in two different locations. The size of the arrowhead is determined by which **Dimension Style** is selected. The characteristics of the line are set up in the **Leader Settings** window. And the arrowhead shape can be set in either location. We are going to go at the leader thing in stages. Here we will look at some of the basics; later we will look at more options. You can go to Appendix I—Leaders if you want more detailed information now.

Set the **Dimension** layer current. Open the **Dimension Style manager** (**Annotation** palette or type **dimstyle** <e>). Select the **quarter style**. Click the **Modify** button to the right. Click on the **Symbols and Arrows** tab. Where it says **Leader** click on the **downward arrow**. Select **Closed filled**. The **Arrow size** should be **1/8"**. **OK**.

Back in the **Dimension Style** window select the **Quarter** scale and click on the **Set Current** button. It will read Quarter in the box below the diagram. **Close**.

Type **qleader**. **Read the prompt**. It says: **specify first point, or (Settings)**. **Type: s <e>**. This will open the **Leader Settings** dialog box (**Fig 3-25**).

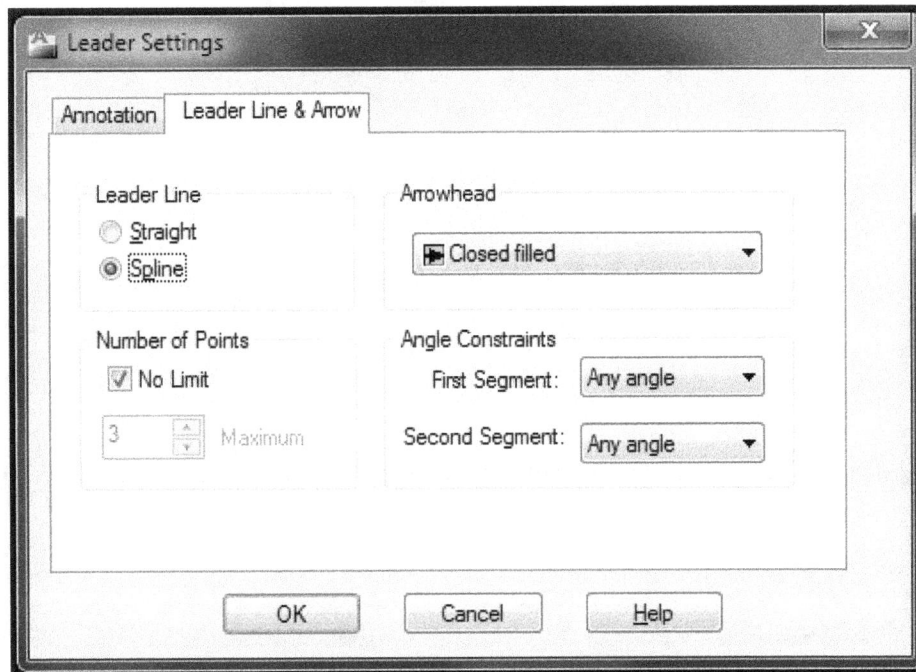

Fig 3-25

Set it as shown. You can see that there is the option to change the arrowhead shape here also, but not the size of the arrowhead. The **Leader Line** is asking you if you want a straight line or if you want to be able to draw a line with the spline tool. The number of points refers to how many points you will set on your leader (spline) line. This becomes important when you have the text function turned on. For now you want no limit.

Click on the **Annotation** tab. Set it as shown in **Fig 3-26**. Set **Annotation Type** to **None**. We want to set the **Annotation Reuse** to **None** also. **OK**.

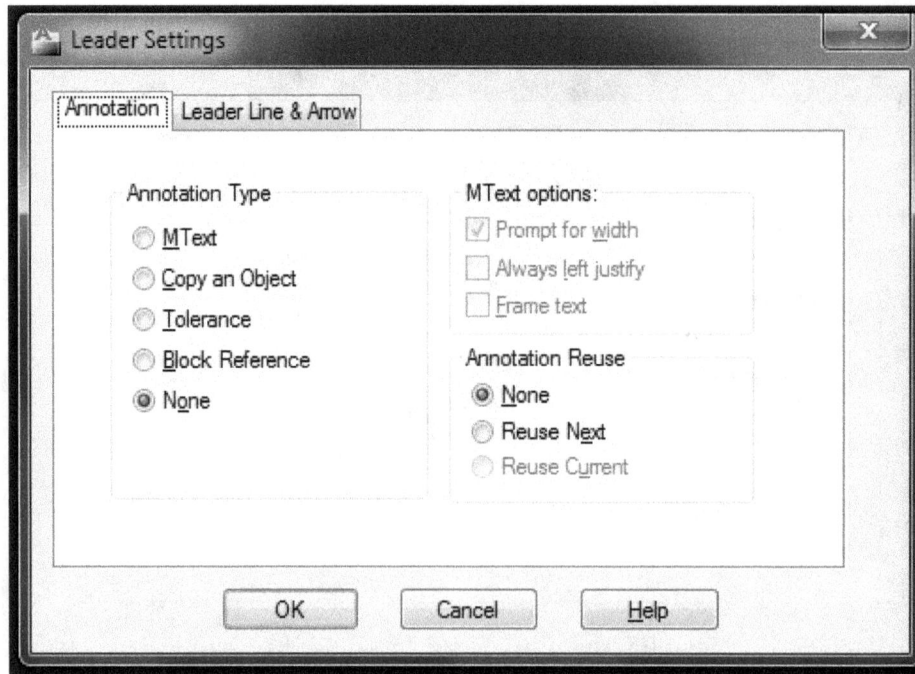

Fig 3-26

You can set up leaders so that they automatically open a text box at the end of the leader. This would require that you click on the MText button in Fig 3-26 (this type of button is called a radio button). Then you set the leader to straight, or set the number of points in the spline. When you use the leader, after you click the number of points you have designated, the text box opens automatically and you just type. I never use this because I find it ungainly and limiting. You can play around with it and you may like it for some uses. I type the text then I add the leader separately. That is how we set it up for this drawing.

There is a Multileader Style button in the drop down menu found when you click the down arrow next to the word Annotation in the Annotation palette. I always use Qleader and can see no downside to that.

The **prompt** at the command line should now be asking you for a **first leader point**. **Click** on one of the points of the arrows shown in **Fig 3-24** (these are set by eye—don't worry about the exact placement for now). The leader begins at the arrowhead point.

Pull the spline out and **click** where you want it to **start bending**. **Click a second point** about two thirds of the way to the text then a **third point** approximately where you see it end in **Fig 3-24** and **Esc**. Three spline points are usually fine, sometimes you will need more. I used four for the leader pointing to the j bolt. Too many points on a leader can make it look uneven. Use the minimum and you will create smoother leaders.

You must pull out the leader line a minimum distance for the arrowhead to appear—3x the arrowhead length.

If you turned off the **hatch layer,** turn it back **on**.

This is it for this chapter. See Chapter 15 Section 15.4 for the other foundation details if you want to draw them now (or wait until Chapter 15).

Chapter 4—Plot Plan

4.1 Plot Plan

You now have most of the basic drawing skills you need for 2D drawing. This chapter demonstrates some advanced drawing skills and introduces plotting scales.

Plot plans (see Fig 4-13) are usually printed in smaller scales than the plan views and elevations because they represent a much larger area. A very large object (like a whole parcel of land) often will not fit on a sheet in ¼" scale. Common scales for plot plans are 1/8 = 1', 1/16 = 1', or scales that are represented by ratios like 1" = 20'.

What determines the scale is usually the largest that will fit on the paper being plotted. Very large parcels (acres of land area) often require two drawings: a very large scale plot plan to show the whole parcel with a smaller plot plan image that encompass just the area around the building site and various components in the vicinity thereof.

In this chapter we are going to use the scale of 1/16" = 1'. The lot size that we will depict will be 100' x 60'. That size of lot will print out on an 8.5 x 11 piece of paper at the 1/16 scale. Later in the book we will scale this same plot plan view to print on architectural size sheets of paper (36" x 24") at 1/8 scale.

First, let me show you what my workspace looks like at this stage. Look at Fig 4-1. Compare it to your drawing page by typing **z** <**e**> then **a** <**e**> (this is zoom all). Your screen will look different, maybe very different. The objects can be anywhere on the workspace screen; it doesn't matter. Later we will organize the material by page.

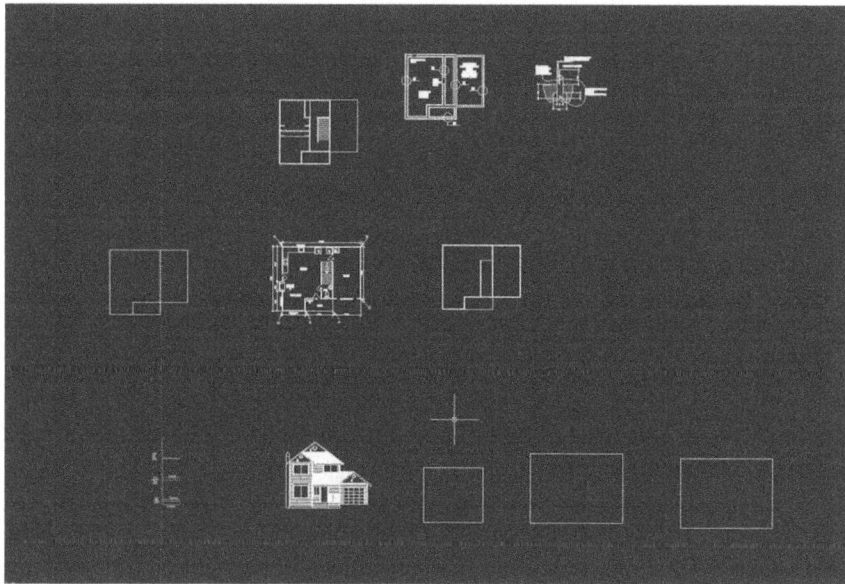

Fig 4-1

Draw a **100' x 60' rectangle** at the top of the drawing space. Use the **rectangle** tool and follow the prompts. The first measurement is always the horizontal, the second vertical (as is common in construction).

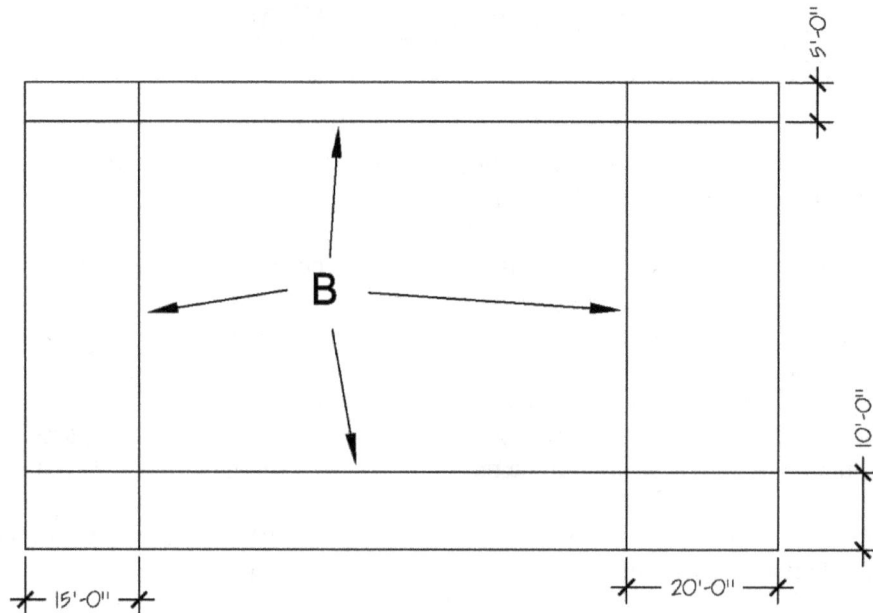

The outer rectangle is 100 ft x 60 ft

Fig 4-2

Create the **offset** lines shown as **B** in **Fig 4-2** using the **Offset** tool.

Click on the **Offset** tool, enter **20'** for the offset and **click** on the new **rectangle** then **click inside**. **You will not see Fig 4-2**. Instead you see a 60' x 20' rectangle in the center (20' offset on all sides). This is because the system recognizes the rectangle as one object—not as four separate sides. If you run your cursor over the rectangle you will see that it highlights as one object. We must break the rectangle into four separate lines. Undo or **erase this offset** (60' x 20' inner) rectangle.

4.2 Explode

We need to turn the outer rectangle into **four separate lines** so we can offset them separately. Click on the **Explode** button on the **Modify** palette (above the Offset button to the right of the palette). Now **click** on the 100 ft x 60 ft **rectangle** and <e>. This separates the components of the selected object, in this case the four sides of the rectangle, into separate objects.

Now if you run the cursor over the four lines of the 100 x 60 rectangle you will see that it selects them separately. It now recognizes them as **four separate lines**.

Now **offset** the **lines** as shown in **Fig 4-2**. **Twenty feet** in from the right vertical line, **five feet** from the top horizontal line, **ten feet** above the bottom horizontal line, and **fifteen feet** in from the left vertical line. These are the **setback lines** (generally, this is the area where no building is allowed).

Create a new line type with the **Layers Properties Manager**. Name it **dashed large**. Make it **green**. Click on the **linetype** where it says **continu...** (as you did in Chapter 3). The **Select Linetype** box appears. Click on the **Load** button. You will see the **Load or Reload Line types** box as in **Fig 4-3**. Scroll down until you see **DASHEDx2 (A in Fig 4-3)**. The one that says **Dashed (2x)** to the right, click on it then click **OK**.

In the **Select Linetype** window **highlight** the new **line type**. Click **Ok**.

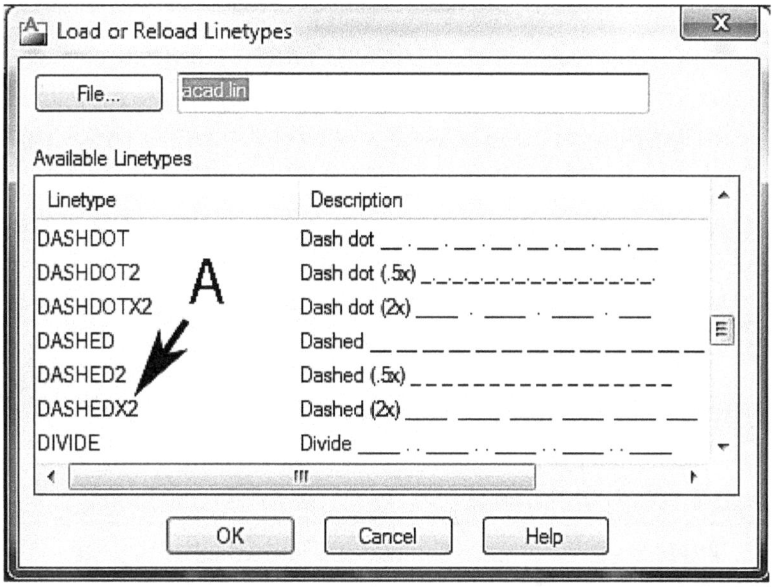

Fig 4-3

Return to the drawing and **select all of the setback lines** as **B** in **Fig 4-2**. In the **Layer Control** drop down menu select the **new dashed large layer (green)**. **Click** on it and the new **lines** will **change** to the **green layer**.

If you do not see a dashed line then see Appendix I—Dashed Lines for troubleshooting.

Press **ESC** on your keyboard. **Click on one of these new dashed lines (B)**. When it shows the little blue grip boxes **right click** the mouse to bring up the drop down box and select the **Properties** box (see Appendix I—Properties if you need help).

Where it says **Linetype scale** click on the number (it should be 1.000). Type **10** in this box (it will read 10.000 or something like that). Close this box. **ESC**.

Now click on the **Match Properties** button on the Properties palette at the top of the screen. With the pick box that appears **click** on the **line that you just changed to 10.000 scale**. Now **click** on **the other three green lines**. They will all change to reflect the new line type scale 10.

This is a roundabout way of getting these lines. There are faster routes, but this path shows you several of the different operations that you can use to manipulate the appearance of your dashed or broken lines.

Now we will place the outline of the house on the lot. Go back to the copy you made of the building outline (as shown in **Fig 1-9**) and **copy** the outline of the house. Bring it over to the space above our plot plan, click to set it in open space, and **rotate** it **90 degrees**. **Place it** as in **Fig 4-4**. Use the osnap on the corner of the house outline and snap it to the intersection of the two setback lines as shown in Fig 4-4.

Different jurisdictions (building/planning departments) require different depictions of the house on the plot plan. Some will want a simplified roof frame plan view to show which way the roof slopes. Some may want the actual floor plan. Since everything is initially drawn in actual full size scale we can add any of the views that we draw to the plot plan. Here we will just show the outline of the house.

We are going to add some topography to the lot behind the house to demonstrate a few more skills. We will add a slope upwards from the house.

4.3 UCS and Coordinates

Remember the **UCS** icon that we turned off in Chapter 1? Now we are going to turn it back on, only this time we are going to set it in a particular location. By doing this we can use it as a reference to locate points on the drawing using x and y coordinates.

In the **View** ribbon click on the **UCS Icon** button. On the **Coordinates** palette* select the **Origin** button (in the middle—hover the cursor over the buttons until you see Origin). Back in the drawing area **click** on the lower left corner of the plot. (C in Fig 4-4—Osnap must be on). You will see the UCS appear at the lower left corner of the rectangle.

The lines of the UCS are over the lines of the lot so they don't show well, but they are there.

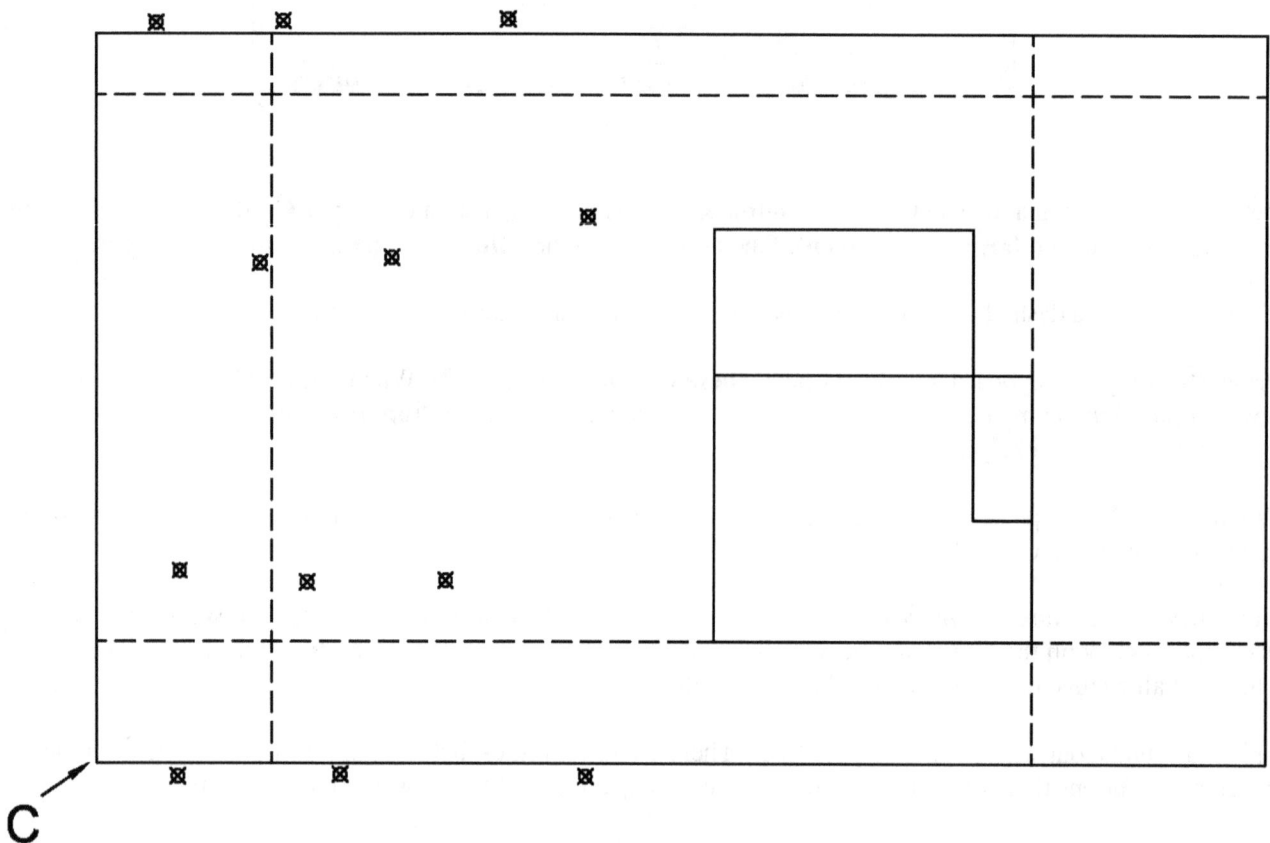

Fig 4-4

Now we are going to set some points (or nodes for Object snaps). Look at Fig 4-4 and Fig 4-5.

Fig 4-4 shows a bunch of points set on the plot plan. I have made mine very large so you can see them.

*If the Coordinates Palette is not on your View ribbon right click anywhere on the ribbon and select Show Panels.

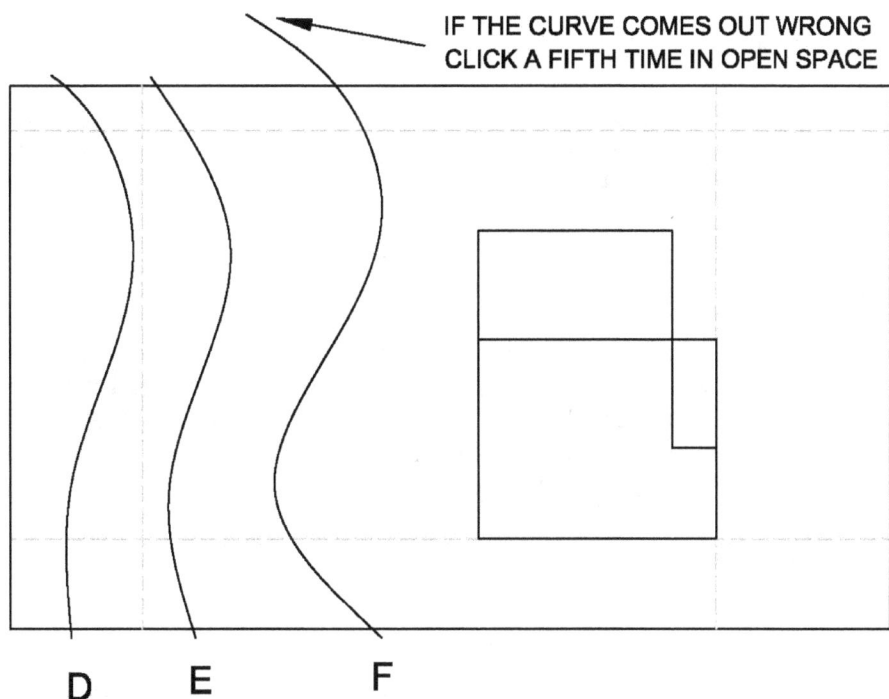

IF THE CURVE COMES OUT WRONG
CLICK A FIFTH TIME IN OPEN SPACE

D   E   F

Fig 4-5

Fig 4-5 shows these points connected by using the **spline** tool to create **topographical lines** (topo lines). These lines show the elevation of the land. They connect **points** of **equal elevation**. Everywhere along each line is the same elevation. You do not need to understand all of this—it is the drawing process that is important.

First let's create a certain kind of point. On the **Utilities** palette (Home tab) click on the down arrow next to Utilities and select **Point Style...**

The **Point Style** box will appear. Click on the **large cross** (third from left on the top row). Click the **radio button** (round button) that says **Set Size in Absolute Units**. Set the units to **5** (remember that inches are the default in the Architectural Units unless you set a different default). Click **OK**.

Select the **Construction** layer from the **Layer Control** drop down list.

Click the **Point** button on the **Draw** palette (click on the down arrow next to Draw and select **Multiple Points**). (You can also type: point.) **Type: 7',-1' <e>. You must type the comma.** A point will appear 7' to the right of the UCS and 1' below. Now repeat this process with the following combinations of numbers: **7',16' <e> / 14',41' <e> / 5',61' <e>**. You do not need to click on the point button each time. When you are finished **<ESC>**.

Set the **layer to the 0 layer**. Click on the **Spline** tool (Spline Fit found with the down arrow next to Draw on the Draw palette). **Start at the bottom** and **click** on **each** of these **four points**. You should see line **D** in **Fig 4-5**. **Node** osnap must be turned on for this procedure.

Repeat the process with the next four points. Type the coordinates: **21',-1'<e>/ 18',15' <e>/ 25',42' <e>/ 16',61' <e>**. Use the **Construction layer for the points** and the **0 layer for the spine**. Use the **spline** and connect them **starting** at the bottom point **E**. Turn off the Ortho for this.

One more time with the points: **42',-1 / 30',15' / 42',45' / 36',61'**. Then **Spline** on **0 layer**. You will see Fig 4-5.

If the last section curves in the wrong direction then erase the spline and try again only this time click a fifth time beyond the fourth point as in Fig 4-5.

Now **turn off the 0 layer** in the **Layer Control** (click on the little light bulb to turn it off). **Select all of the points you just set for the splines and erase them**. Try erasing several of them at the same time using the **blue selection window**.

You have been using the green selection window which is a selection window created by clicking in the drawing and moving the mouse to the left. The blue selection window is created with a click and then movement to the right. The blue selection window will select only objects that are **completely enclosed** in the selection window (the green selects everything that it touches). So here is a perfect example of where to use this function. You can erase the points with two selections/erases if you do not to include the entire green vertical set back line in either selection. You can Undo and try it again if there is a problem.

Trim the **spline** lines to the lot lines as in **Fig 4-6**.

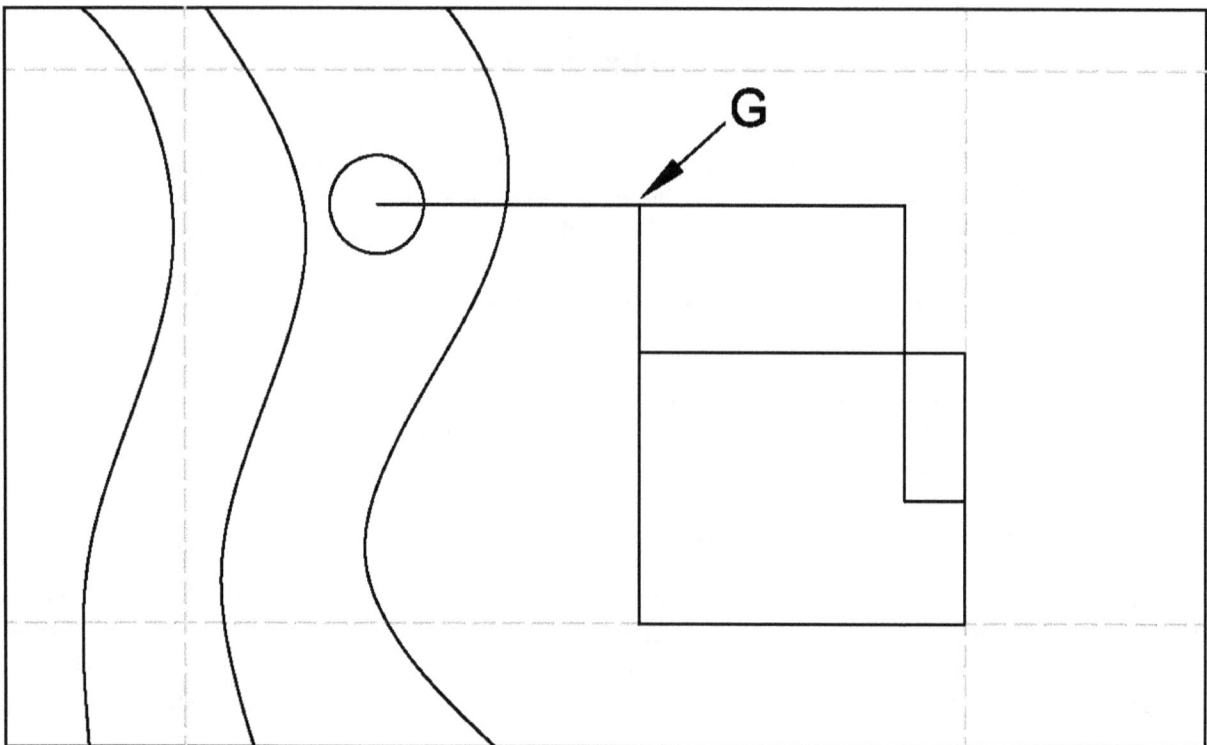

Fig 4-6

110

This type of data entry—using the placed UCS and specifying specific points is useful for curved lines that must be precisely set in an open area of the drawing. Especially if there are a lot of points.

Another spline object that we drew was the top of the fireplace. There we used a grid of temporary construction lines. That spline line was a single curve so it was easier to draw with a grid. But the grid is just another way of locating coordinate points.

For the earth hatch we used the spline freehand, without set nodes or a grid.

The type of leader we used in the foundation detail is also a spline.

There are a lot of different ways to locate a particular point (coordinates) on the plans.

Let's try another method and draw the water tank.

Turn the **Ortho on** and draw a **line** from the upper left corner of the garage (**G** in **Fig 4-6**) to the left. Snap it to the garage corner and pull the line out a ways to the left and then type: **22' <e>**. This is a temporary reference line.

Now use the **circle** button and place a **4' diameter** circle at the end of this line then **erase the reference line**. Read the prompts and you will be reminded of the steps.

Place a square around the circle using the **rectangle** button. Make the rectangle **5'** square and place it around the circle **by drawing a temporary diagonal line** as we did with the water heater in Chapter 1. The proper osnaps will need to be set (ie center of circle). This represents the concrete pad under the water tank.

Read the prompts when you create the **rectangle** and make sure you enter the **d** when it asks for **dimensions**. If you miss this step it will still create a rectangle but it will be the wrong size. You have to click what seems an extra time to get the rectangle to stay on the screen.

For the **circle select** the **d** option also. Here **d** means diameter (as opposed to r for radius).

There is a multitude of information that can be required on a plot plan depending on the jurisdiction where the plans are to be submitted. I am going to keep this plot plan simple because it is the drawing skills that we are seeking (not a discussion of building departments and their requirements—these vary immensely).

4.4 Driveway and Flatwork

Draw the driveway **lines** as shown at **H** in **Fig 4-7**. These are drawn from the corners of the garage (See Fig 4-11 if you need a reference).

Draw a **line 2'** inside the front property line at **K**.

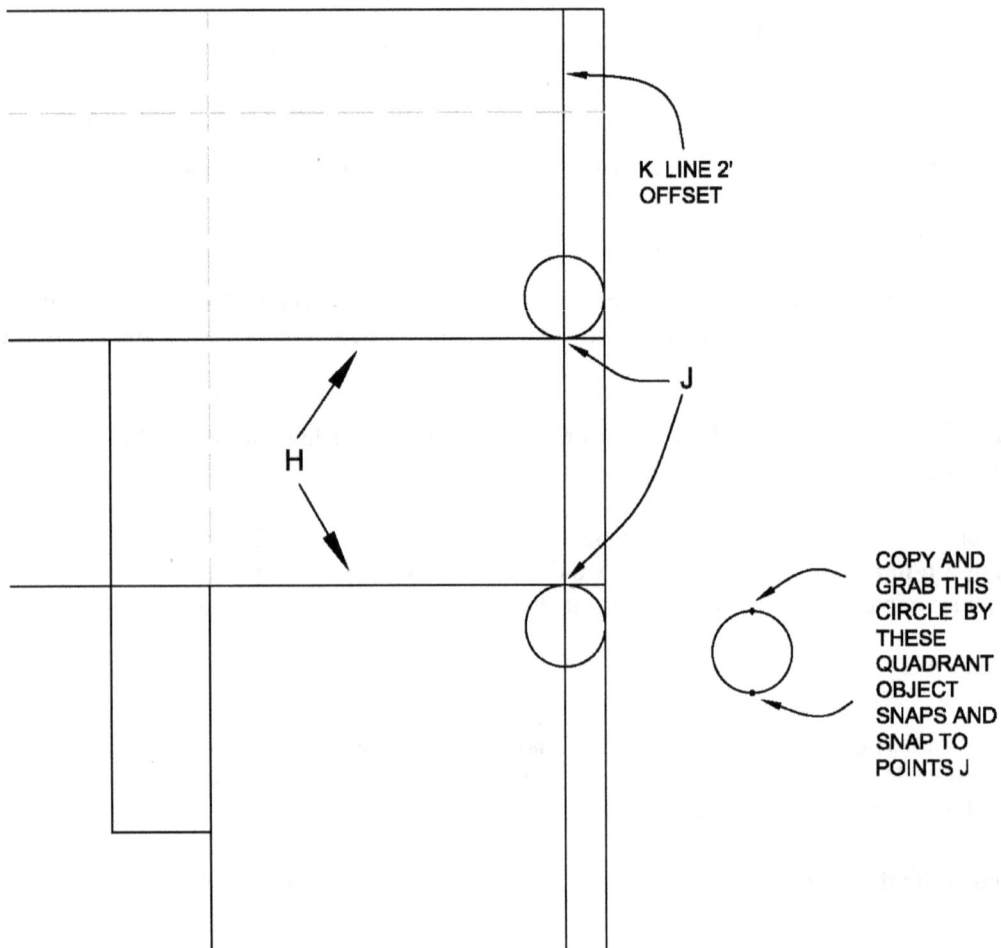

K LINE 2'
OFFSET

J

COPY AND
GRAB THIS
CIRCLE BY
THESE
QUADRANT
OBJECT
SNAPS AND
SNAP TO
POINTS J

H

Fig 4-7

Use the **circle** tool to create the radius at the street (**J**). Draw a circle—**set the radius to 2'**—then attach **copies** of the **circle** to **points J** using the **quadrant object snap** (Osnap settings) as the base point to grab the circle and snap the circles to the intersection of the lines shown at J. **Trim** the **circles** and **erase line K** to show **Fig 4-8**.

We could have used the Fillet tool to get these radii, but, once again, we have used a more complicated method as a way to learn more techniques.

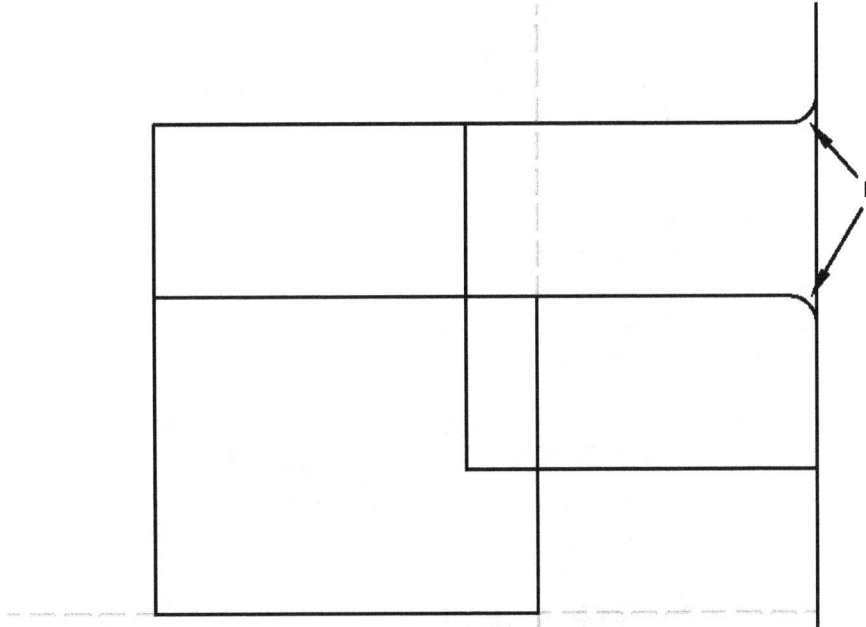

Fig 4-8

Let's suppose that the curve we have drawn at the street side of the driveway is not what we want. Perhaps we want a curve that is more like Fig 4-10. We can use the **arc** tool.

Erase the **curves** at **L** in **Fig 4-8**.

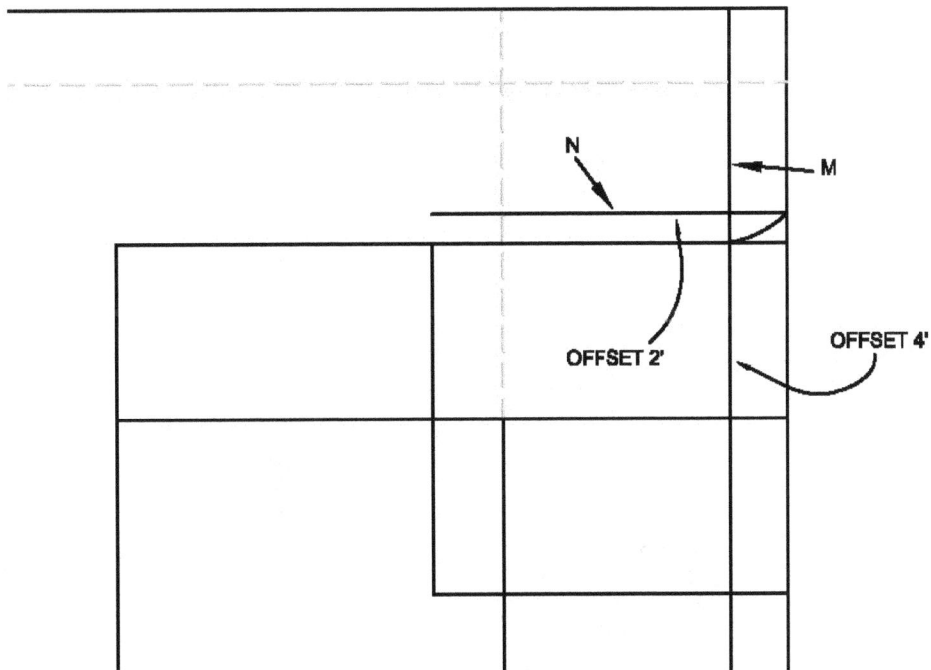

Fig 4-9

Create the **reference lines M** and **N** in **Fig 4-9** using the **Offset** tool. **M** is offset **4'** and **N** is offset **2'**.

Turn on the **Dynamic Input** using the button at the bottom of the screen (same status bar as Ortho and Object Snap). If the button is not there turn it on by clicking on the Customization button at the lower right of the screen that has three horizontal lines (Fig 1-1). This opens the Status bar customization menu. Click to add a check mark next to Dynamic Input to turn it on. A Dynamic input button will appear on the status bar at the bottom of the screen.

Click on the **3-Point Arc** tool on the **Draw** palette (find it in the selection of Arc tools by clicking on the down arrow below Arc). **Click on point O** in **Fig 4-10**. **Click on point P**. An **Arc** will appear. **Pull** the **arc line** out to the **right** and **move** the **cursor** around. See how the arc is affected. The **Dynamic Input** tells you the degrees of arc and the length of the line. Pull it out until it is **approximately 10'** long (**Length** in **Fig 4-9A**) and **80** degrees (**Degrees** in **Fig 4-9A**). Type **10' <e>**. **Click**. This will over write the length in the window.

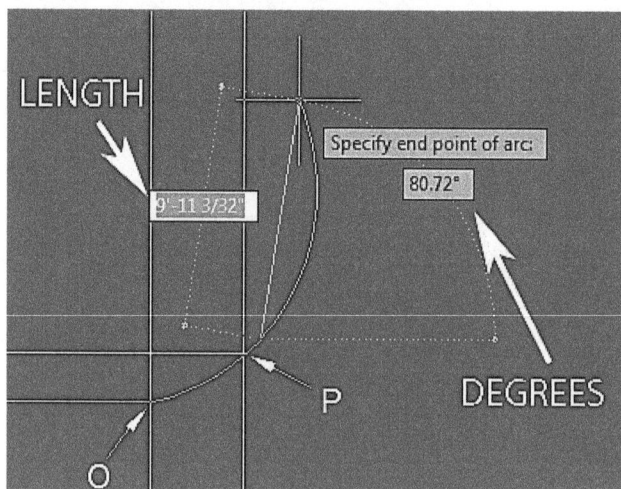

Fig 4-9A

Trim it to look like the upper arc between points O and P in **Fig 4-10**.

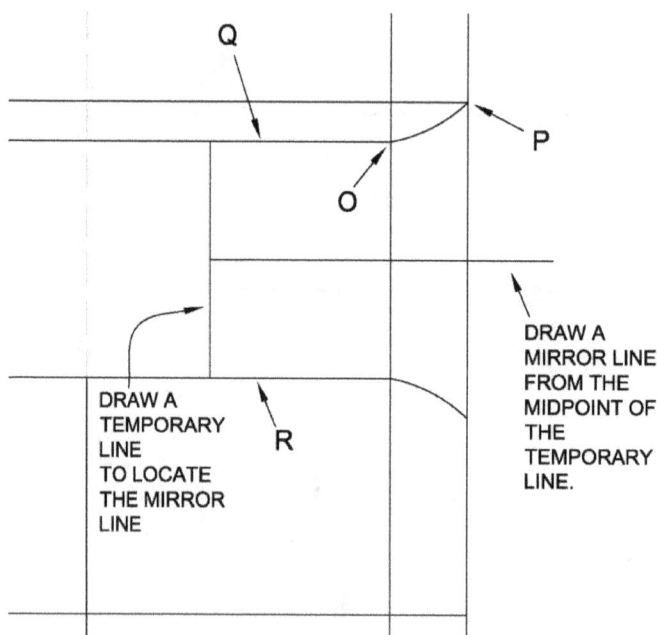

Fig 4-10

This is a good way to create an arc by eye when you are uncertain as to what exactly you want. If you need to make an accurate arc based on this "by eye" arc, use the Properties palette to find its radius, then use the Start,End,Radius option in the drop down arc menu (click the down arrow under the Arc button to find this). Click on the two points, pull out the arc a bit and then type the desired radius and <e>. Try this to see how it works.

Use the **mirror** tool to **create** the mirror image of the **arc**. First draw a temporary line between line **Q** and line **R** in **Fig 4-10**. Use the **midpoint** on **Q** to **start** the **line** and the **perpendicular** osnap on line **R** as the **end point** of this temporary line.

Turn the **Ortho on**. Draw another **line** (see the MIRROR line in Fig 4-10); use the **midpoint** of the **line** between **Q** and **R** for the **starting point** of this line, then **click** in the **approximate** location shown in **Fig 4-10** for the **end point**.

Click on the **Mirror** tool. **Read the prompts. Select** the **arc** as the **object** then <e>. Use the **left end** of the line you just drew as the **first point** of the mirror line; when prompted for the **second point** click on the **right end** of this mirror line, then <e> (**Fig 4-10**). This will create the second, lower, arc as in Fig 4-11.

I will **turn off the Dynamic Input** now. Some people like it on all the time—it drives me batty. I only turn it on for specific objects.

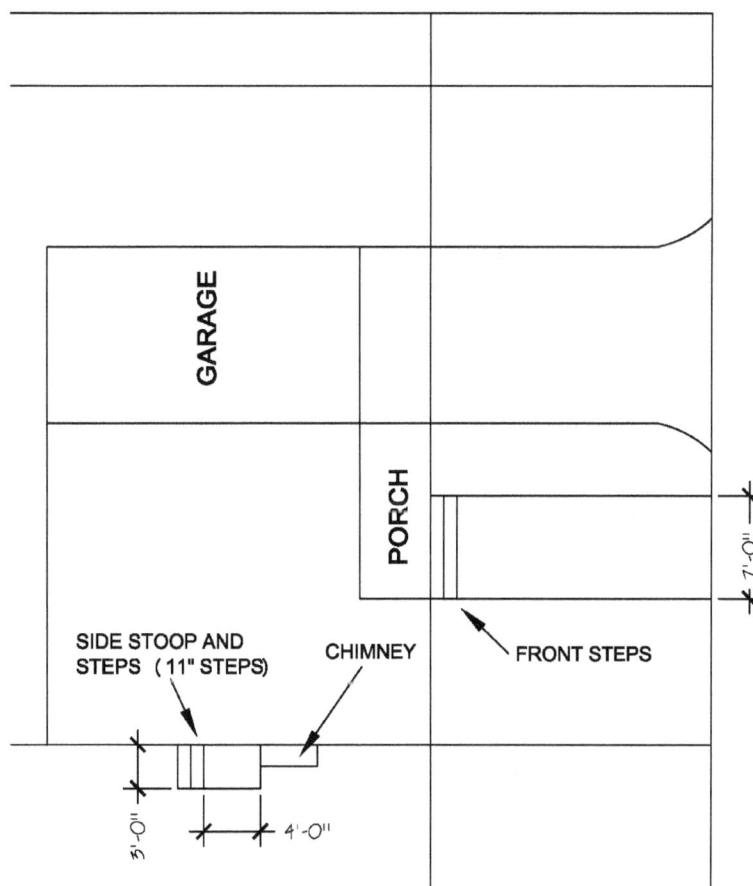

Fig 4-11

Erase the **temporary lines** you drew and **trim** the **driveway lines** at the curve to see **Fig 4-11**.

Draw two **steps** down from the **front porch (10"** each) and the 7' walkway as in **Fig 4-11**. Don't get too caught up in exact measurements. It is the concepts that we are concerned with.

Add the chimney it is **4' x 18"** and it is located **8'** from the lower right corner of the house.

This house has a **side** door that needs a **stoop** and **stairs**. This is shown in **Fig 4-11**.

4.5 Dimensions and Notes

We need to add notes and dimensions.

Since we are going to print this view in 1/16 scale we need to size the letters, numbers and leaders to that scale.

In AutoCAD the initial drawing is always actual size. When we draw a house the program sees the drawing at full scale. Inside the program the floor plan that we drew is 34' x 27'. That may seem strange because we can see it on the screen in a much smaller version. But it really makes perfect sense. The program only knows what you tell it and we use actual dimensions to draw.

So, in theory, if we didn't tell the program that we wanted to print out in a smaller scale it would just print it out at full size. You can actually do that. You could print the whole house out at actual scale on many separate pieces of paper and glue all the pieces together to make a full size drawing of the house. While that might make a good de Cristo art piece, it would be impractical for house plans (and the building department would probably not appreciate it).

We must *tell* the program to plot our drawing at a scale that fits on our paper.

The most common size paper for architectural plans in the United States is 36 x 24 paper. On that size of paper **floor plans, elevations, electrical plans, foundation plans**—most house size objects—show up well at ¼" = 1' (1/48). You can see enough detail to build what is represented in the drawing and use a measuring tape to read the important information. So the pages on the plans that show these views are commonly plotted in AutoCAD at the scale of ¼" = 1'. Each ¼ inch as measured on the plans is equal to 1 foot of the actual building.

The **Plot plan** will be set up at a different scale because it is several times larger than the house. In order to fit it on 8.5 x 11 paper we must scale it to **1/16" = 1'**.

Don't worry if you don't get this all at once. Many people find the scaling thing to be confusing at first. It will become clear as we proceed.

Since the drawing in AutoCAD is actual size, the scale of the printed version does not affect the basic lines and shapes of the objects. They will simply appear larger or smaller according to the plot scale. But the **text, leader arrowheads, dimension text** and **dashed lines** all **need to be adjusted** so as not to be either too large or too small. These must be **fitted** to the **plotted scale** of the drawing.

The layout of text is a bit of an art form. How it is laid out, positioned, and scaled is important to the "readability" of the plans (the ease of comprehension). Placing text in the right position allows the eye to quickly understand the drawing. If it is cramped or set in an awkward position, it can confuse the person reading the plans.

If you need more info right now see Chapter 13. It covers scales in detail. But you can just follow along, all the information required to continue is presented as needed. It becomes clear as the drawing progresses.

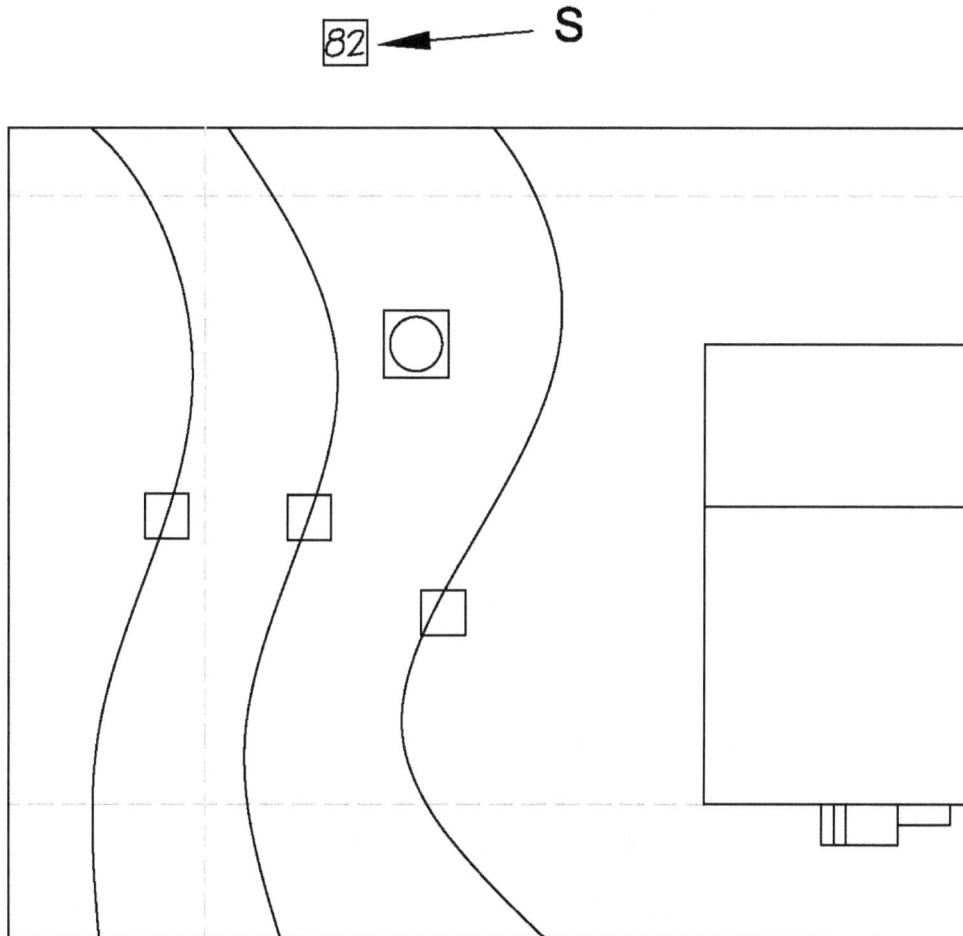

Fig 4-12

First we will add the references to the topo lines designated by **T** in **Fig 4-13**. **Type mt <e>**. In the open space next to the plot plan (as **S** in **Fig 4-12**) open the text window. **Select style 9** from the **Style Palette** that opens with the mtext window. Set the text height to **24"**. Click the **Bold** button. **Type** the text: **82** as shown in **Fig 4-12**. Click **Close Text Editor** to the far right of the text editor ribbon on the **Close palette.** (Or, if you have the Text Formatting toolbar set to display, you can just click OK. See Text—Appendix I)

Make a **square** rectangle around this number. The dimensions are 36 x 36. Copy this rectangle to the points shown in **Fig 4-12** (approximate). **Just the rectangle not the number 82.**

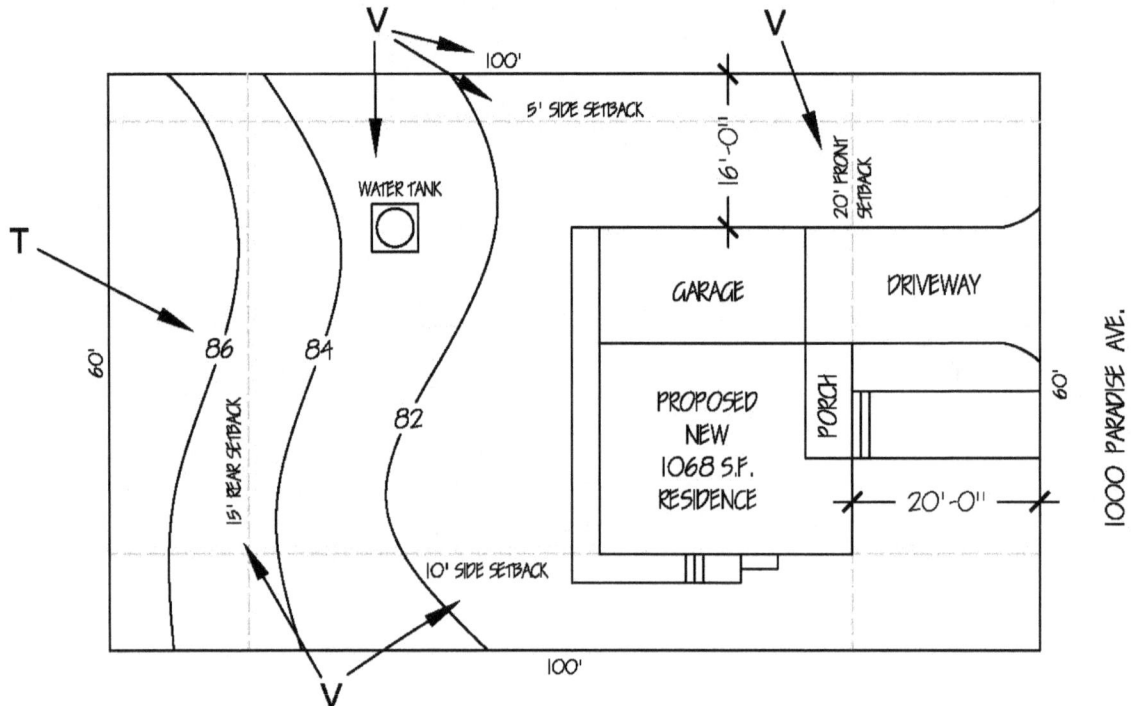

Fig 4-13

Trim the **spline** lines inside the boxes then **erase** the **boxes**.

Copy the **82** text to where the center of the rectangles were (approximately) as in **Fig 4-13**. Set them by eye.

Now click on the **texts**, highlight them, and **edit** them to read as in **Fig 4-13**. Or just type each number separately if you find that easier.

Now **add** the rest of **text** as shown in **Fig 4-13**. The main text is **24"**.

The text for the **numbers**, the "**WATER TANK**", and the **set back notes** are **18"** (as shown at the **V**'s in **Fig 4-13**).

Turn the **Object Snap off** when you set this text. If you have the Object Snap on it will try to snap to something. I set this type of text by eye—just make it look good. As before, I create one of the texts, copy it to the different locations then click on it and edit the text. This is faster than opening a mt box each time. You can do it any way you choose.

Now add the dimensions. First create a new dimstyle (autocad lingo for dimension style).

Click on the **Dimension Style** button on the **Annotation** palette on the Home ribbon. Click **New**. Name it **sixteenth**. Click the **Continue** button.

Select the **Fit** tab. In the box that is titled: **Scale for dimension features,** click on the button that says **Use Overall Scale of, highlight** the **number** in the box and **overtype** it with: **192**. This is the 1/16 scale stated as a ratio. There are 192 sixteenths in 12" (16 x 12—more on this later). The **Annotative** should be **unchecked**. Under the **Primary Units** tab set the **Scale Factor** to **1**. Review section 1.23 if you have forgotten the steps.

Check to make sure that it says **Architectural** in the **Unit format** box. Click **Okay**. Then **Set Current**. It will say **sixteenth** now in the Description box. **Close**.

Add a new osnap object. **Right click** on the **Object Snap button** at the bottom. Turn **on** the **Nearest** object snap.

Click on the **Linear** dimension button. Attach this dimension to the garage first (where it reads 16'-0"). Slide the cursor to the right and left and you will see how the nearest function works. It will now attach the dimension to anywhere on this line. Click somewhere near what you see in Fig 4-13 and then, at the property line, attach it to the **perpendicular** snap object point (you need to have the **perpendicular Osnap** setting turned **on**). This is how you snap to a line where there is no other osnap reference point (endpoint, midpoint or intersection).

Add the other **dimension** shown (**20'-0"**).

Take a moment and check out the **Area** measure tool. It is on the **Utilities** palette (click on the down arrow below Measure). Click on the **Area** button and then click on the four corners of the lot (the 100 x 60 rectangle). Start with the lower right corner, click on the corner osnap icon, then click on the other three corners counter clockwise. Then <e>. It will calculate the square footage inside the shape you define. Read the command line to see the measurements.

Try it with other areas—the residence, the porch. If you use it on the driveway you must click on both of the ends of the arcs. This is very useful—especially when the shapes to be measured are complex.

This is it for the Plot Plan.

There is often much more information on a plot plan, check with the local building/planning department. But you should now be able to draw anything they require. If you need to add trees you can pick them up in the **Design Center** (where you got the toilet and the sink) under the landscape.dwg selection and then Blocks.

As always remember to save your work.

Chapter 5—Cross Sections

5.1 Cross Section

By now you should be able to draw most 2D objects with AutoCAD. The methods you have learned so far are not always the fastest, because the purpose of this book is to acquire the drawing skills in the shortest possible time frame. You can learn faster methods of drawing later.

This chapter is explained in less detail than the beginning chapters. I no longer describe how to draw each line, rectangle, circle—every object—step by step. You have already learned the basic procedures for many of these commands. So, for the most part, you will be directed to simply make the drawing look like mine, except when the command or procedure is new. Refer to the **Index** to find the **instructions** for **each command**.

This chapter will demonstrate a few more drawing techniques, but the main new information is about scales.

Cross sections and details, as you will create in this chapter, are drawn in a number of different scales—½" = 1', ¾" = 1', or 1" = 1' scale. Sometimes even larger scales are used (2" or 3" or larger) depending on the size of the object: the smaller the object, the larger the scale. Often several different objects, drawn in **different scales**, are **displayed** on the **same page**.

You can see what this looks like by looking at the Cross Section/Detail page of the plans. Take a moment and look at page six of the finished plans (see Appendix IV—Page 6). The drawing of this page presents an opportunity to explore some of the different scales and demonstrate how to place them together on the same page. This chapter explains one way to do this. Chapter 14 explains an alternative method.

On Page 6 of the plans you have:

- a **cross section** of the entire house at ½" **scale**.
- a **garage roof section** at ¼" **scale**.
- three **sheer transfer details** at ¾" **scale**.
- a **garage tie-in detail** at 1" **scale**.

Four different views, each plotted at a different scale, drawn on one 36 x 24 inch piece of paper.

There are basically two ways to achieve this multiple scale on one page thing. This chapter demonstrates a method wherein you print the entire page out in one viewport (this is called a single viewport). The alternative method involves creating different delineated sections on the page and scaling them individually (called multiple viewports). The multi-viewport method will be covered in Chapter 14.

You can draw everything in this chapter, or you can skip through the Figures, pick out what you want to learn, and then follow the instructions in **Section 5-4 Scaled Detailed Views**.

This chapter has a lot of Figures but the actual time to draw it all is not much. The text (written instructions) in this chapter can be read in about twenty minutes.

In Chapter 2 you were asked to create a copy of the front elevation (**Fig 2-17**). **Copy** this it to a new area of the drawing space (anywhere). **Trim** and **erase** lines until you see **Fig 5-1**. We are going to use this as the basic drawing for the cross section that you see in the finished plans (also see Fig 5-34). Don't worry too much about making the drawing exactly precise, because, once again, the purpose here is to learn AutoCAD skills, not to create a perfect drawing. You can perfect your drawings later.

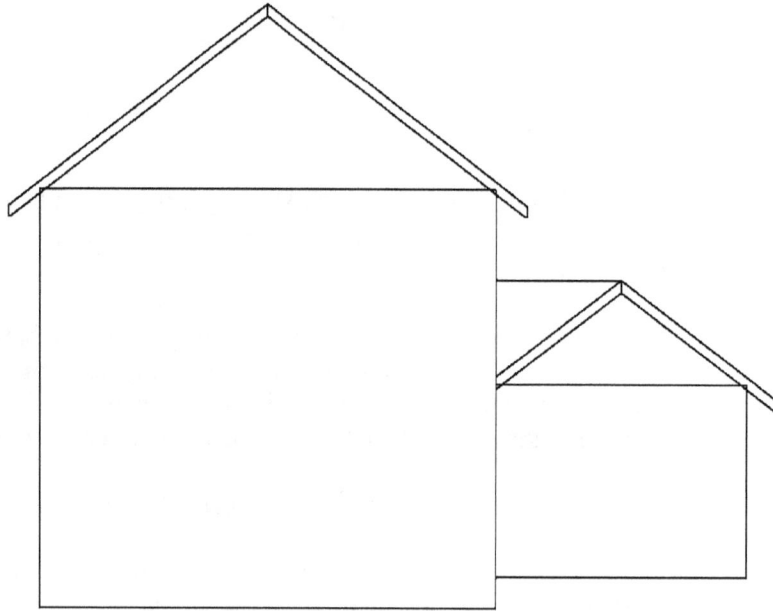

Fig 5-1

Set your layer to **0 layer**.

Extend the **line** out at **A** in **Fig 5-2 five feet** (approximate) from the building. Click on it and use the blue grip box on the end, with the **Ortho on**, pull it out a ways and type **5' <e>**.

Copy the **Story Pole** from Chapter 2 and attach it to line **A** as shown in **Fig 5-2**.

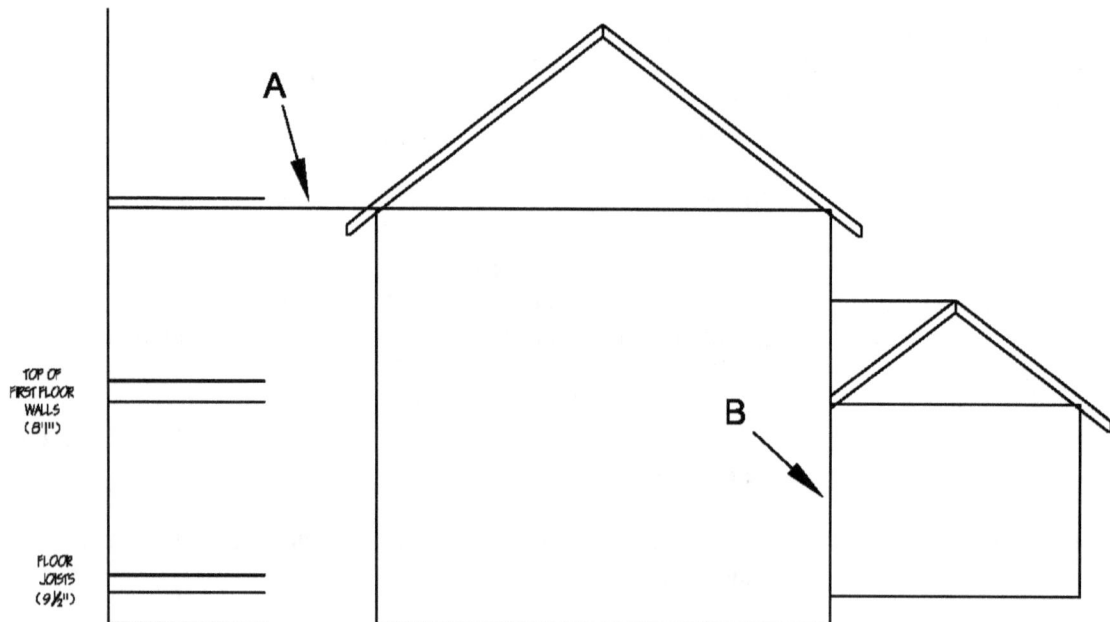

Fig 5-2

Now we will use an alternative **Extend** method (alternative to what we have been doing so far) to draw the other lines through as in Fig 5-3.

Click the **Extend** button (**do not enter this time**). Read the prompts. When it says: **Select objects:** click on line **B** in Fig 5-2 <e>. Now **select** the **lines** to be carried through from the story pole (**Fig 5-3**) and <e>. You can click on the story pole lines individually or you can select them with a green selection window.

You should see Fig 5-3.

As you can see, this is an alternative to the extend method we have been using so far. It seems counter-intuitive in that it prompts you to select objects when it means the line to be extended to. Then it prompts for the fence or crossing when it means the objects to be extended.

The extend command can be persnickety. If it doesn't work at first, escape and try it again. See Appendix I— Trim and Extend if you have problems.

The **top line** (line **C** in **Fig 5-3**) will not be included in the extension of the other lines (it is above line B). So extend it using the original method: **click** on **Extend** and **enter immediately**, then **click** on **line C** several times.

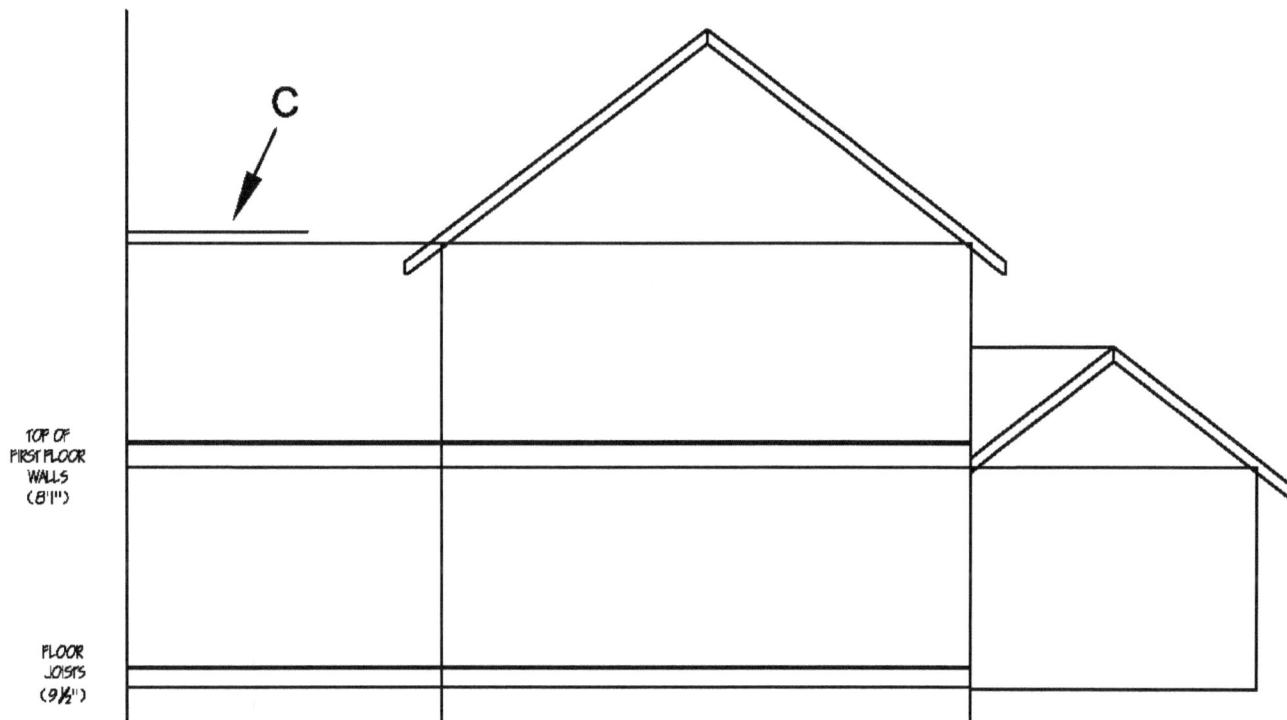

C

TOP OF
FIRST FLOOR
WALLS
(8'1")

FLOOR
JOISTS
(9½")

Fig 5-3

Now try an alternate way of using the **Trim** command. Click **Trim** (**do not enter**). **Read the prompt**. When it reads "**Select objects**" click on the left side of the house (line **D** in **Fig 5-4**) and <e>. Create a green selection window and **select the lines to be trimmed** as in **Fig 5-4**. This method, as with the extend command, can be persnickety. You may have to escape and do it more than once before it works.

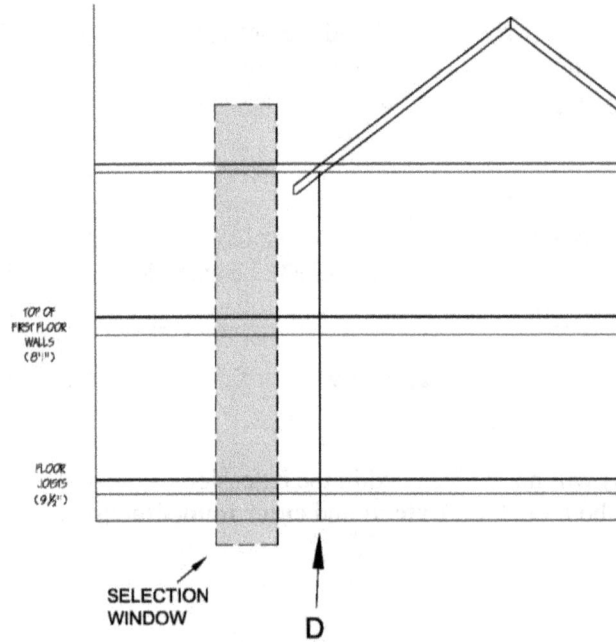

TOP OF
FIRST FLOOR
WALLS
(8'1")

FLOOR
JOISTS
(9½")

SELECTION
WINDOW

D

Fig 5-4

This will not trim the line at the top. **Escape** and **trim** and **erase** it to see **Fig 5-5**. Select all of these new lines then click on the **Layer Control** and **select** the **0 layer** (They were on the Construction layer).

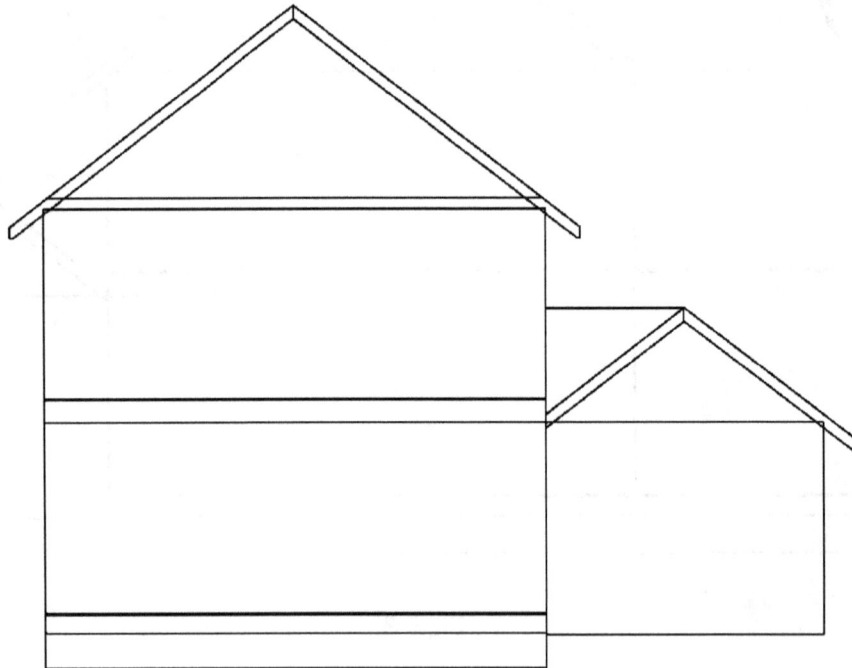

Fig 5-5

You can now **erase** what is left of this copy of the story pole.

Use the **offsets** as shown in **Fig 5-6** to create: the wall thickness at **E**'s (**3.5"**), the ridge at **F** (**7.5"**), the top of the ceiling joist at **G** (**7.5"**), and the roof plywood at **H** (**5/8"** or **.625"**).

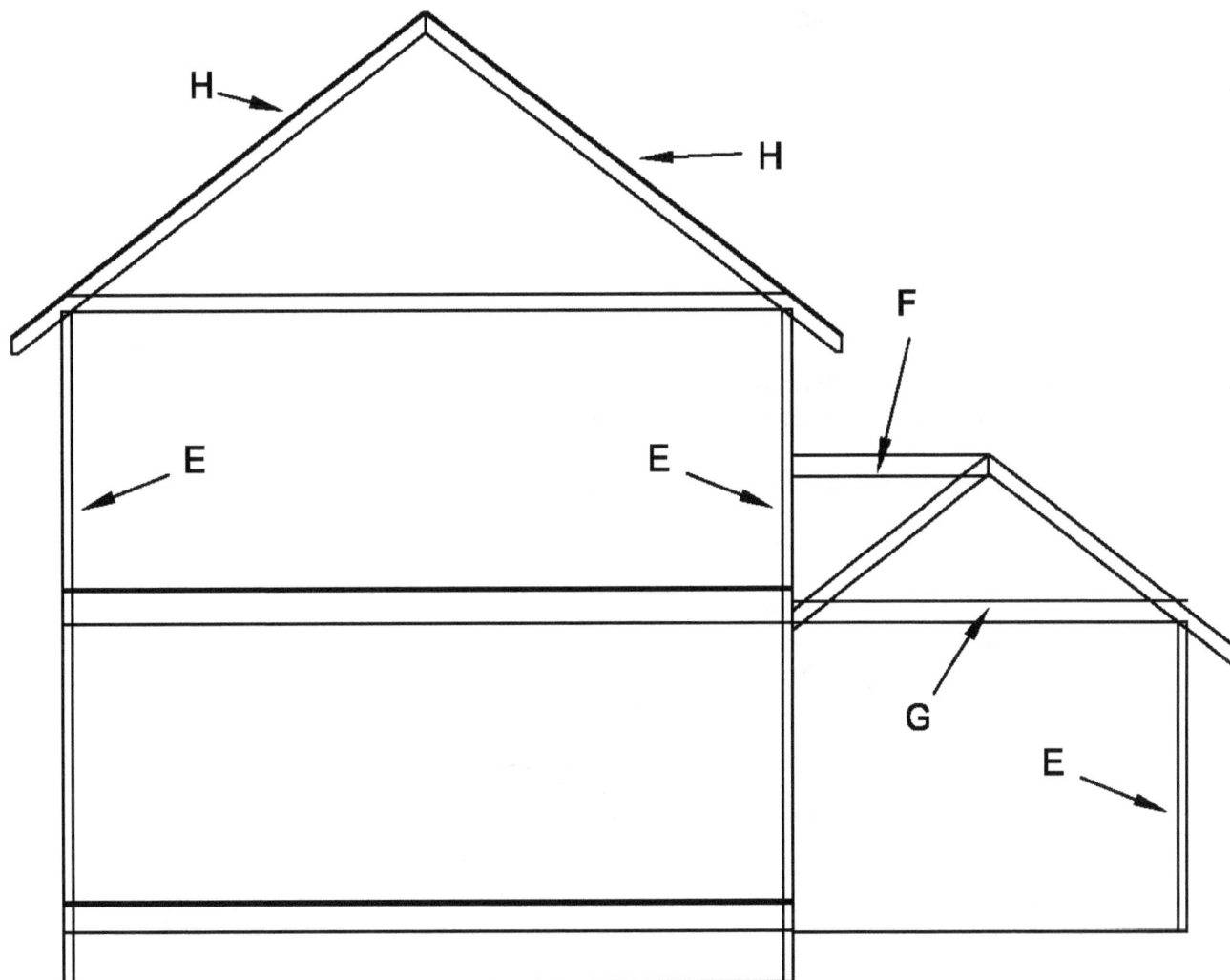

Fig 5-6

Draw the end cut for the ceiling joist as detailed in **Fig 5-7**. Use **1.5" offset** for line **J**. Use **Extend** and **Trim** to get the right hand drawing.

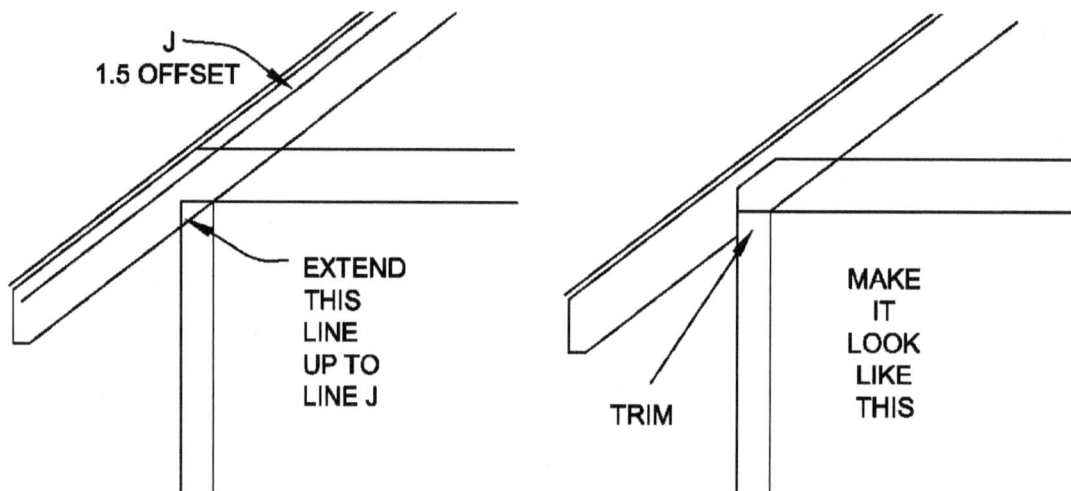

Fig 5-7

5.2 Draw Details

We will now draw some of the details. These will be described to a certain degree in the step by step format, but the majority of these details you will draw using the skills you have already learned. Don't sweat the precision factor too much, you can figure out accuracy later, for now concentrate on the techniques.

Look at **Fig 5-8**. It will be our **reference** for the **next several steps**. The instructions will refer to the different areas shown in Fig 5-8 as Ref L, Ref M, Ref K, etc.

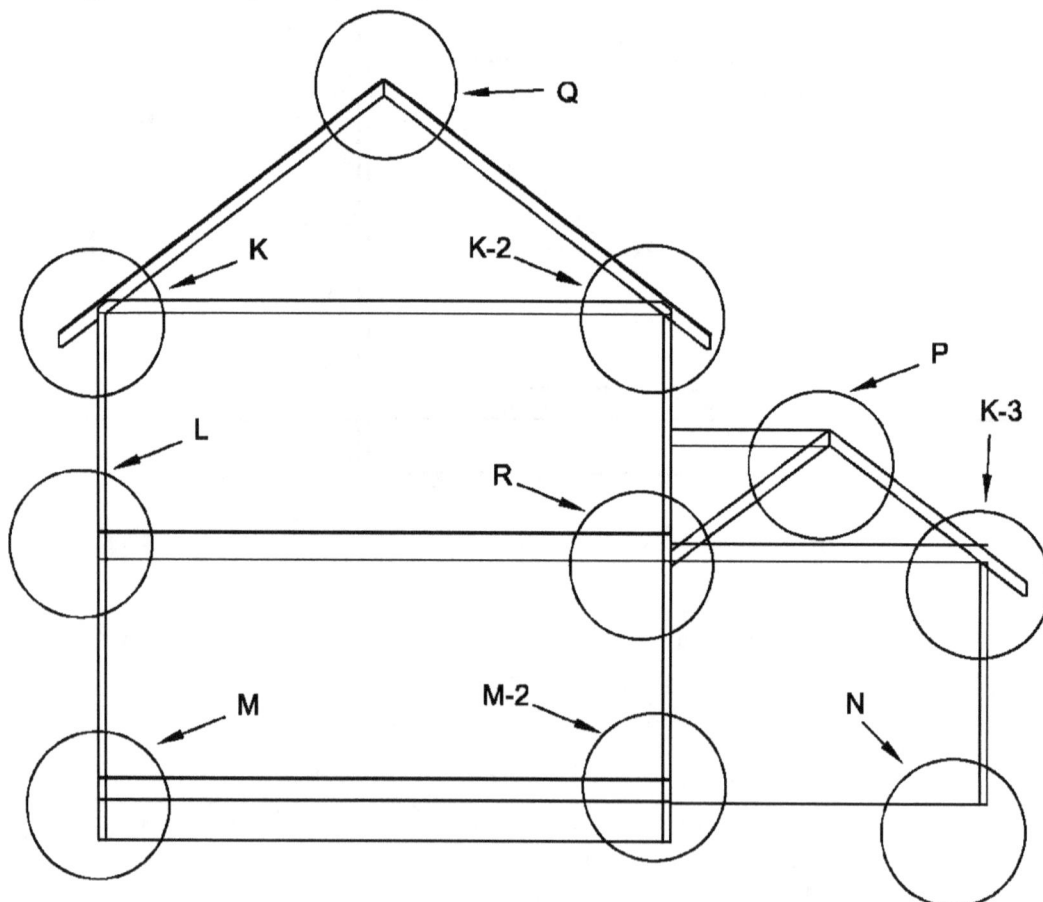

Fig 5-8

The purpose of the **cross section** drawing is to provide a graphic image of some of the important components of the building.

Start with Ref's **L** and **M**. Create line **S** offset from **T 1.5"** as in **Fig 5**-9. Trim this line at the **X**'s shown.

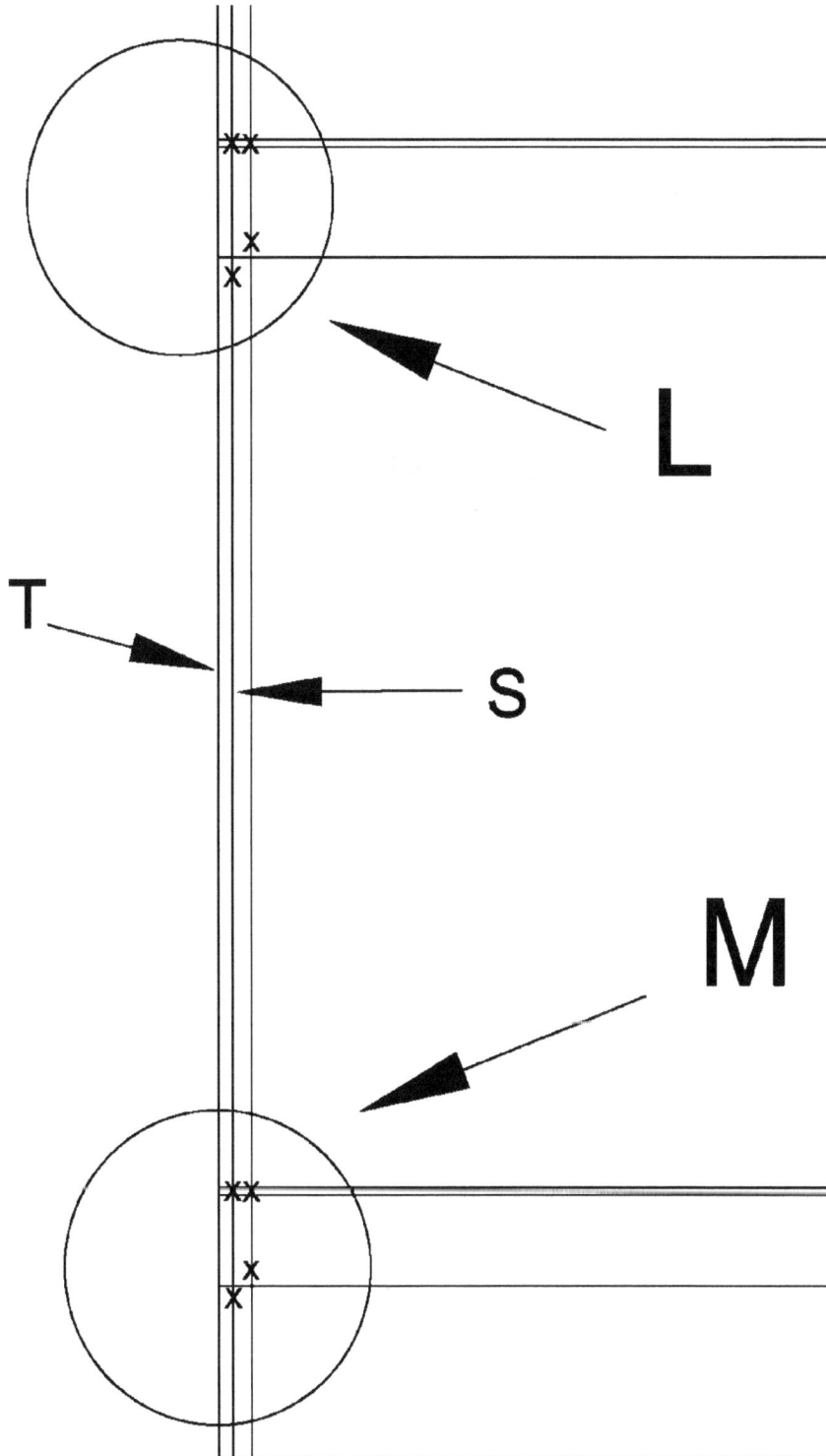

Fig 5-9

Create the diagonal **lines** shown in **Fig 5-10**.

Draw the new lines shown at **U** and **V** in **Fig 5-10** use **1.5" offset** and **trim**. Again, you can create one pair of diagonal lines and copy them (instead of drawing each line separately).

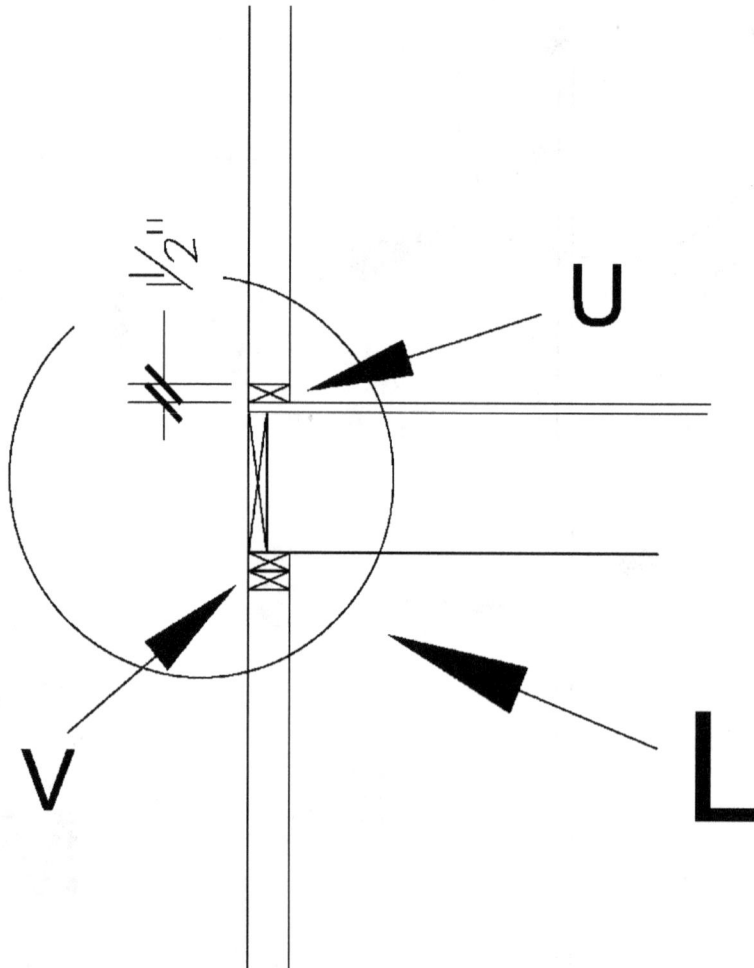

Fig 5-10

Next at **Ref K copy** the **lines** from **V** in Fig 5-10 to create the lines at **W** as shown in **Fig 5-11**.

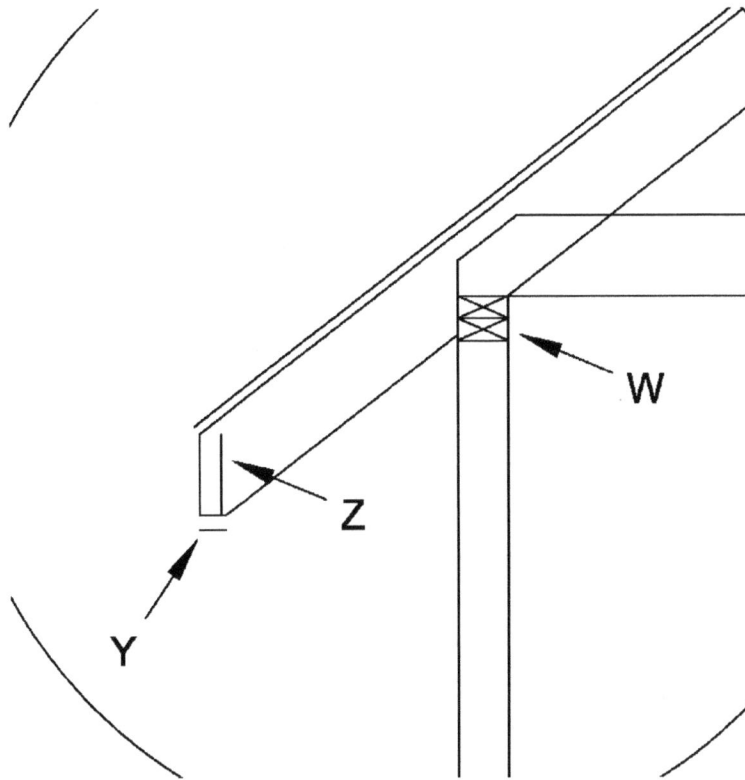

Fig 5-11

Draw **line Z** with **1.5"** offset and line **Y** with **1"** offset.

Extend the lines as shown in **Fig 5-12** (Z up to the ply and down to meet Y). **Trim** at the **X**.

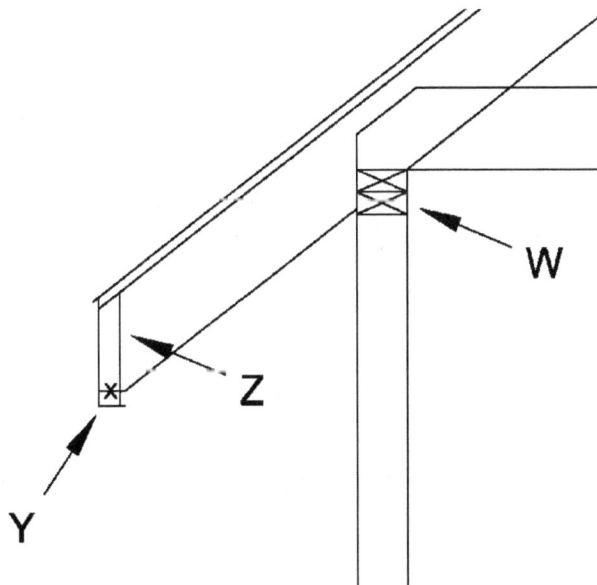

Fig 5-12

Finish off **Ref K** to appear as in **Fig 5-13**.

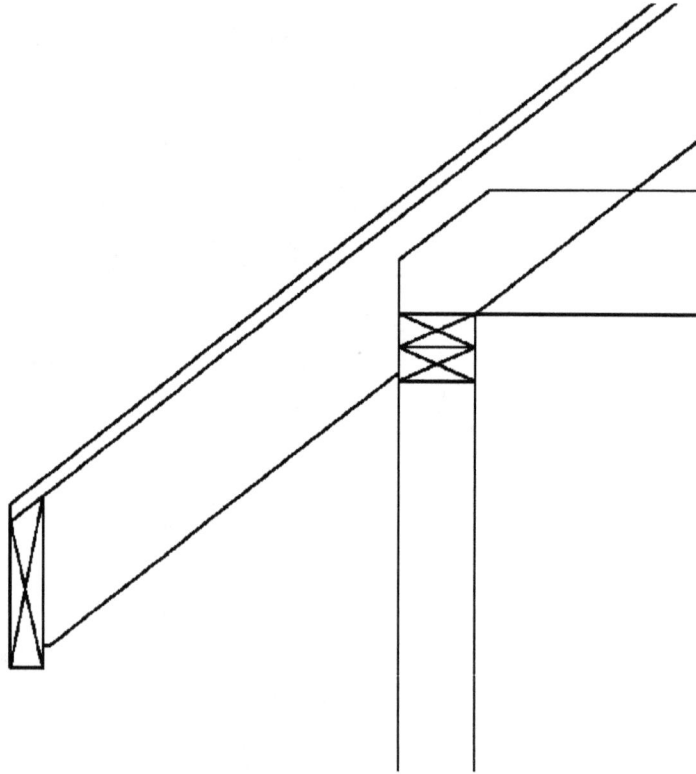

Fig 5-13

Add the **lines** to **Ref M** as shown in **Fig 5-14**. The lines are offset **1.5"**.

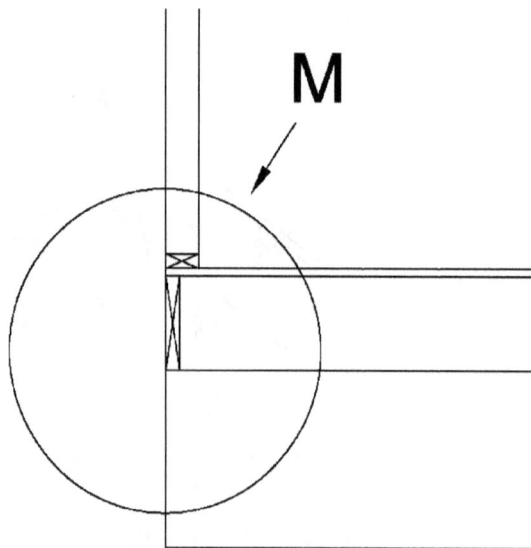

Fig 5-14

In Chapter 3 you copied the foundation detail (Fig 3-17). Copy this **to Ref M** as shown in **Fig 5-15**. **Move** the foundation detail **close** first, and **clean it up** by **erasing** everything **above A** to look like what you see in **Fig 5-15**. Then **copy** and **attach** it to point **A**.

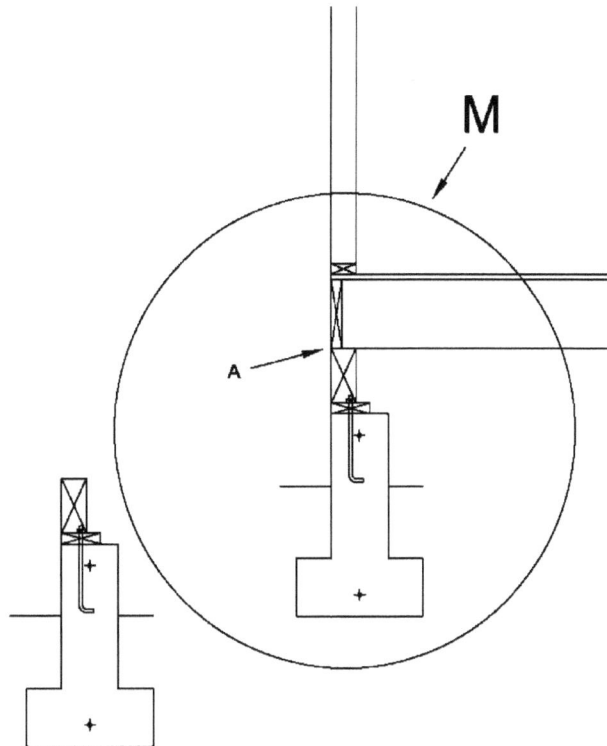

Fig 5-15

At **Ref K-2 erase** the lines marked with the **O**'s in **Fig 5-16**. This will **erase** the **entire right side wall**.

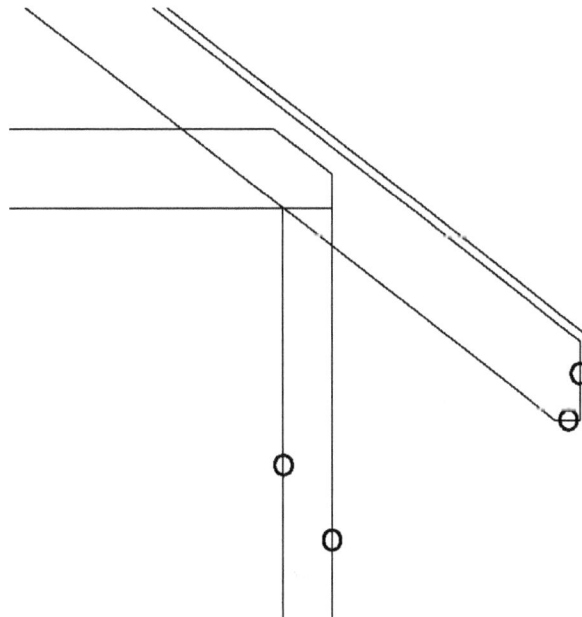

Fig 5-16

Now use the **mirror** tool to mirror everything that we have added to the **Ref's** so far in this chapter as in **Fig 5-17**. This includes the lines added to Ref K and the foundation. If you miss something the first time you can mirror it separately.

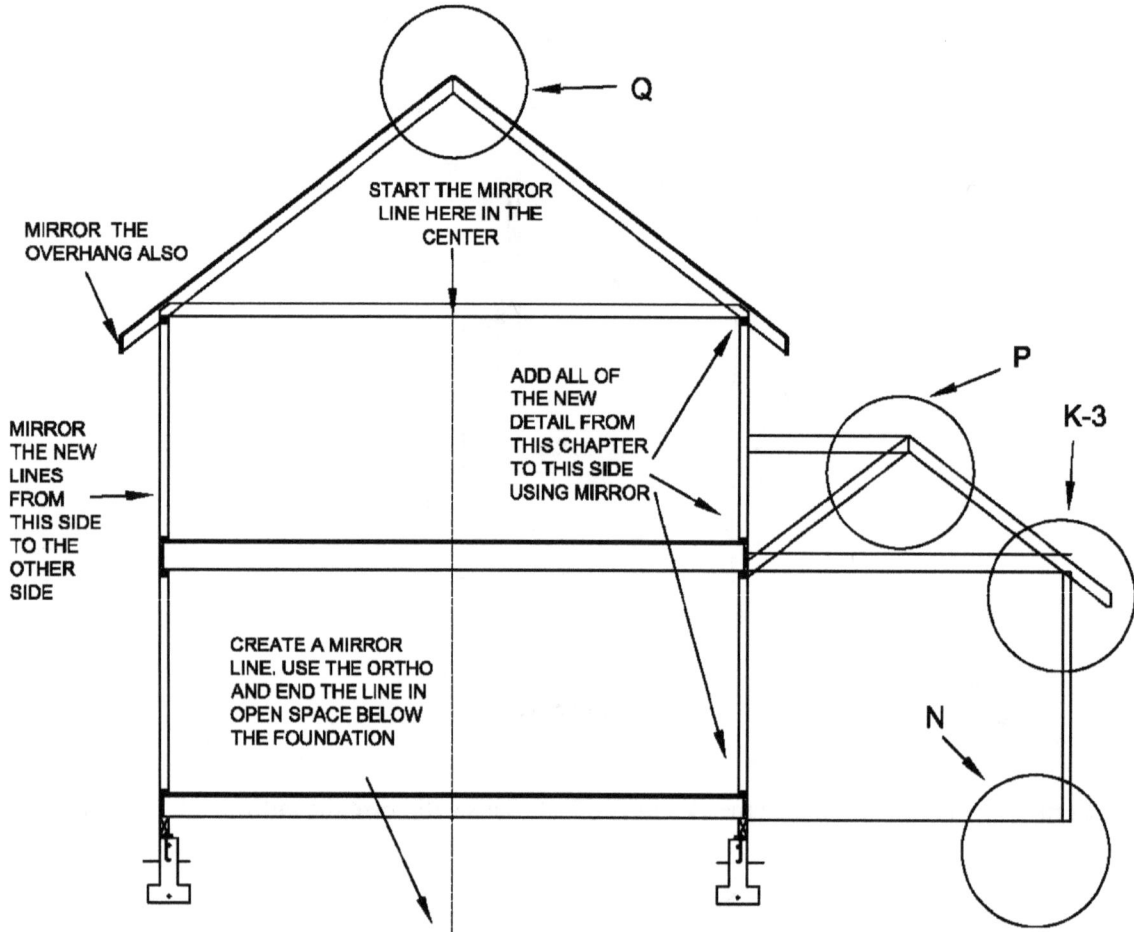

Fig 5-17

At **Ref K-3** clean up the drawing to show **Fig 5-18** on the right. Then copy the pertinent detail from **Ref K-2**. So the overhang looks like the mirror image of **Fig 5-13**.

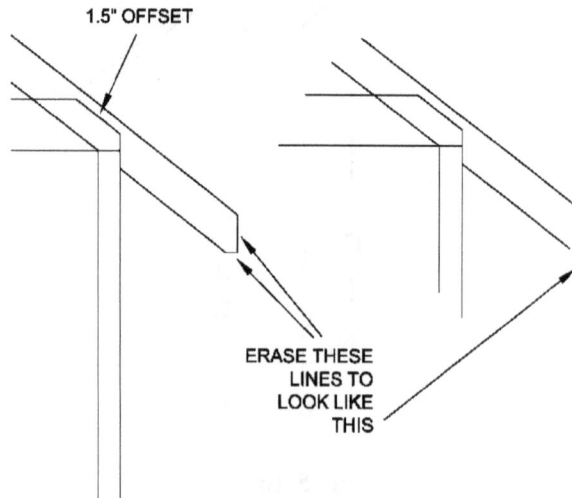

Fig 5-18

At **Ref Q** we are going to draw the ridge board. **Erase** the **line** at **C** in **Fig 5-19**. Then redraw it **7.5"**long. Use the **Ortho**.

Start the **line** at the **top, pull it down** an unspecified distance, and type the measurement **7.5. Enter twice.** Offset this line **both ways** by ¾". Add the bottom **horizontal line** and **trim** to look like **Fig 5-20**.

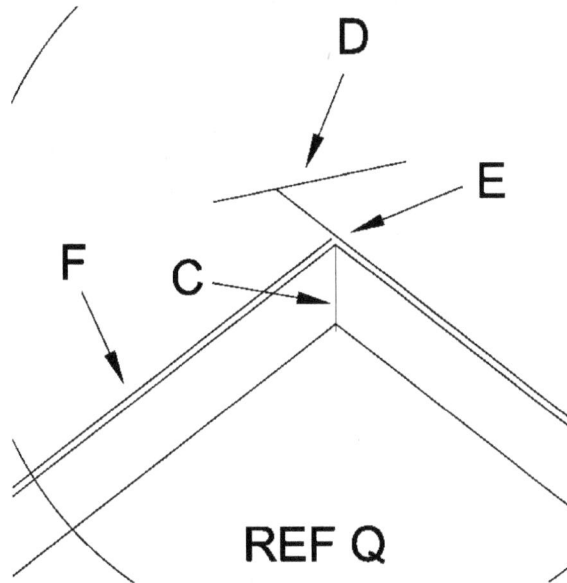

Fig 5-19

Also in Fig 5-19 create a **temporary line** at **D** (approx.) and **extend line E** to meet it then **extend line F** to meet **E. Trim** it all to look like **Fig 5-20**.

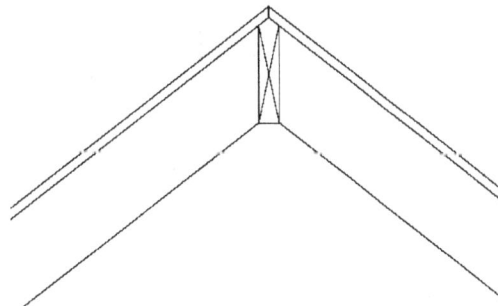

Fig 5-20

Finish off **Ref P** as shown in **Fig 5-21**. The ridge board (with the x in the middle) is **7.5"** long and **1.5"**. Follow the same steps as at Ref Q. Don't worry about exactitude, you can figure out the details of all this later.

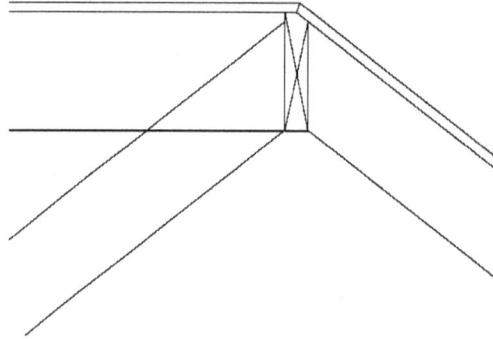

Fig 5-21

Finish off **Ref R** to look like **Fig 5-22**. Everything filled with diagonal lines (x's) is **1.5" thick**.

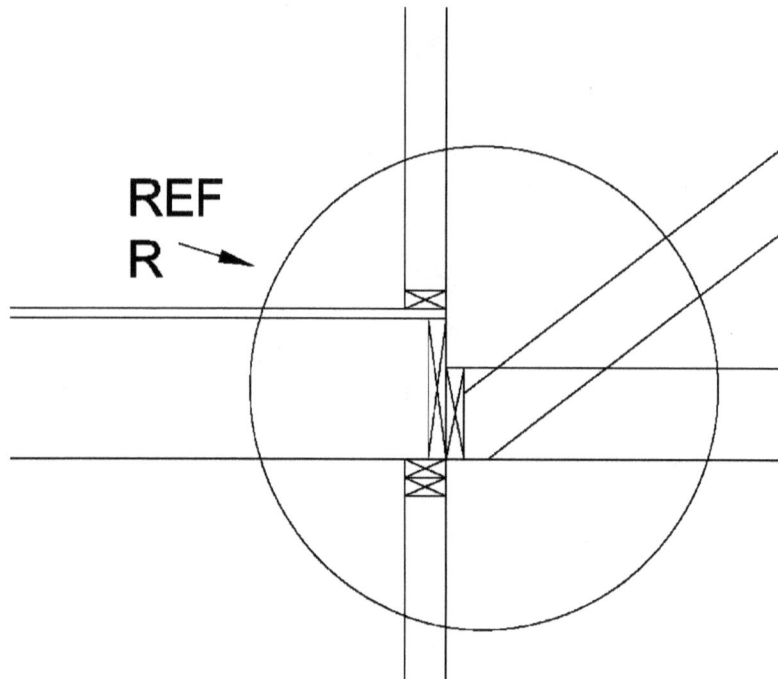

Fig 5-22

We are going to leave some of the details out for now. This view is completed in Chapter 15 (see section 15.6).

5.3 Insulation

We are now going to create a symbol for insulation. Follow the **steps** shown in **Fig 5-26**.

Create a **2" diameter circle**. Turn on the **Quadrant Osnap** setting for attaching the circles to each other (right click the Osnap button for settings). Follow the directions in **Fig 5-26**.

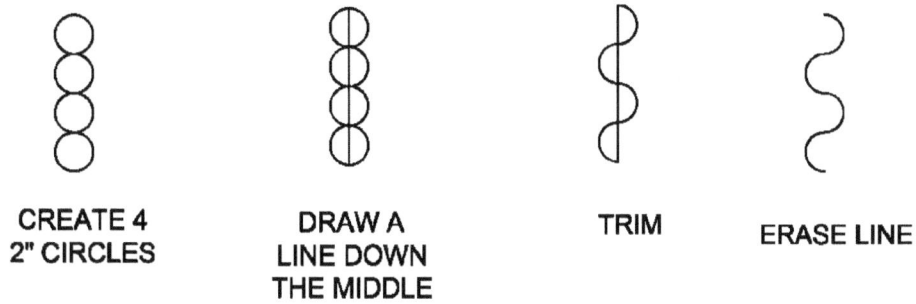

CREATE 4	DRAW A	TRIM	ERASE LINE
2" CIRCLES	LINE DOWN		
	THE MIDDLE		

Fig 5-26

Draw an **eight** foot **temporary line** and create a chain of the curved line as shown in **Fig 5-27** by copying this squiggly line to itself (baseline at the bottom then snap to the top). Copy two then esc and copy that end to end and repeat.

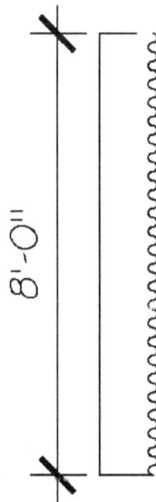

Fig 5-27

Copy this twice (original and two copies) and **scale** one copy up, using the **Scale** tool, use a **scale factor** of **1.5**.

Scale the other copy by a **scale factor** of **2** as shown in **Fig 5-28**. Read the prompts as you scale.

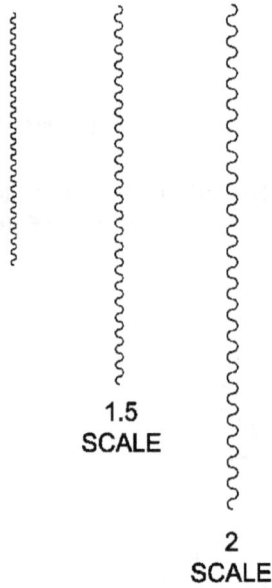

1.5
SCALE

2
SCALE

Fig 5-28

Copy these all again and **rotate** them **90 degrees** so that you have both vertical and horizontal versions.

Copy these to the places shown in **Fig 5-29**, where **O** equals the original size. **Copy** the **1.5 scale** into the **bottom** joist bays as shown (use the rotated copy). **Copy** the **2** scale to the **ceiling joists** as shown. This is not meant to be exact so place them in the center of the spaces approximately. Make them longer by adding more arcs where needed and **trim** them. They do not have to exactly touch both ends. They are very much pictorial.

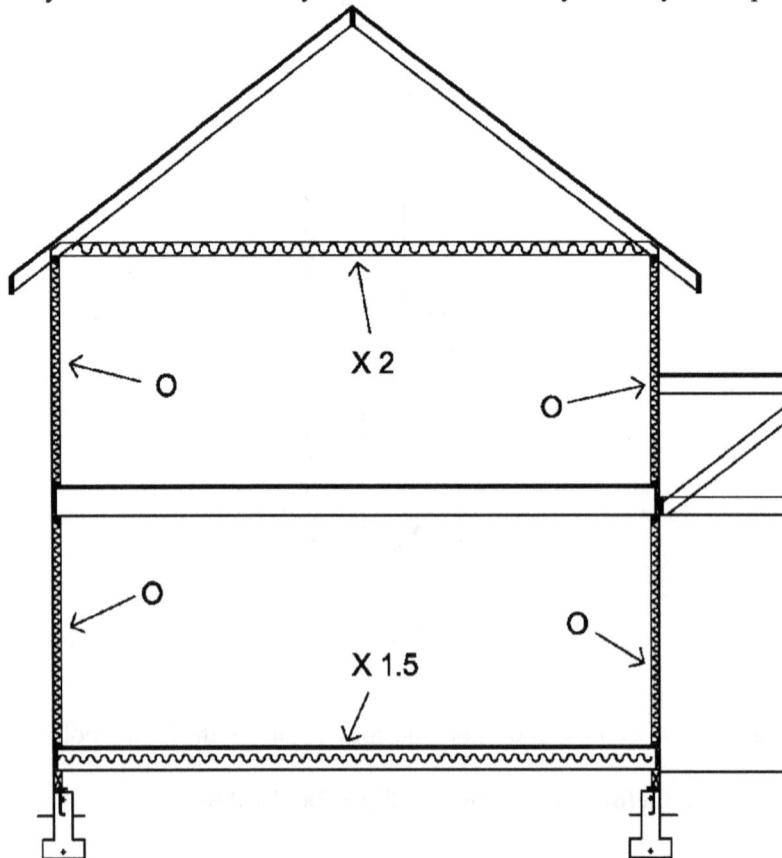

Fig 5-29

Try using the mirror to duplicate the insulation from one side (the O) to the other side.

5.4 Scaled Detail Views

Now we will copy different parts of this cross section to create the different detail views.

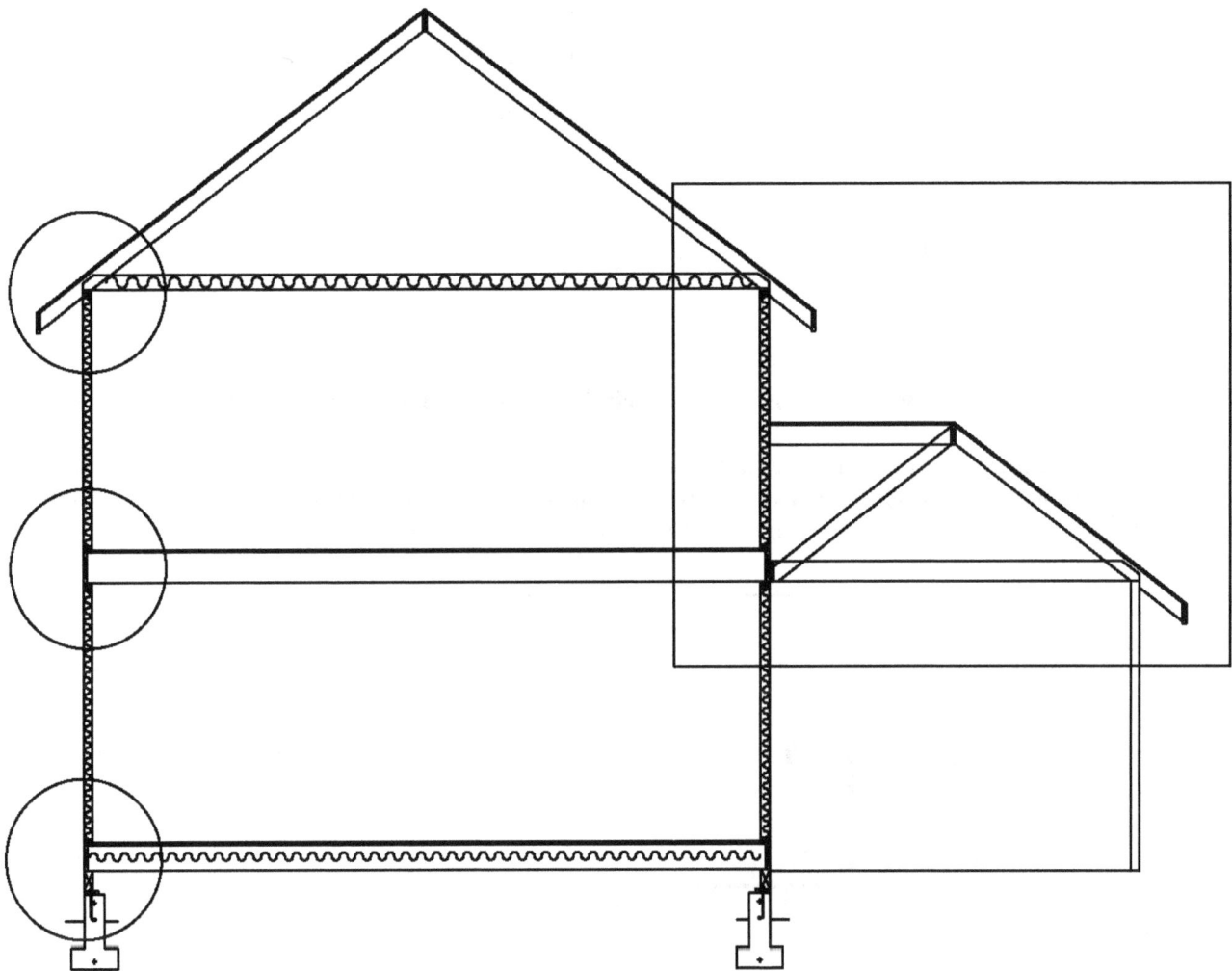

Fig 5-30

Fig 5-30 shows the cross section with three circles and a rectangle. Create the **circles** with **5' diameters** and place them in the **approximate locations**. Do not worry about exact location. Create the **rectangle** shown. It is **18' by 15'**. Center it approximately on the ridge of the garage (the pointy part).

Make a **Copy** of this entire cross section (everything in Fig 5-30) to the side in open space and use the **trim** tool and **erase** to create what you see in **Fig 5-31.**

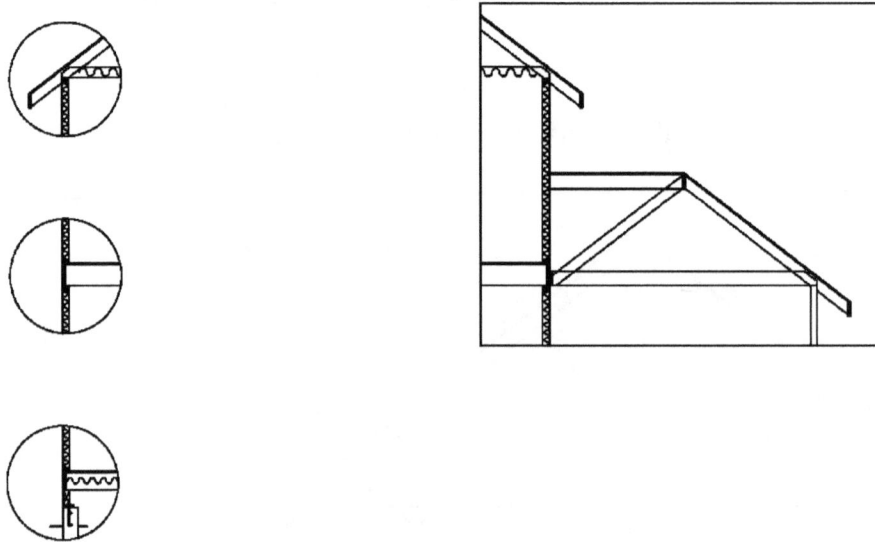

Fig 5-31

You are **trimming** and **erasing everything** outside the **circles** and the **rectangle** in this copy of the cross section.

My trim keeps erasing too much of the line so if you have that problem you may have to recreate some lines by using the extension tool, the offset tool, and re-trimming. This is one of the glitches in the system that I mentioned in the introduction. See Appendix I—Trim for more details on trim problems.

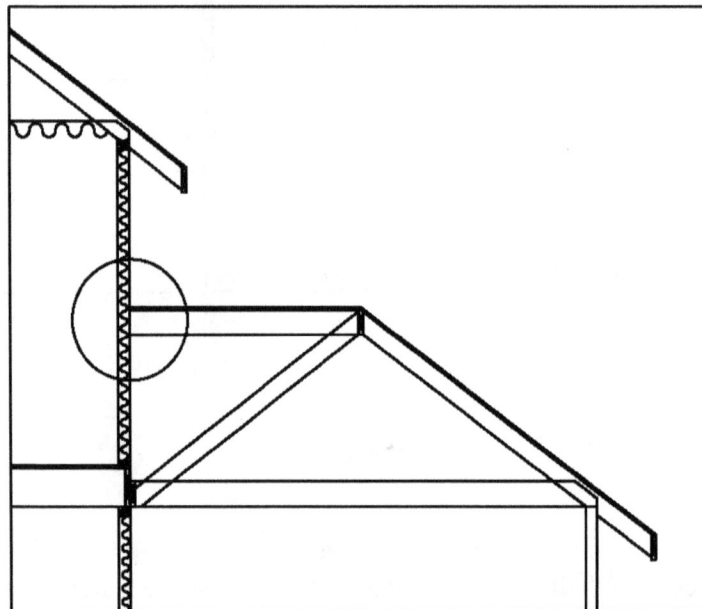

Fig 5-32

Make another **copy** of the area **within** the **rectangle,** as shown in **Fig 5-32**, and **create** another **circle** as shown. The circle is **3'** in **diameter** and it is placed **approximately**.

Trim and **erase** this new copy to look like **Fig 5-33**.

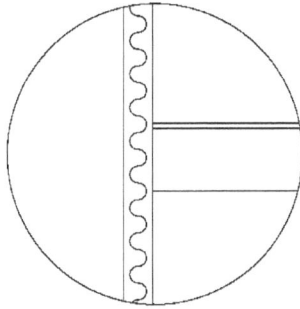

Fig 5-33

Now we are ready to scale everything.

We are going to use the smallest scale as a base point. That is ¼" = 1'. Everything will be scaled in relation to that scale.

The first view we will scale is the cross section. It will be plotted (printed) at twice the base scale.

We will plot the cross section at the **scale of ½" = 1'**.

Make a **copy** of the cross section in open space as in **Fig 5-34**. Use the **Scale** tool to make it **2 x** the original size as shown in **Fig 5-34**. Follow the prompts. The **scale factor** is **2**.

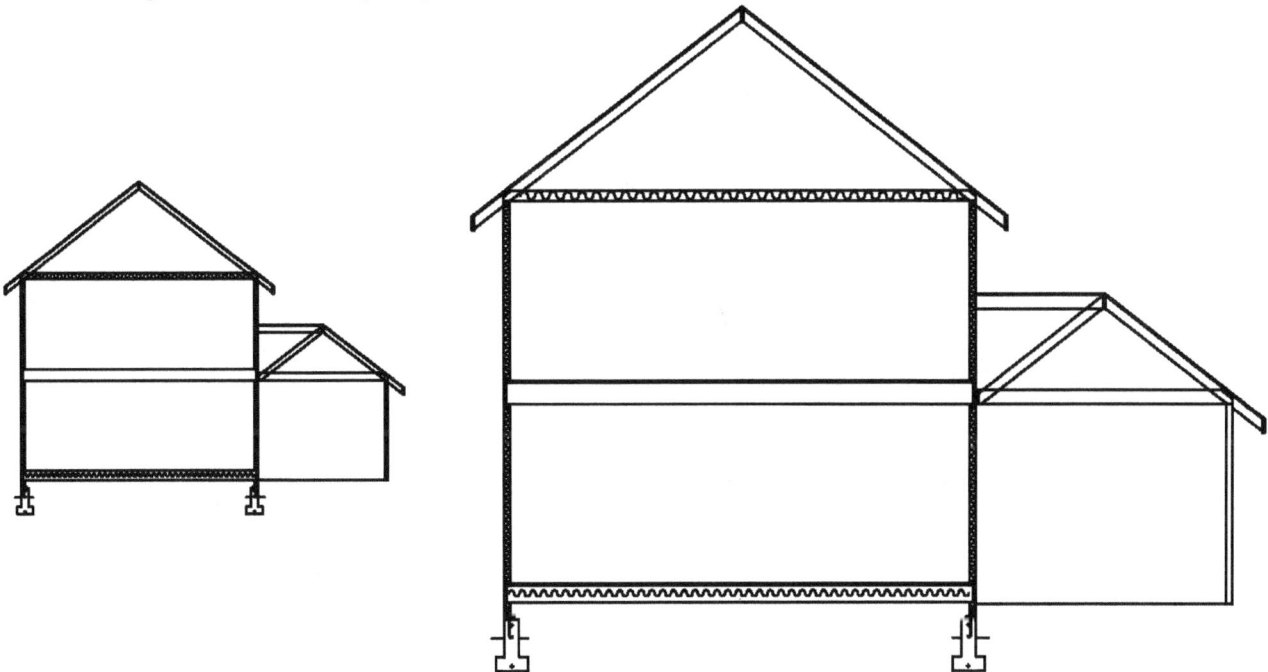

Fig 5-34

Fig 5-35 shows the next group of details that we will **scale** to ¾" = 1' on our plotted page. This is three times the base scale. Make a **copy** of these three details, then use the **scale** tool and use a **scale factor** of **3** as shown in **Fig 5-35**.

The three details on the left are original size and the three on the right are scaled up using a scale factor of three.

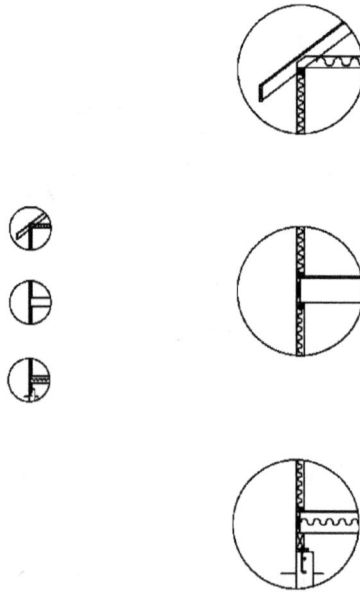

Fig 5-35

For the last figure we need take the drawing we created at Fig 5-33 and erase the insulation. Then add some more lines as shown in **Fig 5-36**. Line **R** is **11.5** inches from **Q**. Then add the diagonal lines shown.

Make a **copy** and use the scale tool with a **scale factor** of **4** to get the 1" = 1' scale for our plotted page.

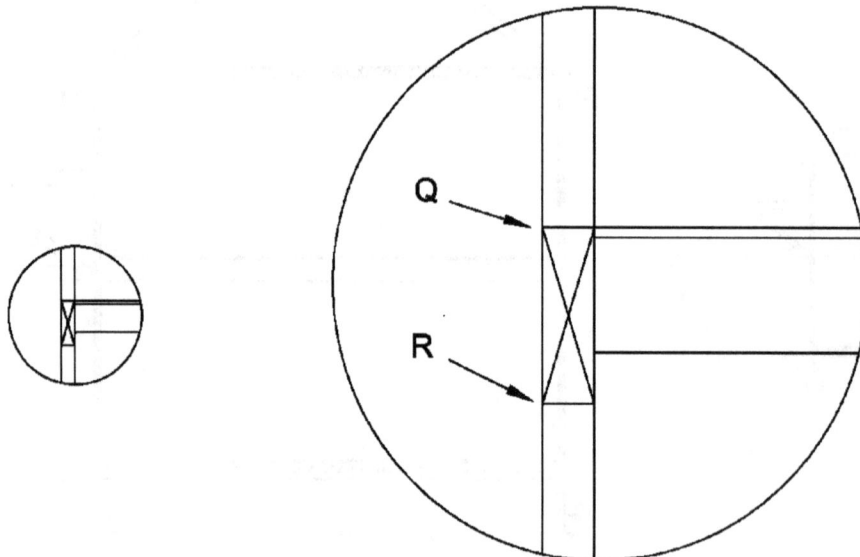

Fig 5-36

That is the end of this chapter. You can see the results of this scaling by looking at the finished page in Appendix IV—Page 6. There are notes and dimensions on that sheet. We will add these as we prepare the page for plotting.

Chapter 6—Plot the Elevations

6.1 Prepare the Elevations Page

With what you have learned so far you can draw a full set of house plans. You should be able to draw just about anything. There are still a number of procedures and drawing tools that are useful and make drawing faster and easier, but the basics that you have learned so far are enough to produce most drawings.

Now you need to know how to print, email and plot your plans. This chapter and the next five chapters are all about printing, plotting and sending PDF copies of your drawings. These are short chapters, but altogether there is a lot of information. Plotting and printing is one of the most complex parts of AutoCAD. Fortunately you will not need to know everything about this subject—just enough to do your job.

In this chapter we will prepare the Elevation page of the drawings. It is the simplest of the pages because it depicts four views that are basically the same size and shape and the entire page is plotted at ¼" = 1' scale (commonly called **quarter inch scale or quarter scale**).

First we are going to produce a 36" x 24" page. This is the most common size for use in the construction industry. In addition to the 36 x 24 pages we will set up for 11 x 8.5 printing. This is a handy size for mailing and carrying to meetings. It is also a common size for mechanical drawings and engineering details. Finally we will produce PDF files of the plans that can be attached to emails.

A number of the methods demonstrated in this book illustrate unique ways of producing drawings (my own personal techniques). The production of the 36 x 24 sheets, as demonstrated here, falls into that category. It describes a specific technique for producing printed/plotted drawings that is fast and simple. You can use this method for now and then design your own style and procedure later.

Fig 6-1

Look at Fig 6-1. It represents a completed page of the Elevation plan (Page 2 of the plan set) to be plotted on 36 x 24 inch paper. It includes the title block with a border around the edge of the sheet and the four elevation views with titles. Here we will prepare and plot just the views; the title block and border are added in chapter nine.

After we plot this page you will be able to use a measuring device (a measuring tape, a ruler or a scale) and each ¼" measured on the page will equal 1 foot of the actual building.

Let's create a rectangle of the appropriate sized area on our AutoCAD workspace. Off to one side in your workspace draw a **rectangle 128' x 92'**. Use the **Construction layer** for this rectangle. Now copy the four different elevations into this rectangle as shown in **Fig 6-2**.

For those of you have not drawn all four elevations, copy the front elevation that you drew to all four locations, just to block out the spaces (the important information here is the layout of the page not the completed elevation views). See Fig 6-17 to see what this looks like.

Fig 6-2

This area represents the part of the 36 x 24 paper that is inside the borders—the paper size minus a small border area and the title block. We will draw the border and title block later.

The page will look better if the four elevation views are lined up. So draw a line at the bottom of the two lower views and set your drawings so that they are **in line with each other**. Do not worry about exact placement. You can set them by eye. The idea is that the page should look balanced and neat.

Draw another line and **align** the two top views. See **Fig 6-3**.

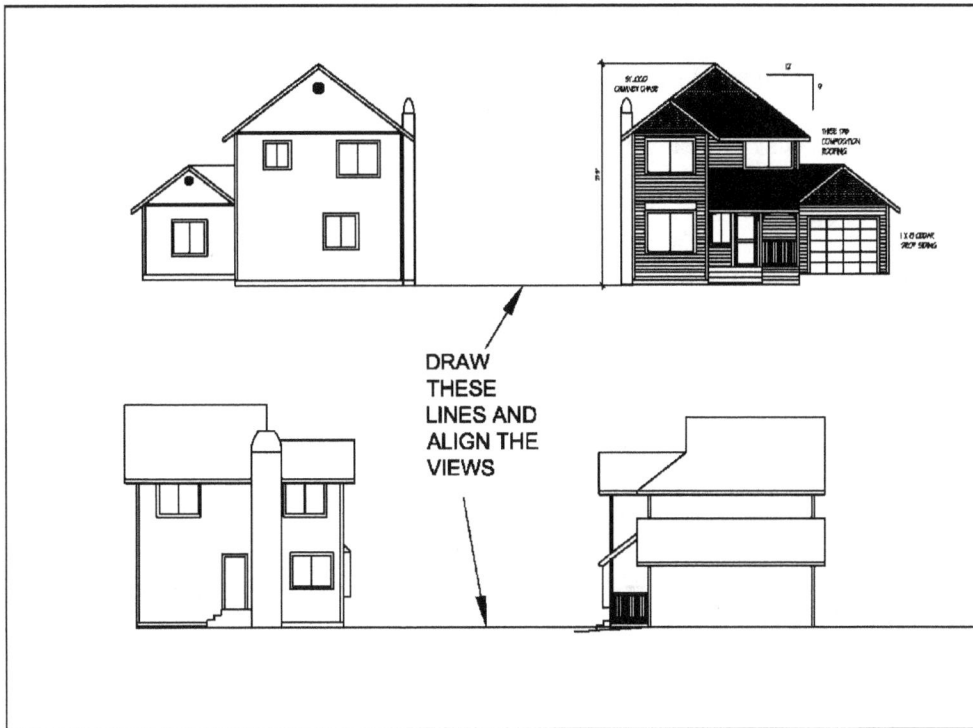

Fig 6-3

Now we need to draw the view titles (see Fig 6-1). **Fig 6-4** shows the **lines** and **layout**.

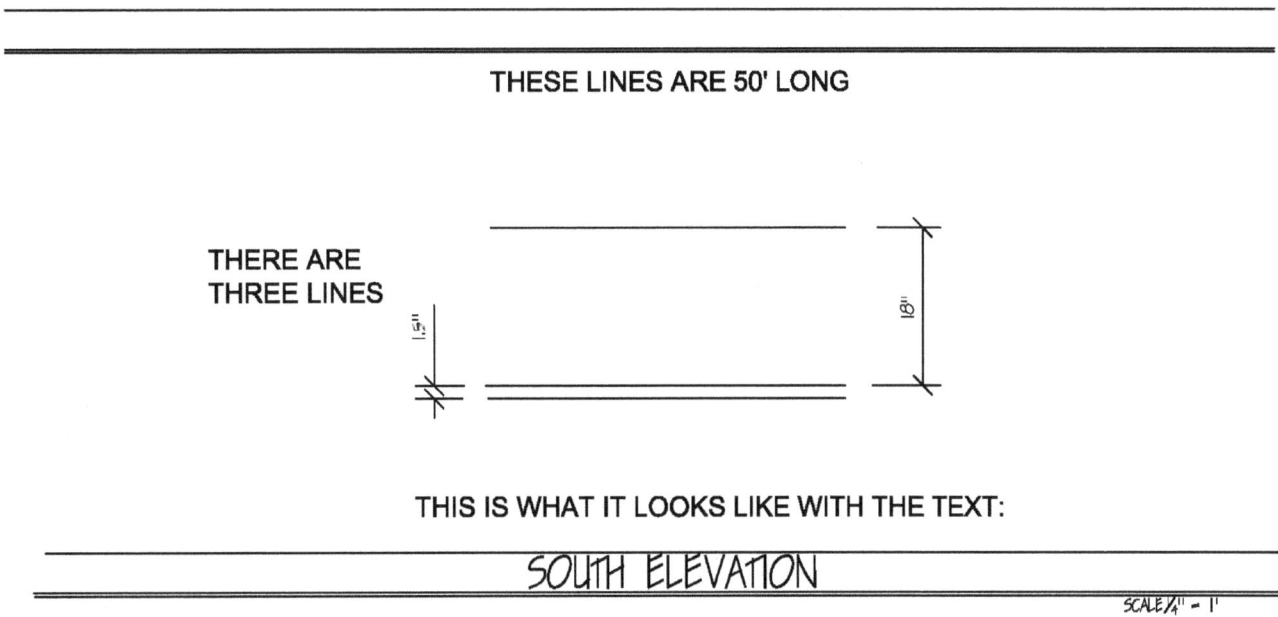

THESE LINES ARE 50' LONG

THERE ARE
THREE LINES

THIS IS WHAT IT LOOKS LIKE WITH THE TEXT:

SOUTH ELEVATION

SCALE ¼" = 1'

Fig 6-4

Beneath the upper right elevation, draw a line **50 feet** long. **Offset** it by **18"** (below) and again by **1.5"** as shown in **Fig 6-4**. Use the **Text layer**.

In the **Object Snap** settings turn on the **Insertion** osnap. This creates a base point for text.

In open space off to the side open an **MText** box (type **mt <e>**). Set the **font style** to **City Blue**. Set the **text height to 18"** and use **Bold** print. **Type** the words: SOUTH ELEVATION (use two spaces between the words—titles look better with two spaces between words). Use **Middle/Center** for the **justification** (use the justification button on the Paragraph palette that opens when you open a Mtext box or see Appendix I—Text). This means centered both horizontally and vertically.

Draw a **diagonal line** as shown in **Fig 6-6**.

Highlight the **text** (SOUTH ELEVATION), **grab** it by the **center** blue **grip** box, and **move** it to the **midpoint** of this **diagonal line** as in **Fig 6-6**. **Erase** the diagonal line.

This is an alternate method of **moving text**: type it, click on the OK in the text formatting bar or Close Text Editor on the ribbon. Highlight the text by clicking on it or select it with a selection window, then move it by the center blue grip. It is a good way to **center text between two lines**.

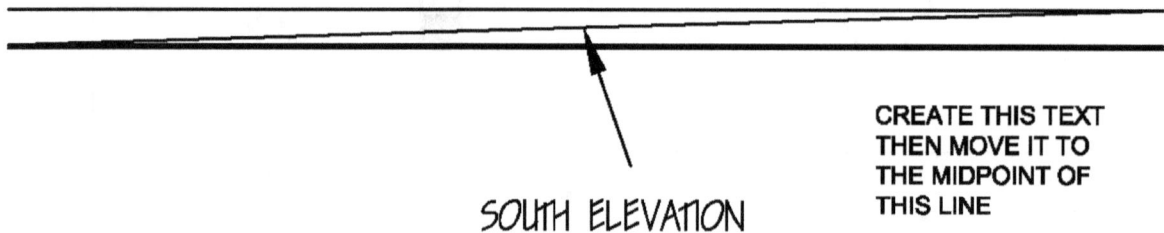

SOUTH ELEVATION

CREATE THIS TEXT
THEN MOVE IT TO
THE MIDPOINT OF
THIS LINE

Fig 6-6

Now open the **Mtext** box again and set the text height to **6"** (I always use bold for light weight font texts like City Blueprint). **Type: SCALE ¼" = 1'**. Use a space both sides of the equal sign. **Copy** this to the approximate space shown in **Fig 6-4 and Fig 6-7**. Set it by eye for now.

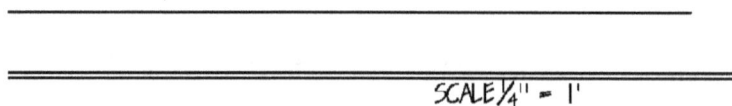

SCALE ¼" = 1'

Fig 6-7

Copy this title to the other **three locations** shown in **Fig 6-1**. Set them by eye or you can create temporary construction lines as you choose. **Highlight** and **edit** the **text** to read the different compass directions (**NORTH**, **EAST**, and **WEST**) shown in **Fig 6-1**.

To give our view titles a little flair we may want to make the lines uneven as you see them in Fig 6-7. Highlight the lines and with the Ortho turned on, use the blue grip boxes to stretch them out or shrink them a bit. This is strictly per eye, there is no formula (and not all drafters do this). You will need to turn off the Osnap or the line will want to keep snapping back to the original end point.

6.2 Page Set up

Now we are ready to plot.

At the bottom of the workspace you will see the **Model** and **Layout** tabs (**1** in **Fig 6-8**).

> If the **Layout tab**(s) **do not display** on your screen then type: Options/ then Display/ and check the box that says: Display Layout and Model tabs.

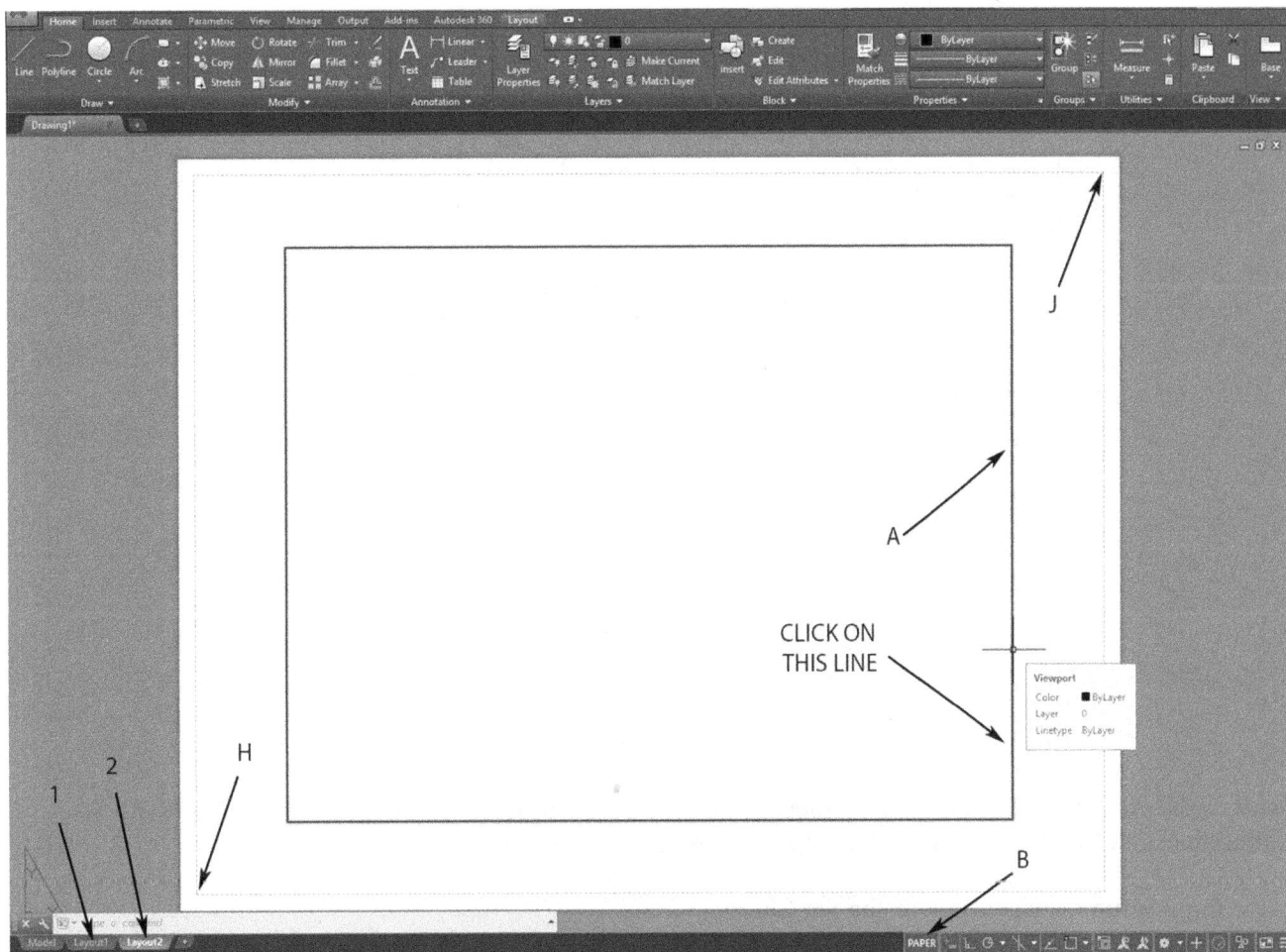

Fig 6-8

Right click on the first **Layout** tab (1) select: **New Layout**. A new Layout tab will appear to the right (**2**).

Click on this **new tab** (You may have more tabs than shown in Fig 6-8, just click on the one furthest to the right). This will bring up a white section. This can vary a lot in how it appears, but it is supposed to represent a piece of white paper. **Click** on the tab at **B** in **Fig 6-8** and you will see that it switches between **Model** and **Paper**. **Set** it to **Paper.** Type **z** <e> then **a** <e> (zoom all) to see the entire sheet of paper.

There will be an inner **rectangle** as at **A** in **Fig 6-8**. **Click** on rectangle **A**.

You may have to highlight rectangle A before you can select it (depending on your system settings). It can be difficult to highlight so move your cursor slowly back and forth across it until the line becomes bold (this means it is highlighted) and click. When it is selected (it will show **blue grip boxes** at the four corners when it is selected) **erase** it (remember you can use the **delete** on your computer keyboard to erase).

Now back at the **Layout** tab (your new layout tab), **right click,** and select **Page Setup Manager**… from the menu that appears. You can also type Pagesetup in the command line.

A **Page Setup Manager** box will open. Select **New**. When the **New Page Setup** box opens type **36x24** for the **new name**, **click** on the **OK**. The box shown in **Fig 6-9 will open**.

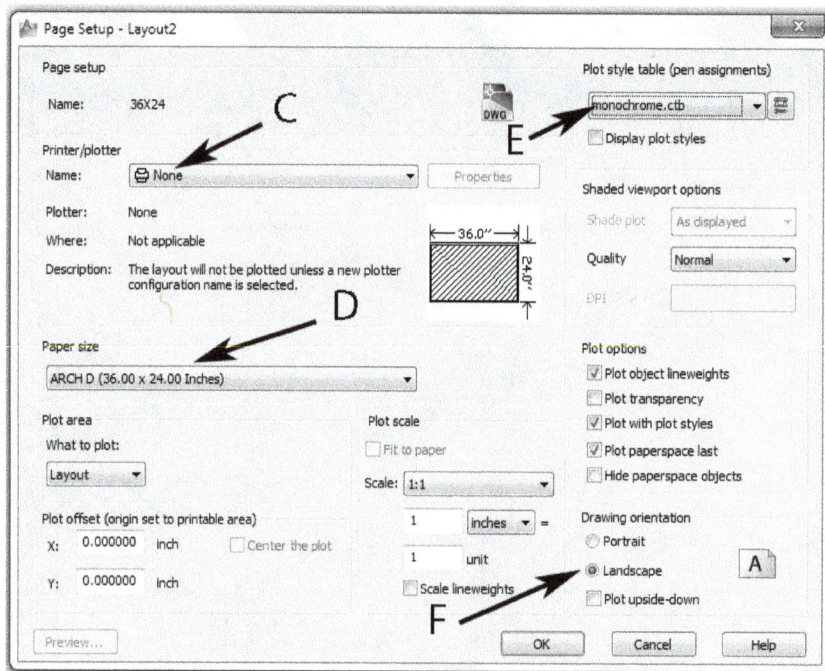

Fig 6-9

Set it as shown in **Fig 6-9**. At **C** set it to **none**. At **D** set it as shown. At **E** set it to **monochrom**.ctb. Set **F** to **Landscape**. Click on **OK**. **Close** the **Page Setup Manager** dialog box.

In the **Page Setup** manager **click** on the **Set Current** button.

Right click again on the **new Layout tab**, and from the **menu**, select **Rename**. The name in the tab will highlight blue. Type: **36x24 <e>**. This new name will appear in the layout tab.

Create a **new Layer** in the **Layer Properties Manager**. Name it **viewport** and make it **black**. At the **Printer icon** as **shown** in **Fig 6-9A**, turn **off** the **printer** (click on it). Now this layer will not print. Set this **layer current**.

TURN OFF THE PRINT LAYER

Fig 6-9A

Select the **Layout** ribbon and click on the **Rectangular** button (it is co-located with the polygon and object button—Fig 6-10) on the Layout Viewports palette (this only appears when a Layout tab is selected). Now click on point **H** in **Fig 6-8** then click on point **J**. It may take a few moments or even a minute to **regenerate** the **Model**. Then a **viewport will open**. This is a view through the paper into the model space behind.

> When you open a viewport, it is as if the paper has become transparent and you are holding it up to the model workspace screen on your computer: you are looking through the paper at model space.

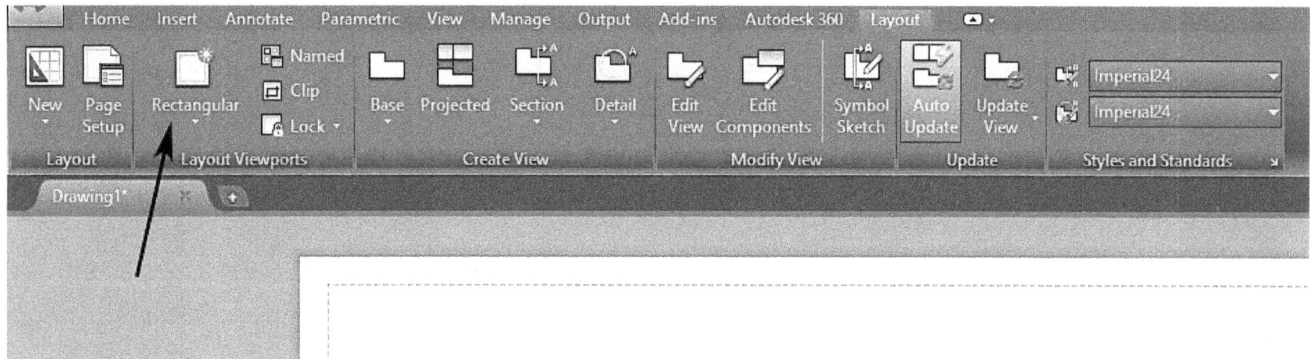

Fig 6-10

Double click in the center of this paper space and the Model/Paper button at the bottom will switch to **Model** (Or click on the Paper/Model button at the bottom of the screen so that Model is displayed—B in Fig 6-8).

Type **z <e>**. then **a<e>** (that is Zoom All). You should now see your entire workspace (everything on your model space screen—called the work space).

Find the elevations as in Fig 6-11. We want to center them in the middle of our paper viewport. Try using the Zoom window (the zoom window button or type **z <e> w <e>**). Then **open** a **selection window around** the **four elevations**.

Use the center mouse wheel to move the four elevations around and place them in the approximate center of the paper as in **Fig 6-11**.

> There is the possibility of confusion between Model space and Paper space as selected by the Model tab and the Layout tab and the Model/Paper space button. You can see these in Fig 1-1. Fig 6-8 shows the Layout tabs next to the Model tab designated 1 and 2 and the Paper/Model space button designated as B.
>
> The tabs take you to Model space or Paper space. The Paper/Model button sets the Layout to either the paper or the model space behind (within) the paper. When it is set to Paper this allows you to open a viewport, adjust the settings for the viewport, set the size, lock the viewport, and scroll in and out on the paper. The Model setting opens model space inside the viewport. Now when you scroll in and out you zoom in and out in model space. This allows you to select what you want centered in the viewport and set it to the desired plotting scale.

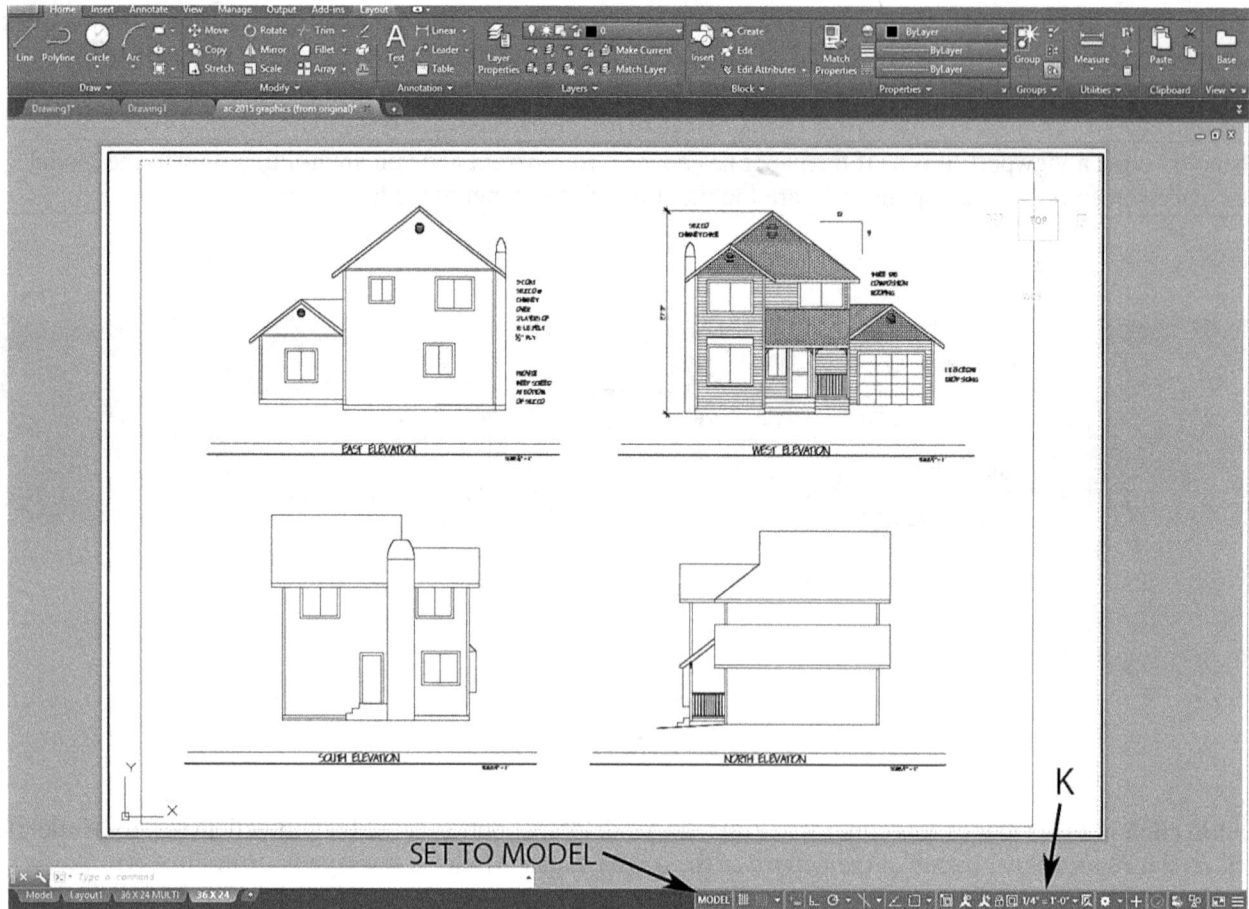

Fig 6-11

Down at the bottom right of the computer screen click on the down arrow in the button shown at **K** in **Fig 6-11** and **Fig 6-12**. This is the **Viewport scale**. A list of scales will appear in a box as shown in **Fig 6-12**.

Find the **1/4" = 1' scale** (at **L** in Fig 6-12) and **click** on it (You may need to scroll down by using the scroll bar to the right of this window (it is thin and hard to see so run your cursor over the right edge until it highlights). Your drawing will adjust to fill the page. It is now ¼" scale (short for ¼" = 1' scale). Center your four elevations drawing in the viewport by grabbing it with the mouse center button and moving it where you want it. Don't worry too much about exact placement just yet.

After you position the drawing in the viewport set the scale again as it can change a tiny bit while you are panning with the mouse wheel. This is important when the scale must be exact.

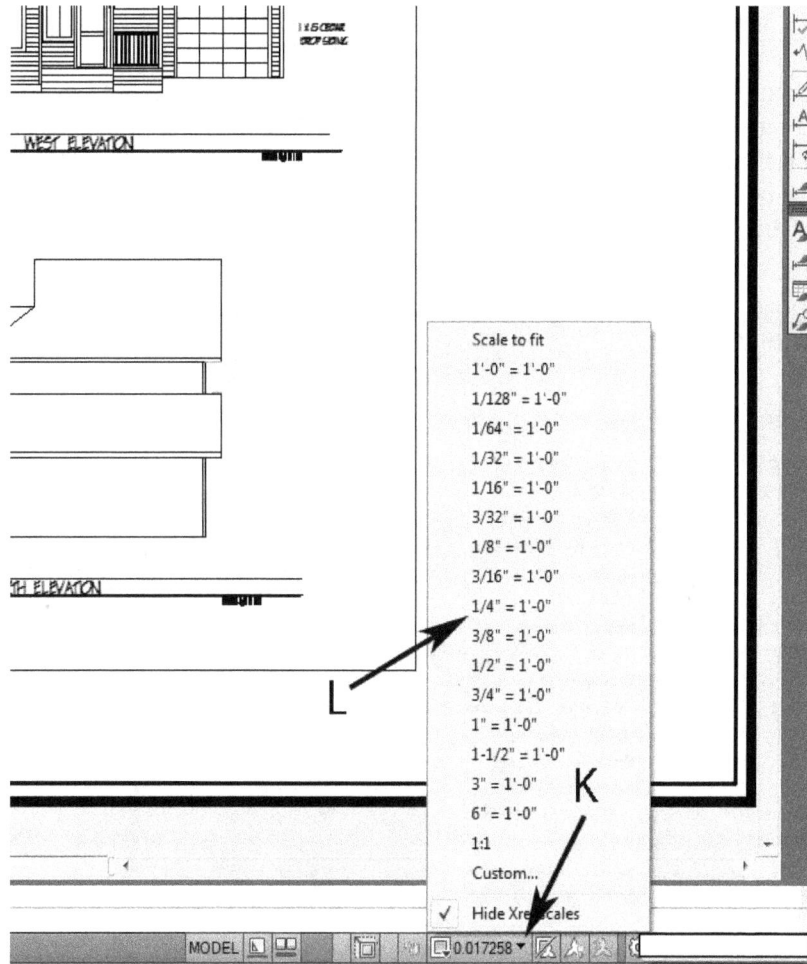

Fig 6-12

This page is ready to plot.

You can **lock** the scale (1/4" = 1') in place by setting the space to **Paper** (use the button at the bottom of the screen: B in Fig 6-8). Select the viewport by clicking on the line of the viewport, when it highlights with the blue grip boxes, right click. Where it says **Display locked** click on the down arrow next to the No and change it to Yes.

Note: the **broken lines** shown in Fig 6-8 are **not** the **viewport**. They are the margin lines—the limits that the printer will print. Printers usually have a small space around the edge of the paper where they will not print.

The lines of the viewport and the paper space can become altered, sometimes spontaneously. See Appendix I—Viewport if this happens and you wish to change it back.

If you decide to lock the viewport, remember that it is locked when you want to change the view in the future. You must **unlock** it before you can **make** any **changes**.

Okay so we are ready to plot, but we need to tell AutoCAD what printer we are going to use.

We must set up a plotter.

6.3 Plotter Setup for 36 x 24

Click on the **Output** ribbon tab. Select **Plotter Manager**. The box shown in **Fig 6-13** will open (you can type plottermanager). Select the **Add-A-Plotter Wizard** by double clicking on it (as shown in Fig 6-13). If double clicking does not open it then highlight it, right click and select Open. Now a series of windows will open that have three buttons at the bottom. It is the **Next button** that we are most interested in. The first box will be titled "**Introduction Page**". Click **Next**. The "**Begin**" page will open. Select the **My Computer radio button**. Click **Next**.

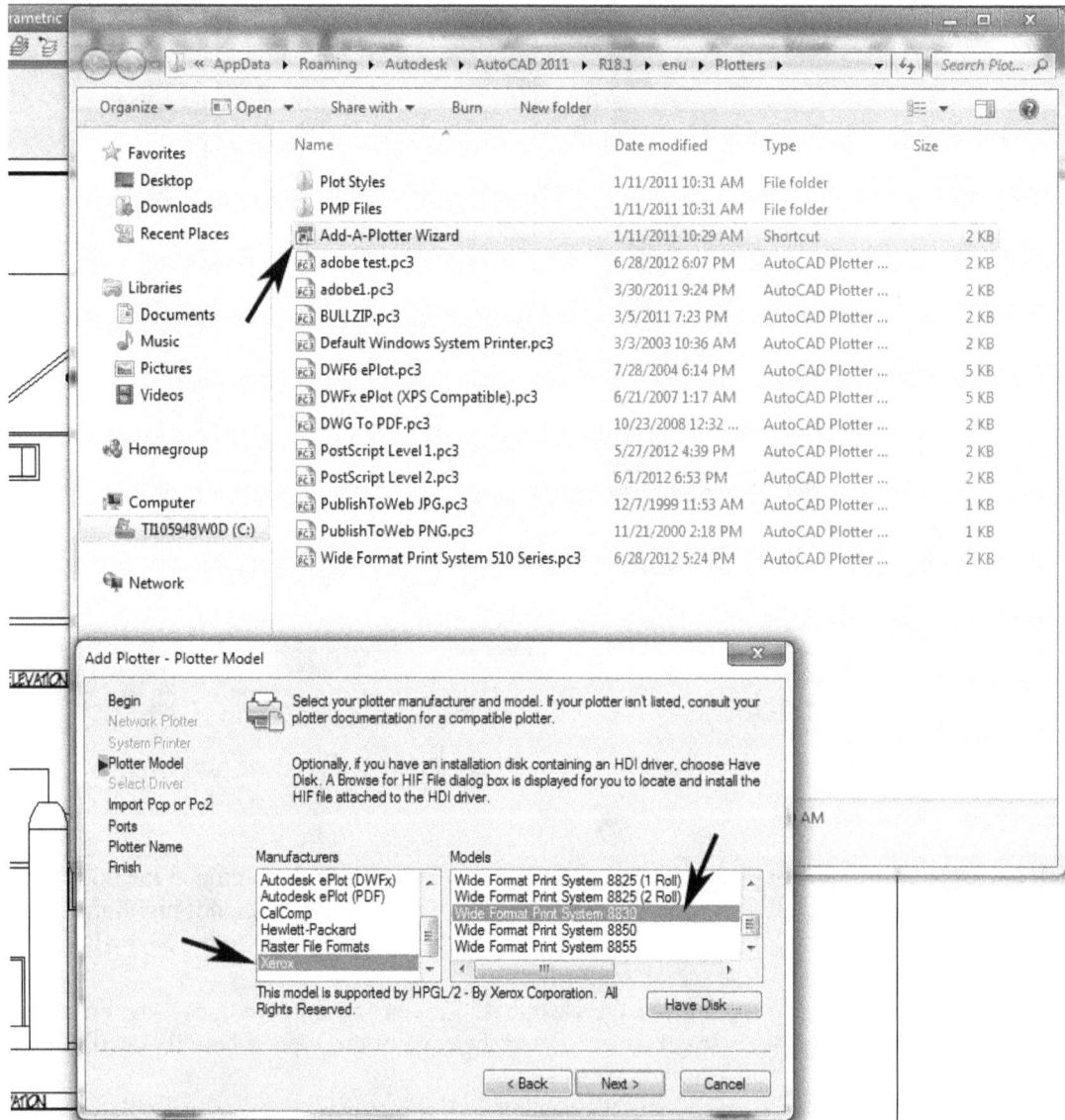

Fig 6-13

This is the "**Plotter Model**" page. You will need to select a **Manufacturer** and **model** of a **Plotter**. This is the plotting machine you will use to print out the 36 x 24 inch copies. Every sizable town has a blue print office where you can have your plans printed (also copy shops, like Kinkos, will often print this size). You will need to call and find out what kind of copier/plotter they are using. They will tell you the model and you can **enter** that **information** by selecting it from the list of Manufacturers and Models shown in Fig 6-13.

My local blue print office uses a **Xerox 8830 Wide Format** print system plotter. That is what I have selected in **Fig 6-13**.

> If you do not know the name of the local plotter (the model used locally), then you can use the settings in this book for now and set up another plotter later (you can set up as many plotters and copiers as you want).

Click **Next**. This is the "**Import Pcp or Pc2**" page. We don't need to deal with this for now. Click **Next**.

This is the "**Ports**" page. Click on **Plot to File** at the top center. This is going to create a plot file on your computer that you can send over the internet as an email attachment, or copy the file onto a disc (or flash drive) and carry it to the office where the plotter/copier is located.

> It is easy to miss this setting the first few times you set up a plotter and it can drive you a bit nuts trying to figure out why your plotting is not producing a file. So remember to check this step if you have a problem.

The next page is the "**Plotter Name**". The model of the printer that you selected should appear here or you can add it. Click **Next**.

Click **Finish**.

You will see that the **printer/plotter** that you set up **is now listed** in the **Plotter manager** box. **Close** this box.

Back at the work space **right click** on the **36x24 layout tab** at the bottom of the screen (**2 in Fig 6-8**).

Click on Plot. A **Plot window will open**. You should have everything set from Fig 6-9 except the selection of the printer. To do this, **select the printer** that you just set up in the window shown at **C** in **Fig 6-9**. Where it says **Name**, you can name the page Xerox or the name of your chosen plotter. Check the other settings as in Fig 6-9.

> Check out the little **window expansion arrow** all the way down in the lower right corner. This collapses and expands the window . Which, again, raises the question: why half a window?

At the bottom where it says **Apply to Layout**—**click**. Then **click** on the **preview button** to see what the page will look like when plotted. **Close** the **preview** (x at the top of the screen) and click **OK**.

A box will open that allows you to **name the plot file**. **Name it: paradise3.PLT** (Paradise is the street name of our fictional project and this is the third page of the plans) and select a destination. Save it on the **desktop** for now if you don't have a preference.

> Eventually you will want to create a document folder for all of your AutoCAD drawings and PLT files. You can do this now if you want and store everything there. Go to Documents on your computer and create a new folder. Name it AutoCAD or whatever.

Minimize AutoCAD and **look at the desktop** (or in your new folder); you should **see** your **PLT file** there. If not then you will need to go back through the steps again and see if you missed anything. See Appendix IV—Plotting for further assistance.

Now you can copy this PLT file on to a **disc** and take it to the local office where they have the printer and they will print it out for you. Or wait until we add the title block in chapter 9. You can also attach it to an **email** and send it to the printer.

Now we will set up another layout, for printing on your copier/printer at home or in the office.

6.4 Plotter Setup for 11 x 8.5

We will essentially follow the same steps as the process in **6.3 Plotter Set up for 36 x 24.** Review that section if you need to refresh your memory.

In order to plot to your **home** or **office printer** you may need to have the **driver** for the printer/copier **installed** on your computer. If the driver is not installed it may not show up in the list of plotters when you get to that step. In that case you will need to install the driver. Your printer/copier most likely came with a disc that contains the driver. You can insert the disc and follow the instructions. **If you do not have the driver disc then go online** to the website of the manufacturer of your copier/printer and they will have the driver online that you can download. Before you do that, go through the steps that follow and see if your copier printer shows up in the list of plotters already listed.

Connect you computer to your printer/copier as you would normally to print off the computer.

Create a new **Layout tab** by **right clicking** on the **36x24** Layout tab (**2 in Fig 6-8**). This will create a new layout tab to the right.

Click on the newly created **Layout** tab. It may take a minute to load.

Once the new layout is added, **right click** on the tab and select the **Page Setup Manager** (just as before). Click **New. Name** it **11x8.5**. In the **Page Set-up** box set everything as in **Fig 6-14**. In the **Printer/plotter** window scroll down until you see your printer/copier and select it. Set the **paper size** to **Letter** (most important). Set the **Plot Style Table** (pen assignments) to **monochrome.ctb**. Then select the **Landscape** setting at the bottom right. **OK**.

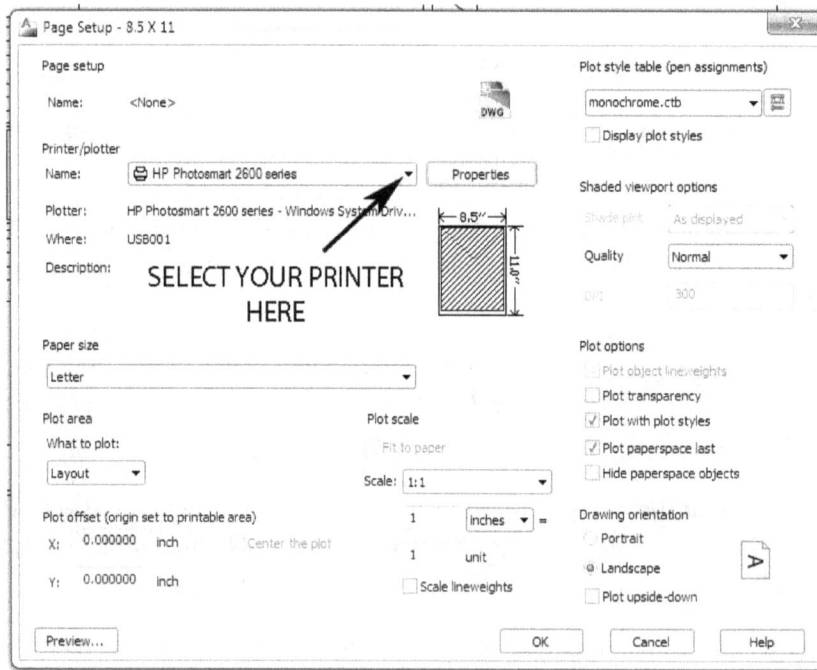

Fig 6-14

Right click on the new layout tab and **name** it **11x8.5**. A new 11 x 8.5 inch paper space "piece of paper" will replace the 36 x 24. It will have a viewport in the middle (not the dashed lines—those represent the margins for the selected printer).

As before, **erase** the **viewport** (set the **space** to **Paper** and move the cursor slowly over one of the viewport lines until it highlights then select it and erase).

Create a **new single viewport** that covers the entire page (or between the dashed lines if they are showing). This is shown at H and J in Fig 6-8.

Select **Model** space from the Model/Paper button at the bottom of the screen (B in Fig 6-8). Select the east view elevation drawing by using the mouse wheel to move it. Place this in the center of the viewport and **set the scale to ¼" = 1'**.

Move the elevation around to see (approximately) as in **Fig 6-15**. Some of the text is off the page but that is okay for now (you can reposition the text and place it on the page).

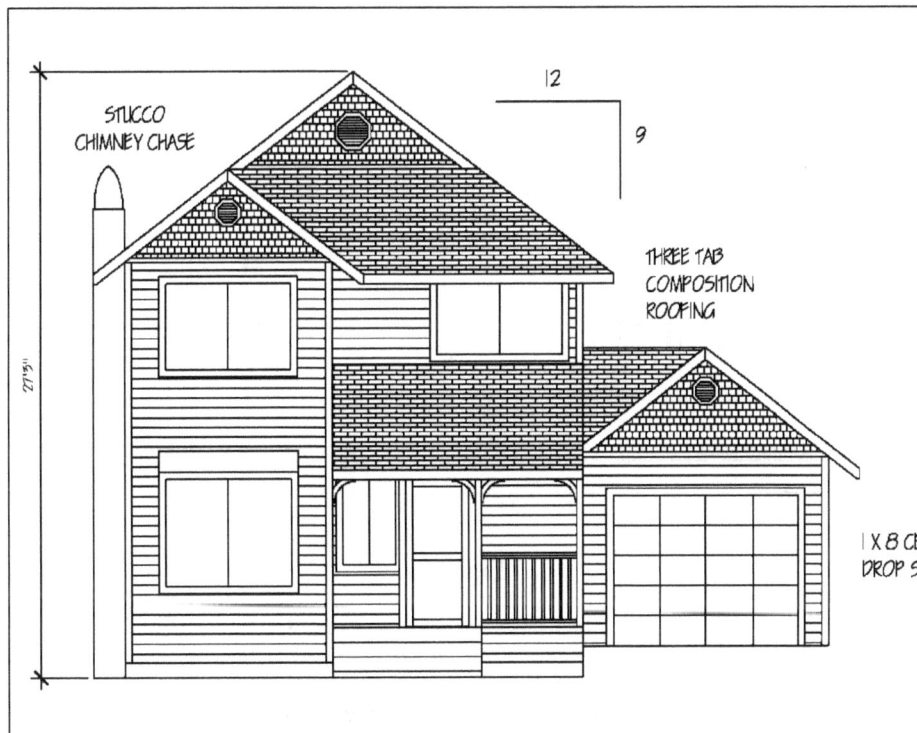

Fig 6-15

Right click the **11x8.5 tab** again and go to **Page Setup Manager**. **Highlight the 11x8.5** and click **Modify**. **Check** the **settings**. They should look like Fig 6-14. If they have changed then reset them. Click **OK**. This layout is ready to print out on your copier.

Close the **Page Setup Manager**. **Right click** on the **11x8.5 tab**. Select **Plot** and **OK**. You can look at the Preview before you print (close it after the preview then click OK).

Now you can see why the house was designed to the size that it is—each view fits on an 8.5 x 11 piece of paper when printed at ¼" = 1' scale. The same is true with the floor plan and the details.

Try a different scale. In paper space select Model from the Model/Paper (B in Fig 6-8) button space and this time select the 3/32 = 1' scale. You will see Fig 6-16 (more or less). Set the scale back to ¼" for printing of the single elevation.

Fig 6-16

6.5 Plot a PDF

Now we will create a **PDF** file that you can attach to an email or send in a disc to someone through the mail.

In order to create a PDF that is larger than letter size you must have a **PDF creating program installed on your computer** that creates the size that you want or use the DWG to PDF.pc3 setting in the Printer/Plotter menu shown in Fig 6-14. There are a number of free PDF creating software programs available on the internet. If you do not see the DWG to PDF.pc3 option in the Printer/Plotter selection list, add it by following the instructions at the end of this chapter.

Basically you will follow the same steps as in Section 6.4. The only difference is that you will select the one of the **PDF settings** in the **Plotter/printer** window as in **Fig 6-14** (you do not have to use the Add-A-Plotter Wizard). You do not need to name this Layout at the top. When you click **OK** you will see the **"Save PDF File As"** screen; **name** the file and send the PDF file to the desktop (or your new folder).

You can now open the PDF file (if you can't then you will need to download Acrobat Reader from the internet).

You can send this as an attachment to an email.

That is it for this chapter. The next several chapters deal more with the printing and plotting process.

Fig 6-17 shows what the page looks like if you have not drawn all four elevations. The front elevation is used in all four locations as a place marker; these can be replaced with the real elevations if they are drawn.

Fig 6-17

Add the DWG to PDF.pc3 Plotter.

1. Open the Add a Plotter Wizard (see Plotter Setup page 150).
2. Select Autodesk ePlot (PDF).
3. Click Next and use the default settings, continue until Finish.

You should now see this selection in the Printer/Plotter list.

There is also a DWG to PDF button that creates PDF's without the need to plot.

Chapter 7—Plot the Detail Page

7.1 Page Set Up

In this chapter we are going to set up and plot the **detail page**. We drew all of the different detail views seen on this page in chapter 5. Now we will place them on the page, add text, add dimensions, and plot/print.

The detail page is different than most of our pages because it contains drawings of **varying scales**. This chapter covers one method for page layout when there are views plotted in different scales on the same page. Chapter 14 covers another method.

The method demonstrated in this chapter is: we take the **scaled up** drawings that we created in Chapter 5 and we place them on the page, we then add **text**, **dimensions**, and **leaders**. The page will look the same in model space as it will appear when we plot it.

The method detailed in Chapter 14 utilizes multiple viewports on the same page—one for each detail (each detail has a different viewport—more on this later).

Both methods have their pros and cons. I use the method described in this chapter most of the time. It is simpler. Its main drawback is that the page scale cannot be changed without modifying the drawings somewhat. This is generally not a problem because we (usually) print out a set of plans in one size only (36 x 24 for example). If multiple sized sheets of plans are needed, then the multi-viewport method may be a better choice.

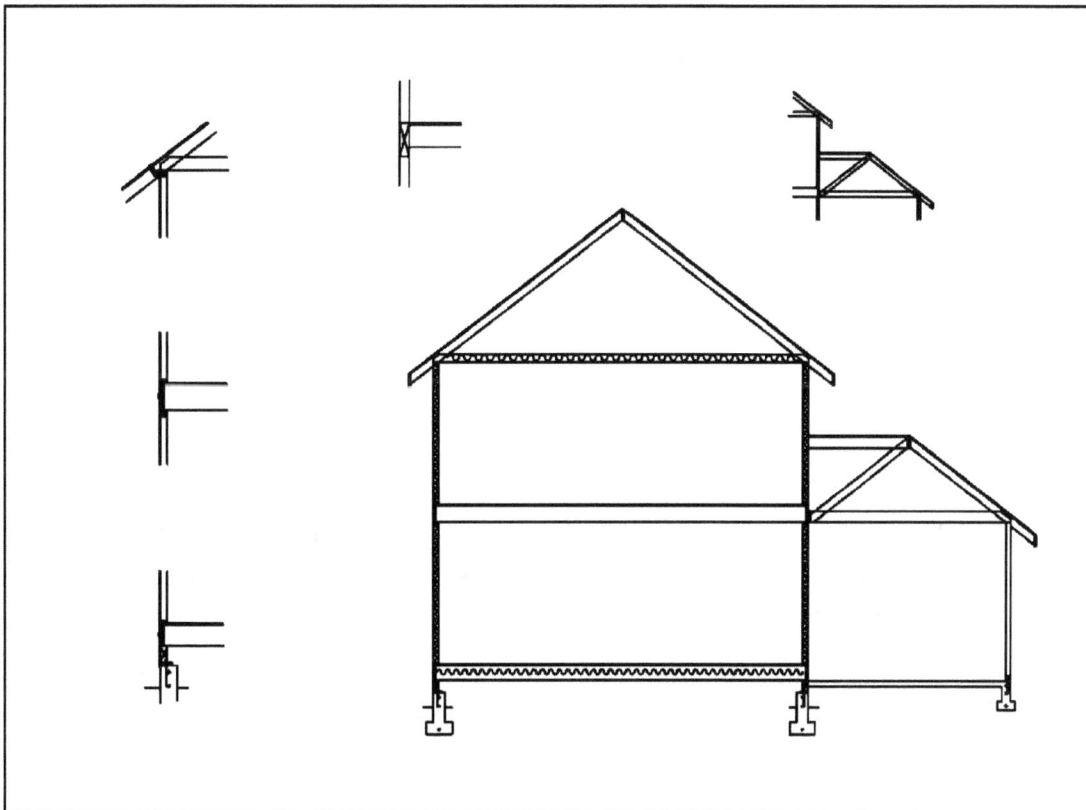

Fig 7-1

In chapter 5 we created a series of details and some of these you **scaled up to larger sizes** (Figures 5-34, 5-35 and 5-36). We will now place these scaled up copies together on a single 36 x 24 page as we did the elevations. Make a copy of your **128 x 92 foot rectangle** (or draw a new rectangle that size) and **copy** your **details** into this rectangle as shown in **Fig 7-1**. These are the scaled up copies (scaled larger by 2,3 and 4 times), except the upper right detail which we did not scale up.

We are not going to spend time on the exact placement. This is something that you can figure out on your own later. Just place them roughly where you see them and you can shift them around later if necessary.

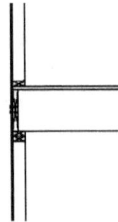

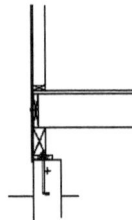

Fig 7-2

This is the final sizing for each drawing so we can use the same size text and leaders for everything on the page. We are going to print this entire page at ¼ scale (just as we did the elevations in the last chapter) so the text will be the same size that we would use for any ¼ scale drawing.

Let us start with the **sheer** transfer details shown in **Fig 7-3**. You have not drawn the sheer ply and the nails yet (this is added in Chapter 15, Section 15.6), but write in the text now for the practice.

Set the **Layer** to **text**. Type **mt** and set it to the **style 9** text that you created. Make the text **7.5 in height** in the **Text Editor** ribbon or the **Text Formatting** bar (see Appendix 1—Text for help). Do this before you begin typing or it will not take. Use **bold**. **Add** the **notes** as shown in **Fig 7-3**.

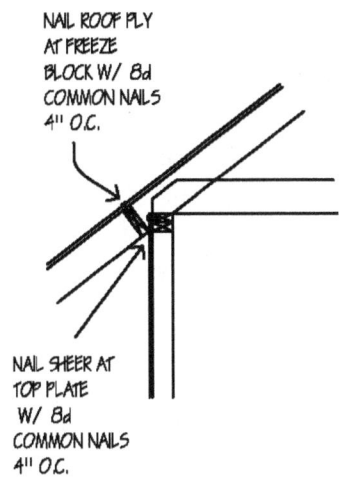

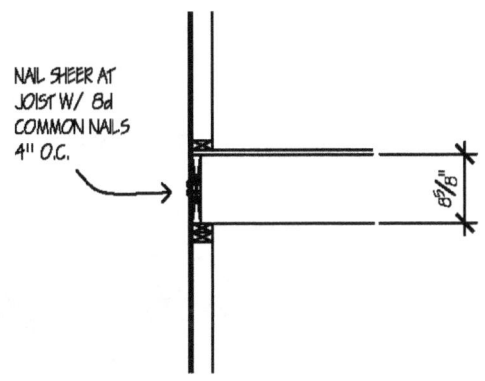

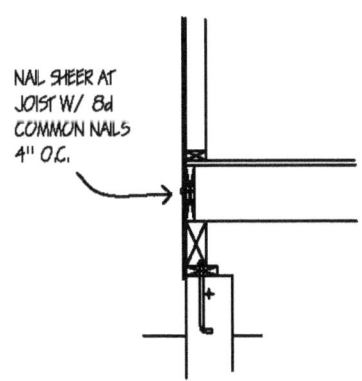

NAIL ROOF PLY
AT FREEZE
BLOCK W/ 8d
COMMON NAILS
4" O.C.

NAIL SHEER AT
TOP PLATE
W/ 8d
COMMON NAILS
4" O.C.

NAIL SHEER AT
JOIST W/ 8d
COMMON NAILS
4" O.C.

8⅝"

NAIL SHEER AT
JOIST W/ 8d
COMMON NAILS
4" O.C.

Fig 7-3

7.2 Leaders

Now we will add the **leaders** (lines with arrowheads). **Leader sizes are set up with dimension styles**. Open the **Dimension Style Manager** as in **Fig 7-4** (on the Annotation palette—click the down arrow next to Annotation—or type: dimstyle). **Select** the **quarter** inch style then click the **Modify** button. The **Modify Dimension Style Quarter** box will open. Select the **Symbols** and **Arrows** tab at the top shown in **Fig 7-4**. Set the **Leader** window to **Right angle** as shown in **Fig 7-4**. Set the **Arrow size** to **3/16"**. **OK**. Then back at the Dimension Style Manager click the **Set Current** button and **Close**.

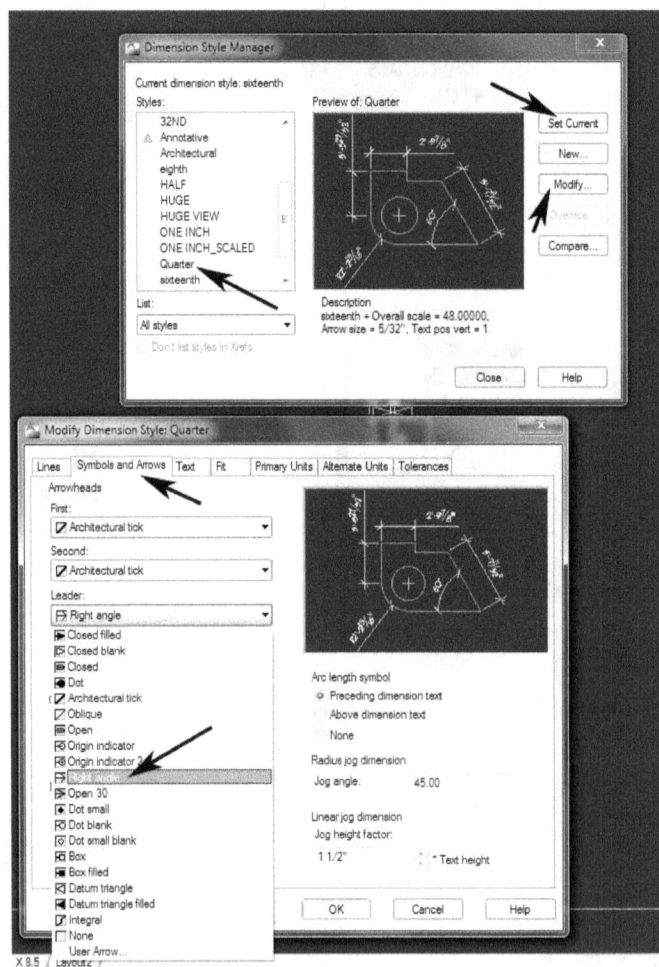

Fig 7-4

Type **qleader <e>**.

At the prompt type: **s <e>**. The **Leader Settings** box will open as shown in **Fig 7-5**.

Select the **Leader Line & Arrow** tab and set it as shown in Fig 7-5.

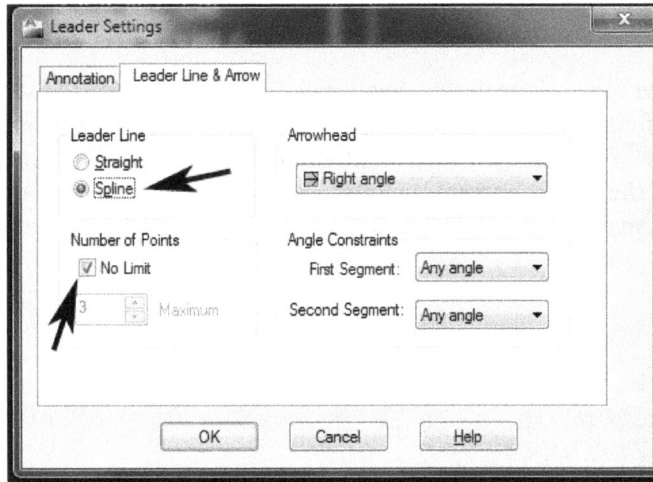

Fig 7-5

Now select the **Annotation tab** at the top and set it as shown in **Fig 7-6**. **OK**.

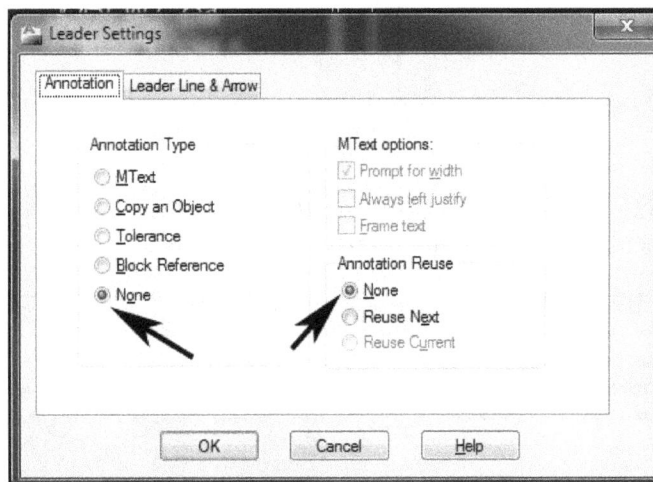

Fig 7-6

Start your leaders at the **arrowhead end** and create the spline shown by clicking on three points along the line. Experiment a bit to see how this works. ***You must pull the first section of the spline out until the arrowhead appears*** (the leader spline needs to be a certain length before the arrowhead appears—3x the arrowhead length).

These leader splines are usually created by eye, they are going to be different every time; it is all about placing the leader and text neatly so that the information conveyed is clear and easy to read. Three or four spline points usually looks best (a lot of points can make the line jagged). **After** the **final spline point** (at the text end of the spline line) you must <e> to set it (sometimes you need to enter two or three times—an AutoCAD conundrum).

I like to copy my text from one place to another and edit it in the new location instead of opening a new mtext box each time. We did this in Chapter 1 with the room titles. But you can open a mt box each time if you prefer. Make it look (generally) like **Fig 7-3**.

In the final drawing we will add more text but for now this is sufficient to demonstrate the method.

7.3 Scaled Dimensions

Now we are going to add some dimensions to this detail section to demonstrate the settings. While the text and leaders use the same settings for all four of our scales on this page, the **dimension settings** must be **different** for each scale. To demonstrate this, click on the **Linear** button on the **Dimensions palette**. Pick the dimension points shown in **Fig 7-7**. The **size of the text is correct**, but read the **dimension (it is wrong)**. It reads 2' -10 ½". That is three times the actual size because we scaled up the drawing by a factor of three. Let's set the dimension style so it reads correctly.

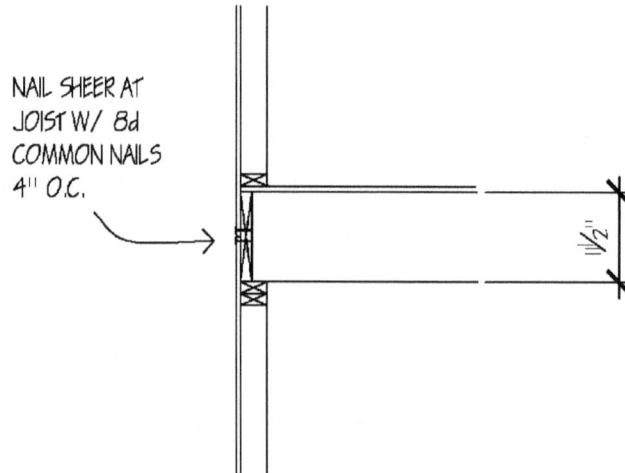

Fig 7-7

Open the **Dimension Style Manager** again. Select the **quarter** style. **Click** on the **New** button. When the **Create New Dimension Style** box opens, **name** this style: **quarterx3**. **Continue**.

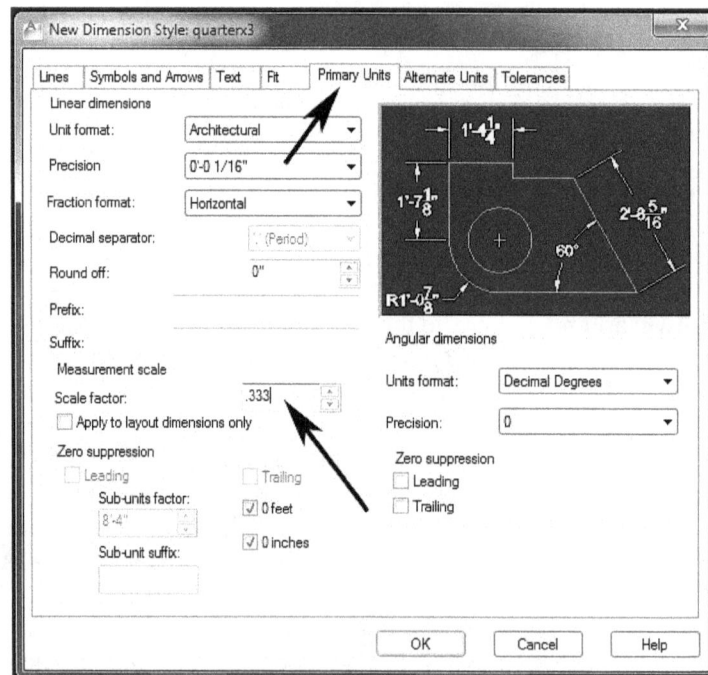

Fig 7-8

In the box that opens (New dimension Style: quarterx3) highlight the 1.0000 in the **Scale factor** window as shown in **Fig 7-8** and over **type** it to read **.333**. **OK. Set Current. Close.**

Erase the **dimension** that reads **2' 10 ½"** and **redo** the **linear dimension**. You will see that the dimension text now reads **11 ½"**.

> If you only have one or two dimensions to change you can use the **properties** box (highlight the object—in this case the dimension—and right click) and use the text override as we did with the height dimension at the end of chapter 2. Otherwise you will need to create a new dimension style for each of the scaled views that you create.

We are going to do the same basic thing with each scaled detail. I won't go through every step again, but let's go through each detail quickly to see what is different with each view.

The next view shown in **Fig 7-9** is **1" scale** (1" = 1'). This view is scaled up by four times. So the **dimension style** must be set to a **Scale factor** of **.25**.

Create a **new dimension** style from the **quarter**. **Name** this new dimension style **quarterx4**. Set the **Scale factor** to **.25** (see **Fig 7-8**). Leave everything else the same. Set this **Current** and **create** the dimension shown in **Fig 7-9**.

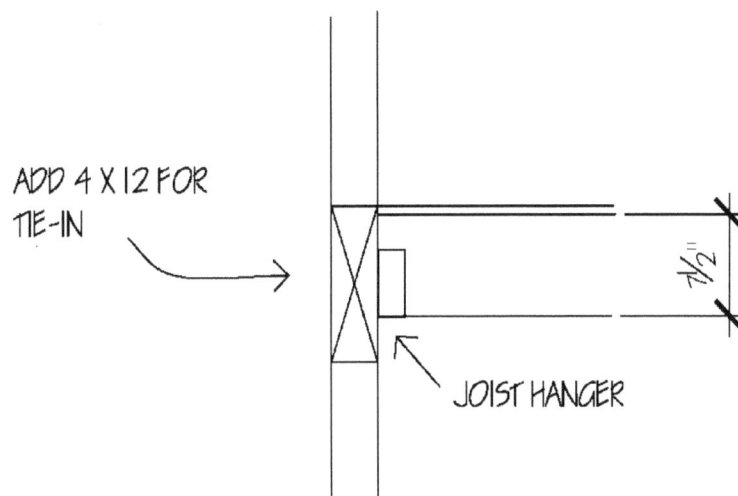

Fig 7-9

You can see that I have added a joist hanger (2" x 5" then scaled up x 4). Draw it then place it by eye as shown (turn off the Osnap to set it). You will have to scale it by a factor of 4 to match the scale of the detail.

The text size will be the same as before. The leaders will be the same also. The **scale factor does not affect the leader size**. It only affects the dimension text (the value of the numbers, not the height of the numbers).

The next section shown in **Fig 7-10** is scaled to **½" = 1'** (called 1/2 scale). So we will need to set up a new **dimension style**. **Name** it **quarterx2** and set the **Scale factor** to **.5**. Set it **current**.

Add the **dimension** shown at the bottom of the cross section in **Fig 7-10**. In this view we have two different sizes of text: **9"** for the ceiling height notes (CEILING 8') and **7.5** for everything else. Type **mt <e>** and set the text height in the bar that opens.

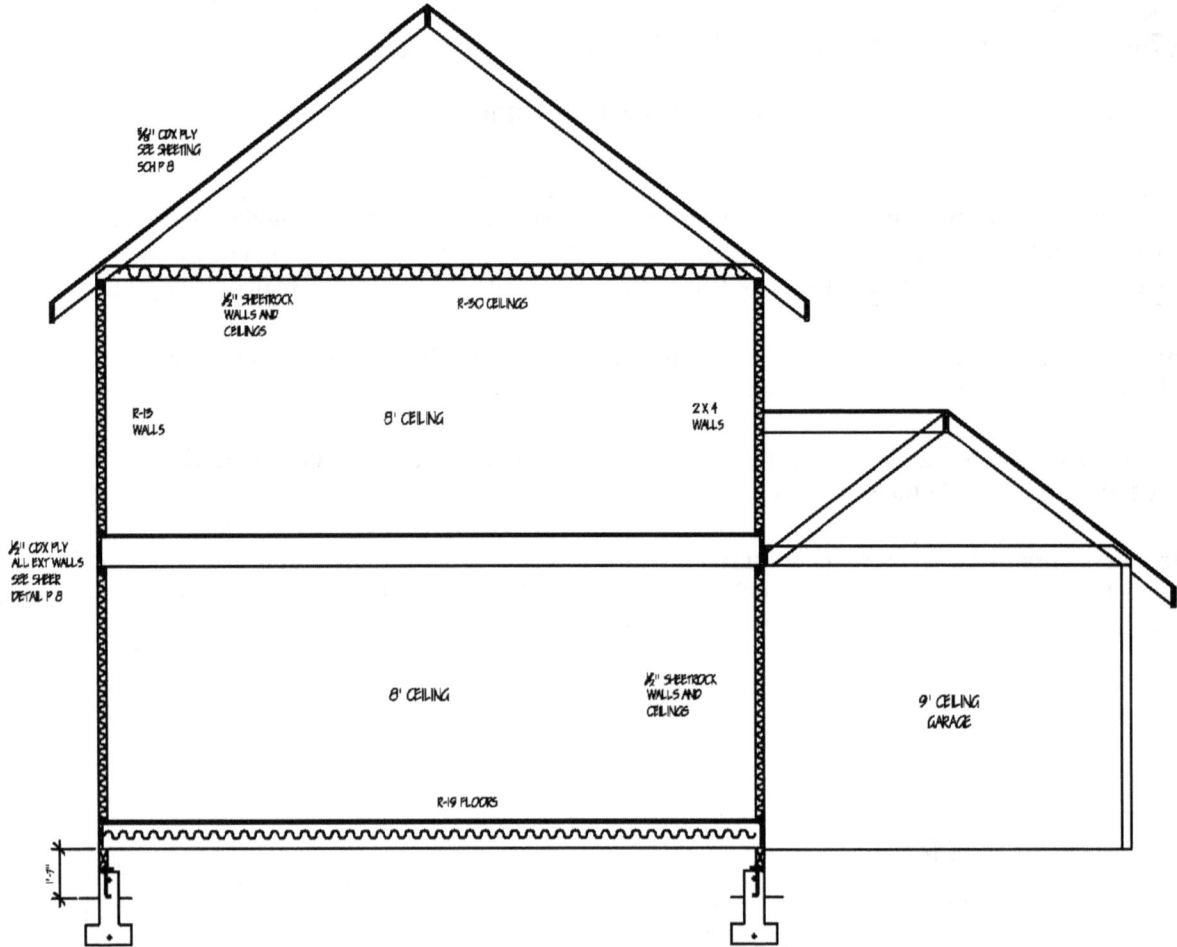

3/4" CDX PLY
SEE SHEETING
SCH P 8

1/2" SHEETROCK
WALLS AND
CEILINGS

R-30 CEILINGS

R-13
WALLS

8' CEILING

2 X 4
WALLS

1/2" CDX PLY
ALL EXT WALLS
SEE SHEER
DETAIL P 8

8' CEILING

1/2" SHEETROCK
WALLS AND
CEILINGS

9' CEILING
GARAGE

R-19 FLOORS

1'-7"

Fig 7-10

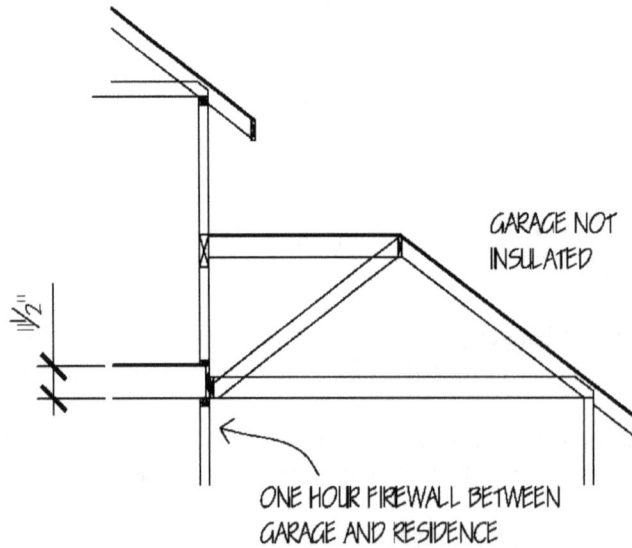

GARAGE NOT
INSULATED

1 1/2"

ONE HOUR FIREWALL BETWEEN
GARAGE AND RESIDENCE

Fig 7-11

Finally use the **quarter** scale **dimension style** to create the **dimension** in **Fig 7-11**. Add some text as shown. Once again I have added a dimension just so you can see how it works.

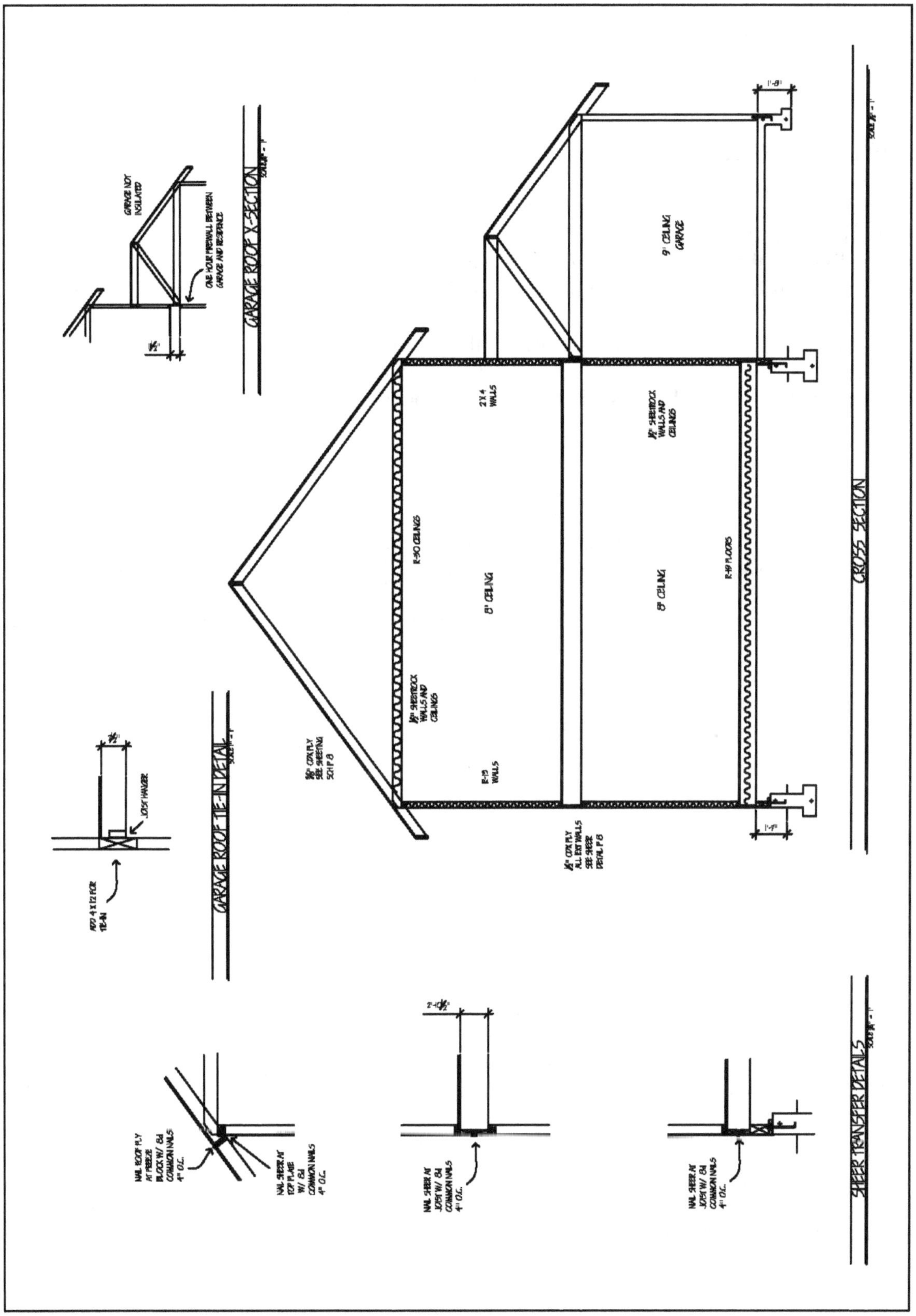

Fig 7-12

Copy one of the view titles **from** the **elevations** (NORTH ELEVATION with the lines and the scale ¼" = 1').
Copy it to all four locations and **adjust** its **length** as shown in **Fig 7-12**. Now highlight the text in each view title
and edit it to read as you see. Then do the same for the scale factors (GARAGE ROOF SECTION is 1/4" = 1'/

CROSS SECTION is ½" = 1'/ SHEER TRANSFER is ¾" = 1'/ GARAGE ROOF TIE-IN DETAIL is 1' = 1') as shown. Adjust the position of the text and the length of the lines.

Now we are ready to plot this page.

7.4 Plotting the Detail Page

Click on the **36 x 24 layout** tab and open the paper space. With the Paper/Model space set to **paper**, type **z <e> a <e>** (zoom all). Place the paper in the middle of the screen about like what you see in Fig 7-13. You must be able to see the limits of the paper in order for this to work, so zoom out until you see the entire piece of paper and then keep the edges visible. Make sure that the **viewport** is **unlocked**—you must do this in Paper space.

Now set it to **Model** space (Fig 7-13). Roughly center the page you just created as shown in **Fig 7-13** (anywhere near the center is fine). **Select** the ¼" = 1' in **Viewport Scale** window. The drawing will fill up the viewport. **Adjust** the drawing in the space by using the **center button** on your **mouse** (hold it down and position the drawing).

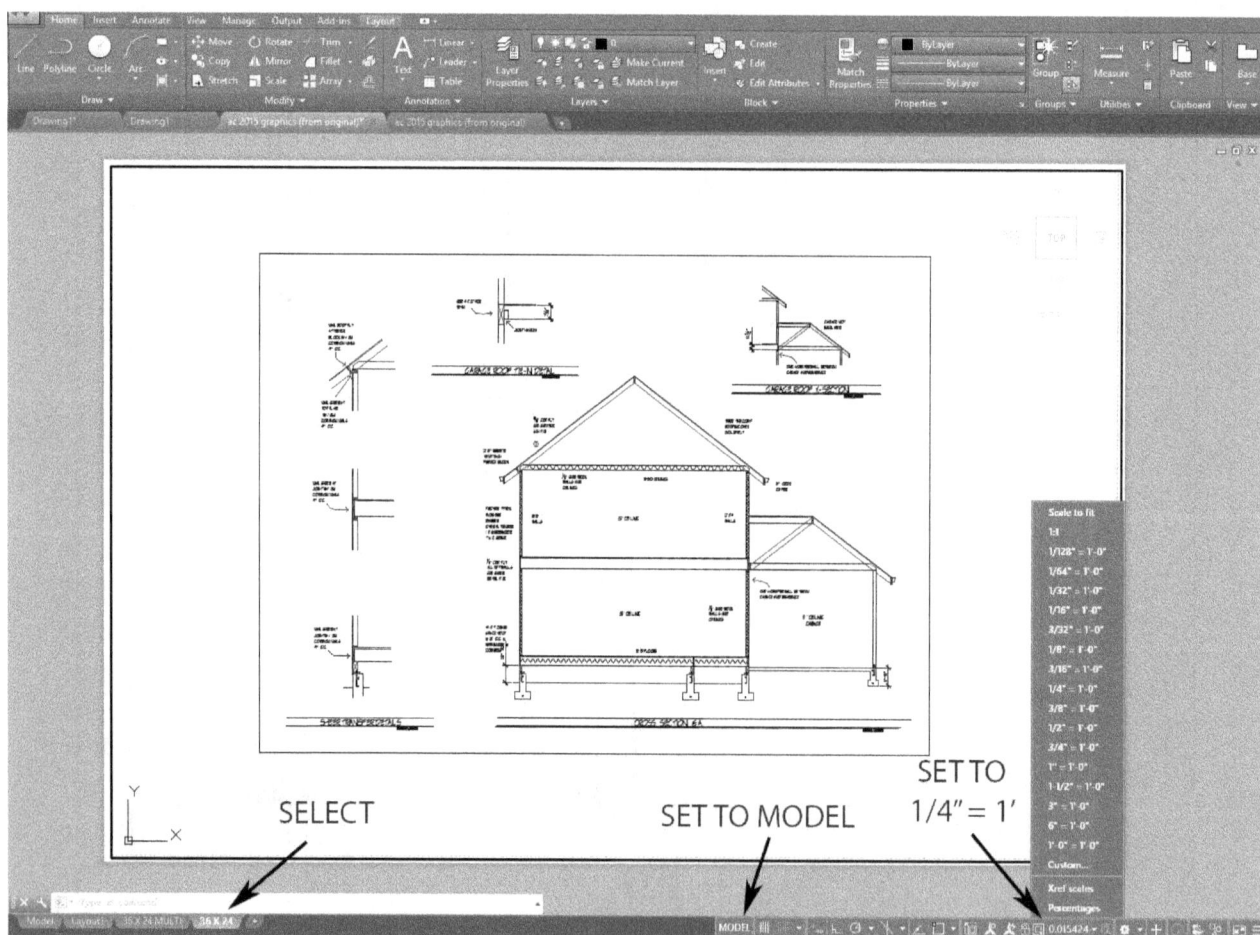

Fig 7-13

Now **right click** the **36 x 24** layout tab as in **Fig 7-13** (where it says SELECT—your tab may be in a different position). Select **Plot**. **Check** to make sure that the right **plotter** is selected (in this example that is the Xerox wide format plotter shown in Fig 7-14).

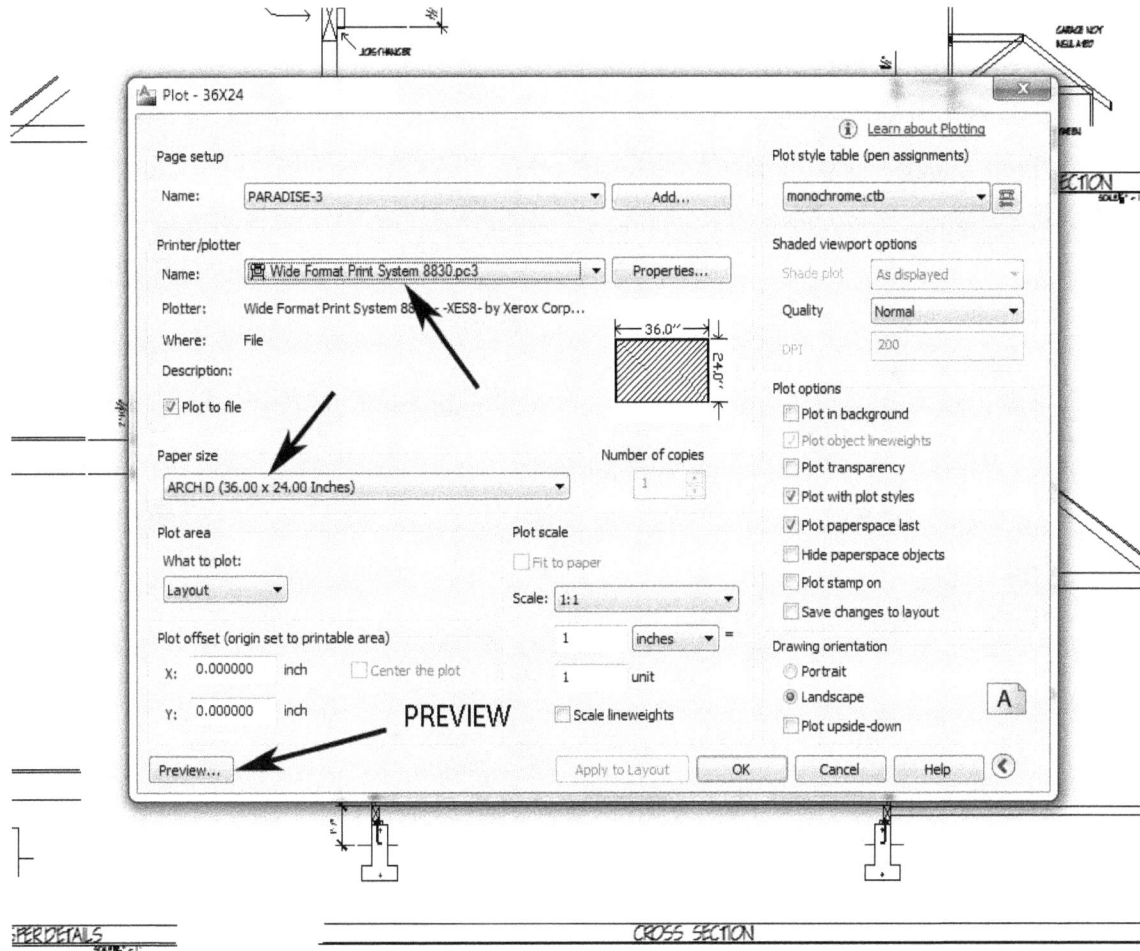

Fig 7-14

Click on the **Preview** button in the lower left hand corner.

Here you will see the page as it will plot out with the four different scaled details . **Close** the **Preview** and **OK**. **Save** it to the desktop or your AutoCAD folder.

Note that you cannot open the PLT file and look at the drawing. This is a file of coded information for the plotter/printer to read.

You can copy this to a disc or email it to your local print shop and they will print it out for you.

You can also print it on your home or office printer. Use the 11 x 8.5 layout tab. If you want you can print out six different parts of the drawing and lay them together to see what the full size drawing will look like.

The concept of scales is discussed in Chapter 13.

The two most important bits of information (when it comes to scaling) in the **Dimension Styles** settings are the **"Scale factor"** (under the **Primary Units** tab) and the **"Use Overall Scale of:"** (**Fit** tab).

The scale factor is what recognizes that you have scaled a drawing (made it larger or smaller) in model space for the purpose of plotting. The parts of the house that have been scaled will not be built two, three, or four times larger. They are just being printed larger so that you can see the detail.

The "Use Overall Scale of:" setting determines the height of the dimension text. The Scale factor affects the number that the dimension reads.

You don't need to fully grasp this yet. It comes clear with time and more examples. One of which we will cover in the next chapter.

Chapter 8—Plot the Plot Plan

The title of this chapter is confusing because the word plot has two different meanings. The Plot Plan is the drawing of the subject parcel; it is called a plot of land. To plot (the verb) means to print out a copy.

8.1 Page Setup for Plot Plan

This is the third chapter that deals with setting up a page for plotting. In Chapter 4 we drew the plot plan. Now we will place it on a page, add some addition items, and plot the page.

This page will be set up to plot at the **scale of 1/8" = 1'**. So all of the text will be sized for that scale—twice the size of what we used on the two previous pages (1/4" scale). The other important new information in this chapter is the importation of raster files and the plotting of dashed lines (or any broken line).

To begin let's create a rectangle that represents the printable part of the page, as in the last chapter, but larger.

Set the **Construction Layer current** and **draw** a **rectangle 256' x 184'**. **Copy** your **plot** plan into the rectangle as in **Fig 8-1**.

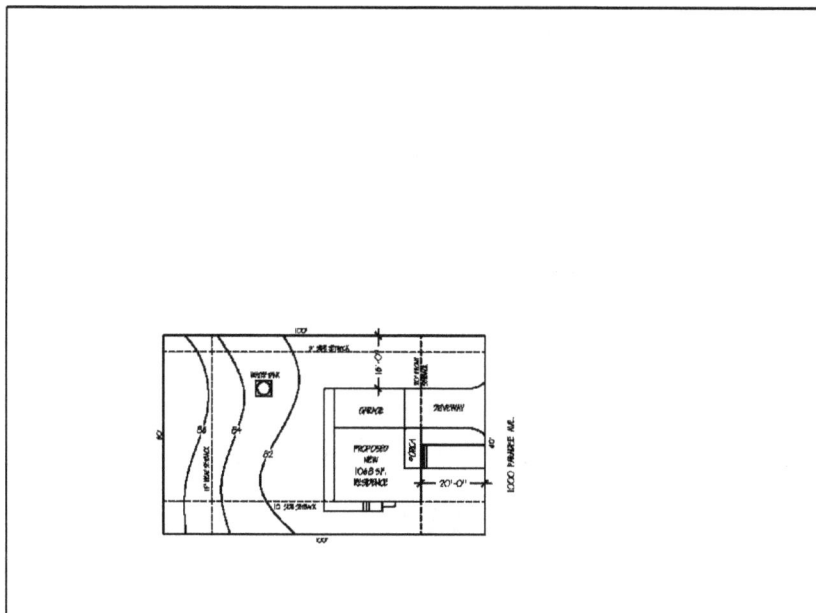

Fig 8-1

8.2 Raster File Import

This section is an exercise in how to import a picture or a graphic (in this case a Map) and then trace over it to duplicate some of the lines in that picture or graphic. There are a lot of variables in this process and they differ a lot from one computer system to the next. So don't get too caught up in the process for now. Give it a try and see if it works for you. If you have a lot of problems, skip over it; you can come back and work it out it later, if you need it.

We are going to create a **vicinity map**. Many building departments require a map on the first page of the plans that shows where the property is located. This map does not need to be "to scale" and it does not need to be a perfect depiction. The purpose is to provide a visual depiction of the location; so the vicinity map can be rather **rough** in nature as long as it tells the person reading the plans how to get to the site.

There is an easy way to do this with the internet and AutoCad. **Start** by **drawing** a **line** as in **Fig 8-2**. This line is **70 feet** long. Place it near the bottom of your workspace and zoom in or out until it starts at one side of the screen and ends at the other side. The purpose of this is to set your workspace to a defined dimensional area.

You can use the **zoom window** to get this 70' line to fit in the screen as shown: **z <e> w <e>** then create a window around the line. Or you can use the mouse.

You can **reset** the **zoomfactor** of your **mouse** by typing: **zoomfactor** and setting the value to a lower number (try **5** and then you can set it back to 40 or 50 after this exercise).

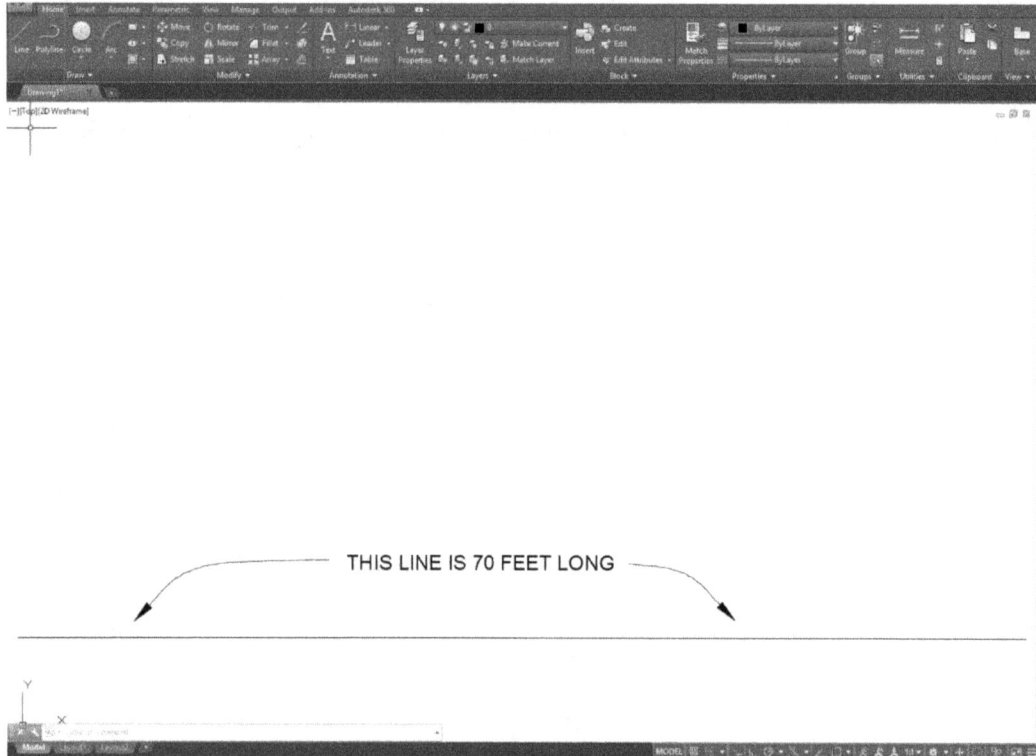

THIS LINE IS 70 FEET LONG

Fig 8-2

Now **go online** and go to **Google Maps**.

Type in the address of the subject property. As an example here we will use the **Presidio in San Francisco, California**. Type that into your **Google Maps search** window. Use the little sideways arrow as shown in **Fig 8-2A** to expand the screen (it is shown expanded, yours might be compressed). Zoom in or out and create a map **size** that is **approximately** what you see in **Fig 8-2A**.

When you create your own maps you will want to adjust the map size so that it includes an area the appropriate size for your specific location. The purpose is to create a map that covers an area large enough so the location of your project is clear. You are guiding people to the site. There really is no set rule for how large of an area to cover with the map.

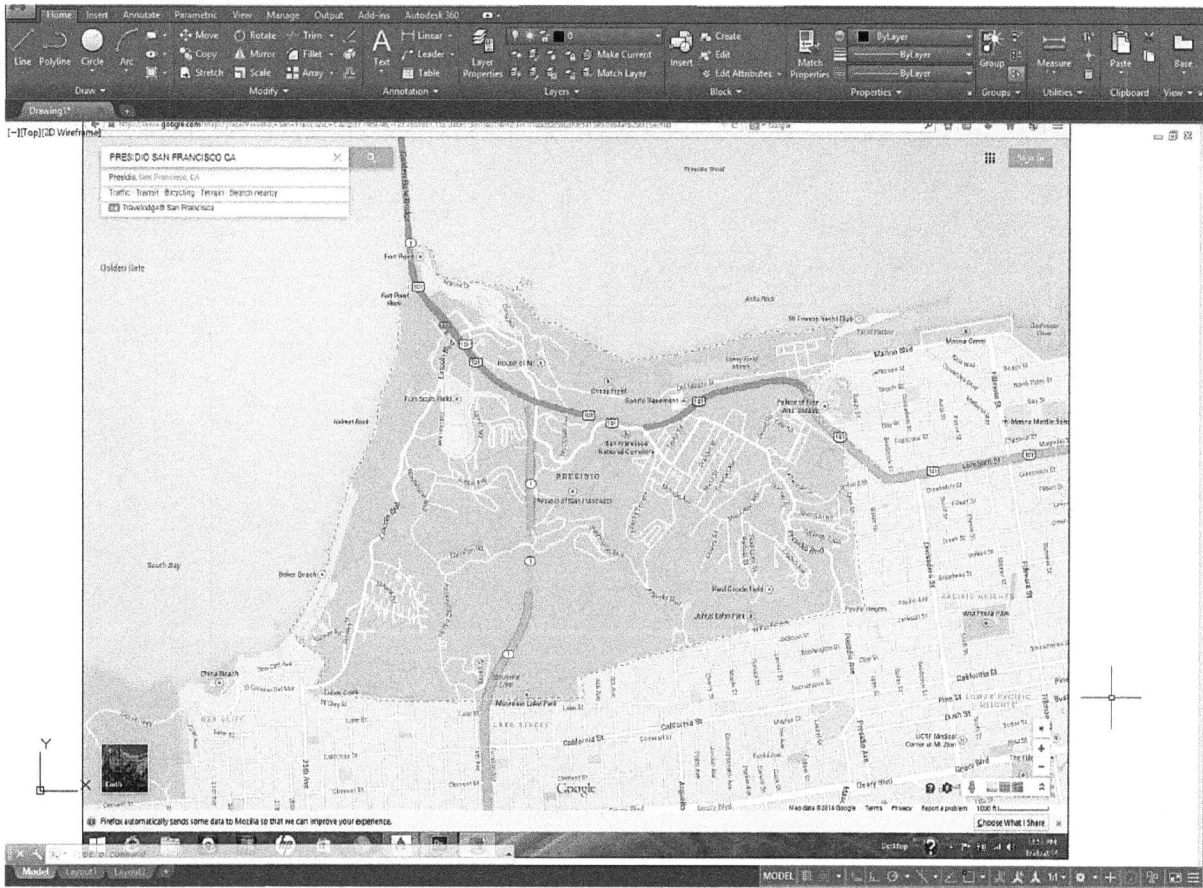

Fig 8-2A

Take a **screen shot** of the map (see **Appendix I—Screen shot** for help), then in your AutoCAD workspace, type: **Ctrl V** on your keyboard. Place your **cursor** on the **left end** of the 70 foot **line** and **click**.

Fig 8-2A shows what my workspace looks like after I have imported the map from Google maps. I cannot tell you how to import this map at an exact scale; it seems to vary from one computer to the next.

This imported map image is called a **raster file**. That is a term that deals with the format of the image. Go online and read about raster files if you are curious about this.

> The size of the copy in your space may be very different. The size of space that you set in the workspace, as we defined with the 70' line, determines the size of the imported image. Do not get caught up in this too much. It is not a skill that is important enough to spend a lot of time figuring out right now.

Set the **0 Layer** current. Then use the **spline fit** tool and draw lines over the main roads that define the Presidio location (**trace** right over the roads on the map). Start with Highway 101. Click a first spline point at the top and then at points along the highway to roughly trace the shape of the highway. Fig 8-3 shows what it looks like after you erase the google map. You won't be able to see the spline lines very well, but you can see them faintly. Don't try to make this very accurate, that is not the point of the vicinity map, it can be rather crude. Click on enough points to get a rough trace of each road shown in Fig 8-5.

After you have traced the roads shown in Fig 8-5 **turn off the 0 Layer** and **erase** the **Google map** (Use a green selection window and encompass the lower right corner of the map then erase). Then **turn the 0 layer on again**. Fig 8-3 shows what my tracing looks like after the erasure.

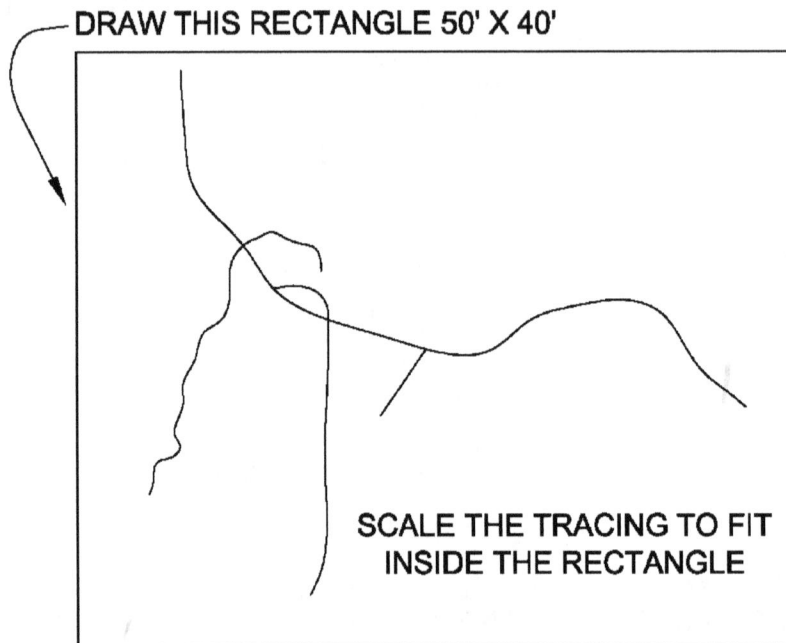

Fig 8-3

Next we have to size the sketch of roads to the approximate size for our plans. Draw a rectangle 50 feet by 40 feet. **Scale the tracing** up or down until it more or less **fills the rectangle**. **Erase the rectangle**.

Once you have a sketch of the roads that is about the right size, use the **offset** tool and **add a second line** to each road as shown in **Fig 8-4**. Use different offsets to signify the relative importance of the roads. The main road on this map is Highway 101. So I will offset it by 10". Lincoln Blvd is a major street so I will offset it by 5". Veterans Blvd is a smaller road so offset it by 3". This is what you see in Fig 8-4.

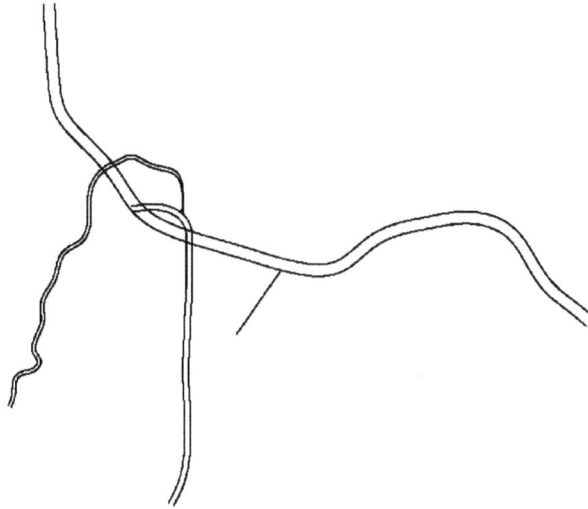

Fig 8-4

Now **add the road names** to the Highway and streets. When you do a map like this you will have to experiment with offsets and text sizes because the vicinity map is going to be a different size for each set of plans (it will depict a different size area).

Use the **text layer** (set it current) and use the following text sizes to create what you see in Fig 8-5: Highway 101 is 8". Lincoln and Veterans Blvds are 7". Presidio St is 6". Create the text then use the **Rotate** tool to align it with the various streets. Use the move tool to place it so that it looks neat. (I always use Bold for light weight font text). See Appendix I—Text if you need help with the settings.

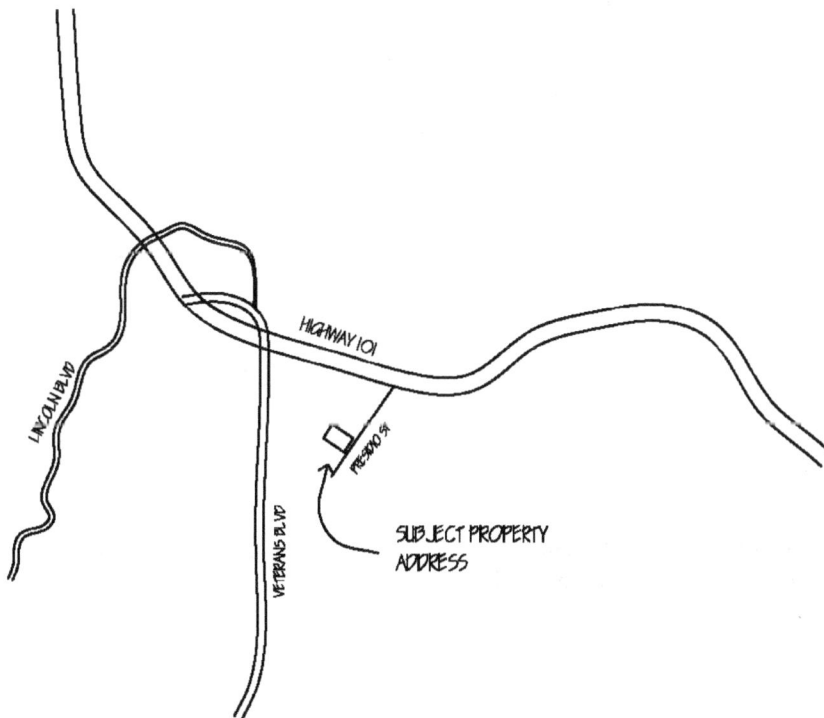

Fig 8-5

Draw a **rectangle** that represents the Subject Property Address (Fig 8-5). This will not be to scale—in fact it is better if the size is exaggerated so that it is easy to see. Remember this is just for directions, not an engineered drawing.

Rotate the rectangle (that depicts the lot) and place it by eye. Use 10" text for the "SUBJECT PROPERTY ADDRESS" leader text. Use the **quarter** scale **dimension style** for the leader (set it current before using qleader).

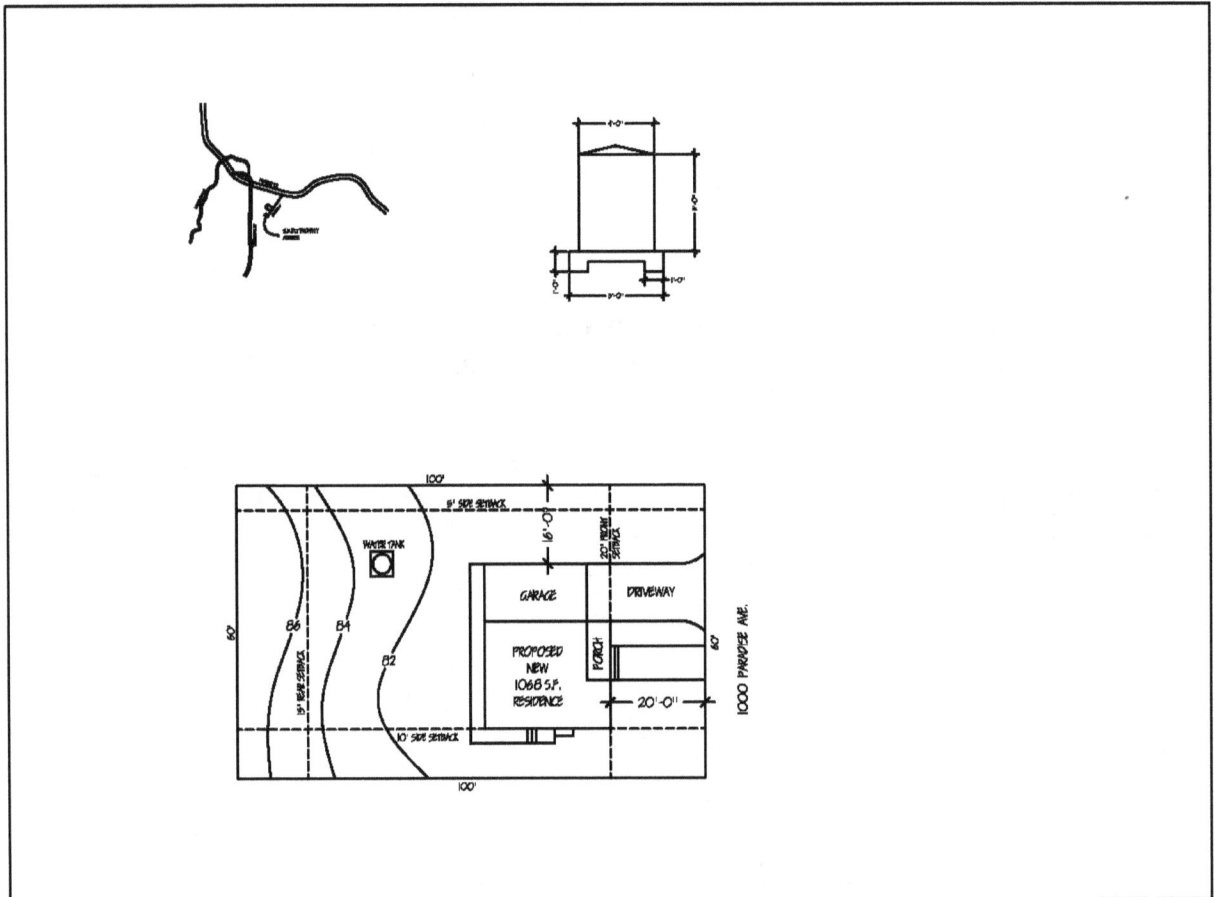

Fig 8-6

Now **copy** this vicinity map to the approximate location shown in **Fig 8-6**.

8.3 Water Tank X-Section

I am going to add a **water tank cross section** so that we have some different scales on the page. Draw the tank as shown in **Fig 8-7** and **scale** it up **by a factor of 4**.

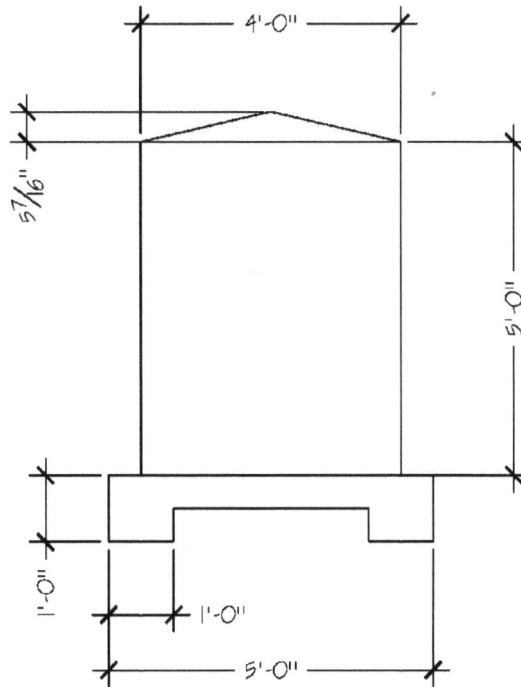

Fig 8-7

Create a new **dimension style**. Make it a **copy of quarter**. Name it **eighthx4**. Under the **Fit** tab set the **Use Overall Scale of**: **96**. Under the **Primary Units** tab set the **Scale factor** to **.25**. See Fig 7-8 if you need to refresh.

Now use the **Linear** dimension tool and add the dimensions shown.

Copy this tank (or your rectangle) onto the page as shown in **Fig 8-6**.

8.4 Text on Plot Plan

Now we will add some **text** as shown in **Fig 8-8**. Start by **drawing** a **line** as at **A**. It is **80 feet** from the right side of the rectangle. Use this line to align the different blocks of Text.

The text you see was created using a series of mtext boxes. The SCOPE OF PROJECT is one mtext box and the listed items under that title are in a different mtext box. The APN is in a different box. The **text sizes** are shown in **Fig 8-9**.

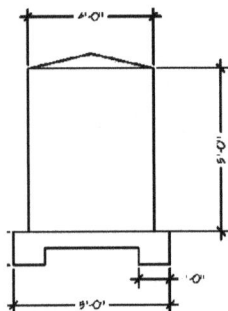

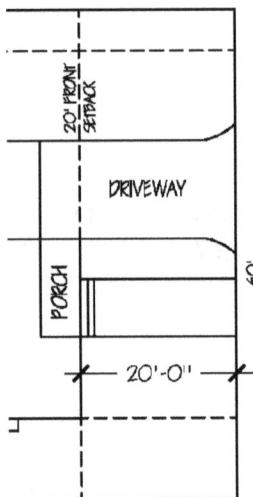

SCOPE OF PROJECT

BUILD 1008 S.F. RESIDENCE WITH 264 S.F. GARAGE ON CURRENTLY VACANT 100' X 60' LOT.

PROJECT INCLUDES ONE FULL AND ONE HALF BATHROOM, WASHER AND KITCHEN SINK.

TOTAL GROUND COVERAGE = 858 S.F.

TOTAL PAVED AREA = 604 S.F.

TOTAL IMPERMEABLE SURFACE = 1462 S.F.

EXPRESSED AS PERCENTAGE = 24`% OF LOT.

PROJECT TO BE FIRE SPRINKLERED

APN
000-000-00

CONTACT INFO

OWNER: DESIGNER:
WINNIE AND BOB OWNER   DESIGNER'S NAME
STREET ADDRESS   CITY, STATE, ZIP CODE
CITY, STATE ZIP CODE   PHONE NUMBER
PHONE NUMBER

ENGINEER:
ENGINEER'S NAME
CITY, STATE, ZIP CODE
PHONE NUMBER

TABLE OF CONTENTS
PAGE 1: PLOT PLAN
PAGE 2: FLOOR PLANS AND ELECTRICAL PLAN
PAGE 3: ELEVATIONS
PAGE 4: FOUNDATION PLAN AND DETAILS
PAGE 5: FLOOR FRAME, ROOF FRAME PLANS
PAGE 6: CROSS SECTION AND DETAILS
PAGE 7: DETAILS AND WINDOW SCHEDULE
PAGE 8: SHEER PLAN AND ENGINEERING DETAILS
PAGE 9: NOTES

A

Fig 8-8

This is an example of how text might look on a plot plan but there is no set standard for this. Different architects and designers have their own style. The important thing is that there is a variation of text sizes, this helps the eye to organize the information.

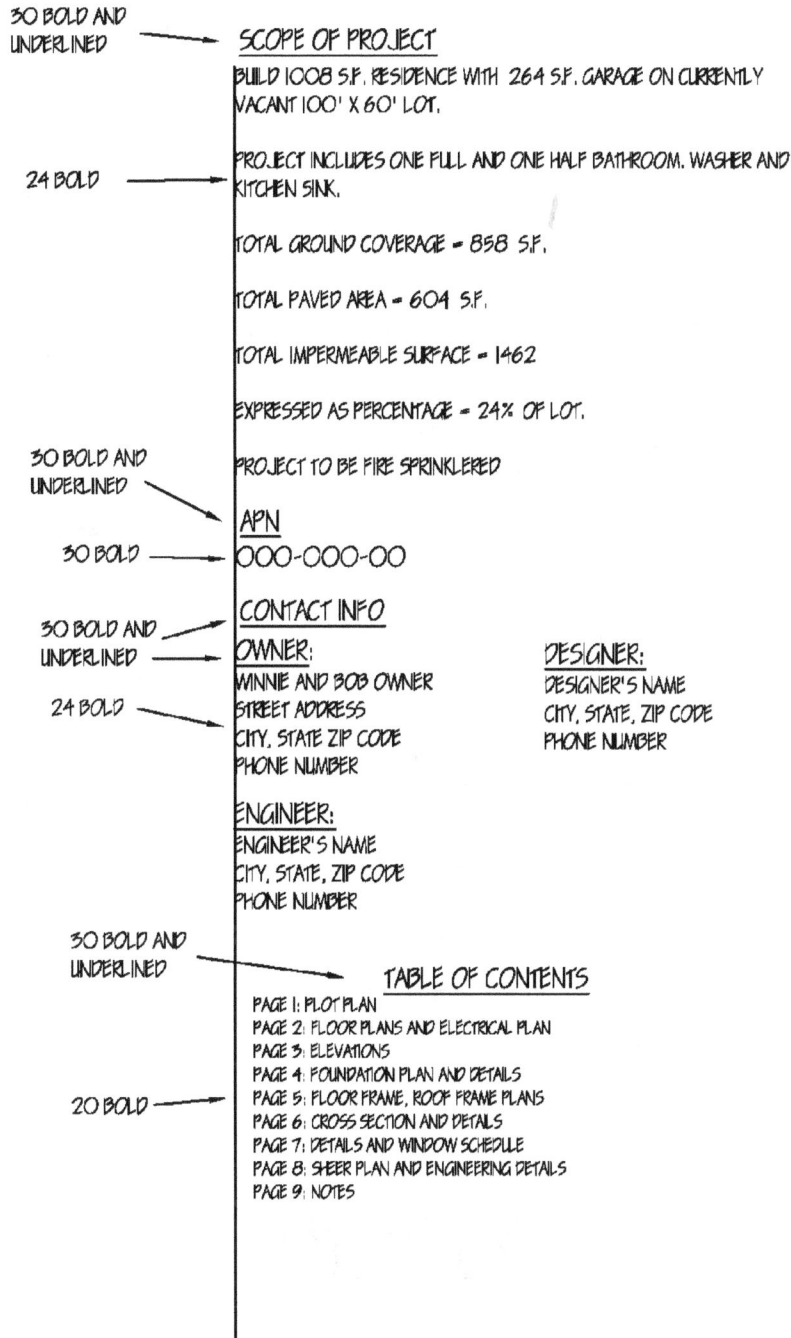

30 BOLD AND UNDERLINED →

SCOPE OF PROJECT

BUILD 1008 S.F. RESIDENCE WITH 264 S.F. GARAGE ON CURRENTLY VACANT 100' X 60' LOT.

24 BOLD →

PROJECT INCLUDES ONE FULL AND ONE HALF BATHROOM. WASHER AND KITCHEN SINK.

TOTAL GROUND COVERAGE = 858 S.F.

TOTAL PAVED AREA = 604 S.F.

TOTAL IMPERMEABLE SURFACE = 1462

EXPRESSED AS PERCENTAGE = 24% OF LOT.

PROJECT TO BE FIRE SPRINKLERED

30 BOLD AND UNDERLINED →

APN

30 BOLD → 000-000-00

CONTACT INFO

30 BOLD AND UNDERLINED →

OWNER:	DESIGNER:
WINNIE AND BOB OWNER	DESIGNER'S NAME
STREET ADDRESS	CITY, STATE, ZIP CODE
CITY, STATE ZIP CODE	PHONE NUMBER
PHONE NUMBER	

24 BOLD →

ENGINEER:
ENGINEER'S NAME
CITY, STATE, ZIP CODE
PHONE NUMBER

30 BOLD AND UNDERLINED →

TABLE OF CONTENTS

PAGE 1: PLOT PLAN
PAGE 2: FLOOR PLANS AND ELECTRICAL PLAN
PAGE 3: ELEVATIONS
PAGE 4: FOUNDATION PLAN AND DETAILS
PAGE 5: FLOOR FRAME, ROOF FRAME PLANS
PAGE 6: CROSS SECTION AND DETAILS
PAGE 7: DETAILS AND WINDOW SCHEDULE
PAGE 8: SHEER PLAN AND ENGINEERING DETAILS
PAGE 9: NOTES

20 BOLD →

Fig 8-9

You do not need to create all of this text. A few lines will suffice for practicing the concepts.

Once you have the text you want on the page, **erase** the **line A**.

To add the view titles make a **copy** of the **NORTH ELEVATION title** and copy it into open workspace. **Scale** it up **by a factor of 2**. Then place it as shown in **Fig 8-10**. **Overwrite the titles** and the **scales** (see Figures 8-11) to match Fig 8-10. The plot plan scale is 1/8" = 1'. Note that when you enter the 1/8" in place of the ¼" that you must also type the inches (") sign and then hit the spacebar on your keyboard in order to get the diagonal stacking of the numbers. See Appendix I—Fraction Stacking for details. The Vicinity Map scale note reads NTS (Not to Scale) as it is not a scaled view. Adjust the length of the title lines so they are proportional to the views.

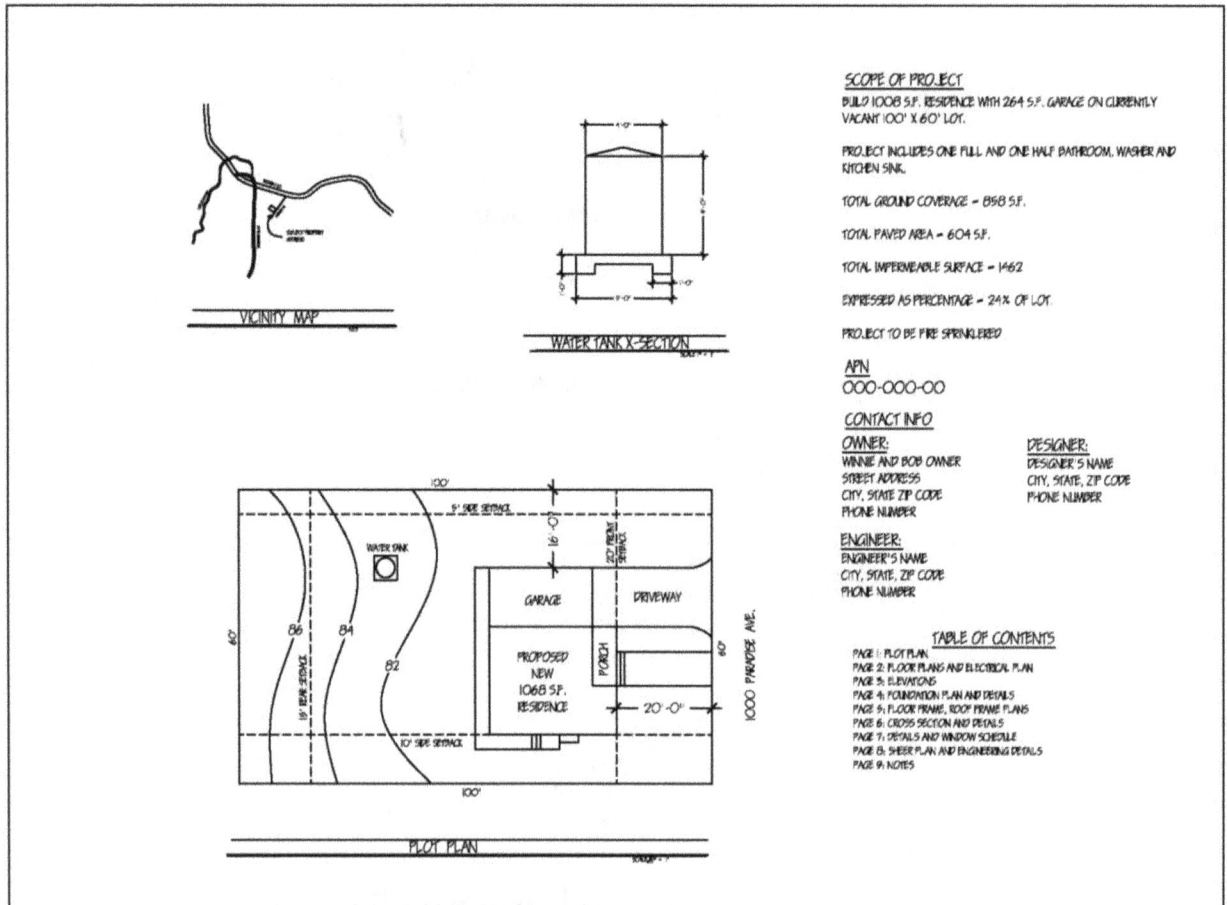

Fig 8-10

Fig 8-11 shows the view titles up close.

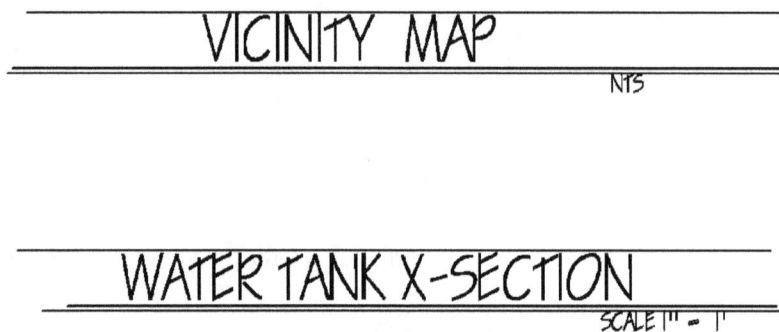

Fig 8-11

This Plot page does not look exactly like the finished Plot page that you see in Appendix IV. There is more information on that page and there is some adjustment to the plot plan. That is all covered in Chapter 15. For now we want to get on to the plotting of the page.

8.5 Plotting Dashed Lines

Click on the **36 x 24 layout tab**. Set the **Model/Paper** button at the bottom of the screen to **Model**. Center (more or less) your plot plan page in the paper space as in Fig 8-12. **Scale the view to 1/8" = 1'**. Review the last two chapters if you need to refresh. You need to see the entire piece of paper on the screen. You can type: z <e> a <e> when the Model/Paper button is set to Paper to see the entire paper space.

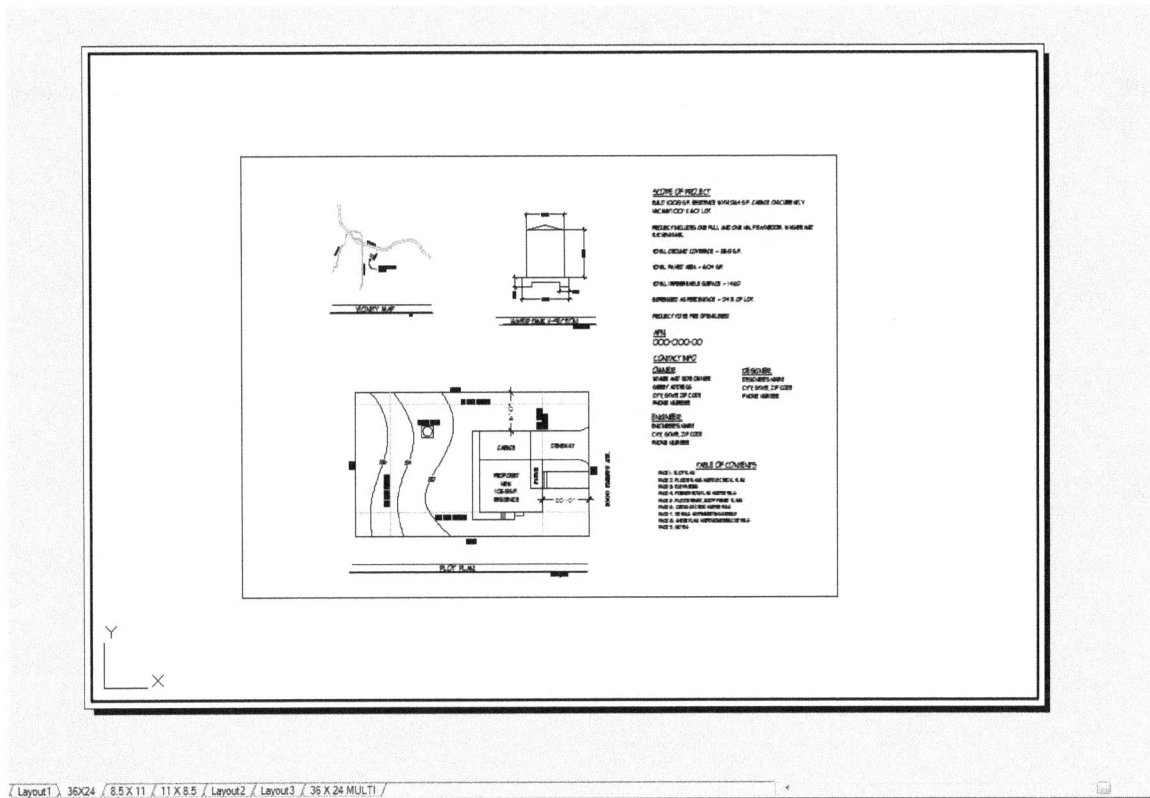

Fig 8-12

Use the center wheel button of your mouse to move the drawing into position. If you have to do this without a mouse button, you can use the zoom tools (**zoom all** then **zoom window**) to center your drawing in the paper space.

Your drawing may now show the dashed line in the plot plan (in model space) as a solid line in paper space. When you have this problem you must reset the **paper space line type scale**. To do this type **psltscale <e>.** When it prompts you to enter a new **value** type **0** and <e>.

Type: **Regenall**. Wait a minute and the drawing will regenerate. The line should now show as a dashed line (see Appendix I—Dashed Lines for help).

You can plot this now as you did in the previous two chapters—right click on the 36 x 24 Layout tab and select Plot. Set the printer for this size paper (the Xerox was set for this in my example) if it is not already selected. Then plot the page.

It will **plot to a file**, so you will need to name it and designate where you want it to be stored on your computer. Name the file. Paradise-1 is a good choice (this is page one of the plans).

You can print out parts of this page (or all of it) on your printer at home or work. Use the 11 x 8.5 Layout tab that we created and print out the different views separately (the plot, the vicinity map, the tank). The plot plan will not print out completely on this size paper at 1/8" scale, but you can print it out at 1/16" scale if you want it all on one page.

That is it for this chapter. Now we will set up the title block and then we are ready to print out the final copy of these pages of the plans. After that you are pretty well ready for any drafting project. The rest of the book is a round-up of various techniques and the discussion of scales.

If you are going to skip (or skim) the rest of the book, I suggest you take a few minutes and look at **Chapter 12 Tables** and the section in **Chapter 14 on text spacing**.

Chapter 9—Title Block

This chapter is going to be very brief. There are not even any subsections. The title block that we are going to create is shown in Fig 9-1.

Fig 9-1

Click on the Model tab (bottom of screen next to the Layout tabs) to **open** the **Model workspace**. Create a **new Layer** and name it **Border**. Make it **green**. **Set it current**.

Start by creating the page border. It is a **rectangle** that measures **140' x 92'**. Use the **Fillet** tool and set the **radius** to **3'** to create the curved corners.

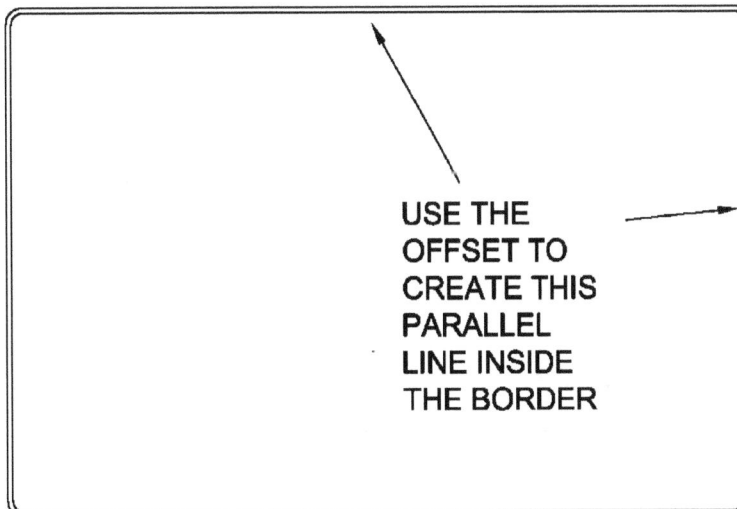

USE THE
OFFSET TO
CREATE THIS
PARALLEL
LINE INSIDE
THE BORDER

Fig 9-2

Use the **offset** tool to create a line inside this border at a **1'** offset as you see in **Fig 9-2**.

Draw line **A** in **Fig 9-3** at **11'** (it starts at the midpoint of the offset border line). Then draw **line B** from the end of line A up and attach it at the top. Use the **extend** tool to extend it to the **bottom**. **Trim** at **C** to create **Fig 9-4**.

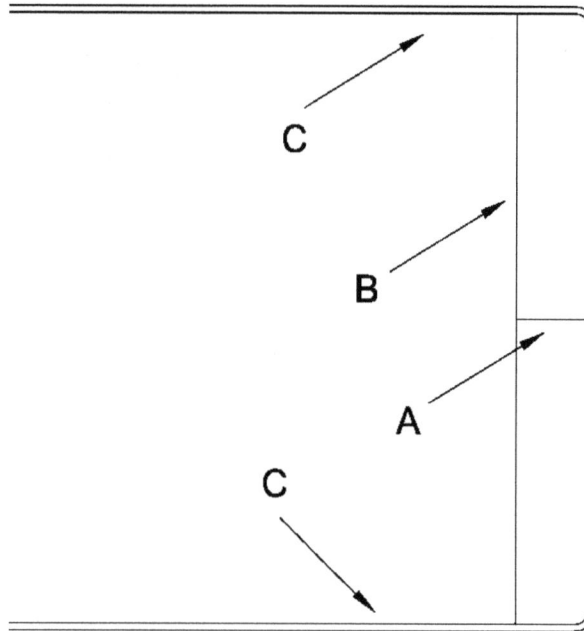

Fig 9-3

Erase what is left of this inside line on the left side of the drawing and you will see **Fig 9-4**. **Erase line A**.

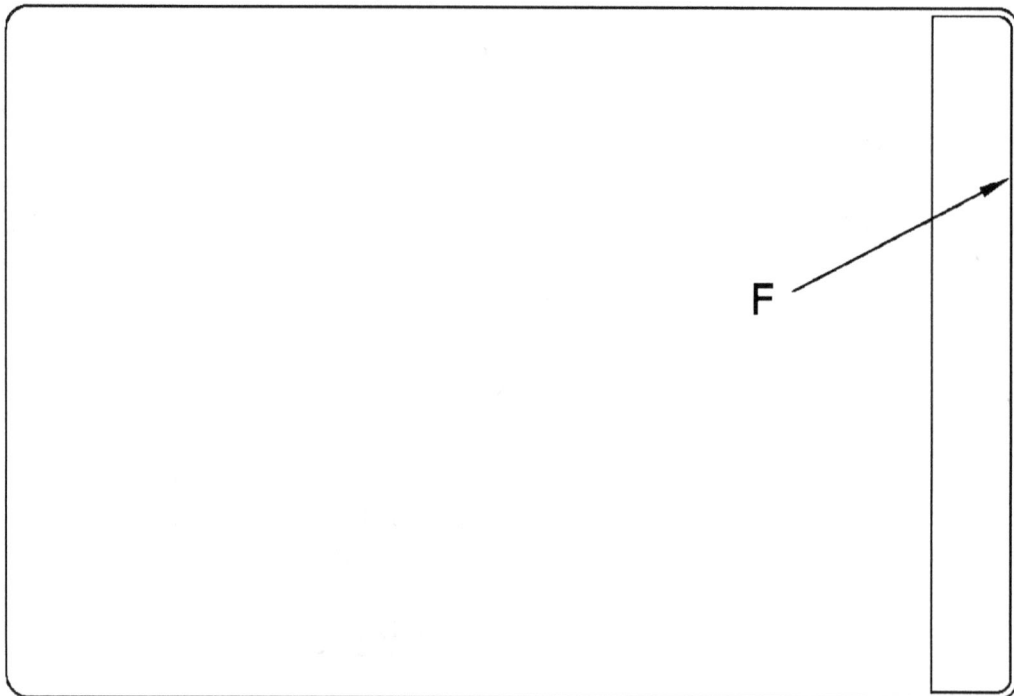

Fig 9-4

Click on the **Explode** tool (or type explode) then click on point **F** in **Fig 9-4** and <e>. This will make the lines and the fillets into separate objects (they were one object: a rectangle with fillet corners).

Create the lines shown in **Fig 9-5**. Use the **offset** tool from the top line—it will not be full length because of the radius corner—use the **extend** tool to connect it to the right. Then use the offsets shown to create the other lines as shown. The first offset is 29', the second offset is 29', the third offset is 5', the fourth is 15', and the fifth is 5'.

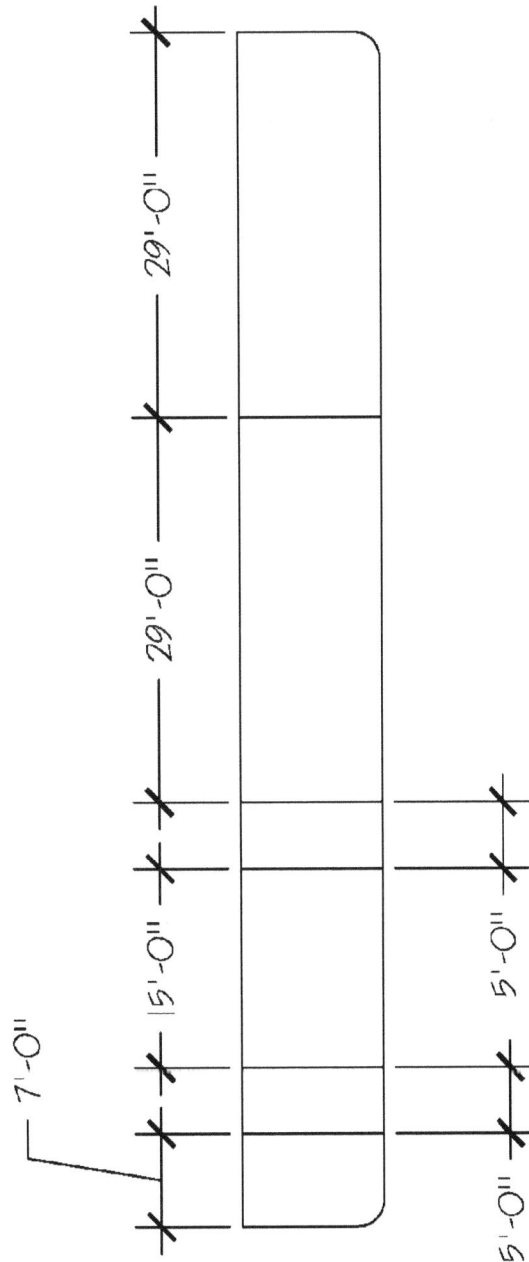

Fig 9-5

Draw the lines shown in 9-6 using the offset tool set to 1'3". This divides the 5' sections into four sections each.

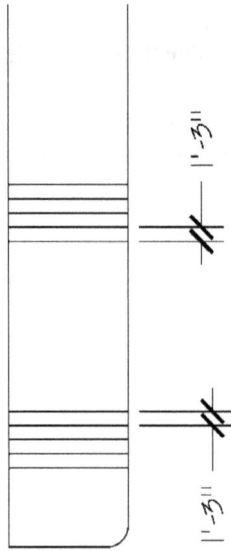

Fig 9-6

Draw the **lines** shown in **Fig 9-7** using the offsets shown. These are located in the upper 5' section (see Fig 9-1).

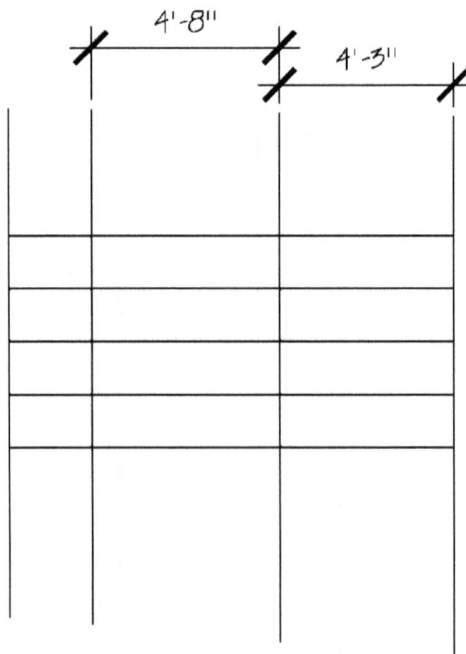

Fig 9-7

Draw the two **diagonal lines** as shown in **Fig 9-8**.

Set the **Text layer current**. Type the text shown in two separate blocks of **mtext**. Make the text **1'3"** in height and use **bold**. **Center** and **Middle justify** the text (see Appendix I—Text for help). After you have typed each text block, **close** the **Text Formatting bar** by clicking on the **OK**. **Rotate** the text **90 degrees** with the rotate tool. Now click on one of the text blocks to bring up the blue grip boxes. The text must be selected to do this—move the cursor around until you see the text change to a highlighted text (sometimes text can be hard to select and it is best to use a green selection window). Once the grip boxes have appeared you can grab the block of text by the **center blue grip box** (text must be **center/middle justified** to get the center grip box to appear) and place it in the center of the rectangle by snapping them to the center of the diagonal lines. With this method you **do not use** the **Move** or **Copy tool**. You just grab the text by the center blue grip box and move it. Erase the diagonal lines after you have placed the text. If you use the Copy or Move tool you must turn on the **Insertion** Osnap (in the Object snap settings).

Try another method: erase the lower of the two texts (PROPOSED NEW RESIDENCE, ETC.) and create a **mtext window inside** the **rectangular space** (from corner to corner instead of the diagonal line). **Type mt**, then **click** on the **lower left corner** of the rectangle, **right click** the mouse and select rotation. **Set** the **rotation angle to 90**. **Then click** on the **upper right** corner. The text window will open; set the **justification** for **middle/center**. Type the text and it will center the text automatically.

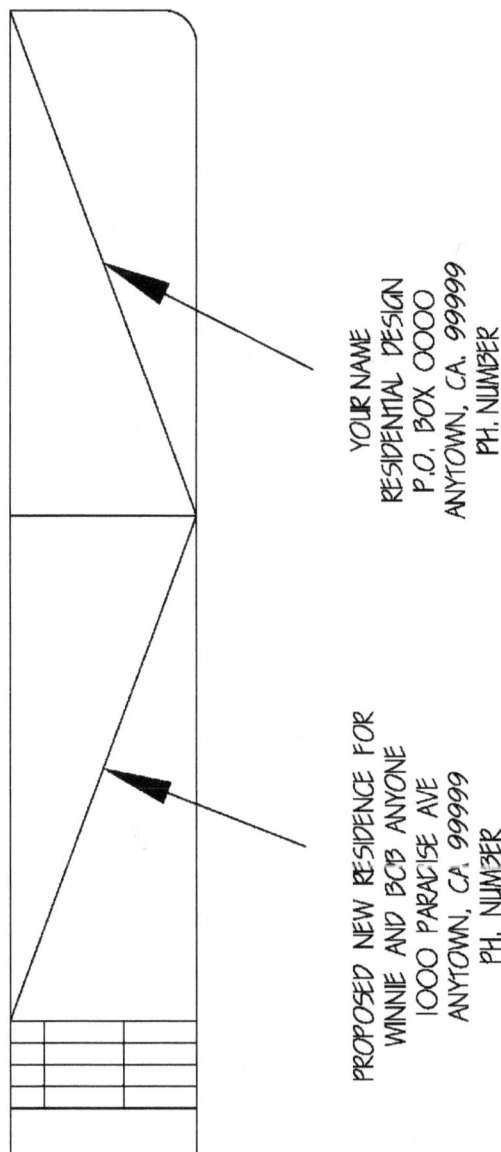

Fig 9-8

Repeat this process for the **text** shown in **Fig 9-9** (minus rotation). Create the text in three separate mt blocks. Make this text **6"** in height, center/middle justify it, and move it to the center of the diagonal lines shown. Erase the diagonal lines.

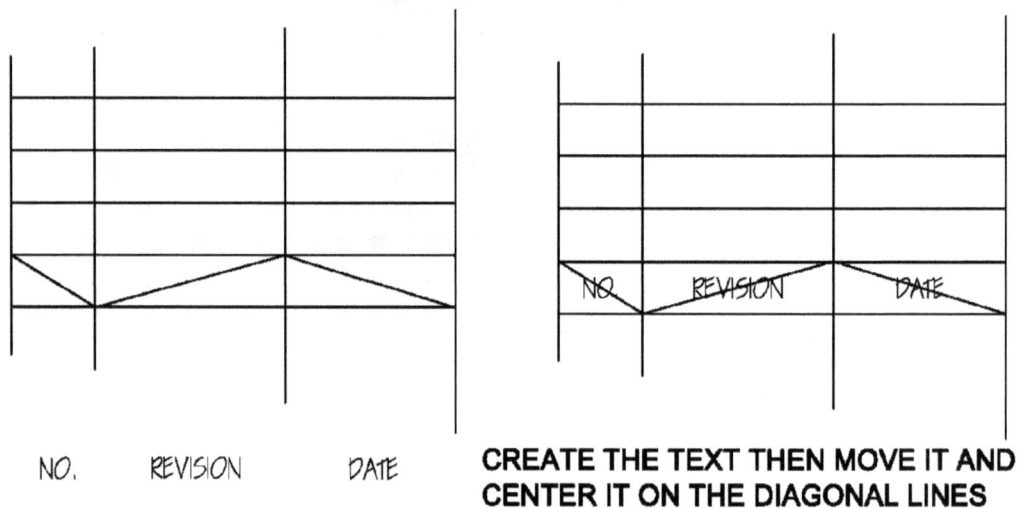

NO.   REVISION   DATE

CREATE THE TEXT THEN MOVE IT AND CENTER IT ON THE DIAGONAL LINES

Fig 9-9

Create the **text** shown in **Fig 9-10**. Set the **Text layer current**. Use the text sizes shown. Make the number **2** five feet in height (**5'**). For now **set** this **text** by **eye**. We could set up grids or other reference lines to place each piece of text precisely but you should be able to set it by eye so that it looks good—turn off the Ortho and the Osnap to do this.

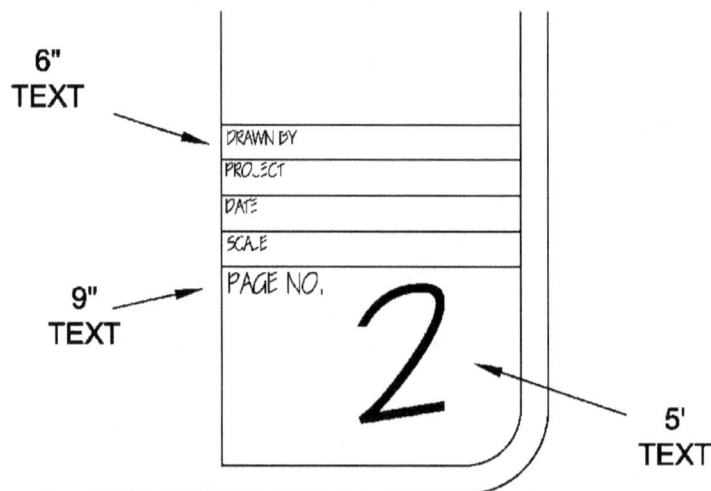

Fig 9-10

Now round off the lower left corner using the **fillet** tool set to a **2'** radius as in **Fig 9-11**. Repeat the process at the top of this line.

That's it for the title block and border. It should look like Fig 9-1. Don't worry if it is not exact—you will probably create your own customized block in any event.

Fig 9-11

This border and title block is sized for plotting at the scale of ¼" = 1'. The other scale we will be plotting is 1/8" = 1'. So let's make a **copy** and **scale** it up by a **scale factor** of **2**. Select the entire copy and use the **scale** tool. The **scale factor** is **2**. This is shown in Fig 9-12.

Fig 9-12

Sometimes when you scale up text it blows up into a strange configuration. If you have this problem you may have to erase and re-enter some of the text in the larger size.

We are now ready to print out a few pages in their completed form. That we will do in the next chapter.

Chapter 10—Plot Sheets

This is going to be another quick chapter with no sub sections. In Chapter 9 we created the title block, now we will use it to create a complete set of plans. Fig 10-1 shows a completed title block.

Fig 10-1

There are many different styles of title blocks. You will probably design your own or use one that is designated by the boss. What is important here is to see how to create different sized title blocks to plot out with the different scaled drawings.

What follows is my personal technique. I prepare the entire page with the title block in model space and then print it all in one viewport. Most designers probably create a separate viewport for the title block and another for the drawings.

There are a number of reasons why I like this method. The most important reason is that it creates a graphic image of what the finished pages of the plans will look like. You can see all the pages laid out side by side. They can be adjusted and fine tuned—details and views can be moved from one page to another to create a set of plans that is balanced, logical, and easy to read.

The first step is to create one title page for each page of the plans. This is demonstrated in **Fig 10-2**. Here you see eight title blocks scaled for ¼" = 1' plotting and one laid out for 1/8" plotting. They are copies of page 2 except the large one at the top, it is the scaled up version that you created in Chapter 9.

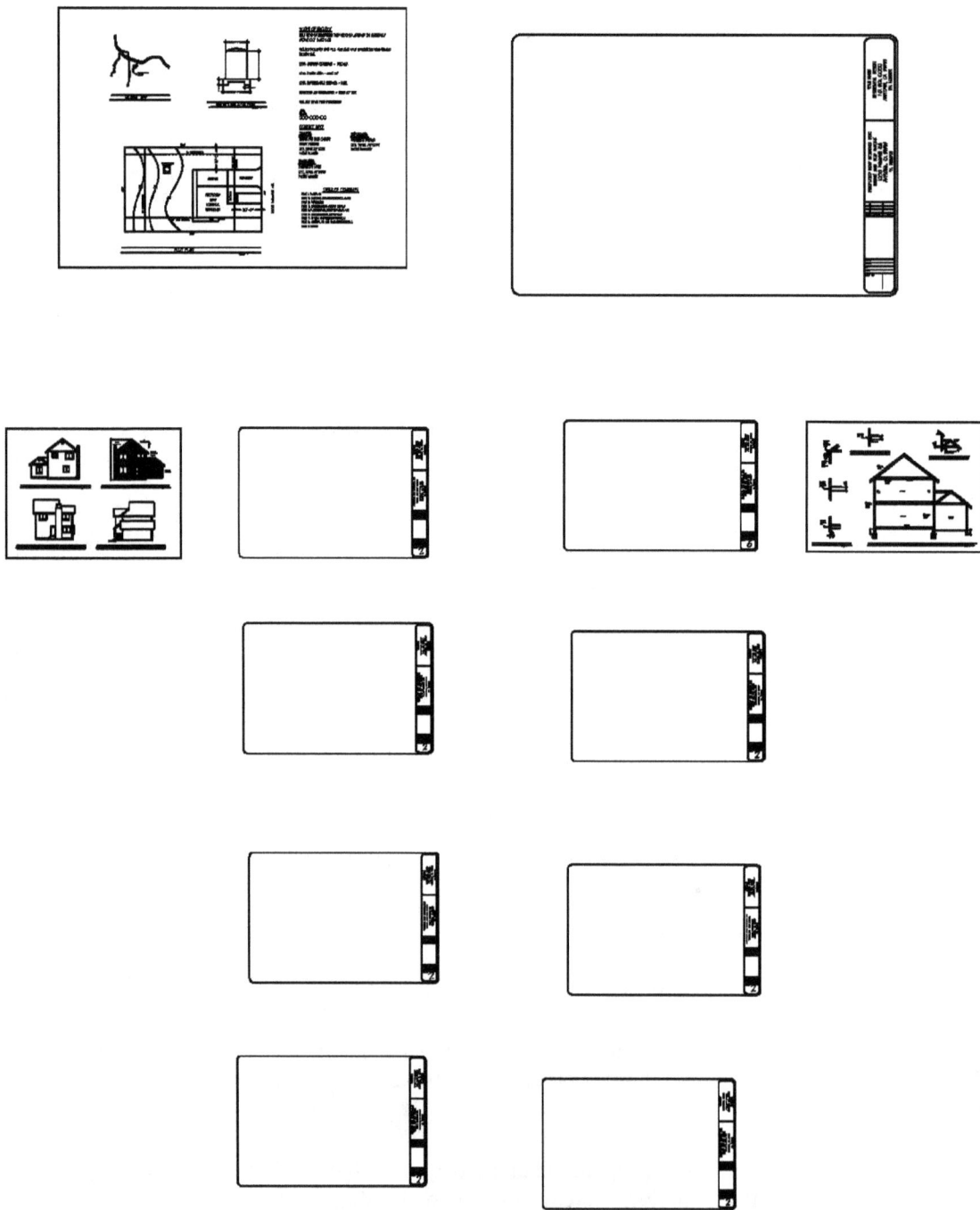

Fig 10-2

Also in Fig 10-2 you see that I have copied the pages we have already prepared for plotting—the elevations (chapter 6), the Cross Section and Details page (Chapter 7) and the Plot Plan (Chapter 8)—and placed them alongside their respective title blocks.

The large title block at the top of Fig 10-2 is for the Plot Plan page because that page will be plotted at 1/8" scale or half the scale of the ¼" pages. So it needs to be twice the size. More on this in Chapter 13.

Copy the block for the elevations into the border as shown in **Fig 10-3**.

Before you copy the block, check the large rectangle (A) surrounding the elevations drawing to make sure that it is on the construction layer. If not, place it on that layer by clicking on A then selecting the construction layer.

Now **copy** it into the title block border as shown in **Fig 10-3**. Click the **Copy** button then select the whole elevation block, **Grab** it at **A** and snap it to **B** (both midpoints). Osnap must be on for this.

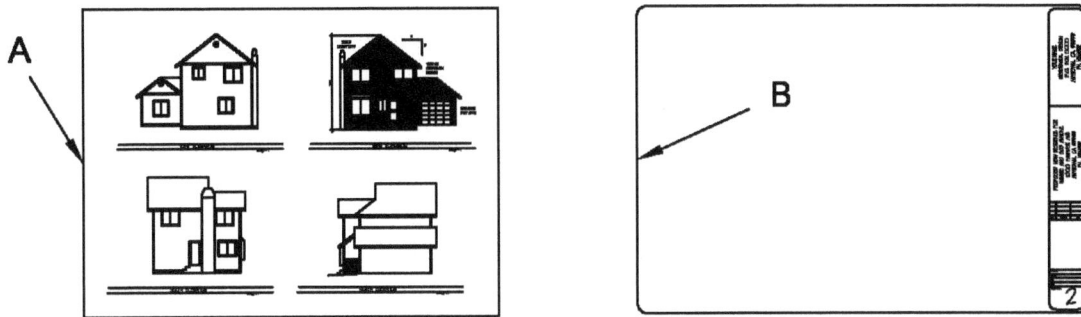

Fig 10-3

Erase the **construction layer rectangle** (A in Fig 10-3).

Now we are going to add a bit more text to the page. Use **mtext** and create the text shown in **Fig 10-4** then move it to the center of the diagonal line as shown. Make this text **18"** in height and **bold**.

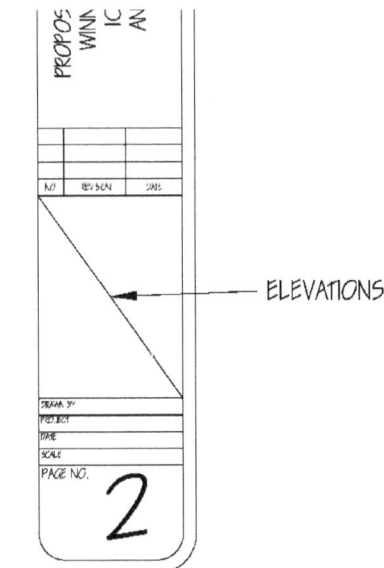

Fig 10-4

The page number (**2**) is **5'** in height.

Now create the other **text** shown in **Fig 10-5** and set it by eye. Make this text **9"** in height.

Fig 10-5

Now we will prepare the **Plot Plan** page as shown in **Fig 10-6** (the large **page 1** at the top). All the text is twice the height as page 2. Use **36"** height text for the page title (PLOT PLAN), 10' for the page number (1), and **18"** text for the rest of the added text.

Fig 10-6

To create the title block for page 6 (below and to the right of page 1 in Fig 10-2), copy all of the new title block text from page 2. You can copy it **all at one time** by using the **copy** tool, then **selecting all** the new **text** and <e>. Use any osnap icon for the **base point** (the midpoint on the right border is a good choice), then snap it to the same relative point on the page 6 border/title block that you see in Fig 10-2.

Once you have copied it, edit the text as necessary. Change the **number** to **6** and the **title** to read as in **Fig 10-6A**.

Fig 10-6A

Now we are ready to plot these pages. Go to the **36 x 24 layout** (click on the layout tab). Set the **space** to **Paper** and **type z <e> a <e>**.

Set the space to **Model** and approximately center the Elevations **page (2)** you just created. Select the ¼" = 1' **scale** from the **Viewport scale** window (see Figures 6-11 and 6-12).

Adjust the drawing to be centered as in **Fig 10-7**.

If the viewport is not large enough—if you can't see the entire border—you can click on the line that represents the viewport (you must be in paper space to select the viewport) then right click to bring up the **Properties** window. Reset the width and height as needed. The paper is 3' x 2', so your viewport can be anything under that. Our border is ½" all around so the **viewport** needs to be **2' 11 ¾" x 1' 11 ¾"**.

Don't confuse the margins lines with the viewport lines. The margins lines are broken (sometimes the settings change spontaneously); they show the limits of the printing area for the printer.

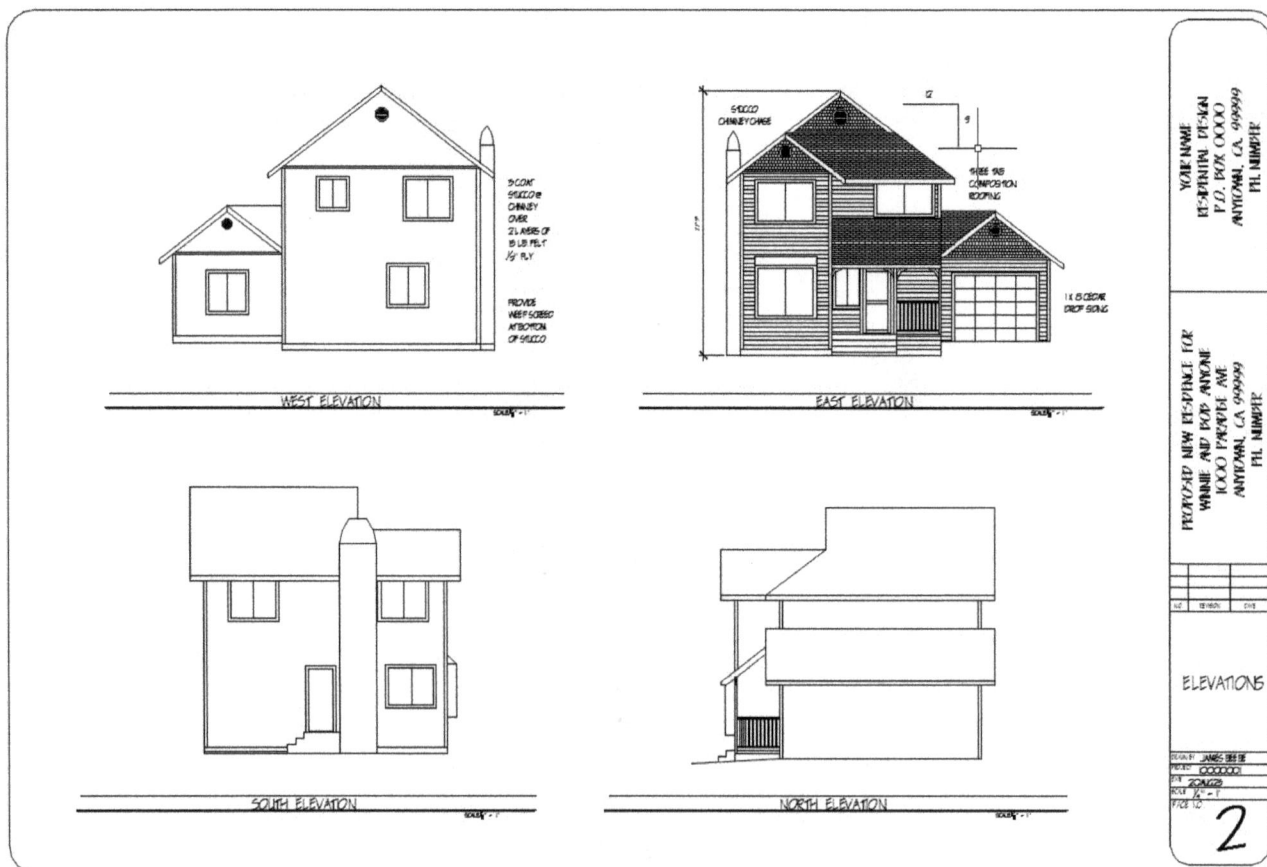

Fig 10-7

This time when we plot we will check to make sure that the **viewport layer** is **turned off** in the Layers Properties Manager dialog box—click on the printer icon so it has a red mark on it (see Fig 6-9A).This is an easy one to miss and you won't see the extra line until they plot your pages at the printer (bummer alert!)—so check it every time before you begin to Plot.

And while you are in the Layers Properties Manager make sure that nothing is turned off that you want to print. Sometimes there are glitches in the system and layers get turned off by the cyber pixies.

Now you can plot this to file (if you so choose) and save it somewhere on your computer where you can find it.

Now center the **Plot Plan** page (1) in this same 36 x 24 viewport and select the **1/8" = 1' scale** from the viewport scale window. Center it and it is ready to plot.

Well there you have it—if you can do this then you are ready for drafting. The next few chapters wrap up some details. Two import details to look at are the **Text spacing adjustment** (Chapter 11) and **Tables** (Chapter 12).

Chapter 11—Line Spacing and Shading

This chapter covers two **essential** skills. We will draw the second story joist framing view of the plans to demonstrate them. Figure 11-1 shows a partially completed Second Story Floor Framing Plan.

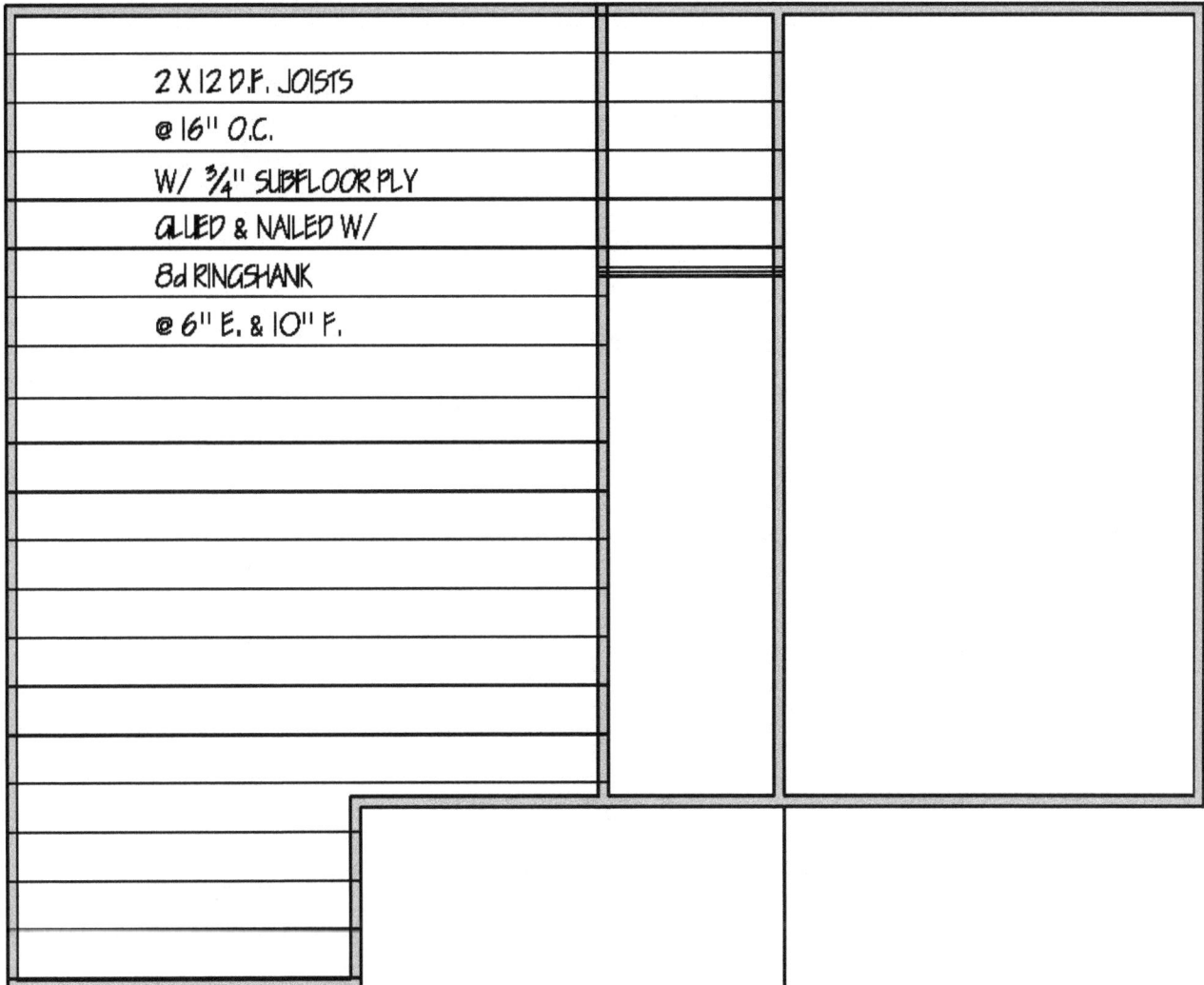

2 X 12 D.F. JOISTS
@ 16" O.C.
W/ ¾" SUBFLOOR PLY
GLUED & NAILED W/
8d RINGSHANK
@ 6" E. & 10" F.

Fig 11-1

Use the **copy** of the Floor plan that you made in Chapter 1 (Fig 1-15) and make another copy for this drawing.

Often shading is used in drafting to help create a quicker understanding of what is being depicted in a drawing.

We covered shading a bit in Chapter 3, here we will review it briefly.

Set the **Hatch layer current**.

Click on the **Gradient** tool and open the **Hatch Creation** ribbon. Select the **Solid tab** at the top (Fig 11-2). Click on the down arrow next to the **Use Current** button (co-located with By Layer and By Block).

Now click on the button shown at **C** . That will open the **Select color box** shown in **Fig 11-3**.

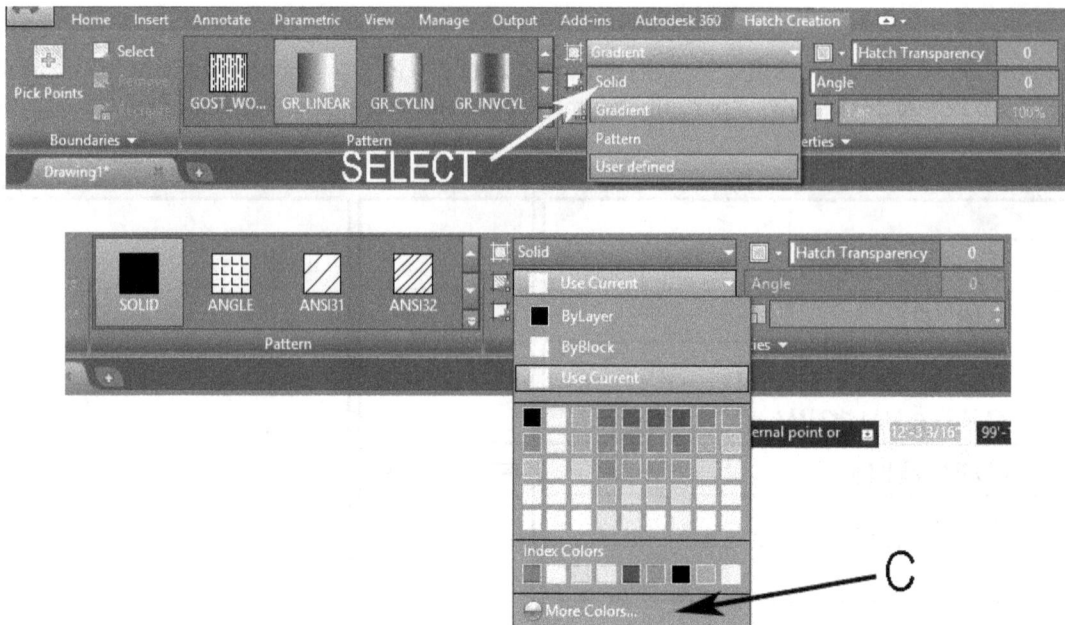

Fig 11-2

In the **Index Color tab** select the **blue** color as in **Fig 11-3**.

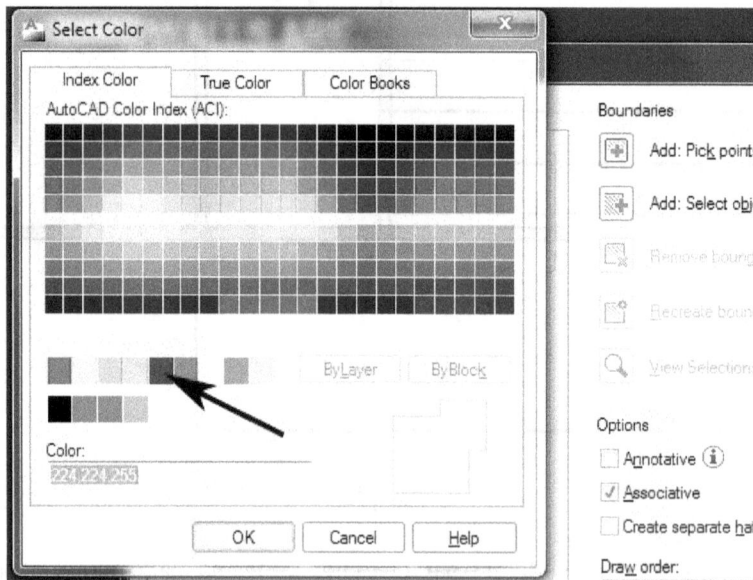

Fig 11-3

Now open the **True Color** box and set the **Luminance** to **97** as in **Fig 11-4**. **OK**.

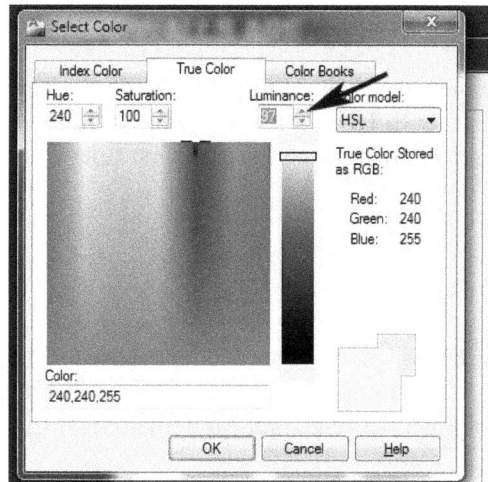

Fig 11-4

You need to set the luminance to very light if you want a shading, anything below about 95 may print out as solid black and you will not be able to see the lines that cross the shading. You printer may work in a different manner so you will need to run a test sheet to find out what luminance setting works.

Click on the **Pick points** button .

Back at your drawing, **select** any point **inside** the 3.5" **walls** (they are all one space) as in **Fig 11-5**. The space between the wall lines should fill with a very light shade of blue. If this does not work see Appendix I—Gradient.

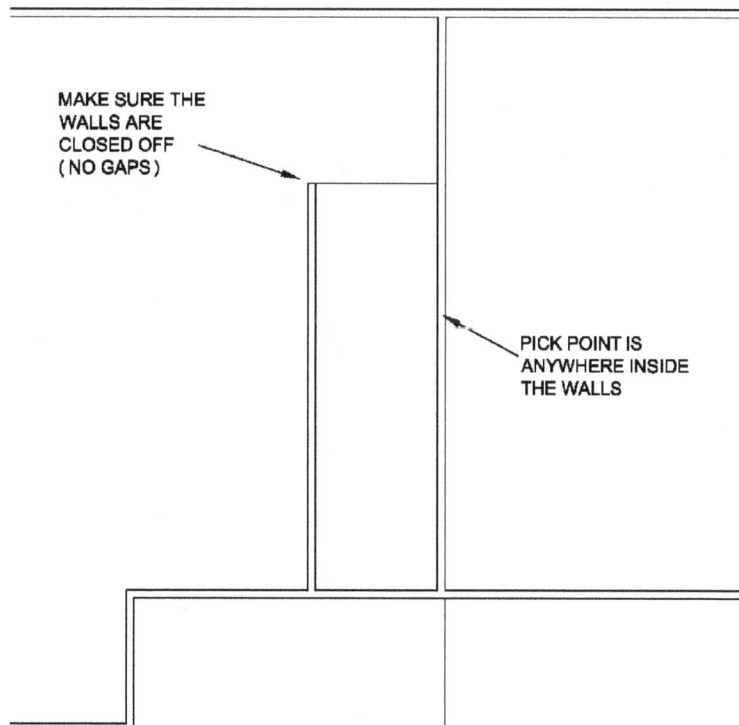

Fig 11-5

197

Turn off the **Hatch layer**.

Set the **0 layer current** and draw the lines that represent the joists (don't draw the three short lines at the stair well). Start at the top and use the **offset** set to **16"**. Read the prompts and use the **Multiple** option so you can just click for each line without having to select anything. Offset the first time from the top horizontal line.

Turn the **Hatch layer on**.

Now we will add the text. Turn **off** the **Osnap**.

Set the **Text layer** current. Above the drawing a bit, **type** the text shown in **Fig 11-6**. Use **7.5"** for the **text height** and **bold**. **Copy** as shown by placing the first line halfway between two lines (place this by eye). The rest of the text will run into the lines as shown in Fig 11-6. We want each line of text to be centered between two lines.

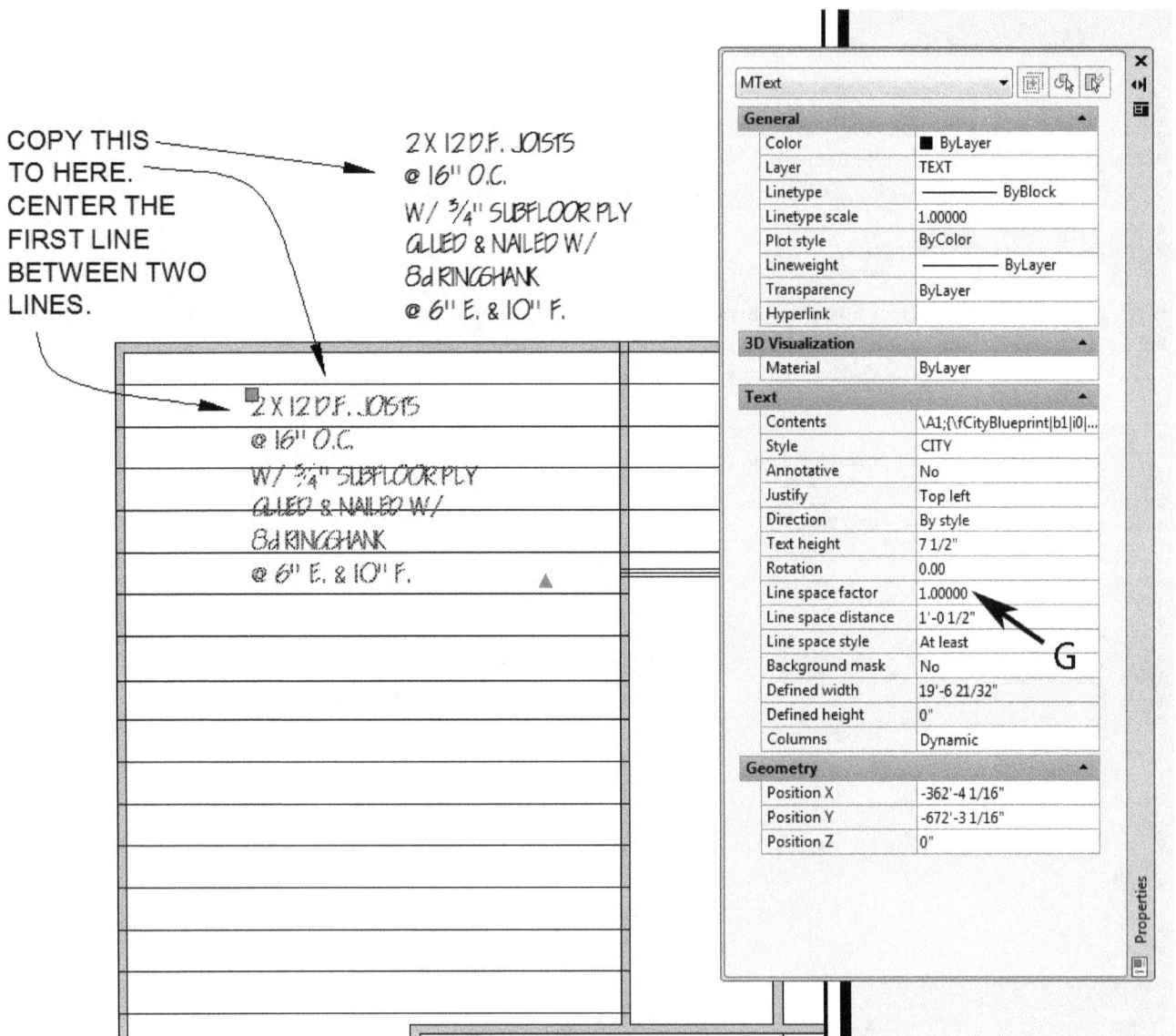

Fig 11-6

198

In order for the text to fit as in Fig 11-1 we must **adjust** the **spacing**.

Click on the **text** and then **right click** the mouse. In the drop down box select **Properties**. In the properties box, scroll down to **Line Space Factor** as in **Fig 11-6**. Change the setting to read **1.25** and <e>.

Now you will see the text as it appears in **Fig 11-1**.

That is it for this chapter. These are relatively simple tasks when you know how to perform them, but they can be difficult to figure out.

Chapter 12—Tables

12.1 Tables

There is a lot of information that is best displayed in table format. The Tables tool makes this easier because it automatically draws the lines and centers the text in each cell.

One of the most common tables on a set of plans is the window schedule. That is what we will create in this chapter. It is shown in Fig 12-1.

WINDOW SCHEDULE					
ROOM	SIZE	S.F.	TYPE	MATERIAL	GLAZING
LIVINGROOM	2-6 X 4-0	10	SLD	VYNYL	DUAL
	6-0 X 5-0	30	SLD	VYNYL	DUAL
	5-0 X 4-0	20	SLD	VYNYL	DUAL
KITCHEN	4-0 X 3-6	14	SLD	VYNYL	DUAL
UPSTAIRS HALL	6-0 X 3-0	18	SLD	VYNYL	DUAL
BEDROOM 1	6-0 X 4-0	24	SLD	VYNYL	DUAL
	5-0 X 4-0	20	SLD	VYNYL	DUAL
BEDROOM 2	5-0 X 4-0	20	SLD	VYNYL	DUAL
	5-0 X 4-0	20	SLD	VYNYL	DUAL
UPSTAIRS BATH	3-0 X 3-0	9	SLD	VYNYL	DUAL
GARAGE	4-0 X 4-0	16	SLD	VYNYL	SINGLE

Fig 12-1

In model space click on the **Table** button on the **Annotate** ribbon. This will open the **Insert Table** box shown in **Fig 12-2**.

In the lower right area you see the **Set cell styles** section. You can see that the first row is set to Title, the second to Header, and the third to Data. The Preview window to the left shows what this looks like.

The Title designation creates a full open row with a larger size font. The headers are the same width as the data columns but taller to accommodate a larger font size than the data entries. You can see how this looks in Fig 12-1. There are three different font sizes. The headers are the top row below the title.

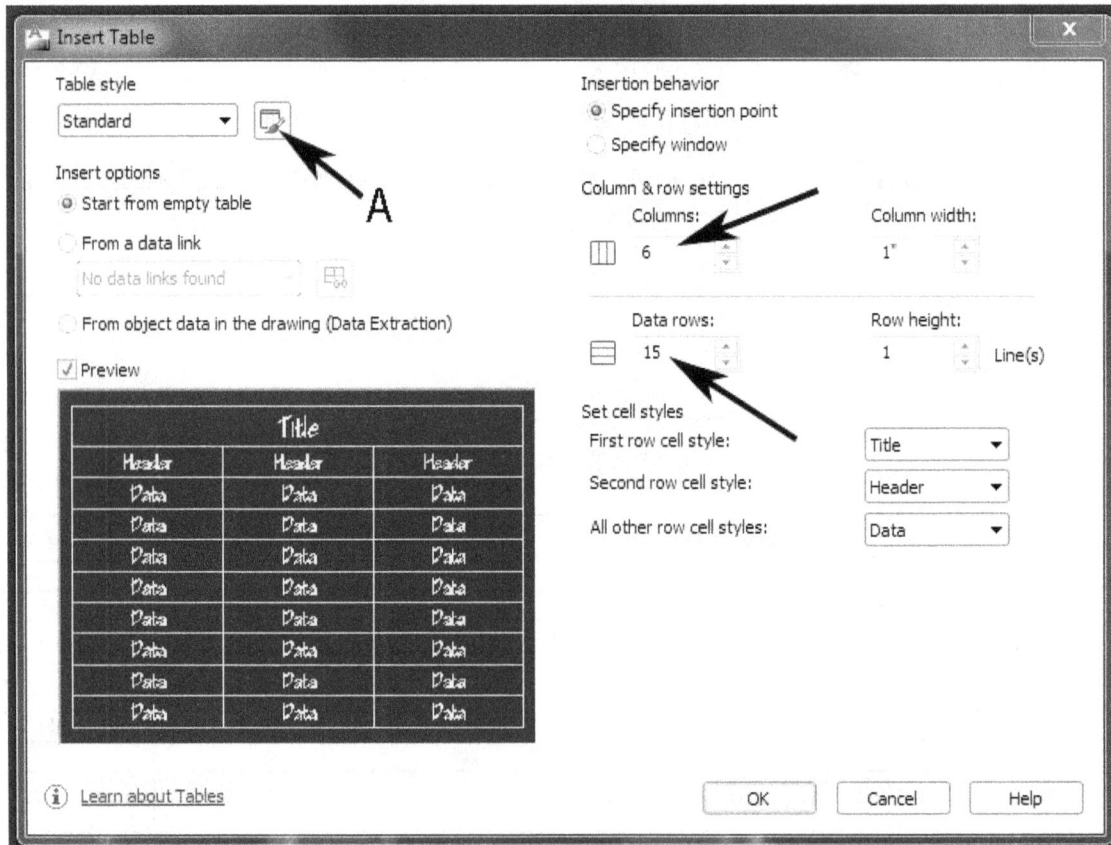

Fig 12-2

Set the **columns** to **6** and the **rows** to **15** as shown in **Fig 12-2**. You can double click on the number and over write it. Set the **column width** to **2.5"**. Click on the button shown at **A**. The **Table Style** dialog box will open and click on **New**. Name the new style **window** then **Continue**. The **New Table Style** window will open. Here is where many of the basic settings are to be found. Click on the three different tabs (General, Text, Borders) and explore the options. The **Format** (under the General tab) is important because it will determine how numbers are displayed (set it to General for now). **Text style** should be set to **City Blueprint** (click on the button next to the Text Style window to find the fonts). Under the **Borders** tab set borders to the **First button** on the **left** for borders all the way around (in the row of buttons that show the border style options). **OK**. Then **Set Current**. **Close**.

Recheck the column and row numbers in the first window. There seems to be a glitch that changes them as you go back through the dialog boxes.

Click on the workspace screen and a table will appear—it will be very tiny so pay attention to where you click, so that you can find it later. Zoom in.

You will need to add some rows to your table (this is for practice—obviously you would set the correct amount in the set up). You can do this with the **Insert Row** button on the **Rows Palette** as shown to the left side of **Fig 12-3**. **Click** on the **table** once, then wait and click on the table again to open this palette. Table is a strange function. One of the oddities is that clicks will bring up one of four different Palette/windows. Two rapid clicks will bring up the Properties palette if you are clicking on a line and it will bring up the Text Editor ribbon (and Text Formatting palette if you have it set to show up) if you click in a cell. A bit tricky and you will have to experiment to see how it works. If you click once on a line you bring up the grips and you can change the cell sizes manually (turn off osnap). When you click once inside a cell it opens the Table Cell formatting ribbon.

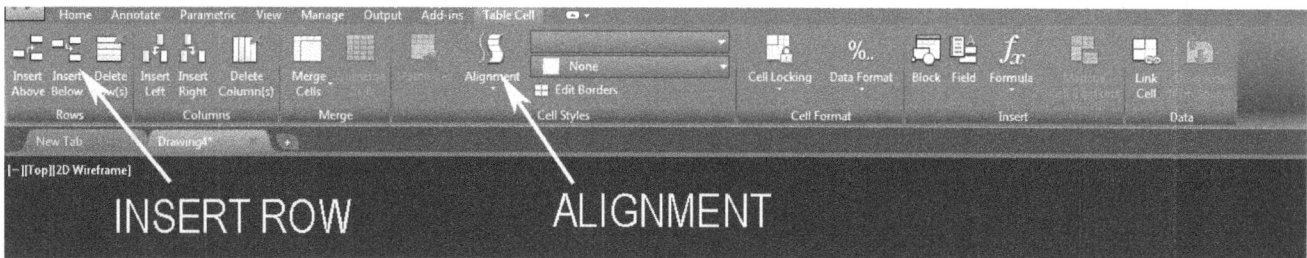

Fig 12-3

Click inside a cell and then the Insert Below button on the Rows palette.

Now **fill in the cells** as shown in **Fig 12-1**. To bring up the **Text Formatting** ribbon/palette you have to double click in the cell to get it to come up. Use **bold**. To use bold text (best with City Blueprint or other light fonts) you need to set it each time you type into a cell. Or use the Match Properties function described below.

You don't need to fill them all for this exercise; just a few will suffice for learning.

You can use the arrow buttons on your computer keyboard to toggle around the table.

When you put the numbers in the **SIZE column** they may want to justify to the right. To center them in the cells click on the table, then on the letter at the **top** to select the entire column (as in C in Fig 12-4). Then on the **Table palette/bar** select **Alignment** (Fig 12-3) and select the **Middle Center** setting—the entire column should justify to center.

	A	B	C	D	E	F
1	WINDOW SCHEDULE					
2	ROOM	SIZE	S.F.	TYPE	MATERIAL	GLAZING
3						
4	LIVINGROOM	2-6 X 4-0	10	SLD	VYNL	DUAL
5		6-0 X 5-0	30	SLD	VYNL	DUAL
6		5-0 X 4-0	20	SLD	VYNL	DUAL
7						
8	KITCHEN	4-0 X 3-6	14	SLD	VYNL	DUAL
9						
10	UPSTAIRS HALL	6-0 X 5-0	18	SLD	VYNL	DUAL
11						
12	BEDROOM 1	6-0 X 4-0	24	SLD	VYNL	DUAL
13		5-0 X 4-0	20	SLD	VYNL	DUAL
14						
15	BEDROOM 2	5-0 X 4-0	20	SLD	VYNL	DUAL
16		5-0 X 4-0	20	SLD	VYNL	DUAL
17						
18	UPSTAIRS BATH	3-0 X 3-0	9	SLD	VYNL	DUAL
19						
20	GARAGE	4-0 X 4-0	16	SLD	VYNL	SINGLE
21						

Fig 12-4

Double click on the word **ROOM** to bring up the **Text Formatting** ribbon. **Highlight** the **text** (ROOM) and **change** the **text height** to ¼" on the **Style palette** and <e>. Click on the **Close Text Editor** (right of ribbon) to exit text formatting (or OK on the Text Formatting toolbar if you have it turned on).

Click on the **word Room** again to highlight this cell and **right click** and select the **Match Cell** option. Now **click** on the **other column titles** (with the text: SIZE, S.F., TYPE, etc...) they will change to the new text height. There is also a Match Cell button on the Table Cell ribbon.

Let's make the title a bit larger. **Double Click** on the text that says: **WINDOW SCHEDULE**, this opens the **Text Formatting** palette, **highlight** the **text** and **set the height to 3/8"** <e>. The border around the cell adjusts automatically to the larger size. You must click into open space or enter again to exit the text formatting ribbon.

If you want the **cell** block to be **taller** you can highlight it (you must click on the line not in the cell) and use the **grip box** at the top center to pull the box up (the grip box must be red to move it—click on the blue box to change it to red). Turn the Osnap off and the Ortho on when you do this or else it will want to snap back on itself.

Sometimes you will want to add a **subtitle** to the middle of the table; to do this, **click** on the table then **right click** on the row number as shown at **H** in **Fig 12-5**. Select the **Cell Style** and then **Title** as shown in Fig 12-5. This will give you a full open row for use as a subtitle or just as a space. Sometimes you will get a selection menu instead of the window shown, just close it and try again.

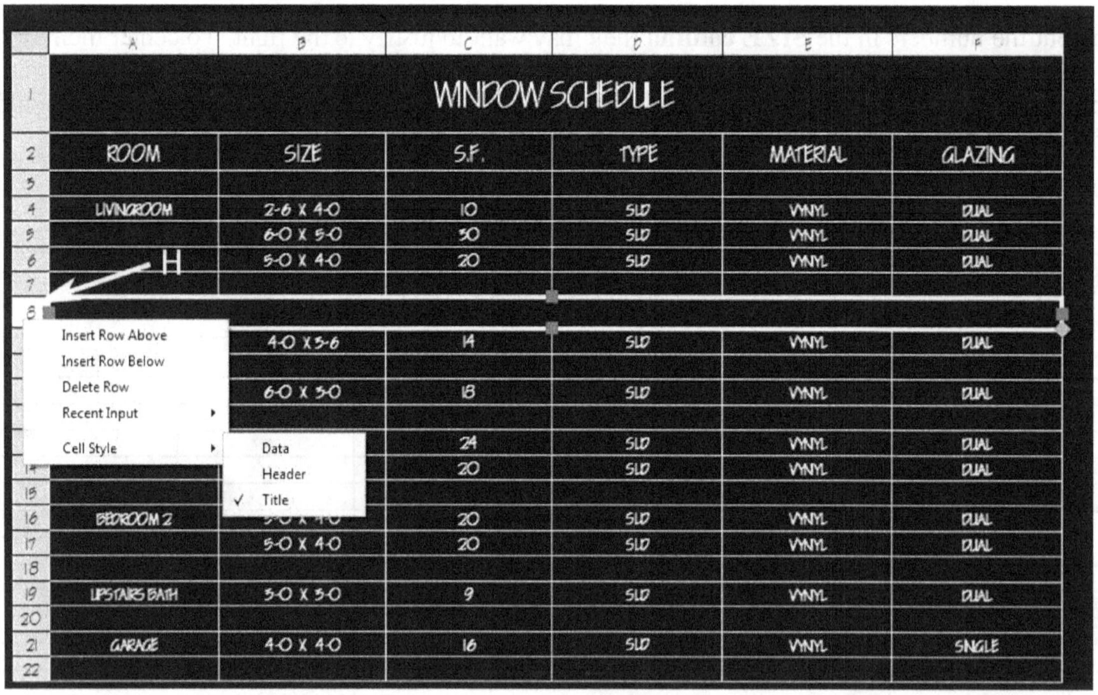

Fig 12-5

Check out the other settings in the Table Cell ribbon bar and also in the Table style dialog box. There are a number of options. The most important having to do with borders. Sometimes you won't want borders all the way around each cell. Play around with the options a bit, you can always Undo if you get into trouble.

If you click on a cell or a column or row heading then right click a box will open with a number of options. The Properties selection is at the bottom. The **Data Format** selection opens a Table Cell Format box where you can select the format for your cells. Try the different settings to see what this means. There is a monetary setting, text setting, and options for justification. Some settings will turn numbers into calendar dates or other automatic formats that you do not want. When this happens this is where you will find the solution.

You can also alter the cells and overwrite the text in the **Properties** box. Spend some time with the properties box to see what you can do—a lot.

Now we have our Window Schedule Table. Draw a large rectangle around it to mark it. Otherwise you may have a bit of trouble finding it on the screen as it is very small in relation to everything else you have drawn so far. Make the rectangle 10' x 10'.

Open up your **36 x 24 Layout** tab and find your table. Try some different scales to see what you have. 1:1 scale will place it on the page in its actual size. It is tiny at this scale.

How you scale any particular table will depend on what scale you will be using for the entire page.

We are going to place our table on page 7.

Make a copy and scale it up by a scale factor of 24. This page is going to be plotted at the ¼" = 1' scale. Look at Appendix IV—Page 7 to see what it looks like on the page.

There are a lot of settings and options in the Table function. The basics covered in this chapter should meet most needs. The best way to learn more about Tables is create some practice tables and spend some time exploring the settings.

Chapter 13—Scales

Scales can be rather confusing at times. The problem is compounded by the use of **imperial units** because they use **fractions** of an inch. Then, just to confuse things, the scales are described as ratios expressed as fractions of an inch to feet. So you can get a ¼" object scaled to ¼" = 1'. Even some mathematicians might have to stop and think about that.

You can use the **Annotative Text, Dimension and Leader** features. Annotative text is described in Chapter 16. Sometimes it is easier to use (for some purposes), but not always. In some cases it is easier to do the scaling manually. In any event, some understanding of scales as described in this chapter is important for most drafters. If you think that you will be using annotative text all the time, you may want to just skim through this chapter to get the general drift.

13.1 Scales, scales, scales

Scales in cad drawings only refer to the scale at which something is being printed or plotted. That's it. The size of the object is always the actual size. **The drawing is in actual size**. So the house we are drawing in the CAD program is 28 feet 3 inches tall and 34 feet wide. If you could step into model space, you would see a full sized building in there (not recommended). It is only the **printed picture** of your object that is **smaller**. Just as if you took a photo of your house from fifty feet away and then another from one hundred feet way. The house did not change size for the second photo, only the image size of the house in the photo is different.

You could get a large piece of cardboard and write on that cardboard in three foot high letters the word "TEXT". Then get your friend to stand next to the house and take a picture of the house at fifty feet away and another at one hundred feet. The letters are going to be much smaller in the photograph taken at one hundred feet. But **the proportion of the letters to the house will remain the same**.

1/8" = 1' Scale

Fig 13-1A

This is most of what we are dealing with in scales: the proportion of the text to the graphic drawing.

Figures 13-1A and 13-1B are a graphic depiction of this. 13-1A is printed at 1/8" = 1' and 13-1B is printed at ¼" = 1' (These are not exact because this is a word processing program, plotted they would be exact).

¼ " = 1' Scale

Fig 13-1B

This dashing character holding the sign is just under six feet tall in the actual size drawing space in AutoCAD. He is holding a sign that is 5' x 3' and the text letters are 12" in height.

If I print it again in 1/16" = 1 foot, it will look like Fig 13-1C. You can see that this guy's head is approximately level to the center of the window in all three views. Everything is proportionally the same.

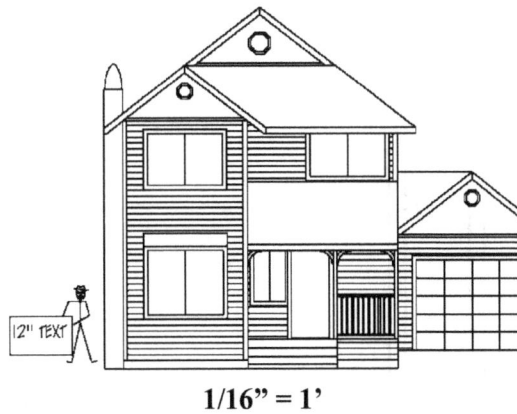

1/16" = 1'

Fig 13-1C

The text looks good in the 1/8" scale, but it is way small here in the 1/16" scale. Some people might want the text to be the size that it is in the ¼" scale; but no matter what size we prefer the text, we want it to be consistent on all the pages of our plans. We don't want little tiny letters on one page and huge letters on another.

Drawings typically use several different sizes of text on each page. The smallest is for detail notes like the window sizes on the floor plans. The next size up will be for notes like the joist and plywood notes that we spaced for the floor joist plan. The third size might designate room usage as in the floor plans; and then there is the size that is used for the view titles (NORTH ELEVATION, PLOT PLAN, etc...).

So say we want to use the following sizes of text on our plotted sheets: 1/8", 3/16", 1/4" , and 3/8". We want those four sizes of text on all of our pages even if they are to be plotted at a variety of scales.

When we create 12" text in the workspace it will plot or print at one quarter inch height when plotted at ¼" scale as shown in Figures 13-1B.

Don't stop here to think about this too long, keep reading and it will become clearer.

On the 1/8" scale the 12" text will be one eighth inch as in Fig 13-1A.

On the 1/16" scale the 12" text will be one sixteenth inch (Fig 13-1C).

You can see this on your Layout in Paper Space. Open a layout tab and center a drawing—use the floor plan—then select various scales for comparison. Select model space and use the Viewport scale to set various scales. Try ¼" = 1'. Then try 1/8" = 1'. Try 1/16" = 1'. You can print these from your 11 x 8.5 Layout and look at them in real plotted scale on paper.

So, in order for the text to be the same size on different scaled drawings we must adjust the size of the text; starting with the **1/4" = 1'** scale as a **base** point, we must make the text on the **1/8" = 1'** scaled drawing **twice** the size, and the text on the **1/16" = 1'** scaled drawing **four times** the size.

Fig 13-2 demonstrates this. The drawing is shown in three different scales but the **text is the same size**. Everything remains the same except the size of the sign and the letters on that sign. Compare this to 13-1A, 13-1B and 13-1C. As the house gets smaller on the printed page the proportional size of the letters must increase.

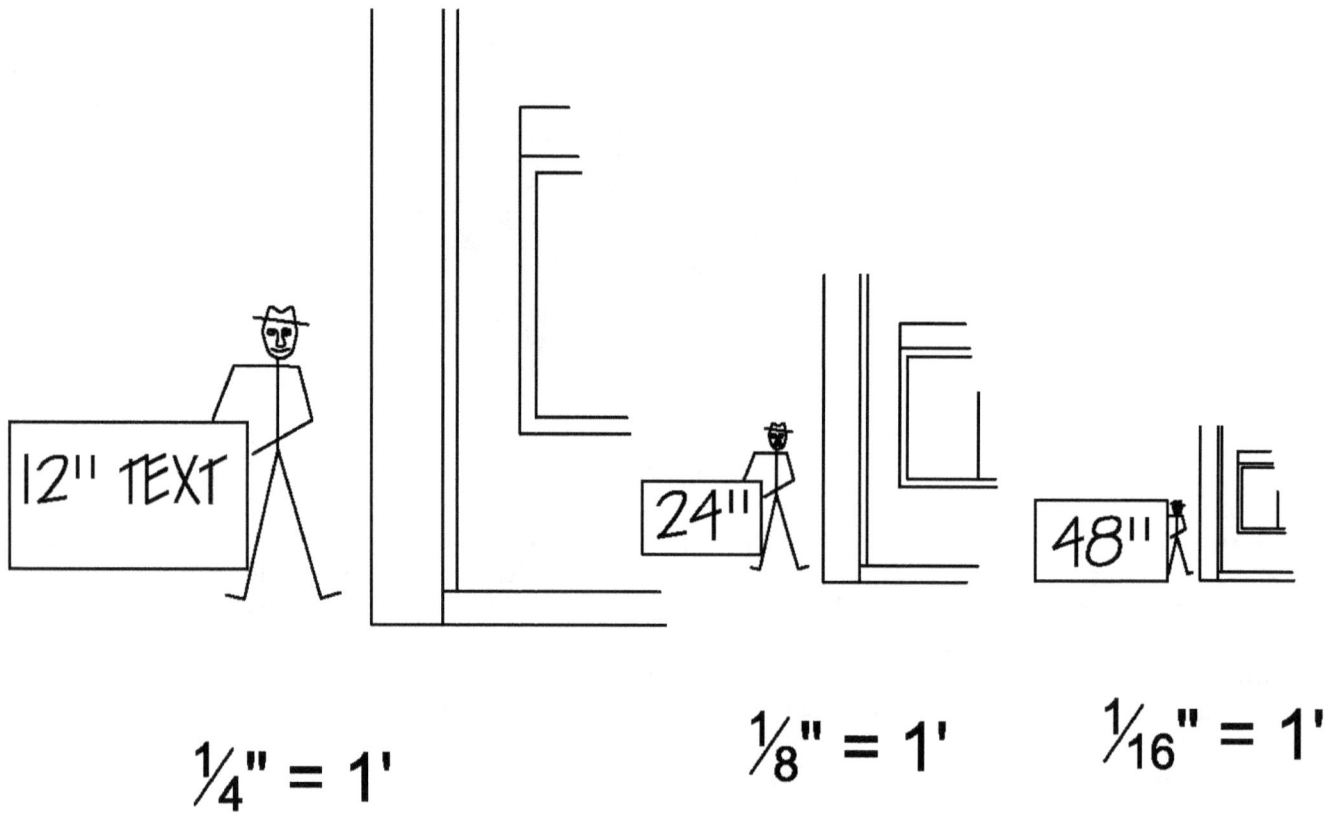

¼" = 1'   ⅛" = 1'   ¹⁄₁₆" = 1'

Fig 13-2

Figures 13-3 A, B, and **C** show another example of this using the same three scales **with no adjustment of the text**—the same scaling is used for the graphic and the text in these drawings.

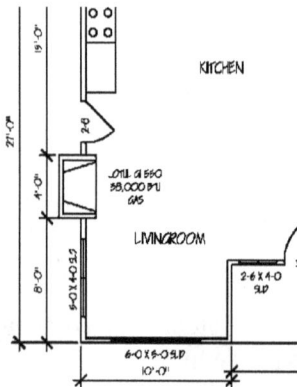

Fig 13-3A

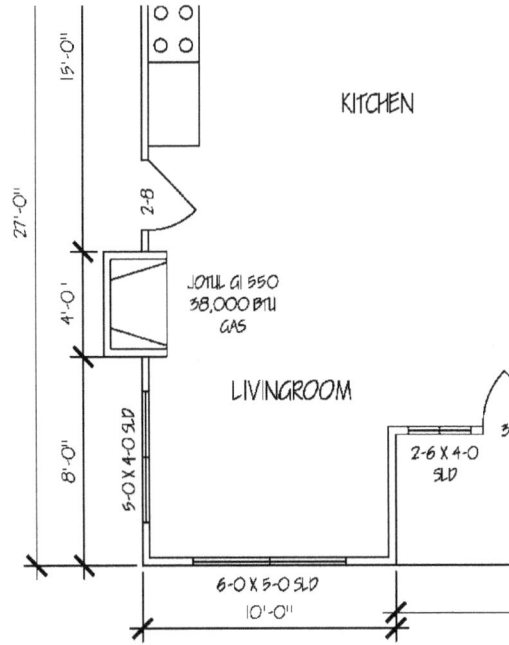

Fig 13-3B

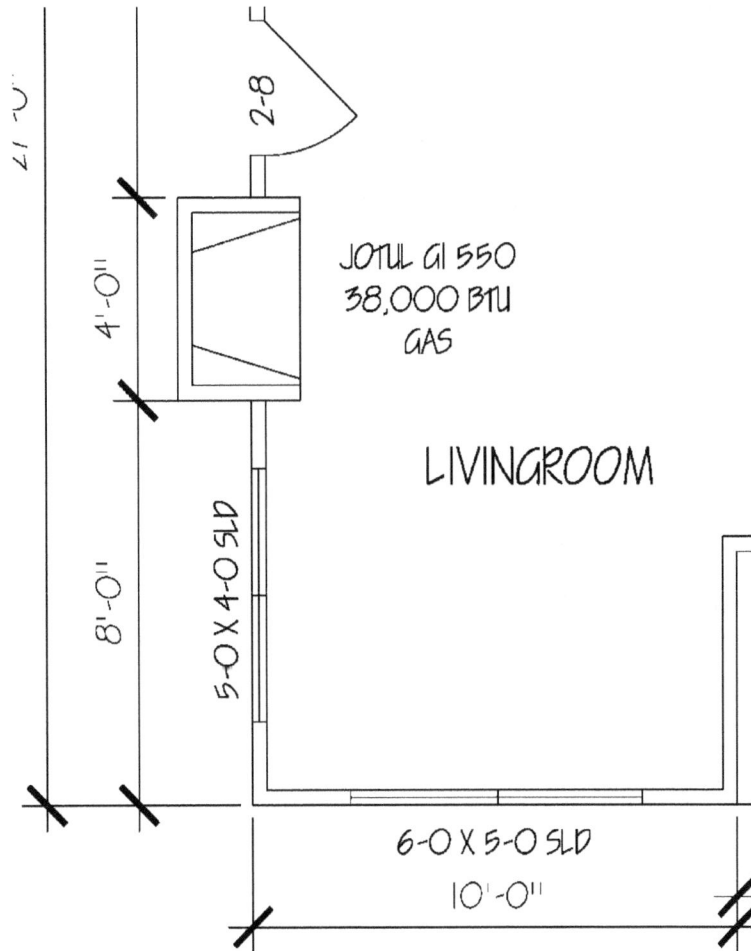

Fig 13-3C

These drawings are printed to scale here in the book (once again they are not exact because of the word processing software).

Fig 13-4 shows what this would look like on Page 7 of our plans, where we have four different scales on the same page, if we did not adjust the text height for each scale. Here the text is scaled at the same ratio as each graphic. The cross section is 2x the garage roof section, the sheer details are 3x, and the garage roof tie-in detail is 4x.

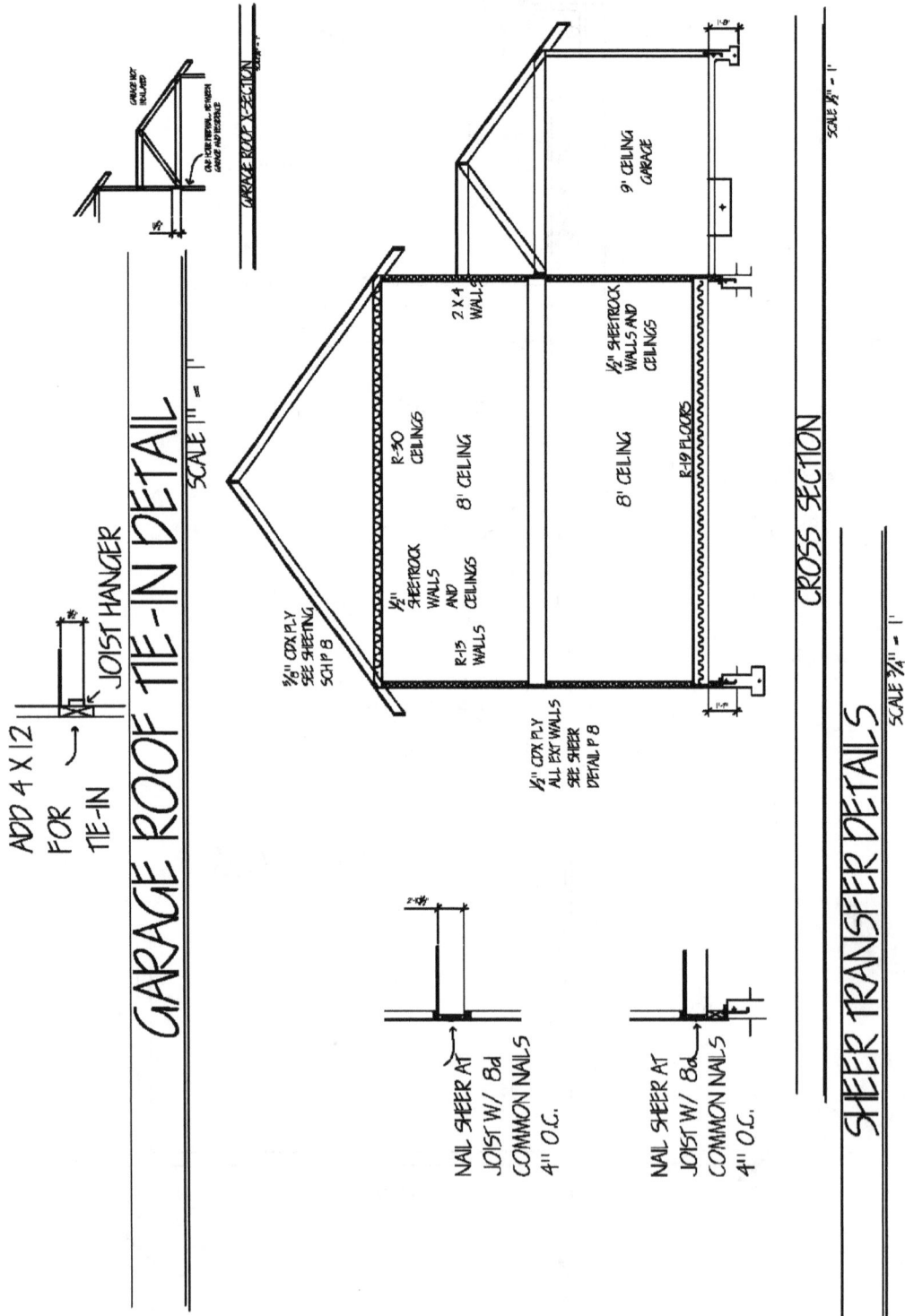

Fig 13-4

We want the text to be uniform for all the views as shown in Fig 13-5. Here the text is the same size in each view. Compare 13-4 and 13-5. So the **ratios** of the text size to graphic must be different for each view.

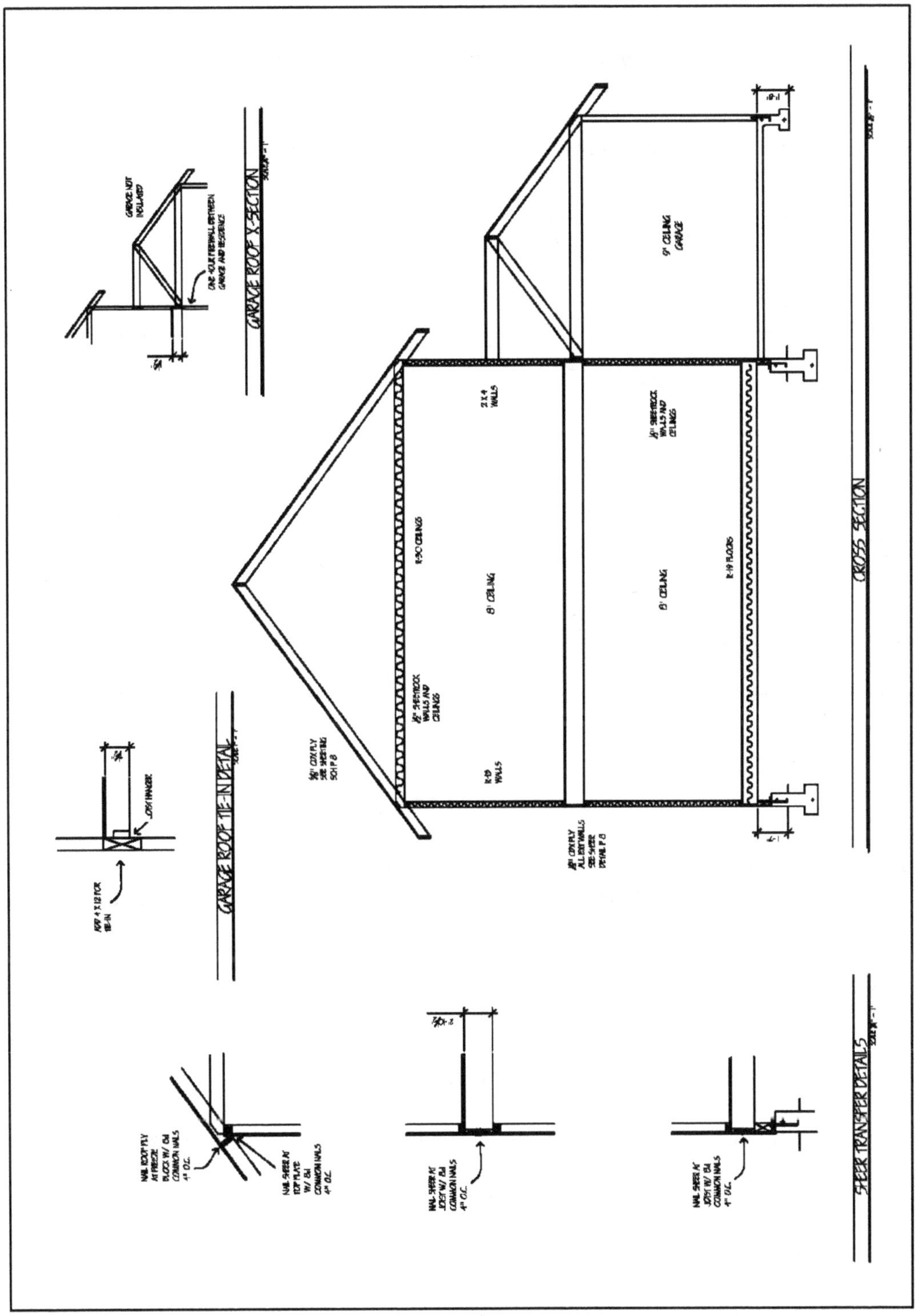

Fig 13-5

The same is true one page to another. We want the text on our plot plan (scaled at 1/8" = 1') to be the same as the elevation page (1/4" = 1').

The size of the text in the drawing area on the computer workspace must be proportional to the **scale** size **of the** *plotted drawing*. This requires that we know at what size the view or detail is to be plotted.

Fig 13-6 shows the height of text (**in inches**) used in the (actual size) workspace drawing to obtain the various plotted text size (on paper) in some of the more common architectural scales.

If you want text that is **1/8"** in a drawing that is **plotted** at ½" = 1' use **3** inch text in your model space. Read down the **column** that is titled **1/8" TEXT** until you come to the **row** that is titled ½" = 1', read **3**.

If you want 3/8" text in your final drawing that is to be printed at ½" scale, use 9" text in the workspace drawing.

TEXT HEIGHT (IN INCHES) BY SCALE						
	⅛" TEXT	³⁄₁₆" TEXT	¼" TEXT	⅜" TEXT	½" TEXT	1" TEXT
SCALE						
$\frac{1}{16} = 1'$	24	36	48	72	96	192
⅛" = 1'	12	18	24	36	48	96
¼" = 1'	6	9	12	18	24	48
½" = 1'	3	4.5	6	9	12	24
¾" = 1'	2	3	4	6	8	16
1" = 1'	1.5	2.25	3	4.5	6	12

Fig 13-6

It is easier to think of these ratios if you think of the 1 foot in the scales as 12 inches. ¼" = 1' is the same as ¼" = **12"**. In that way you can see the ratio. There are **four** ¼" in 1". There are **48** one **quarter inches** in **12 inches**. 4 x 12.

So, as you can see, we are talking about ratios. The **ratios** of all the scales shown here are the same as the numbers in the **1" TEXT column** in **Fig 13-6**.

To figure out the size of any text use the following formula:

Size of Plotted Text x Ratio of Scale = Text Height in Drawing

Translated to examples:

1/8" (.125 desired printed size of text) x 48 (ratio-1/4" = 1') = 6" (Typed Into Drawing)

3/8" (.375 Printed Text) x 24 (ratio for ½" = 1' scale) = 9" (Typed into Drawing)

The table has these already calculated for many sizes, but you will need to be able to figure out other sizes. Try it with some other ratios.

Let's say we have a drawing that will be plotted at 3" = 1'. And we want text that is ¼" in height. Use the formula shown. There are **four** 3" in 12" (1 foot). So our ratio for this scale is 4 (because 4 x 3 = 12).

¼" (.25 printed text size) x 4 = 1"

Drawings using the **metric system** work in the same way. Use the ratio of the scale to determine the printed text size just as you do in imperial.

In the metric system we simply scale everything to a ratio. For example a scale in metric that is relatively close to the ¼" = 1' scale would be 1:50 (1/4" = 1' is a ratio of 1:48).

So we use that number (50) in our formula to determine the printed text size in that scale of drawing.

Fig 13-7 shows the metric scale next to the imperial scale. This image is enlarged for clarity—it is not actual size.

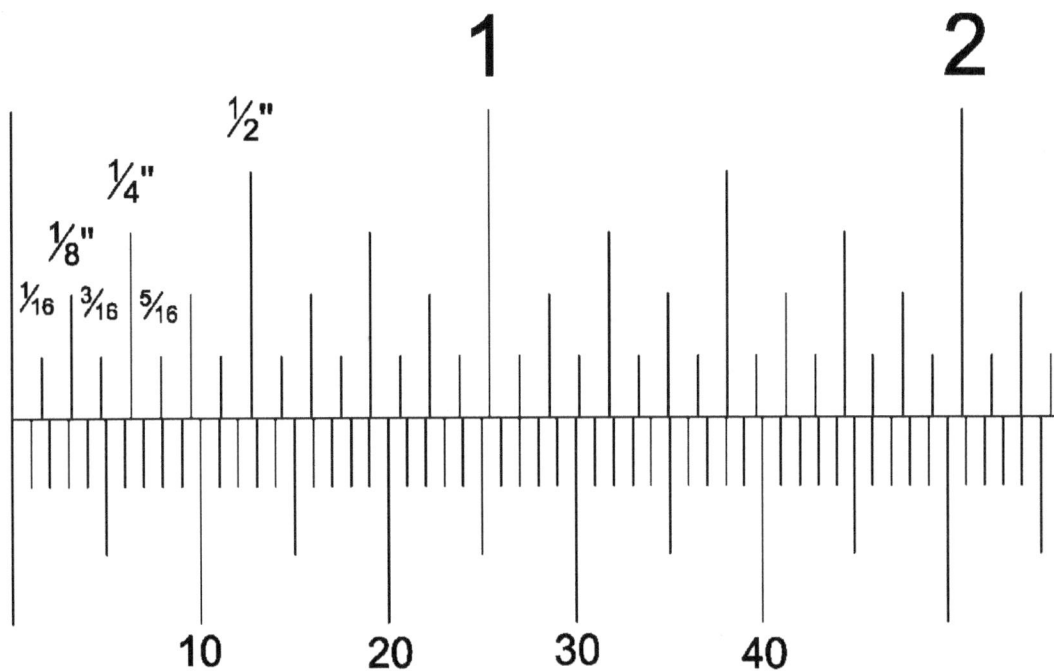

Fig 13-7

As you can see ¼" is close to **6 millimeters**. So if we want text that is similar to ¼" in a metric drawing depicted at a 1:50 scale we would make it 6 mm.

Now we can use the same formula as with imperial.

6mm (printed text) x 50 (scale ratio) = 300 mm (in model space)

The conversion from inches to metric is 25.4 mm = 1 inch. So let's check our numbers. 300 divided by 25.4 equals **11.81** inches. In the ¼" scale it was **12** inches, so we can see that is pretty close and just what we are looking for.

13.2 Leaders and Dimensions

I said at the beginning of this chapter that scales mostly affect text size, but they also affect **dashed** (or broken) **lines**, **leaders** and **dimensions**.

In the next chapter you can clearly see what this means in relation to leaders. The arrowheads become so small in some scales that you can't even see them. They must be scaled up or down to be the same size in each view, consistently, throughout the plans.

Leader sizes are set with the **dimensions styles.**

Dimensions must also be proportional to the scale of the plotted page, so you can **set the leaders** and the **dimensions** at **the same time.**

The most important information about setting up **dimensions styles** is this: the **"Use Overall Scale of "** setting. The number entered here must be the same number as the **ratio** of the scale to be plotted (this is the scale you will use in the viewport).

So for a page that is going to plot at ¼" = 1' use a ratio of 48. We already did this and you have a **quarter scale dimension style** already set up that we have been using.

The ratios for some other scales are the same as the 1" text column in the text size chart (Fig 13-6). For scales not on the chart you can figure them by dividing the number on the right side of the equal sign by the number on the left. ½" = 1' would be 24, because there are **24** one-half inches **in 12 inches** (one foot).

It is important to be able to figure out the ratio of any given scale because you will be confronted from time to time with less common scales like 1" = 10', 1" = 20', 1" = 40' or scales that are expressed as a ratio as in 1:5, 1:10.

Of course the scales expressed as ratios (1:5) *are* **the ratios** that you need for the text conversion.

These are not difficult once you understand the concept.

The ratios for the scales expressed as 1" = 20' are just the same. Twenty feet equals 240 inches (20' x 12" = 240). So the ratio for this scale is 240.

These are the numbers that you enter into the **Use Overall Scale of** window as shown in **Fig 13-8** at **V.**

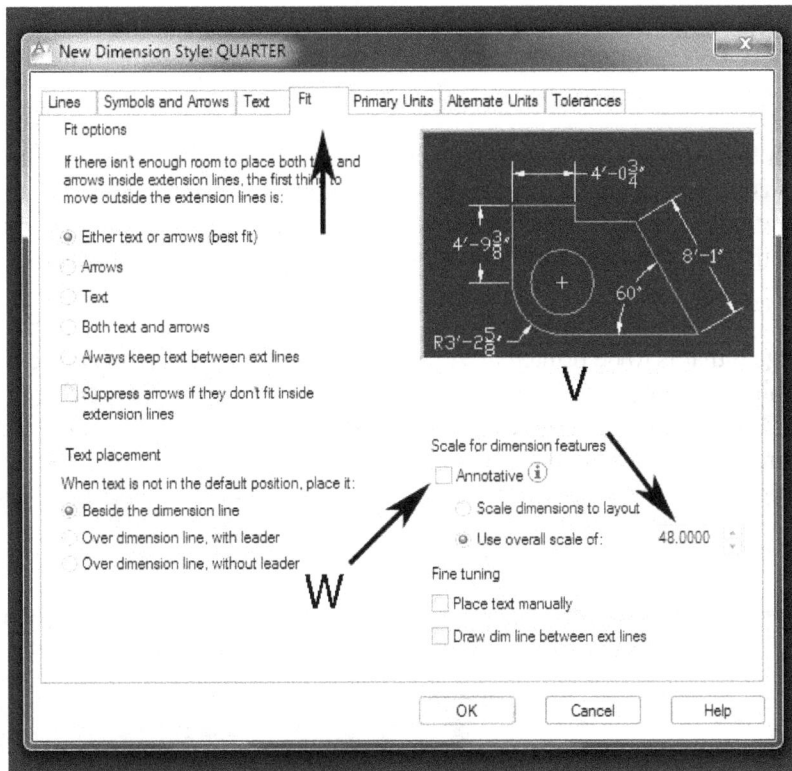

Fig 13-8

There are **two different ways** to **scale** a **drawing**.

Most often scaling is done in **paper space**. You set up a **paper space layout** for each different size of paper, and open a viewport on that layout. Then you **scale** that **viewport** (just as we have done in the chapters 6 through 10).

The other type of scaling is done in **model space** using the **scale tool**. That is what we did in chapter 7. The reason for doing it this way is to be able to plot the entire page in one viewport. The scaling up (or down) in model space is in relation to the **viewport scale** of that page.

This model space scaling was covered in chapter 7. But just to review a bit, when you scale in model space and you wish to add dimensions or leaders you must set the **Use Overall Scale of** to the **plotted scale**—the **scale** you will use in the **viewport**. Then, for the correct measurement to appear in the dimensions, you must adjust the **Scale factor** in the **Primary units** tab as shown in Fig 13-9. The scale factor entered there is the **inverse** of the **scale** used with the **Scale tool**. If we use the Scale tool and scale a drawing up in model space by a factor of 2, then the scale factor entered in the Primary units window will be .5. **Multiply the two numbers and you get a product of 1** (2 x .5 = 1). That is what you want every time.

Fig 13-9 shows the scale factor that we used in chapter 7 to create the dimensions for the ¾" = 1' detail on page six of our plans. We are plotting the entire page using the ¼" = 1' scale. Then we are scaling up three of the views in model space so they will print out larger and show more detail. Because we are **plotting** the **entire page** in one viewport at the ¼" = 1' scale, **everything** on that page is **scaled in relation** to the ¼" = 1' **scale**. The three quarters detail view was scaled up by **3** (3 x ¼ = ¾).

We need to use the **inverse** of that **ratio** in the **Scale of** window. We scaled the view up by 3 so we need to set the scale factor to the inverse or .333 to get a product of 1 (shown in **Fig 13-9**).

That is how the program knows the **dimension text** is the measure of the original size (actual size or real size) and that the scaled up version is merely for printing purposes. Otherwise, in this example, all the measurements will be three times the actual size.

You can experiment with this. Make a 12" rectangle. Add dimensions to it and then scale it up by a factor of 2. The dimension will read 24". Now open the dimension style box and change the Scale of: to read .5. Make sure to set this style current. Now erase the dimensions and redo the linear dimension; it will still read 12". You have informed the cad system that the scaling is for plotting purposes only and you have not simply decided to draw a 24" rectangle.

The **cross section** on **page 6** that is to be printed at ½' = 1' was scaled up in model space by a factor of **2** (2 x ¼ = ½). The house in this cross section is no longer 34' wide (the actual size), it is twice that size—68' wide— and that is how AutoCAD will measure it. The **dimension text will read 68'**unless you tell it, heh, this is just for printing purposes—we are not going to build a double sized building. So we set the scale factor in this case to .5. Then the program realizes that the measurement is actually one-half (.5) of the scaled up version and the text reads 34'.

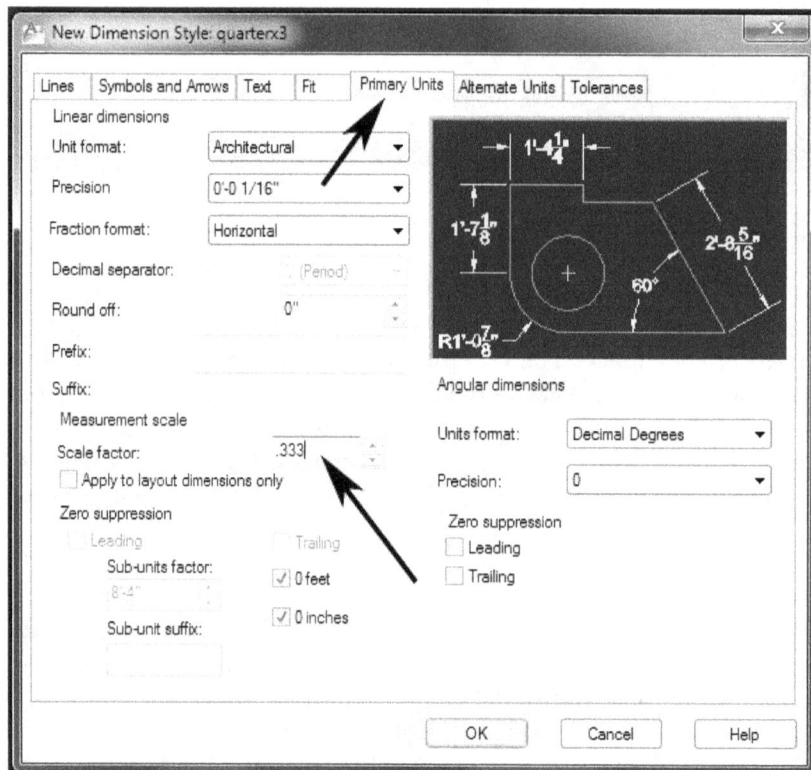

Fig 13-9

If you are only going to scale the drawing in a **paper space viewport,** not in model space, then you will set the **Scale factor** to one (1). Only use a number other than 1 in the **Scale factor** window if you are **scaling in model space**.

13.3 Dashed Lines

The other item that needs to be scaled is broken or dashed lines. The gross scale of a line can be set in the **Layer Properties manager** box. You can set up a new layer with a broken or dashed line and select one of several lines from the list. These lines vary in dimension.

You can then adjust that scale factor by using the **properties** box and adjust the **scale factor** for individual lines. You can use the **match properties** tool to transfer the scale to other lines (as opposed to opening the properties manger box for each line).

Remember that to print out dashed lines the **paper space line type scale** must be set to zero (**0**). You will want to **make a note of this** and remember it—it is one of those things that will drive you batty if you forget it and the dashed lines keep plotting as solid lines. Always check the Preview before you plot, it is frustrating to get your plans back from the printer and find all your dashed lines have been printed as solid.

If your dashed or broken lines are showing up as solid lines in paper space (or when you print them) type **psltscale** and enter **0** as the factor. Then **regen** the plans (very important to remember also). Type: regenall.

This is all you really need to know about scaling. It can seem a bit confusing at times. It is good to experiment a bit. Draw a rectangle and then use the scale tool to create a few sizes. Then set some different dimension styles and use the linear dimension tool and qleader. Print these out at different scales.

Try different settings on the **Fit tab** under **Use Overall Scale of:** and, under the **Primary Units** tab, try different settings for the **Scale factor**. With enough experimentation you will see the light.

In the next chapter we will go through a few more exercises to clarify these concepts.

For those of you who do not have a printer, you can set the paper space to the width of a piece of 8.5 x 11 paper. This will allow you to see what things look like when they are printed.

To do this, hold a piece of paper up to the screen and set the paper space to that width. You may need to change the setting on your mouse wheel to get the right size paper space. Type **zoomfactor** and set the factor to 5. This will allow you to fine tune zooming. Reset the zoomfactor to a larger number (40 or 50 is good) when you are done.

Even after you understand scales they can be confusing at times (for some of us). If things get confusing, go back to the concept of the printed/plotted page and the ratio between the plotted page and the **real size of the object**, then work things out from there. That should lead to clarity.

The next chapter deals with scaling in multiple viewports.

Chapter 14—Mulitple Viewports

This chapter demonstrates an alternative method of plotting a page with multiple views displayed in different scales. The method covered in Chapter 7 put everything on page 6 of the plans in one viewport, then we scaled that viewport to one scale (1/4" scale).

Now we are going to create a different viewport for each of the details and the cross section.

Start by creating a **new layout**; **right click** on the **36 x 24 layout tab**. On the menu that pops up click on "**New layout**". Wait, it sometimes takes a minute for the new tab to be created. **Click** on this **new tab** (it will be the tab furthest to the right). Once it opens **right click** on the **tab** and select the **Page Setup Manager. Click** on **New**. The **New Page Setup** window will open. **Name** the new layout **36 x 24 Multi**. In the **Page Setup** window that opens **set it** to look **like Fig 14-1**. Most of the settings will already be set from the 36 x 24 layout.

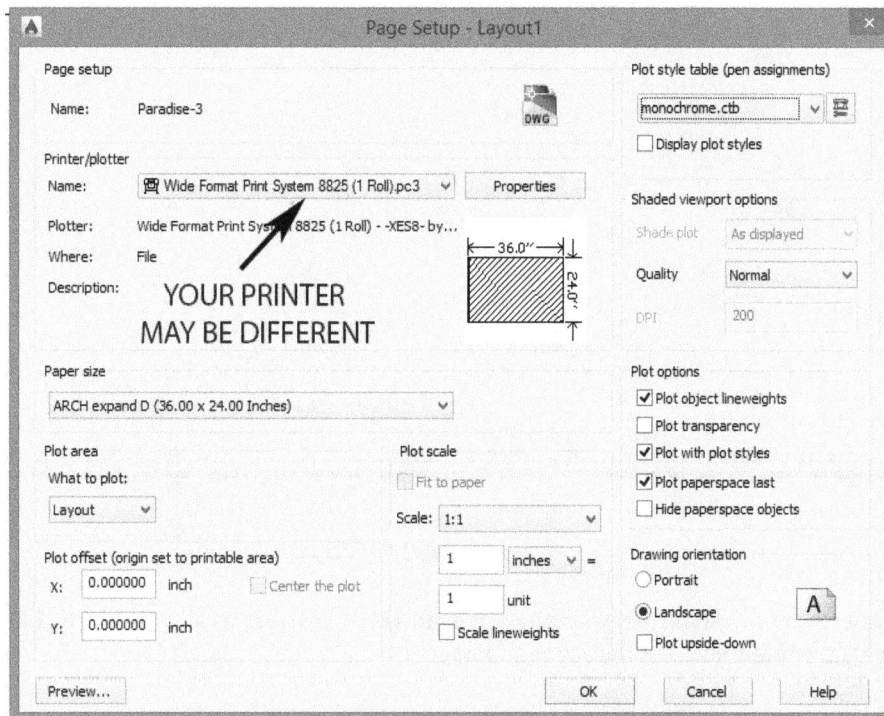

Fig 14-1

Your plotter setting may be different (if you set it up for your local print shop). This new page should have the same settings in the Page Setup as were used for your 36 x 24 layout. **Click** the **OK** button at the bottom. **Close** the Page Setup Manager.

Set the Model/Paper button space to **Paper** (B in Fig 6-8). **Type z <e> a <e>. Erase** the **viewport** that appears. Click on the viewport to select it (blue grip boxes appear) and erase.

Set the **viewport layer** current in the Layer Control at the top of the screen (Fig 1-1).

Create a new viewport that covers the entire page and center the **title block** and **border** as shown in **Fig 14-2**. To do this click on the Layout tab at the top of the screen and select Rectangular from the Viewports selection (or type vports and select Single). Rectangular is co-located with the Polygon and Object buttons. Scale this viewport to ¼" = 1'. If the entire border doesn't show then resize the viewport by clicking on it, then right click and select the Properties palette, here you can adjust the height and width. Switch to Model space to get the title block.

Fig 14-2

Now we are going to create **four separate viewports within this viewport** as shown in **Fig 14-3**. Each one is labeled (A,B,C and D) for reference. Set the space to Paper.

Start with **viewport A**. **Click** on the **Rectangular Viewport** button on the Layout Viewports palette (on the layout ribbon), then **click** in the **approximate location** that you see the **lower left hand corner** (the blue grip box in the lower left corner of the new viewport) in **Fig 14-4**. Don't worry about the exact location; we are going to resize it. Draw the viewport up and **click** in approximately the place where you see the **upper right hand corner** (again anywhere near this point is fine). The lines for this viewport must be inside the page borders and not touching the title block lines. If the viewport lines are over the border lines they will be blocked out by the viewport.

Now **click** on one of the new **viewport lines**—when it is selected you will see the **blue grip boxes** on each corner (as shown in Fig 14-4). **Right click** the mouse to bring up the menu and select **properties**. In the Properties box change the **height** to read **1'-4 ¾"** and the **width** to read **1'-8 ½"** as shown in **Fig 14-4** and <e> and **close** the **properties** box. **ESC**.

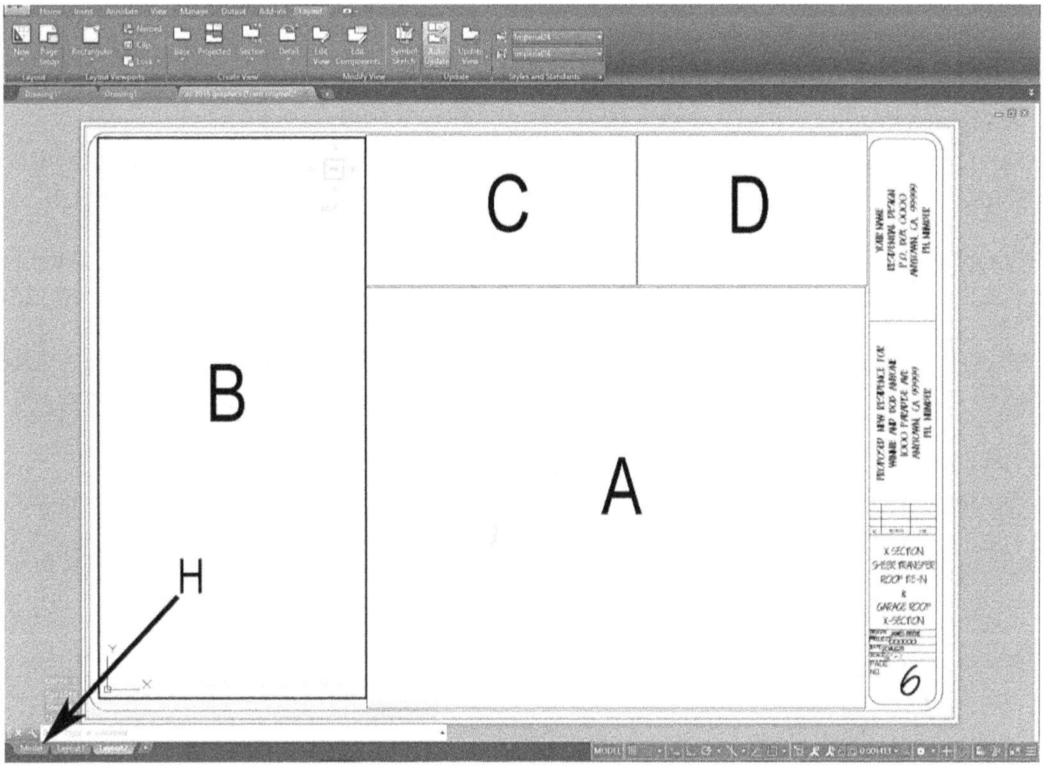

Fig 14-3

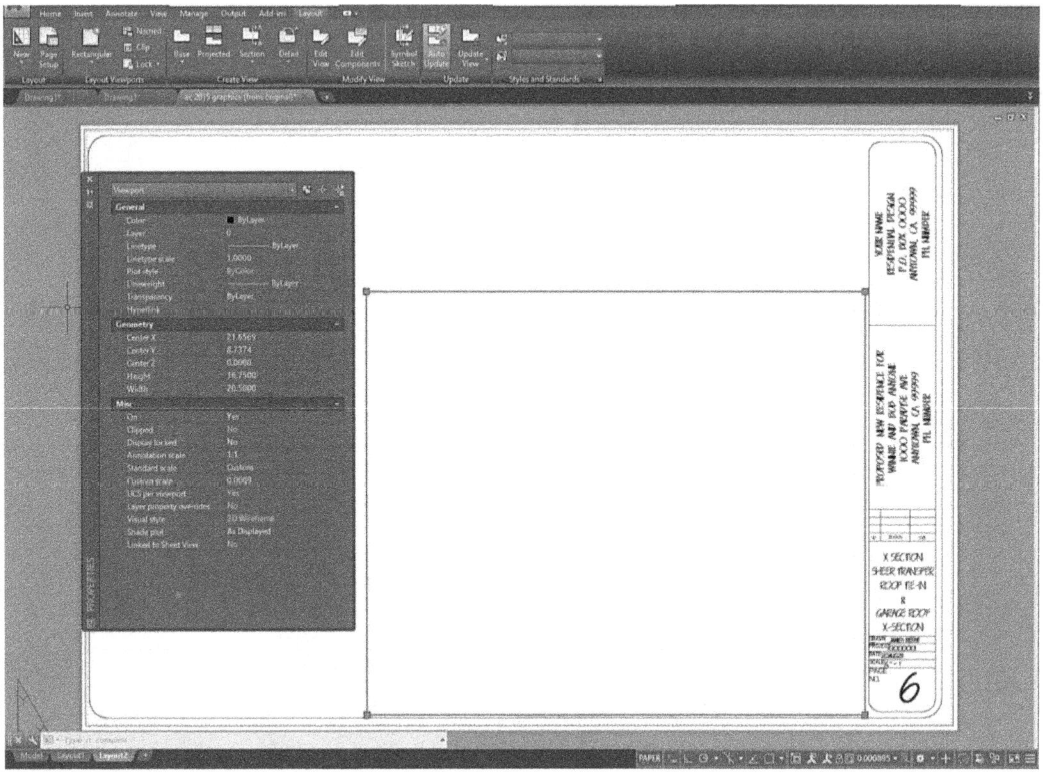

Fig 14-4

Use the **Move** tool to position this viewport within the borders and so that it doesn't cover the title block outline (click the Move button and then the line of the viewport A).

Once you have viewport A set, create **viewport B** by filling up the space to the side—**click** on the **Rectangular Viewport button** again and set it by eye. Make sure that it doesn't cover the borders or the edge of viewport A.

Now create **viewport C** to look approximately like **Fig 14-3**. **Click** on one of the lines of this **viewport** and right click to bring up the **Properties** palette again. Change the **height** to read **6"** and the **width** to read **11"**.

Use the **move** tool to place it so that it doesn't overlap the border or the other viewports. You may have to move viewport A down a bit. Don't sweat the details, don't try to make this perfect, we are just learning the concepts for now.

Now create **viewport D**. Do this by eye and just fill up the space that is left to look approximately like **Fig 14-3**.

Each of these viewports is going to be filled separately, with actual size (not the scaled) drawings from model space.

In chapter 5 we drew the four different views shown in Fig 14-5.

Go to **Model** space (H in fig 14-3).

In order to organize this setup **create** a large **rectangle** that is **128' x 92'**. Do this off to the side in open workspace. Now place **copies** of the **original details** and **cross sections** inside this rectangle as in **Fig 14-5** (placement is approximate). You will find the drawings where you copied them as shown in Fig 5-32 through Fig 5-35.

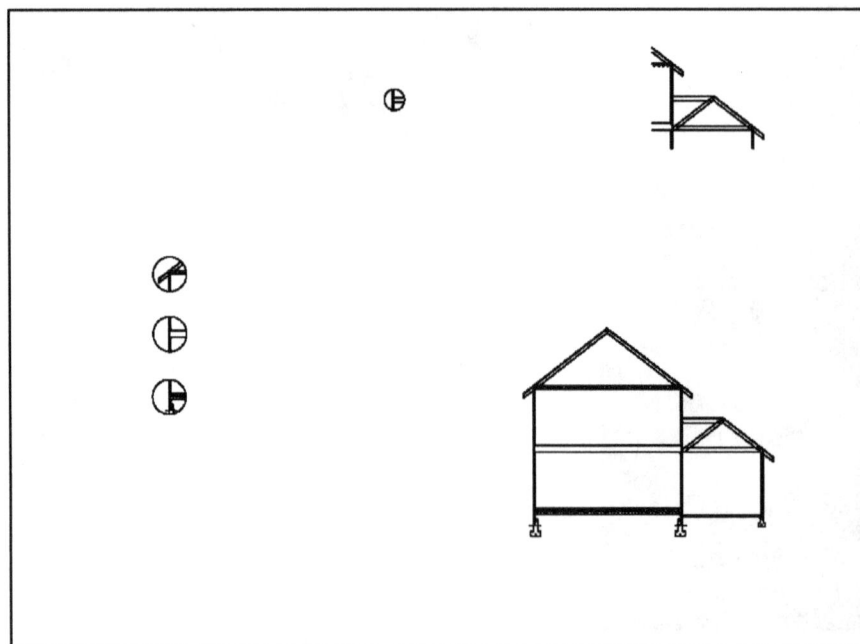

Fig 14-5
These are all the original drawings (the original/actual size) before we scaled up copies.

We are not going to redraw the entire page because we have already created it using the single viewport method. But we will add some text and dimensions to these drawings to see how this multiple viewport method works.

Create the **text** shown in **Fig 14-6**. Do this in **model space**, anywhere in open workspace. Use the text sizes shown.

12" TEXT

9" TEXT

6" TEXT

3" TEXT

Fig 14-6

Place this group of text (copy it) as shown by the arrows in **Fig 14-7**. This placement is approximate.

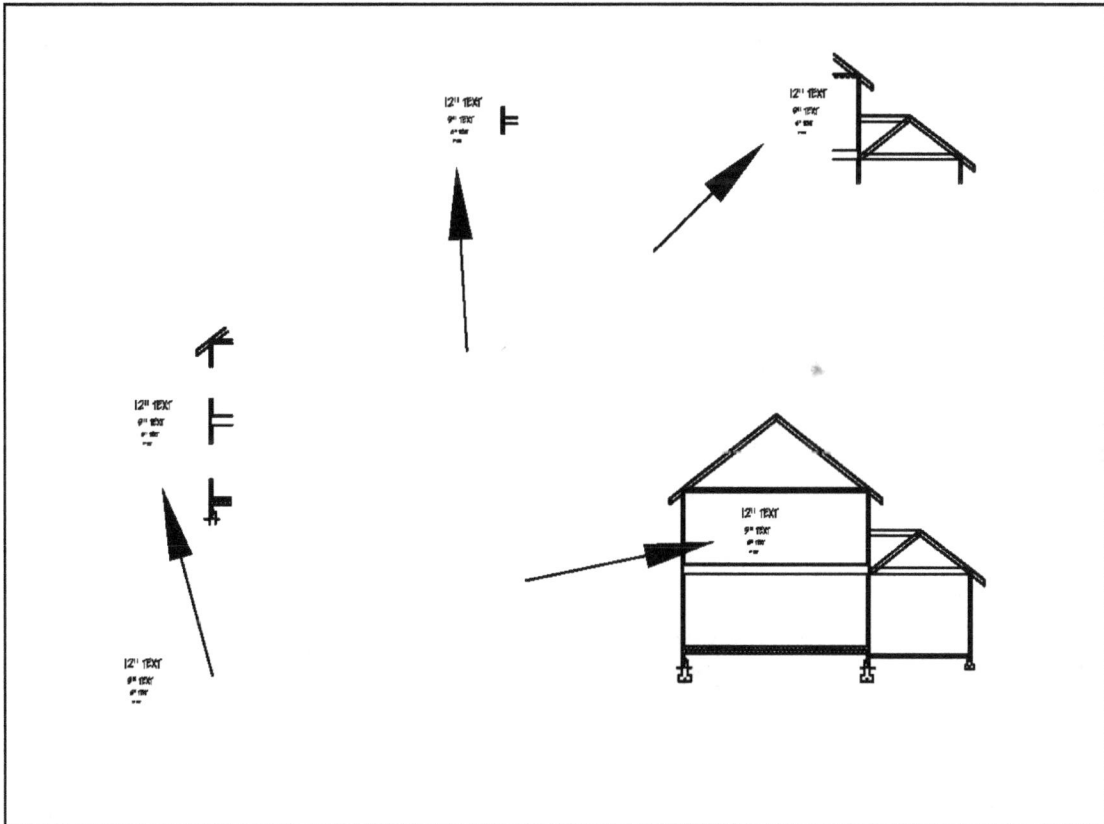

Fig 14-7

Now **open** the **36 x 24 multi layout** tab (**E** in **Fig 14-8**). Set the Paper/Model space to **Model** space (**F** in **Fig 14-8**).

Use **CTRL + R** to toggle from one viewport to another (hold down the CTRL key and press the R key on your keyboard). Select **Viewport A**. Position the cursor inside viewport A and use the mouse wheel to zoom out. Find the cross section drawing in the lower right corner of Fig 14-7.

Place the image in the viewport as shown in Fig 14-8. Then set the viewport scale using the **viewport scale** window (**G** in **Fig 14-8**). Repeat this for each viewport (CTL + R to toggle between the viewports). Set the viewports to the scales (at G in Fig 14-8) shown here:

Viewport A is ½" = 1'.
Viewport B is ¾" = 1'.
Viewport C is 1" = 1'.
Viewport D is ¼" = 1'.

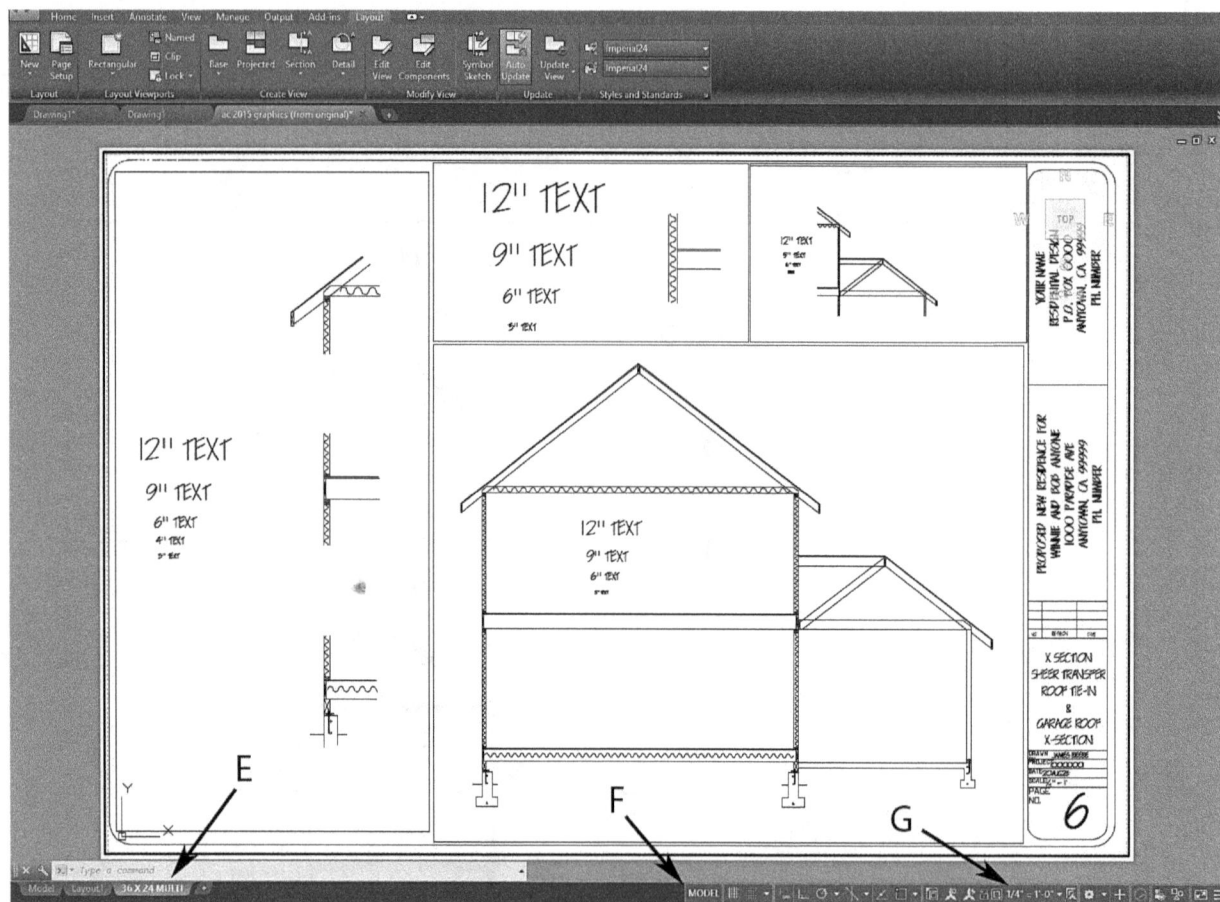

Fig 14-8

Because this is a 36 x 24 sheet you won't be able to view it at its actual size unless you print it out (unless of course you have 48" monitor). But you can see the relative sizes of the text.

The twelve inch text will plot out at ¼" in viewport D. In viewport A the six inch text will plot at ¼". This makes sense because the scale is ½" = 1' in viewport A: twice the size as the scale (¼" = 1') in viewport D.

The three inch text will plot out at ¼" in viewport C. The three inch text will print out at 3/16" in viewport B (we would need 4 inch text to print out at ¼" in viewport B).

We want the text to be consistent for the entire page. So when we use multiple viewports we must use different sized text for each scale. These are the **text sizes listed in the chart in Chapter 13**.

Now let us add some **dimensions** and **leaders** to these drawings to see how they function.

Back in **model** space (H in Fig 14-8) we need to create some new dimensions styles. Open the **Dimension Style** box. Select the **quarter** style, click **New**. Name this new style **half**. Set the **Use Overall Scale of** to **24** and check the **Primary Units** tab to be certain the **Scale factor** is **1**. Remember the scale factor is always 1 when there is no scaling in **model** space.

Create two more dimstyles:

Create a ¾ **dimension style**: use an **overall scale** of **16**. **Name** it **Three Quarters**. Use scale factor of 1.
Create a **1" dimension style**: use and **overall scale** of **12**. **Name** it **One**. Use scale factor of 1.

Now, somewhere off to the side, in open workspace, **draw** the **leaders** that you see in **Fig 14-9** (type qleader).Set the quarter dimension style and draw a leader (not too long—say three feet long). Now do the same with the **Half dimension style** set current, then the **Three Quarters**, and finally the **One**.

Next **draw** a **rectangle 18" x 18"**. Set the **quarter dimension style current** and use the linear dimension tool to create the first 1'-6" dimension as shown in **Fig 14-9**. **Repeat** this with the other **three dimension styles** as shown. Set the Half dimstyle current and use the linear dimension tool to create the second dimension shown in Fig 14-9. Then use the Three Quarters dimstyle and the linear dimension tool again, then the One dimstyle.

You can see that the dimension text and the leader arrowheads are smaller each time.

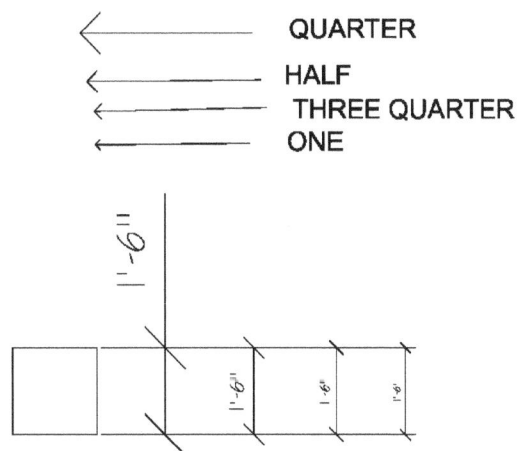

Fig 14-9

Place this **graphic** into each of the four views as in **Fig 14-9A**. This placement is approximate.

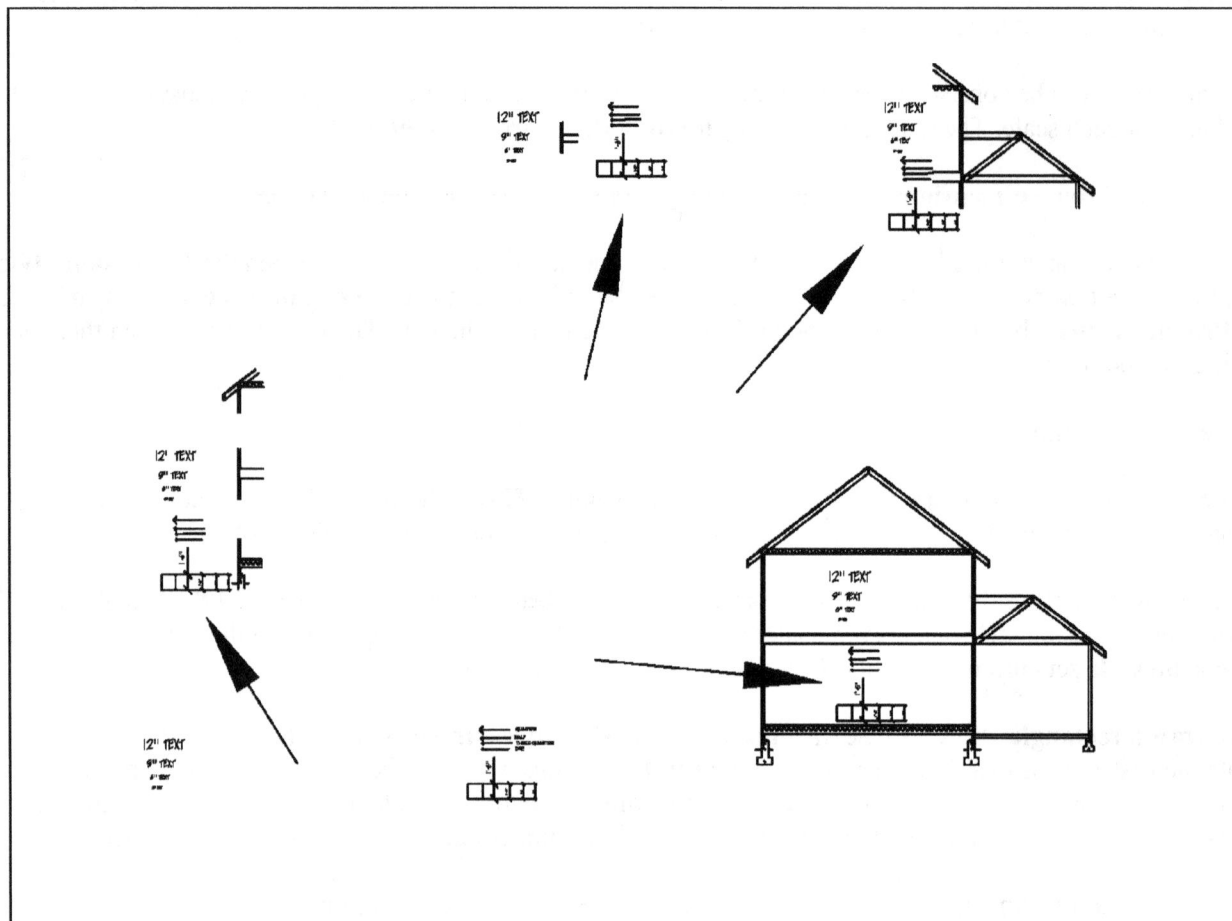

Fig 14-9A

Back in the **36 x 24 Multi layout** look at what you get in the different scaled viewports.

You will have to toggle to viewport C and pan over to see the dimensions because the scale is large and the window viewport is relatively small. Hold down the **CTRL** and type **R** until you get there (the Paper/Model space must be set to Model to toggle into the different viewports).

Once again we want all of the leaders and text for the dimensions to be the same for the entire page. So we would use the corresponding **dimension style** for each viewport: Quarter for Viewport D, Half for viewport A, Three Quarter for Viewport B, and One for viewport C.

If you erase all the dimensions and leaders in each view, except the *correct* dim style for that view, you will see they will be uniform on the entire page. This is difficult to explain because there are several sized texts in each view; but the leader text, for example, is usually one size, and labels are usually a larger size—we want these to be uniform from one view to the next.

We are not going to fill in all the text and dimensions because we have already created this page using the single viewport method. This chapter is just to show you how you can create the same plotted page with multiple viewports.

You may see why I prefer the single viewport method—it is less complicated and faster. But there are times when multiple viewports are preferable. For example, when you have to print out the plans in various sizes—say one for the jobsite, and another for the architectural review committee—on a different size paper for each purpose.

To finish this chapter I am going to recreate this multiple viewport page using a trick.

You don't have to do this, but follow along. If we go to the completed page 6 that we prepared in Chapter 7 (see Fig 7-13), we can make a copy of this drawing. Copy it to one side in open workspace and then reduce all of the views back to **actual size** using the **Scale** tool. To do this we use scale factors that are the inverse of what we used to scale them up for this page (Fig 7-13).

Use a scale factor of .5 for the Cross section in the lower right.

A scale factor of .333 for the details to the left.

A scale factor of .25 for the upper left detail.

This reverses the (up) scaling that we used in chapter 5, and returns each of these drawings to the original (actual) size. You will see Fig 14-10.

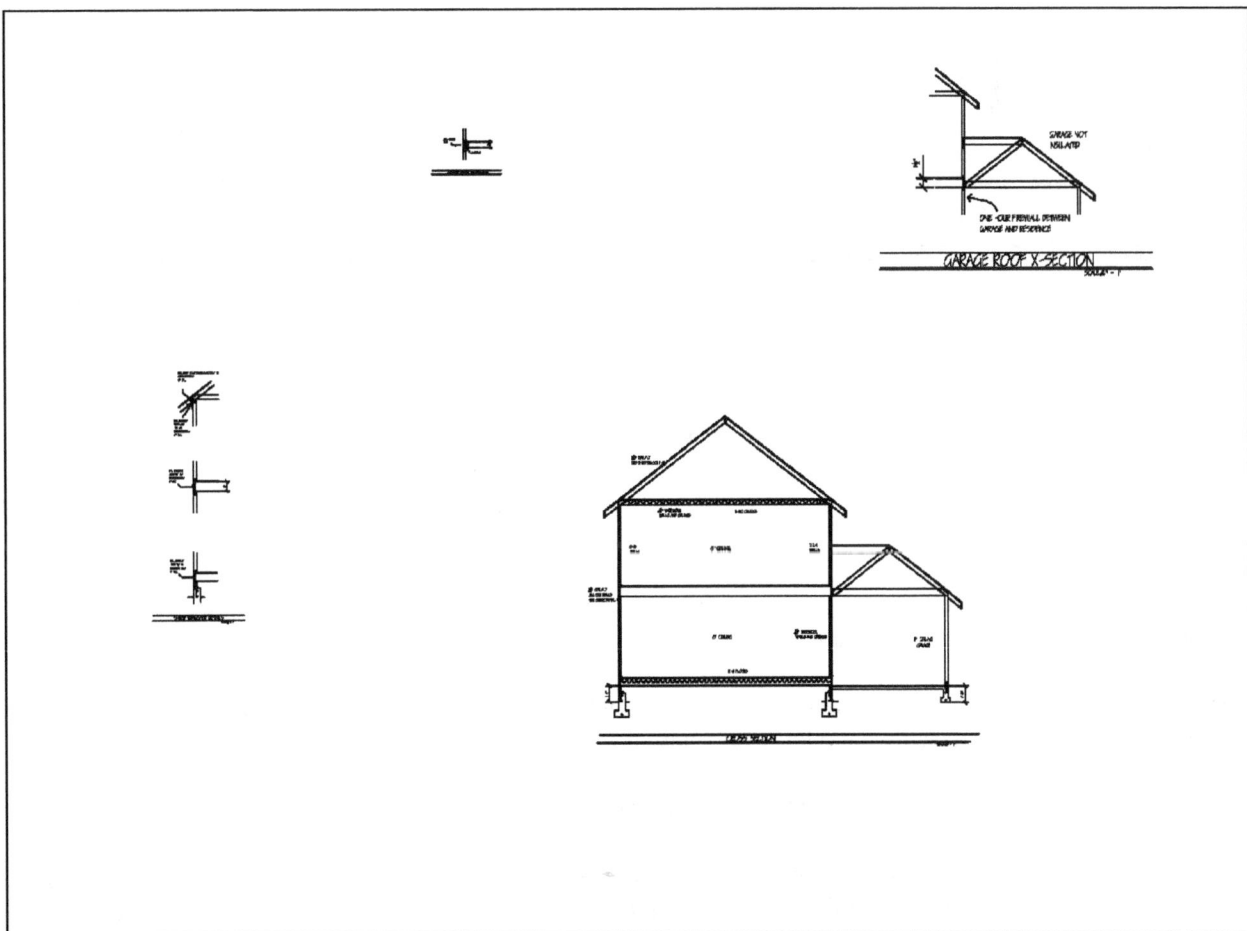

Fig 14-10

Notice the size of the text, leaders and dimensions. They are different for each view.

We have scaled the text to the sizes that we would select from our text chart if we were to use the multiple viewport method. The leaders and dimension styles are the same as if we set them with the different dimension styles we just created.

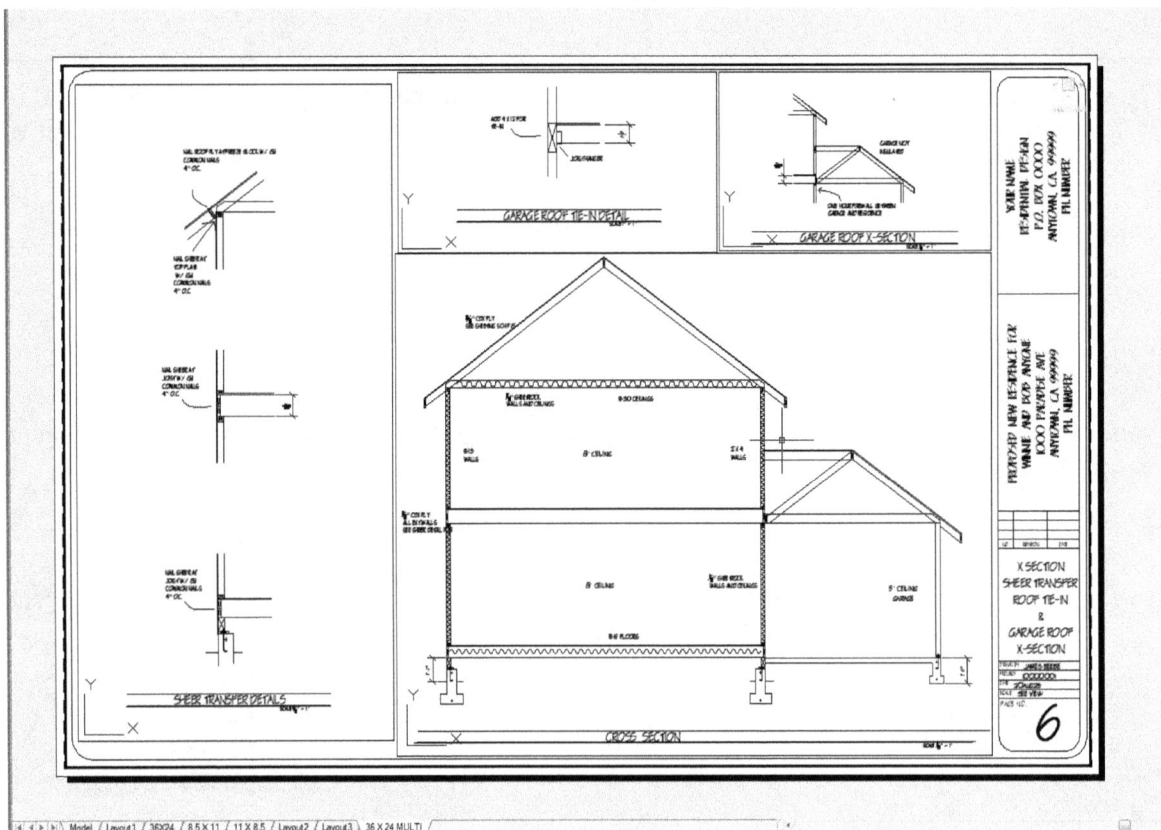

Fig 14-11

Now we can open the different viewports in the **36 x 24 multi layout**, center each of these drawings in its respective viewport, and scale each of the viewports appropriately: A is ½, B is ¾, C is 1" and D is ¼". V*iola!* We have the page back just as it was in the single viewport. We have just gone around full circle. It looks like Fig 14-11.

So in chapter 5, we scaled each of the details and cross sections up. We placed these scaled drawings on our page. Then we added the text dimensions and leaders to the entire page using the same size for the entire page.

Here we scaled them back to their original in model space which reduced the text, leaders and dimensions. Then we used the viewport scale to scale them back up again.

This is a good exercise for understanding the scaling concept.

Remember, when you plot, always **turn off** the **viewport layer for printing in the Layer Properties Manager**, or the viewport border (the line that defines the viewport) will show on the printed page. This not fun if you discover it after going to the print shop and paying for a bunch of pages.

Chapter 15—Complete Plans

In this chapter we will finish the complete set of plans. This is, mostly, for those who intend to do architectural drafting. If you are going to draft architectural plans it is a good idea to draw a complete set of plans prior to offering AutoCAD design services to your clients or employer. In this way you know that you can deliver the goods.

In this chapter there is little in the way of detailed drawing instructions. You have already learned how to draw everything presented here, so each view is displayed with a few notes to point out any new techniques, some alternative methods, and some general notes on architectural drafting.

You can skim through the drawings quickly, draw some, all, or none of the details, depending on your needs.

The completed title blocks for each page are displayed in Appendix IV. A full set of plans can be viewed at **www.AutoCADin20Hours.com**. There you can zoom in for greater detail.

The amount of information on a set of plans can vary considerably. In some rural areas the building department will require only the barest of plans; and if a small contractor is going to build the building, doing most of the work in-house, there may be only a sketch of the building represented on the plans.

On the other hand, large cities or densely populated counties often require extensive details and notes. The notes and details can vary widely depending on what information is deemed most important by each jurisdiction. Some require lots of notes (mostly sections of building code and local code) written on the plans.

There is no way to draw a standard set of plans that will satisfy every situation. Most building departments have handout sheets that detail their requirements.

I have been designing buildings since 1976 and during that time I have submitted plans to over a dozen jurisdictions. This set of plans is detailed enough to pass all of those jurisdictions, with some additional information tailored to each building department. Engineering is often required.

Text size is a matter of personal choice. There are no exact standards. Every set of plans should have several different sizes of text for different purposes. You don't need to be too concerned about the sizes of text here—you will develop your own style or your employer will dictate style.

We are now going to look at each page of the plans starting with the **Plot Plan** on **page 1**.

15.1 Page 1

For our complete set of plans we will reduce the text size on the Plot plan (on page 1). This is because we drew it in Chapter 4 to be printed on a standard 8.5 x 11 printer for people who want to print it on a home or office printer. It must be printed at 1/16 scale in order to fit on 11 x 8.5 paper.

Our complete set of plans is to be plotted on sheets of paper that are 36 x 24. For that size sheet the plot plan on page 1 of our plans will be plotted at 1/8 scale. Sixteenth scale is too small for this size of paper. Eighth scale is a much better fit for the larger paper and easier to read.

The **new text sizes** are shown in **Fig 15-1**. Try using the match properties function: change one piece of text and use the **Match properties** to change the others of that size that are oriented in the same direction. Play around with this a bit and get some more experience with the match properties function.

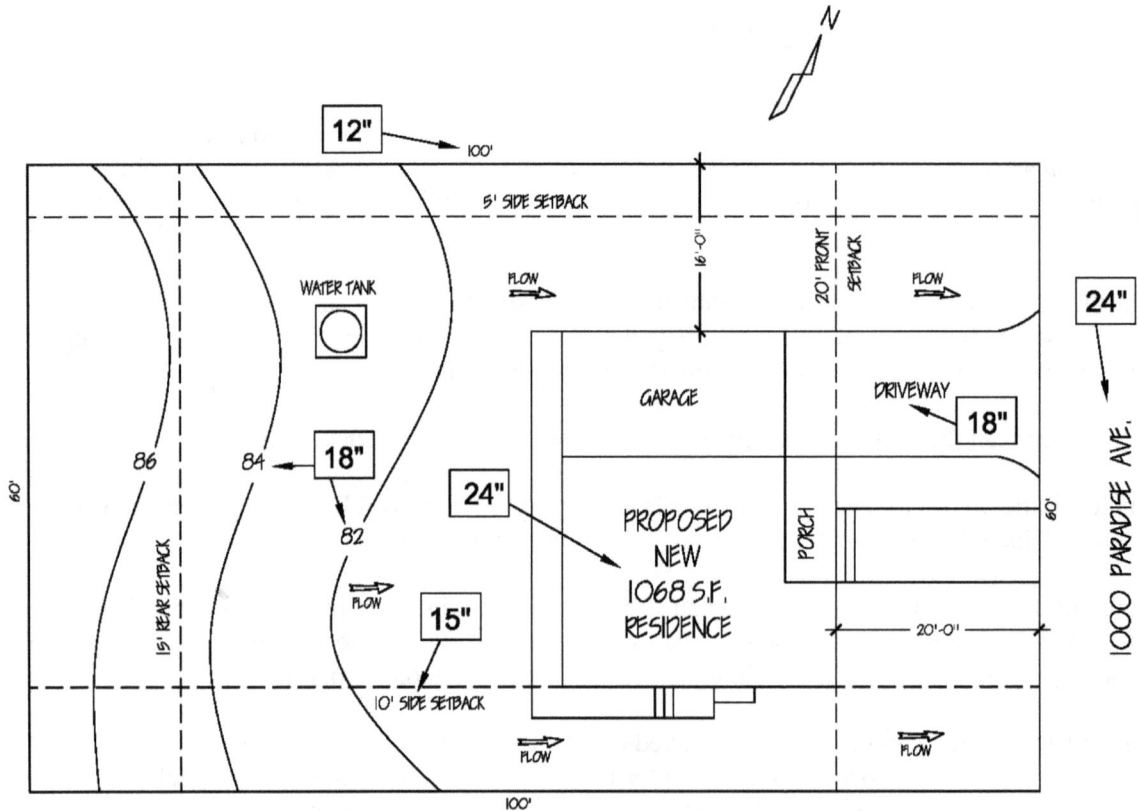

Fig 15-1

Create a new **dimension style**. It will be for **1/8" = 1'** plotting. Under the **Fit** tab set the **Use Overall Scale of** to: **96**. The **Scale factor** is **1**. **Name** this dimension style **Eighth**. Change the dimensions on the plot plan to this new Eighth style using the **Properties** box and the **Match properties** tool.

There is a **North Arrow** located at the top of the plot plan (Fig 15-1) as shown in **Fig 15-2**. The center line of the north arrow is **8 ft** and orientated at **65 degrees** (**type: @8'<65**). Don't worry about the exact shape; these arrows are done in many different styles, and you can make up your own, as long as it is clear which way is north. Use Fill (**Solid** selection with Hatch/Gradient settings), set to a very light value, to fill the spaces you create. The text **N** is **24"**. Rotate it by eye or enter the degrees of rotation at the prompt.

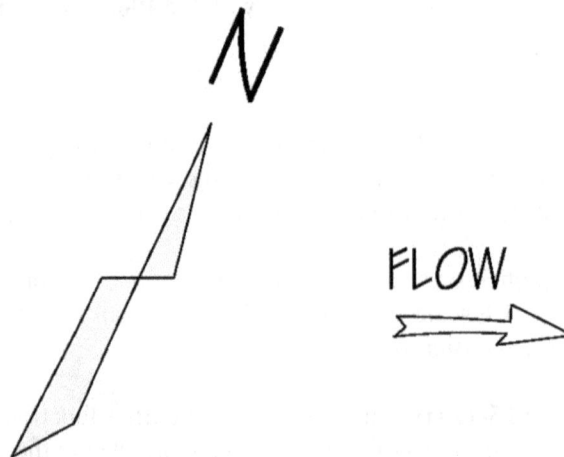

Fig 15-2

Fig 15-2 also shows the flow arrows. Once again don't be concerned with the exact shape—make your own using the **spline** tool and the **line** tool. These are about 3' long. The **text** is **12"**. There are two **mirrored** versions, one curves up, and the other down. Place them by eye.

Fig 15-3 shows some **erosion control notes** that are commonly required. These will vary considerably from one jurisdiction to another. The **title** is **30"** and the body of the **text** is **18"** (use Bold).

EROSION CONTROL & DRAINAGE NOTES

- ROOF TO DRAIN INTO DOWNSPOUTS ONTO
  SPLASH BLOCKS.
- GRADE LOT TO PROVIDE FOR RUNOFF TO STREET.
- HOSES TO BE EQUIPPED WITH SHUT OFF NOZZLES.
- SITE RUNOFF TO BE CONTROLLED DURING CONSTRUCTION
  BY THE INSTALLATION OF WATTLES OR EQUIVALENT
  MEASURES.
- PROVIDE 2% SLOPE IN FIVE FEET FROM FOUNDATION.

Fig 15-3

I **moved** the **Vicinity Map** a bit up and to the left to make some room for this text. When you create bullets like this you have to use the space bar at the beginning of each line that does not have a hyphen, for some reason it doesn't want to let you begin a line with a space. See Appendix IV for the placement of these notes.

That is it for Page 1.

15.2 Elevations

Page 2 is shown complete in Appendix IV. I have not put in all the hatches on all the views because it is clearer for this demonstration. They aren't always put on every elevation on every set of plans in any case.

Use the story pole. Finish the Second Story floor plans before you draw all of the elevations. In that way you can use it for reference to get the windows. Rotate the floor plans and use them as we did in Chapter 2 for the front elevation. Review that chapter if needed.

15.3 Page Three

The **First Story Floor Plan** on **Page 3** of the plans has some added text, a refrigerator, and the cross section reference graphic that shows where the **6A Detail cut line** is located as shown in **Fig 15-4**. The **text** for this is **12" and bold**. The four inch bollard has been added in the garage with notes.

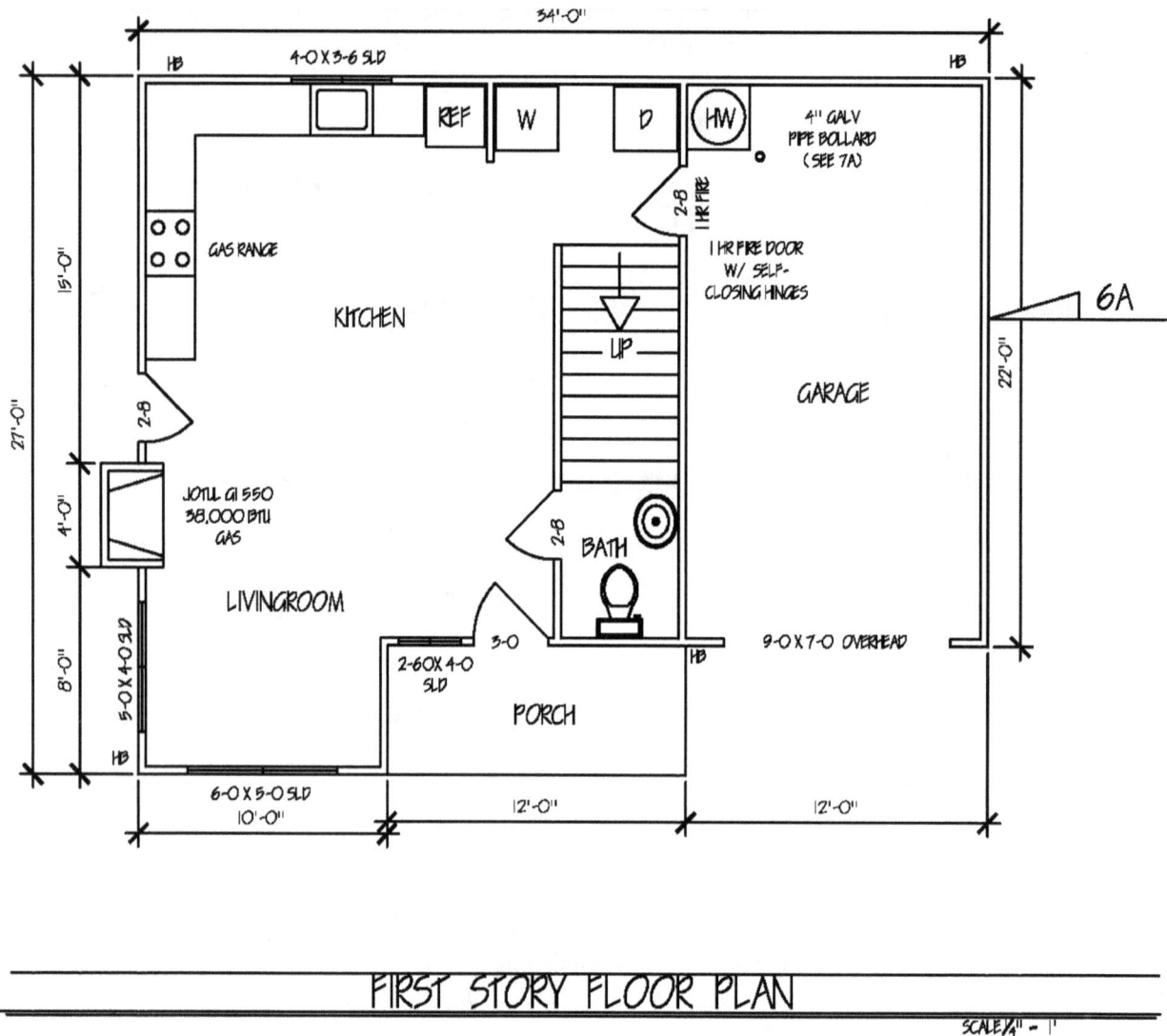

Fig 15-4

Fig 15-5 shows the finished **2ⁿᵈ Story Floor Plan**. The bedroom closets are both the same dimensions. The closet openings are 9'. The closet in the hall is 20" deep inside.

The door to bedroom 2 is centered in the wall section shown and the door to bedroom 1 is six inches off the corner.

You don't need to make the plans perfect, as long as you know that you can draw everything, you are there.

Try using the **Stretch** function to elongate the tub. See Appendix I—Stretch for instructions.

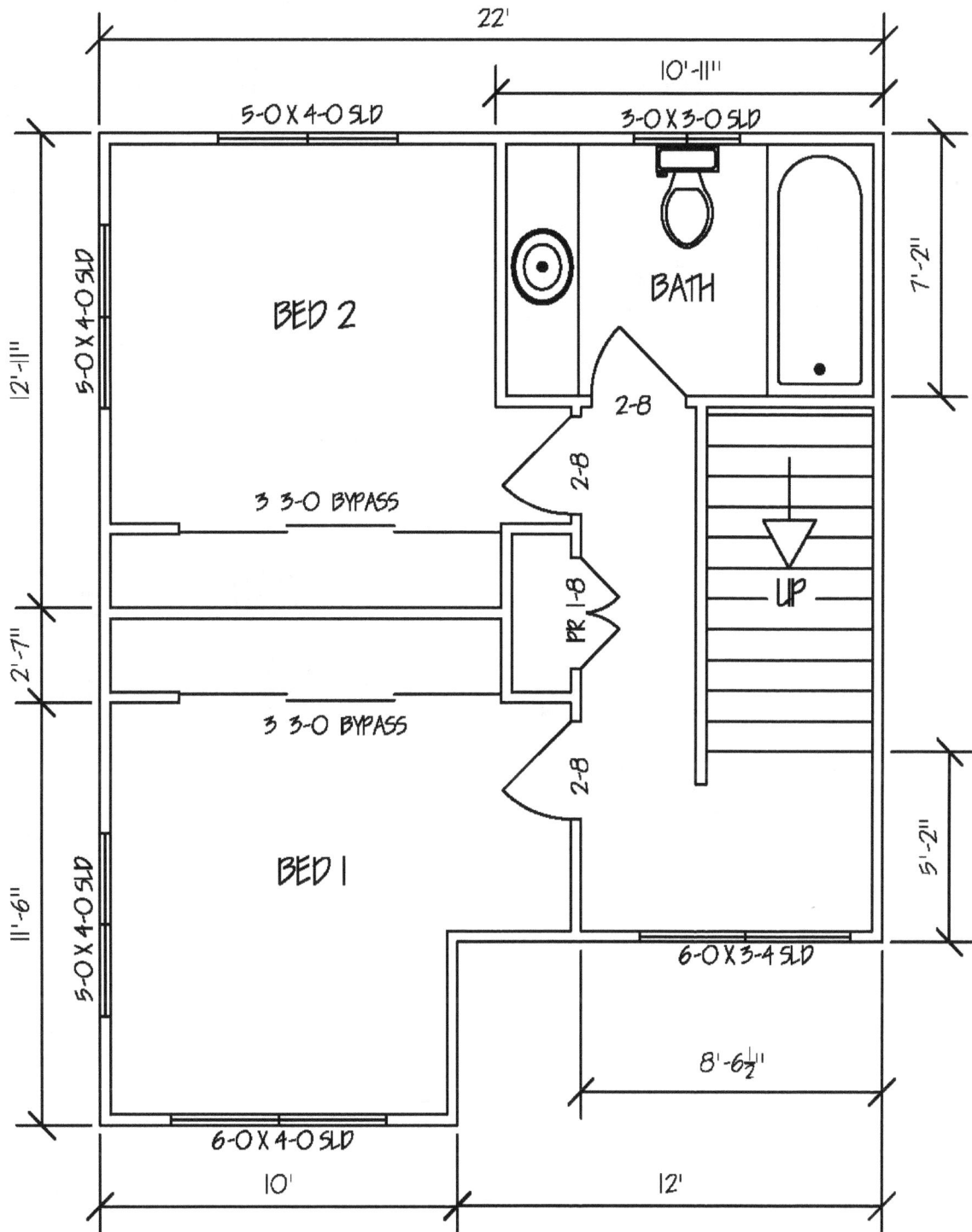

2ND STORY FLOOR PLAN

SCALE 1/4" = 1'

Fig 15-5

Fig 15-6 Shows the **First Story Electrical Plan**. Create the symbols for the outlets and the light fixtures using a 6" diameter circle. Use the offset tool to create another temporary circle for the lengths of the lines (a 1.5" offset was used here). Place the parallel lines on the outlets 2" apart. Create a temporary line 1" from the end of these parallel lines and use the midpoint of that line as the base point when you copy the outlets (one inch off the walls—use **nearest** osnap to position them along the walls). The symbols are shown in larger scale in Fig 15-6A.

ALL BRANCH CIRCUITS THAT SUPPLY 125-VOLT, SINGLE PHASE, 15 AND 20 AMP OUTLETS SHALL BE PROTECTED BY AFCI BREAKERS EXCEPT CIRCUITS REQUIRING PROTECTION BY GFI PER CEC 210-12(B) AND CEC 210.8(A)

ALL 15 AND 20 AMP OUTLETS TO BE TAMPER RESISTANT

ALL EXT. LIGHTING TO BE HIGH EFFIFCIENCY AND EQUIPTED W/ PHOTO SENSOR AND MOTION DETECTOR

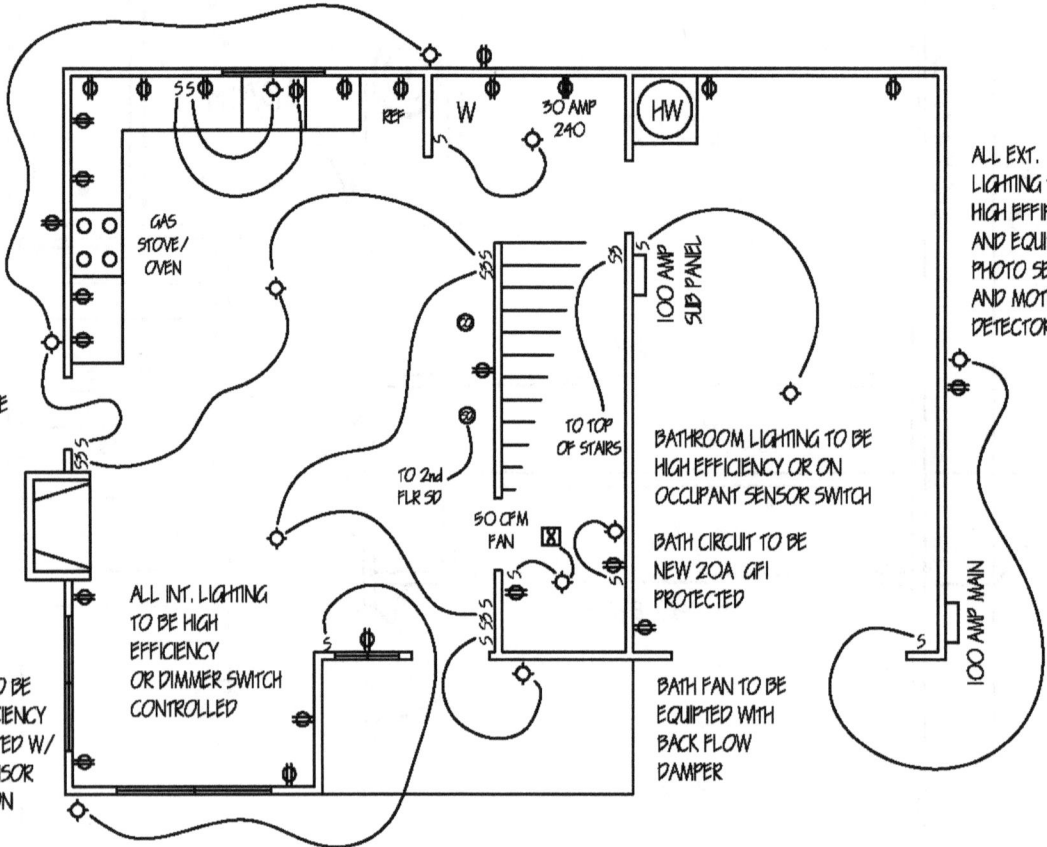

GAS STOVE/ OVEN

REF   W   30 AMP 240   HW

100 AMP SUB PANEL

ALL EXT. LIGHTING TO BE HIGH EFFIFCIENCY AND EQUIPTED W/ PHOTO SENSOR AND MOTION DETECTOR

TO TOP OF STAIRS

TO 2nd FLR SO

50 CFM FAN

ALL INT. LIGHTING TO BE HIGH EFFICIENCY OR DIMMER SWITCH CONTROLLED

BATHROOM LIGHTING TO BE HIGH EFFICIENCY OR ON OCCUPANT SENSOR SWITCH

BATH CIRCUIT TO BE NEW 20A GFI PROTECTED

BATH FAN TO BE EQUIPTED WITH BACK FLOW DAMPER

100 AMP MAIN

FIRST STORY ELECTRICAL PLAN

SCALE ¼" = 1"

Fig 15-6

If you need help with these symbols see **Appendix I—Electrical Symbols**. See Appendix IV for more detail.

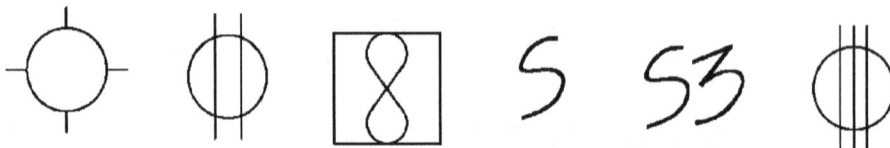

Fig 15-6A

The **spline** tool is used to show which switch goes with each light. The text size for the **S**'s and **S3**'s is 6" (S3 is a three way switch: it operates from two different locations—don't ask why it is not called two way; three locations is called four way).

For the fans: draw the fan box (**rectangle**) at **8"**, then create two **3" circles**. Use the **Quadrant** osnap as a base point and copy the circles inside the rectangle. Use the line tool and the **Tangent Osnap** to draw the lines that cross in the middle. Add the text as shown. The text sizes are the same as used in the Floor Plan text sizes.

Fig 15-7 shows the **2nd Story Electrical Plan.**

ALL BRANCH
CIRCUITS THAT
SUPPLY 125-VOLT,
SINGLE PHASE, 15
AND 20 AMP
OUTLETS SHALL BE
PROTECTED BY AFCI
BREAKERS EXCEPT
CIRCUITS REQUIRING
PROTECTION BY GFI
PER CEC 210-12(B)
AND CEC 210.8(A)

ALL 15 AND 20
AMP OUTLETS TO BE
TAMPER RESISTANT

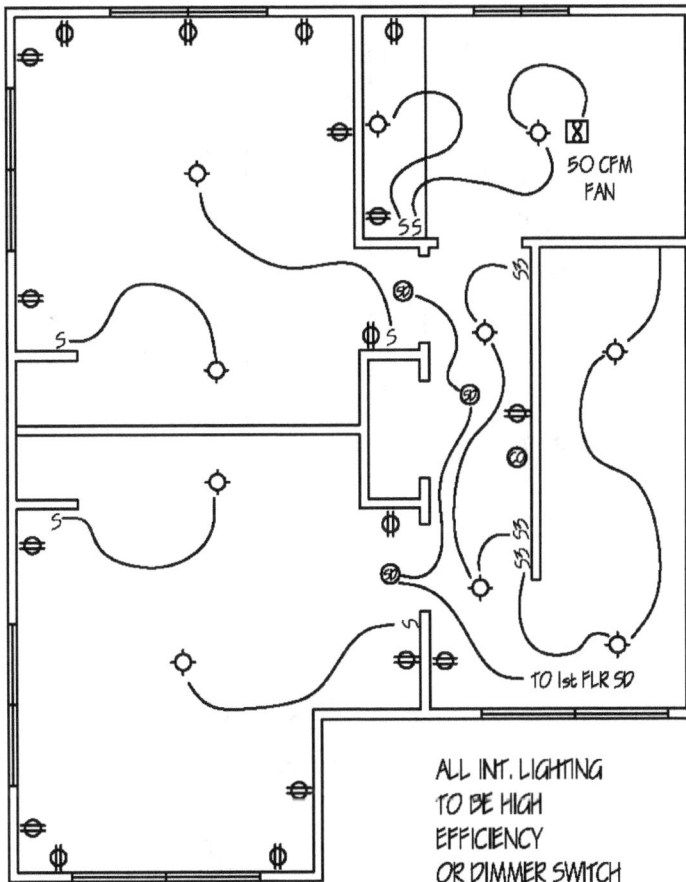

BATHROOM LIGHTING TO BE
HIGH EFFICIENCY OR ON
OCCUPANT SENSOR SWITCH

BATH CIRCUIT TO BE NEW
20A GFI PROTECTED

BATH FAN TO BE
EQUIPTED WITH
BACK FLOW
DAMPER

50 CFM
FAN

TO 1st FLR SD

ALL INT. LIGHTING
TO BE HIGH
EFFICIENCY
OR DIMMER SWITCH
CONTROLLED

2ND STORY ELECTRICAL PLAN

SCALE¼" = 1'

Fig 15-7

When you use the spline tool to make the wiring diagram, try to use as few points as possible. The lines look smoother with fewer points, and you can adjust them with the grip boxes if there are not too many. Sometimes you will need more points to get around tight spaces. It takes some practice to create smooth lines.

15.4 Page Four

Next we move on to page 4. **Fig 15-8** shows the complete **Foundation Plan**. The **bollard** has been added (7A).

We also need an access to the area under the front porch (the lower 30" x 18" ACCESS).

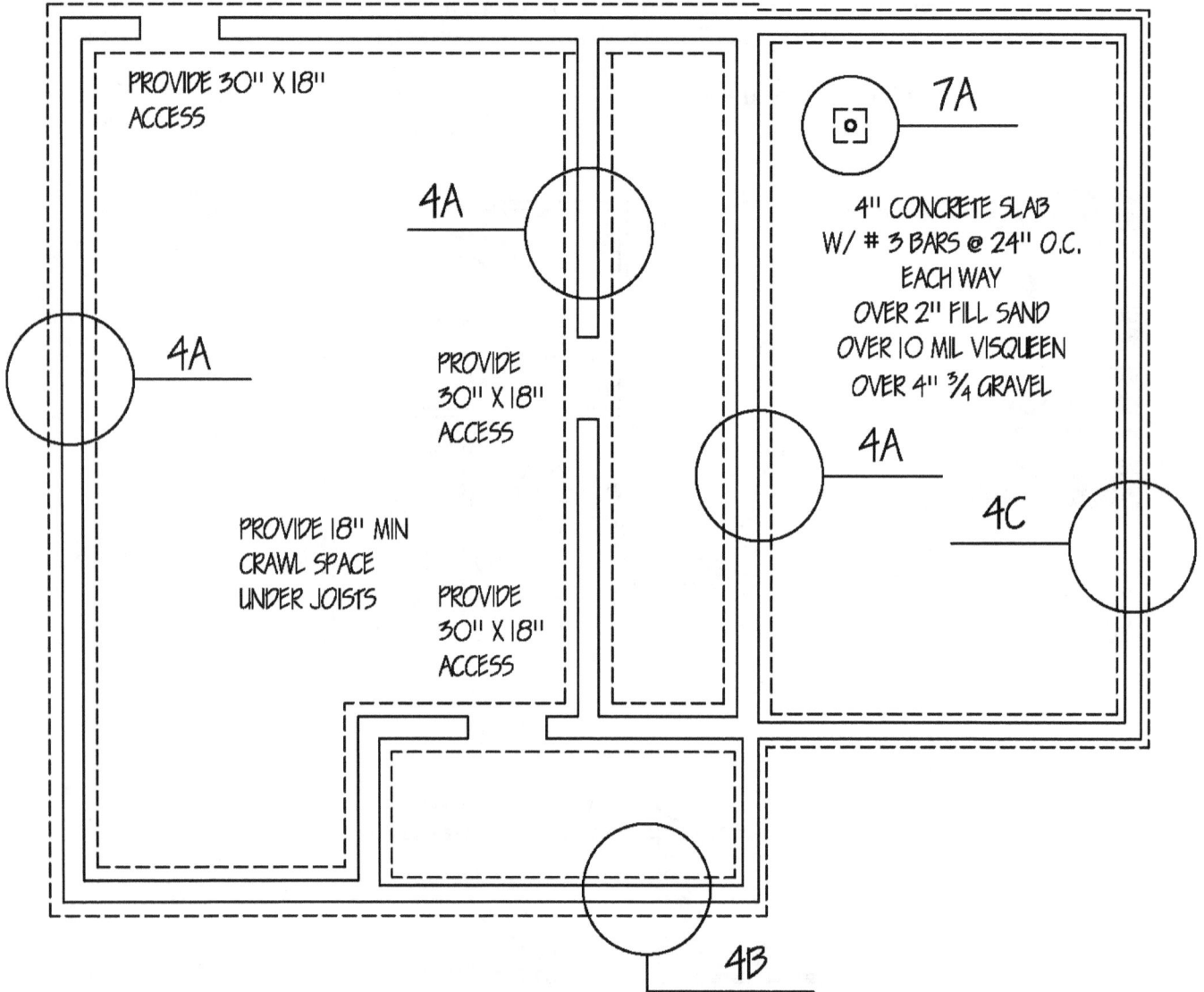

PROVIDE 30" X 18" ACCESS

4A

4A

7A

4" CONCRETE SLAB
W/ # 3 BARS @ 24" O.C.
EACH WAY
OVER 2" FILL SAND
OVER 10 MIL VISQUEEN
OVER 4" ¾ GRAVEL

4A

4C

PROVIDE 30" X 18" ACCESS

PROVIDE 18" MIN CRAWL SPACE UNDER JOISTS

PROVIDE 30" X 18" ACCESS

4B

Fig 15-8

Fig 15-9 shows the completed **Detail 4B**. The wall is 6"; the footing is 12" x 6" and 12" deep (into the earth).

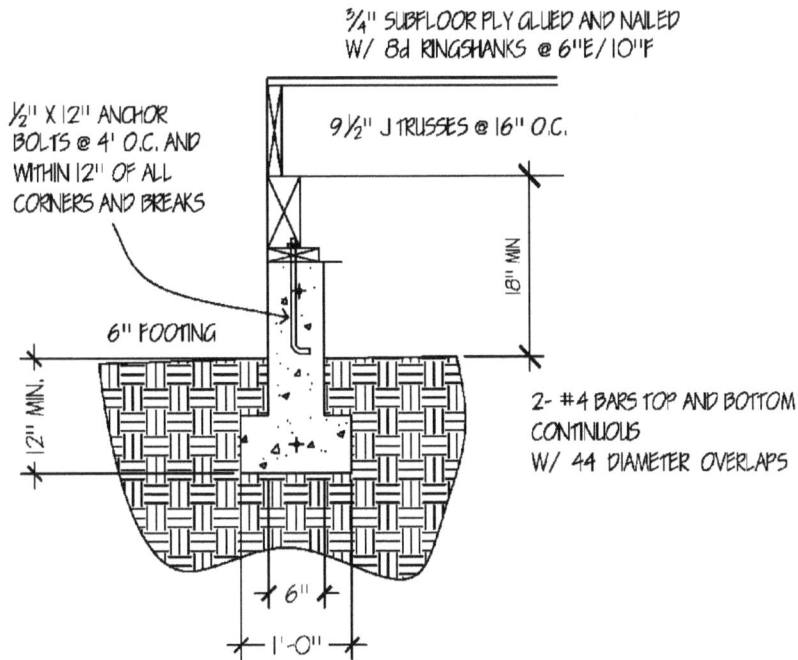

¾" SUBFLOOR PLY GLUED AND NAILED
W/ 8d RINGSHANKS @ 6"E/10"F

½" X 12" ANCHOR
BOLTS @ 4' O.C. AND
WITHIN 12" OF ALL
CORNERS AND BREAKS

9½" J TRUSSES @ 16" O.C.

18" MIN

6" FOOTING

12" MIN.

2- #4 BARS TOP AND BOTTOM
CONTINUOUS
W/ 44 DIAMETER OVERLAPS

6"

1'-0"

Fig 15-9

Fig 15-10 shows the completed **Detail 4C**.

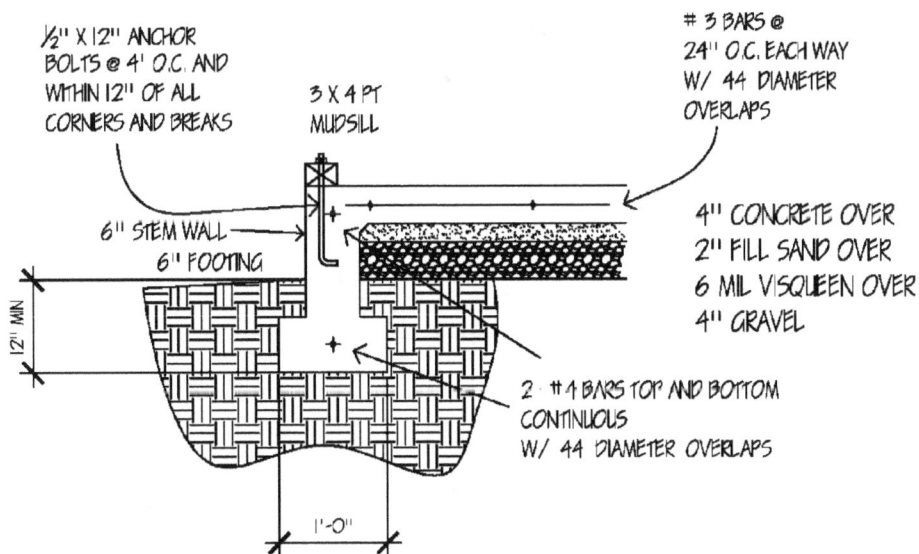

½" X 12" ANCHOR
BOLTS @ 4' O.C. AND
WITHIN 12" OF ALL
CORNERS AND BREAKS

3 X 4 PT
MUDSILL

3 BARS @
24" O.C. EACH WAY
W/ 44 DIAMETER
OVERLAPS

6" STEM WALL
6" FOOTING

4" CONCRETE OVER
2" FILL SAND OVER
6 MIL VISQUEEN OVER
4" GRAVEL

12" MIN

2 #4 BARS TOP AND BOTTOM
CONTINUOUS
W/ 44 DIAMETER OVERLAPS

1'-0"

Fig 15-10

15.5 Page Five

Fig 15-11 shows the finished **First Story Floor Frame Plan**. The second of the double joists are added over the foundation walls.

Remember you can set the text **line spacing** in the **properties** box (review Chapter 11 if needed). You can see that I have not used the gradient to add shading to the walls in this view. It is easier to read for this demonstration (and not always required). **Text size** is **7.5"**. The number in the **hexagon** is relating to the **Ply Schedule** on **page 8** of the plans (and copied from there). The ply schedule is demonstrated further in this chapter.

PROVIDE 14 X 7 CRAWL SPACE VENT
8' O.C. & 32" FROM EACH CORNER

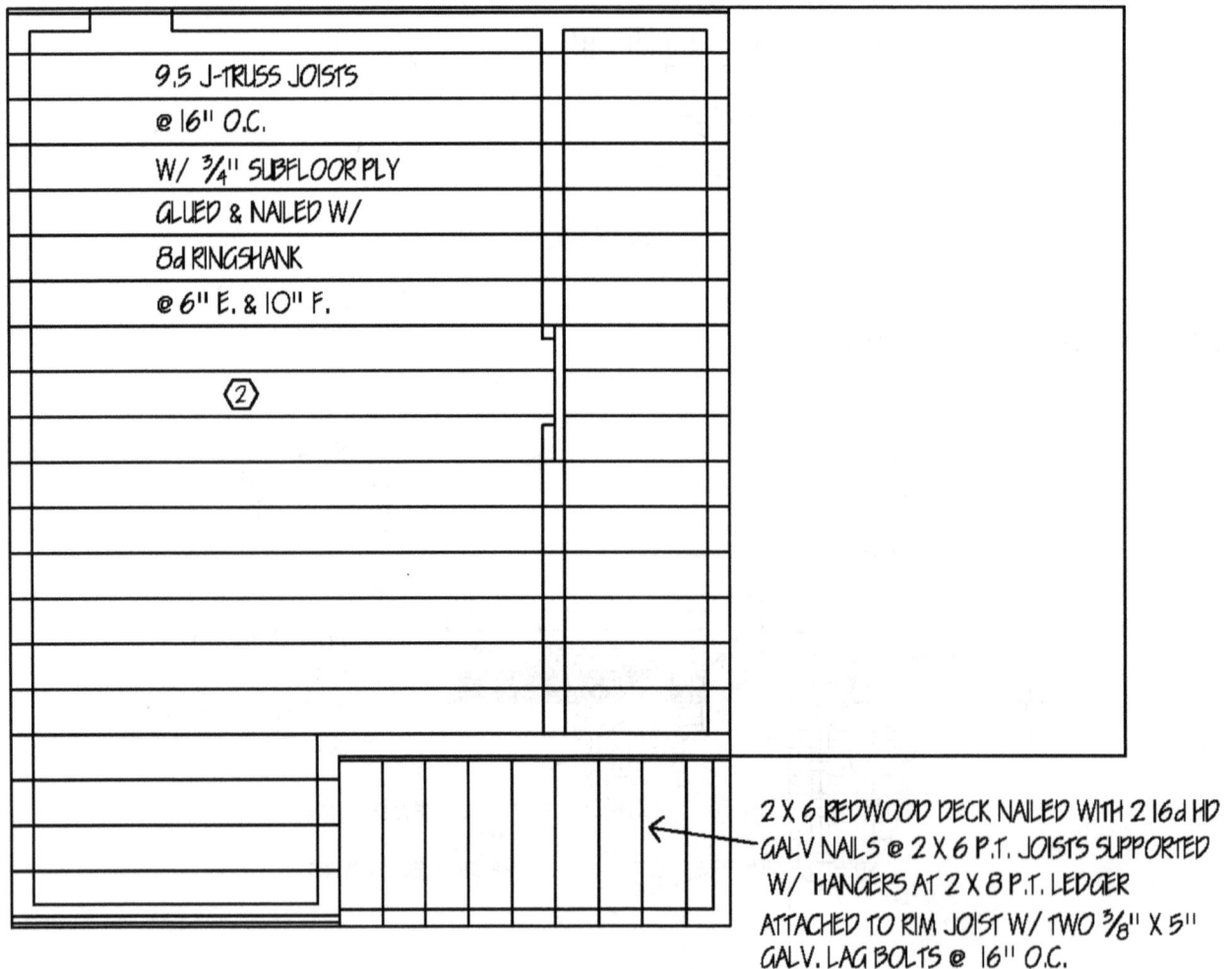

9.5 J-TRUSS JOISTS
@ 16" O.C.
W/ 3/4" SUBFLOOR PLY
GLUED & NAILED W/
8d RINGSHANK
@ 6" E. & 10" F.

②

2 X 6 REDWOOD DECK NAILED WITH 2 16d HD
GALV NAILS @ 2 X 6 P.T. JOISTS SUPPORTED
W/ HANGERS AT 2 X 8 P.T. LEDGER
ATTACHED TO RIM JOIST W/ TWO 3/8" X 5"
GALV. LAG BOLTS @ 16" O.C.

Fig 15-11

Fig 15-12 shows the **2ⁿᵈ Story Floor Frame Plan**. This is drawn using the first story walls (below the joists). I added some notes to the drawing we created in Chapter 11 and added some lines to represent the joists required under the walls that run parallel to the joists.

You can use the 2ⁿᵈ Story Floor Plan to locate the center line of the parallel walls; add a line .75" to each side of the center line. You may notice that I erased the inside of the garage wall line and eliminated the gradient. You could draw this without the garage at all because there is no second story in the garage, but it helps to quickly orientate the drawing.

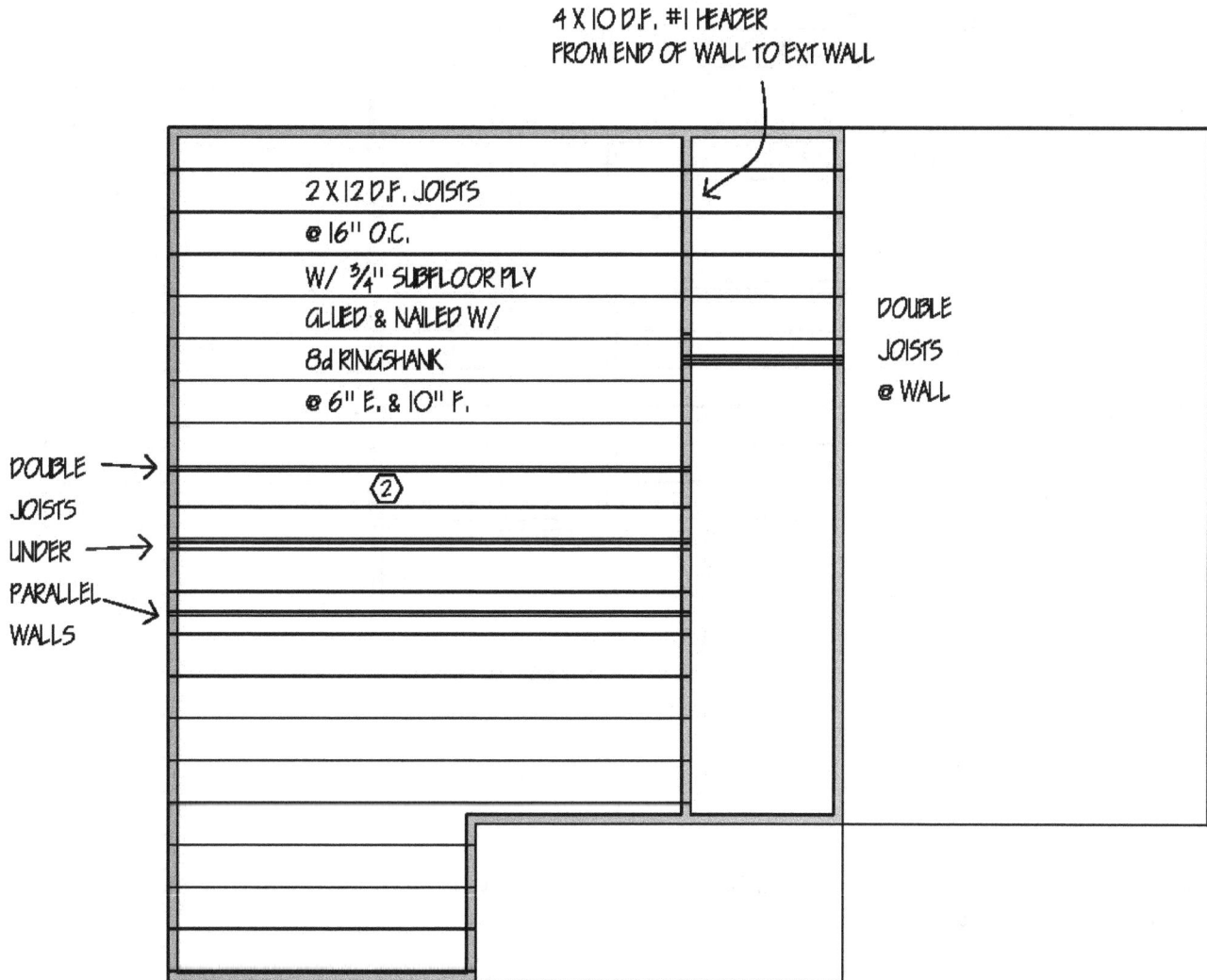

Fig 15-12

Fig 15-13 shows the **Ceiling Frame Plan**. There is some detail around the chimney for the tie-in (see Appendix IV for a larger view). The lines that indicate the **MST's** are **40mm lines**. Highlight them and change the weight of the line using the **Line Properties** windows as shown in **Fig 15-14**.

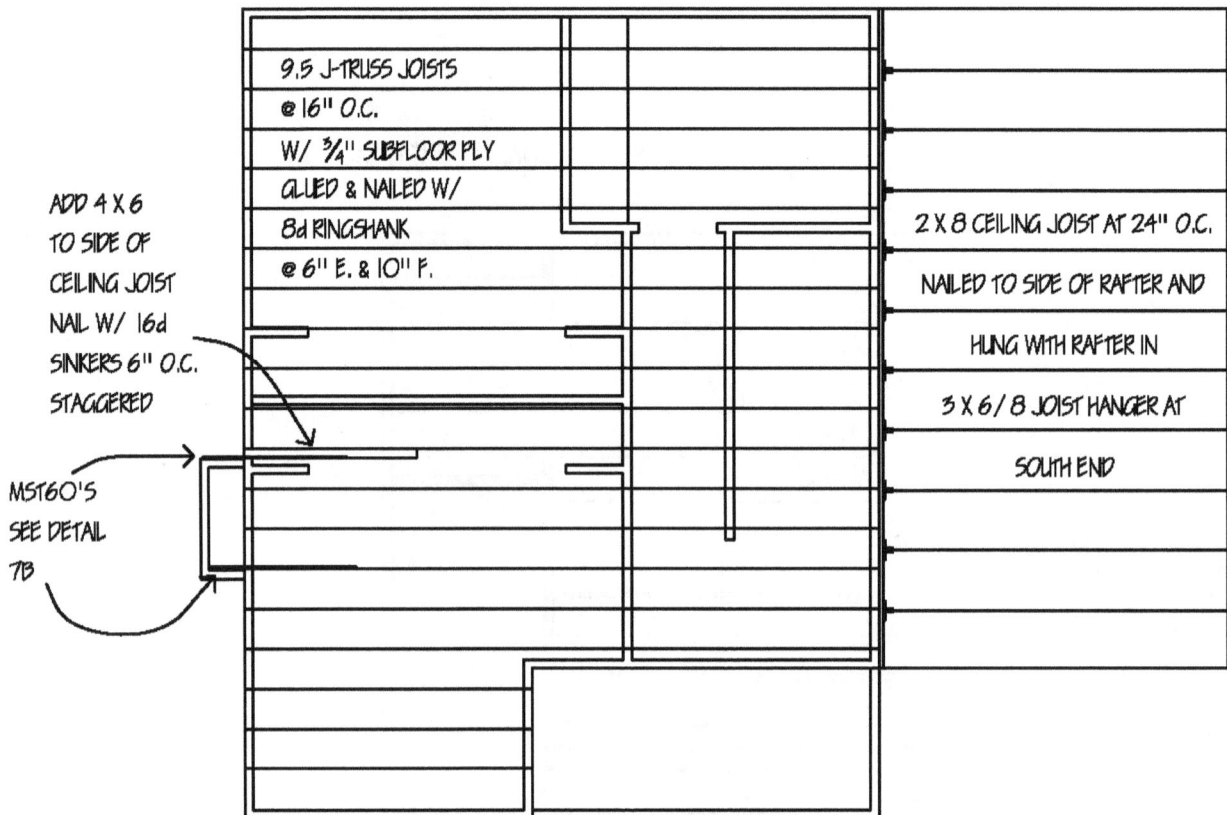

ADD 4 X 6
TO SIDE OF
CEILING JOIST
NAIL W/ 16d
SINKERS 6" O.C.
STAGGERED

MST60'S
SEE DETAIL
7B

9.5 J-TRUSS JOISTS
@ 16" O.C.
W/ ¾" SUBFLOOR PLY
GLUED & NAILED W/
8d RINGSHANK
@ 6" E. & 10" F.

2 X 8 CEILING JOIST AT 24" O.C.
NAILED TO SIDE OF RAFTER AND
HUNG WITH RAFTER IN
3 X 6 / 8 JOIST HANGER AT
SOUTH END

Fig 15-13

The spacing for the **garage ceiling joists** is **24" O.C.** so you will have to **space** the **text lines** further apart than you did with the 16" spacing.

The joist hangers are 3" x 3" lines, mirrored with 1.5" between the two sides (Fig 15-13A). Set them using a base point that is 1" from the center of the back side and space them off the building 1"—otherwise you can't see them. These brackets are not that size in reality but this type of graphic is best displayed as a representational graphic rather than a realistic depiction—it is clearer, easier to see and understand this way.

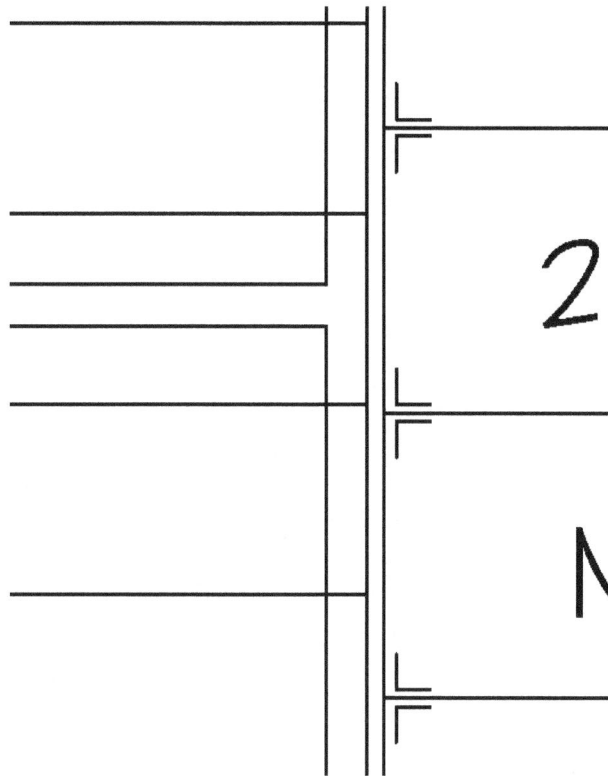

Fig 15-13A

ADJUST LINE WEIGHT HERE

Fig 15-14

Fig 15-15 shows the **Roof Framing Plan**. The line that represents the **overhang** is **18"** (just as you see in the elevations views).

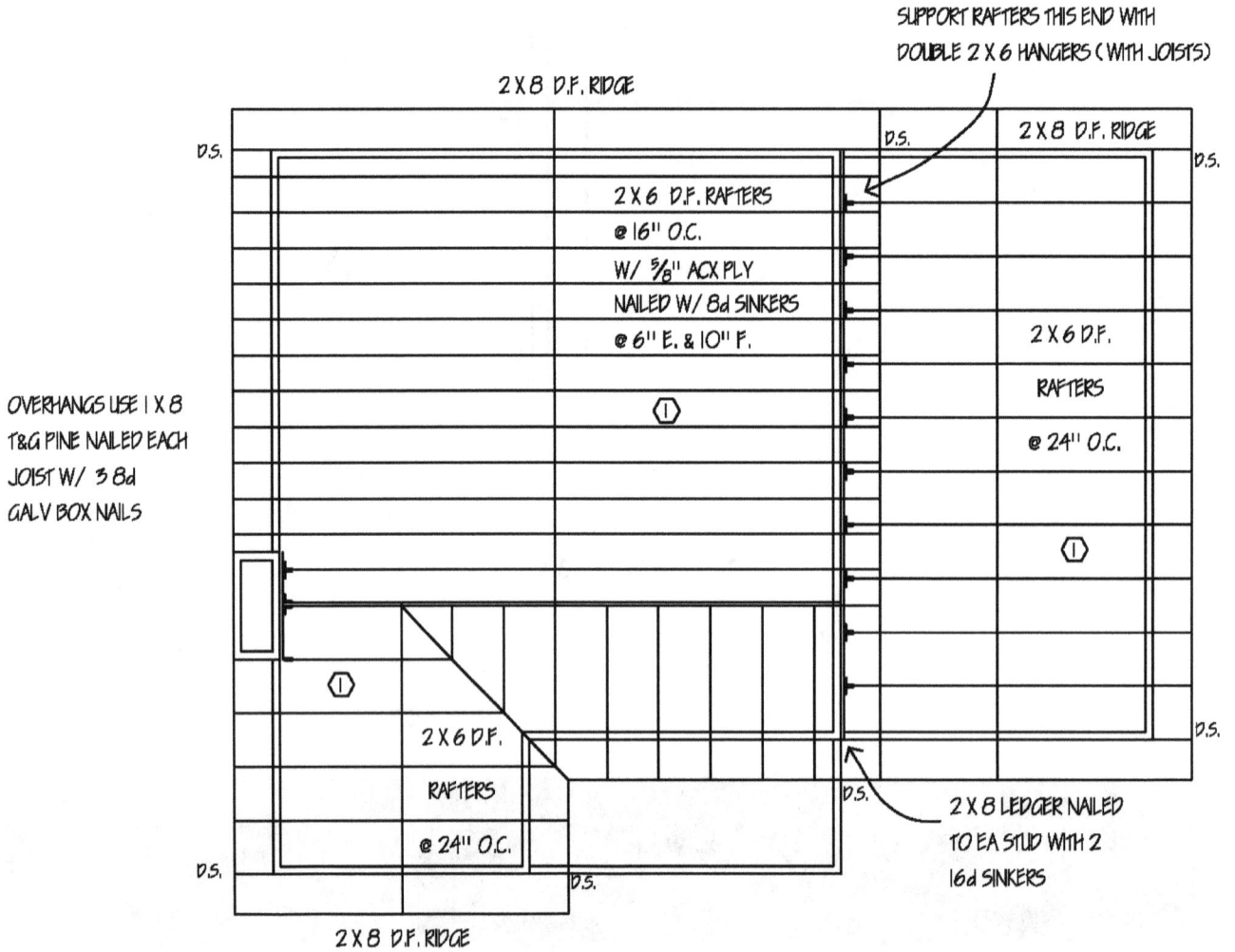

SUPPORT RAFTERS THIS END WITH
DOUBLE 2 X 6 HANGERS (WITH JOISTS)

2 X 8 D.F. RIDGE

D.S.

D.S.

2 X 8 D.F. RIDGE

D.S.

2 X 6 D.F. RAFTERS

@ 16" O.C.

W/ 5/8" ACX PLY

NAILED W/ 8d SINKERS

@ 6" E. & 10" F.

2 X 6 D.F.

RAFTERS

@ 24" O.C.

OVERHANGS USE I X 8
T&G PINE NAILED EACH
JOIST W/ 3 8d
GALV BOX NAILS

2 X 6 D.F.

RAFTERS

@ 24" O.C.

D.S.

D.S.

D.S.

2 X 8 LEDGER NAILED
TO EA STUD WITH 2
16d SINKERS

D.S.

2 X 8 D.F. RIDGE

Fig 15-15

Fig 15-15A shows the **Roof Framing Plan** in more detail.

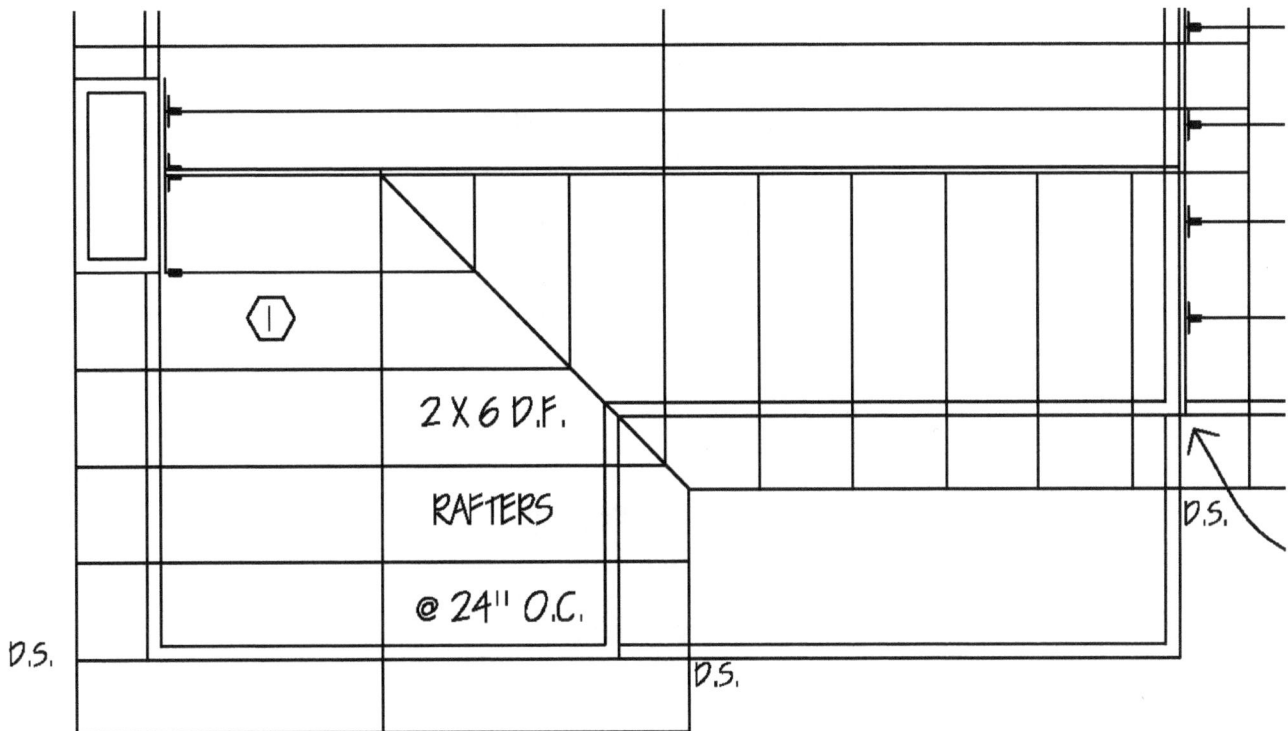

Fig 15-15A

The Forty-five degree line represents the valley where the two roof sections meet. You can locate it on the elevations or from where it intersects (draw a 45 degree line until it intersects) the ridge line of the 10' wide gable roof section. The ledger at the top of the 45 degree (the double line) line is 5' back from the exterior wall line (half of 10').

The ledgers are offset 1.5 inches from the walls or each other. The double rafters are 1.5" apart.

I have added some **D.S.** notes for the **downspouts** (6" text).

Fig 15-16 shows the **Porch Roof Framing Plan**. The joist hangers are the same as in Fig 15-13A.

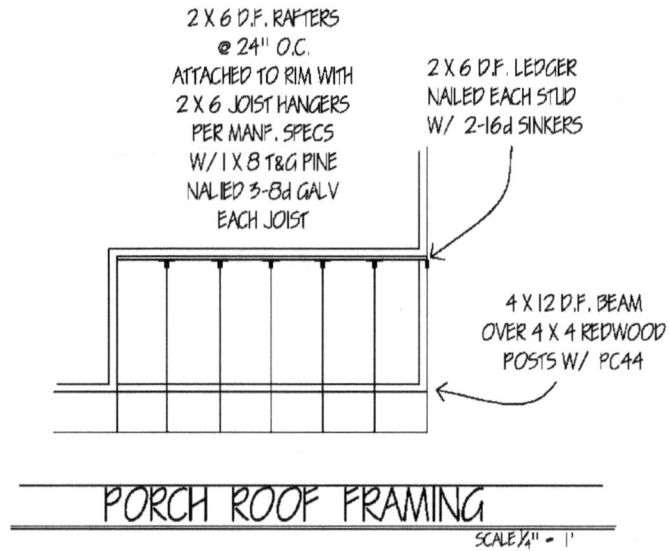

2 X 6 D.F. RAFTERS
@ 24" O.C.
ATTACHED TO RIM WITH
2 X 6 JOIST HANGERS
PER MANF. SPECS
W/ 1 X 8 T&G PINE
NAILED 3-8d GALV
EACH JOIST

2 X 6 D.F. LEDGER
NAILED EACH STUD
W/ 2-16d SINKERS

4 X 12 D.F. BEAM
OVER 4 X 4 REDWOOD
POSTS W/ PC44

PORCH ROOF FRAMING

SCALE ¼" = 1'

Fig 15-16

Fig 15-16A shows closer detail of the ledger and hangers in the porch roof framing.

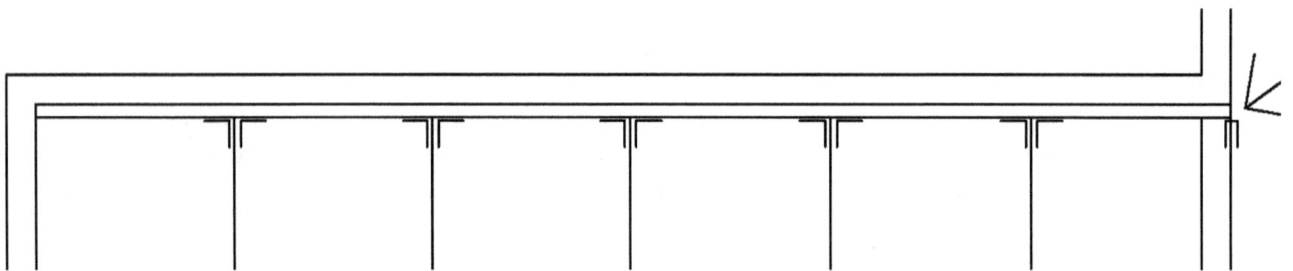

Fig 15-16A

Fig 15-17 shows the **Garage Roof Cricket Framing** plan. The cricket is framed over the garage roof after it is sheeted (sometimes called farmer framed).

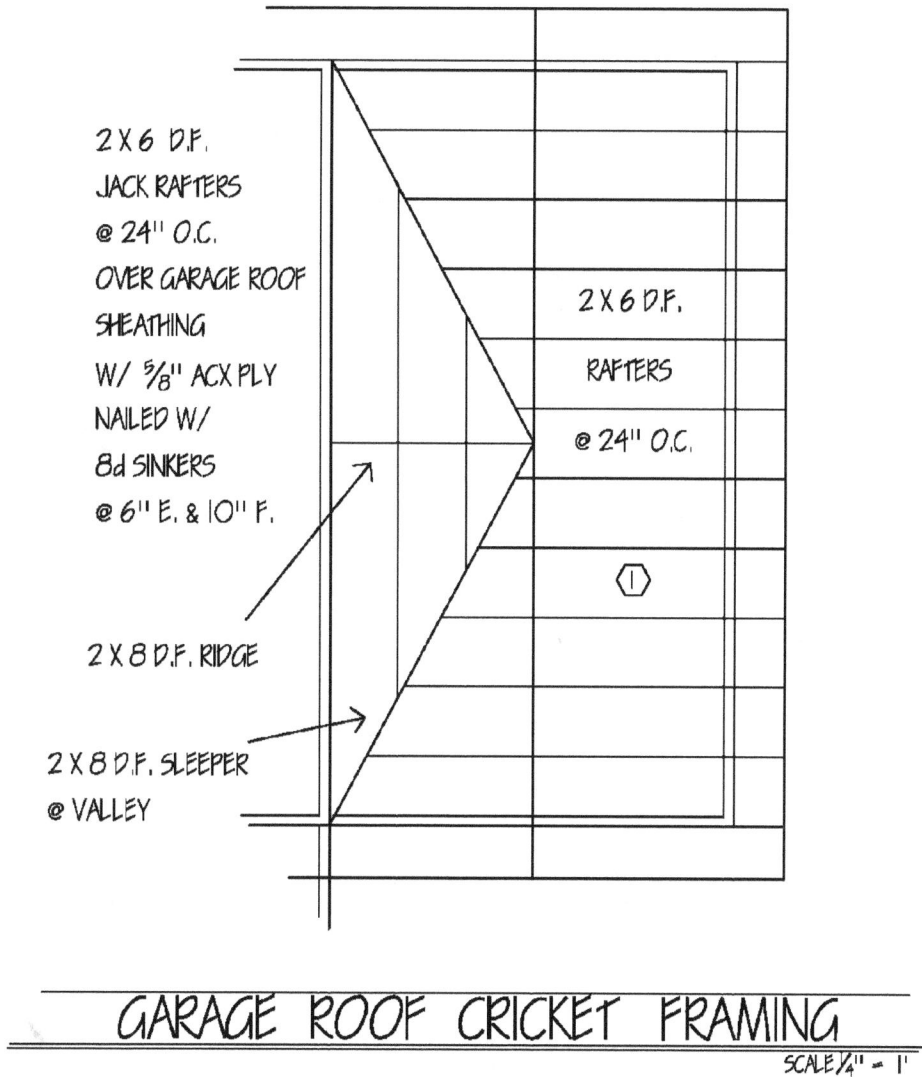

2 X 6 D.F.
JACK RAFTERS
@ 24" O.C.
OVER GARAGE ROOF
SHEATHING
W/ ⅝" ACX PLY
NAILED W/
8d SINKERS
@ 6" E. & 10" F.

2 X 8 D.F. RIDGE

2 X 8 D.F. SLEEPER
@ VALLEY

2 X 6 D.F.

RAFTERS

@ 24" O.C.

GARAGE ROOF CRICKET FRAMING

SCALE ¼" = 1'

Fig 15-17

15.6 Page Six

Page 6 is already close to completion. The **Cross Section** has a few **added notes** for the roof and the exterior walls. I have added more **foundation detail** to the **cross section** (see **Fig 15-18**). Copy the foundation and place it 10' from the edge of the garage wall (because this view has been scaled up by a factor of 2, the actual measurement is 5'—see the foundation plan). Add the garage foundation from Fig 15-10.

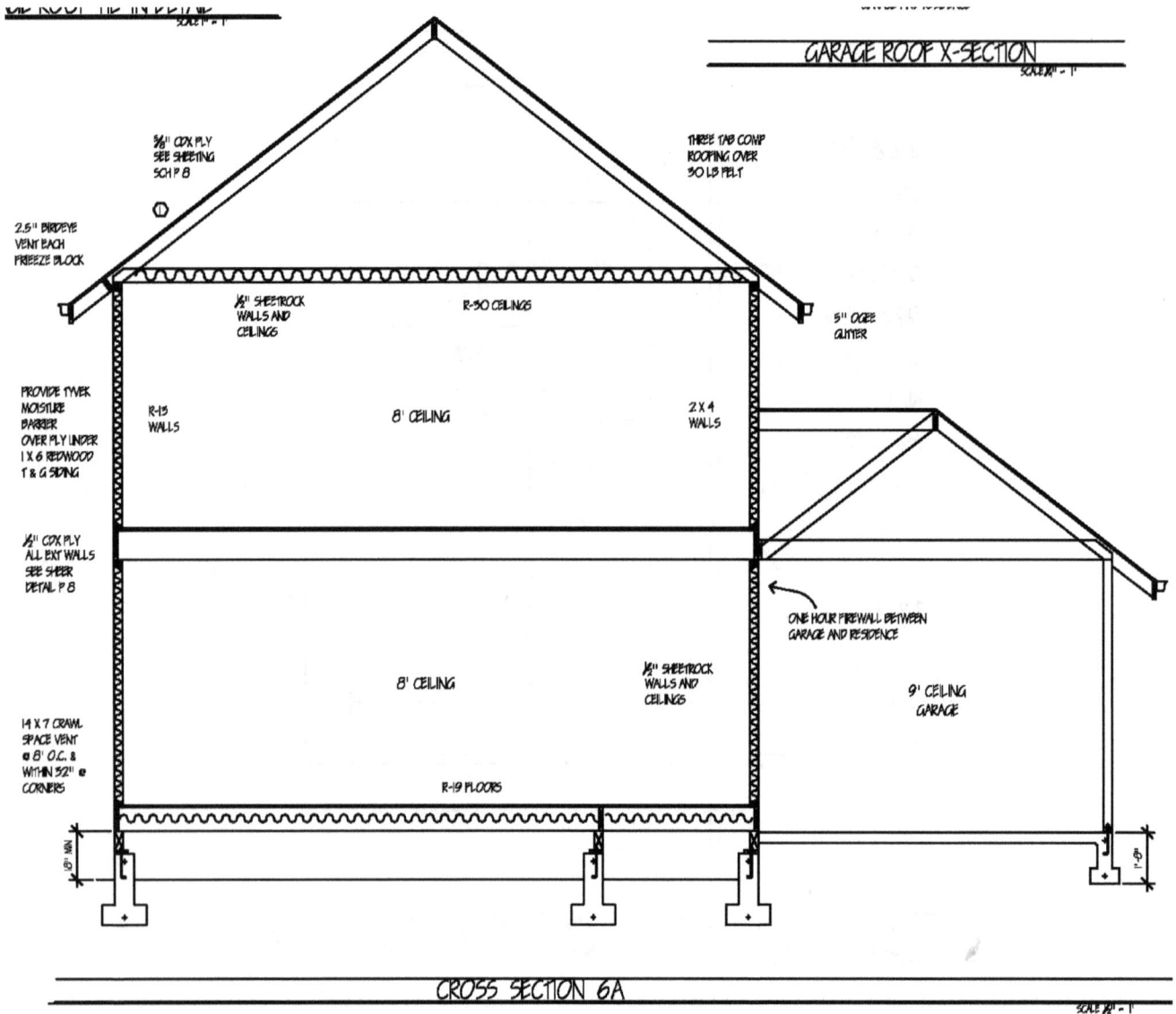

Fig 15-18

I have also used the **text override function** in the Properties drop down box (highlight the object and right click to select the properties box) to override the **dimension text** on the left to read as shown (18" MIN).

I have added the **gutter** shown in Fig 15-19. This is an ogee gutter. I used a temporary grid and the arc tool to create the ogee. Create a grid for the two arcs as shown.

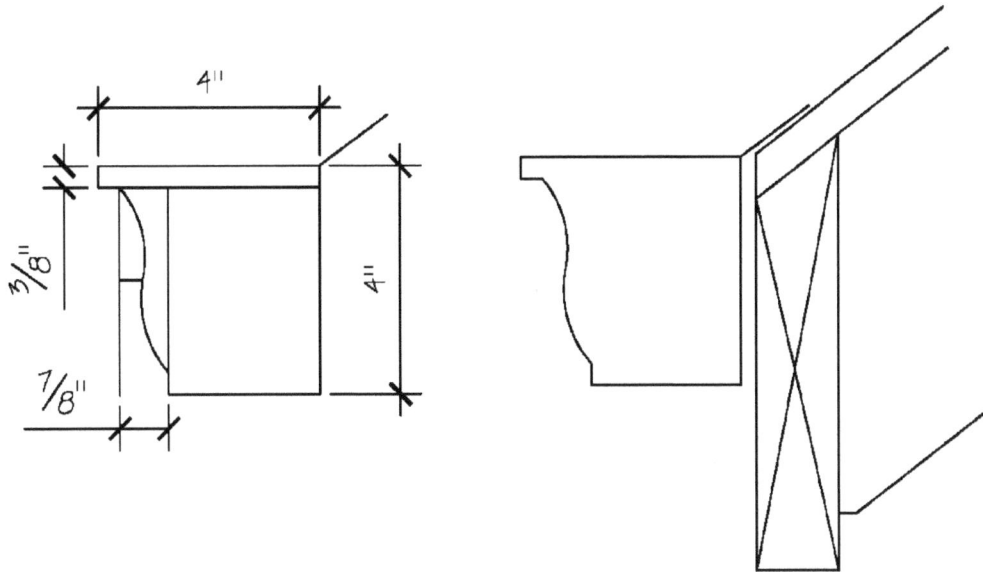

Fig 15-19

Figures 15-19A, B and **C** show the **sheer transfer details** on page 6 with the addition of the ½" plywood and the nails required for the sheer transfer. These nails are not actual size—they are representational so that they can be seen. They are 6" long in this scaled up drawing; the nail heads are 2.25", the lineweight is 40. Set the lineweight using the properties palette (click on the lines after you draw them, right click to bring up the properties menu, set the lineweight). Because this drawing is scaled up by a factor of three, the plywood will be 1.5" thick (3 x ½").

NAIL SHEER AT
JOIST W/ 8d
COMMON NAILS
4" O.C.

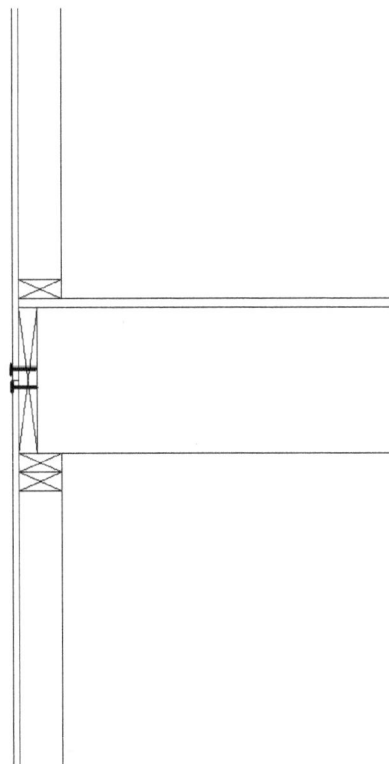

Fig 15-19A

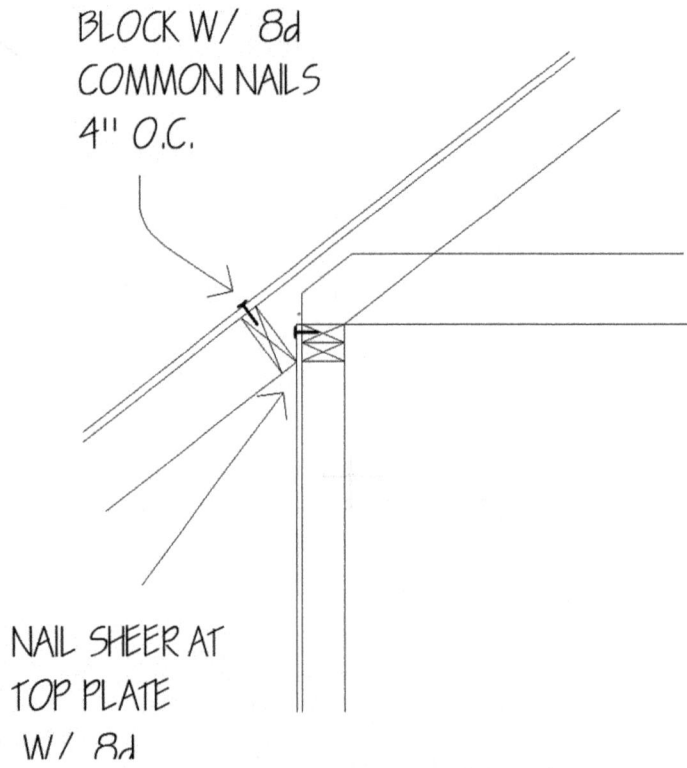

BLOCK W/ 8d
COMMON NAILS
4" O.C.

NAIL SHEER AT
TOP PLATE
W/ 8d

Fig 15-19B

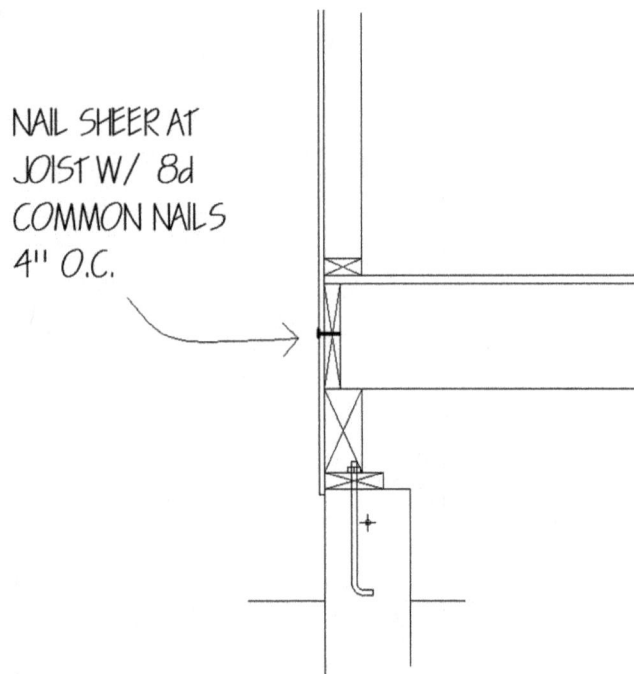

NAIL SHEER AT
JOIST W/ 8d
COMMON NAILS
4" O.C.

Fig 15-19C

15.7 Page Seven

Page 7 of the plans already contains the window schedule that we created. We add some more detail drawings here. See the finished page in Appendix IV to determine how they fit on the page.

Fig 15-20 shows the **Chimney Attachment Detail 7B**. This view, as with all the views on this page, is scaled up in model space (this page was set up using the single viewport method—review Chapter 7 for this). For this new detail the scale factor is 4. After you scale up the drawing add the text. The **text** here is **7.5"** and the **leader** is set with the **quarter dimension style**.

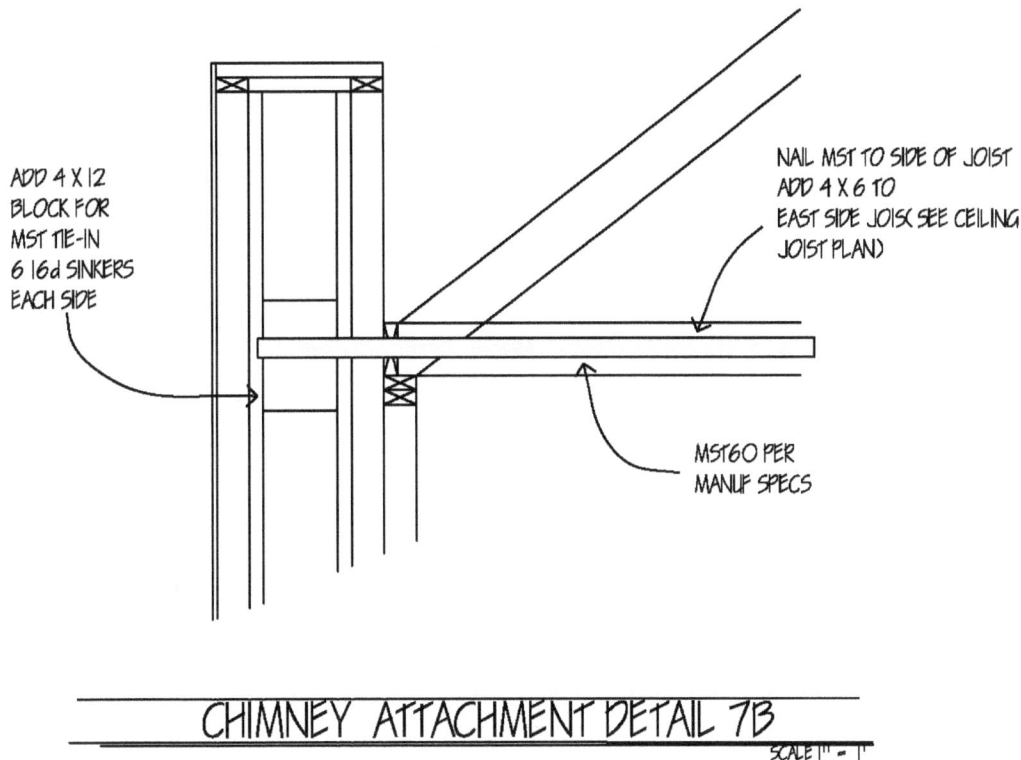

ADD 4 X 12
BLOCK FOR
MST TIE-IN
6 16d SINKERS
EACH SIDE

NAIL MST TO SIDE OF JOIST
ADD 4 X 6 TO
EAST SIDE JOIST SEE CEILING
JOIST PLAN)

MST60 PER
MANUF SPECS

CHIMNEY ATTACHMENT DETAIL 7B
SCALE 1" = 1'

Fig 15-20

Draw it in real scale first (without the text), use the **scale** tool and scale it up by a **factor of four**. Then add the text. This may seem a bit weird because there is nothing on the page that is actually scaled to ¼ scale, but, you will recall the title block and border that we created for all (but one) of the pages is scaled to 1/4. So everything is either plotted in that scale or scaled up in relation to that scale (except page 1 which is eighth scale).

The MST strap is filled in with a fill. The **Solid** fill for the **MST** strap is set to blue and the luminosity to 97. If you set the color luminosity too dense (lower than 95) it may plot out solid black (depending on the plotter/printer), which doesn't look good on the plans: it shows up as a solid black mass of ink. Your printing or plotting experience might be different so do a trial before you print a whole bunch of sheets with a fill on them.

Figure 15-21 shows the **Bollard Detail**. Draw it in real scale, then **scale** it up by a **factor of 4** to get the **1" = 1'** scale. For the dimensions use the **Quarterx4 dimension style** (Primary Units tab: Scale factor set to .25). This will measure the objects with a scale factor of .25. The dimension will read correct even though you have scaled it up to four times its actual size.

You will have to create temporary lines to close up the space that contains the hatch pattern. Try a few different hatch scale factors to see how they look.

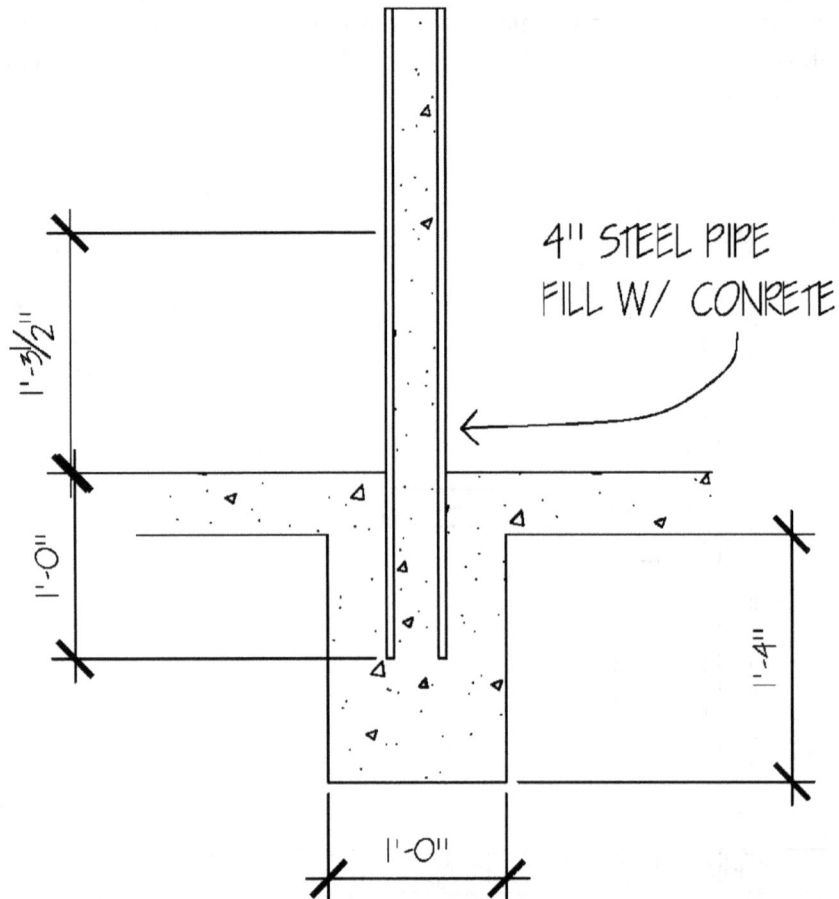

Fig 15-21

Fig 15-22 shows the **hand rail** cross section. It is to be plotted at **2" = 1'**. This is a good scale for objects that are small and would not show up at even the 1" scale very well. I used a **spline** line and **Mtext** to create the dimensions text shown. It is a very tight space for dimensions and they come out clearer this way.

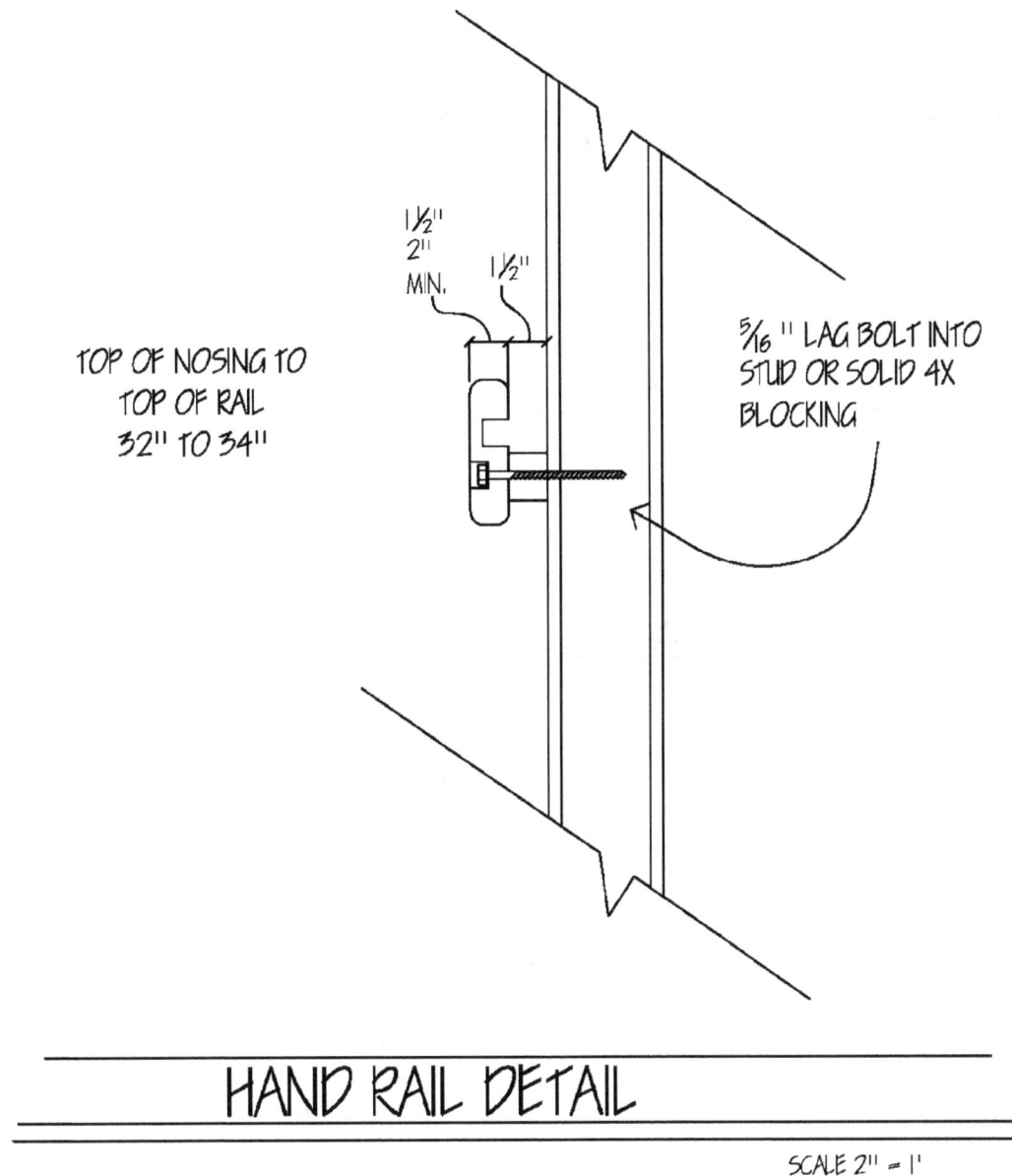

TOP OF NOSING TO
TOP OF RAIL
32" TO 34"

1½"
2"
MIN.

1½"

5⁄16" LAG BOLT INTO
STUD OR SOLID 4X
BLOCKING

HAND RAIL DETAIL

SCALE 2" = 1'

Fig 15-22

Fig 15-23 shows a close up of the **lag bolt**. It is not necessary to draw something this elaborate. But if you take the time to draw something like this you will always have it and can copy it into future drawings. Create a rectangle for the shaft that extends the full length of the shaft and threads, then draw the first angled line (30 degrees), offset the angled line to create all of the 30 degree lines, use the arc tool to create the curves for the thread between the end of the angled lines. You can use the mirror tool for the arcs to create the other side and move this mirrored copy into place.

Fig 15-23

There are some fasteners in the **design center** (where we got the sink and toilet). No lag bolts, however. And there are a lot of objects (called **blocks** in AutoCad) available on the internet. You can import them into your drawings.

15.8 Page Eight

Page eight complete is shown in Appendix IV. **Fig 15-24** shows the **First Floor Sheer Plan**. Fig 15-24A shows some closer detail of this. The lines and the text that reads HDU5-SDS2.5 are set to 45 degrees. The hexagons are relating to the Ply Schedule shown in Fig 15-28. They can be copied from there. The lines that designate the sheer panel sections are double lines (see Fig 15-24A). They are 1 inch offset from each other and 2" offset from the wall line.

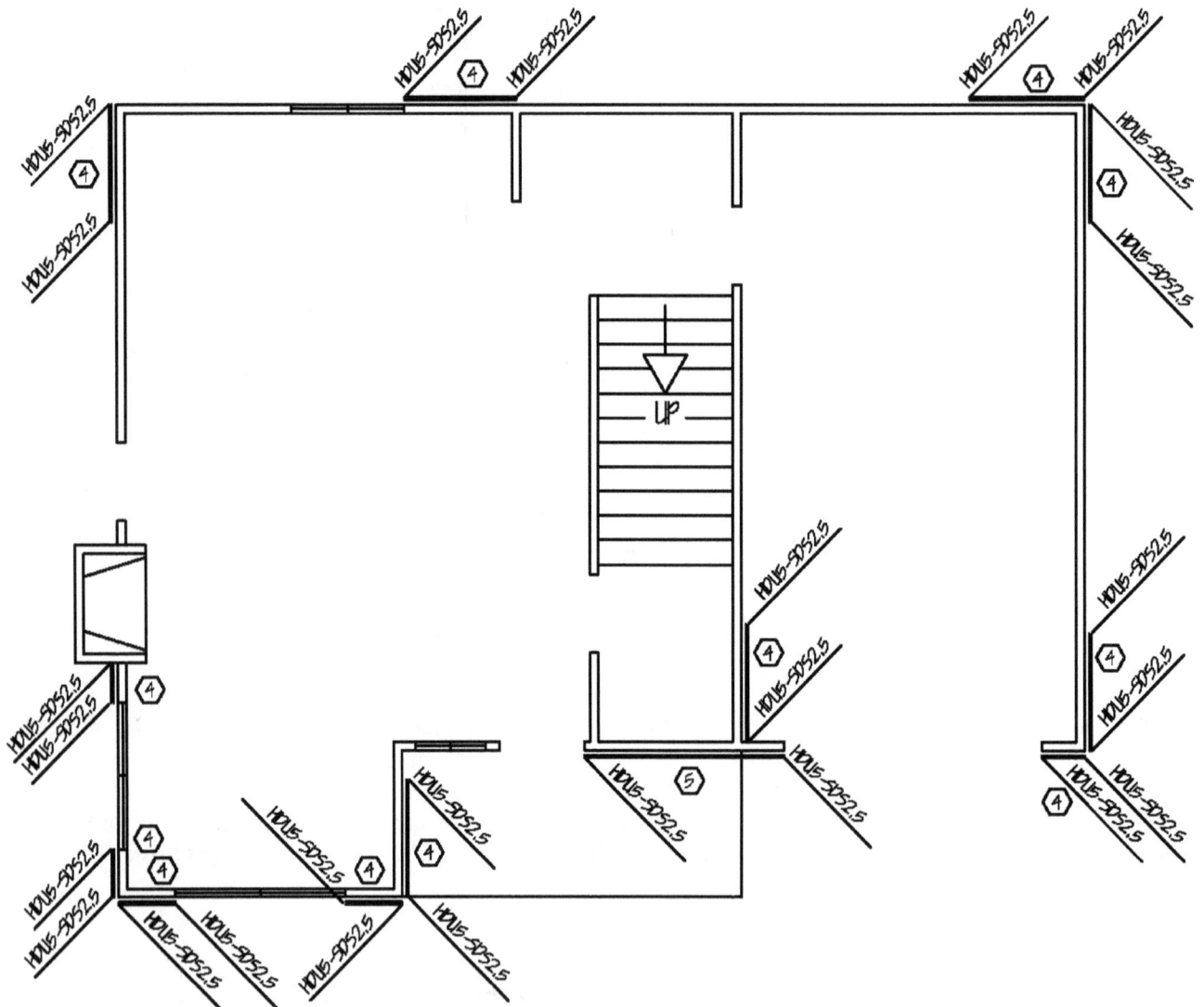

Fig 15-24

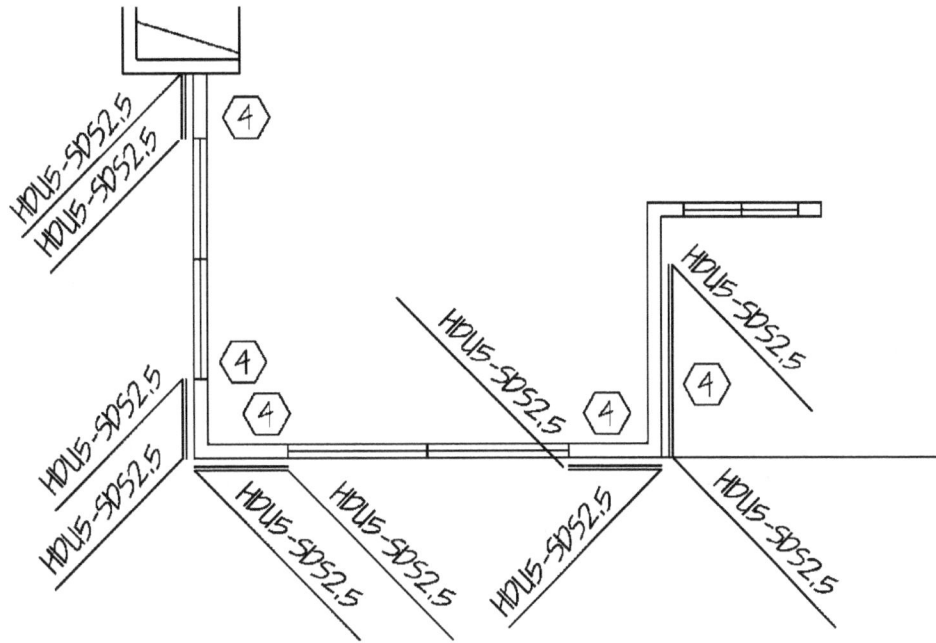

Fig 15-24A

Fig 15-25 shows the **Second Story Sheer Plan**. The lines that designate the sheer panel sections are double lines. They are 1 inch offset from each other and 2" offset from the wall line. The hexagons, once again relate to the **Plywood Schedule** on this same page and they are copied from there.

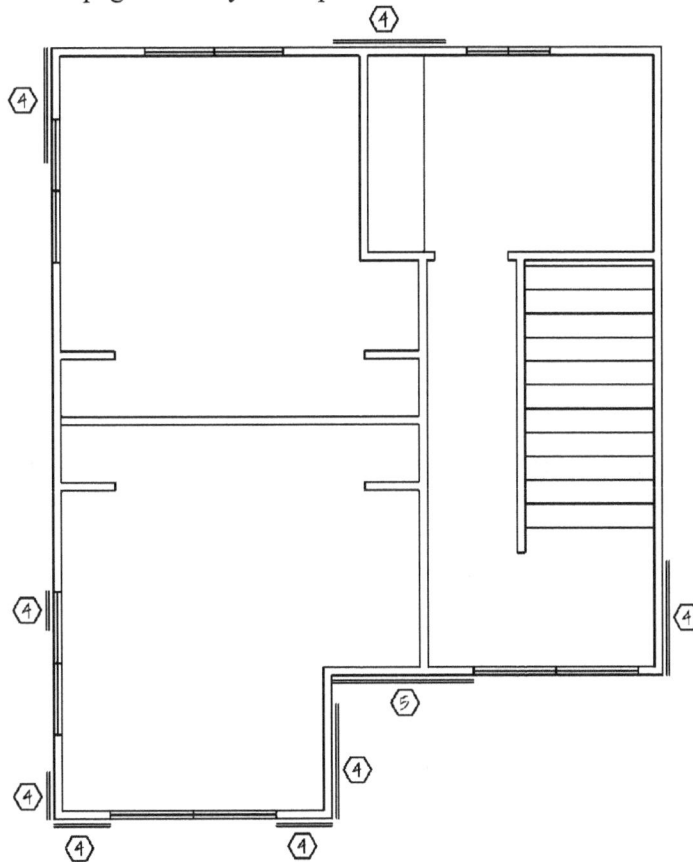

Fig 15-25

Fig 15-26 is **Sheer Detail 8A**. The scale is ½" = 1'. Draw it and scale it up by a factor of 2. Use the dashed line layer for the dashed lines, then **re-scale the line** using the **properties** box to get something similar to what you see in the drawing.

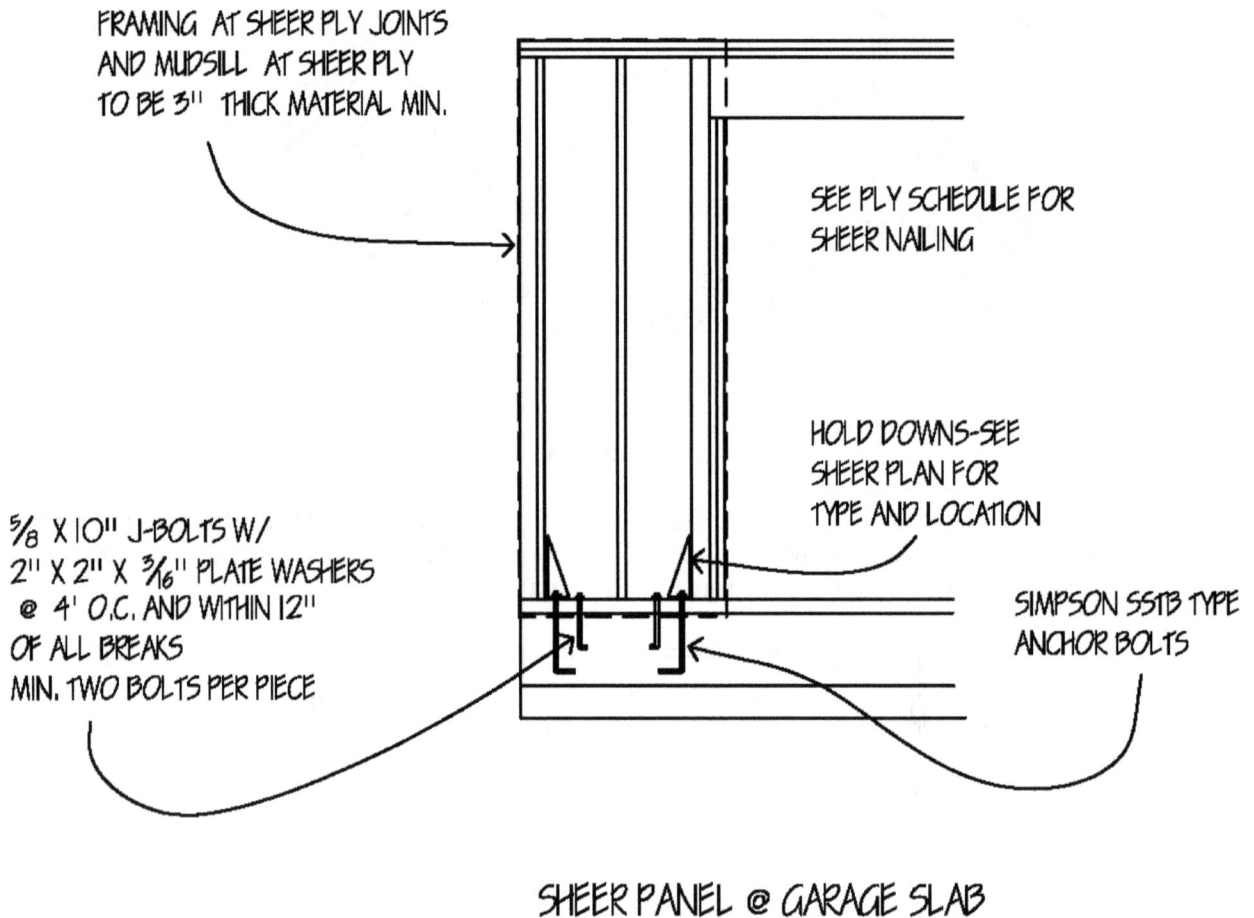

FRAMING AT SHEER PLY JOINTS AND MUDSILL AT SHEER PLY TO BE 3" THICK MATERIAL MIN.

SEE PLY SCHEDULE FOR SHEER NAILING

HOLD DOWNS-SEE SHEER PLAN FOR TYPE AND LOCATION

⅝ X 10" J-BOLTS W/ 2" X 2" X ³⁄₁₆" PLATE WASHERS @ 4' O.C. AND WITHIN 12" OF ALL BREAKS MIN. TWO BOLTS PER PIECE

SIMPSON SSTB TYPE ANCHOR BOLTS

SHEER PANEL @ GARAGE SLAB

Fig 15-26

Fig 15-26A shows closer detail of this section. The long **bolts** are **16" x ¾"**. The **hold downs** are not drawn to true scale as they are representational. Here they are **4" x 12"**.

This wall section represents the sheer panel construction for the walls on the garage concrete slab. The **walls** in the **garage** are **9 feet** tall. The width of the panel is not the same as the front of the garage because this is a typical drawing that is used on all my plans. It is representational to the extent that the wall section can be varying widths.

The anchor bolts are the same as shown in the foundation details and can be copied from there.

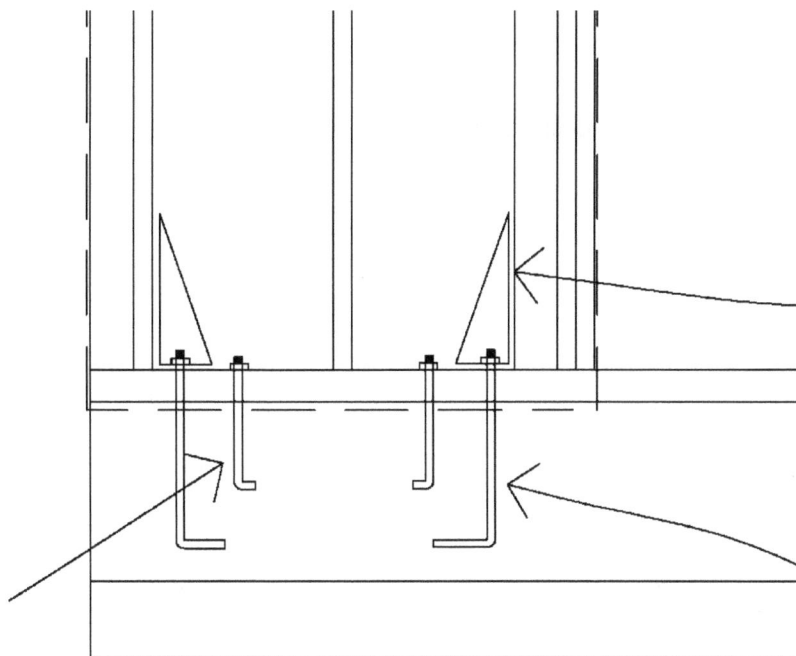

Fig 15-26A

Fig 15-27 is **Sheer Detail 8B**. The wall height here is 8' 1". The lines at the bottom are: the bottom plate of the wall, below that is the floor joist, then the rim girder, with the foundation below. The measurements can be taken off the foundation details (Page 3 of the plans).

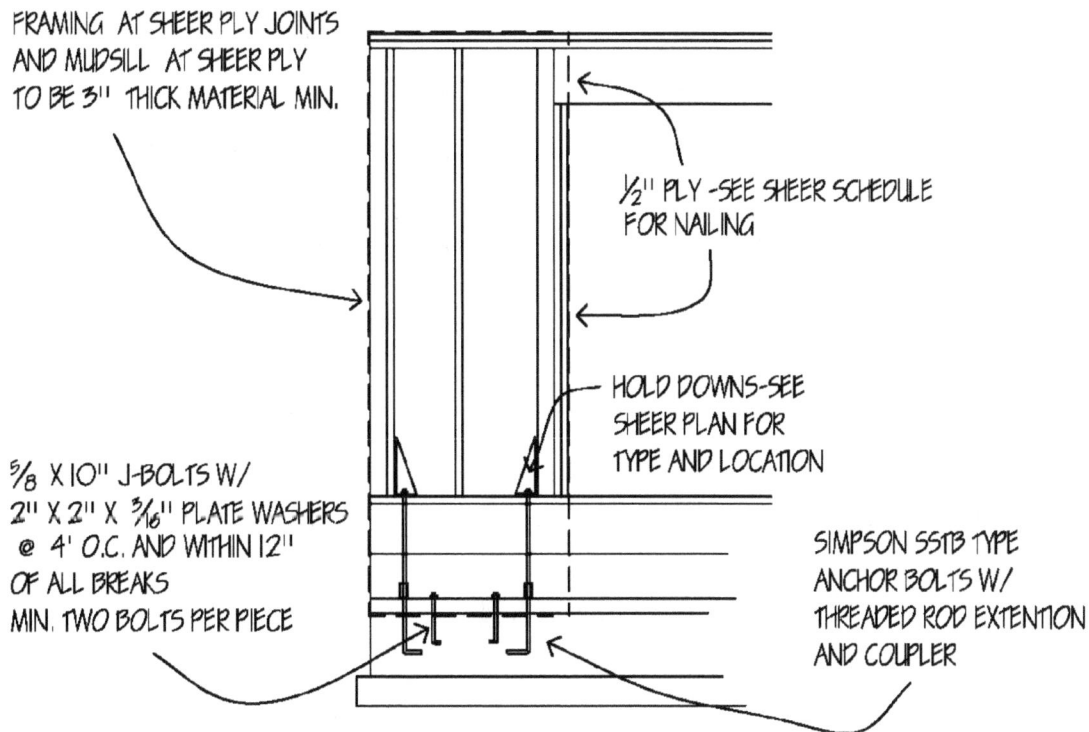

FRAMING AT SHEER PLY JOINTS AND MUDSILL AT SHEER PLY TO BE 3" THICK MATERIAL MIN.

½" PLY -SEE SHEER SCHEDULE FOR NAILING

HOLD DOWNS-SEE SHEER PLAN FOR TYPE AND LOCATION

⅝ X 10" J-BOLTS W/ 2" X 2" X 3/16" PLATE WASHERS @ 4' O.C. AND WITHIN 12" OF ALL BREAKS MIN. TWO BOLTS PER PIECE

SIMPSON SSTB TYPE ANCHOR BOLTS W/ THREADED ROD EXTENTION AND COUPLER

SHEER PANEL @ FRAMED FLOORS
Fig 15-27

Fig 15-27A shows a larger image of this detail. Here the long bolt is 33" long with a rectangle that represents a coupler. It is 1 ¾" x 3".

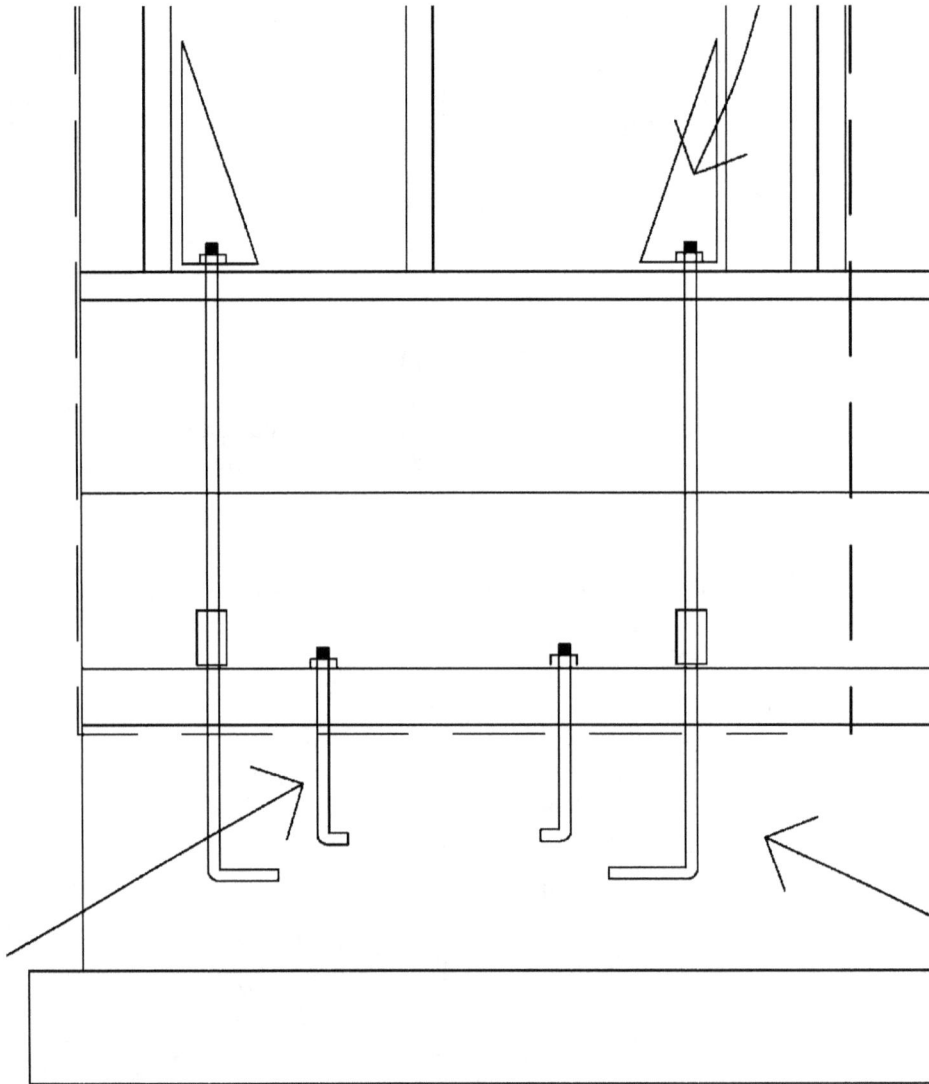

Fig 15-27A

Fig 15-28 is the **Ply Schedule**. This is a table. I am going to let you figure this out on your own using the information from **Chapter 12**. Review the steps for the window schedule if you need to refresh. The text in this table is 1/8" and the tile is 5/16". The hexagons are drawn to the side, the numbers added, then copied into the table.

PLYWD KEY	PLY THICKNESS	PLYWOOD RATING	COMMON NAIL SIZE	PANEL EDGE NAIL SPACING	FIELD NAIL SPACING	DENOTED EDGE BLOCKING REQD
①	5/8"	APA RATED COX	8d	6	12	
②	3/4"	APA RATED LL	8d	6	10	T & G
③	1/2"	APA RATED COX	8d	6*	12	B
④	1/2"	APA RATED COX	8d	4*	12	B
⑤	1/2"	APA RATED COX	8d	2*	12	B
⑥	3/8"	APA RATED COX	8d	2*	12	B

- EDGE FRAMING AND SILL PLATE AT ADJOINING PANEL EDGES TO BE 3X FRAMING MINIMUM WITH NAILS STAGGERED 1" MINIMUM

- DOUBLE TOP PLATES AT WALLS TO BE LAPPED 4' MIN.

HOLD DOWNS: USE SSTB16 ANCHORS

Fig 15-28

15.9 Page Nine

Finally we come to the last page—**Page 9**. This is a page for **notes** (Fig 15-29). I have not added a lot of notes. Often the notes page will be filled completely. These are specific instructions for the different trades, specifications, and codes that are required to be printed on the plans by different jurisdiction. Here are a few of the more common notes.

GENERAL CONSTRUCTION NOTES

1-CURRENT APPLICABLE CODES: 2010 CBC, 2010 MECH, PLUMB & ELECT CODES.

2-PLUMBING FIXTURES SHALL COMPLY WITH THE FOLLOWING STANDARDS

      -TOILETS TO BE HIGH EFFICIENCY = 1.6 GALS/ FLUSH MAX

      -SHOWER HEAD = 2.5 GALS./ MIN MAX.

      -LAVATORY FAUCET = 2.2 GALS./ MIN. MAX.

3-ALL DOORS AND WINDOWS TO BE CHAULKED FOR SEAL FOR DRAFT BARRIER

4-ALL EXT DOORS TO BE WEATHER STRIPPED

5-CHAULK ALL VENTS AND PIPES AT PERFERATION OF EXT. MEMBRANE.

6-PROVIDE TYVEK TYPE MOISTURE BARRIER AT EXT. WALLS UNDER SIDING.

7-ALL EXT FASTENERS TO BE OF CORROSION RESISTENCE EX: GALV, ANODIZED, STAINLESS OR ALUMINUM.

8-ALL CONSTRUCTION LUMBER TO BE #2 & BTR DF UNLESS SPECIFIED.

9-ALL WOOD EXPOSED TO THE WEATHER TO BE PT OR APPROVED NATURALLY DECAY RESISTANT SPECIES.

10-ALL MEASUREMENTS TO BE FIELD VERIFIED.

11-PROVIDE 12" X 12" REMOVABLE ACCESS PANEL FOR ALL PLUMBING FIXTURES W/ CONCEALED SLIP JOINT CONNECTORS.

12-SHOWER ENCLOSURE TO BE TEMPERED GLASS.

13-PROVIDE NON-REMOVABLE BACK FLOW DEVICES AT ALL HOSE BIBS.

Fig 15-29

We are finally done with the complete plans. Congratulations are in order. You are now ready to draw architectural plans professionally with AutoCAD.

The next and final chapter is about annotative features and some miscellaneous odds and ends.

Chapter 16—Annotative Text, Dimensions, Leaders, and Misc. Stuff

You now have the basic skills to draw 2d objects. There are a lot of features in AutoCAD that are not covered in this book. The object of this book was to get you drawing as quickly as possible. As you go forward from this point you can learn more features and discover new methods that you may prefer. A few of those features are covered in this chapter.

One of the features that you may want to learn is the Annotative features for Text, Dimensions and Leaders. This feature is essentially a calculator that sizes these things for you. The system is similar for each of these three categories but enough different that each needs to be described separately.

16.1 Annotative Text

Annotative text sets the height of text automatically. You tell the system the height you want your text to plot or print, you then tell it at what scale you will be plotting, and it sets the height of the text automatically.

Go to the **Text Style** dialog box and under **Styles** select **Annotative** then click on **New**. **Name** the new style **Annotative City**. Set the **Font Name** to: **CityBlueprint**. Set the **Paper Text Height to 3/16"**. Check the **Annotative** box. Set **current** and **close**.

Back in the workspace window set the **Annotative Scale** at the bottom of the screen (**Fig 16-1**) to ¼" = 1'.

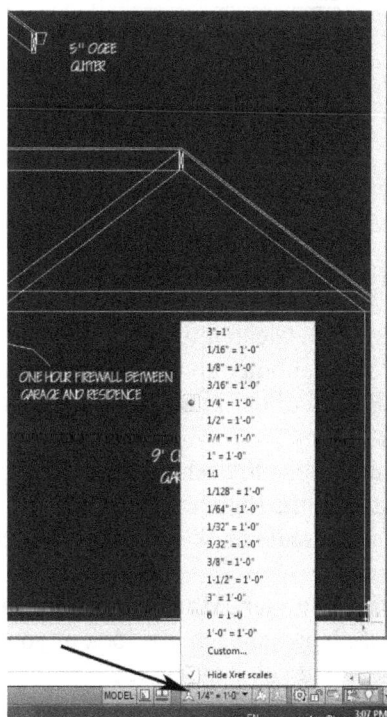

Fig 16-1

Zoom in on the Cross Section in Page 6 of your plans and use the **Mtext** function to type some temporary text on the page. Next to the **8' CEILING** text type **8' CEILING** again. You will see that it automatically creates text that is the same height as the 9" text we created before. It is setting the **scale factor** automatically to print out at 3/16" when plotted in a viewport set to ¼" = 1' scale. It is automatically selecting the size from a text size chart as in Chapter 13.

If you want a different size text in the ¼" = 1' scale, you can set this in the **Text Editor ribbon** or the **Text Formatting toolbar** (the same way we did manually) if you set it to open with mtext or you can set it on the Text Editor ribbon that opens with mtext. With the annotative feature, the number that you enter will be the plotted text size (1/8", 3/16", 1/4", etc).

You must remember to change the Annotative Scale (Fig 16-1) in model space to whatever scale you intend to plot/print (the scale you will set in the viewport). This must be done before you create the text. Set the annotative scale in model space to match the viewport scale that you intend to use for plotting for each separate view.

16.2 Annotative Dimension

To see how annotative dimension functions, let's try an example. Click on your **DimStyle** button. You have a preset style on the left for **Annotative**, click on this. Click **Modify**. In the **Text** tab set the height of your text to **1/8"** (**uncheck** the box that says: **Draw frame around text**). In the **Fit** tab make sure the **Annotative** button is **checked**. In **Primary Units** tab make sure that you have the **Unit format**: set to **Architectural**. **Ok** and **Set Current**. At the bottom of the screen click on the **Annotation Scale** arrow and set it to ¼" = 1'. Click back in the workspace to close the scale setting window.

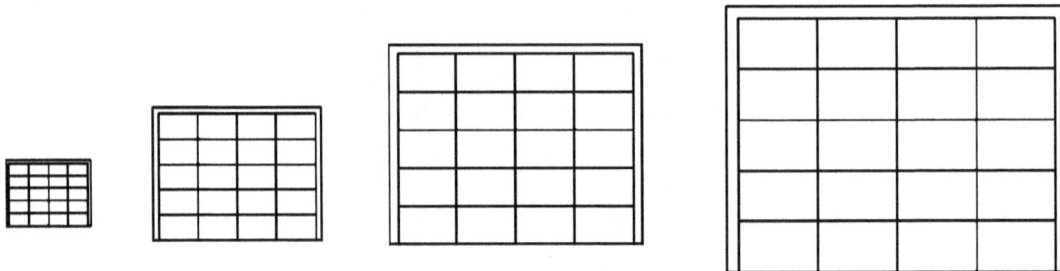

Fig 16-2

Make a **copy** of the **garage door** as in **Fig 16-2**. Clean it up and make **four copies**. Now use the **scale** tool to scale up one copy by a scale **factor of 2**. Scale another up by a **factor of 3**. And a third by a **factor of 4**. These are the same scale factors that we applied to Page 6 of our plans.

Use the **linear dimension** tool and add dimensions to each of these. They will read (the heights) 7', 14', 21' and 28'. The size of the dimensions—the text size, the lines, etc—is good for plotting at ¼" = 1'. The height of the text is going to plot at 1/8" when plotted at the scale of ¼" = 1'. But only the first dimension (7') is correct.

To fix this go back to the **Dimension Style Manager. Modify** the **Annotative Dimension Style** and under the **primary units** tab set the **scale factor** to **.5**. Now go back and look at your measurements. The second copy has the correct measurement because it was scaled up by a factor of 2.

You might see that this is very similar to what we did in our drawings for multiple scales printed in a single viewport.

To make this work you will need to set up a **different Annotative Dimension Style** for **each scale factor** on the page. Just as we did before these scales would be .5, .333, and .25 respectively. Call them Annotative2, Annotative3, and Annotative4.

If you do this you can use them for the four different garage doors and you will then get a dimension of 7' for all of them.

If you are going to plot in the scale of ½" = 1', you would set that dimstyle current and then change the annotative scale in the window at the bottom of the Model space screen.

Leaders will be **set with** these **dimension styles** just as before.

When you create dimensions on a page to be printed in any particular scale, set the annotative scale at the bottom of the screen to that scale before you add the dimensions and leaders.

This is handy and relatively easy compared to using size charts and manually setting dimension styles. Some may ask: why did we did not do the whole set of plans using this feature, and just skip all of the discussion of the non-annotative method. That is a reasonable question. I think that it is important to understand scales and not simply have the computer do the work without an understanding of what it is doing. For some this won't ever matter. For others it will be very important.

16.3 The Classic Interface

We have used the **ribbon** set up for the workspace. Many people prefer the old classic interface which was titled: **2D Drafting & Annotative** setting for Workspace. There are fewer clicks to get the same results.

You can set up the screen as the classic screen by using the CUI. Type cui to see this dialog box. You can find instructions on the internet. Basically you add toolbars and dock them in the old configuration and then turn off the ribbons. You must save your settings to a file or you will have to reset them every time you open a new file.

16.4 Set up Page

It is a good idea to create a **Setup Page** file that you can copy and open for a new drawing. This page will have the workspace set up the way you like it. It will have everything (like units) set up and ready to go; your layers will be preset, layouts, palettes, etc…

The other thing that you can do with the setup page is **copy your title block and border** to that file so you will only have to fill in the blanks.

To do this, make a copy of your drawing file using the **Save as** function on your screen under the **AutoCAD icon** at the upper left.

Click Save As…and when the screen comes up save the file where you will be storing your AutoCad drawings; **name** it **Standard Setup** (or any other name you prefer). **Open** this file (it should open automatically) and **erase everything except** for the **title block** and **border**. **Save** the file and **Close** it.

When you **start a new drawing open this file** and **save a copy** using the **Save as** function; **rename** the new copy for your new project. This will create a copy and leave the setup page unchanged to be used again. Now you have your title blocks ready to use and all of your settings.

16.5 Plotter Settings

There are a lot of options for plotting. Right click on a Layout tab and select Plot. When the Plot window opens click on the **Properites** button next to the **Plotter/printer Name** window. Here you will see a lot of settings including custom paper sizes.

You can print banners or super large full scale plans by creating custom paper sizes. On some printers you can print 36" by any length. I created a full scale 14' x 7' set of plans for a steel gate that had many custom curved metal parts. I then took it to the metal fabricator; they spread it out on the floor, and bent the metal to match the plans.

Type **Options**, then select **Plot and Publish**. Here are more settings.

Blocks and Copying from One Drawing to Another

The easiest way to copy objects from one drawing file to another is to simply go into the drawing file that contains the objects to be copied, highlight the objects, and then use **Cntl C** (hold down the Control button on your keyboard and press C). Now open the destination file and copy using Cntl **V** (hold down the Control key and press V). The cursor will flicker a bit and you can click anywhere in your drawing to set it in the workspace.

There are a number of other options. One is to **create** a **block** which is essentially an AutoCad file with the object stored on a drawing by itself. You create a block by typing **wblock** and selecting the object you wish to save. You insert a block by typing **insert** and selecting the block, then setting the object onto your screen.

You can get some weird stuff happening with the blocks thing. One of the main problems is that the layers come with it and you may have those **layers turned off**. Check this first. If you can't see the block item after you insert it, look around on the page, it may have set it to some strange point on your drawing.

You can always just copy it with Ctl C and Ctl V (aka: copy and paste).

Xrefs

Xrefs is another way of saving your objects. Both the blocks and the xrefs can be set so that if you change the master drawing it will change the objects in all the places where you have inserted it. This is very useful for very large projects. Say, as an example, you are designing a large apartment building with dozens of bathrooms that are all the same; if you need to change something in the bathrooms, you can just change the master drawing and it will change all the bathrooms automatically.

This is a lot less helpful for residential design, because the blocks that you want to copy will often be altered a bit from drawing to drawing. Say to reflect a code change. You won't want to change it in old drawings. You can isolate the xref so that they don't all change together, but then you are really just copying and pasting—so, in those cases, you can just copy and paste. Or use a block.

Clouding

Clouding is used to show changes that have been made to the plans since the last revision. Clouding is used to clearly call out these changes for the building or planning departments per the items on their correction notices. It is quite easy to use. Click on the **Cloud** button on the draw palette or type **cloud,** click on the approximate point you want to begin the cloud, then encircle the object to be enclosed in the cloud. The **settings** come up when you first hit the cloud button (or type cloud); **set** your **cloud arc size** at the prompt. Try a few settings for different sized arcs and you will quickly grasp the idea.

Wipeout

Occasionally you will need to block out something on the screen. This is useful when adding text to an area that is filled with hatch or gradient. Type **wipeout** and follow the prompts. Pick an area inside a hatch and see how it works. You can then type text into the area that has been wiped out.

Measure tool

The Distance tool on the Utilities palette can be used to check linear measurements.

Options

Check out the Options selections. Type: **options** and the options dialog box will open. Look through all the different tabs. There are dozens of settings. You can change the color scheme of your workspace.

If you don't like the black background in model space, you can change it to white or any color.

You can change how the mouse clicks function under Preferences. Under lineweight settings you can adjust how the lines display on the screen. Under Drafting you can change the appearance of the cursor and the pick boxes. And a lot more.

Appendix I   General Information

General help under alphabetic categories

Arc

If you turn on the Dynamic Input function (located with the Ortho and Osnap buttons at the bottom of the screen) you can see the length and angle of the arc that you are creating using the 3-Point. You can get it close to what you want, and then customize the arc using the properties palette or one of the other Arc tools. Which too depends on what parameters are important. Radius is a common definition used. The Start,End,Radius Arc tool is good for this. Look at the list and try out the different options to see which tool is best for each parameter.

Cursor settings

You can customize the settings for your cursor and selection boxes. Type **options** to open the **Options** dialog box. Click on the **Drafting** tab. This will open a dialog box where you can change the size of your cursor and Osnap icon size.

Chamfer and Fillet

Both chamfer and fillet can be set by reading the prompts and making selections as you go through the set up process. Watch for the **Multiple** option and type m. This will allow you to fillet or chamfer a series of corners without having to go through the whole process each time.

Command Line

If you lose the command line press Ctrl 9. If this doesn't work try typing: commandline. The command line can be expanded or reduced by grabbing the border with the cursor (it will turn into a little H grip) and sliding it up or down. It can be placed in different places on the screen by using the grip in the upper left corner.

Dashed Lines

Model Space Problems: if your dashed lines do not show as dashed lines in model space. Check your settings for ltscale, msltscale, celtscale.

Ltscale sets the scale for all lines in the drawing. Type ltscale to set the value. Try some experimental lines using different linetypes (set them as different layers). Then try different scales and see what you get.

Celtscale sets the linetype value for the next object drawn (and everything after that until you reset it) without changing the overall scale that is set with the ltscale setting. The properties palette can also be used for this.

Msltscale sets the linetype to annotative. A value of 1 makes the linetypes annotative, 0 is non-annotative. See Chapter 16 for the discussion of annotative features.

Properites palette can be used to change the line characteristics for individual or groups of lines.

Paper Space Problems: Dashed lines can be a bit difficult at times. A common problem is when they do not show up as dashed lines in the **paperspace** viewport or when plotted/printed. If you have this problem the first thing to do is to reset your **paperspace linetype** scale. Type: psltscale and set the value to **0**. Then **regen** the drawing and they should appear. To regen type **Regenall**. Wait a bit, it can take some time.

You can easily change the scale of your dashed or broken lines by using the **Properties** palate. Click on a line to select it then right click on choose the **Properties** option. Change the line type scale.

Set up linestyles in the Layer Properties Manager (Appendix II). When you click on the linetype (where it says Continu…) you bring up the **Select Linetype** window. Click on **Load** and the **Load or Reload Linetypes** window will open. The size of the dashes that will appear on your drawing is determined by which of these lines you select and then by the linetype scale for the entire drawing that is set by typing **ltscale** and setting a value. You will need to play around with this a bit to find the setting that you want.

There are only five standard dashed lines listed, but you can rescale any of these using the **Properties palette** in the model workspace. Use the **match properties** to change all of the lines that you want to be the same scale.

Design Center

The design center can be difficult to navigate. Follow the directions in Chapter 1, Section 1.19 for an explanation of how to find the preset graphics.

In this book we only use the most basic function of the design center. That is to import graphics. You can find a lot more graphics by going online.

Many companies that sell construction products also have cad graphics of their products that you can import into your drawings. As an example go online and search for kohler cad drawings. There you will find lists of cad drawings of their plumbing products that can be imported into your drawings. You can copy and paste these drawings. Select the graphic with a selection window, then use Ctrl+C, go to your drawing and place it with Ctrl+V.

Dimensions

Dimension styles are set in the **Dimension Styles Manager** dialog box. You can access it by clicking on the Dimension Style manager button in the Annotation palette or type: **dimstyle**. You start out with a Standard and an Annotative Style preset.

To **create** a **new style**: click on one of these two (depending on if you want annotative or not) and then the "**New**" button. This is all detailed in Chapter 1 Section 1.23. Also read Chapter 13 for a discussion of scales and then Chapter 16 Section 1.1 for a discussion of Annotative dimensions.

Whether you use the Annotative feature or set your dimension style manually, you will need to know what scale you intend to plot to (or print out). Determine this before you create dimensions or text on your drawing. The ratio of that scale is then entered into the **Use Overall Scale of** window under the **Fit** tab when you are using a non-**annotative dimstyle**. Read Chapter 13 for a complete discussion of this.

Chapter 16 (section 16.1) describes how to use the **annotative** feature.

If an object is **scaled in model space** then the **inverse** of that **scale** must be **entered** into the **Scale factor** window under the **Primary Units** tab. Experiment with this a bit and you will understand how it works. Follow the steps in Chapter 14 to understand how this works.

The other settings in Dimstyle are easy to understand and the display window shows you the results of changing the settings.

Angular dimensions (not 90 degree vertical or horizontal) are added with the **Aligned** dimension tool on the Annotation palette (co-located with the Linear button).

Electrical Symbols

Fig A-1 shows the progression of the electrical symbol for a light. Draw a 6" circle, offset it to the outside by 1.5". Next draw the lines by using the Quadrant Osnap. Erase the outer circle and trim to see the light symbol.

Fig A-1

Fig A-2 shows the progression of the outlet drawing. Start with a 6" circle. Draw a 9" line and place its midpoint on the center of the circle using the Center Osnap. Offset this line to each side by 1". Erase the middle line and draw a line between the two end points of the two outside lines. Offset this line by 1". Now copy this symbol (but not the short horizontal line). Use the midpoint of the short horizontal line as your base point for copying. Remember that when you copy or move an object the base point (the point you will use to snap to an Osnap icon) doesn't need to be a part of the object you copy. You can use any point on the workspace as your base point.

Fig A-2

Fig A-3 shows the electrical symbols enlarged. The main text in Chapter 15 Section 15.3 explains how to create the fan.

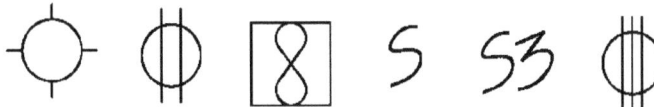

Fig A-3

Extend

Extend is one of the commands that can be difficult. It doesn't always work the first time. Often it is necessary to **double click** on the command button in order for the system to recognize the command. See **Trim and Extend** later in this appendix for a discussion of Extend.

First Line

UCS sometimes interferes with the identity of the first line. To turn it off click on the View tab then on the UCS icon to the far left.

The UCS can be placed anywhere on the workspace. See Chapter 4 (section 4.3) for an explanation of this. Also read Line in this appendix, if you still have problems with the Line command.

Fraction stacking.

Fractions can be typed in various styles. Type the fraction then **highlight it** with the cursor. **Right click** on the highlighted text and choose **Stack or Unstack**. There is also a button on the Text Editor ribbon and the Text Formatting bar.

Glitches

AutoCad has a lot of glitches in the system. I have experienced numerous glitches with several different editions (years) and different computers. This is an impossible subject to cover here because there are so many variables, but if strange things happen, you can look in the different headings in this appendix to see if a specific glitch is covered.

One pesky glitch is that the system will start up and tell you that your settings were not saved. Then it will open, and many of your settings will be gone. You can look for a back up file, these are **.bak** files. You may be able to open a bak file to restore and save your settings. Look for the bak files in your computer files. You may not find them by clicking on Open in your AutoCad program.

If you cannot find the bak file, you will have to recreate your settings: layers, dimension and text styles. If you have a set up file you can copy and paste your drawing into a copy of that to restore your settings. Type units and make sure the system has not changed unit settings.

It seems as though many of the system settings can change on their own. Unfortunately this is one area that cannot be covered because there are too many different forms that this can take. Usually this means resetting the settings one by one. Many of the settings are found in the Options window under the Tool tab at the top of the screen.

If you are trying to do something in this book, and it just doesn't seem to work, you may need to consider that certain settings have been altered. Try saving your file, exiting AutoCad and restarting your computer. Then restart AutoCad and see if that fixes the system. Check any settings that may be associated with the function that is not working.

There is a system reset (reset to defaults). This is found on your computer. Go to start (often just an icon in the lower left corner of your screen), go to All Programs, find AutoDesk and find: **Reset Settings to Default**. This will set everything back to the way it came out of the box. This can resolve some of the stranger system errors that occur from time to time. My 2016 version doesn't have this option. You may need to uninstall and reinstall.

Gradient

Hatch and Gradient function the same basic way. See Chapter 2, Section 2.10 for the steps involved with Hatch/Gradient. Then see Chapter 3, Section 3.3 for more on Gradient settings.

Hatch is a pattern and Gradient is a color fill (or two colors). The color can be a gradient between two colors or a gradient from light to dark. This is set with the **one** or **two color** setting. Use Solid to get a single color fill.

The best way to understand Gradient is to create a rectangle of say 10 ft x 10 ft and then try the different settings. First try one color and see what you get. Then try two colors and see what you get.

The biggest problem with Hatch and Gradient is selecting the **Pick points**. Quite often the system fails to recognize the enclosed space that you select. The reason for this is usually that there are micro openings in the corners. The Hatch/Gradient needs a completely enclosed space in order to function. Otherwise it would spill out and fill up the entire workspace (it doesn't do this—you get an error window).

AutoCAD will create gaps in the corners that were previously closed. This can be very difficult to find because they can be microscopic. The tolerances for AutoCad are extremely minute. See Hatch in this appendix for more on this.

Hatch

Sometimes Hatch locks up and the system becomes **unresponsive**. If this happens use the **Esc** key and try again. Give it a minute (or two) to respond. You may need to do this several times.

The biggest problem with hatch is that it requires that the space to be filled with the hatch or gradient must be completely enclosed—there can be **no gaps** between the enclosing lines. Sometimes you think an area is completely enclosed by lines but it is, in fact, not.

AutoCAD operates to very minute tolerances and you can have a **microscopic gap** where two lines meet. Use the extend tool to make sure the corners are all enclosed if you find that Hatch or Gradient cannot define the space to be filled.

Sometimes **gaps will open after you have them closed**. This is a glitch in the system and it can really throw you for a loop. If the system says it cannot define the space then you must go back to all the corners and make sure they are closed. Even the extend feature will not sometimes close up entirely. So if you really cannot seem to get the system to define the enclosed space you may try drawing the lines beyond the point where they intersect and then trim them back—they won't trim unless they are crossing (and that means closed). You can also try adding more lines and subdivide the area into smaller sections. This will help isolate the problem area.

Another irritating problem with hatch and gradient is that sometimes AutoCAD will not select the hatch or the gradient for editing (or erasing). You can try to zoom in and select a large area with the green selection window. Sometimes you just have to keep trying different zoomed parts of the Hatch until you can highlight it.

If you find that the program simply won't recognize the hatch for selection, you can turn off the other layers around the hatch. Then try to select the entire hatch with a selection window. If all else fails you can turn off all the other layers and erase the hatch or gradient, and replace it.

Keyboard

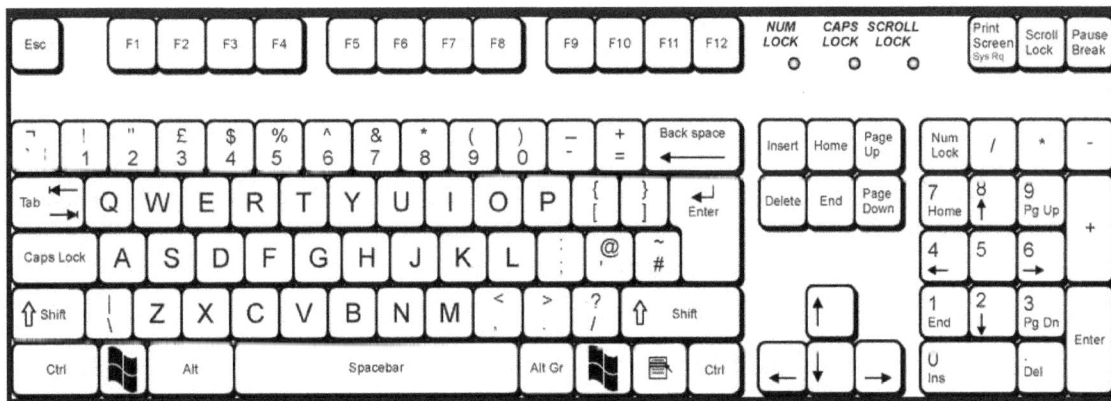

Fig A-4

The F keys are the top row. F3 toggles **Osnap** and F8 toggles **Ortho**.

Enter in this book means hit the enter button on the keyboard (also: <ent> or just <e>).

For some operations you must hold down the **Control** key while you press another key at the same time. Here the control key can be seen in the lower left hand corner marked **Ctrl**.

Cap locks are on the left side.

Layers

Make certain to turn off the plot setting for layers that you do not want plotted/printed before you plot (see Fig 6-9A). This will usually mean the Viewport Layer, but also any construction lines or temporary line layers.

Layers are set and controlled in the **Layer Properties Manager**. Here you can create a new layer with a dedicated line type. See Chapter 1 Section 1.18 (Fig 1-37) for details on setting up Layers. Chapter 4 Section 4.2 deals with dashed lines.

Layer Control sets the current layer and allows you to change the layer of an object (select the object then click on the layer in the Layer Control you want to change it to). Here you can also turn specific layers off or on (the little light bulb symbol), freeze or thaw layers, and lock the layers so they can't be altered.

Leaders

This book only deals with **Qleaders**.

Leaders have to be a **certain length before the arrowhead shows**. This is about 3 times longer than the arrowhead.

The settings for leaders are found in two different places. See Chapter 3, Section 3.5 for instructions.
The **size** of leaders is set with the **Dimension Style Manager**. If you want to change the size of the leader you must change the current dimension style. Set the dimension style for the scale you will be plotting before you draw the leader.

Most of these plans are plotted at ¼" scale. For those pages you would set the quarter dimension style which is set up to print at the scale of ¼" = 1' (see Chapter 1, section 1.23).

The **arrowhead size** and some other aspects of the leader are set in the **Symbols and Arrow** tab. Click on the **Dimension Style Manager** button on the Annotation palette or type **dimstyle <e>**. Chose a style and click on the Modify button. There you will see the Symbols and Arrows tab.

Some of the **leader settings** are **located** in **another location**. Type **qleader**. Read the prompts in the command line. When it reads: specify first point, or [Settings] <Settings>: **type s** and hit the **enter** key. (This is the way a lot of commands work: all you need to do is type the first letter of a word that is listed in the prompts). When you do this, a **Leader Settings** box opens. There you can set your annotation. For this book you set it to **None**. Then under the leader line and arrow you can set the line to either straight lines or spline (curved lines). Set the number of points that determine the shape of the spline (**no limits** for this book), Angle restraints (**Any angle** for this book), and the shape of the leader arrowhead. **Okay**.

Annotative leaders will be set with the Dimension Style manager. They will self adjust to the scale set in the Annotation Scale window at the bottom of the Model workspace screen. See Chapter 16 Section 16.2.

Line

If you are trying to draw the first line of a drawing and it just won't draw a line, it may be that the **units** are **not set correctly**. AutoCAD has a glitch in the system whereby it does not always set the system units when you set them in the page setup. Type: **units**. Then make certain that your settings are correct (for this book you want **Architectural** and **inches** as the insertion scale).

Lines, like most objects display **grip boxes** when you select the line as shown in Fig A-5.

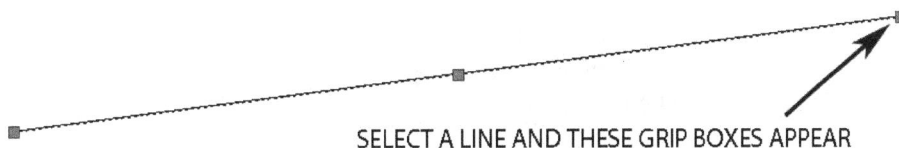

SELECT A LINE AND THESE GRIP BOXES APPEAR

Fig A-5

You can turn these on by clicking on the line (selecting it). Blue grip boxes will appear. If you click on one of the blue grip boxes it will turn red. If you do this to the end of the line you can stretch the line. You can pull it out a ways and enter in a number for the extension that you desire. You can also rotate it from the end box. If you grip it in the middle it will move the entire line.

This can be a good way to trim and extend lines when those functions are not responding properly.

There are a number of ways to draw lines. **Angled lines** can be draw with a **written description** in the command window. Click **line** then, then specify the first point (start of the line), then enter the description of where the line goes from that first point. You enter the **length** first and then the **angle**. The format is as follows for a 10'6" line that is at an angle of 45 degrees: type **@10'6<45** (enter).

Most often it is easiest to start a **right angle** line by specifying a first (starting) point, pull a ways in the direction you wish to draw the line (with the **Ortho** on) and then type the length.

If you are drawing a lot of lines with a certain degree you can use polar tracking and set the accuracy to include the angle you will draw. Set this by right clicking on the **Polar Tracking**. See Polar Tracking in this Appendix.

Lines can also be drawn using coordinates. These reference the UCS origin point. You can set a UCS origin point anywhere in the drawing and then type line coordinates. Enter the horizontal measurement first, then the vertical. Both points on the line (the start and end) will have two coordinates. This is not especially helpful, but is good to keep in mind for certain applications.

Linetypes
See Dashed Lines

Mirror
Mirror is a simple tool to use. The only complicated part of it is that the mirror line between the two (right and left) views of the object is not a line that you draw with the line tool. It is a line that you create in the process of the Mirror command. Try this to see what this means. Use the mirror tool. Turn the ortho on. Select an object to mirror. Read the prompts. When the prompt says: Specify first point of mirror line, click on the empty space next to and above your object (that you want to mirror). Then pull the line that appears down. This is the mirror line. So, as you can see, you do not need to draw a line with the line tool.

The other thing about mirror is that you almost certainly want to use the **ortho** when creating a **mirror line**. If you experiment with this command for a few minutes you will see how it works.

Mouse settings
The mouse can be set to function in various ways. Of course the functions will depend on the type of mouse that you have. Find the mouse settings under **Options**. Type Options and then select the user **Preferences** as shown here in A-6. The right click options will come up and you can customize them.

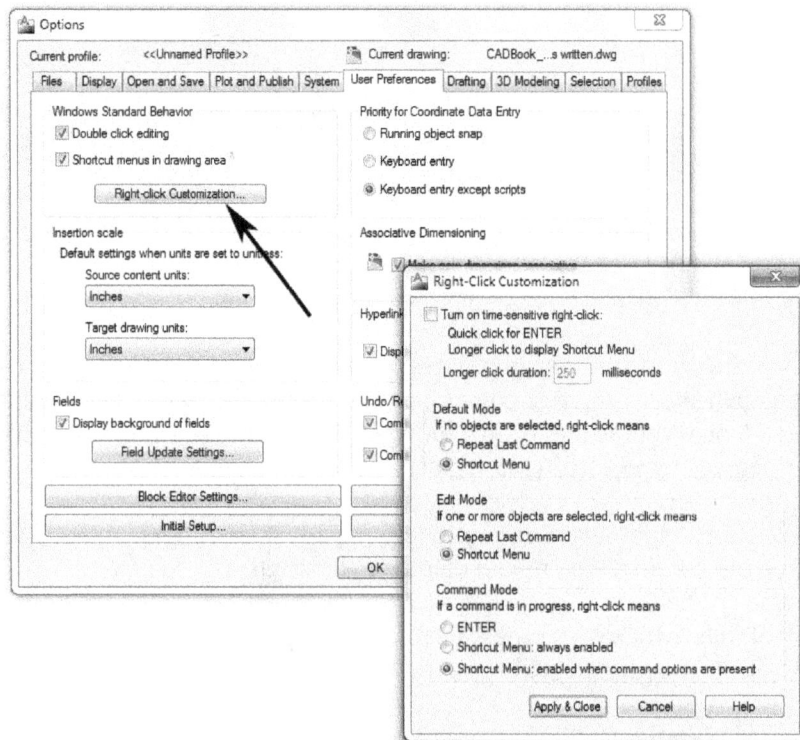

Fig A-6

The size of your grip boxes and your pick boxes can be set under the **Selection** tab.

To set how quickly the mouse wheel zooms in and out type **zoomfactor** and enter a number to determine how fast the mouse wheel zooms in and out. For most operations a setting of 40 to 60 is best.

Enter can be done with a right click of the mouse for many commands. Use the trial and error method to figure out which. That is easier than explaining each variation. As always, use the Undo button if you get into trouble.

There are a variety of right click options and the best way to discover them is to right click at various times during the different functions and see what happens. You can always undo if you get into a weird place.

Mouse Wheel
The mouse wheel is used for moving around in the drawing and zooming in and out. Holding the wheel down allows you to move the drawing (called panning or to pan), turning the wheel zooms in and out.

Nodes and Points
See Chapter 4, Section 4.3 for the discussion of points and nodes. They are basically the same thing. You can set the style of the point or node in the **Point Style** settings box. Type ptype to open this box. You can alter **individual points** with the **Properties palette**.

Ortho

Ortho restricts the movement of objects (and the drawing of lines) to 90 degree angles: vertical and horizontal. Use the **F8** button on the keyboard to toggle this on and off, or click on the button at the bottom of the workspace screen.

Object snap

Object snap pinpoints a particular point for attaching lines or other objects. If you type in Osnap, a **Drafting Settings** window will open. Set the points where you want the Osnap to automatically attach objects.

You can turn the Osnap function on and off with the **F3** button on your keyboard. Or use the button at the bottom of the screen (shown in Fig 1-1)

It is important to understand that when you are moving or copying an object that the **base point** you use to grab that object (and osnap it to where you are copying or moving it) can be **anywhere** on the screen. **It does not have to be located on the object itself**. This you will use quite often.

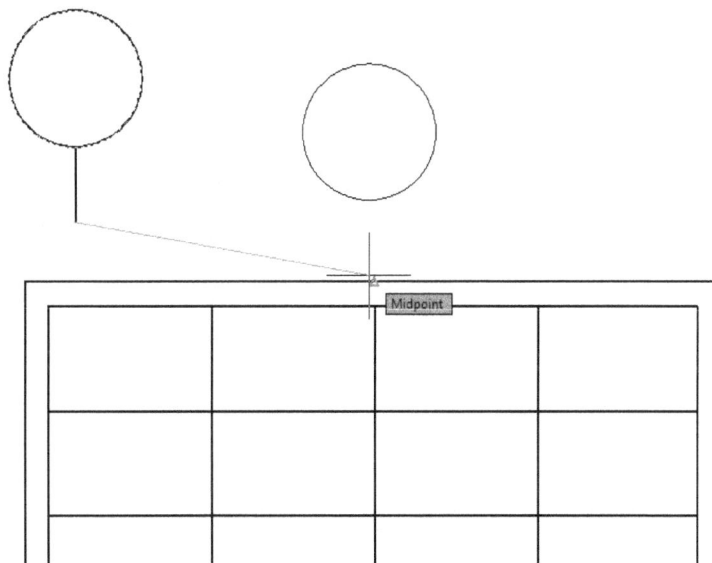

Fig A-7

Fig A-7 demonstrates how this functions. The circle was drawn at the upper left. To copy it we select the circle, but **do not select the line**. **Enter**. When prompted for a **base point**, click on the **lower end** of the **line**. *This will copy the circle but not the line*. It will snap the circle to the midpoint shown, but it will be copied to a point offset from the midpoint by the distance equal to the length of the line.

It would be the same if you copied the circle and line, then erased the line.

Object snap settings

To set object snaps (called osnaps) **right click** on the **Osnap button** at the bottom of the screen. The osnap settings window will come up. Here you can select the osnap points that you want to snap to.

Page Setup (first time)

First time page set up is detailed in Chapter 1. That is the quick start version, however, and much of the setup is scattered throughout the book. Here is the setup in order of steps.

You must set the **units**. You can type units and select the Architectural selection. Insertion scale should be inches. Angle will be Decimal Degrees. Precision can be set to 0.00 (that is close enough for this type of drawing—of course other types of drafting will require more precision).

In some templates AutoCad asks that you set up Extents. I have always ignored this and cannot find any downside to that. But if you wish you can set the limits of the drawing area (type: limits). If you are drawing something small then this can be the size of your paper (the paper size you will print on). Something large, like a house with many views will require a huge area for drawing. You can change it later. But it should be many times larger than the house. If you do not set the extents, the **program automatically recognizes the extent of what you have drawn** at any particular stage in the drawing process; so when you zoom all the way out it will always show just what you have drawn. The Zoom All button will do this automatically (or type z <e> a <e>).

You will eventually need to set up Text Styles, dimension styles, and layers. But you can start drawing at this point.

Text Styles are set by clicking on the Text Style button on the Annotation palette (click the down arrow next to Annotation) or type **style <e>**. Pick a font (set it as regular for now in the Font Style window); set the height of the text (this can be altered, later, in the Text Editing ribbon that opens when you use the Mtext function). See Chapter 1, 1.21.

If you want to use **Annotative text**, set the height to the size of text that you will want to print out on paper. See Chapter 16.

If you do not want to use annotative text, you must set the actual size of the text in relation to your drawing. Chapter 13 is a complete discussion of this concept. These sizes also can be changed in the Text Editor ribbon that opens each time you use Mtext (it opens when you open a mtext box). Set your style **Current**.

Open a Mtext window (type mt and enter, then click on the screen in two points to open a box) and look through the options available in the Text Editor ribbon.

You can turn on the Text formatting Toolbar by clicking on the arrow next to More in the Options panel of the Text Editor ribbon. Select Editor Settings then Show Toolbar.

Dimension styles are set in the Dimension Styles Manager dialog box. You can access that by clicking on the Dimension Style manager button in the Annotation palette or **type: dimstyle**. You start out with a Standard and an Annotative Style preset. To create a new style: click on one of these two and then the "**New**" button. This is all detailed in Chapter 1 Section 1.23. Also read Chapter 13 for a discussion of scales and then Chapter 16 Section 1.2 for a discussion of **Annotative** dimensions.

Whether you use the Annotative feature or set your text height manually, you will need to know what scale you intend to plot to (or print out). Determine this before you create dimensions or text on your drawing.

Leaders are set with the dimension style, except you must also set the leader settings under the **Leader Settings** (see Leaders in this appendix for details).

Layers are used to create different line styles (dashed for instance) and to create different layers that can be turned on or off. Many architectural drafters use many (sometimes many, many) layers. There are reasons for this, but for simple house plans, eight or ten layers is enough. Use a text layer, a dimension layer, and set up a construction line layer for temporary reference lines that you do not want to be part of the final drawing. Use a Hatch layer for hatch and gradients.

The set up for layers is through the **Layer Properties Manager**. You can see a graphic of this in Chapter 1, Section 1.18. Dashed lines setup is discussed in Chapter 4 Section 4.2. You can alter the properties of any object by using the **Properties** palette—select an object then right click and select Properties to open the palette. This is especially useful for setting the dashed lines to the right scale. It is also very useful for overriding text in the dimensions (Chapter 2, Section 2.11).

This is most of what is involved in the initial setup. But you can just follow along with the book and it will guide you through all of this as it is required.

Panning
Use the center mouse wheel. Press down and hold. You will see a little hand. Use the hand to move around in the drawing. If you don't have a mouse with a center wheel, buy one. If you won't or cannot then your best option is using the different Zoom commands to move around in the workspace. Try out the different settings. **Zoom All** shows everything on the screen. **Zoom Window** zooms in on the area you select. These two work well in combination. The **Zoom Dynamic** is very helpful for this, also.

Plotting
The book walks you through the set up for plotters and printers. This begins in Chapter 6 where most of the details are explained.

Plotting a variety of scaled drawings on the same page is detailed in Chapters 7 and 14.

An important thing to remember is that you have to **plot to file** if you are not going to print out directly to a printer. So if you are going to take your drawing to a blueprinter and have it printed out (called plotting in the jargon of drafting), then you need to create a file that can be emailed or copied onto a dvd or flashdrive.

Find the setting for that in the **Plotter Setup wizard**, which you open by selecting the **Output** tab and then: **Plotter Manager**. Select: **Add-A-Plotter Wizard**. As you go through the windows in the wizard you will come to the **Add Plotter-Ports** page. At the top you will see a radio button for **Plot to File**. That is what you want. You are plotting on a particular printer but not directly through a wire—rather you are delivering the file to the printer via disc, email or flash drive. Make sure you save the file to some place on your computer where you can find it—the desktop works well while you are working on the project.

Make sure to turn off any layers that you do not want to be plotted or printed. Do this in the **Layer Properties Manager**. Click on the little **printer icon** so that it has a red circle with diagonal line in it.

Dashed lines sometimes show up as solid lines in the viewport (and plot as solid lines on paper). If you don't see your dashed lines in the viewport you can check in the print preview. If they are not there you need to reset your paper space line type scale. Type **psltscale** and set the value to **0**. Then type: **Regenall**. The lines should appear dashed. If not see dashed lines in this appendix.

Points
See Nodes.

Polar Co-ordinates
Polar co-ordinates refer to the degrees of arc from the **starting point** (0) which is set by default as left to right horizontal on the screen. Fig A-8 shows how this works. When you draw lines by using coordinates this is the system that is used for the angles of the lines. This is, also, the system that is used for rotation. As you can see it is counter clockwise in its orientation. You can enter negative numbers to get a clockwise rotation.

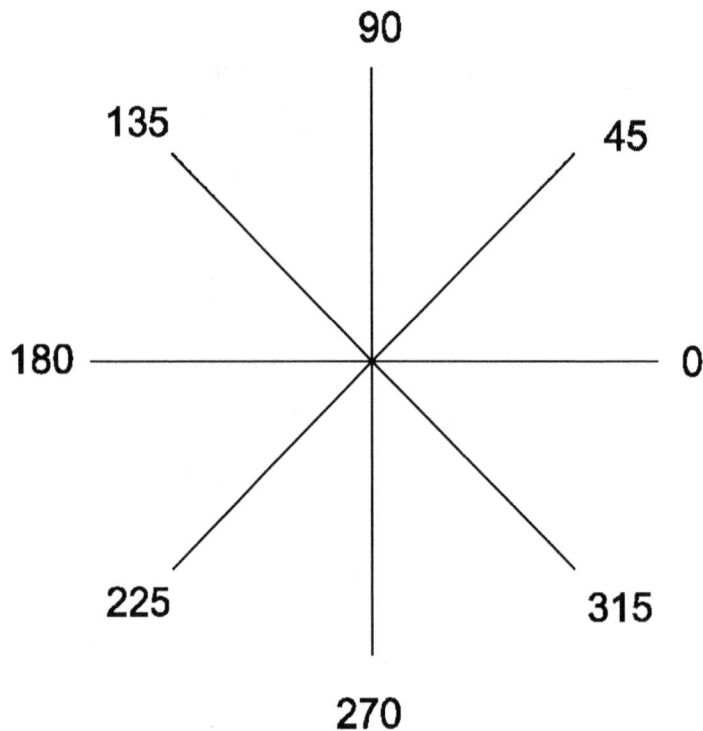

Fig A-8

Polar Tracking

Polar Tracking can be set from the Draft Settings window. You can set the number of degrees that you want it to recognize. This is useful for drawings with a lot of angles and especially for isometric drawings. Try it to see how it works. Right click on the Polar Tracking button at the bottom of the screen (next to osnap) to get at the settings.

If it is not there click on the Customization button on the Status bar (three horizontal lines to the far right in the bottom of the screen). Turn on the status bar buttons you want.

Printer Driver

Many office or home printers require a driver. You must download the driver to the computer that you are using. Many printers come with a disc that contains the driver. If that is not available you may need to go online and search for your driver on the website of the company that manufactures the printer.

Properties palette

Properties is very useful for a plethora of things. You can make adjustments to any object here. This is especially useful for the purpose of overriding text in dimensions, you can change the scale of your dashed lines, you can alter line spacing, and all manner of other adjustments.

To open the Properties palette, select an object, then right click and select Properties from the window that appears. You can also type **properties** or find it on the Properties palette—click on the little arrow in the lower right corner.

Saving

The system saves automatically (newer versions). You can change the time between saves. Type **Options** then the **Open and Save** tab.

Screen shot

Screen shots are copies of what you see on the computer display (screen) at the time you record the screen shot. The method for creating a screen shot is different for each brand of computer. The most common is to hold down the **function key** and press the keyboard button that says **screen shot**. These are often blue or a light colored designation on the keyboard, so look closely.

You may have to consult the user manual for your computer or look online for the method that works with your computer.

To **place** the **screen shot** in the destination drawing use **Ctrl+V**. Hold down the Ctrl button on your keyboard and press V. Then click on the screen where you want to insert the screen shot.

If it is a very small item, relative to the overall drawing, then you must keep track of where you place it or you may have difficulty finding it later.

Selection window

Selection windows cover areas of the drawing for selection (for example to copy) as opposed to clicking on a single object (for example: several lines as opposed to one single line).

There are two types of selection windows. The **green selection window** opens when you click on the screen and move the cursor to the left. The **blue selection window** opens when you click on the screen and move the cursor to the right.

The **green** selection window selects **everything touched by** the green shading (even if it doesn't completely encompass the object).

The **blue** selection window only selects items that are **located completely within** the blue shading.

So, to select a line: it must be completely covered by the blue shading to be selected, but only touched by the green shading to be selected.

There are now (finally) two ways to use the selection windows. One is to click, let go of the mouse button, move the mouse and click again on the opposite corner to create a rectangular selection window. The other method is to click on the screen and hold the left mouse button down to create an irregular selection window. Try it both ways to see how this functions.

Figure A-9 shows a green selection window (the blue window works in the opposite direction):

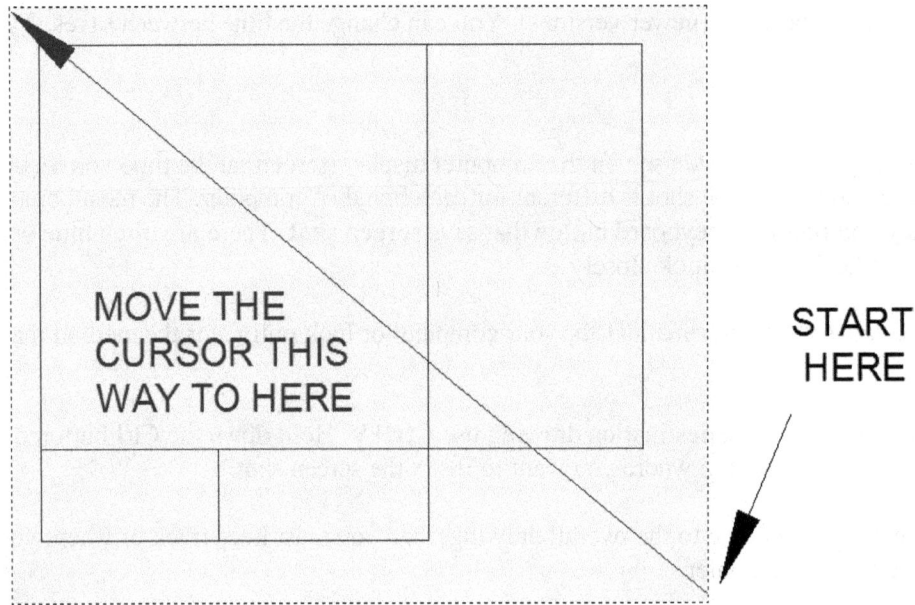

Fig A-9

Fig A-9 shows how to use the green selection window. In this case it completely covers the objects to be copied (the house plan layout), but, in fact, it only needs to touch each element to select it.

The blue selection window works in the opposite direction—start at the left and pull toward the right.

Selection problems
Sometimes a glitch in the system will change the settings so that you cannot select objects. If this happens you should type: **Selectionpreview**, set it to **3**.

Sometimes AutoCAD will not recognize an object in the drawing. This seems to happen most often with text, especially text that has been copied into a drawing. If this happens you may need to move your drawing objects away from the unrecognized object and then you may be able to select and erase the offending unrecognizable objects and replace them. Or you can leave them off to the side of your drawing area. Of course this will mean you must redraw the objects, so this is the last resort when all else fails.

Setup Page
It is a good idea to create a standard page that is already setup with all of your settings for any particular type of drawing (say one for architectural and another for mechanical drawings). Read Chapter 16 Section 16.4 for instructions.

Snap From
Snap from is essentially an offset tool. Use it when you want to start a line where there is no Osnap icon (some place other than the end of a line, or intersection of two lines, or a midpoint, etc).

Snap from is demonstrated in Chapter 1, Section 1.11.

Snap from only works if you do **not click** for the **second point** of the **offset**. Read the prompts as you use this command.

Click for the first point, but the second point is entered numerically. Fig A-10 shows how this functions.

Draw a line 20' long. Then click on the **Line** button, hold down the shift key on your key board and right click to open the Osnap menu. Select **From**. **Click** on the **Endpoint** icon as in **A** in **Fig A-10**. Now **hover** over the midpoint icon at **point B**—**do not click** on it. **Type 7.5' <e>**. The icon at point B must be highlighted when you type 7.5' and <e>. Now move the cursor down until you see the line that starts at point C and click. We are not concerned with the length of this line.

If the icon at B is not visible when you enter the 7.5', the new line (which starts at C) will not be attached to the first line. It may look like it is attached but it will (most likely) be off just a tiny bit. Sometimes you will highlight the icon (as at point B) but, when you let go of the mouse to type, it will shift a bit and the icon will disappear. This will not work. The icon must be visible when you type the offset and enter.

The procedures for Snap From are very precise. If you vary them at all, it will not work.

In spite of this, Snap From is a very useful tool.

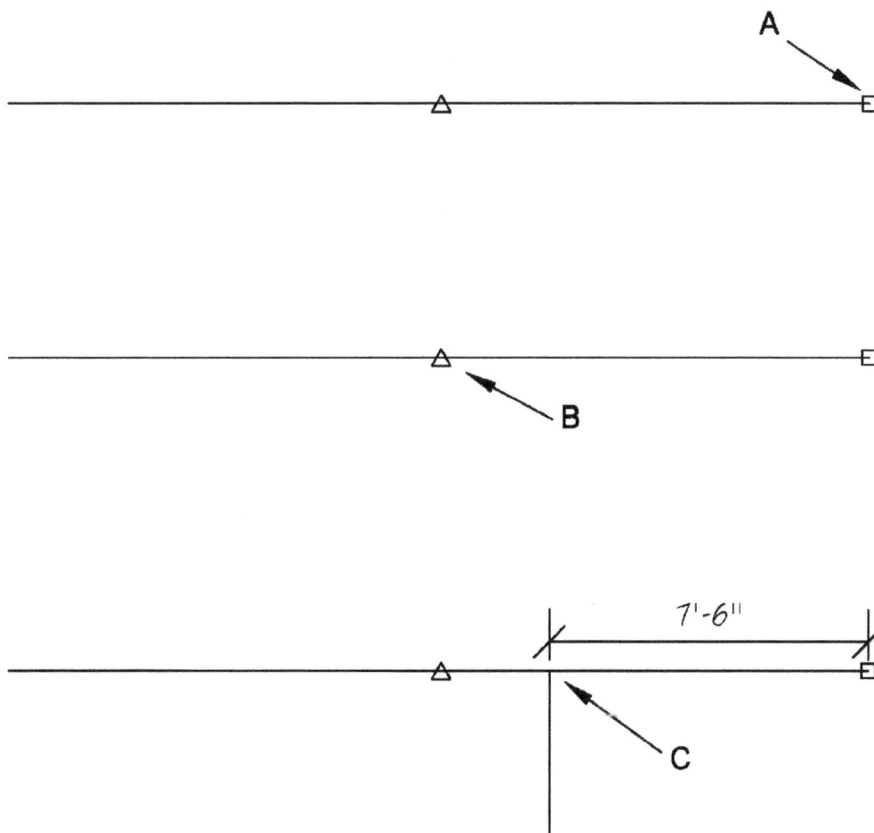

Fig A-10

Spline
Splines are set by pressing the **enter** key on the keyboard **after clicking to set the last point** of the spline. After you set the last point pull the spline line beyond the last point. Pull it way out and move the cursor around to see how it affects the spline. When you see what you want hit the **enter** on your keyboard.

Splines sometimes take a hook at the end when you try to terminate the spline line. You must not move the cursor (as much as that is possible) after you click on the last point of the spline. You can also pull the line way out into space (but no click) before you **enter** to prevent this hook thing from happening.

Start up instructions
See Page Setup for start-up instructions. Or simply start with the introduction and follow the text as all the setup is contained in the lessons.

Stretch
Stretch is one of the most difficult commands to use. It involves understanding what AutoCAD sees as an object. A good way to understand this is to stretch the bathtub that we imported in Chapter 1. Make a copy of the tub. Now click on the **Stretch** button on the **Modify palette**. It will prompt you to select objects. Make a green selection window around the right half of the tub, enter, click on the right side of the tub, and then try to stretch it to the right. Nothing happens. This is because AutoCAD sees the tub as one object.

Now use the **Explode**. Type: explode and enclose the entire tub in a selection window and enter.

Now try the Stretch command again. Create a **green selection window** around the **right half** of the **tub, enter, click** on the **right side** of the tube and **pull** the cursor out to the **right. Click.**

With the explode function you have broken the tub into a series of lines and curves. Now AutoCAD sees these separately and can distinguish which are to be stretched. You have to select only half (or a section of) the object to be stretched. Otherwise the system doesn't know which lines to stretch and which to leave unaltered.

Try this again with a blue selection window—it won't work. This is because the blue selection window only selects objects that are completely covered with the blue shading. Stretch must be used with the green selection window and the green shading can only cover half (or a portion) of the object.

Tables
Tables are explained in Chapter 12. I had a glitch with tables where it would not set the correct cell size. I shut down AutoCAD and restarted it and it worked properly. If your table is odd shaped, check the font size. The cell height will adjust to the font size. For the instructions in this book set the height to 3/16".

Text
Text Styles are set by clicking on the **Text Style** button on the **Annotation palette** or type **style** (enter). The setup is explained in **Chapter 1 Section 1.21**. Pick a font (set it as regular for now in the Font Style window); set the height of the text (this can be altered in the Text Formatting bar that opens when you use the Mtext function).

If you set up the **Text Formatting Toolbar** (Fig A-11) to open it will open when you use Mtext. To turn on the text formatting tool bar type **mtexttoolbar** and set the variable to **1**. Or set it on the **Text Editor** ribbon that opens when you open a Mtext window. Find it on the **Options** palette under **More/Editor Settings/Show Toolbar**.

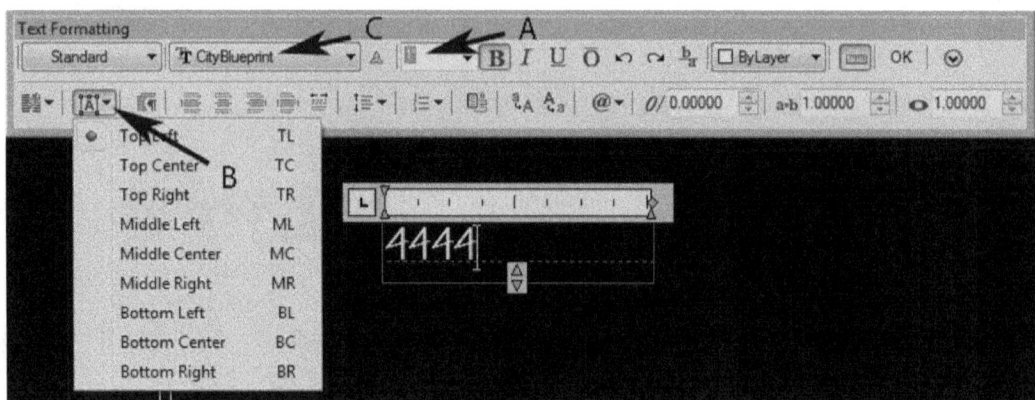

Fig A-11

Sometimes the **text box** and **ruler** are **huge** and run off the screen out into infinity. If this happens type: **mtextcolumn** and set the value to 0. If it still persists with the huge box then type **mtextfixed** and set the value to 0. If it still persists then open a mtext box and in the Options palette (Text Editor ribbon) click on More, then Editor Settings, then turn on the Always display as WYSIWYG. This means: what you see is what you get (no I am not joking).

If the **Text Formatting** bar is in the way, **move it** with the blue strip at the top: position the cursor on the blue bar and hold down the left mouse button to grab it and move it.

Set the **height** of the text in the window **A** in **Fig A-11**. Set the **style** at **C**. The **justification** can be set at **B**. You can also set this on the Text Editor ribbon.

If you are going to edit text that is already there, you must highlight the text first. Click at the beginning or the end of the section of text you wish to edit and run the cursor over the text while you hold down the left mouse button, then to shade it. Then make the changes you desire.

HUGE TEXT Problem: If you are getting **huge text,** when you do not want to get huge text, then the problem may be that the Annotation Scale in the window at the bottom right of your screen is set to some scale. You want it to read 1:1 with non-annotative text styles. Set it thusly and that should fix the problem.

If you want to use **Annotative** text, set the height to the size of text that you will want to print out on paper (1/8" for example).

If you do not want to use annotative text then you must set the actual size of the text in relation to your drawing. Chapter 13 is a complete discussion of this concept. These sizes can be changed in the Text Formatting bar (Fig A-11) that opens each time you use Mtext or on the Text Editor ribbon that also opens with the Mtext window.

When you set a new text style set that style **Current** in the **Text Style** window.

Everything about text cannot be explained here. Most of it is simply typing like any word processing program. The only thing that is difficult is the size (or scale) of the text. See the appropriate sections of the book: Chapter 1 Section 1.21, all of chapter 13 and, for annotative text, see Chapter 16 Section 16.1.

Trim and Extend

Trim and Extend can be a bit difficult at times. They don't always function properly. As with a lot of commands at certain times (especially it seems when files get real large—as they tend to do with architectural plans) the buttons don't respond very well. In this case it helps to **double click.** That usually get the message through.

Trim and Extend both work pretty much the same. You can use them two ways. The method that is the most useful is to click on the button then **immediately** hit the **enter** key on your keyboard. This creates a cutting tool for trim that trims everything you click on back to any line that crosses it. For Extend it extends everything you click on to the next crossing line or object.

But extend doesn't always work this way because it may not recognize which side of the line you are extending and it might not recognize the crossing line that you want to extend to.

Extend won't work unless there is a line (or object) in the crossing plane of the line to be extended. It must run into another line or object.

And trim won't work if there is not another line or object crossing the line you are trimming.

This can be difficult to determine because AutoCAD works to extremely fine tolerances and it can appear that two lines are touching when they are not. So if trim is not working, zoom way in to see if the lines are crossing.

The other way to use trim and extend is to click on the button and then follow the prompts (do not enter immediately). Trim will ask you to select objects. This is the reverse of what many might think, it is asking for the trim line, not the line to be trimmed. Then you enter and click on the line to be trimmed.

The same for extend. When you click on the Extend button, and do not enter right away, it will prompt you to select objects. This is the line to which you want to extend to. Then enter and click on the line you want to extend.

If you forget just try it both ways and you will rediscover what the prompts are referring to.

Typing Commands

All of the commands can be typed instead of using the buttons. But if you do this you must **type** the **command** and then **enter**. These two steps are the same as clicking on the button. Or to put it another way, clicking a button equals typing the command and then pressing the enter key on the keyboard.

This can lead to a bit of confusion because the commands in this book are just clicking on the button. As an example, the Trim (and Extend) functions two different ways. One way involves clicking on the button and then hitting the enter key immediately. This creates a trimming tool. But if you **type** Trim you must **enter twice** immediately to get the trim to function this way—once to set the Trim command, and once to set the trimming tool function.

The buttons equal the **typed command *and* enter**. So if the procedure calls for clicking a button and entering, to type that same command you must type the command, enter, and enter again. This is difficult to explain but easy to see if you try it. The button sets the command in motion. A typed command just sits on the command line until you press enter to set the command in motion. Try this a few times to see how this works.

UCS

The UCS is a point of orientation on the work space. In two dimension drawing it has two axes—X and Y. This can be used to set points in the workspace; it can also be used to draw lines or place objects based on co-ordinate input. In other words you can type in a pair of co-ordinates for the starting point of a line and another pair for the end point. This is not very efficient for most objects, but it is an excellent way to place points in an open field (as we do with the plot plan in Chapter 4).

The origin of the UCS is the point from which everything is measured. It can be set anywhere in the workspace or it can be left in the lower left corner of the drawing area (this is called World UCS). Either way it works basically the same. To set a point (or node) click on the **Point** button (on the Draw palette) or type po and read the prompts. It asks for co-ordinates and these can be entered as a distance from the origin point of the UCS—horizontal first, then a comma, then vertical. See Chapter 4, Section 4.3 for details.

Lines are the same: type two co-ordinates for the start of the line and two for the end.

The **settings** for UCS are on the **Coordinates** panel on the View ribbon. Turn it on or off with the UCS button to the far left of the View ribbon.

Set it to a particular point on your drawing by clicking on the **Origin** button in the middle of the coordinates panel on the View ribbon and then click on the point in your drawing where you want to set an origin point. Now you can use this to enter co-ordinates for many different objects.

Viewports

Viewports can be locked so they do not accidentally get altered. In the Layout tab that you are using set the Model/Paper button to Paper. Now run the cursor over the line that represents the edge of the viewport, it will highlight—click on it when it is highlighted to select it. Do not confuse the margin line for the viewport line. When the viewport line is selected (the blue grip boxes will appear) right click. There you will see the setting for locking the viewport. Remember that it is locked if you need to change things later.

The lines of the paper space can change, sometimes spontaneously (a glitch). The settings to get it back are in the Options dialog box. Type options and click on the Display tab and then the box next to Display paper background.

Chapter 6 covers the basics of viewports and Chapter 14 covers the subject in more detail.

Units

Set the units by typing **units** or access it from the **Format tab** at the top of the page. Often AutoCAD **does not set the units correctly in the Startup box**. So if you have problems set it here, it should stick.

Zoom

There are a number of zoom options in AutoCad. They are as follows:

Mouse wheel set the zoomfactor (how fast it zooms in and out) by typing **zoomfactor** and enter a number.
Zoom Window—the area enclosed in the selection window (that you create) fills the screen.
Zoom Dynamic—zooms out and then creates a box that can be adjusted in size and then enter to zoom in. This is essentially like using Zoom All and Zoom Window together in one command.
Zoom Scale—uses some complicated formula.
Zoom Center—pinpoint a spot on the workspace and enter a number that represents the size of the zoom area.
Zoom Object—zooms in on selected object.
Zoom in—zooms into the current screen.
Zoom out—zooms out in the current screen.
Zoom All—zooms out to show the entire workspace in use.
Zoom Extents—zooms out to show the entire area covered in the extents that have (maybe) been set (how is this different from Zoom All?)

Type z <e> and then the **first letter** of the **zoom command** type as in **A** for Zoom **All** (**z** <e> then **a** <e>) or **W** for Zoom **Window** (**z** <e> then **w** <e>). There are also buttons in the lower right corner of the Navigate panel on the View ribbon, but it is easier just to type these commands.

Appendix II—Location of Buttons and Settings

Most of the buttons and command paths can be found in the Help menu. Click on Help at the top of the screen or press the F1 key. From the menu at the left of the screen select Commands. An alphabetical list will come up and then follow the links to the command you are trying to find.

Many of the command buttons are co-located with other command buttons. The Rectangle command button is co-located with the Polygon button; the Linear dimension command button is co-located with other dimension command buttons. So when you are looking for a button on a particular palette, and do not see it, click on the down arrow next to the visible buttons to see what appears.

Remember that all commands and settings can be done by typing in the command line. The typed command can be found in the Command Reference as referenced above. The most common are often the first letter of the command, sometimes the first two or three letters will do, but you can usually type the whole word.

A number of commands are available upon right clicking the mouse. Right click on the open screen and see what comes up. At the bottom you will see Options. This is a quick way to get at the options should you need to switch back and forth a bit. Try right clicking at different points in any given command process to see what is available.

Also the most recently used commands can be accessed from the menu that you get from a right click when no command is in process.

You can add or remove ribbon tabs and palettes by right clicking anywhere on the ribbon. There you will find the Show Tabs selection menu and the Show Panels menu (Panels and Palettes are the same).

AutoCad Appendix IV—Plan Set

This appendix is the complete set of plans and a few close-up details. All of the views are in the body of the text of this book. Chapter 15 contains a lot of the views with close-up details for clarity.

Of course it is difficult to get good detail on this size (8.5 x 11) paper when the subject is meant to be displayed on paper that is 36 x 24 inches. A house is a large object to draw. The graphics necessary to draw these plans are included in the corresponding chapters. For an expandable view go to the website. There you will find a **full set of plans available in PDF format**. These can be zoomed and all the detail is very clear in that format.

www.autocadin20hours.com

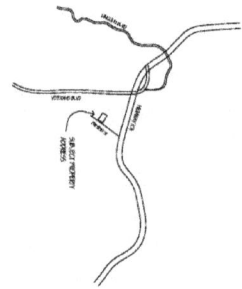

VICINITY MAP

EROSION CONTROL NOTES

- ROOF TO DRAIN INTO DOWNSPOUTS ONTO SPLASH BLOCKS.
- GRADE LOT TO PROVIDE FOR RUNOFF TO STREET.
- HOSES TO BE EQUIPPED WITH SHUT OFF NOZZLES.
- SITE RUNOFF TO BE CONTROLLED DURING CONSTRUCTION BY THE INSTALLATION OF WATTLES OR EQUIVALENT MEASURES.

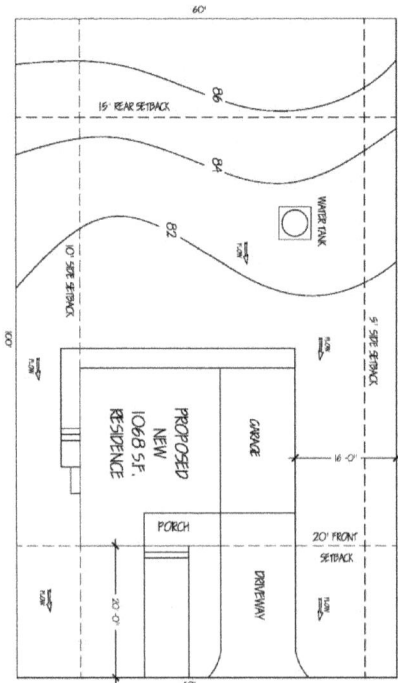

PLOT PLAN
SCALE: 3/16" = 1'

60'
15' REAR SETBACK
86
84
82
WATER TANK
10' SIDE SETBACK
100'
5' SIDE SETBACK
100'
PROPOSED NEW 1068 S.F. RESIDENCE
GARAGE
15'-0"
PORCH
20'-0"
DRIVEWAY
20' FRONT SETBACK
60'
N

1000 PARADISE AVE.

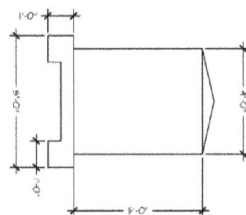

WATER TANK X-SECTION
SCALE: 1/2" = 1'

SCOPE OF PROJECT
BUILD 1068 S.F. RESIDENCE WITH 264 S.F. GARAGE ON CURRENTLY VACANT 100' X 60' LOT.

PROJECT INCLUDES ONE FULL AND ONE HALF BATHROOM, WASHER AND KITCHEN SINK.

TOTAL GROUND COVERAGE = 858 S.F.

TOTAL PAVED AREA = 604 S.F.

TOTAL IMPERMEABLE SURFACE = 1462

EXPRESSED AS PERCENTAGE = 24% OF LOT.

PROJECT TO BE FIRE SPRINKLERED

APN
000-000-00

CONTACT INFO

OWNER: DESIGNER:
WINNIE AND BOB ANYONE   DESIGNER'S NAME
STREET ADDRESS   CITY, STATE, ZIP CODE
CITY, STATE ZIP CODE   PHONE NUMBER
PHONE NUMBER

ENGINEER:
ENGINEER'S NAME
CITY, STATE, ZIP CODE
PHONE NUMBER

TABLE OF CONTENTS
PAGE 1: PLOT PLAN / EROSION CONTROL / VICINITY MAP
PAGE 2: FLOOR PLANS AND ELECTRICAL PLAN
PAGE 3: ELEVATIONS
PAGE 4: FOUNDATION PLAN AND DETAILS
PAGE 5: FLOOR FRAME, ROOF FRAME PLANS
PAGE 6: CROSS SECTION AND DETAILS
PAGE 7: DETAILS AND WINDOW SCHEDULE
PAGE 8: SHEER PLAN AND ENGINEERING DETAILS
PAGE 9: NOTES AND ENERGY CALCS

PROPOSED NEW RESIDENCE FOR	YOUR NAME
WINNIE AND BOB ANYONE	RESIDENTIAL DESIGN
1000 PARADISE AVE	P.O. BOX 0000
ANYTOWN, CA 99999	ANYTOWN, CA. 99999
PH. NUMBER	PH. NUMBER

PLOT PLAN
SCOPE
AND
CONTENTS

DRAWN BY: JAMES PRITZKER
PROJECT: 10000001
DATE: 20MAY25
SCALE: SEE VIEW
PAGE NO.

NO. REVISION

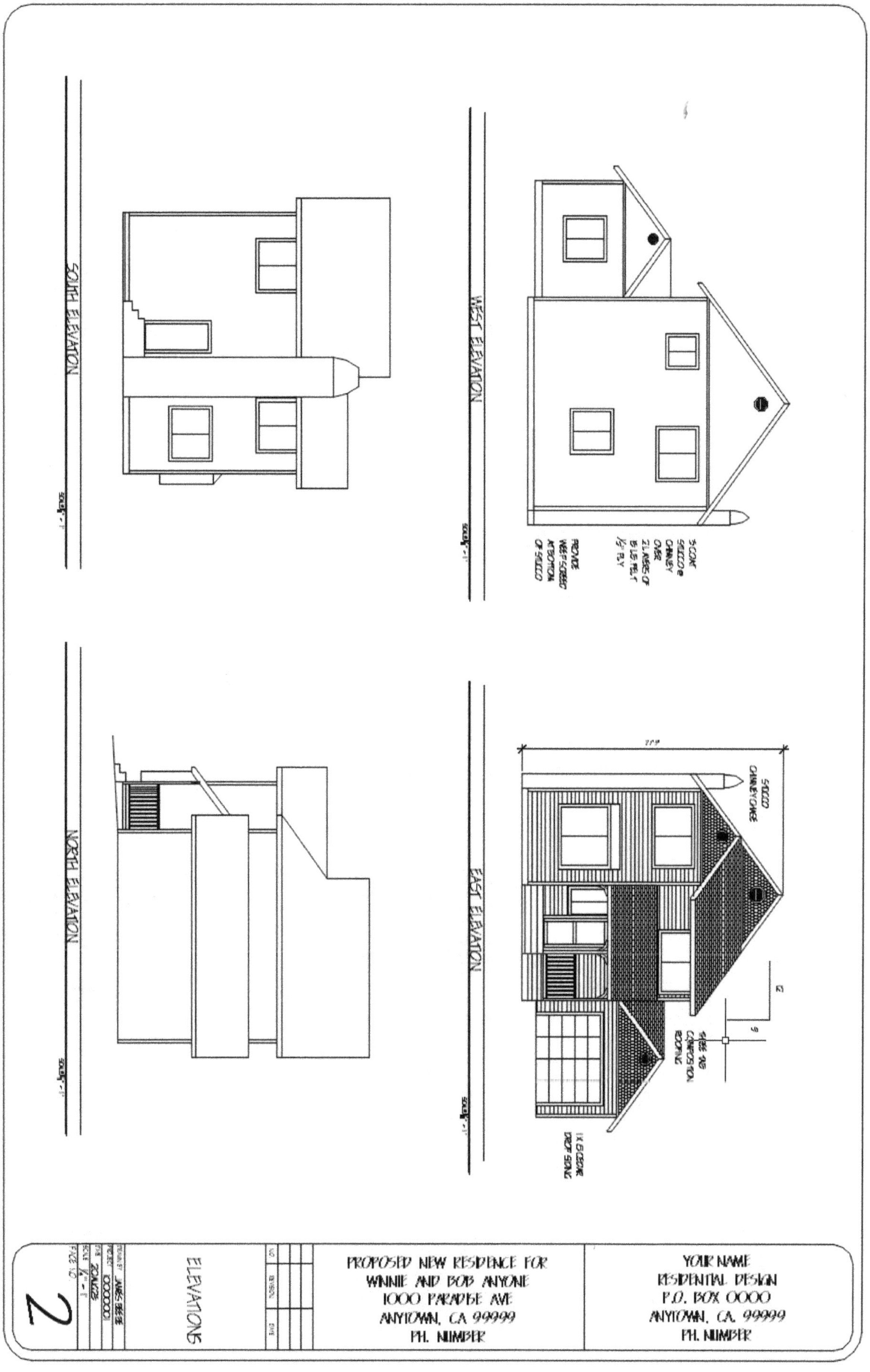
SOUTH ELEVATION
NORTH ELEVATION
WEST ELEVATION
EAST ELEVATION
PROPOSED NEW RESIDENCE FOR
WINNIE AND BOB ANYONE
1000 PARADISE AVE
ANYTOWN, CA 99999
PH. NUMBER
YOUR NAME
RESIDENTIAL DESIGN
P.O. BOX 0000
ANYTOWN, CA. 99999
PH. NUMBER
ELEVATIONS
2

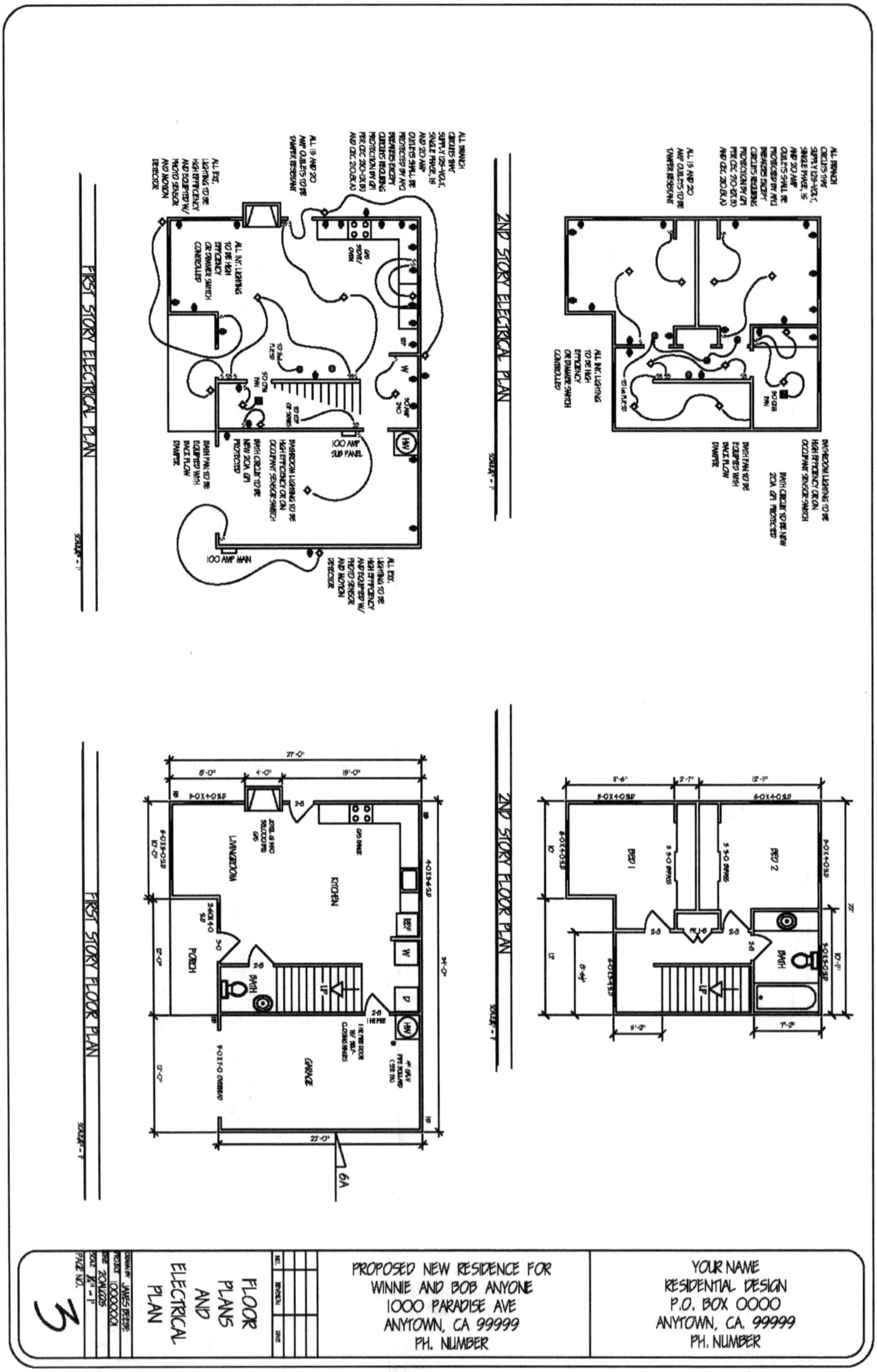
FIRST STORY ELECTRICAL PLAN
2ND STORY ELECTRICAL PLAN
FIRST STORY FLOOR PLAN
2ND STORY FLOOR PLAN
PROPOSED NEW RESIDENCE FOR
WINNIE AND BOB ANYONE
1000 PARADISE AVE
ANYTOWN, CA 99999
PH. NUMBER
YOUR NAME
RESIDENTIAL DESIGN
P.O. BOX 0000
ANYTOWN, CA. 99999
PH. NUMBER
FLOOR
PLANS
AND
ELECTRICAL
PLAN
3

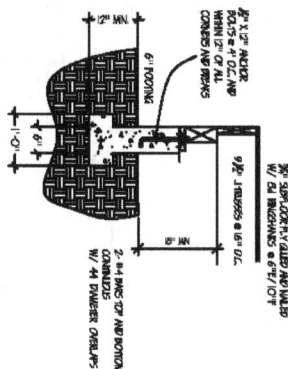

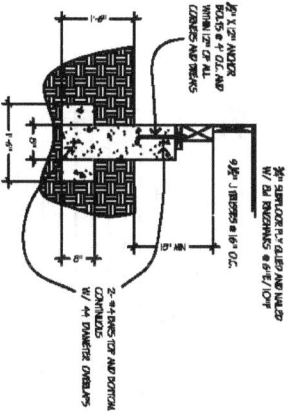

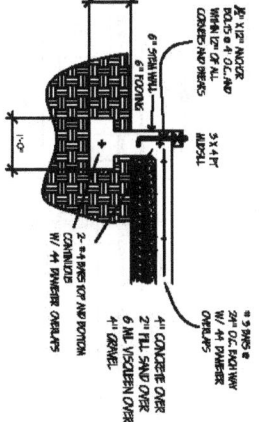

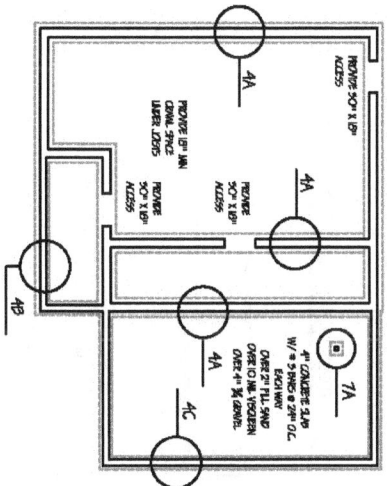

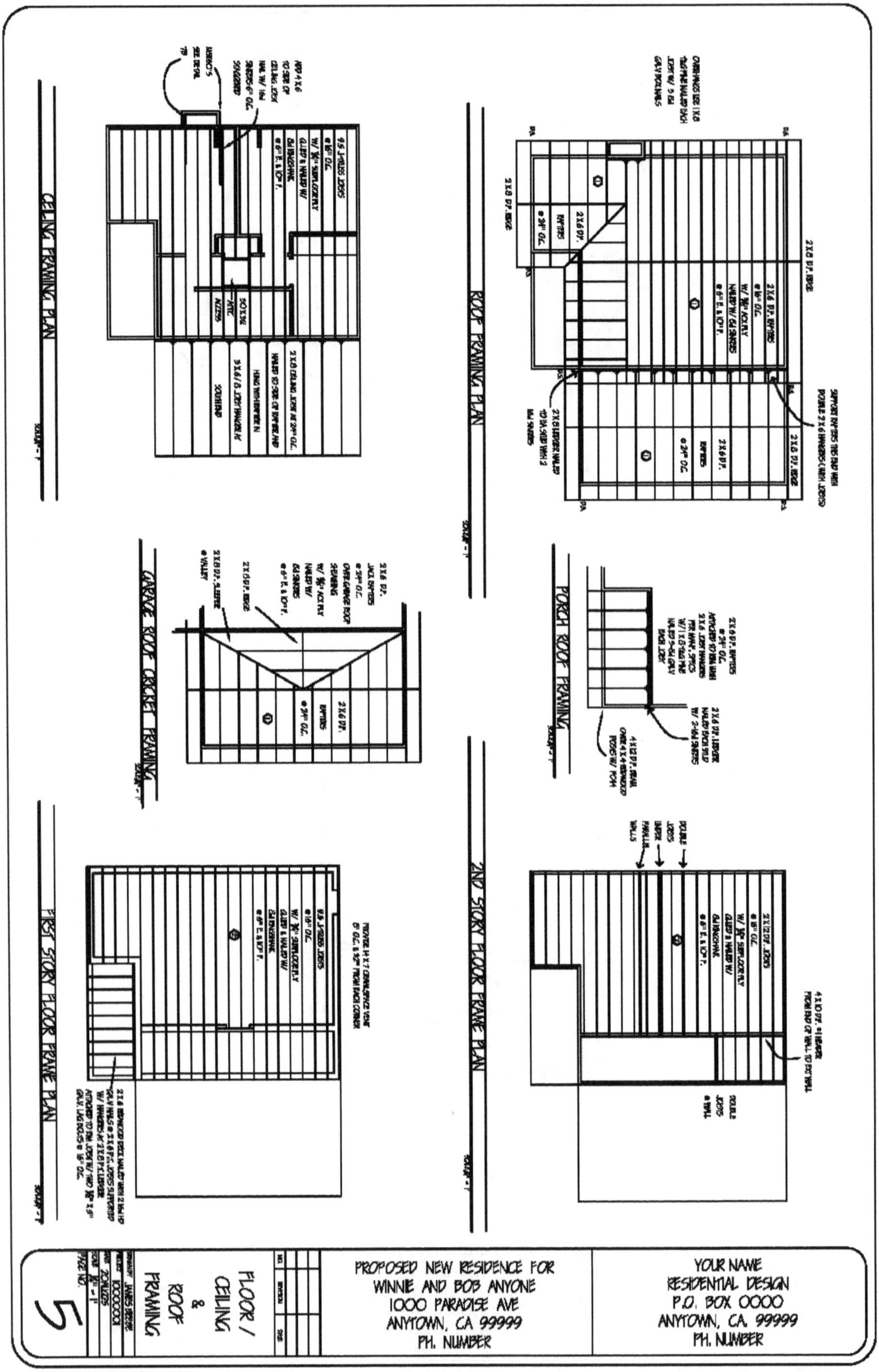

CEILING FRAMING PLAN
ROOF FRAMING PLAN
GARAGE ROOF CRICKET FRAMING
PORCH ROOF FRAMING
FIRST STORY FLOOR FRAME PLAN
2ND STORY FLOOR FRAME PLAN
PROPOSED NEW RESIDENCE FOR
WINNIE AND BOB ANYONE
1000 PARADISE AVE
ANYTOWN, CA 99999
PH. NUMBER
YOUR NAME
RESIDENTIAL DESIGN
P.O. BOX 0000
ANYTOWN, CA. 99999
PH. NUMBER
FLOOR /
CEILING
&
ROOF
FRAMING
5

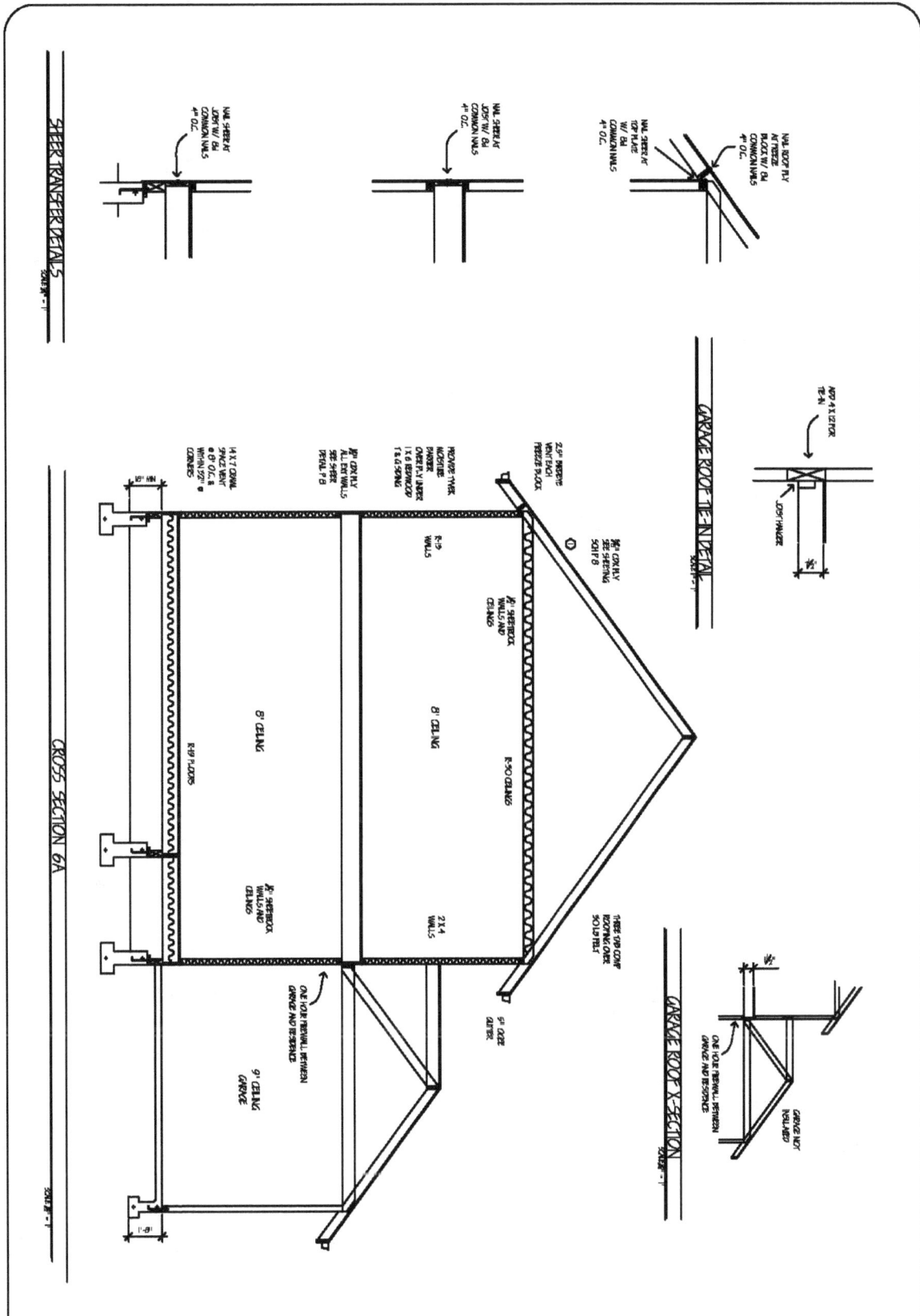

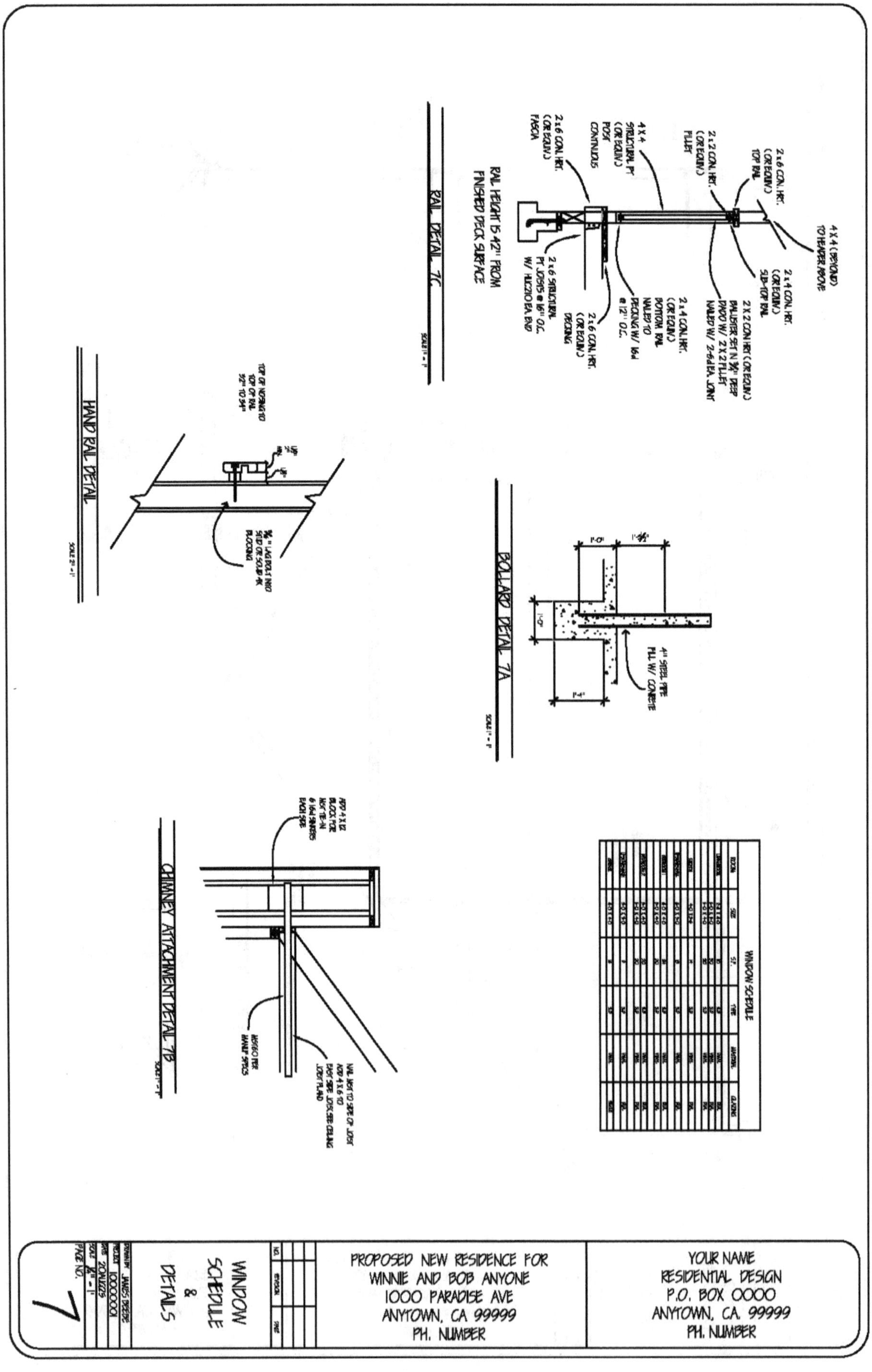
RAIL DETAIL 7C
RAIL HEIGHT IS 42" FROM FINISHED DECK SURFACE
HAND RAIL DETAIL
BOLLARD DETAIL 7A
4" STEEL PIPE FILL W/ CONCRETE
CHIMNEY ATTACHMENT DETAIL 7B
WINDOW SCHEDULE
PROPOSED NEW RESIDENCE FOR
WINNIE AND BOB ANYONE
1000 PARADISE AVE
ANYTOWN, CA 99999
PH. NUMBER
YOUR NAME
RESIDENTIAL DESIGN
P.O. BOX 0000
ANYTOWN, CA. 99999
PH. NUMBER
WINDOW
SCHEDULE
&
DETAILS
PAGE NO.
7

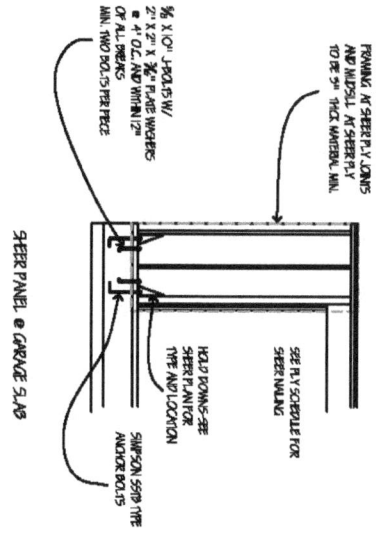

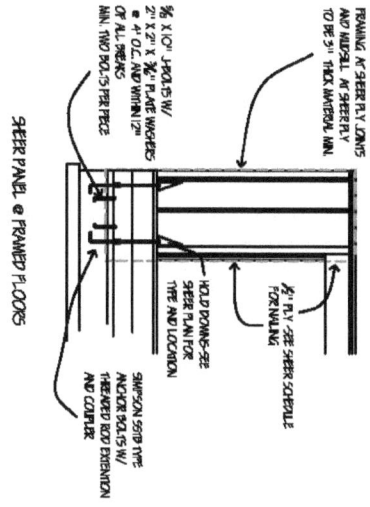

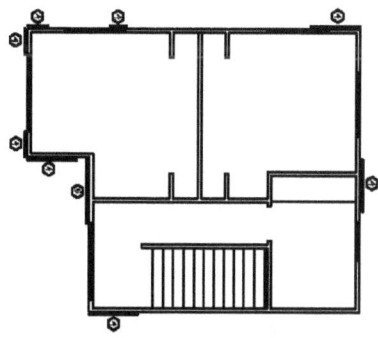

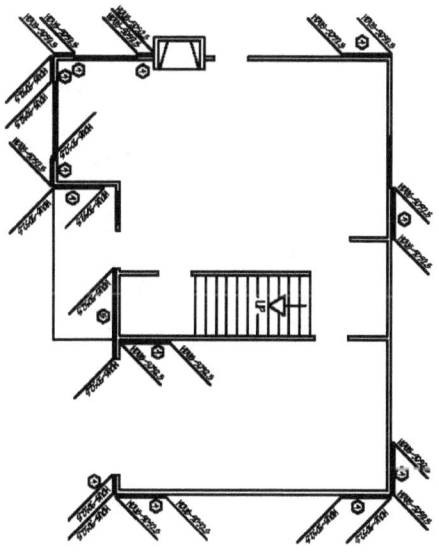

GENERAL CONSTRUCTION NOTES

1 - ALL BLDG'S APPLICABLE CODES, 2010 CBC, 2010 MECH, PLUMB & ELECT CODES.
2 - PLUMBING FIXTURES SHALL COMPLY WITH THE FOLLOWING STANDARDS
 - TOILETS TO BE HIGH EFFICIENCY - 1.6 GALS / FLUSH MAX.
 - SHOWER HEAD - 2.5 GALS / MIN MAX.
 - LAVATORY FAUCET - 2.2 GALS / MIN. MAX.
3 - ALL DOORS AND WINDOWS TO BE CAULKED FOR SEAL.
4 - ALL EXT DOORS TO BE WEATHER STRIPPED.
5 - CAULK ALL VENTS AND PIPES AT PENETRATION OF EXT. MEMBRANE.
6 - PROVIDE TYVEX TYPE MOISTURE BARRIER AT EXT. WALLS UNDER SIDING.
7 - ALL EXT FASTENERS TO BE OF CORROSION RESISTANCE BY GALV, ANODIZED, STAINLESS, OR ALUMINUM.
8 - ALL CONSTRUCTION LUMBER TO BE #2 & BETTER UNLESS SPECIFIED.
9 - ALL WOOD EXPOSED TO THE WEATHER TO BE PT OR APPROVED NATURALLY DECAY RESISTANT SPECIES.
10 - ALL FASTENERS INTO PT LUMBER TO BE HOT DIPPED ZINC COATED GALVANIZED, ANODIZED, OR STAINLESS STEEL.
11 - ALL MEASUREMENTS TO BE FIELD VERIFIED.
12 - PROVIDE 12" X 12" REMOVABLE ACCESS PANEL FOR ALL PLUMBING FIXTURES W/ CONCEALED SLIP JOINT CONNECTIONS.
13 - SHOWER ENCLOSURE TO BE TEMPERED GLASS.
14 - PROVIDE NON-REMOVABLE BACK FLOW DEVICES AT ALL HOSE BIBS.
15 - PROVIDE WEEP SCREED AT BOTTOM OF ALL STUCCO SECTIONS.

		PROPOSED NEW RESIDENCE FOR	YOUR NAME
NO.	REVISION	DATE	WINNIE AND BOB ANYONE	RESIDENTIAL DESIGN
		1000 PARADISE AVE	P.O. BOX 0000
		ANYTOWN, CA 99999	ANYTOWN, CA. 99999
		PH. NUMBER	PH. NUMBER

DRAWN BY: JAMES PEESE
JOB #: 10000001
DATE: 2010\025
SCALE: ¼" = 1'
PAGE NO.

6

NOTES

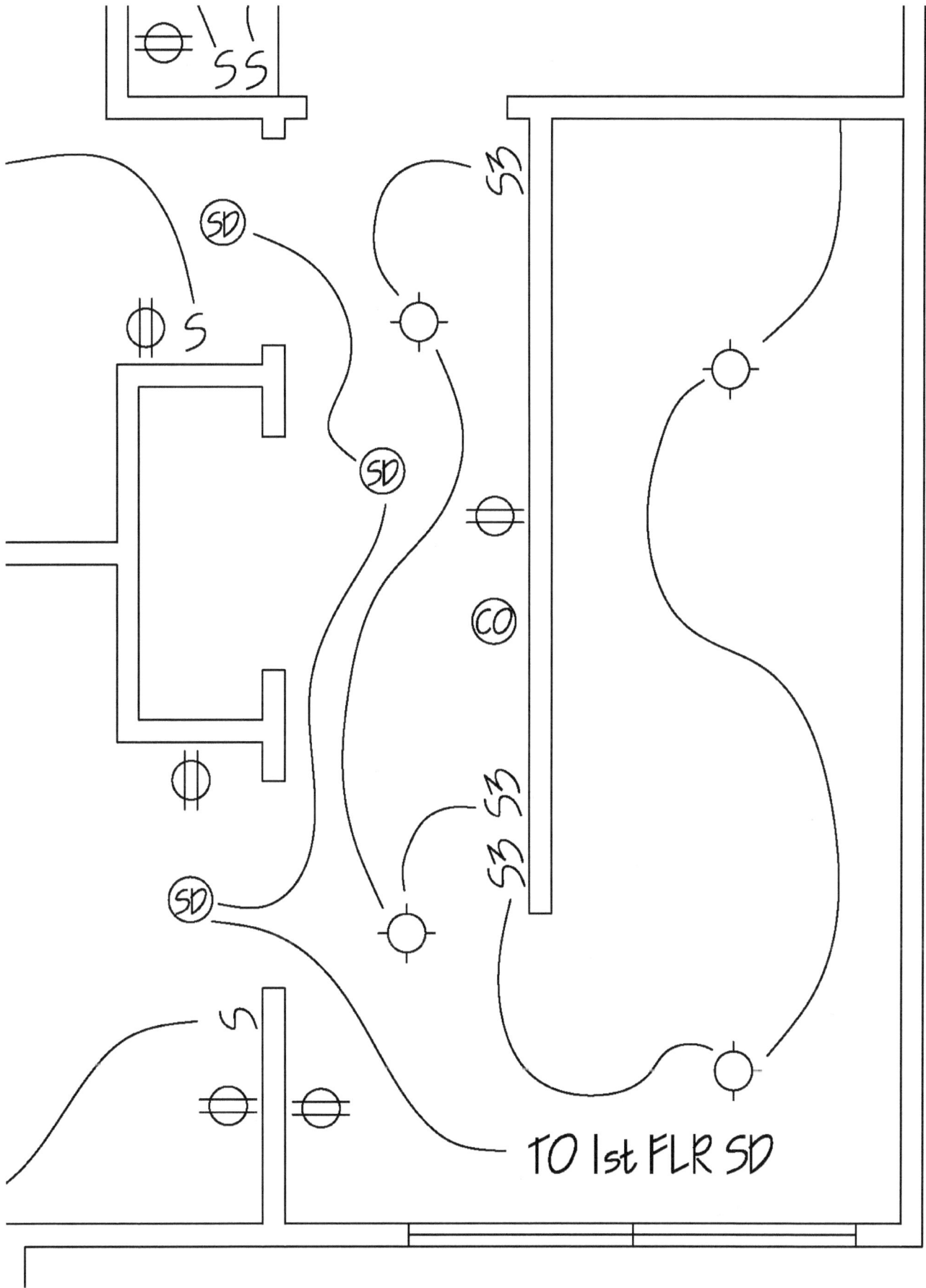

TO 1st FLR SD

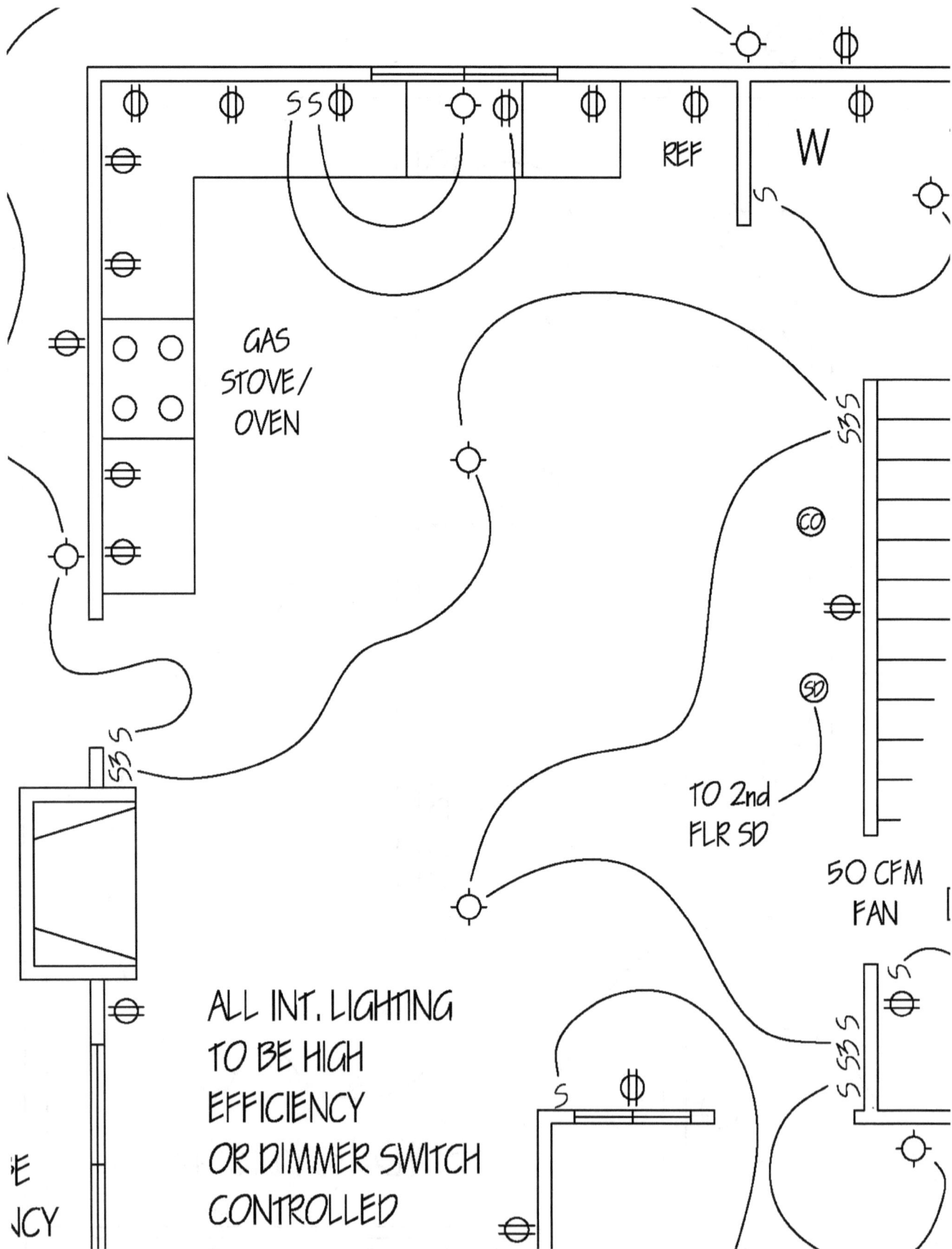

GAS
STOVE/
OVEN

REF

W

CO

SD

TO 2nd
FLR SD

50 CFM
FAN

ALL INT. LIGHTING
TO BE HIGH
EFFICIENCY
OR DIMMER SWITCH
CONTROLLED

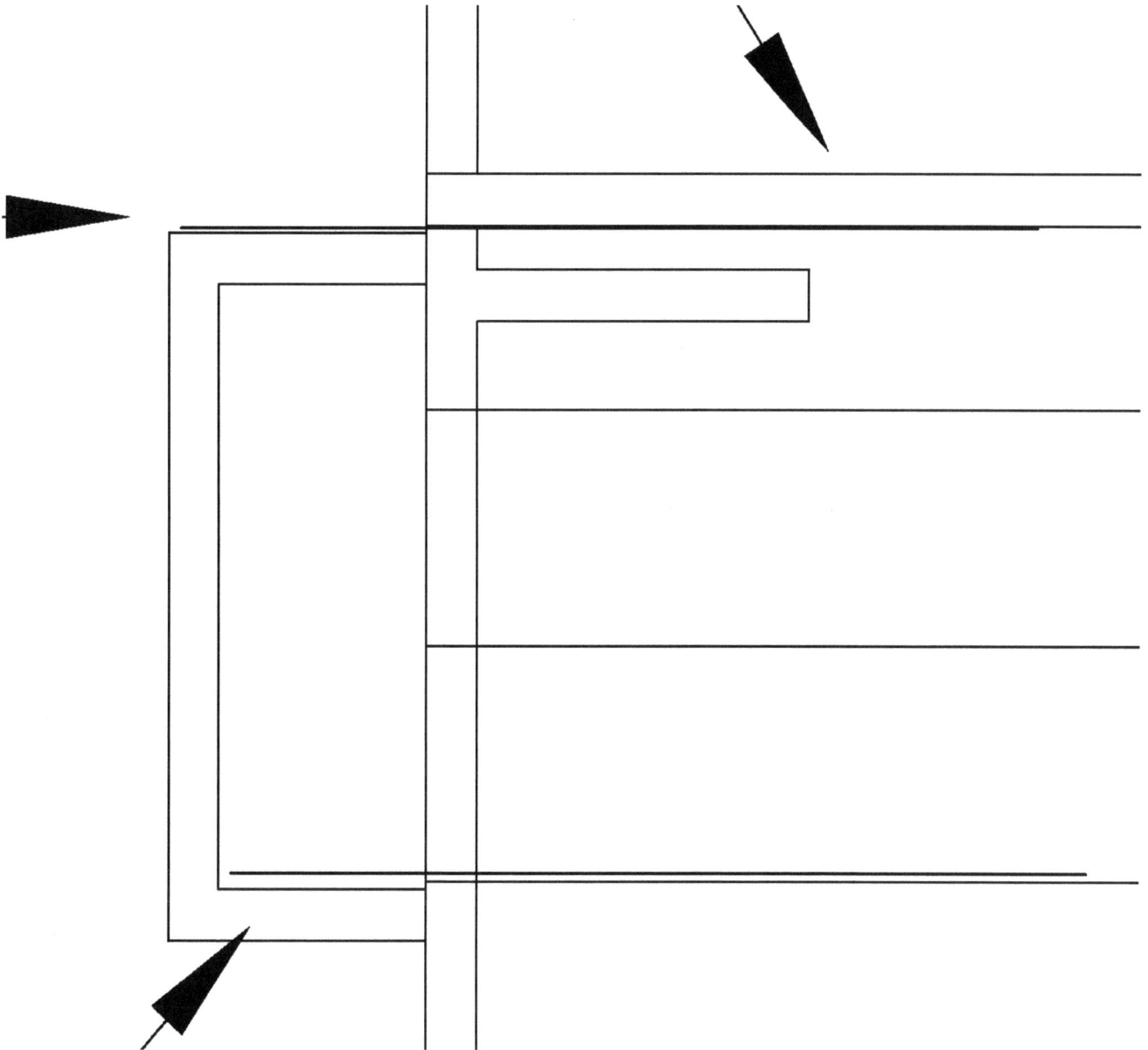

Detail of Chimney Tie-in from Page 7

Index